STUDIES PRESENTED

to

ROBERT D. BIGGS

Robert D. Biggs. Photograph by Fred Donner

From the Workshop of the Chicago Assyrian Dictionary

Volume 2

STUDIES PRESENTED

to

ROBERT D. BIGGS

June 4, 2004

Edited by

Martha T. Roth
Walter Farber
Matthew W. Stolper
and
Paula von Bechtolsheim

THE ORIENTAL INSTITUTE OF THE UNIVERSITY OF CHICAGO

2007

Library of Congress Control Number: 2007937366
ISBN: 978-1-885923-44-8
ISBN: 1-885923-44-9
ISSN: 0066-9903

The Oriental Institute, Chicago

Assyriological Studies No. 27

Series Editors

Leslie Schramer
and
Thomas G. Urban

Printed by Edwards Brothers, Ann Arbor, Michigan

The paper used in this publication meets the minimum requirements of American National Standard for Information Services — Permanence of Paper for Printed Library Materials, ANSI Z39.48-1984.

∞

TABLE OF CONTENTS

FOREWORD

Robert D. Biggs joined the staff of the *Chicago Assyrian Dictionary* (*CAD*) in 1963 after receiving his Ph.D. from Johns Hopkins University. In June 2004, he celebrated his seventieth birthday and retired from the University of Chicago as Professor of Assyriology in the Oriental Institute and the Department of Near Eastern Languages and Civilizations; his service to the *CAD*, however, will continue until the final volume appears. To acknowledge and honor his forty-one years of extraordinary service to the *CAD* as collaborator, Associate Editor, and Editorial Board member, contributions from some of his former and current *CAD* colleagues are assembled into the volume, *Studies Presented to Robert D. Biggs, June 4, 2004*, From the Workshop of the Chicago Assyrian Dictionary, vol. 2. It is fitting to revive this series, as the first volume, *Studies Presented to A. Leo Oppenheim, June 7, 1964*, From the Workshop of the Chicago Assyrian Dictionary, appeared forty years ago, and Bob's contribution there was his first published article.

The contributions range over the several areas to which Bob has contributed: Akkadian and Sumerian, texts and archaeology, literature and medicine, philology and lexicography. The common thread throughout this volume is that every contributor has enjoyed the privilege of discussing her or his scholarly work with our esteemed colleague Robert D. Biggs in the fertile field of the *Chicago Assyrian Dictionary*.

The editors are grateful for the support of Gil Stein, Director of the Oriental Institute of the University of Chicago. We also wish to acknowledge the invaluable technical and editorial assistance of Linda McLarnan, the Manuscript Editor of the *CAD*, and of Leslie Schramer and Katie L. Johnson of the Oriental Institute Publications office.

MARTHA T. ROTH
Professor of Assyriology
Editor-in-Charge, *Chicago Assyrian Dictionary*

EDITORIAL NOTE

Whenever possible, texts and monographs cited in the articles in this volume have followed the most recent list of bibliographical abbreviations of the *Chicago Assyrian Dictionary* (vol. Ṭ). All other citations, as well as the punctuation and presentation, have generally followed the editorial style of the *Journal of Near Eastern Studies*.

For the four contributions in German, it was decided to keep the old spelling and word-division and not to follow the guidelines of the controversial, and still not universally observed, language reform, the *Neue Rechtsschreibung*. To date (May 2006), the rules for this language reform are still being revised.

PAULA VON BECHTOLSHEIM
Managing Editor, *Journal of Near Eastern Studies*

MY CAREER IN ASSYRIOLOGY AND NEAR EASTERN ARCHAEOLOGY*

Robert D. Biggs, The University of Chicago

My father's grandparents and great-grandparents crossed the vast American plains in wagons drawn by teams of oxen from Arkansas to the Walla Walla area of Washington Territory in 1870 in a typical pattern of western migration in America before the coming of the railroads to the West. My mother's parents, on the other hand, were immigrants from Denmark in 1901. Like many other immigrant families from Scandinavia, they settled in a farming community peopled mainly by fellow Danes, first in Colorado, and subsequently near St. Andrews in central Washington State.

My interest in languages arose early. My Danish grandmother, who was in her mid-thirties when she came to America, learned to understand English and to speak a heavily accented English, but never learned to write in English. In the days before many farm families had telephones, family members wrote to one another a couple of times a week. My grandmother wrote, of course, in Danish, which was my mother's first language and which she had learned to read and write in summer Danish schools in her rural community. While still in elementary school, I wanted to learn to read my grandmother's letters myself. With the help of a small Danish-English dictionary and an elementary grammar that my mother had, I learned Danish vocabulary and Danish grammar well enough to understand her letters. By the time I was in high school, I had developed an interest in family history, so I began to write to my grandmother's sister and my grandfather's brother and sisters who had remained in Denmark. At that time, hardly anyone—certainly not of their generation or even the next—in rural Denmark studied English, so I attempted to write to them in Danish. I certainly made many mistakes, but apparently they were able to understand what I wrote, and I could understand their responses.

In 1943 my parents moved from the small town of Hunters (near the Columbia River and across the river from the Colville Indian Reservation) to a 240-acre farm in Spokane County, Washington. We had no electricity or running water (water was pumped from a well by a windmill or by a hand pump). We children attended the local two-room school that was two miles away, but in 1945 our school district was split

* This article appeared in the *Journal of Assyrian Academic Studies* 19/1 (2005): 5–27. We would like to thank Robert Paulissian, M.D., and the journal's Editorial Board for granting us permission to republish the article. This version includes a few minor corrections.

and consolidated with two schools in nearby towns. Our new school in Medical Lake was still small—two grades to each room. In high school, I had an opportunity to study Spanish—the only language offered at first. This was a lot of fun. The next year several of us who were interested asked the teacher of Spanish if she would also offer Latin. I did not realize at the time what an added burden that was, but she took it on cheerfully and offered us two years of Latin. In my junior and senior years, the same teacher offered German to a small class of about five of us, with textbooks that used the old German Gothic script.

I knew that I did not want a future life as a farmer. Especially in retrospect, I treasure some of the experiences of farm life, but the drudgery of twice-a-day milking and feeding of cows, the care of other animals, the discomforts of putting up hay in the summertime, the dustiness of planting and tilling and wheat harvesting, building barbed-wire fences, and such did not appeal to me. I definitely wanted something different in my future.

Having a younger brother and three sisters, I realized that there was no question of any family financial support for college, but as valedictorian of my high school graduating class in 1952 at Medical Lake, Eastern Washington College of Education (subsequently Eastern Washington University) in the town of Cheney offered me a scholarship of $100 that paid most of my student fees. At that time, it was possible to get part-time work on campus that paid enough to cover room and board (the pay was 80 cents an hour). One year I worked in the college library, the next year on the grounds crew (raking leaves, chipping ice off sidewalks, digging ditches, etc.), and then did janitorial work in the college elementary school. I also earned extra money by editing and typing the term papers of other students for fifty cents a page.

I was excited by the opportunities to study languages in college. My Spanish was good enough that I could immediately take advanced classes. In my first year, I also began the study of French and Russian. Russian seemed a timely language to study, and, indeed, the leader of the Soviet Union, Joseph Stalin, died in 1953 during the year I studied Russian. Unfortunately the professor of Russian (he was a native of Russia, but taught in the economics department) did not return the following year, so I had to give up on Russian. Hoping to be able to teach Spanish and French at the high-school level, I pursued a degree in education.

Summers in my college years (and part of my graduate school years as well) were spent working in the Green Giant pea cannery in Dayton, Washington, the area where my father's family had settled in 1870. Most of the men working in the pea harvest were from Mexico (they were called *braceros* in Spanish), and I got acquainted with several of them. They appreciated having an American who was reasonably fluent in their language and who enjoyed the Mexican music with them on the jukebox in one of the local taverns.

In my first years at Green Giant, I had relatively low-skill jobs such as handling the empty wooden boxes that the peas were hauled to the cannery in. Eventually I had a much more responsible job—processing the peas in huge retorts with steam. About a dozen of these retorts were arranged in a circle. A crane lowered three large steel baskets filled with cans of peas into each retort, which was then clamped shut. My job was to turn on the steam, bring the temperature to a certain degree, and to cook the peas for a specified length of time. So it was a matter of keeping an eye on six or eight retorts at a time, both for temperature and timing, all a few minutes apart. Luckily, I never blew the top off a retort or overcooked a load of peas. To this day, the smell of canned peas reminds me of my years working for the Jolly Green Giant.

When the pea-canning season was finished, I usually drove a truck in the wheat harvest for farmers in the area hauling a truck load of threshed wheat to the nearest grain elevator, about 20 miles away, thus earning money for clothing and books for the coming college year. Driving a wheat truck is not as easy as it sounds. The threshed wheat is held in a large hopper on the combine until it is nearly full. A man on the combine signals the truck driver, who drives so that an augur moves the wheat through what looks like a huge spout and into the bed of the truck. So as not to lose any time, the combine does not stop or slow down, so the truck must keep the same speed. The driver has to be careful to keep the spout over the bed of the truck and also not to drive into the combine. This gets tricky on the rolling hills of the Dayton area. The combine has a leveling device that keeps the body of the combine level even on a hillside (and they do tip over occasionally nevertheless), but it can be a bit scary for a truck driver. Depending on the distance to the grain elevator and whether there was a line of trucks waiting to unload, there was often some time to read a bit between runs. Thus I had a chance to read several French novels, the memoirs of Simone de Beauvoir, and Shakespeare plays while I waited.

For recreational reading in my college years, I followed up on a youthful interest in ancient Egypt and its pyramids and mummies. At some point I had read Edward Chiera's *They Wrote on Clay* (Chicago, 1938, reprinted 1957), which was my introduction to the world of Babylonia and Assyria and its mysterious cuneiform script. I was fascinated by the thought of someone being able to read cuneiform and to read something that no one had read in thousands of years. It was also then that I first read W. F. Albright's *From the Stone Age to Christianity* (Baltimore, 1940, second edition 1957) and it opened up to me a new window on the ancient Near East. I wondered if I was foolish to think of trying to study the ancient Near East seriously.

I became active in student government, particularly in my junior and senior years. In the summer of 1955 I was a delegate to the national meeting of the National Student Association at the University of Minnesota in Minneapolis. The plenary sessions lasted late into the evening, with especially heated discussions on foreign policy matters. One of the hottest topics was whether the China seat on the Security Council of the United Nations should be the Nationalist government in Taiwan or the People's Republic of China. In 1956 I applied to attend a six-week seminar of the organization devoted to issues of foreign policy as they affected students. I was among those selected to attend the seminar, held at Harvard University. It was only many years later that it was disclosed that these seminars were secretly funded by the United States government through the Central Intelligence Agency.

In my senior year of college, my French teacher encouraged me to apply for a Fulbright Scholarship to study for a year in France. The Dean of Students urged me to apply also for a Danforth Fellowship (funded by the founders of the Ralston-Purina Company in St. Louis). To my great surprise, I was awarded both a Danforth (to pursue a higher degree) and a Fulbright. Since the Fulbright was for only one year, it was agreed that I should take up the Fulbright first. Thus, for the 1956/57 academic year, I was assigned to Toulouse in southwestern France (a city, I confess, I had never heard of before). I crossed the Atlantic from New York City to Le Havre, France, on the 1936 Cunard ocean liner, the original "Queen Mary," a wonderful Art Deco ship (now docked in Long Beach, California, as a tourist attraction). Once in Toulouse, it was made clear to me that I was not obliged to pursue the course of study originally proposed, so I registered for a course in Greek and Roman art, and then I learned that across town there was the Institut Catholique where one could study Hebrew, Arabic, and even Akkadian! Abbé Maurice Baillet welcomed me warmly in his courses of Hebrew and Akkadian, and I started Arabic with another faculty member. While I kept up with the other students in the classes, I have to confess that I did not learn a great deal beyond the scripts and rudimentary grammar.

Hebrew and Arabic use alphabetic scripts, so the script is not a real hurdle to learning the languages. Cuneiform is another matter. As the name implies, the script is made up of wedge-shaped marks. In the case of clay, the wedges are made with a reed stylus in the damp clay. In the case of stone, the wedges need to be chiseled into the stone. Cuneiform is a script that has been used to write many different languages, the first of which was Sumerian, the language of ancient Sumer that is unrelated to any other known language. Later, it was adapted, and somewhat modified, to write Akkadian (the term used to include both Babylonian and Assyrian). The script utilizes several hundred signs.

While I was in Toulouse, I had an opportunity to meet with Professor Georges Boyer, an elderly historian of law who was also a scholar of cuneiform. He was then preparing an edition of legal texts discovered by French excavators at the Syrian site of Mari and which appeared in 1958 as *Textes juridiques* in the series Archives Royales de Mari. He was the first professional Assyriologist I ever met.

Being in Europe meant it was possible to make brief visits to other areas of France. I was also able to make two trips to Spain, one to central Spain where there were lots of remnants of the Roman period. In the spring I hitchhiked with a German girl to Barcelona where we were able to get a boat to Palma de Mallorca. In the long Easter recess, I took a train to Denmark to visit my mother's relatives for the first time.

Even though the Fulbright paid enough for living expenses and a bit of travel, more extensive travel required other strategies. At that time, it was quite common for students to hitchhike (called "auto-stop" in some European languages) throughout

Europe, so I decided I would hitchhike to Greece or as far as I could get, stopping at night in youth hostels or inexpensive hotels. I especially wanted to visit the Roman ruins across southern France (Narbonne, Arles, Nimes, Fréjus, etc.). In Trieste, Italy, I was able to get a visa to travel through Yugoslavia. I had no concept of how little traffic there would be in Yugoslavia—the main north-south highway was cobblestones, and so little traveled that grass grew in the roadway. Yugoslavia was then still only slowly recovering from World War II. I saw many people walking barefoot along the roadway carrying their shoes, obviously to prevent unnecessary wear. Cars were few and far between, and I even had a few rides on donkey carts. Somewhere south of Belgrade, a young Greek man driving a German car stopped for me. I soon realized that he had a double purpose—not only to have someone to talk to for the long trip, but also to have an accomplice in his smuggling operation. He asked me to hide a number of wristwatches and women's nylon stockings in the bottom of my knapsack to smuggle into Greece. But his main purpose was to smuggle the car into Greece by having documents altered and the serial number filed off at a small town near the border. The customs agent gave up searching my knapsack before he got to the watches and nylons under my loaf of bread. My friend had no problem with the car. We crossed the border into Greece and drove on to Athens where I stayed with his family for several days. He also took me to Mycenae and Epidaurus (famous in the history of Greek medicine). Of course I visited the Parthenon and other famous sites (including the Areopagos where the Apostle Paul had preached) before taking an overnight boat to the island of Crete.

I had had a year of Classical Greek in college, but that was not much help with Modern Greek, though of course I could read the street signs perfectly well.

After a few days in Crete, during which I got to visit the site of Knossos (about 1600 B.C.), home of the legendary King Minos, I was able to go on to the Island of Rhodes for a few days and then to get passage on a tiny fishing boat to the small fishing village of Marmaris on the southwestern Turkish coast. Marmaris is now a tourist center, but it certainly was not at that time. I was able to find a small hotel. The sheets had obviously been slept in before, but there really was not much choice. I asked why the legs of the bed were sitting in cans of water. I was told that the water prevented bedbugs from getting into the bed. Maybe this worked—I did not get any bedbug bites! After a day or so there, I took a bus to Istanbul, where I stayed in an inexpensive hotel while I visited Hagia Sophia, the Blue Mosque, the Topkapı Palace Museum, the covered bazaar, and other major sites in Istanbul. But I wanted to go inland as well, so I took a bus to Ankara, the capital in central Anatolia, which had a fine museum of Hittite culture. I had hoped to visit the ruins of the ancient Hittite capital, Hattusha, but time was running out, so I took a train back to Istanbul and then to Western Europe. But the time in the Moslem areas of Yugoslavia and in Turkey had given me a foretaste of the Middle East.

The Danforth Fellowship paid not only tuition but also a stipend for living expenses and books. I applied to several graduate schools, but I really wanted to go to Johns Hopkins in Baltimore to study with W. F. Albright, whose book *From the Stone*

Age to Christianity had so excited me some years earlier. After a cross-country trip by Greyhound bus from Spokane, Washington, to Baltimore, I showed up at Johns Hopkins. Albright was Chairman of the Oriental Seminary (now called the Department of Near Eastern Studies), so, of course, I had to see him. He was interested that I had just spent a year in France, so he began to speak to me in French. I had read of his great language prowess and of the many languages he could speak, so I was curious to hear how good his spoken French was. It was only a couple of years later that I learned that this conversation was my language exam in French, which I had passed! I did not know in advance that 1957/58 was Albright's final year and that he was retiring, but I was glad to have had his courses in ancient Near Eastern history and Palestinian archaeology as well as a seminar on the Dead Sea Scrolls. I stayed in touch with him until he died.

In 1957/58, an advanced graduate student, Edward Campbell, taught Akkadian at Johns Hopkins. The next year, as I recall, Thomas Lambdin taught the second-year course. But fortunately for me, the following year, 1959, Johns Hopkins hired a full-time Assyriologist, W. G. Lambert, who, though originally from Birmingham, England, had been teaching in Toronto. His Toronto student, Kirk Grayson, followed him to Baltimore, so there were two of us who were serious about Assyriology.

The Johns Hopkins tradition was the study of a number of languages. Everyone took several years of Biblical Hebrew. Most of us took two or three years of Classical Arabic. I also had a couple of years of Egyptian hieroglyphics, as well as Ugaritic, the language written in an alphabetic cuneiform script in the area of ancient Ugarit on the coast of Syria. The only one of these languages that I have followed up on or that has proved particularly useful is Arabic, though the Classical Arabic we studied is a far cry from the Iraqi Arabic heard on the streets of Baghdad or spoken by our workmen. Nevertheless, I can usually get the gist of a radio news broadcast or a newspaper article in Modern Standard Arabic, which is based on Classical.

I wrote my Ph.D. dissertation under Lambert on Babylonian potency incantations, of which he had identified and copied new fragments, particularly in the British Museum (the dissertation was published in an expanded version in 1967 as *ŠÀ.ZI.GA: Ancient Mesopotamian Potency Incantations*). Kirk Grayson and I both were awarded our doctorate degrees on the same day in June 1962. While Grayson had been recruited for work on the *Assyrian Dictionary* in Chicago, Lambert had supported my application to the Baghdad School of the American Schools of Oriental Research for a fellowship to study Sumerian incantations in the Iraq Museum in Baghdad. Dr. Vaughn Crawford of the Metropolitan Museum in New York, who was a member of the Baghdad School Committee, had arranged for me to stay at the British School of Archaeology in Baghdad with whose expedition he had worked several seasons at the old Assyrian capital Nimrud (ancient Kalhu, Calah of the Old Testament). When passing through Chicago that summer, I visited the Oriental Institute and met with Professors Leo Oppenheim and Erica Reiner, but I also met Donald Hansen, who was a member of the Oriental Institute expedition to Nippur. He urged me to pay a visit to Nippur while I was in Iraq.

In late summer 1962 I headed for Iraq, traveling on the Norwegian ship "Stavengerfjord" to Copenhagen, where a cousin met me and traveled with me to Jutland, the peninsula which is the mainland of Denmark, where I was to visit Danish family (I stayed with my grandfather's youngest brother and his family). While there, I fell ill with hepatitis, conjectured to have been contracted from eating contaminated shellfish in Baltimore. I spent a month in a hospital in Skive, the principal town in that part of Jutland, and then recuperated with cousins before I was strong enough to continue by train to Baghdad, stopping each night to spend the night in a hotel to rest. After a couple of days of rest in Istanbul, I boarded a train bound for Baghdad. On the platform I heard the news that Eleanor Roosevelt, the much-admired widow of President Franklin Roosevelt, had died. The slow train (I think it was an extension of the Simplon Orient Express, though certainly not the luxurious one made famous by Agatha Christie) made frequent stops across Turkey, where passengers could get off and buy provisions or buy from vendors on the platform who crowded near the train windows at every station. Among the passengers in my compartment was an elderly Iraqi couple traveling to Baghdad. They had a small primus that they lit occasionally to brew tea, which they shared with me. The further we traveled, the more the sights and smells became Middle Eastern—the calls of the muezzin, the herds of camels, the sound of spoken Turkish and then Arabic. As the sun rose on the last morning, I caught sight through the train window of the Malwiyah (the spiral minaret in Samarra which I recognized from having seen it on a series of Iraqi postage stamps). After the long dusty overland journey, it was a relief to arrive at the British School where I heard native speakers of English for the first time in a long while. Despite the horrors we associate with Baghdad these days, it seemed then to be a magical moment, the culmination of a long dream.

The British School of Archaeology was then headquartered in an old Ottoman Turkish house on the bank of the Tigris directly across the river from the Zia Hotel (I believe it is called the Tia Hotel in Agatha Christie novels) where archaeologists had traditionally stayed in Baghdad. The house had the typical central courtyard, surrounded by rooms on the ground floor and on the second floor (first floor in British terminology).

Among the young British who were at the School that year was Julian Reade, who has become well known as an authority on Assyrian sculpture and on British excavations in Assyria. He went to the Iraq Museum each morning, so he showed me what bus would drop me right across the street from the Museum and he introduced me to officials and young colleagues there. This was the original Iraq Museum, not its successor on the other side of the Tigris that was looted in the aftermath of the 2003 invasion of Iraq. The old museum was small and there were no special facilities for visiting researchers, but the Director of the Museum, Faraj Basmachi, had a small table set up for me in his office near a window so I had good natural light for reading cuneiform tablets. He facilitated my getting the cuneiform tablets I wanted to study.

The Iraq Department of Antiquities was without doubt one of the most professional of any in the Arab world. When I arrived in Baghdad, the Director General of Antiquities was Taha Baqir, and the Director of Excavations was Fuad Safar (a Christian). Both had graduate degrees from the University of Chicago. Taha Baqir retired from his position and died a number of years ago, but Fuad Safar remained a towering presence and the intellectual center of the Department until his tragic death in 1978 in an automobile wreck when en route to visit a site in an area of salvage excavations.

In November 1962 there was a bit of excitement at the British School when they got word of the impending visit of the British archaeologist Max Mallowan and his wife Agatha Christie. We were all told that we were to address her only as Mrs. Mallowan and that we were not to mention her mystery novels or her plays. As it happened, when they arrived, they had just the night before attended a celebration of the fifteenth year of her play "The Mousetrap" in London, and they were still wearing the clothes they had worn to the celebration the evening before. Due to turbulence en route, a flight attendant (they were called stewardesses then) had spilled a whole tray of Coca-Cola on her but, unfazed, she soaked her skirt in a bathtub and changed. The next day (a Friday) a trip had been planned for Babylon, so I finally got to see fabled Babylon. It was a disappointment to find that the Tower of Babel was now a deep, water-filled hole in the ground and that no one knew for sure where the Hanging Gardens of Babylon had been located. However, there was a wonderful tranquility walking among the groves of date palms along the slowly moving Euphrates. Now, so many years later, the phrase that comes to mind when I think of Babylon is from Psalm 137, "By the waters of Babylon, there we sat down and wept."

At the School, all residents had breakfast on their own schedule, but lunch and dinner were taken together in the ground-floor dining room. The Brits apparently all learn at school the art of telling amusing stories, and we heard a good many, but I felt somewhat out of my element. One evening at dinner, Mrs. Mallowan good-naturedly called me "Robert-the-Silent," and it is true that I was rather silent. Following British custom, tea was served every afternoon around 4:30 in the second floor sitting room, usually with small cookies that the Persian cook, Ali, had baked. Mrs. Mallowan was often sitting there reading a murder mystery or knitting.

Tea might be the traditional British black tea or what is called *chai hamuth* (literally "bitter tea"), which is made from dried crushed Basra limes (*numi Basra*). The latter is nearly always sweetened with sugar. Both *chai hamuth* and regular tea are served in Iraqi teahouses in small glasses called *istakhan*. If one does not specify, the tea will be served with several teaspoons of sugar added. I always found it necessary to say "*kullish qalil*, very little."

Normally at meals (and especially at breakfast), the local Iraqi flat bread (called *khubuz*) was served. The local Iraqi wine (from northern Iraq) was not especially good, and was only rarely served, but one could get Lebanese wine occasionally. Each person could keep a personal bottle of alcohol in the bar in the sitting room for a cocktail before dinner. The local drink was *araq* (the Iraqi version of Turkish *raki*, Greek *ouzo*, etc.), an anise-flavored alcoholic drink to which water is added. Unique to Iraqi varieties of *araq*, as far as I know, is one called *mastaki* that tastes, to most non-Iraqis, like turpentine.

When I was first in Iraq, the value of the Iraqi dinar was tied to the British pound. In fact, the banking system was really a holdover from earlier British influence in Iraq, even to banks being closed on Boxing Day (the day after Christmas). Across from one of the main banks, the Rafidain, were the small stands of the money changers where most of us changed currency as needed.

One of the pleasures of living in Baghdad was visiting the *suq* (the Arabic word for what is elsewhere called a bazaar). Different areas were specialized in different things. The silver *suq* was dominated by elderly men with long beards (they were predominantly members of a religious group known as Mandaeans, whose religious rites, focused heavily on water, we could often see from the British School on the bank of the Tigris). Here one heard the gentle taps of the smiths' small mallets on the silver as they made the typical Iraqi *niello* work (napkin rings, cigarette cases, sometimes whole tea sets) decorated with scenes of boats on the Tigris, camels, and mosques. The copper *suq* was a very noisy place, with a great deal of hammering as the coppersmiths made copper pots and pans and other household utensils. There one had to shout to be heard over the din of the hammering. There was also a carpet *suq*. In the cloth *suq* one could choose a fabric, have measurements taken, and come back in a day or so to pick up a *disdasha* (the long dresslike garment traditionally worn by men) or a warm wool *abba* (very welcome for warmth in unheated rooms). This is the old, traditional part of the *suq*, between the Tigris and Rashid Street, one of the main thoroughfares of old Baghdad. On the other side of Rashid Street is the Shorjah, the spice *suq*, the area where one buys tea, coffee, pots and pans, and kitchen wares, but also the area where used Western style clothing was sold (an inexpensive place to buy warm clothing for wearing on archaeological digs). A report I first saw on April 20, 2005, says that the Shorjah has been destroyed by fire. Baghdad, along with Aleppo, had one of the great old *suq*s, largely unmodernized, except for dangling electric light bulbs. I think it is a cultural calamity that any part of it be lost.

It had been arranged that in late December I would go south to Afak to visit the Oriental Institute excavations at Nippur. I took a train to Diwaniyah, where the Nippur driver, Jabbar, was to meet me with the expedition Land Rover. The expedition had rented a house beside the canal and a few feet from the *suq* in Afak (and drove daily to the site, some seven miles away). There I met Donald Hansen again and the Field Director, Carl Haines, as well as Giorgio Buccellati, a student at the University of Chicago who was that season's epigrapher (responsible for finds of cuneiform texts). I greatly enjoyed visiting the site and participating in the work. I spent Christmas with the Nippur Expedition, but I then returned to Baghdad so Robert McCormick Adams, the new Director of the Oriental Institute, could have what had been my room.

In the early spring of 1963, I took a train north to Mosul so I could visit the British excavations at Nimrud. While I was there, they arranged a Friday outing to visit some of the Christian monasteries in Assyria, including Mar Behnam, one of the best-known monasteries and which is still in active use. A couple of the monks gave us a tour of the monastery. Especially in view of the very early establishment of Christianity in Assyria and its continuity to the present and the continuity of the population, I think there is every likelihood that ancient Assyrians are among the ancestors of modern Assyrians of the area.

In 1981 I was able to visit additional monasteries on a trip to the north arranged by the Directorate General of Antiquities. On this occasion they had arranged for the whole group to have lunch at a monastery. We were served some of the local wine. The extent and importance of Christianity in northern Iraq is probably little recognized in Europe or America. An excellent study (of which I own a set) is J. M. Fiey, *Assyrie chrétienne: Contribution à l'étude de l'histoire et de la géographie ecclésiastiques et monastiques de l'Iraq* [Christian Assyria: Contribution to the study of ecclesiastical and monastic history and geography in northern Iraq], 3 volumes (Beirut, 1965–68). Fiey also wrote a separate volume on Christian Mosul. Unfortunately, I have never had an opportunity for independent travel to Christian towns and villages in Iraq. In Baghdad I knew the Assyrian scholar, Donny George, former Director of the Iraq Museum. Ironically, most Assyrian Christians I know I met in Chicago, beginning with the late Fred Tamimi in the 1970s; subsequently his brother-in-law, Robert Paulissian, M.D.; the Northeastern Illinois University linguist Edward Odisho; Daniel Benjamin; and Norman Solkhah of Chicago, who founded a Mesopotamian museum in Chicago, to name only a few with whom I have had long and most cordial friendships.

In 1962/63 there were relatively few foreigners in Baghdad, and most were in the diplomatic corps, though several were there as commercial representatives (such as an American, who was married to an Italian woman, who was head of the Pan American Airlines office). I was readily integrated into the Anglophone group (which included a Danish couple who lived at Abu Ghraib—at that time, the center for dairy research). One of the frequent activities was a Friday picnic outing to visit various ancient sites reachable from Baghdad. This was a wonderful opportunity to get a feel for the geography and the climate and to see the native wildlife. The picnics usually featured bread and cheese, sometimes canned hams, and one couple regularly brought a thermos of martinis. But there were also frequent dinner parties at the homes of various diplomatic personnel where there was vivacious discussion of current political events, particularly in British homes where the men in the group separated from the women, usually for cigars and brandy after dinner. Later that year, and in subsequent years, many of these people used their Fridays for visits to our excavations, invariably bringing fresh fruits and vegetables that we could not get locally and occasionally an imported Danish ham. When the weather was hot, a cooler of beer such as Pilsner Urquell (or the excellent Iraqi beer, Ferida) was especially welcome.

Circumstances—and probably just plain luck—triggered events that were to lead to extraordinary finds of cuneiform tablets. Oriental Institute Director Robert Adams had decided that at the close of the season at Nippur, the Nippur Land Rover (owned by the Oriental Institute) should be used by the Oriental Institute's expedition at Choga Mish in Iranian Khuzestan (southwestern Iran), directed by Pinhas Delougaz and Helene Kantor, two of the senior professors of archaeology at the Oriental Institute. Adams asked Donald Hansen to drive it there and agreed to Donald's request that I accompany him. Due to Iraqi customs regulations, we were not allowed to take the Land Rover out of the country without posting a security deposit (something like $1,500 as I recall), which Adams authorized the Oriental Institute in Chicago to wire to Baghdad (wiring funds was perfectly easy in the banking system then in use). We got our Iranian visas and then drove to Basrah and spent the night, but then there was a heavy rain, so we spent another night hoping the mud that lay between Basrah and the Iranian border would have dried sufficiently. Despite being bogged down in the mud several times, we made it to a sleepy border crossing where we crossed into Iran and made our way to Ahwaz, where we spent the night before going on to Choga Mish. We had been in Iran only a couple of days when we got word that there had been a revolution in Iraq, and the Leader (*al-zaʾim*), Abd al-Karim Qassem, had been killed (February 9, 1963) and the borders of Iraq had been closed. I spent ten days or so participating in the excavations at Choga Mish. I was also able to visit the nearby site of Jundi Shapur, well known as the location of one of the Nestorian (also called the Assyrian Church of the East) schools that had a leading role in preserving (in Syriac) Greek writings on medicine, astronomy, and mathematics. There is a new book by Raymond Le Coz, *Les médecins nestoriens au Moyen Âge: Les maîtres des arabes* [The Nestorian physicians in the Middle Ages: The teachers of the Arabs] (Paris, 2004). He has an excellent discussion of the medical school at Jundi Shapur on pp. 53–66. I also took advantage of being in Iran to visit Persepolis, Shiraz, Isfahan, and then Tehran, before joining a busload of Shiite pilgrims en route to Baghdad.

When Donald Hansen returned to Iraq, he found that the security deposit could not be refunded and taken out of the country. He then made a bold proposal to Director Adams. There was a site a few miles from Nippur that he had visited several years before where the surface of the tell was littered with pottery of the Early Dynastic period (mid-third millennium B.C.) and earlier, levels that lie many meters below the surface at Nippur. He proposed using that money for a brief sounding at the site of Abu Salabikh. The Department of Antiquities approved the request and loaned us two or three large canvas tents that served as work areas, dining room, and sleeping quarters. I was listed as epigrapher. Vaughn Crawford was to join us later from his season with the British at Nimrud and was to be the photographer. Donald Hansen hired as a cook an elderly man from India who had come to Iraq in the time of World War I. He had cooked for various foreign families in Baghdad and, in spite of our limited facilities, was innovative in serving us good meals with locally available products (in the spring it seemed to be mostly zucchini squash, tomatoes, and onions, though we could buy eggs and live chickens from local farmers). Iraq had good plants for processing jams made from local fruits—especially figs, though they also made jam from carrots. Dates were always available and very cheap. From the Nippur Expedition we had borrowed cots, mattresses, sheets, pots and pans, and dishes (the English-made set that had been used by the Oriental Institute in its excavations at Megiddo in Palestine in the 1930s). We also borrowed their refrigerator, which operated by burning kerosene. Kerosene lamps provided our lighting. Some of these lamps used mantles (defined by the dictionary as "a lacy hood or sheath of some refractory material that gives light by incandescence when placed over a flame"). Such lamps had to be pumped up constantly to maintain enough pressure to provide a good light. The disadvantage of such light is that it attracts vast numbers of insects, making it a challenge to do much work at night by lamplight.

People who live in cities can have no idea of how much more of the heavens are visible at night when there is no light pollution at all. It is easy to understand that the rise of astronomy should have occurred in such a land.

At the highest point of the mound was an area where heavy burning had turned the soil a reddish color. We decided to start our excavations there. We soon found that mud-brick walls had been so thoroughly baked in a conflagration that they were baked red. In the first few days, two cuneiform tablets were discovered, both baked hard, apparently in the huge fire that consumed the building. They had to be soaked for days in changes of water to dissolve the accretion of salt on their surface. Later, a number of small, unbaked fragments of tablets began to turn up in the debris. Vaughn Crawford took these to Nippur, where he baked them in the Nippur kiln (fueled by diesel). It was soon obvious to me that some of these fragments had lists of geographical names and that others appeared to be literary. One very thick tablet had a colophon on the back (giving the name of the scribe). Amazingly, the names were Semitic, that is, of the same language group as Babylonian and Assyrian, rather than the unrelated Sumerian language expected in the mid-third millennium. Adams, back in Chicago, seemed sufficiently impressed with the finds that he sent some additional funding, so we were able to continue until early June, when it became much too hot for fieldwork in southern Iraq.

We wanted to return to the site, but were not able to arrange it until January 1965. Almost immediately, in the same area, we came upon a huge pile of unbaked cuneiform tablets, obviously thrown into a rubbish pit along with broken pottery, fish bones, and bones of slaughtered animals. Selma al-Radi, the representative of the Iraqi Department of Antiquities, and I spent the next several weeks with the help of one Sherqati workman (Sherqat is the modern village near the ancient site of Assur; men from the village were trained by the Germans excavating Assur early in the twentieth century in the art of excavating mud-brick; their descendants have been the traditional skilled workmen on most archaeological expeditions until comparatively recently) carefully excavating the tablets—several hundreds of fragments, and some very large tablets with hundreds of lines of writing. It soon became obvious that some of these were truly literary in the sense of *belles lettres*. Selma has given an account of the adventures—and misadventures—of this season in her article, "Digging with Donald," in Erica Ehrenberg, ed., *Leaving No Stones Unturned: Essays on the Ancient Near East and Egypt in Honor of Donald P. Hansen* (Winona Lake, Indiana, 2002), pp. ix–xii.

After the close of the brief season, we transported the tablets to Nippur to the newly constructed expedition house where, for the next couple of months, I labored daily at baking and cleaning the tablets (along with Selma al-Radi). So that I could bake every day, I constructed a second kiln, for after firing, the tablets need to cool in the kiln for a day or so before they are cool enough to handle.

Before turning the tablets over to the Iraq Museum, I made Latex molds of most of them so that they could be cast in plaster of Paris in Chicago for study. Back in Chicago, with access to books, I was able to identify some of the literary texts as the same compositions known from copies from hundreds of years later. I spent several years of evenings and weekends working on my drawings of the inscriptions—a slow and laborious task. This involved several trips to the Iraq Museum to compare my drawings with the originals so I could further revise them. One of these visits was a month in the summer of 1972. Summer temperatures in Baghdad are often in the 120 to 140 degrees Fahrenheit range. The Iraq Museum had its air-conditioning system turned to the maximum, so I was more comfortable wearing a sweater in the museum, but one was hit with a blast of hot air when stepping outside. At the time, only a couple of luxury hotels had air conditioning. Most hotels had only an overhead fan. I decided then not to plan another summer visit to Baghdad.

Thus the site of Abu Salabikh (ancient name still unknown), and its tablets, whose discovery was due to fortuitous circumstances, revealed an important, and unexpected, aspect of mid-third-millennium literature and scholarship and demonstrated that people speaking a Semitic language, rather than being simple herdsmen tending their flocks, were deeply immersed in a center of Sumerian learning. I published these texts in a thick volume in 1974 (*Inscriptions from Tell Abū Ṣalābīkh,* Oriental Institute Publications, vol. 99 [Chicago, 1974]). Several compositions were present in a number of fragmentary or somewhat damaged copies, and it was possible for me to reconstruct several compositions in virtually complete form and to present them in transliteration. The conventions for writing Sumerian were substantially different in the mid-third millennium than in the texts from several centuries later that are more familiar to us. While some passages we can translate with reasonable confidence, and can present tentative translations of others, some still defy us, though a great deal of progress has been made (mainly by other scholars) since I first published these texts more than thirty years ago.

Because of my extensive experience with texts of the mid-third millennium B.C., I was in a unique position to appreciate the importance of an extraordinary discovery in the mid-1970s of tablets of similar age by an Italian expedition from the University of Rome at the ancient site of Ebla (modern Tell Mardikh) near Aleppo in Syria. Initial reports, both in the popular press and in scholarly journals, caused great excitement among Bible scholars who were hearing that the names of Abraham, Sodom and Gomorrah, and a wealth of other names familiar from the Old Testament were found in these new tablets. Several of us, including my late colleague Ignace J. Gelb, who were experienced in the peculiarities of third-millennium cuneiform spelling conventions, were skeptical. Gelb's initial analysis was published as "Thoughts about Ibla: A Preliminary Evaluation, March 1977," *Syro-Mesopotamian Studies* 1, pp. 3–30 in 1977. In 1978 I was invited to discuss these finds in a lecture to the Chicago Society of the Archaeological Institute of America. Then I was asked to give my perspective on the topic in an article in *Biblical Archeologist* ("The Ebla Tablets: An Interim Perspective," *Biblical Archeologist* 43 [1980]: 76–87), which is an updated and shortened version of my 1978 lecture. About that time, a film was produced for airing on PBS stations. It was called "The Royal Archives of Ebla" and included interviews with both Gelb and me. Such was the frenzy in some biblical circles that a well-known radio evangelist included Ebla on his Holy Land tours! In the end, sober scholarship prevailed and the question of Ebla and the Bible is now a dead issue.

In 1982 I had an opportunity to visit the site of Ebla. I had accompanied two Chicago couples and a couple from Australia on a trip to Yemen and Syria that spring. While the others terminated their visit in Damascus, I wanted to stay on to visit Ebla, since it had been a focus of a lot of my scholarly activity for several years. The Syrian ambassador to Washington (whom I had met when he was in Chicago) had urged me to present myself at the Department of Antiquities. Indeed, I found that because of my publications and lectures concerned with the disputes about the Ebla tablets, my name was well known to the Director General of Antiquities and other officials, and they received me most cordially.

It was easy to get a ticket on a modern bus going to Aleppo. En route we passed through the ancient city of Hama (especially famous for its water wheels) and saw with our own eyes the recent devastation of the city caused by the putting down of a local uprising. In Aleppo I stayed at the Baron Hotel, the same hotel where archaeologists normally stayed in the 1930s (Agatha Christie and her husband Max Mallowan were regular guests during their years in Syria) and which had been little modernized since then. That year Chicago friends and colleagues, Paul Zimansky and his wife Elizabeth Stone were in Aleppo, so we jointly hired a car and driver to take us to Ebla and to some of the Roman and medieval ruins in the area. The Italian team had not yet arrived at Ebla for that season's work, but we were able to visit the site and get a good idea of the architecture of the third-millennium palace where the tablets had been discovered.

I now backtrack in time and geography to Washington State. As a child and teenager, I attended the only local church, the Evangelical United Brethren (a denomination that subsequently merged with the United Methodist Church). Our exposure to other Christian denominations, even Protestant ones, was limited, and I doubt that many of us were even acquainted with any Roman Catholics. College was a bit more diverse but not much. It was not until I lived in France that I had regular contact with Roman Catholics. One was a fellow Fulbright Scholar with whom I planned a trip to Italy during the Christmas vacation. He had a cousin who was a priest in Rome and who was able to get us tickets for a "semi-private" audience with Pope Pius XII. The Pope who succeeded Pius XII was John XXIII, whom I came to admire greatly. In June 1963 I was ready to leave Baghdad, so I reserved a seat in a shared taxi to go to Jerusalem. Because of the extreme heat in the daytime, the taxi traveled across the desert at night. Upon arriving in Damascus the next morning, we learned that Pope John had died during the night. After a change of taxis in Damascus, it was on to Jerusalem. At that time, the Old City of Jerusalem was under the control of Jordan and could be reached easily from Damascus. Because I was a Fellow of the American Schools of Oriental Research that year, I was able to stay at their facility in Jerusalem for a modest charge. In Jerusalem it seemed that everyone was talking about the Pope's death, and church authorities announced that there would be a High Pontifical Mass in the Church of the Holy Sepulchre, which I was able to attend and which I found very moving.

While in Jerusalem, I took a day's trip to visit Bethlehem. Whether the Church of the Nativity covers the real birthplace of Jesus or not, it is very moving for anyone raised a Christian to visit the site so long associated with his birth.

I made my way from Jerusalem to Beirut and then on to Istanbul where I visited the archaeological museum. This museum has a fabulous collection of Near Eastern antiquities since, when Middle Eastern countries were still part of the Ottoman Empire, the government's share went to the capital, Istanbul. I met colleagues there, including Muazzez Çığ, who was in charge of the collection of cuneiform tablets, as well as Veysel Donbaz, who is now the head of the collection. I went on to Berlin to study some of the tablets in their collection from the German excavations at Assur. At that time (and for a number of subsequent visits in the next years) one found a pension or hotel in West Berlin and made the daily crossing of the Berlin Wall at Checkpoint Charlie into East Berlin. Colleagues there (among them Liane Jakob-Rost and Evelyn Klengel-Brandt) were warmly welcoming.

I eventually got to London, where the annual meeting of Assyriologists (Rencontre Assyriologique) was being held. The Rencontre, normally an annual event, was held mostly in Western Europe in the earlier years, but in 1967 it was held in Chicago for the first time in the U.S. In 2004 it was held in South Africa, and the 2005 meeting again was held in Chicago. It is a collegial gathering of scholars of ancient Mesopotamia and nearby lands, whether philologists, archaeologists, or art historians. At the 1963 London Rencontre I was able to meet (or at least see and listen to) some of the leading scholars whose books and articles I had studied. Although I have returned frequently to the British Museum to study cuneiform tablets, for the duration of the conference, the Students' Room was closed to visitors, so I was not able to study any tablets at that time.

While still in Baghdad, I had received an offer of an appointment as a Research Associate on the *Chicago Assyrian Dictionary*, which I eagerly accepted, as my first employment as an Assyriologist. The annual salary of $5,000 sounded good to someone who had never had a salaried job. I arrived in Chicago in the fall of 1963 to find a small apartment and to take up my appointment at the University of Chicago. I soon found a congenial group of people, mostly either graduate students or Assistant Professors, who were approximately in my age group and who shared an interest in the ancient or modern Middle East or the Mediterranean area in general. Every couple of weeks one of us would host a small party, sometimes enlivened by a young American woman who had learned to play the Turkish *saz* (a stringed instrument) very well and who had a beautiful singing voice. One such gathering turned out not to be a party, but rather a solemn gathering of mourners, the day after the assassination of President John F. Kennedy.

One of the young women in our group worked in the Oriental Institute administrative office. She advised me that, if I expected to get a better salary, I would stand a better chance if I had a job offer from elsewhere. As it happened, my Johns Hopkins classmate Kirk Grayson had been teaching at Temple University in Philadelphia but had been appointed to a position in his native Canada. I applied for his position and received an offer. This resulted, in 1964, in my receiving a modest salary increase but also an appointment as Assistant Professor of Assyriology in the Department of Oriental Languages (as it was then called, for it included Chinese and Japanese) and an appointment as Associate Editor of the *Assyrian Dictionary*.

An administrative peculiarity of the Oriental Institute is that it is a research institution that grants no degrees. Degrees in its subject matters are offered through what is now called the Department of Near Eastern Languages and Civilizations, which is one of the departments in the Humanities Division. So this meant that I was then in a tenure-track position. Several years later, when I received an offer of an appointment at Johns Hopkins, I was promoted to Associate Professor (with tenure).

I enjoyed my work on the *Assyrian Dictionary*, but I was also eager to follow up my own research interests. I often returned to the Oriental Institute in the evenings after supper and usually came in on weekends as well, either to use the vocabulary files of the *Assyrian Dictionary* or to use the library.

It was exciting to be working with some of the top scholars in the field of Assyriology, and they fostered an attitude of expanding one's scholarly horizons. We young Research Associates were encouraged to sit in on courses, especially the courses in Sumerian, the very ancient non-Semitic language of Mesopotamia. There was also a tradition of weekly reading sessions where we collectively read through newly published volumes of texts that had been published only in drawings of the cuneiform (a practice several of us continue, even in our retirement). It was partly an effort to document new occurrences of words that would be cited in future volumes of the *Assyrian Dictionary* but also, for us young Assyriologists, to develop our skills at reading a variety of genres of texts.

In 1963 the first volume of Franz Köcher's *Die babylonisch-assyrische Medizin* was published. While it was his intention to follow up the publication of his hand drawings of the cuneiform with transliterations and translations, at his death in 2002 only the six volumes of his drawings had been published. Babylonian medical texts are a special challenge to read, as they include a great many names of plants (mostly unidentified) whose Babylonian names are often hidden behind the Sumerian words that served as sort of an abbreviation. In addition, the texts are filled with technical vocabulary for the procedures of preparation of medications and their administration. But I was determined to learn to read these texts, so I plunged in, reading and rereading as I became more familiar with the genre. Babylonian medical texts have been one of my principal specialties within the vast domain of cuneiform studies. In 2004 I was appointed to the two-member editorial board of the series Die babylonisch-assyrische Medizin published by de Gruyter in Berlin.

Another interest I developed was Babylonian divination, that is, the "science" of foretelling events from omens. There are vast collections of such omens of many different kinds. The Babylonians believed that the gods wrote messages on the livers and other organs of sheep that experts could interpret. In the first millennium B.C. astrology became increasingly important, especially for the Assyrian Court. Monstrous births (such as a three-legged chicken or a two-headed lamb) were considered very bad omens that might affect the king. I have made a particular study of the liver omens, which, like medical texts, form a highly technical genre.

Leo Oppenheim and Erica Reiner were very flexible about the months I spent working on the *Assyrian Dictionary*, thus permitting me to serve as epigraphist on the Oriental Institute's Nippur Expedition in 1964/65, 1976, 1977, 1981, and 1985. Nippur, the ancient religious capital of Sumer, was first excavated by Americans from the University of Pennsylvania in 1888. In 1948 the Oriental Institute, in collaboration with the University of Pennsylvania (and at times other institutions) resumed excavations there. By far the greatest proportion of Sumerian literature known to us has been recovered from the excavations at Nippur, principally those carried out by the University of Pennsylvania at the end of the nineteenth and beginning of the twentieth centuries.

In 1964 en route to Iraq I stopped in Jordan to visit my Johns Hopkins friend and colleague, Ray Cleveland, who was living in Jericho. A friend of his from the Jericho refugee camp joined us on an overnight trip to visit Petra. We got up the next morning to snow, the first the young man had ever seen. Despite rain, we spent an enjoyable day visiting the spectacular site. Back in Jericho we were able to visit the Dead Sea and the area of the caves where the Dead Sea Scrolls had been discovered.

Occasionally when we had visitors at Nippur, we would arrange for camel rides (there were plenty of camels in the area). On one occasion a member of the Oriental Institute Visiting Committee and her daughter were visiting, and a camel ride to the nearby (several miles) site of Drehem was planned. Camels have notoriously bad breath and can be rather contrary, not to mention providing a rather rough ride, and we were all rather sore by the time we got back to the expedition house.

One of the facts of life in southern Iraq is the occurrence of sandstorms, sometimes lasting several days at a time. On the excavation site wearing goggles helped somewhat, but nevertheless, one's hair and clothing were soon full of fine sand. To minimize the amount that filtered in between gaps between windowpanes in my room at the expedition house, I employed the old technique of wetting newspapers and stuffing every crevice as tightly as possible. While this helped some, fine sand was always ubiquitous on tables, chairs, and in one's bed.

In addition to my several seasons at Nippur, I was able to join Donald Hansen and Vaughn Crawford as epigraphist and archaeologist on the Metropolitan Museum-New York University, Institute of Fine Arts Expedition to al-Hiba in 1968/69 and 1970/71. Each year a student from the University of Chicago accompanied me, first Elizabeth Carter, now a professor of archaeology at the University of California at Los Angeles, and in the second year Abdullah Masry, who returned to his native Saudi Arabia to a position in the Department of Antiquities.

The site of al-Hiba, first mentioned above, is now known to be ancient Lagash, the capital of one of the Sumerian city-states of the third millennium B.C. It was a low mound that lay on the very edge of one of the great marshes of southern Iraq. The nearest town was Shaṭra, but the site could be reached then only by canal, meaning a couple of hours by a motorized boat. The people in the area lived much as their Sumerian predecessors did thousands of years ago, for ecological conditions had changed little. In excavations, we find baked clay model boats that look just like the ones called *tarada* that are the means of locomotion in the marshes, propelled by long punting poles.

The only practical building material in the area was reeds from the marshes, so all our structures for sleeping quarters, work areas, dining, etc., were made of reeds by local workmen accustomed to building with reeds. (For illustrations of such reed structures and the process of constructing them, see Ochsenschlager's book cited below. Such structures very closely resemble depictions on ancient cylinder seals from Mesopotamia.) To our chagrin, we discovered that in their first year of use, reed houses leak when it rains, which it did a lot! The marshes were an area of incredible beauty and tranquility, teeming with waterfowl and fish. Flocks of storks often flew overhead. Occasionally, especially after a heavy rain, we also saw a wild boar. The local economy was largely dependent on reeds and water buffalo. They provided milk, and their dung was collected and mixed with straw for fuel for baking bread. The way of life of these people, before many modern developments reached them, and before Saddam Hussein largely destroyed their way of life by draining the marshes, has recently been documented by Edward Ochsenschlager in his book *Iraq's Marsh Arabs in the Garden of Eden* (Philadelphia, 2004). A great many of his photographs were taken in the late 1960s and early 1970s.

Although not easily accessible for residents of Baghdad, at Christmas 1968 our Danish friends from Abu Ghraib, Kirsten and Hans "Bielle" Bielefeldt, came to visit with their two children. Although we could not have a traditional Christmas tree, we fashioned one from a dried shrub and decorated it with small red and white Danish flags and some foliage from the marshes. On Christmas Eve, following Danish customs, we sang and danced out one end and in the other of the reed house that served as our living room and dining room. Such are the memories of Christmas in the marsh area of Iraq, far from the Santas and the commercialism of an American Christmas.

Our workmen were entirely from local villages, and there needed to be a certain delicacy in hiring men from the various sheikhs' groups. This is a very conservative area, and there was a discreet request, made through the representative of the Iraqi Department of Antiquities, that the female members of our staff cover their lower extremities more carefully (this was the era of the mini-skirt!). Nevertheless, at lunch break, there would often be someone who played a drum and someone else a flute. One small elderly man, obviously something of a "character" among the group, sang and danced with many lewd gestures, much to the merriment of the other workmen. Our 1970/71 season at al-Hiba ended tragically. While I and a couple of others stayed behind to close up camp, the first boatload of our expedition members and some of the household staff left to return to Baghdad. Another boat speeding on the canal in the opposite direction rammed their boat, and Roberta Lewis was killed instantly.

I decided in 1968 that en route to Iraq, I would visit Afghanistan, a country that held a great fascination for me, especially the small area that used to be known as Kafiristan, "Land of the Heathens," for the area had never been converted to Islam until forced to convert in the nineteenth century, when it was renamed Nuristan, "Land of Light." Afghanistan's national airline had flights to Kabul from Beirut, so I went, staying in an old and somewhat decrepit hotel in Kabul. One of the young managers there spoke quite good English and offered to accompany me if I hired a car and driver to an area in the south where his uncle owned a number of villages. It happened that the uncle was away, but the family welcomed us, and we slept on mats in the small building that served as the compound's mosque. We spent a couple of days walking to the various villages, always warmly welcomed with tea or fresh watermelon. Here in these villages I could see traditional craftsmen at work making rope, making bullets, and watched a woman weaving on a large flat loom. Returning to Kabul, I hired another car and driver to take me to Bamiyan in the heart of the Hindu Kush Mountains. En route, we passed great numbers of nomads coming down from the mountains for winter, with small children, chickens, and lambs tied to loaded camels. The women in particular were dressed in colorful clothing. At Bamiyan there was a rest house that offered beds and a simple meal for visitors. From there I could look across the valley and see the two giant statues of the Buddha carved into the cliff and which I was able to explore in detail the following day—the same Buddhas that the Taliban destroyed several years ago. Unfortunately, because of political tensions, no foreigners were allowed in Nuristan. However, I was able to purchase in Kabul a Nuristan harp that very closely resembles harps played in Sumer thousands of years ago. After getting an export authorization from the National Museum, I was able to have it sent to me in Chicago, where it still sits, unplayed, in my Chicago home.

One of the pleasant aspects of my years in Baghdad was the possibility of accompanying Iraqi friends for an evening in a *casino* along the bank of the Tigris. An Iraqi *casino* is not a gambling establishment, but a sort of outdoor café. These are located along Abu Nuwas Street, named for the Abbasid poet Abu Nuwas (born about A.D. 756) from the time of the Caliph Harun al-Rashid when Baghdad was at the height of its glory. At street level, one can choose a live fish (called *mazquf*) from several held in a tank of water. The fish will later be roasted over wood. In the meantime, one descends to a lower level where tables are set up fairly far apart in a grassy area. Here one can order *araq* or beer and typical appetizers such as pistachios, *jajik* (a yogurt and cucumber dip), or fresh fruits in season (such as plums). Typically songs sung by Umm Kalthum, a famous Egyptian singer who was much loved throughout the Arab world, would be played from tape recordings. Especially in hot weather, this is probably the coolest place in Baghdad and certainly provides a relaxing evening.

In all my years in Iraq, I never felt I was in the slightest danger (except on the two-lane highways where Iraqi drivers take death-defying risks constantly, especially when behind a slow-moving truck). In fact, I used to say that I felt safer on the streets of Baghdad than I did in Chicago. Our expeditions have been in Iraq at various times of international crisis, including the 1967 Middle East war, but we never felt that we were personally at risk.

In 1971, at the death of Keith Seele who had been Editor since 1948, I was appointed to the editorship of the *Journal of Near Eastern Studies*. William Rainey Harper, who was later to become the first President of the University of Chicago, had founded its predecessor journal, *Hebraica*, in 1884. The *Journal of Near Eastern Studies* is one of the principal journals in America devoted to the Near and Middle East, though its coverage is generally prehistory to the end of the Ottoman Empire about 1918. I have served now (2005) as its editor for 34 years, but anticipate being relieved of the responsibility within a year or so. For most of those years I have had the expert help of Paula von Bechtolsheim, who is now Managing Editor. Her background in studying Turkish and other modern Middle Eastern languages has been an invaluable complement to my own studies of the ancient Near East, and her knowledge of German and French has also proved to be important.

My editorial experience has been put to use in several other publications. My friend and colleague McGuire Gibson organized a symposium at the Oriental Institute on seals and sealing practices in the ancient Near East. I did most of the editorial work (and in the days before most of us had computers, it involved a lot of retyping on a manual typewriter and cutting and pasting by hand); it was published as *Seals and Sealing in the Ancient Near East* in Malibu in 1977 as a volume of the series Bibliotheca Mesopotamica. He also organized another symposium, this one on bureaucracy in the ancient Near East, for which I again did a lot of the editorial work. It was published as *The Organization of Power: Aspects of Bureaucracy in the Ancient Near East* by the Oriental Institute in 1987 (it went out of print so quickly that a slightly revised version was published in 1991). In between these two symposiums, the Chicago Rug Society, of which I was a member, decided to mount an exhibition of Kurdish weavings at the Block Gallery at Northwestern University. I served as Editor for the beautifully illustrated book that accompanied the exhibition and symposium, *Discoveries from Kurdish Looms* (Evanston, 1983). Among the participants and authors was William Eagleton, an American diplomat who had spent considerable time in Iraqi Kurdistan and whom I knew from his posting at the American embassy in Baghdad. I saw him again in Damascus in 1985 where he was then the American ambassador.

In 1974 I was asked by the chief editor of the Time-Life series Great Ages of Man to be their principal consultant for the book *The Birth of Writing*. While the actual writing was done by one of their professional writers, they employ scholars as consultants to advise on factual matters, questions of emphasis, on sources for photographs, and to advise on other areas to explore. This involved a number of visits to their headquarters in New York City and even a trip to upstate New York to consult on the premises of their artist, who was doing the drawings and paintings for their illustrations. Their pay at the time was $100 a day, which earned me a nice supplementary income that year, plus giving me the satisfaction on working on a worthwhile project. Later I was asked to advise them on the second edition of *The Cradle of Civilization* (about ancient Mesopotamia).

While the Oriental Institute was not able to follow up its soundings at Abu Salabikh in 1963 and 1965 with full-scale excavations, the British School of Archaeology, recognizing the site's great potential to provide information on the third millennium in that part of Iraq, decided to undertake excavations. In 1976 Nicholas Postgate, the Field Director of the expedition, invited me to join the expedition as epigraphist, which I was happy to do. Once again, it was a matter of living in tents, though this time it was the fall of the year, so instead of the weather getting hotter and hotter as in 1963, this time it got colder and colder. Late in the fall, at the time of a fairly long religious holiday, Postgate allowed several of us to take the Land Rover for a trip of a couple of days into Kurdistan, an area that had generally been largely inaccessible to foreigners. So for the first—and only—time I got to visit Kurdish towns and villages whose names were then largely unknown to most people in Europe or America.

In 1981 the Iraqi government invited me (and several other colleagues from Chicago and other American and European universities) to attend the Third International Symposium on Babylon, Assur, and Himrin in Baghdad in November. It was well organized, with copious lunches and dinners. The tours included a two-day trip to northern Iraq, including a stop in Haditha. One of the overnight stays was in large tents. Evening entertainment that day included singing and dancing by Iraqi gypsies (singular *Kawli*, plural *Kawaliyyah*) such as we had seen a number of times in southern Iraq. Weather in northern Iraq was getting decidedly cold, so we had a certain amount of discomfort, but the hospitality was warm and generous, typical of the Iraq I knew.

In 1984 the international meeting of Assyriologists was held in Leningrad (whose name was subsequently restored to St. Petersburg). This provided an opportunity for me to visit the Soviet Union for the first time. I went a couple of days early to visit museums (such as the Hermitage) and various other attractions in the city. My Toronto friend and colleague Grant Frame had earlier suggested that we sign up for a two-week guided tour of Soviet Central Asia (this was the only practical way to visit this area at the time). I eagerly jumped at the chance. Following the Rencontre in Leningrad, we spent several days in Moscow, where our tour was leaving from. We had two young women as our tour guides. They were very friendly and congenial on the tour buses, but they were not allowed to sit with us at meals. At each stop, local guides gave detailed talks. Seeing the Islamic monuments in Samarkand and Bukhara was especially interesting. Tblisi, in Soviet Georgia, was quite different, for here one saw churches rather than mosques. It was interesting to find that one could buy Danish beer more cheaply in Central Asia than in Copenhagen, where I had a day's layover en route to Chicago.

In the 1985 season at Nippur, few cuneiform tablets were found, and I was not normally needed on the excavation, so I took over the responsibility of driving to Afak to buy the canisters of cooking gas we needed, to do shopping, and to pick up bread. I stood in line at the bakery to buy bread hot from the oven. That year we had not hired a local cook, and Beverly Armstrong, wife of staff member James Armstrong, did most of the cooking. However, I made the rice for both lunch and dinner, preparing it Iraqi style with a golden crust on the bottom. Among our guests that year were James Akins, the American ambassador to Saudi Arabia in the Nixon administration, and his wife Marjorie (Marney) who had been great friends of the Nippur Expedition when they lived in Baghdad in the early 1960s. I drove us one day to visit the nearby site of Isin, which had been excavated by a German expedition. The site has since the invasion of Iraq in 2003 been totally destroyed by looters.

That year my Danish friends from early Baghdad years, the Bielefeldts, were living in Bahrain and they had invited me to visit them at the close of our season. Kirsten had maintained her interest in archaeology, so she drove me to visit various sites. On a Friday the three of us took a picnic lunch and drove to the other end of the island. From Bahrain, I went on to Damascus, where I had been invited to give a series of lectures at Damascus University.

The looting of the Iraq Museum in the immediate aftermath of the invasion of Iraq caused great anger and outrage among members of the archaeological community and, indeed, caused embarrassed consternation in the U.S. State Department. In an effort to take some kind of remedial action, a meeting was called of people from the State Department, the Department of Homeland Security, U.S. customs officers, law enforcement agencies from European countries, representatives of international cultural organizations such as UNESCO, and international police. The meeting was held at INTERPOL headquarters in Lyon, France. To aid these people in recognizing the kinds of antiquities they should be on the lookout for, several scholars were invited to give illustrated talks. The State Department asked me to make the presentation on cuneiform tablets. I would like to think that our efforts have helped in the recovery of some of the stolen antiquities.

While I would never claim any professional qualifications as an archaeologist, I have greatly enjoyed my many seasons on expeditions in Iraq and my many visits to ancient sites, both in Iraq and in other countries. Because of my interest in archaeology, I joined the Archaeological Institute of America in the 1960s. In 1985 I was elected President of the Chicago Society of the Archaeological Institute and remained president until 1992, so my terms in office included my presiding over the celebrations for the centennial of the Chicago Society in 1989. I remain a member of the Executive Committee.

My years at the University included teaching courses frequently, most often in Babylonian literature, Babylonian divination, Babylonian medicine and other scientific texts, as well as Babylonian religious texts, and, occasionally, a course in Old Akkadian, the Semitic language of Babylonia in the third millennium B.C. But I decided that I would take retirement in June 2004, just short of my 70th birthday—at least retirement from teaching and from committee responsibilities, though I continue (for now) as Editor of the *Journal of Near Eastern Studies*. I continue my commitment to the *Chicago Assyrian Dictionary* and will help with verifying the references for the final volume, U/W.

I am truly grateful to the Oriental Institute and to the many friends, colleagues, and students who have made my long tenure here so professionally and personally rewarding. I hope that my contributions to accomplishing the mission of the Oriental Institute and to the field of Assyriology and the study of the ancient Near East in general have justified the confidence shown by my appointment more than forty years ago. As a late colleague said a few days before his death, "It's been fun!" But I expect my fun to continue for a while. It is my hope that eventually some of my ashes can be scattered at Nippur, reuniting me in a sense with a land I came to love and whose ancient culture has been the focus of my professional life.

BIBLIOGRAPHY OF PUBLICATIONS BY ROBERT D. BIGGS

Charles E. Jones, The American School of Classical Studies at Athens and The University of Chicago
and
Paula von Bechtolsheim, The University of Chicago

In addition to his authorship of the monographs, articles, and reviews listed in this bibliography, Bob has influenced and contributed to the scholarship of the field by his service as Editor of the *Journal of Near Eastern Studies* from 1971 to the present, as Associate Editor for the *Chicago Assyrian Dictionary* since 1965 (Vols. B, A/2, K, L, M, N, Q, S, Š/1, Š/2, and Š/3), and as a member of the *CAD*'s Editorial Board since 1996 (Vols. R, P, T, Ṭ, and U/W)

1964

Editor, with John A. Brinkman. *Studies Presented to A. Leo Oppenheim, June 7, 1964*. From the Workshop of the Chicago Assyrian Dictionary. Chicago: The Oriental Institute.

"An Inscription of Ilum-Gāmil of Uruk." In *Studies Presented to A. Leo Oppenheim, June 7, 1964*, edited by Robert D. Biggs and John A. Brinkman, pp. 1–5. From the Workshop of the Chicago Assyrian Dictionary. Chicago: The Oriental Institute.

Review of *The Sumerians: Their History, Culture, and Character*, by Samuel Noah Kramer (Chicago, 1963). *Technology and Culture* 5: 445–46.

1965

"A Chaldaean Inscription from Nippur." *Bulletin of the American Schools of Oriental Research* 179: 36–38.

"A Letter from Kassite Nippur." *Journal of Cuneiform Studies* 19: 95–102.

1966

"The Abū Ṣalābīkh Tablets: A Preliminary Survey." *Journal of Cuneiform Studies* 20: 73–88.

With Miguel Civil. "Notes sur des textes sumériens archaïques." *Revue d'assyriologie et d'archéologie orientale* 60: 1–16.

"Le lapis-lazuli dans les textes sumériens archaïques." *Revue d'assyriologie et d'archéologie orientale* 60: 175–76.

1967

"Semitic Names in the Fara Period." *Orientalia*, n.s., 36: 55–66.

"More Babylonian 'Prophecies'." *Iraq* 29: 117–32.

ŠÀ.ZI.GA: Ancient Mesopotamian Potency Incantations. Texts from Cuneiform Sources 2. Locust Valley, New York: J. J. Augustin.

1968

"An Esoteric Babylonian Commentary." *Revue d'assyriologie et d'archéologie orientale* 62: 51–58.

Note brève to "Notes sur des textes sumériens archaïques." *Revue d'assyriologie et d'archéologie orientale* 62: 95–96.

"The Sumerian Harp." *The American Harp Journal* 1: 6–12.

Review of *Ur Excavation Texts VIII: Royal Inscriptions, Part II*, by E. Sollberger (London, 1965). *Journal of Near Eastern Studies* 27: 145–46.

1969

With Giorgio Buccellati. *Cuneiform Texts from Nippur: The Eighth and Ninth Seasons*. Assyriological Studies 17. Chicago: The University of Chicago Press.

"Babylonian Wisdom Texts, Oracles, and Prophecies." In *Ancient Near Eastern Texts Relating to the Old Testament*, 3d ed., edited by J. B. Pritchard, pp. 592–607. Princeton: Princeton University Press.

"Early Dynastic List A: The Abū Ṣalābīkh Sources." In *The Series lú = ša and Related Texts*, edited by Miguel Civil et al., pp. 8–12 and pl. 2. Materials for the Sumerian Lexicon 12. Rome: Pontificium Institutum Biblicum.

"Early Dynastic List E." In *The Series lú = ša and Related Texts*, edited by Miguel Civil et al., pp. 16–21. Materials for the Sumerian Lexicon 12. Rome: Pontificium Institutum Biblicum.

"A propos des textes de libanomancie." *Revue d'assyriologie et d'archéologie orientale* 63: 73–74.

"*Qutnu*, *maṣraḫu* and Related Terms in Babylonian Extispicy." *Revue d'assyriologie et d'archéologie orientale* 63: 159–67.

"Medicine in Ancient Mesopotamia." *History of Science* 8: 94–105.

Review of *Schriftarchäologie der altmesopotamischen Kultur*, by Kurt Jaritz (Graz, 1967). *Bibliotheca Orientalis* 26: 207–9.

Review of *Cuneiform Texts from Babylonian Tablets in the British Museum*: Part XLVII: *Old-Babylonian Nadītu Records*, by H. H. Figulla (London, 1967). *Journal of Near Eastern Studies* 28: 133–35.

Review of *Cuneiform Texts from Babylonian Tablets in the British Museum*: Part XXII (reprinted 1966), Part XXIII (reprinted 1967), Part XXIV (reprinted 1967), Part XXV (reprinted 1967). *Journal of Near Eastern Studies* 28: 135.

1970

Review of *Heidelberger Studien zum alten Orient: Adam Falkenstein zum 17. September 1966*, edited by D. O. Edzard (Wiesbaden, 1967). *Bibliotheca Orientalis* 27: 26.

Review of *Ur Excavation Texts VI: Literary and Religious Texts, Second Part*, by C. J. Gadd and S. N. Kramer (London, 1966). *Journal of Near Eastern Studies* 29: 58–59.

Review of *Das akkadische Syllabar (2., völlig neubearbeitete Auflage)*, by Wolfram von Soden and Wolfgang Röllig (Rome, 1967). *Journal of Near Eastern Studies* 29: 137–38.

Review of *XVe Rencontre Assyriologique Internationale 1967: La Civilisation de Mari*, edited by J.-R. Kupper (Paris, 1967). *Journal of Near Eastern Studies* 29: 293–94.

1971

"Ašgi (*Ašširgi) in Pre-Sargonic Texts." *Journal of Cuneiform Studies* 24: 1–2.

"An Archaic Sumerian Version of the Kesh Temple Hymn from Tell Abū Ṣalābīkh." *Zeitschrift für Assyriologie* 61: 193–207.

Review of *Ancient Musical Instruments of Western Asia in the British Museum*, by Joan Rimmer (London, 1969). *American Journal of Archaeology* 75: 94–95.

Review of *Gestirn-Darstellungen auf babylonischen Tontafeln*, by Ernst Weidner (Vienna, 1967). *Journal of Near Eastern Studies* 30: 73–74.

Review of *Cuneiform Texts from Babylonian Tablets in the British Museum: Part XLIX: Late-Babylonian Economic Texts*, by D. A. Kennedy (London, 1968). *Journal of Near Eastern Studies* 30: 158.

1972

Review of lišan mitḫurti: *Festschrift Wolfram Freiherr von Soden zum 19. VI. 1968 gewidmet von Schülern und Mitarbeitern*, edited by W. Röllig (Kevelaer and Neukirchen-Vluyn, 1969). *Journal of Near Eastern Studies* 31: 50–51.

Review of *Toward the Image of Tammuz and Other Essays on Mesopotamian History and Culture*, by Thorkild Jacobsen, edited by William L. Moran (Cambridge, Massachusetts, 1970). *Journal of Near Eastern Studies* 31: 134.

Review of *The Sumerian Problem*, by Tom Jones (New York, 1969). *Journal of Near Eastern Studies* 31: 223–34.

Review of *The Art of Ancient Mesopotamia: The Classical Art of the Near East*, by Anton Moortgat, translated by Judith Filson (London and New York, 1969). *Journal of Near Eastern Studies* 31: 235–36.

1973

"On Regional Cuneiform Handwritings in Third Millennium Mesopotamia." *Orientalia*, n.s., 42 (I. J. Gelb Festschrift): 39–46.

"Pre-Sargonic Riddles from Lagash." *Journal of Near Eastern Studies* 32: 26–33.

Review of *Akkadische Zeichenliste*, by Rykle Borger (Kevelaer and Neukirchen-Vluyn, 1971). *Journal of Near Eastern Studies* 32: 258.

Review of "Miscellanées d'ancient arabe," Vol. 2, by A. Jamme (Washington, D.C., 1971). *Journal of Near Eastern Studies* 32: 279.

Review of *Near Eastern Studies in Honor of William Foxwell Albright*, edited by Hans Goedicke (Baltimore, 1971). *Journal of Near Eastern Studies* 32: 341.

1974

Inscriptions from Tell Abū Ṣalābīkh. Oriental Institute Publications 99. Chicago: The University of Chicago Press.

"A Babylonian Extispicy Text Concerning Holes." *Journal of Near Eastern Studies* 33: 351–55.

Review of *Cuneiform Texts from Babylonian Tablets in the British Museum*, Part 50, *Pre-Sargonic and Sargonic Economic Texts*, by E. Sollberger (London, 1972), and *Cuneiform Texts from Babylonian Tablets in the British Museum*, Part 51, *Miscellaneous Texts*, by C. B. F. Walker (London, 1972). *Journal of Near Eastern Studies* 33: 177.

Review of *In Memoriam Eckhard Unger: Beiträge zu Geschichte, Kultur und Religion des alten Orients*, edited by Manfred Lurker (Baden-Baden, 1971). *Journal of Near Eastern Studies* 33: 177–78.

Review of *Essays on the Ancient Semitic World*, edited by J. W. Wevers and D. B. Redford (Toronto, 1970). *Journal of Near Eastern Studies* 33: 178.

Review of *A Bibliography of Mesopotamian Archaeological Sites*, by Richard S. Ellis (Wiesbaden, 1972). *Journal of Near Eastern Studies* 33: 423.

Review of *Gratz College Anniversary Volume on the Occasion of the Seventy-fifth Anniversary of the Founding of the College*, edited by Isidore D. Passow and Samuel T. Lachs (Philadelphia, 1971). *Journal of Near Eastern Studies* 33: 426.

1975

"GAN-GAN+GAM in an Inscription of Entemena." *Revue d'assyriologie et d'archéologie orientale* 69: 185–86.

"An Ur III Agricultural Account from Nippur." *Studia Orientalia* 46 (Armas Salonen Festschrift): 21–30, with additions and corrections *Studia Orientalia* 48/3 (1977): 3.

Review of *A Basic Bibliography for the Study of the Semitic Languages*, edited by J. H. Hospers (Leiden, 1973). *Journal of Near Eastern Studies* 34: 296–97.

1976

Inscriptions from Al-Hiba—Lagash: The First and Second Seasons. Bibliotheca Mesopotamica 3. Malibu, California: Undena Publications.

"Enannatum I of Lagash and Ur-Lumma of Umma – A New Text." In *Kramer Anniversary Volume: Cuneiform Studies in Honor of Samuel Noah Kramer*, edited by Barry Eichler, pp. 33–40. Alter Orient und Altes Testament 25. Kevelaer: Butzon & Bercker.

"Texts and Fragments." *Journal of Cuneiform Studies* 28: 98–100.

1977

Editor, with McGuire Gibson. *Seals and Sealing in the Ancient Near East*. Bibliotheca Mesopotamica 6. Malibu, California: Undena Publications.

Review of *Die Schlussklauseln der altbabylonischen Kauf- und Tauschverträge*, 2d ed., by Mario San Nicolò (Munich, 1974). *Journal of Near Eastern Studies* 36: 160.

Review of *The Healing Hand: Man and Wound in the Ancient World*, by Guido Majno (Cambridge, Massachusetts, 1975). *Journal of Near Eastern Studies* 36: 302–3.

Review of *Studien zur altorientalischen und griechischen Heilkunde: Therapie – Arzneibereitung – Rezeptstruktur*, by Dietlinde Goltz (Wiesbaden, 1974). *Journal of Near Eastern Studies* 36: 303–4.

Review of *Handbuch der Keilschriftliteratur*. Vols. 2 and 3, by Rykle Borger (Berlin, 1975). *Journal of Near Eastern Studies* 36: 304–5.

Review of *Altsumerische Wirtschaftstexte aus Lagasch*, by Josef Bauer (Rome, 1972). *Journal of Near Eastern Studies* 36: 305–6.

Review of *Road to Babylon: Development of U.S. Assyriology*, by C. Wade Meade (Leiden, 1974). *Journal of Near Eastern Studies* 36: 306.

1978

With Donald Eugene McCown and Richard C. Haines. *Nippur II: The North Temple and Sounding E: Excavations of the Joint Expedition to Nippur of the American Schools of Oriental Research and the Oriental Institute of the University of Chicago*. Oriental Institute Publications 97. Chicago: The University of Chicago Press.

"Babylonien." In *Krankheit, Heilkunst, Heilung*, edited by Heinrich Schipperges, Eduard Seidler, and Paul U. Unschuld, pp. 91–114. Veröffentlichungen des "Instituts für Historische Anthropologie e.V." 1. Freiburg and Munich: Verlag Karl Alber.

With J. N. Postgate. "Inscriptions from Abu Salabikh, 1975." *Iraq* 40: 101–17.

Review of *Babylonian Historical-Literary Texts*, by A. K. Grayson (Toronto and Buffalo, 1975). *Journal of the American Oriental Society* 98: 144–45.

Review of *Travels in the World of the Old Testament: Studies Presented to Professor M. A. Beek on the Occasion of His 65th Birthday*, edited by M. S. H. G. Heerma van Voss, Ph. H. J. Houwink ten Cate, and N. A. van Ushelen (Assen, 1974). *Journal of Near Eastern Studies* 37: 67.

Review of *The Engraved Tridacna Shells*, by Rolf A. Stucky (São Paulo, 1974). *Journal of Near Eastern Studies* 37: 350.

1979

Review of *Cuneiform Texts of Varying Content*, by J. J. A. van Dijk (Leiden, 1976). *Journal of Semitic Studies* 24: 109–10.

Review of *Spätbabylonische Texte aus Uruk: Teil 1*, by Hermann Hunger (Berlin, 1976). *Journal of Near Eastern Studies* 38: 53–54.

Review of *Wirtschaft und Gesellschaft im alten Vorderasien*, edited by J. Harmatta and G. Komoróczy (Budapest, 1976). *Journal of Near Eastern Studies* 38: 217–18.

Review of *Semitic Writing: From Pictograph to Alphabet*, 3d ed., rev., by G. R. Driver (London and New York, 1976). *Journal of Near Eastern Studies* 38: 311–12.

Review of *İstanbul Arkeoloji Müzelerinde Bulunan Sumer Edebî Tablet ve Parçaları-II*, by Samuel Noah Kramer (Ankara, 1976). *Journal of Near Eastern Studies* 38: 312.

1980

"The Ebla Tablets: An Interim Perspective." *Biblical Archeologist* 43: 76–87.

Review of *Dictionnaire illustré multilingue de l'architecture du Proche Orient ancien*, edited by Olivier Aurenche (Lyon, 1977). *Journal of Near Eastern Studies* 39: 225.

Review of *XIX. Deutscher Orientalistentag, vom 28. September bis 4. Oktober 1975 in Freiburg im Breisgau: Vorträge*, edited by Wolfgang Voigt (Wiesbaden, 1977). *Journal of Near Eastern Studies* 39: 225–26.

1981

"Ebla and Abu Salabikh: The Linguistic and Literary Aspects." In *La lingua di Ebla: Atti del convegno internazionale (Napoli, 21–23 aprile 1980)*, edited by Luigi Cagni, pp. 121–33. Series minor, Seminario di Studi Asiatici 14. Naples: Istituto Universitario Orientale, Seminario di Studi Asiatici.

"Kopfkrankheiten." *Reallexikon der Assyriologie und vorderasiatischen Archäologie* 6, pp. 210–11.

Review of *Biblisches Reallexikon*, 2d ed., edited by Kurt Galling (Tübingen, 1977). *Journal of Near Eastern Studies* 40: 66.

Review of *Pottery and Ceramics: A Guide to Information Sources*, by James Edward Campbell (Detroit, 1978). *Journal of Near Eastern Studies* 40: 148–49.

1982

"The Ebla Tablets: A 1981 Perspective." *Bulletin of the Canadian Society for Mesopotamian Studies* 2: 9–24.

Review of *On Trees, Mountains, and Millstones in the Ancient Near East*, by M. Stol with a chapter by K. van Lerberghe (Leiden, 1979). *Journal of the American Oriental Society* 102: 659–60.

Review of *Die babylonisch-assyrische Medizin in Texten und Untersuchungen*. Vols. 5 and 6, by Franz Köcher (Berlin, 1980). *Journal of Near Eastern Studies* 41: 312–13.

1983

Editor of *Discoveries from Kurdish Looms*. Evanston, Illinois: Mary and Leigh Block Gallery, Northwestern University.

With Matthew W. Stolper. "A Babylonian Omen Text from Susiana." *Revue d'assyriologie et d'archéologie orientale* 77: 155–62.

"Lebermodelle. A. Philologisch." *Reallexikon der Assyriologie und vorderasiatischen Archäologie* 6, pp. 518–21.

"Lepra." *Reallexikon der Assyriologie und vorderasiatischen Archäologie* 6, p. 605.

Review of *Death in Mesopotamia: Papers Read at the XXVIe Rencontre Assyriologique Internationale*, edited by Bendt Alster (Copenhagen, 1980). *Journal of Near Eastern Studies* 42: 314–15.

1984

"Hebraica, American Journal of Semitic Languages and Literatures, Journal of Near Eastern Studies 1884–1984." *Journal of Near Eastern Studies* 43: 1–8.

Review of ZIKIR ŠUMIM: *Assyriological Studies Presented to F. R. Kraus on the Occasion of his Seventieth Birthday*, edited by G. van Driel, Th. J. H. Krispijn, M. Stol, and K. R. Veenhof (Leiden, 1982). *Journal of the American Oriental Society* 104: 366–68.

With Dennis Pardee. Review of *La Statue de Tell Fekherye et son inscription bilingue assyro-araméenne*, by Ali Abou-Assaf, Pierre Bordreuil, and Alan R. Millard (Paris, 1982). *Journal of Near Eastern Studies* 43: 253–57.

1985

"The Babylonian Prophecies and the Astrological Traditions of Mesopotamia." *Journal of Cuneiform Studies* 37: 86–90.

Review of *Societies and Languages of the Ancient Near East: Studies in Honour of I. M. Diakonoff*, edited by M. A. Dandamayev, I. Gershevitch, H. Klengel, G. Komoróczy, M. T. Larsen, and J. N. Postgate (Warminster, 1982). *Journal of Near Eastern Studies* 44: 155–56.

Review of *M.A.R.I.: Annales de Recherches Interdisciplinaires*. Vols. 1 and 2, edited by Jean Margueron and Jean-Marie Durand (Paris, 1982 and 1983). *Journal of Near Eastern Studies* 44: 227.

1986

"Ancient Mesopotamia and the Scholarly Traditions of the Third Millennium." *Sumer* 42: 32–33.

Review of *Documents cunéiformes de la IVe Section de l'Ecole Pratique des Hautes Etudes*. Vol. 1, *Catalogue et copies cunéiformes*, by Jean-Marie Durand (Geneva and Paris, 1982). *Journal of Near Eastern Studies* 45: 328–29.

Review of *The Late Babylonian Tablets in the Royal Ontario Museum*, by G. J. P. McEwan (Toronto, 1982). *Journal of Near Eastern Studies* 45: 329–31.

1987

Editor, with McGuire Gibson. *The Organization of Power: Aspects of Bureaucracy in the Ancient Near East*. Studies in Ancient Oriental Civilization 46. Chicago: The Oriental Institute.

"Babylonian Prophecies, Astrology, and a New Source for 'Prophecy Text B'." In *Language, Literature, and History: Philological and Historical Studies Presented to Erica Reiner*, edited by Francesca Rochberg-Halton, pp. 1–14. American Oriental Series 67. New Haven: American Oriental Society.

"Liebeszauber." *Reallexikon der Assyriologie und vorderasiatischen Archäologie* 7, pp. 17–18.

"An Old Assyrian Text." *Nouvelles Assyriologiques Brèves et Utilitaires* 1987/96.

1988

"An Old Assyrian Letter." In *A Scientific Humanist: Studies in Memory of Abraham Sachs*, edited by Erle Leichty, Maria deJ. Ellis, and Pamela Gerardi, pp. 33–38. Occasional Publications of the Samuel Noah Kramer Fund 9. Philadelphia: The University Museum.

"The Semitic Personal Names from Abu Salabikh and the Personal Names from Ebla." In *Eblaite Personal Names and Semitic Name-giving: Papers of a Symposium Held in Rome, July 15–17, 1985*, edited by Alfonso Archi, pp. 98–98. Archivi reali di Ebla, Studi 1. Rome: Missione Archeologica Italiana in Siria.

"Early Dynastic Texts." In *Tablets, Cones, and Bricks of the Third and Second Millennia B.C.*, edited by Ira Spar, pp. 3–5. Cuneiform Texts in the Metropolitan Museum of Art 1. New York: The Metropolitan Museum.

Review of *Fragmenta Historiae Elamicae: Mélanges offerts à M.-J. Steve*, edited by L. de Meyer, H. Gasche, and F. Vallat (Paris, 1986). *Journal of Near Eastern Studies* 47: 217.

Review of *Archives and Libraries in the City of Assur: A Survey of the Material from the German Excavations*. Part 1, by Olof Pedersén (Uppsala, 1985). *Journal of Near Eastern Studies* 47: 217–18.

Review of *Traditional Crafts of Saudi Arabia*, by John Topham, Anthony Landreau, and William E. Mulligan (London, 1982), and *Bedouin*, by Wayne Eastep (London, 1986). *Journal of Near Eastern Studies* 47: 232.

Review of *Oikumene: Studia ad historiam antiquam classicam et orientalem spectantia*. Vol. 5, edited by G. Komoróczy et al. (Budapest, 1986). *Journal of Near Eastern Studies* 47: 310.

Review of *Catalogue of Cuneiform Tablets in Birmingham City Museum*. Vol. 1, *Neo-Sumerian Texts from Drehem*, by P. J. Watson (Warminster, 1986). *Journal of Near Eastern Studies* 47: 310–11.

1989

"An Old Akkadian Literary Text from Umm al-Hafriyat." In *DUMU-E$_2$-DUB-BA-A: Studies in Honor of Åke W. Sjöberg*, edited by Hermann Behrens, Darlene Loding, and Martha T. Roth, pp. 33–36. Occasional Publications of the Samuel Noah Kramer Fund 11. Philadelphia: The University Museum.

"A Recut Old Babylonian Seal with a Sumerian Prayer of the Kassite Period." In *Essays in Ancient Civilization Presented to Helene J. Kantor*, edited by Albert Leonard, Jr. and Bruce Beyer Williams, pp. 55–56. Studies in Ancient Oriental Civilization 47. Chicago: The Oriental Institute.

Review of *M.A.R.I.: Annales de Recherches Interdisciplinaires*. Vol. 5 (Paris, 1987). *Journal of Near Eastern Studies* 48: 74.

1990

"Medizin in Mesopotamien." *Reallexikon der Assyriologie und vorderasiatischen Archäologie* 7, pp. 623–29.

With Richard L. Zettler. "Cuneiform Texts in Chicago Collections." *Acta Sumerologica* 12: 15–49.

1991

Editor, with McGuire Gibson. *The Organization of Power: Aspects of Bureaucracy in the Ancient Near East*. 2d ed. with corrections. Studies in Ancient Oriental Civilization 46. Chicago: The Oriental Institute.

"Ergotism and Mycotoxicoses in Ancient Mesopotamia?" *Aula Orientalis* 9 (Miguel Civil Festschrift): 15–21.

Review of *An Index to English Periodical Literature on the Old Testament and Ancient Near Eastern Studies*. Vols. 1 and 2, by William G. Hupper (Metuchen and London, 1988). *Journal of Near Eastern Studies* 50: 61–62.

Review of *The Correspondence of Sargon II*, Part 1: *Letters from Assyria and the West*, by Simo Parpola (Helsinki, 1987). *Journal of Near Eastern Studies* 50: 62–63.

Review of *Astronomical Diaries and Related Texts from Babylonia*. Vol. 1, *Diaries from 652 B.C. to 262 B.C.*, by Abraham J. Sachs, completed and edited by Hermann Hunger (Vienna, 1988). *Journal of Near Eastern Studies* 50: 63–65.

Review of *Woven from the Soul, Spun from the Heart: Textile Arts of Safavid and Qajar Iran 16th–19th Centuries*, edited by Carol Bier (Washington, D.C., 1987). *Journal of Near Eastern Studies* 50: 230.

1992

Inscriptions from Al-Hiba—Lagash: The First and Second Seasons. 2d printing with additions. Bibliotheca Mesopotamica 3. Malibu, California: Undena Publications.

"Ebla Texts." In *Anchor Bible Dictionary*. Vol. 2, edited by David Noel Freedman, pp. 263–70. New York: Doubleday.

"The Babylonian Prophecies." *Bulletin of the Canadian Society for Mesopotamian Studies* 23: 17–20.

Review of *Notae Bibliographicae: Old Babylonian Extispicy: Omen Texts in the British Museum*, by Ulla Jeyes (Istanbul, 1989). *Orientalia*, n.s., 61: 482.

Review of *The Rituals of the Diviner*, by I. Starr (Malibu, 1983). *Aula Orientalis* 10: 170–71.

Review of *Archives épistolaires de Mari*. Vol. 1/1, by Jean-Marie Durand (Paris, 1988), and *Archives épistolaires de Mari*. Vol. 1/2, by Dominique Charpin, Francis Joannès, Sylvie Lackenbacher, and Bertrand Lafont (Paris, 1988). *Journal of Near Eastern Studies* 51: 311–12.

Review of *Mesopotamian Myths*, by Henrietta McCall (London, 1990). *Journal of Near Eastern Studies* 51: 315.

1993

"Ancient and Medieval Western Asia." *Society for Ancient Medicine Review* 21: 30–33.

"'Prophecy Text B' in SAA 8 No. 459." *Nouvelles Assyriologiques Brèves et Utilitaires* 1993/73.

"Descent of Ištar, line 104." *Nouvelles Assyriologiques Brèves et Utilitaires* 1993/74.

Review of *Bibliographie de Mari: Archéologie et textes (1933–1988)*, by Jean-Georges Heintz (Wiesbaden, 1990). *Journal of Near Eastern Studies* 52: 236.

1994

"Šušan in Babylonia." In *Cinquante-deux réflexions sur le Proche-Orient ancien offertes en hommage à Léon De Meyer*, edited by H. Gasche, pp. 299–304. Mesopotamian History and Environment, Occasional Publication 2. Leuven: Peeters.

"Ancient and Medieval Western Asia." *Society for Ancient Medicine Review* 22: 30–31.

Review of *Textes de la bibliothèque: Transcriptions et traductions*, by Daniel Arnaud (Paris, 1987). *Journal of the American Oriental Society* 114: 515.

Review of *Understanding and History in Arts and Sciences*, edited by Roald Skarsten, Else Johansen Kleppe, and Ragnhild Bjerre Finnestad (Oslo, 1991). *Journal of Near Eastern Studies* 53: 224–25.

Review of *Eblaitica: Essays on the Ebla Archives and Eblaite Language*. Vols. 2 and 3, edited by Cyrus H. Gordon and Gary A. Rendsburg (Winona Lake, Indiana, 1990 and 1993). *Journal of Near Eastern Studies* 53: 306–7.

1995

"Medicine, Surgery, and Public Health in Ancient Mesopotamia." In *Civilizations of the Ancient Near East*. Vol. 3, edited by Jack M. Sasson, pp. 1911–24. New York: Charles Scribner's Sons. (Reprinted in *Journal of Assyrian Academic Studies* 19 [2005]: 28–46.)

"Ancient and Medieval Western Asia." *Society for Ancient Medicine Review* 23: 44–45.

Review of *Uruk: Spätbabylonische Texte aus dem Planquadrat U 18*. Part 4, by Egbert von Weiher (Mainz, 1993). *Orientalia*, n.s., 64: 137–38.

Review of *Epilepsy in Babylonia*, by M. Stol (Groningen, 1993). *Bibliotheca Orientalis* 52: 728–30.

Review of *Jardins d'Orient*, edited by Rika Gyselen (Paris, 1991). *Journal of Near Eastern Studies* 54: 52.

Review of *Semitic Studies in Honor of Wolf Leslau on the Occasion of His Eighty-fifth Birthday, November 14th, 1991*, edited by Alan S. Kaye (Wiesbaden, 1991). *Journal of Near Eastern Studies* 54: 311–12.

1996

"A Woman's Plaint in an Old Assyrian Letter." *Wiener Zeitschrift für die Kunde des Morgenlandes* 86 (Hans Hirsch Festschrift): 47–52.

"An Inscription of Enlil-bani of Isin." *Nouvelles Assyriologiques Brèves et Utilitaires* 1996/21.

"Šuʾû, 'King,' in an Omen Text." *Nouvelles Assyriologiques Brèves et Utilitaires* 1996/22.

"Šumma Izbu at Nimrud." *Nouvelles Assyriologiques Brèves et Utilitaires* 1996/103.

"Exploits of Šulgi?" *Nouvelles Assyriologiques Brèves et Utilitaires* 1996/108.

"A Göttertypentext from Nimrud." *Nouvelles Assyriologiques Brèves et Utilitaires* 1996/134.

Review of *Babylonian Topographical Texts*, by A. R. George (Leuven, 1992). *Journal of Near Eastern Studies* 55: 61–63.

Review of *Through Time, across Continents: A Hundred Years of Archaeology and Anthropology at the University Museum*, by Dilys Pegler Winegrad (Philadelphia, 1993). *Journal of Near Eastern Studies* 55: 218–19.

Review of *Konkordanz der Keilschrifttafeln I: Die Texte der Grabung 1931*, by Silvin Košak (Wiesbaden, 1992). *Journal of Near Eastern Studies* 55: 236.

Review of *The Brockman Tablets of the University of Haifa*. Vol. 1, *Royal Inscriptions*, by Raphael Kutscher (Haifa, 1989). *Journal of Near Eastern Studies* 55: 240–41.

Review of *Astrological Reports to Assyrian Kings*, by Hermann Hunger (Helsinki, 1992). *Journal of Near Eastern Studies* 55: 241–42.

Review of *Ah, Assyria...: Studies in Assyrian History and Ancient Near Eastern Historiography Presented to Hayim Tadmor*, edited by Mordechai Cogan and Israel Ephʿal (Jerusalem, 1991). *Journal of Near Eastern Studies* 55: 242–43.

Review of *Natural Phenomena: Their Meaning, Depiction and Description in the Ancient Near East*, edited by D. J. W. Meijer (Amsterdam, 1992). *Journal of Near Eastern Studies* 55: 243–44.

1997

"Šulgi in Simurrum." In *Crossing Boundaries and Linking Horizons: Studies in Honor of Michael C. Astour on His 80th Birthday*, edited by Gordon D. Young, Mark W. Chavalas, and Richard E. Averbeck, pp. 169–78. Bethesda, Maryland: CDL Press.

"Ancient and Medieval Western Asia." *Society for Ancient Medicine Review* 24: 50–53.

With L. E. Wilbanks. "Another Šulgi-simtum text." *Nouvelles Assyriologiques Brèves et Utilitaires* 1997/99.

Review of *Illness and Health Care in the Ancient Near East: The Role of the Temple in Greece, Mesopotamia, and Israel*, by Hector Avalos (Atlanta, 1995). *Journal of the American Oriental Society* 117: 169–71.

Review of *Near Eastern Studies Dedicated to H. I. H. Prince Takahito Mikasa on the Occasion of His Seventy-fifth Birthday*, edited by Masao Mori, Hideo Ogawa, and Mamoru Yoshikawa (Wiesbaden, 1991). *Journal of Near Eastern Studies* 56: 62–63.

Review of *Letters from Assyrian and Babylonian Scholars*, by Simo Parpola (Helsinki, 1993). *Journal of Near Eastern Studies* 56: 63–64.

Review of *Who's Who in Biblical Studies and Archaeology*. 2d ed. (Washington, D.C., 1993). *Journal of Near Eastern Studies* 56: 75–76.

Review of *The Healing Past: Pharmaceuticals in the Biblical and Rabbinic World*, edited by Irene Jacob and Walter Jacob (Leiden, New York, and Cologne, 1993). *Journal of Near Eastern Studies* 56: 123–24.

Review of *Medizinische Omina aus Ḫattuša in akkadischer Sprache*, by Gernot Wilhelm (Wiesbaden, 1994). *Journal of Near Eastern Studies* 56: 230–31.

Review of *La circulation des biens, des personnes et des idées dans le Proche-Orient ancien: Actes de la XXXVIIIe Rencontre Assyriologique Internationale (Paris, 8–10 juillet 1991)*, edited by D. Charpin and F. Joannès (Paris, 1991). *Journal of Near Eastern Studies* 56: 231–33.

Review of *Drinking in Ancient Societies: History and Culture of Drinks in the Ancient Near East: Papers of a Symposium Held in Rome, May 17–19, 1990*, edited by Lucio Milano (Padua, 1994). *Journal of Near Eastern Studies* 56: 233–34.

Review of *Der Tempelturm Etemenanki in Babylon*, by Hansjörg Schmid (Mainz, 1995). *Journal of Near Eastern Studies* 56: 287–90.

Review of *Solar Omens of Enuma Anu Enlil: Tablets 23 (24)–29 (30)*, by Wilfred H. van Soldt (Leiden, 1995). *Journal of Near Eastern Studies* 56: 290–92.

1998

"Nacktheit." *Reallexikon der Assyriologie und vorderasiatischen Archäologie* 9, pp. 64–65.

Review of *Amurru, 1: Mari, Ebla et les Hourrites: Dix ans de travaux*. Part 1, edited by Jean-Marie Durand (Paris, 1996). *Journal of the American Oriental Society* 118: 287–89.

Review of *The Shemshāra Archives 2: The Administrative Texts*, by Jesper Eidem (Copenhagen, 1992). *Journal of Near Eastern Studies* 57: 72–74.

Review of *The Topography of Remembrance: The Dead, Tradition and Collective Memory in Mesopotamia*, by Gerdien Jonker (Leiden, New York, and Cologne, 1995). *Journal of Near Eastern Studies* 57: 74–75.

Review of *M.A.R.I.: Annales de Recherches Interdisciplinaires*. Vol. 7 (Paris, 1993). *Journal of Near Eastern Studies* 57: 75–76.

1999

Review of *Zukunftsbewältigung: Eine Untersuchung altorientalischen Denkens anhand der babylonisch-assyrischen Löserituale (Namburbi)*, by Stefan M. Maul (Mainz, 1994). *Journal of Near Eastern Studies* 58: 146–48.

Review of *Cuneiform Documents from the Chaldean and Persian Periods*, by Ronald H. Sack (Selinsgrove, London, and Cranbury, 1994). *Journal of Near Eastern Studies* 58: 148–49.

Review of *Literary Texts from the Temple of Nabû*, by D. J. Wiseman and J. A. Black (London, 1996). *Journal of Near Eastern Studies* 58: 149–51.

Review of *Arabia Felix: Beiträge zur Sprache und Kultur des vorislamischen Arabien: Festschrift Walter W. Müller zum 60. Geburtstag*, edited by Norbert Nebes (Wiesbaden, 1994). *Journal of Near Eastern Studies* 58: 155–56.

Review of *Catalogue of the Babylonian Tablets in the British Museum*. Vol. 2, by M. Sigrist, H. H. Figulla, and C. B. F. Walker (London, 1996). *Journal of Near Eastern Studies* 58: 290–91.

Review of *Collectanea Orientalia: Histoire, arts de l'espace et industrie de la terre: Etudes offertes en hommage à Agnès Spycket*, edited by H. Gasche and B. Hrouda (Neuchâtel and Paris, 1996). *Journal of Near Eastern Studies* 58: 291–92.

Review of *Tablettes et images aux pays de Sumer et d'Akkad: Mélanges offerts à Monsieur H. Limet*, edited by Ö. Tunca and D. Deheselle (Liège, 1996). *Journal of Near Eastern Studies* 58: 293–94.

Review of *The Ḫabiru Prism of King Tunip-Teššup of Tikunani*, by Mirjo Salvini (Rome, 1996). *Journal of Near Eastern Studies* 58: 294–95.

Review of *Uruk: Analytisches Register zu den Grabungsberichten, Kampagnen 1912/13 bis 1976/77*, by Uwe Finkbeiner and Manfred Robert Behm-Blancke (Berlin, 1993). *Journal of Near Eastern Studies* 58: 295–96.

Review of *Index documentaire d'El-Amarna—I.D.E.A.* Vol. 2, *Bibliographie des textes babyloniens d'El-Amarna (1888 à 1993) et concordance des sigles EA*, by Jean-Georges Heintz (Wiesbaden, 1995). *Journal of Near Eastern Studies* 58: 296.

Review of *Language and Culture in the Near East*, edited by Shlomo Izreʾel and Rina Drory (Leiden, New York, and Cologne, 1995). *Journal of Near Eastern Studies* 58: 297–98.

Review of *The Origin and Ancient History of Wine*, edited by Patrick E. McGovern, Stuart J. Fleming, and Solomon H. Katz (Langhorne, Pennsylvania, 1995), and *In Vino Veritas*, edited by Oswyn Murray and Manuela Tecuşan (London, 1995). *Journal of Near Eastern Studies* 58: 298–300.

2000

"Conception, Contraception, and Abortion in Ancient Mesopotamia." In *Wisdom, Gods and Literature: Studies in Assyriology in Honour of W. G. Lambert*, edited by A. R. George and I. L. Finkel, pp. 1–13. Winona Lake, Indiana: Eisenbrauns.

Review of *The Oxford Encyclopedia of Archaeology in the Near East*. 5 vols., edited by Eric M. Meyers (New York and Oxford, 1997). *Journal of Near Eastern Studies* 59: 36–38.

Review of *The Oriental Rug Lexicon*, by Peter F. Stone (Seattle and London, 1997). *Journal of Near Eastern Studies* 59: 58–60.

Review of *Texts from the Vicinity of Emar in the Collection of Jonathan Rosen*, by Gary Beckman (Padua, 1996). *Journal of Near Eastern Studies* 59: 72–73.

Review of *Uruk: Spätbabylonische Wirtschaftstexte aus dem Eanna-Archiv, Teil II: Texte verschiedenen Inhalts*, by Erlend Gehlken (Mainz, 1996). *Journal of Near Eastern Studies* 59: 73.

Review of *Katalog der beschrifteten Objekte aus Assur: Die Schriftträger mit Ausnahme der Tontafeln und ähnlicher Archivtexte*, by Olof Pedersén (Berlin, 1997). *Journal of Near Eastern Studies* 59: 73–74.

Review of *The Conquest of Assyria: Excavations in an Antique Land, 1840–1860*, by Mogens Trolle Larsen (London and New York, 1996). *Journal of Near Eastern Studies* 59: 126.

Review of *Built on Solid Rock: Studies in Honour of Professor Ebbe Egede Knudsen on the Occasion of His 65th Birthday, April 11th, 1997*, edited by Elie Wardini (Oslo, 1997). *Journal of Near Eastern Studies* 59: 127.

Review of *Mitología y religión del oriente antiguo II/1: Semitas occidentales (Ebla, Mari)*, by P. Mander and J.-M. Durand (Barcelona, 1995). *Journal of Near Eastern Studies* 59: 127–28.

Review of *Miscellanea Eblaitica*. Vol. 4, edited by Pelio Fronzaroli (Florence, 1997). *Journal of Near Eastern Studies* 59: 217.

Review of *The Standard Babylonian Epic of Gilgamesh*, by Simo Parpola (Helsinki, 1997). *Journal of Near Eastern Studies* 59: 217–18.

Review of *Testi amministrativi della III dinastia di Ur dal Museo Statale Ermitage San Pietroburgo-Russia*, by Franco D'Agostino (Rome, 1997). *Journal of Near Eastern Studies* 59: 218–19.

Review of *Flowers Underfoot: Indian Carpets of the Mughal Era*, by Daniel Walker (New York, 1997). *Journal of Near Eastern Studies* 59: 235–36.

Review of *Colours of the Indus: Costume and Textiles of Pakistan*, by Nasreen Askari and Rosemary Crill (London, 1997). *Journal of Near Eastern Studies* 59: 236.

2001

"Nin-Nibru." *Reallexikon der Assyriologie und vorderasiatischen Archäologie* 9, pp. 476–77.

Review of *Archives and Libraries in the Ancient Near East 1500–300 B.C.*, by Olof Pedersén (Bethesda, 1998). *Journal of Near Eastern Studies* 60: 226–27.

Review of *Die orientalische Stadt: Kontinuität, Wandel, Bruch: 1. Internationales Colloquium der Deutschen Orient-Gesellschaft, 9.–10. Mai 1996 in Halle/Salle*, edited by Gernot Wilhelm (Saarbrücken, 1997). *Journal of Near Eastern Studies* 60: 227–28.

Review of *Tablettes cunéiformes de Tello au Musée d'Istanbul datant de l'époque de la IIIe Dynastie d'Ur*. Vol. 2, *ITT II/1, 2544–2819, 3158–4342, 4708–4713*, by Bertrand Lafont and Fatma Yıldız (Leiden, 1996). *Journal of Near Eastern Studies* 60: 228–29.

Review of *Akkadische Rituale aus Ḫattuša: Die Sammeltafel KBo XXXVI 29 und verwandte Fragmente*, by Daniel Schwemer (Heidelberg, 1998). *Journal of Near Eastern Studies* 60: 289–90.

Review of *Uruk: Spätbabylonische Texte aus dem Planquadrat U 18*. Part 5, by Egbert von Weiher (Mainz, 1998). *Journal of Near Eastern Studies* 60: 290–91.

Review of *High Places in Cyberspace: A Guide to Biblical and Religious Studies, Classics, and Archaeological Resources on the Internet*. 2d ed., by Patrick Durusau (Atlanta, 1998). *Journal of Near Eastern Studies* 60: 318.

2002

"The Babylonian Sexual Potency Texts." In *Sex and Gender in the Ancient Near East: Proceedings of the 47th Rencontre Assyriologique Internationale, Helsinki, July 2–6, 2001*, edited by Simo Parpola and Robert M. Whiting, pp. 71–78. Helsinki: The Neo-Assyrian Text Corpus Project.

Review of *Mesopotamien: Späturuk-Zeit und frühdynastische Zeit*, by Josef Bauer, Robert K. Englund, and Manfred Krebernik (Freiburg and Göttingen, 1998). *Journal of Near Eastern Studies* 61: 134–36.

Review of *Ein neuassyrisches Privatarchiv der Tempelgoldschmiede von Assur*, by Karen Radner (Saarbrücken, 1999). *Journal of Near Eastern Studies* 61: 136–37.

Review of *La science des cieux: Sages, mages, astrologues*, edited by Rika Gyselen (Bures-sur-Yvette, 1999). *Journal of Near Eastern Studies* 61: 138.

Review of *The Furniture of Western Asia, Ancient and Traditional: Papers of the Conference Held at the Institute of Archaeology, University College London, June 28 to 30, 1993*, edited by Georgina Herrmann (Mainz, 1996). *Journal of Near Eastern Studies* 62: 138–40.

Review of *Dictionary of Deities and Demons in the Bible*. 2d ed., rev., edited by Karel van der Toorn, Bob Becking, and Pieter W. van der Horst (Grand Rapids and Leiden, 1999). *Journal of Near Eastern Studies* 61: 140–41.

Review of Ki Baruch Hu: *Ancient Near Eastern, Biblical, and Judaic Studies in Honor of Baruch A. Levine*, edited by R. Chazan, W. W. Hallo, and L. H. Schiffman (Winona Lake, Indiana, 1999). *Journal of Near Eastern Studies* 61: 150–51.

Review of *Uzbekistan: Heirs to the Silk Road*, edited by Johannes Kalter and Margareta Pavaloi (London, 1997). *Journal of Near Eastern Studies* 61: 217–18.

Review of *Return to Tradition: The Revitalization of Turkish Village Carpets*, by June Anderson (San Francisco, Seattle, and London, 1998). *Journal of Near Eastern Studies* 61: 218–19.

Review of *Letters from Priests to the Kings Esarhaddon and Assurbanipal*, by Steven W. Cole and Peter Machinist (Helsinki, 1999). *Journal of Near Eastern Studies* 61: 288.

Review of *Dictionary of the Ancient Near East*, edited by Piotr Bienkowski and Alan Millard (Philadelphia, 2000). *Journal of Near Eastern Studies* 61: 317.

Review of *Zwischen Tigris und Nil: 100 Jahre Ausgrabungen der Deutschen Orient-Gesellschaft in Vorderasien und Ägypten*, edited by Gernot Wilhelm (Mainz, 1999). *Journal of Near Eastern Studies* 61: 318.

Review of *If a City Is Set on a Height: The Akkadian Omen Series* Šumma Ālu ina Mēlê Šakin. Vol. 1, *Tablets 1–21*, by Sally M. Freedman (Philadelphia, 1999). *Journal of Near Eastern Studies* 61: 318–19.

2003

"Cuneiform Inscriptions in the Looted Iraq Museum." *IFAR Journal* 6: 46–49.

"Ohr, Ohrenkrankheiten." *Reallexikon der Assyriologie und vorderasiatischen Archäologie* 10, pp. 42–43.

Review of *Damaskus—Aleppo: 5000 Jahre Stadtentwicklung in Syrien*, edited by Mamoun Fansa (Mainz, 2000). *Journal of Near Eastern Studies* 62: 36–38.

Review of *Mesopotamien: Akkade-Zeit und Ur III-Zeit*, by Walther Sallaberger and Aage Westenholz (Freiburg and Göttingen, 1999). *Journal of Near Eastern Studies* 62: 38–39.

Review of *Richard F. S. Starr Memorial Volume*, edited by David I. Owen and Gernot Wilhelm (Bethesda, 1996). *Journal of Near Eastern Studies* 62: 39–40.

Review of *Cities, Seals and Writing: Archaic Seal Impressions from Jemdet Nasr and Ur*, by Roger J. Matthews (Berlin, 1993). *Journal of Near Eastern Studies* 62: 138–39.

Review of *Documentation for Ancient Arabia*. Part 2, *Bibliographical Catalogue of Texts*, by K. A. Kitchen (Liverpool, 2000). *Journal of Near Eastern Studies* 62: 219.

Review of *Historische semitische Sprachwissenschaft*, by Burkhart Kienast (Wiesbaden, 2001). *Journal of Near Eastern Studies* 62: 283–84.

Review of *Astral Sciences in Mesopotamia*, by Hermann Hunger and David Pingree (Leiden, Boston, and Cologne, 1999). *Journal of Near Eastern Studies* 62: 284–86.

Review of *The Induction of the Cult Image in Ancient Mesopotamia: The Mesopotamian* mīs pî *Ritual*, by Christopher Walker and Michael Dick (Helsinki, 2001). *Journal of Near Eastern Studies* 62: 286.

Review of *Démons et merveilles d'Orient*, edited by Rika Gyselen (Bures-sur-Yvette, 2001). *Journal of Near Eastern Studies* 62: 286–87.

Review of *Banquets d'Orient*, edited by Rika Gyselen (Bures-sur-Yvette, 1992). *Journal of Near Eastern Studies* 62: 287–88.

Review of *From Athens to Jerusalem: Medicine in Hellenized Jewish Lore and in Early Christian Literature: Papers of the Symposium in Jerusalem, 9–11 September 1996*, edited by Samuel Kottek and Manfred Horstmanshoff (Rotterdam, 2000). *Journal of Near Eastern Studies* 62: 288–89.

Review of *Herrschaftswissen in Mesopotamien: Formen der Kommunikation zwischen Gott und König im 2. und 1. Jahrtausend v. Chr.*, by Beate Pongratz-Leisten (Helsinki, 1999). *Journal of Near Eastern Studies* 62: 289.

Review of *Adapa and the South Wind: Language Has the Power of Life and Death*, by Shlomo Izreʾel (Winona Lake, Indiana, 2001). *Journal of Near Eastern Studies* 62: 289–90.

Review of *Who's Who in the Ancient Near East*, by Gwendolyn Leick (London and New York, 1999). *Journal of Near Eastern Studies* 62: 290.

2004

"The Babylonian Fürstenspiegel as a Political Forgery." In *From the Upper Sea to the Lower Sea: Studies on the History of Assyria and Babylonia in Honour of A. K. Grayson*, edited by Grant Frame, pp. 1–5. Uitgaven van het Nederlands Instituut voor het Nabije Oosten te Leiden, *voorheen* Publications de l'Institut historique-archéologique néerlandais de Stamboul 101. Leiden: Instituut voor het Nabije Oosten.

Review of *Landscapes: Territories, Frontiers and Horizons in the Ancient Near East*. Vols. 1–3, edited by L. Milano, S. De Martino, F. M. Fales, and G. B. Lanfranchi (Padua, 1999–2000). *Journal of Near Eastern Studies* 63: 47.

Review of *Patavina Orientalia Selecta*, by Elena Rova (Padua, 2000). *Journal of Near Eastern Studies* 63: 47–48.

Review of *The Prosopography of the Neo-Assyrian Empire*. Vol. 1, Part 1, *A*, and Vol. 1, Part 2. *B–G*, edited by Karen Radner (Helsinki, 1998 and 1999). *Journal of Near Eastern Studies* 63: 48–49.

Review of *Ancient Astronomy and Celestial Divination*, edited by N. M. Swerdlow (Cambridge, Massachusetts, 1999). *Journal of Near Eastern Studies* 63: 49–50.

Review of *Dictionnaire des civilisations de l'Orient ancien*, by Guy Rachet (Paris, 1999). *Journal of Near Eastern Studies* 63: 160.

Review of *Correspondance des marchands de Kaniš au début du IIe millénaire avant J.-C.*, by Cécile Michel (Paris, 2001). *Journal of Near Eastern Studies* 63: 210–11.

Review of *The Shemshara Archives*. Vol. 1, *The Letters*, by Jesper Eidem and Jørgen Læssøe (Copenhagen, 2001). *Journal of Near Eastern Studies* 63: 211–12.

Review of *Wettergottgestalten Mesopotamiens und Nordsyriens im Zeitalter der Keilschriftkulturen: Materialien und Studien nach den schriftlichen Quellen*, by Daniel Schwemer (Wiesbaden, 2001). *Journal of Near Eastern Studies* 63: 212–14.

Review of *The Roman Textile Industry and Its Influence: A Birthday Tribute to John Peter Wild*, edited by Penelope Walton Rogers, Lise Bender Jørgensen, and Antoinette Rast-Eicher (Oxford, 2001). *Journal of Near Eastern Studies* 63: 224–25.

Review of *Prophètes et rois: Bible et Proche-Orient*, edited by André Lemaire (Paris, 2001), and *Prophecy in Its Ancient Near Eastern Context: Mesopotamian, Biblical, and Arabian Perspectives*, edited by Martti Nissinen (Atlanta, 2000). *Journal of Near Eastern Studies* 63: 298–99.

Review of *Ur III-Texte der St. Petersburger Eremitage*, by Natalia Koslova (Wiesbaden, 2000). *Journal of Near Eastern Studies* 63: 311–12.

Review of *Der Tell Halaf und sein Ausgräber Max Freiherr von Oppenheim: Kopf hoch! Mut hoch! und Humor hoch!*, by Nadja Cholidis and Lutz Martin (Mainz and Berlin, 2002). *Journal of Near Eastern Studies* 63: 312–13.

2005

"The Birth of Writing, the Dawn of Literature." In *The Looting of the Iraq Museum, Baghdad: The Lost Legacy of Ancient Mesopotamia*, edited by Angela M. H. Schuster and Milbry Polk, pp. 104–21. New York: Harry N. Abrams.

"My Career in Assyriology and Near Eastern Archaeology." *Journal of Assyrian Academic Studies* 19: 5–27. (Reprinted in this volume, pp. ix–xxxi.)

"Medicine, Surgery, and Public Health in Ancient Mesopotamia." *Journal of Assyrian Academic Studies* 19: 28–46. (Reprinted from *Civilizations of the Ancient Near East*. Vol. 3, edited by Jack M. Sasson, pp. 1911–24. New York: Charles Scribner's Sons, 1995.)

"Recent Advances in the Study of Assyrian and Babylonian Medicine." *Journal of Assyrian Academic Studies* 19: 47–50.

"The Theft and Destruction of Iraq's Ancient Past." *Journal of Assyrian Academic Studies* 19: 51–55.

"Potenzerhöhung." *Reallexikon der Assyriologie und vorderasiatischen Archäologie* 10, pp. 604–5.

Review of Ūmē Ṭābūti: *"I giorni favorevoli,"* by Maria Cristina Casaburi (Padua, 2003). *Journal of the American Oriental Society* 125: 149–50.

Review of *Riches Hidden in Secret Places: Ancient Near Eastern Studies in Memory of Thorkild Jacobsen*, edited by Tzvi Abusch (Winona Lake, Indiana, 2002). *Journal of Near Eastern Studies* 64: 71–72.

Review of *Eblaitica: Essays on the Ebla Archives and Eblaite Language*. Vol. 4, edited by Cyrus H. Gordon and Gary A. Rendsburg (Winona Lake, Indiana, 2002). *Journal of Near Eastern Studies* 64: 123–24.

Review of *Umma Messenger Texts in the British Museum: Part One*, by F. D'Agostino and F. Pomponio (Messina, 2002). *Journal of Near Eastern Studies* 64: 124–25.

Review of *Etudes ougaritiques 1: Travaux 1985–1995*, Ras Shamra-Ougarit, vol. 14, edited by Marguerite Yon and Daniel Arnaud (Paris, 2001). *Journal of Near Eastern Studies* 64: 125–26.

Review of *The Standard Babylonian Etana Epic*, by Jamie R. Novotny (Helsinki, 2001), and *The Standard Babylonian Epic of Anzu*, by Amar Annus (Helsinki, 2001). *Journal of Near Eastern Studies* 64: 126–27.

Review of *Hama and Jabla: Watercolours 1931–1961 by the Danish Architect Ejnar Fugmann*, by Alexandra Nilsson (Aarhus, 2002). *Journal of Near Eastern Studies* 64: 222–23.

Review of *Vom Zweistromland zum Kupfergraben: Vorgeschichte und Entstehungsjahre (1899–1918) der Vorderasiatischen Abteilung der Berliner Museen vor fach- und kulturpolitischen Hintergründen*, edited by Nicola Crüsemann (Berlin, 2000). *Journal of Near Eastern Studies* 64: 223–24.

Review of *Vorderasiatische Museen: Gestern, Heute, Morgen: Berlin, Paris, London, New York: Eine Standortbestimmung: Kolloquium aus Anlaß des einhundertjährigen Bestehens des Vorderasiatischen Museums Berlin am 7. Mai 1999*, edited by Beate Salje (Mainz, 2001). *Journal of Near Eastern Studies* 64: 224–26.

Review of *Neue Beiträge zur Semitistik: Erstes Arbeitstreffen der Arbeitsgemeinschaft Semitistik in der Deutschen Morgenländischen Gesellschaft vom 11. bis 13. September 2000 an der Friedrich-Schiller-Universität, Jena*, edited by Norbert Nebes (Wiesbaden, 2002). *Journal of Near Eastern Studies* 64: 226–27.

Review of *Magic and Divination in the Ancient World*, edited by Leda Ciaolo and Jonathan Seidel (Leiden, 2002). *Journal of Near Eastern Studies* 64: 227–28.

Review of *Pazuzu: Archäologische und philologische Studien zu einem altorientalischen Dämon*, by Nils P. Heeßel (Leiden, 2002). *Journal of Near Eastern Studies* 64: 228–29.

Review of *Keilschrifttexte aus japanischen Sammlungen*, by Ozaki Tohru (Wiesbaden, 2002). *Journal of Near Eastern Studies* 64: 229–30.

Review of *Two Lyres from Ur*, by Maude de Schauensee (Philadelphia, 2003). *Journal of Near Eastern Studies* 64: 313–15.

Review of *Literatur, Politik und Recht in Mesopotamien: Festschrift für Claus Wilcke*, edited by Walther Sallaberger, Konrad Volk, and Annette Zgoll (Wiesbaden, 2003). *Journal of Near Eastern Studies* 64: 315–17.

Review of *Legal Transactions of the Royal Court of Nineveh, Part II: Assurbanipal through Sin-Šarru-iškun*, by Raija Mattila (Helsinki, 2002). *Journal of Near Eastern Studies* 64: 317.

Review of iškar šēlebi: *Die Serie vom Fuchs*, by Burkhart Kienast (Stuttgart, 2003). *Journal of Near Eastern Studies* 64: 317–18.

Review of *Historical Dictionary of Mesopotamia*, by Gwendolyn Leick (Lanham, Maryland, 2003). *Journal of Near Eastern Studies* 64: 318–19.

2006

"Appendix 3: The Inscriptions." In *Nippur V: The Early Dynastic to Akkadian Transition: The Area WF Sounding at Nippur*, by Augusta McMahon, pp. 165–69. Oriental Institute Publications 129. Chicago: The Oriental Institute.

"The Human Body and Sexuality in the Babylonian Medical Texts." In *Médecine et médecins au Proche-Orient ancien: actes du colloque international organisé à Lyon les 8 et 9 novembre 2002*, edited by Pierre Villard and Laura Battini, pp. 39–52. Oxford: Archaeopress.

Review of *The Pantheon of Uruk during the Neo-Babylonian Period*, by Paul-Alain Beaulieu (Leiden and Boston, 2003). *Journal of Near Eastern Studies* 65: 141–43.

Review of *The Nimrud Letters, 1952*, by Henry W. F. Saggs (London, 2001). *Journal of Near Eastern Studies* 65: 143–44.

Review of *The God Dagan in Bronze Age Syria*, by Lluís Feliu (Leiden and Boston, 2003). *Journal of Near Eastern Studies* 65: 144–45.

Review of *The Political Correspondence of Esarhaddon*, by Mikko Luukko and Greta Van Buylaere (Helsinki, 2002). *Journal of Near Eastern Studies* 65: 145–46.

Review of *The British Museum: 250 Years*, by Marjorie Caygill (London, 2003). *Journal of Near Eastern Studies* 65: 222–23.

Review of *Prophets and Prophecy in the Ancient Near East*, by Martti Nissinen with contributions by C. L. Seow and Robert K. Ritner (Atlanta, 2003). *Journal of Near Eastern Studies* 65: 304–5.

Review of *Hayim and Miriam Tadmor Volume*, edited by I. Ephʿal, A. Ben-Tor, and P. Machinist (Jerusalem, 2003). *Journal of Near Eastern Studies* 65: 305–6.

Review of *Amarna Studies: Collected Writings*, by William L. Moran (Winona Lake, Indiana, 2003). *Journal of Near Eastern Studies* 65: 306.

Review of *Les lieux de culte in Orient: Jacques Thiry, in honorem*, edited by C. Cannuyer (Ath, Brussels, and Leuven, 2003). *Journal of Near Eastern Studies* 65: 306–7.

Review of *Spät-altbabylonische Tontafeln, Texte und Siegelabrollungen*, by Horst Klengel and Evelyn Klengel-Brandt (Mainz, 2002). *Journal of Near Eastern Studies* 65: 307–8.

Review of *Ur III Incantations from the Frau Professor Hilprecht-Collection*, by Johannes J. A. van Dijk and Markham J. Geller (Wiesbaden, 2003). *Journal of Near Eastern Studies* 65: 308–9.

Review of *Jerusalem in Original Photographs 1850–1920: Photographs from the Archives of the Palestine Exploration Fund*, by Shimon Gibson (Winona Lake, Indiana, 2003). *Journal of Near Eastern Studies* 65: 309.

MASCULINE OR FEMININE? THE CASE OF CONFLICTING GENDER DETERMINATIVES FOR MIDDLE BABYLONIAN PERSONAL NAMES*

J. A. Brinkman, The University of Chicago

In Babylonian texts, beginning in the Middle Babylonian period and continuing for centuries thereafter, personal names were regularly prefixed with a gender determinative: $^{/I/}$ (the vertical wedge) before male names and $^{/f/}$ (the SAL or MUNUS sign) before female names. Though personal names in the very earliest Middle Babylonian documents seem to lack such indicators,[1] the prefixing of personal gender determinatives seems to have become the rule by about 1400 B.C.[2] Through the rest of this period, with the exception of royal names,[3] very few personal names were written without one of these prefatory elements.[4]

---

* I wish to express my gratitude to colleagues who helped in the preparation of this article: Dennis Campbell, who provided updated bibliographical material on Hurrian and critiqued a draft of the Hurrian material in the excursus; Kevin Danti, who sent scans of several University Museum texts to assist with collations; Gene Gragg, who offered comments on the content and wording of the excursus; and Christopher Walker, who collated a passage in BM 82699.

[1] For example, 11 NT 27, published by M. Civil, "Cuneiform Texts," in M. Gibson, ed., *Excavations at Nippur – Eleventh Season*, OIC 22 (Chicago and London, 1975), pp. 131 and 140, no. 19; UM 55-21-62 (= 2 NT 356), published by L. Sassmannshausen, "Ein ungewöhnliches mittelbabylonisches Urkundenfragment aus Nippur," *Bagh. Mitt.* 25 (1994): 447–57.

[2] Ni. 3199 and D 85, legal texts from the reigns of Kadašman-Ḫarbe I and Kurigalzu I, respectively, use such determinatives. The latter text is published by V. Donbaz in "Two Documents from the Diverse Collections in Istanbul," SCCNH 2, pp. 72–75.

[3] Though the masculine personal determinative is used occasionally before names of kings in Babylonian texts written during their throne tenure in the Kassite period, most such names occur without a personal determinative. The writings are cited in detail in Brinkman *MSKH* 1 88–319, passim. In the following Post-Kassite period, down to 722 B.C., the names of Babylonian kings are almost never preceded by a masculine personal determinative in Babylonian inscriptions written during their reigns (references in Brinkman *PKB*, passim), though such determinatives are occasionally added in later copies.

[4] For example, [^{Id}]NIN.IB-SAG DUMU $^{\emptyset}$*šum-ma-li* (Ni. 832:17), ⸢^{I}UD-*šú*-ZÁLAG-*ir*⸣ DUMU $^{\emptyset}$LÚ-^{d}AMAR.UTU UM 29-15-681:26. Lack of personal determinatives is at present confined mostly to patronyms and matronyms. A notable exception to this picture is the work roster Ni. 911, a text without preserved date but clearly from the height of the Kassite period in the fourteenth and thirteenth centuries (because of the distinctive text style and personal names), which lists more than thirty names of living persons without preceding personal determinatives. It may also be observed that, when female sex-age classifications are listed before a personal name in a Middle Babylonian labor roster, the feminine personal

A small group of personal names poses an interesting variation within this framework. These names are written with both the masculine and feminine personal determinatives, in that sequence, for example, ^{If}*ḫu-mur-ti* (gen.)[5] and ^{If}*in-bu-šá*.[6] At first glance, one may be inclined to interpret these as scribal errors or to try to read the SAL sign syllabically (for example, as *sal*, *šal*, or *rak*).[7] But there are now more than twenty-five known examples of this phenomenon among published and unpublished Middle Babylonian texts, and in many instances it is clear that the name following the two determinatives is complete in itself and thus does not require the SAL sign to be read syllabically. Examples of such complete names are:

1. *Amat-Adad* : ^{If}GÉME-^{d}IM (CBS 13253 rev.? 7′)
2. *Ḫummurtu* : ^{If}*ḫu-mur-ti* (gen.; TuM NF 5 29:34)
3. *Ina-Ekur-rīšat* : ^{If}*ina*-É.KUR-*ri-šat* (CBS 3640 rev. ii′ 12′)
4. *Inbūša* : ^{If}*in-bu-šá* (CBS 3640 ii′ 14′)
5. *Mušta'ītu* : ^{If}*muš-ta-i-t*[*i*] (gen.; CBS 3640 rev. i′ 6′)
6. *Napširī-Bēltu* : ^{If}*nap-ši-ri*-NIN (Ni. 1264:8)
7. *Rabât-Gula* : ^{If}*ra-bat*-^{d}*gu-la* (CBS 3640 rev. ii′ 8′)
8. *Rabâtu* : ^{If}*ra-ba-ti* (gen.; BE 15 87:4, 175:15)
9. *Simut-abūša* : ^{Ifd}*si-mu-ut-a-bu-šá* (BM 82699 iv 7′)
10. *Šurānitu* : ^{If}*šu-ra-ni-t*[*i*] (gen.; Ni. 836:13′)[8]

How is one to interpret these double determinatives? It hardly seems necessary to infer that these cases describe persons of biologically ambiguous or indeterminate sex, and the graphic convention /If/ seems unlikely to be argot or an example of scribal

determinative before the name is frequently omitted, for example, BE 14 58:6, 7, 12, and passim (in comparable contexts, the masculine personal determinative is not omitted).

[5] Where textual references to personal name forms ending in an -i are quoted without context in this article and the final vowel in question may result from the fact that the context requires a genitive case, such forms will be marked "gen.," indicating that the name in this instance may be declined for case. (This does not imply that forms not so designated are not serving a genitive function within a clause but just that the ending of the form in context does not seem to be influenced by declension.)

[6] TuM NF 5 29:34; CBS 3640 ii′ 14′.

[7] Clay in the initial publication of BE 15 and PBS 2/2 read such names as ^{If}*ra-ba-ti* as *Rak*(*shal*)-*ra-ba-ti* (for BE 15 87:4, 175:15) and *Rak-rib-ba-ti* (for PBS 2/2 51:3); see also Clay *PN*, p. 120. To explain these, K. Jaritz, "Die kassitischen Sprachreste," *Anthropos* 52 (1957): 885, postulated a Kassite element "rak(ra)" attested only in personal names. Hölscher *Personennamen*, p. 176, retained Clay's readings but queried their accuracy. The possibility that the sign cluster /If/ should be read simply as an epigraphic variant of the SAL sign seems less likely, especially given the co-occurrence of /If/ and /f/ in CBS 3640 as discussed below.

[8] *Šurānitu* seems to be the word for "female cat," hitherto unattested, at least in Middle Babylonian. It occurs also in the name Ø DUMU ⌈^{If}*šu-ra-ni-ti*⌉ in Ni. 6670:17.

esoterica, as it occurs in a variety of pedestrian text types, including administrative lists and memoranda, letters, and legal documents. Thus far unambiguous occurrences of ^{If}PNs are restricted to two patterns: *a*) PN DUMU(.SAL) ^{If}PN, and *b*) Ø DUMU ^{If}PN. For example:

1. ^{I}*ik-ku-uk-ku* DUMU ^{If}*ra-ba-ti* (BE 15 87:3–4)
2. Ø DUMU ^{If}*ia-*⌈*ú*⌉*-ti* (Ni. 6670:11)[9]

There is as yet no unambiguous attestation of ^{If}PN other than in a citation of parentage.[10]

What is the meaning of these occurrences? One hint may be provided by the unpublished text CBS 3640, a roster of servile personnel, which contains an abundance of such names in varying context. Here is one of the better-preserved passages:

Rev. ii′

8′	GURUŠ.TUR	^{I}SUD-*ú-lu-lu*	DUMU ^{If}*ra-bat-*^{d}*gu-la*
9′	⌈*pir-su*⌉	^{I}*mu-šab-šu-ú*	DUMU ^{If}KI.MIN
10′	SAL.TUR	^{f}*li-ta-at-*^{d}*gu-la*	DUMU.SAL ^{f}KI.MIN
11′	DUMU.SAL.GABA	^{f}*ta-ri-ba-tum*	DUMU.SAL ^{f}KI.MIN
12′	GURUŠ.TUR	^{I}*ta-qí-ša-*^{d}*gu-la*	DUMU ^{If}*ina-*É.KUR*-ri-šat*
13′	*pir-su*	^{I}BA-*šá-*^{d}U.GUR	DUMU ^{If}KI.MIN
14′	*pir-su*	^{I}*iz-kur-*^{d}U.GUR	DUMU ^{If}KI.MIN
15′	SAL.TUR	^{f}*ni-ip-pu-ri-tum*	DUMU.SAL ^{f}KI.MIN
16′	SAL.T[UR]	^{f}*muš-ta-i-tum*	DUMU.SAL ^{f}KI.MIN
17′	[ ]	⌈^{f}⌉*tar-ba-tu-šá*	DUMU.SAL ^{f}KI.MIN
18′	[ ]	⌈^{f}⌉*ra-bat-*DINGIR*-sa*	DUMU.SAL ^{f}KI.MIN

Each entry consists of three parts: the sex-age classification of the worker,[11] the name of the worker prefixed with either a masculine or feminine personal determinative, and then the rubric "son/daughter of" followed by the name of the parent. Parents' names are written out in full the first time each occurs, but for subsequent entries the name is

[9] Names of the type Ø DUMU(.SAL) PN are discussed in Clay *PN*, p. 45 (though he broadens the category unduly to include also personal names prefixed with sex-age classifications such as DUMU.SAL.GABA) and in Hölscher *Personennamen*, p. 7.

[10] For a possible exception, see the excursus on Ḫazi and Ḫagi names below.

[11] This classification section contains three subcolumns, the first listing the sex-age classification, the second noting whether the worker had died, and the third recording whether the worker had fled or escaped. In the passage quoted above, the second and third subcolumns are blank for lines 8′–15′, then destroyed for the last three lines. (Sex-age classifications in these rosters have been discussed in J. A. Brinkman, "Sex, Age, and Physical Condition Designations for Servile Laborers in the Middle Babylonian Period," *Kraus AV*, pp. 1–8.)

abbreviated as “the same” (KI.MIN). The full or abbreviated parental name is prefixed by personal gender determinatives: $^{/If/}$ is used when the descendant is male and only $^{/f/}$ is used when the descendant is female. In every case in this passage the name of the parent is a matronym, but the choice of personal determinative(s) before the matronym varies with the gender of the offspring. Other sections of this roster list male and female laborers with patronyms (usually prefixed with $^{/I/}$), with matronyms (usually prefixed with either $^{/If/}$ or $^{/f/}$), or without indication of parentage; and the pattern ^{If}PN is restricted to parents of male descendants.[12]

Even in its present damaged condition, CBS 3640 preserves twelve examples of ^{If}PN that adhere to this paradigm.[13] Outside this text there are at least fourteen further examples of ^{If}PN parentage (i.e., matronym) linked to male descendants: *a*) five of the type ^{I}PN DUMU ^{If}PN; *b*) at least nine of the type Ø DUMU ^{If}PN. Thus far I have seen only one example of a female descendant linked with a matronym written with both the masculine and feminine personal determinatives: [...]-x DUMU.SAL ^{If}GÉME-^{d}IM CBS 13253 rev.? 7′.[14]

Matronyms in Middle Babylonian texts are also written in the more customary way, i.e., with the female personal determinative alone. There are multiple cases of matronyms attested in the following patterns:

- *a*) ^{I}PN DUMU ^{f}PN—e.g., ^{Id}30-*na-ap-ši-ra* MU.NI [D]UMU ^{f}*bi-ri-ri-tum* (D. 85:1–2, published in Donbaz, SCCNH 2, pp. 72–75);
- *b*) ^{f}PN DUMU ^{f}PN—e.g., ^{f}*ina*-AN-⸢*e-nam*⸣-*rat* DUMU.SAL ^{f}*i-la-ti* (CBS 3640 ii′ 18′);
- *c*) Ø DUMU ^{f}PN—e.g., Ø DUMU ^{f}*a-da-ri-ti* (Sassmannshausen *Beitr.*, p. 240, no. 43:14);
- *d*) Ø DUMU.SAL ^{f}PN—e.g., Ø DUMU.SAL ^{f}*ḫi-li-*^{d}*za-an-na-ru* (Ni. 1151:8′).[15]

There are also examples of ^{f}PN DUMU.SAL ^{Ø}PN, in which the parent is a woman, such as, ^{f}KÁ-*ša-ti* DUMU.SAL ^{Ø}*ḫu-zu-ti* (Ni. 1056 rev. ii 23′)[16] and ^{f}*u-bar-*[*t*]*um* DUMU.SAL ^{Ø}*ni-sa-an-ni-ti* (UM 29-16-108:4).

---

[12] But the patterns ^{I}PN DUMU ^{If}PN/^{If}KI.MIN and ^{f}PN DUMU.SAL ^{f}PN/^{f}KI.MIN are not followed exclusively throughout the text. For example, there are two instances of ^{f}PN DUMU.SAL ^{Ø}KI.MIN (ii′ 11′–12′) and one case of ^{I}PN DUMU ^{f}PN (ii′ 22′). So there is hardly a set of inflexible rules being followed here.

[13] I.e., in addition to examples of ^{If}KI.MIN.

[14] Where clearly preserved, the style of worker entries in this text is generally ^{f}PN DUMU.SAL ^{I}PN. The sole exception to this pattern is the line cited here in which the parent's name is preceded by $^{/If/}$. There seems little question that the broken section at the beginning of this line originally contained a female personal name.

[15] Note also the occurrence of Ø ⸢DUMU⸣.SAL ^{f}*bi-it-*⸢*tu*⸣*-um-ma* at Dur-Kurigalzu (O. R. Gurney, “Texts from Dur-Kurigalzu,” *Iraq* 11 [1949]: 145, no. 6:7).

[16] *Ḫuzzu'tu* (*Ḫuzzūtu*) or *Ḫunzu'tu*, “the cripple”; see Hölscher *Personennamen*, p. 86 s.v. Ḫuzzûtu). The name is written ^{f}*ḫu-zu-tum* in

So we are left with the following picture. Current attestations of ^{If}PN occur in a variety of text types written by different scribes. These texts, where they contain a regnal year and a royal name, fall across a range of several decades in the thirteenth century (from 1300 till at least 1232, i.e., from Nazi-Maruttaš year 8 till at least the first year of Kaštiliašu IV).[17] All occurrences discussed thus far are in texts from Nippur, which has provided the overwhelming majority of documentation currently available for the period. The use of the double determinative seems to reflect scribal choice, since the more common way of expressing gender for matronyms by prefixing simple $^{/\mathrm{f}/}$ was also in use at Nippur over the same time range. There is no indication that the women with $^{/\mathrm{If}/}$ determinatives occupied a distinctive social or economic status in the community other than their role as mothers and presumably heads of household (in the absence of citation of a patronym); this is illustrated clearly in the passage from CBS 3640 cited above, where different occurrences of the name of the same woman are sometimes prefixed with $^{/\mathrm{If}/}$ and sometimes with $^{/\mathrm{f}/}$.[18] And it is worth observing that women do occur as household heads in many instances at Nippur in the Middle Babylonian period, chiefly as the principal of a *qinnu* or putative family/clan grouping[19] or as chief representative and primary referent in laborer households where an adult male was lacking.[20] (Under certain circumstances, these two categories may overlap.) Was it felt in some cases by scribes that the prefixing of a masculine personal determinative before a female name marked an elevated status as head of household, a rank customarily reserved for an adult male?

TuM NF 5 34:36′, Ni. 852:14, Ni. 1154 i 10′, and Ni. 11373 i ⌜5′⌝; ^{f}*ḫu-un-zu-ʾ-tum* in CBS 4909 rev. 7′ and Sassmannshausen *Beitr.*, p. 278, no. 96:19 (and partially restored ibid., line 4), ^{f}*ḫu-un-zu-ʾ-ti* (gen.) in Ni. 826:4. It corresponds to the masculine **Ḫuzzuʾu* or *Ḫunzuʾu* (also written ^{I}*ḫu-un-zu-ḫu*); references to *Ḫunzuʾu*/*Ḫunzuḫu* may be found in Hölscher *Personennamen*, p. 85, to which may be added the genitive ^{I}*ḫu-un-*⌜*zu-i*⌝ in Ni. 732:22′. The male form *Ḫunzuʾu* had become an ancestral or family name by the late Middle Babylonian period (see W. G. Lambert, "Ancestors, Authors, and Canonicity," *JCS* 11 [1957]: 2–4, 6–7, and passim); this family was to remain prominent until well into the Seleucid period. In Ni. 1056, the text cited here, the personal determinative is also omitted before the name of a male parent: ^{f}*ša*-KÁ-^{d}*gu-la* DUMU.SAL $^{\varnothing}$ur-^{d}IM (rev. ii 22′).

---

[17] TuM NF 5 29 is dated in Nazi-Maruttaš year 8. The account Ni. 836 covers months I–XII of [MU.x].KAM of Kaštiliašu, hence at least his first year.

[18] Though it may be observed that many of the female names are drawn from servile laborer rosters or ration lists, indicating a relatively low social status. But in some instances there is insufficient information available to draw conclusions about the status of the women.

[19] In which case the *qinnu* is named after them (for example, *qin-ni* ^{f}GAL-*šá*-^{d}*iš-ḫa-ra*, CT 51 19:5). Many, and perhaps most, *qinnātu* attested in Middle Babylonian administrative texts seem to involve persons of servile laborer status.

[20] See, for example, Ištar-bēlī-uṣrī and her family (BE 14 58:12–17), Ina-Akkadi-rabât and her family (UM 29-15-760:6′–8′). Such examples are abundant in worker rosters and ration lists.

A prominent female family head is also attested at Middle Babylonian Ur,[21] where her designation as ancestress/parent also led to scribal inconsistency. The name of Dey(y)ānatu,[22] attested as the ancestress of at least seven males, is written sometimes with a masculine, sometimes with a feminine personal determinative, and—on one occasion—perhaps with both determinatives.[23]

This brief survey has called attention to the existence of Middle Babylonian female personal names prefixed with both the masculine and feminine personal determinatives. A possible explanation for the choice of the /If/ expression and for its significance would focus on the enhanced prominence of the designated women as heads of family or household, though we should bear in mind that the present distribution of attestations of IfPNs solely as matronyms could be due to the accidents of textual survival.[24] Additional data and further research should be able to test the accuracy and relevance of this hypothesis. Even more interesting and fruitful should be a broader study of the roles and influence of women, especially as heads of household, in Middle Babylonian society.

---

[21] For the status of this family, see most recently the remarks by E. Robson, "Technology in Society: Three Textual Case Studies from Late Bronze Age Mesopotamia," in Andrew J. Shortland, ed., *The Social Context of Technological Change: Egypt and the Near East, 1650–1550 B.C.* (Oxford, 2001), pp. 39–57 (especially "The Brewers and Burglars of Ur," pp. 46–50).

[22] The name is written I*da-a-a-na-ti*, f*da-a-a-na-ti*, If?*da-a-a-<na>-ti* (once), and f*di-ia-na-ti* (all gen.) in its fully preserved attestations (references in UET 7, p. 12, supplemented by Gurney *MB Texts*, p. 197; see also n. 23 below). This is a hypocoristic of an original *Dey*(*y*)*ānat-ina*-GN, which became *Dey*(*y*)*ānat* + the case ending *-u*. To judge from the orthography of personal names, the spoken forms for classical *day*(*y*)*ānu* and *day*(*y*)*antu* in the Middle Babylonian period must have been something like *dey*(*y*)*ānu* and *dey*(*y*)*andu*; note the spellings Ø DUMU I*de-e-a-a-ni* (gen.) in CBS 10908:6′, f*de-e-a-an-di-ina*-UNUG.KI in Ni. 1066+1069 rev. ii′ 5′ (cf. SAL *di-ia-an-di-i-na*-UNUG.KI in BE 15 188 rev. iii′ 8′). Personal names formed with Dayyānat-/Dey(y)ānat- are all borne by women in the Middle Babylonian period. Such names are most commonly written in a form such as *Day*(*y*)*ant*(*i*)*-ina*-GN; note the sample of writings for *Dayyant*(*i*)*-ina-Uruk* quoted in Hölscher *Personennamen*, pp. 58–59—and comparable writings can be found for the names *Day*(*y*)*ant*(*i*)*-ina-Akkadi* (Ni. 6713 i 4′) and *Day*(*y*)*ant*(*i*)*-ina-Isin*, though the latter is written SAL *da-a-a-di-i-na-ì-si-in* in Ni. 6874 rev. i′ 15′. These names, which use a stative form, are to be distinguished from names such as f*Day*(*y*)*antī-Bēlet-Nippuri*, in which *day*(*y*)*antī* is the noun *day*(*y*)*antu* with the first-person singular genitive pronominal suffix. (For the use of *dey*(*y*)*ānu* and other occupation/profession names as family or ancestral names in the Middle Babylonian period, see my article "The Use of Occupation Names as Patronyms in the Kassite Period: A Forerunner of Neo-Babylonian Ancestral Names?" in A. Guinan et al., eds., *If a Man Builds a Joyful House: Essays in Honor of Erle Verdun Leichty* [Leiden and Boston, 2006].)

[23] With a masculine personal determinative in UET 7 18:2 and rev. 8, 22:5, 30:3, 33:7, 46:⌈3⌉; with a feminine personal determinative in UET 7 12:4′, 21 rev. 11, 25:8. In UET 7 2 rev. 25, to judge from the copy, the scribe seems to have written both determinatives; note also the comment by Gurney *MB Texts*, p. 28.

[24] For the possible occurrence of one such individual in non-matronym status, see the discussion of NBC 7948 in the excursus on Ḫazi and Ḫagi names below.

Postscript

Other examples of masculine and feminine personal determinatives written before Middle Babylonian matronyms have recently come to my attention, and these in part expand the range of the attestations. In texts from Babylon, there are now at least two such instances in the form ^{I}PN DUMU ^{If}PN; the matronyms in these cases are ^{If}*ba-bi-la-a-a-i-t*[*i*] (gen.) Bab 34300 rev. 3 (no date preserved) and ^{If}*lu-ri-in-di* (gen.) VAT 13210:10 (Kudur-Enlil year 6 [1259]). In a tablet offered at a Bonhams auction in May 2003, a legal text dated in the first year of Kadašman-Turgu (1281) recounts the efforts of Ina-pīša-imrir to buy a young slave-girl as a bride for her son; Ina-pīša-imrir's name is consistently written with the feminine determinative alone (lines 1, 7, 10, etc.) except in the sole case where it occurs as a matronym for her son, Adad-muštēšir—there her name after the DUMU sign is written with both the masculine and feminine determinatives: ^{If}*i+na*-KA-*ša-im-ri-ir* (line 4).[25] Finally, in a legal text dated in Šagarakti-Šuriaš year 5 (1241) in the Cornell University cuneiform collection, another Middle Babylonian matronym is attested in the sequence ^{I}*qu*-⸢*nu*⸣-*nu* DUMU ^{fd}*iš-tar-šar-rat* (Cornell, no. 5:10–11).

EXCURSUS

Ḫazi and Ḫagi Names

There is a small group of personal names that contain the elements ḫazi and ḫagi and are also apparently preceded by the determinative cluster $^{\mathrm{/If/}}$. But, since the interpretation of these names has yet to be adequately established and a syllabic reading for the SAL sign definitively excluded, I am treating these names here separately.

The most common of these names is written ^{If}ḫa-zi-^{d}AMAR.UTU (or ^{I}SAL-ḫa-zi-^{d}AMAR.UTU).[26] It is attested to date in three texts:

1. Ø DUMU ^{If}ḫa-zi-^{d}AMAR.UTU, listed in an entry in a ration text that records fodder for horses (BE 14 56a:23; dated Nazi-Maruttaš, year 13 [= 1295 B.C.]).[27]

---

[25] Bonhams, *Antiquities, Wednesday 14 May 2003, Knightsbridge* (London, 2003), pp. 84–85, no. 235 (with photos). I am indebted to W. G. Lambert, who kindly sent me his transliteration made from the tablet itself, which helped clear up the reading of passages insufficiently visible in the photographs.

[26] I am here provisionally reading the SAL sign as the feminine personal determinative, without implying that this will be the preferred or finally accepted reading.

[27] Clay interpreted this name as *Shal*(?)-*ha-zi-Marduk* (BE 14, p. 52) and *Šal-ḫa-zi-Marduk* (Clay *PN*, p. 128). Hölscher *Personennamen*, p. 200, transliterated ^{m}ŠAL-*ḫa-zi*-^{d}AMAR.UTU and suggested a possible emendation to *Šadḫazi-Marduk*.

2. Ø DUMU.SAL ^{If}ḫa-zi-^{d}AMAR.UTU, mentioned four times in a legal text concerned with real estate described as É *ša* PN (Ni. 1585:5, 9, 12, 17; dated Šagarakti-Šuriaš, year 4 [= 1242 B.C.]).[28]
3. ^{If}ḫa-zi-^{d}AMAR.UTU, mentioned in an undated letter from Itti-Marduk-balāṭu to Esagil-šadûni dealing with livestock and related matters (NBC 7948:13).

The same or a similar name may occur in the administrative text AO 8136 rev. 15 (Durand *Textes babyloniens*, pl. 14): ⸢^{I}⸣^{f}ḫa-zi-⸢^{d}x⸣.[29]

There does not seem to be an appropriate ḫaz or ḫazi element known in either Akkadian or Kassite, but there are numerous attestations of a stem ḫaz, or more precisely ḫaž ("to hear") in Hurrian, which also occurs in personal names. Thomas Richter has observed[30] that the Hurrian consonant /ž/ was written in two principal ways in cuneiform script: either with a sign in the "z" sign-series or with a sign in the "š" sign-series. Ḫažib,[31] a third-person nonergative form of the verb ḫaž, is attested in names written in such ways as Ḫazib-Aranziḫ or Ḫašib-Tešup. Ḫažib written with a "zi" sign is attested generally at Mari and in what at one time constituted the core region of the Mittani state between the Euphrates and Tigris.[32] Written with a "ši" sign, it is attested outside this region, both to the west (for example, Alalakh, Tigunānu) and to the east (Nuzi, Shemshara).[33] The final b of this verb form sometimes assimilates, partially or fully, to a following consonant in such names as Ḫašik-Kewar, Ḫašil-Lumti, Ḫašim-Matka, Ḫašim-Nati, Ḫašim-Nawar, and Ḫašin-Nawar;[34] and the resulting doubled consonant

---

[28] The first of these references occurs in the phrase ⸢*aš-šum*⸣ *mi-ši-iḫ-ti* É *ša* DUMU.SAL ^{If}ḫa-zi-^{d}AMAR.UTU. This seems to be the first attestation of *mišiḫtu* in Middle Babylonian (the term is otherwise known only in first-millennium texts).

[29] Hölscher *Personennamen*, p. 82, reads ^{f}*Ḫa-zi*-⸢^{d}x⸣, but all the personal-name entries in this section of the text begin with a damaged masculine personal determinative (lines 2–7, 9–16). A similar damaged name ⸢^{I}⸣^{f}ḫa-zi⸣[ ] may occur in Ni. 6606:8, a *tēlītu* account dated in year 5 of Kadašman-Enlil II (= 1259 B.C.).

[30] See T. Richter, "Anmerkungen zu den hurritischen Personennamen des *ḫapiru*-Prismas aus Tigunānu" in SCCNH 9, pp. 125–34 (especially pp. 131–33).

[31] Or hažip.

[32] For example, at Chagar Bazar and Rimah. For the situation at Emar, see R. Pruzsinszky, SCCNH 13, pp. 239, 250, and 253. The verb form ḫažib is not yet attested in Emar personal names, but may be represented in apparent hypocoristics such as ^{I}ḫa-zi-ia and ^{I}ḫa-zi (references cited on p. 374 of the text on the compact disk issued with SCCNH 13).

[33] Walter Farber has kindly called my attention to the writing ^{I}ḫa-še-ku-nu in an Old Babylonian PN from Tell ed-Dēr (Edzard *Tell ed-Dēr*, no. 61:17).

[34] These examples are drawn primarily from the Nuzi corpus, and references for the names may be found in *NPN*, pp. 56–57 and Cassin *Anthroponymie*, p. 53, with the exception of Ḫašim-Nawar, which is found in the Tigunānu prism (Salvini, *The Ḫabiru Prism of King Tunip-Teššup of Tikumani*, i 13, ii 15, viii 51). That assimilation does not always take place in such contexts at Nuzi may be seen from such name forms as Ḫašib-Kiaše and Ḫašib-Ninu (Cassin *Anthroponymie*, p. 54). The more restricted corpus of names available from Mari, Chagar Bazar, and Tell Rimah does not seem to favor this assimilation, such as Ḫazib-Nawar (ARM 23 125:5, 160:3), Ḫazib-Kuzuḫ (AOAT 1 217 no. 40:26), ḫa-zi-ib-mu-[ ] (*OBT Tell Rimah* 322 v 36).

can be written singly or doubly, for example, ḫa-ši-lu-um-ti vs. ḫa-ši-il-lu-um-ti, ḫa-ši-na-mar vs. ḫa-ši-in-na-ma-ar.[35] Though hybrid Hurrian-Akkadian personal names are relatively rare,[36] there are a few known examples such as Gimil-Tešup and Ḫašib-Bēl(e)t-ekalli.[37] Ḫazi-Marduk, or perhaps more properly Ḫazi(m)-Marduk (from Ḫažib-Marduk), could theoretically be explained as an example of such a hybrid name.

One drawback to this explanation is that one would have to assume a writing of the Hurrian /ž/ with a "zi" sign at Nippur—which would apparently deviate from the geographic pattern of orthographic distribution sketched above.[38] But there is another more serious objection. At Nippur, the /ž/ in the name Ḫažib-Tilla is written with a "ṣi" sign: ^{I}ḫa-ṣi-ib-til-la seems to be the local orthography for this name, attested in several texts.[39] The situation is further complicated by the presence of a similar name written ^{I}ḫi-ṣi-ib-til-la or ^{I}ḫi-ṣib-til-la in these and other Nippur texts;[40] the initial element of this name seems otherwise unparalleled in Hurrian, though one may ponder the possibility of a derivation from the Akkadian *ḫiṣbu*, "abundance," which is attested in topographical names and at least once in an Old Babylonian personal name.[41] The orthography of Hurrian names at Middle Babylonian Nippur is as yet imperfectly understood,[42] and further research may yield a more nuanced view of scribal practices.

Another aspect of this name, ^{If}Ḫazi-Marduk, which is not yet shared with the ^{If}PNs discussed in the main section of this article, is that in one instance it occurs as the name of a living individual, not just as an ancestor.

There is similar uncertainty about the interpretation of a name written ^{If}ḫa-gi or ^{I}SAL-ḫa-gi, which occurs once as the name of a living individual in an account text

---

[35] JEN 516:15, HSS 16 333:11; JEN 250:31, HSS 16 348:14.

[36] Mauro Giorgieri, "L'onomastica hurrita," *La parola del passato* 55 (2000): 291 under 2.5; see also examples cited ibid., p. 288 under 2.2.1.

[37] *NPN*, pp. 85, 57; Cassin *Anthroponymie*, pp. 82, 54.

[38] Note, however, that Purves in *NPN*, p. 215 s.v. ḫaz, observed that ḫaš "to hear" was written as ḫaz in personal names in documents drafted by Akkadian scribes at Nuzi. He also suggested that ḫaz might be the Akkadian rendering of Hurrian ḫaš.

[39] ^{I}ḫa-ṣi-ib-til-la in CBS 3480 i 39′, CBS 4914 rev. 12′, and CBS 11143 i 25′; ^{I}ḫa-ṣi-ib-til-l[a], ⸢^{I}ḫa-ṣ⸣i-ib-til-la in PBS 2/2 84:22, 35. The spelling ḫa-ši-ib-til-la, cited in Hölscher *Personennamen*, p. 81, is from the Istanbul tablet D 137, which is from Nuzi or a related area, not Nippur (note also the comment by Sassmannshausen, in his review of Hölscher *Personennamen*, in *BiOr* 55 [1998]: 825).

[40] ^{I}ḫi-ṣi-ib-til-la in CBS 3480 i ⸢38′⸣, 42′; CBS 4914 rev. ⸢11′⸣, 15′; CBS 11143 i 24′ (a CBS 3480 reference, with a queried -ṣi-, is cited by Clay *PN*, p. 80); ^{I}ḫi-ṣib-til-la in Ni. 5860 ii 5′, 8′; and Ni. 6470 ii′ 9′. That Ḫiṣib-Tilla is not simply a variant of Ḫaṣib-Tilla seems likely from the fact that these names are used to designate different persons in three of the same rosters.

[41] As noted in *CAD* Ḫ s.v. *ḫiṣbu* A.

[42] One may have to reckon with improvised renderings by local scribes of sounds absent from the customary Babylonian phonological inventory or with traditional writings imported by foreign scribes educated elsewhere. Or, in this case, could the similarity of the non-theophoric elements of the two names (ḫiṣib and ḫaṣib) have influenced the scribal choice of orthography? It may also be noted that work rosters record the presence of foreign scribes at Nippur in the Middle Babylonian period (for example, scribes from Arrapḫa are mentioned in Ni. 1624 ii′ 8′–9′).

dated in year 3 of Šagarakti-Šuriaš (= 1243 B.C.).[43] Insofar as I am aware, there does not appear to be an appropriate element ḫag(i) or ḫak(i) in Akkadian, Kassite, or Hurrian; and there seems to be no obvious explanation of this name.

These names are mentioned here as potential further examples of the /If/ personal-name category, but better and less ambiguous evidence is needed to determine with reasonable certainty how they are to be read and interpreted.

[43] FLP 1338:13, published in Sassmannshausen *Beitr.*, p. 445, no. 463.

EARLY SEMITIC LOANWORDS IN SUMERIAN

Miguel Civil, The University of Chicago

The existence of two successive layers of loanwords (hereafter LW) of Semitic origin in Sumerian has been recognized for a very long time. The first and older one has the ending -a, the second the ending -um. A third, and presumably still older, layer of endingless forms, such as silim, has been of course recognized,[1] but the words belonging to it have so far not been systematically collected and analyzed. The present article is a first attempt to examine, at least partially, this lexical subset. Its existence and importance are not surprising, given the close symbiosis of Sumerians and Semites in southern Mesopotamia since the beginning of historical times. I am pleased to offer this article as a modest homage to my friend and colleague Robert D. Biggs, who presented the earliest convincing evidence for the presence of Semites among the Mesopotamian scribes.[2]

1. This article is a partial result of an investigation aimed at detecting regularities in the phonological shape of the entries of the Sumerian lexicon[3] and the possible relationship of those shapes with semantic sets as well as with historical factors in the formation of the lexicon. The historical aspect will be limited here to the identification of possible Semitic etymologies.[4] To keep the investigation within reasonable limits,

---

[1] See, for instance, the contributions of D. O. Edzard, I. J. Gelb, and A. Falkenstein in "Aspects du contact suméro-akkadien," *Genava* 8 (1960): 301–14, 341–71.

[2] See his pioneering article "Semitic Names in the Fara Period," *JCS* 36 (1967): 55–66 and especially his monumental work *Inscriptions from Tell Abū Ṣalābīkh*, OIP 99 (Chicago, 1974), pp. 34–35. Some of the points discussed in this paper, and related matters, have already been presented by me at the 204th (Madison, Wisconsin, 1994) and 206th (Philadelphia, 1996) Annual Meetings of the American Oriental Society, and at the 48th Rencontre Assyriologique International in Leiden in 2002. I thank my colleagues Gonzalo Rubio and Leonid Kogan for their suggestions and corrections. Of course, all errors are mine. The financial aid of the Institut Català de Recerca i d'Estudis Avançats (Barcelona) is gratefully acknowledged.

[3] The term "lexicon" is taken here as the inventory of the *lexical* (as opposed to *grammatical*) morphemes of a language, but the label "lexical phonology" is avoided because of its associations with particular linguistic schools.

[4] This is not to deny that there cannot be other sources, besides the uncontrollable, unknown languages of the area. Indo-European, for instance, may have provided a certain number of words, such as maḫ "large, great" (competing with gal); cf. Skt. *mah-*, Gk. μέγας, IE **meĝ(h)-*; see also the discussion of d/taraḫ below. To date, published attempts to identify Indo-European words have been rather unfortunate; see G. Rubio, "On the Alleged 'Pre-Sumerian Substratum'," *JCS* 51 (1999): 9–11.

it will be arbitrarily circumscribed to a graphically and phonologically defined lexical subset of words that fulfill the following conditions:

a) the word must have the form $C_1V_1C_2V_2C_3$;[5]

b) $V_1 = V_2$;

c) -V_2C_3 should not be -um, unless it can be proved that this m is part of the radical; otherwise there are no restrictions in the choice of the consonants (including duplicated consonants and clusters);

d) the word, as far as it can be ascertained, should not be the result of a reduplication process nor a (homovocalic) compound of two monosyllabic roots.

The provisional exclusion of heterovocalic CVCVC-forms, such as ḫašḫur "apple" or ḫazin "ax," as well as of items of the form VCVC, such as asal "poplar" (Arabic *aṯal*/ *ʾtl*, Heb. *ešal*, Egypt. *jzsr*.(*t*) "tamarisk") or udun "oven" (Akk. *a*/*utūnu*, Arabic *ʾattūn*, Geʿez *ʾeton*), whose etymology may involve at times initial Semitic "laryngeals,"[6] is due purely to economy of space. Homovocalic variants of words regularly attested as heterovocalic are also omitted, such as ḫubur, variant of ḫe(n)bur "reed shoot"; ḫulup, variant of ḫalup "a kind of tree"; and so on. A further exclusion eliminates Akkadian words given in some syllabaries in the construct state, such as UR = *ka-la-ab* in Proto-Ea 648. Condition *d*) requires (1) that the word not be a transparent compound such as ŋušur "beam" < ŋe/iš "piece of wood" + ùr "roof," with vowel assimilation, or nis(s)ig "vegetable" < níŋ "thing" + sig_7 "green," or the result of vowel harmony: za-pa-ág "shout" < zi "breath" + pa-ág "to emit(?)"; (2) nor should it be an opaque compound (in practice, no confirmation of this fact will be possible in most cases) such as šidim "mason," conceivably from $ši(g)_4$ "brickwork" + dím "to build"; (3) unambiguous reduplicated forms must also be eliminated: babbar "white" < bar + bar, nunus "eggs" < *nus + nus, etc. The rationale behind the choice of CVCVC-forms, besides keeping the length of this article within reasonable limits, is that longer lexical items provide a wider, safer base of comparison and the risk of operating with chance similarities is thus minimized. There are no doubt shorter LWs, but the phonological correspondences will be more solidly established first with the help of the longer ones, so that the results of the study of the $C_1V_1C_2V_2C_3$-forms, as defined above, will be but a first step toward an examination of the whole lexicon.

2. It is not easy to determine the monosyllabic or polysyllabic nature of a Sumerian word. Apparently monosyllabic entries dominate the Sumerian lexicon. Of the 200 most frequent verbal stems, only about 8 percent are graphically bisyllabic; the rest

---

[5] C in this paper includes consonantal clusters.

[6] Other processes may be involved, as in ušum "(mythical) snake" < *wušum < bušum (MUŠ = bù-šúm, in Ebla); cf. Akk. *bašmu*, Ugar. *bṯn*, Arabic *baṯan*.

are monosyllabic. Statistics about nominal stems give similar results: samples from literary texts show 79–82 percent of monosyllabic roots, 10–15 percent of bisyllabic, 7–8 percent of CVCVC-forms. Due to the nature of cuneiform syllabic writing and to various scribal habits, however, the graphic syllabification may not exactly match the phonological one. Syllabic writing cannot directly represent a word-initial or word-final consonantic cluster without the insertion of an epenthetic vowel or the (graphic) elision of one of the consonants, usually the first. At all times, the scribes alternate very frequently, and freely(?), between CVC and CVCV definitions. Thus ŋi-ir "foot" alternating with ŋi-ri may in principle represent /ŋir/, /ŋri/, or /ŋiri/; ka-la-ak "strong" can be /kalk/, /klak/, or /kalak/; and so on. Furthermore, in these cases, as well as in apparently bisyllabic words of the form VCV, such as igi, aga, ugu, etc., the scribe could have used a final vowel to indicate some property of the consonant or of the preceding, not contiguous, vowel, as in the English spellings of the type *ate*, *same*, etc.[7] The sonority hierarchy of the syllable makes it quite likely that in a sequence stop + liquid a vowel in between is a merely graphic epenthesis.[8] Furthermore, a CV graphic syllable can correspond in fact to a CVC syllable, due to the scribal conventions that may delete the graphic representation of syllable-final consonants. Thus one has spellings, such as du-si (/tupsik/) "basket for dirt," written alternatively tu-up-ši-ik (Hh. V–VII 194 Emar) (Akk. *tupšikku)*, with cluster simplification and nonrepresentation of the final consonant. A Sumerian LW in Akkadian, if available, can disambiguate between CVC- and CVCV-forms. In the first case, the LW will end in *-CCu*, in the second with a long vowel *-û*.

3. All the preceding considerations suggesting that the writing CVCVC could occasionally represent a phonologically monosyllabic word do not really affect the outcome of the present investigation. The triconsonantic structure remains in all cases

[7] Note that igi gives the LWs *igu* and *igû* in Akkadian, failing to provide an answer. The long form, however, may be due to the fact that sign names tend to end in a long vowel. Cf., on the other hand, the formation of the so-called *marû*-forms of the Sumerian verb by the addition of the suffix -e, which may simply signal a change in the stem vowel. Finally, and as a corollary, traditionally accepted CVCV-forms may be in fact CVC: dumu "son" could very well be /dum/. The syllabaries give equal chances to both forms, and the frequent parallelism dam // dum(u) could, perhaps, be an indication that the short form is preferable. Note, however, the Emesal spelling du_5-mu (that could nonetheless be taken as an indication of an Emesal reading */duŋ/) and the Greek transcription δωμο in S. M. Maul, "Neues zu den 'Graeco-Babyloniaca,'" *ZA* 81 (1991): 92:7.

[8] This phenomenon is not limited to obstruent + liquids. An epenthetic vowel may be present in words of the form $C_1iC_2a(C_3)$, where C_1 is a sibilant and C_2 a stop or a lateral. Examples include šita "mace," šitan "small ditch," sila "street," silà "measure," sipad "shepherd," and many others. The hypothesis that phonologically they are /šta/, /sla/, /spat/, etc., is extremely likely. Equally likely is the assumption that the syllabary definitions of the word for "bread" (ni-in-da, in-da, ni-da, i-da, and ì-da) are attempts to represent /nda/ or /nta/. Note that such phenomena do not need to be purely graphic; Spanish *cruz* "cross," for instance, gives *ruz* in Chol Mayan and *kurus* in Tzotzil Mayan.

intact and can thus always be compared with a presumed Semitic original. Once a credible relationship between a Sumerian word and a Semitic counterpart has been established, the problem of the direction of the borrowing should be tackled. Given the lack of information about the early stages of Akkadian and the uncertainties about archaic Semitic, the whole resting on a background of unknown linguistic entities, clear answers often will be impossible. Even if it can be established that two words are cognates, the direction of a borrowing often cannot be ascertained. The possibilities are many. A word (1) may have entered the Sumerian lexicon from what one could call Proto-Akkadian, in which case the word may or may not have survived into the historical stages of Akkadian, (2) it may have been borrowed from a Semitic language other than Akkadian, or (3) Sumerian and Semitic/Akkadian may both stem from a common, unknown source. In the opposite direction, (4) a Sumerian word may have been borrowed by a Semitic language. For instance, the name of the šutur-garment may be a derivation of the root *str* "to cover, to hide," well attested in Semitic but not in Akkadian (except perhaps in Old Assyrian *šitru*). The words zú-lum and *suluppu* "date," like other terms related to the date palm, both come in all likelihood from an unknown language spoken in the Gulf area, according to botanists the location of the origin of the date palm. The other Semitic languages have a different word for the date: Arabic *tamr*, *tummūr*, and parallels.[9] Backborrowings are also possible: Arabic *bunẓur* (and vars.) "female sex organ," a common Semitic term, became b/penzer in Sumerian but seems to have reentered Akkadian as (*u*)*pinzer* "cobweb" and *bunzirru* "hunting blind." One case where the direction of borrowing is clear is Akk. *us*/*zqāru* "crescent moon": Sumerian shares saḫar (with var. s/šakar) "moon" with Semitic (*šaḫr*) and adds u_4 to the form u_4-sak/ḫar. The Akkadian initial *u*- and the -*q*- show that the term was borrowed from Semitic through Sumerian.

4. From the examination of the list of CVCVC-words in the Appendix (see below), one can draw the conclusion that a sizable number of them have a Semitic etymology, creating the presumption that the words of unknown origin in the same list may very well be in their majority, if not Semitic, at least foreign. As for more specific details about the form of the LWs from Semitic, as well as about the borrowing process, one can draw here only very provisional conclusions, since the evidence has been restricted, in an arbitrary way, to a particular homovocalic form. Additional evidence, from long, heterovocalic forms, as well as from shorter words,[10] will be required for safer, more general, conclusions. One can, nevertheless, already formulate a few conclusions.

---

[9] Cf. also Arabic *ṯamar* "fruit" and the name of the date palm: Sum. nimbar, Akk. (*giš*)-*šimmar*.

[10] It is likely, however, that the number of Semitic LWs is much higher among the CVCVC- and VCVC-words than among shorter ones, due to the high frequency of triconsonantism in Semitic stems.

4.1. Writing and Phonology

It must be remembered that the writing system is markedly underdifferentiating, as easily seen in (2) below and in the well-known case of stops and sibilants (not examined here).

(1) Many of the words in the list are always, or at least very frequently, written syllabically in texts with standard orthography and in the vocabularies.

(2) [H]-signs, very frequent in the list, correspond to a wide range of Semitic sounds: ʾ, ʿ, ḫ, ḥ, ġ. In some cases, however, the Semitic consonant is omitted altogether.[11] In any case, the opinion that Akkadian lost these sounds due to Sumerian influence is in need of revision.

(3) [H] alternates with [R] in Sumerian apparently only in words of Semitic origin (besides šuḫ/ruš "root," šuḫ/ruz "to set on fire," note ḫ/rus "angry," Akk. *ezzu*), pointing to a fricative uvular pronunciation of the rhotic,[12] contrasting with the "flap" pronunciation suggested by the common graphic alternation <r/d>.

(4) Alternations between [L] and [R] are frequent (including metathesis), as well as between [N] and [L]; there are also some infrequent alternations between [D] and [S].

(5) Alternations between /bu/ and /gu/ are shown to be an internal phenomenon of Sumerian; words with etymological /b/ have variants with /g/.

(6) [S] would correspond exceptionally to /ṣ/ in saḫar and *salam.

(7) The typological issue of the excessive number of u-vowels in Sumerian is evident in the list (a = 33.8 percent, i = 26.7 percent, but u = 39.4 percent). It cannot be discussed here other than to say that it can already be detected in the Ebla Sign List: ù-su-ru_{12}-(um) for e-sír "sandal" (96), ù-ru_{12}-š(úm) for ereš "lady" (30), ù-šu-wu-(um) for anše "donkey" (85), and so on. It may be due to a variety of reasons ranging from the presence of an undetected (and undetectable) additional back vowel to a possible use of /u/ as a "neutral" vowel in citation forms.

[11] Resulting in a VCVC-word; for instance, a-ga-am "doorkeeper's helper"; cf. Arabic *ʾaʿgama* "to close the door," Soqoṭri *ʿegom* "barrer, obstruer"; see W. Leslau, *Lexique Soqoṭri (Sudarabique moderne) avec comparaisons et explications étymologiques* (Paris, 1938) (hereafter [*LS*]), p. 297.

[12] But in what language, Sumerian or Semitic? Note that in the first example Sum. h/r corresponds to Sem. *-r-* (*šrš*); in the second it corresponds to *-ḥ-* (*ʾḥḏ*) and in the last to *-z-* (*ʿzz*).

4.2. Morphology

(1) Verbal roots are mostly conjugated according to the regular rules of Sumerian: they are provided with normal verbal affixes and subject to reduplication.

(2) There are, however, a number of cases that use a periphrastic conjugation with the auxiliaries ak, dug_4/e, or dù.

(3) Plural/totality is at times indicated by reduplication.

(4) The assimilated verbal stems with initial šu- (mostly causative š-forms) are reanalyzed as native compound verbs with šu; the remaining part can then be given the status of independent stem. Note also some nouns with initial /ša/ interpreted as šà-.

4.3. Lexicon

(1) A borrowing process often results in "doublets":[13] the new, foreign word does not eliminate a semantically close native one that is retained, but whose meaning may be readjusted, taking on a more specialized (or conversely more generic) sense: kaskal and ḫar-ra-an "road, caravan"; ŋír and ba-da-ra "knife, sword"; me and ŋarza "legal/religious duties" (both Akk. *parṣu*, Arabic *farḍ*);[14] agar and ašag/k "cultivated field"; and so on.

(2) A group of words sharing a concrete phonological pattern may belong to the same semantic field. The best-known example is the pattern C_1aC_2in, which includes almost exclusively terms related to cereal culture and brewing. The pattern C_1aC_2ur designates trees (ḫašḫur "apple tree," ḫalup "a type of oak," etc.) and is, perhaps, of "Caucasic" origin. In the present list one can easily detect the well-known pattern $C_1aC_2aC_3$ in words common to Semitic designating professions. Conversely, the members of one borrowed semantic field may have no common phonological pattern. The names of equids in Sumerian would seem to be all foreign, but they show no common pattern. No phonological structure, for instance, is common to two borrowed words related to land tenure: temen "reserved plot in a field" (hence "perimeter of a sacred area") and agar "agricultural field," presumably related to τέμενος and 'άγρος respectively. The linguistic origin of the semantic fields has a historical and cultural significance. Provisionally, it is worth pointing out the apparent southern origin of the names of some containers and, curiously, of some anatomical terms.

---

[13] U. Weinreich, *Languages in Contact* (The Hague, 1963), pp. 55–56.

[14] The close semantic resemblance between the Sumero-Akkadian and the Arabic terms would seem worthy of close study.

5. The time of entry of these LWs into the Sumerian lexicon cannot be determined with any satisfactory degree of accuracy. Nor is there any evidence that they arrived all at once within a limited period of time. The majority are words of extremely low frequency, or even *hapax legomena*, and the kind of texts in which they would be expected are practically nonexistent before the eighteenth century B.C. Note, however, cases such as šu-dug$_8$-ùr, already in Early Dynastic lists. An indication of an early date would be the morphological adaptation, reflected in the normal verbal affixes and reduplication, and the reanalysis of verbs with šu- as compound verbs. Both could take place only, it would seem, at a period when Sumerian was very much a living language. It is possible, however, that at some relatively late time LWs were introduced as a sort of literary fashion. This would apply, for instance, to periphrastic forms with dù (instead of the expected dug$_4$/e or ak), such as ga-ba-al-dù or sikil-dù-a, typical forms in Old Babylonian Edubba texts.

6. In conclusion, there are a number of Semitic lexical borrowings in Sumerian, many of them apparently coming directly from a language other than Akkadian, even when they also appear in historical Akkadian. Their number is moderate, far from the number of Arabic words in Spanish, or French words in Middle English, and clearly lower than the number of borrowings from Sumerian into Akkadian but, nevertheless, significant and consonant with the coexistence of Sumerian- and Semitic-speaking populations that must have taken place from the dawn of history. Every presumed LW requires a detailed study of its individual history, something for future investigation by others. The purpose of this article is just to establish the existence of this phenomenon, as a starting point for further investigation.

APPENDIX: CHECKLIST OF CVCVC-WORDS IN SUMERIAN[15]

This appendix includes most of the homovocalic CVCVC-words of the Sumerian lexicon (a few possibly *lexicalized* reduplications, for example, kinkin or gigir, and some borderline cases have been included). Discussion and nonessential references have been kept to a minimum. To justify in detail a single entry would often require an article-length study. The headword in the individual entries is given in transcription, followed by the essential evidence from the syllabaries and other graphic data and an

[15] No references are given for the lexemes found in the more usual dictionaries, such as L. Koehler and W. Baumgartner, *The Hebrew and Aramaic Lexicon of the Old Testament*, rev. ed. (Leiden and New York, 1994); E. W. Lane, *Arabic-English Lexicon* (Edinburgh, 1863); H. Wehr, *A Dictionary of Modern Written Arabic* (Ithaca, New York, 1961). Abbreviations for lexical references: [*DRS*] = D. Cohen, *Dictionnaire des racines sémitiques* (Paris, 1970–99); [*LGz*] = W. Leslau, *Comparative Dictionary of Geʿez (Classical Ethiopic)* (Wiesbaden, 1987); [*SED*] = A. Militarev and L. Kogan, *Semitic Etymological Dictionary I: Anatomy of Man and Animals*, AOAT 278/1 (Münster, 2000).

English gloss. The Akkadian translation and Semitic parallels then follow. If the Akkadian translation is not etymologically compatible with the headword, it is separated by a semicolon. If the Semitic relationship of a word is apparently well established on the basis of a single language, no effort has been made to include all the information about the distribution of this word within the Semitic family (e.g., in Ugar., Aram., etc.). Morphological information (Morph.) about inflected forms, if attested, some literary passages (Lit.), and occasional comments may be added at the end. The entries have been kept as brief as possible; as a rule, information about the sources that can be found easily in the syllabaries and customary dictionaries is not given. The entries are grouped in three sublists, according to their vowel, *e* and *i* being grouped together (except in words where they are consistently attested as different, as in geštin "vine, wine"). Personal and geographical names are excluded from the list.

CaCaC

001. balaŋ (BALAG: ba-la-áŋ, ba-la-ag, bu-lu-un, bu-lu-ug) "a musical instrument" Akk. *balangu*. Most likely onomatopoeic.
002. bandar (syll. ba-dar; ḪA-*tenû*: ba-an-dar) "dagger" (or the like) Akk. *patru*. Var. of ba-da-ra, but cf. Akk. *patarru* (back loan?).
003. baraḫ (syll. ba-ra-aḫ) "brawl?" *PSD* B 19b s.v.; possibly a form of the verb ra-aḫ. Cf. gaba-ra-aḫ "rebellion."
004. b/parak (bará-g-) "to filter (oil)"; Akk. *ḫalāṣu*. Morph. bará-ak. Cf. Sem. *f/prq* "to separate." See parak n.
005. daban (syll. da-ba-an, da-ban; KU_7: da-ba-an) "a leather part of the horse harness"; Akk. *šardappu*.
006. dakan (syll. da-ga-n-; dag-ga-n-, da-gan; KI.GIŠGAL: da-ka-an) (1) "part of a building, private room(?)" Akk. *dakkannu*. Cf. perhaps Arabic *dukkān*, Soqoṭri *dekkān* "store, shop" [(questionable) *LS* 127]; (2) "ligament"; Akk. *riksu* "ligament, sinew"; (3) "totality"; Akk. *kullatu* A.
007. d/taraḫ (DARÀ, $DARA_4$: da-ra-aḫ, du-ra-aḫ) "ibex" Akk. *turāḫu* (not common Sem.). Cf. perhaps Gk. δορκάς.[16]
008. gabal (syll. ga-ba-al) "quarrel" Akk., Sem. *qbl* "battle"; Akk. *gerû* "to fight" (mostly in a lawsuit). Morph. ga-ba-al—dù/dug_4/ak.
009. ganam (LAGAB×GUD+GUD and vars.: ga-nam) "sheep" Arabic *ġanam* "sheep" (collective); Akk. *immertu*, *laḫru* "ewe."

[16] Note, however, the widespread opinion that the original Indo-European form was closer to the ιορκος of Hesiod (and the ιορκες of Hesychius) because of sporadic Greek spellings with initial ζ (ζορξ) and common Celtic **york-*; see, for example, P. Chantraine, *Dictionnaire étymologique de la langue grecque: histoire des mots* (Paris, 1968–80), p. 293.

010. garaš (GÁ×ḪÚB: ga-ra-aš) "?"; Akk. *tibnu* "straw," lexical *hapax*.

011. gašam/n (NUN.ME.TAG: ga-šá-am) "artisan, expert"; Akk. *mudû* "expert" and syn.

012. gašan, Emesal form of nin.

013. ḫalam (syll. ḫa-lam, Emesal /geleŋ/, ḫe-le-eŋ) "to destroy"; Akk. *ḫalāqu*. Cf. Heb., Ugar. *hlm* "to hit."

014. ḫarran (syll. ḫar-ra-an) "road" Akk. *ḫarrānu*, Soqoṭri *ʿorim* (better *ʾorim*), Mehri *ḥōrem* "road" are unlikely cognates.

015. kalak (syll. ka-la-ak-k-, ka-la-k-; KAL: ka-al complement -g-) "strong"; Akk. *dannu*.

016. kal/nam (syll. ka-na-m-, ka-na-ŋ-, ge-ne-m- Ebla; UN: ka-nam, ka-lam, ka-la-ma; Emesal ka-na-áŋ) "homeland"; Akk. *mātu*. Despite the traditional transliteration with -l-, the form with -n- is lexically better attested. Perhaps a compound ki + X.

017. kamar (syll. ka-mar, ki-mar Pre-Sar.; NI: ga-mar) "a fish trap" Akk. *kamāru* A. A compound of ki, in view of the Pre-Sar. var. ki-mar.

018. kankan (KÁ: ka-an-ka-an, a-ga-an, a-ka-an, a-ka, ka-a) "gate"; Akk. *bābu*. Perhaps a redupl. of /(a)kan/. The form akan is the better attested against traditional transliteration ká.

019. kapar (syll. ga-ab-bar, gáb-ra; PA.DAG.KISIM$_5$×KAK: [ka]-bar/pár) "a shepherd" Akk. *kaparru*. The spelling gáb-ra, which looks like an active participle of the type ga-b-R, is based on folk etymology and is not the source of the Akkadian form.

020. kapas (syll. ka-pa-z-) "sea snail" Akk. *kapāṣu*, from *kapāṣu* "to curl"; Sem. *qpṣ* in *AHw*.

021. k/garan (syll. ga-ra-an) "a bunch of fruits" Akk. *karānu* "grapes"; also *inbu*. See also girin.

022. karaš A (KI.KAL.IDIM: ka-ra-áš, ga-ra-áš) "army camp" Akk. *karašu* A. Could be a compound ki + X.

023. karaš B (wr. as in garaš A) "disaster" Akk. *karašû*, Arabic *karraṯa*, with chronological and semantic problems.

024. karaš C (syll. ga-raš) "leek" Akk. *karašu* B, Arabic *kurraṯ*. Cf. Gk. πράσον.

025. karam (GÁ×UD: ka-ra-am) "ruin" Akk. *karmu*.

026. katam (syll. ga-dam) "cover" Akk. *katammu*.

027. laban (EZEN×LA: la-ba-an) "a sheep disease"; Akk. *pismu*. See also libin and lubun.

028. labar (syll. la-bar Emesal), (1) "servant"; Akk. *ardu*, (2) "cantor"; Akk. *kalû*, (3) "minister"; Akk. *sukkallu*. Could be main dialect written NU-bar = la$_9$-bar. Like libir, labar has a wide range of meanings in need of clarification.

029. lagab (LAGAB: la-ga-ab) "block"; Akk. *upqu* and related terms.

030. lagar A (SAL.ME: la-ga-ar, lu-ku-ur) "a religious/social class of women"; Akk. *nadītu*.

031. lagar B (syll. nu-gú-l- Ebla; LAGAR: na-ga-al, la-gal, la-ga-ar) "a kind of priest" Akk. *lagarru*.

032. lagar C syn. of labar (3).

033. laḫan (syll. la-ḫa-da-m- Ebla, la-ḫa-an) "jug" Akk. *laḫannu* "a type of bottle." Cf. λεκάνη (*AHw.*)?

034. laḫar (syll. na-ḫi-r- Ebla; LAGAB×GUD and vars.: la-ḫar, la-aḫ-rù) "ewe" Akk. *laḫru*, Sem. *rḫ̮l* (metathesis).

035. laḫtan (NUNUZ.ÁB×LA/SILÀ and vars.: laḫ-ta-an) "a jar for brewing" Akk. *laḫtanu*. The lex. texts make a careful distinction between laḫan and laḫtan; the relation between the two is unclear.

036. laraḫ (syll. la-ra-aḫ) "narrowness, distress"; Akk. *pušqu*.

037. madal (BU: ma-da-al, mu-du-ul, ma-ad-la, mu-ud-la, ma-al-la, mu-ul-la) "a pole to carry loads"; Akk. *maššû*, *makkû* "a pole."

038. makkaš (AŠ, DIŠ: ma-ak-kaš, ma-ka-áš) "scream"; Akk. *ikkillu*.

039. malaḫ (syll. má-laḫ$_5$) "boatman" Akk. *malāḫu*. A native compound or popular etymology?

040. masap (syll. gi.ma-sá-ab) "a type of basket" Akk. *masabbu/masappu*, Soqoṭri *msefi*, Amharic *masob* [*LS* 289].

041. masar (syll. ma-sa-ar, ma-sa-r-, ma-sar) "pile, large amount(?)." Lit. šà du-lum-ma ma-sa-re dug$_4$, ma-sa-ar lugud dé-a dug$_4$, Edubba D 235–36; (offerings) ma-sar-re-eš im-mi-in-tùm, Enlil Hymn 92. Cf. zar "stack of sheaves," Akk. *s/zarru*.

042. maškan (syll. maš-gán) "place, settlement" Akk. *maškanu*, Arabic *maskan*.

043. nagar (syll. na-ga-l- Ebla; NAGAR: na-ga-ar) "carpenter" Akk. *naggāru*, Sem. *nqr* "to drill, to hew out." Cf. ma-an-ga-ra "chisel."

044. naŋaḫ (syll. na-gá-aḫ) "stupid"; Akk. *nuʾû*. Cf. perhaps Arabic *ḥağğa*, Soqoṭri *nohog* "jouer, s'amuser."[17]

045. nanam (ŠÀ×NE: na-nam, ni-ni-im) "jealousy"; redupl.? Akk. *qinû*.

046. paḫal (syll. pa$_4$-ḫal) "thigh" Akk. *paḫallu*, Arabic *faḥl* "male," Syr. *paḫalta* "testicles," Soqoṭri *fáḥal* "penis" [*SED* no. 210]. Other Akk. mngs. secondary (e.g., *zittu* "portion," false graphic etymology).

---

[17] Perhaps derived from a gentilic, compare *nuʾû/nuwāʾum* "Anatolian native" in Old Assyrian texts. Note Soqoṭri *mangainaḥ*, *manqaynaḥ* "fou" (from *gnḥ*, derived from *n-gnn* "être, devenir fou"). The change *gnn* > *gnḥ*, however, is specifically Soqoṭri.

047. paḫar (syll. ba-ḫa-r- Ebla; DUG.SILÀ.BUR, BAḪÁR: ba-ḫa-ar, pa-ḫa-ar) "potter" Akk. *paḫāru*.

048. palak (syll. ba-la-g-, ma-la-g- Ebla; BAL: ba-la) "spindle" Akk. *pilaqqu*, Heb. *pelek*.

049. papaḫ (syll. pa-pa-aḫ) "inner room" Akk. *papāḫu*. Redupl.?

050. papal (syll. pa-pa-al) "shoot, tendril" Akk. *papallu*. Redupl.?

051. parak n. (BARÁ: ba-ra, pa-ra-ak) (1) "curtain of separation" (around the area reserved to the king and royal family or to a deity in a temple), fig. "royal person, royal abode" Akk. *parakku*, Sem. *f/prq* "to separate," Akk. *parāqu* (but cf. also *parāku* "to put an obstacle on the way"),[18] (2) "a package made with sackcloth"; Akk. *bašamu*, *saqqu*.

052. parak v. (DAG: ba-ra, ba-ar, pa-ár, complement -g-) "to spread out (a net, a bedspread, etc.)"; Akk. *šuparruru*.

053. paraš (syll. ba-ra-aš) "to fly." Cf. Akk. *naprušu*. Morph. ba-da-ab-ra-aš, mu-e-ši-ba-ra-aš.

054. sabad (GÁ×SIG$_7$: sa-bad) "battle" or "middle part?";[19] Akk. *qablu*. Var. /sad/ with slightly different signs.

055. s/šabar (syll. si-in-bar, síg-bar, ši-bar; ŠEG$_9$.BAR: sa-bar, še-en-bar) "wild ram" Akk. *s/šapparu*, Heb. *šōpar*.

056. saŋŋar (syll. sag-gar) in sag-gar—ak "to spin"; Akk. *ṭamû*.

057. saḫab (syll. sà-ḫé-ab, zé-ḫe-b-; ŠU.DIŠ, ŠU.DI.EŠ: su-ḫu-ub) "bolt." Cf. Arabic *saḥaba* "to pull out," "to draw"; Akk. *mēdelu*.

058. saḫar (SAḪAR: sa-ḫa-ar) "sand" Arabic *ṣaḥārā* "desert," *aṣḥar* "of the color of the desert sand"; Akk. *ṣēru* "steppeland,"[20] *eperu* "soil, loose earth."

059. saḫ/kar (SAR: sa-kar, šá-kar, var. sa-ḫar) (1) in u$_4$-sakar "crescent moon" Akk. *usq/kāru*, South Arabic and Sem. *šahr* "moon"; (2) "a vessel" Akk. *šaḫarratu*.

060. *salam "statue, figure," assuming an interpretation sa$_7$-alam or ^{sa_7}alam, Akk. *ṣalmu*; otherwise *bunnannû*, etc.

061. samak (URUDA×U, UM/DUB, and vars.; sa-ma-ak, su-mu-uk) "mole, wart"; Akk. *šullu*, *umṣatu*.

062. saman (ÉŠ.SUD.NUN.ÉŠ.TU and vars.: sa-ma-an, su-mu-un) "leading rope" Akk. *šummannu*, Arabic *zimām* "rein, halter."

---

[18] Cf. Heb. *parōket* "dividing curtain in the temple" and Arabic *frḵ/k/q* "l'énorme enceinte de toile qui dans les pays musulmans entoure la vaste tente du souverain," R. Dozy, *Supplément aux dictionnaires arabes* (Leiden, 1881), p. 1:1.

[19] Lex. *hapax*, cannot be decided to which of the two *qablu* homonyms it belongs.

[20] [*SED* no. 284] would separate, against *AHw*. and *CAD*, *ṣēru* "back" from *ṣêru* "desert," the latter belonging originally to the root *ṣḥr*.

063. sandan (GAL.NI: sa-an-ta-na, šá-an-da-an) "chief gardner" Akk. *šandanakku*. A genitive compound (sag + X) as shown by the Akk. form.

064. šagan (U.GAN: sa-ka-an, sa-ma-an, šá-gan) "a vessel"; Akk. *šikkatu* A.

065. šaŋar (KA×GAR: ša-gá-ar; Emesal šà-mar) "hunger" Soqoṭri *śáqar*, *śágar*, with Kushitic parallels; Akk. *bubūtu* A and syns.

066. šakal (syll. šà-kal) "a tree" Akk. *šakkullu*.

067. šamaḫ (syll. šà-maḫ) "large intestine" Akk. *šammāḫu*, *šamaḫḫu* (also *irru kabru)*, Geʿez *semāh/ḥ/ḫ* "spleen" [*SED* no. 247].

068. šarag (syll. ša-ra-g-, -š-ra-g-; SAR-g-) "to dry up, to shrink"; Akk. *ubbulu*, *muṭṭû*. Morph. ba-da-an-ša-ra, mu-(un)-ša-ra-ge, nam-ba-ša-ra-ge-en, nu-ša-ra-ge.

069. šaraḫ (syll. šà-ra-aḫ) (1) "to knead (clay)," (2) "to double a reed plaiting" Arabic *saraʿa* "to braid, plait"; Akk. (1) *pasālu*, *pisiltu*, (2) *eṣēpu* "to twine."[21]

070. šaran (DAG.KISIM$_5$×Ú+GÍR: ša-ra-an, šá-ri-in, šu-ri-in) "an insect"; Akk. *ṣarṣaru* and vars.

071. šatam (syll. šà-tam) "a functionary" Akk. *šatammu*.

072. taḫab (syll. ta-ḫab, ta-ḫáb) "to soak"(?). Morph. ta-ḫab, ta-ta-ḫab = *ṭuḫḫudu* (*ša šamni*) "to soak with fat," im-ta-ḫab = *rušumtu* "excessively wet clay, morass."

073. taḫar (syll. ta-ḫa-ar) "distended (belly)(?)"; Akk. *ṣemru*. Cf. Arabic *ṭaḥīr* "coliques, contorsions dans le ventre" (A. de Biberstein-Kazimirsky, *Dictionnaire arabe-français*, vol. 2 [Paris, 1860], p. 60).

074. tamkar (syll. dam-gàr) "merchant" Akk. *tamkāru*. Cf. Heb. *makar*, etc.

075. zabar (UD.KA.BAR: za-ba-ar) "bronze" Akk. *siparru*.

076. zagar (syll. za-gàr) "tower" Akk. *zaqāru* "to be high, pointed." Cf. *ziqqurratum*, also Akk. *dimtu*.

077. zaḫal (syll. za-ḫa-al) "to disappear" Arabic *zaḥala* "to go away." In za-ḫa-al—ak; Akk. *ḫalāqu* "to disappear."

078. zaḫam (syll. za-ḫa-am, za-ḫa-an) "a mineral"(?); Akk. unknown. Lit. kù-babbar-zu níg-za-ḫa-am(var. -an)-šè ḫé-sa$_{10}$-sa$_{10}$ Agade 243; the context requires the name of a mineral or metal of a value between that of silver and that of copper. As a verb: za-ḫa-am-ma-mu-dè Inanna-Abzu col. ii 19 (broken context). Cf. perhaps Arabic *saḥ/ḫam* "black." One could propose manganese oxide ("kohl") for the noun and "to make up (the eyes)" for the verb.

---

[21] The translation *ša libbi eṣpu*, in Hh. VIII 310 (revised) and parallels, shows that it was understood as a compound: šà + ra-aḫ.

079. zaḫan (U.GA: za-ḫa-an) (1) "a cereal concoction" Akk. *zaḫannu*, also *diktu*, (2) "a saucer"(?). Cf. perhaps Arabic, Jibbali *ṣaḥn*, Soqoṭri *ṣaḥen*.

080. zaḫaš (syll. za-ḫa-áš) "leg"; Akk. *purīdu* "leg," also *pušqu* "narrowness, difficulty."

081. zalag/k (UD: za-la-ag) "clean, shiny, bright"; Akk. *ebbu* and syns. Cf. *zlg/k* [*DRS* 733, 742].

082. zalaḫ (syll. za-la-aḫ) "to slip through an opening (said of a draft, a ghost)" Arabic *zalaʿa* "to slide along, to slip"; Akk. *zâqu*. Morph. mu-un-za-la-aḫ-(ḫe)-e-ne, nam-ba-za-la-ḫe-en.

083. zalam (syll. za-lam) in za-lam-gar "tents." Cf. perhaps Arabic *zlām* "members of a clan/tribe"?

084. zapaḫ (syll. šu-paḫ Early Dynastic; MAŠ: zi-pa-aḫ; ŠU.BAD: za-pa-aḫ) "span" Heb. *ṭpḥ*, Amharic *ṭeffi* "palm of the hand," Sem. *ṭpḥ*; Akk. *ūṭu*.

085. zaraḫ A (syll. za-ra-aḫ, and KI.SAG.SAL for [2]) (1) "female genitals" (or a disease thereof); cf. perhaps Soqoṭri *zirho* "saleté"; Akk. *laqlaqqu*, (2) "a bird name"; Akk. *igirû* "heron"(?) and *laqlaqqu* "stork."

086. zaraḫ B (SAG.PA.LAGAB: za-ra-aḫ, also LU.KI.KAK, KU.KI.SAG) "grief"; Akk. *nissatu*. Cf. perhaps Akk. and Arabic *ṣrḫ*, if the grief is expressed with sounds.

CiCiC/CeCeC

087. b/penzer (syll. pe-en-ze_2-er, be_5-en-ze_2-er, bì-in-zi-ir) "the female sex organ, or part thereof" Akk. *biṣṣūru*, Arabic *baẓr*, *bunẓur*, with vars. [*SED* no. 37]; Sum. also "cobweb," by semantic extension.

088. birig (syll. bi-ri-ig) "to sneer at"; Akk. *ganāṣu*.

089. dikbir (KI.NE.AN.MÙŠ: di-ik-bi-ir) "?"; Akk. *aṣur pindi* and vars. Perhaps < *X + kibir, since the Akk. term seems to have something to do with fire or coal.

090. dilim A (di-li-NE Ebla; LIŠ: di-li-im) "shallow dish, bowl, spoon, skull" Akk. *tilimtu* but more frequently *itquru*, *itqurtu*. It is possible, in view of the distribution of the different forms, and despite their different Akkadian translations, that dilìm = *itquru*, silím (KAL) = *ḫub/pšašû*, and ti-lim-(da) = *karpatu*, represent one and the same word.[22] Cf. also lim_x(BUR) "bowl" Akk. *lummu*. Var. silim/silím in Dialogue 1:35.

---

[22] For the consonantic alternation, cf. d/s/tal = *rapāšu*.

091. dilim B (LAGAB×IM: di-li-im, and vars.) "oven." Part of a group of vars. of šu-rin "oven" with r > l and final -m/n (*JCS* 25 [1973]: 173); influenced by dilim A?

092. dilip A (KA×ŠID: di-li-ib) "woman"; Akk. *amīltu*. In a series of metonymic terms for woman. Cf. perhaps the following entry.

093. dilip B (ŠID, SAG×ŠID: di-li-ib) "head of hair"; Akk. *uruḫḫu*.

094. diŋir (syll. ti-ḫi-ir Susa, ti-in-ki-r Bogh.; AN: di-gi-ir, di-mi-ir, di-in-gír, di-me-er, di-mi-ir; dìm-me-er Emesal) "deity"; Akk. *ilu*.

095. dinik A (syll. di-ni-g-; KI.NE: di-ni-ig) "crucible, brazier"; Akk. *kūru* B.

096. dinik B (LÚ.(ME).EN, LÚ.LAGAB: di-ni-ig) "important person"; Akk. *šapṣu*.

097. dirik (syll. di-ri-k-; SI.A: di-ri, complement -g-) "to be more, to surpass"; Akk. (*w*)*atāru*.

098. gibil (NE-*šeššig*: gi-bi-il) "new"; Akk. *edēšu*, *eššu*.

099. g/kibir (ŠÚ.AŠ: ki-bi-ir, gi-bi-il, gi_4-bi-ir) "firewood" Akk. *kibirru*; also *qilûtu*.

100. gidim (gé-dím) "an ax" Sem. **gdm*, Akk. (Mari) *qudūmu*; otherwise, Akk. *agû*, *titennu*. The relationship with aga/àga = *gur-di-mu* (Emar), *gur-du-mu-um* (Ebla),[23] and cognates (Aram., Tigre, etc.) is not completely clear.

101. g/kid/tim (syll. gi-dim, ki-ti-im, -ga-t[i]-m- Ebla) "ghost of a dead person"; Akk. *eṭemmu*. The form with k- is the better attested. The Akkadian word is probably related, but it is not clear how, perhaps kit/dim < ki + idim. For another case of the loss of initial k-, see kešeg.

102. gigir (LAGAB×U and vars.: gi-gi-ir) "wagon"; Akk. *narkabtu*. Redupl.

103. $gili^{m}b$ (GI_4×GI_4: gi-li-im, ki-li-im, gi-ib) "to put crosswise, to obstruct"; Akk. *parāku*, *egēru*, etc.

104. ŋilip (KA×LI: gá-li, gi-li, me-li, mi-li, mi-ri, mi-li-b- UET 6 354:3; me-li Hh. XV 31b; gi-ri VAT 9523 ii′ 8′; KA×RU: mi-li-ib; KA×NÍG+ŠÀ+A: me-li; KA×Ú: me-li) "melodious voice." Cf. Akk. *ḫalālu* B "to pipe, wheeze," Geʿez *ḫ*ᵉ*llat*, Heb. *ḥālīl* "flute"), also Akk. *maʾlatu*, *mallatu*, *nemlû* "throat, or part thereof." There could be two words, one */ŋili/ or */ŋilli/, root *ŋll, the other /ŋilip/.

105. girim (syll. gi-ri-m-; A.ḪA.KUD.DU; PÉŠ: gi_4-li-in, ki-li-im, and vars.) "?"; see M. Krebernik, *Beschwörungen aus Fara und Ebla* (Hildesheim, 1984), pp. 233 ff.

106. girin A (gi-ri-in, gi-rin; LAGAB: gi-ri-im, gi-ri-in, gi-ri_4-in) "flower" Akk. *girimmu*, *girinnu* (from Sum.); also *illuru*, *inbu* and syn. In Sumerian contexts,

---

[23] G. Conti, *Il sillabario della quarta fonte della lista lessicale bilingue Eblaita*, Miscellanea Eblaitica 3, Quaderni di semitistica 17 (Florence, 1990), p. 138, no. 477.

the meaning is "flower" rather than "fruit." The word belongs to an apparent Ablaut set with gurun "fruit" and garan "a bunch of fruits."

107. giriš (BIR: gi-ri-iš) "butterfly" Arabic *faraša*; Akk. *kurṣiptu*.

108. ŋiskim (IGI.DUB: giš-gi-im, giš-ki-im, i-is-ki-im; Emesal mu-uš-ki-im) "sign, signal" Akk. *giskimmu*; usually *ittu* A. A compound of ŋiš.

109. ḫibis (syll. ḫi-pi-is; TUR.DIŠ: ḫi-bi-is; AL×UŠ: ḫi-bi-is) (1) "?"; Akk. *ruššû* A "to act in contempt(?)"; (2) *aplu* "son," and cf. ḫibis-kar = *mēlulu* "to play." There are a number of textual problems in the lexical sources, and in the various Akk. translations, concerning this word.

110. ḫilip A (NAGA: ḫi-li-ib, ḫé-li-ib) "to thrive, flourish" Akk. *elēpu*, Soqoṭri *ʿolif* "pousser (feuilles)" [*LS* 311]; Akk. also *šamāḫu* "to flourish" and *nâḫu* "to (be) calm."

111. ḫilip B (IGI.KUR: ḫi-li-ib) "netherworld."

112. ḫenzer n. (IGI.DIM: ḫe-en-zèr, ḫe-e[n-z]e-ru) "small, infant."

113. ḫenzer v. (syll. ḫe-en-zé-er) in šu-ḫe-ḫe-en-zé-er "to extend, to open wide"; Akk. *muṣṣû*.

114. ḫirin A (*LAK* 175: ḫi-ri-in) "spikenard"; Akk. *lardu*.

115. ḫirin B (KI.KAL: ḫu-rí-in, ḫe/ḫé-rí-in, ḫu-ra-nu) "a weed"; Akk. *arantu*, *sassatu*. Akk. *ḫirinnu* (*CAD*), *ḫerīnu* (*CAD*) are not attested. Perhaps heterovocalic: /ḫurin/.

116. ḫirin C (KU_7: ḫi-ri-in) "waterskin" Akk. *ḫirinnu*, as a foreign word in Malku; also *zim/nbuḫaru* Ea IV 194. The ususal Akk. term is *nādu*.

117. kikkin (ḪAR: ki-in-ki-in, ki-ik-ki-in) "millstone"; Akk. *erû*. Possibly onomatopoeic redupl. < kin-kin.

118. kilib (LAGAB, LAGAB.LAGAB: ki-li-ib, ki-lib, ki-líb) "totality"; Akk. *napḫaru*.

119. kilim (PÉŠ: gi-li-im, ki-li-im) "animal"; Akk. *nammaštu*.

120. kirid (KÉŠ: ki-ri-id, ki-ri-is) "pin, needle" Akk. *kirissu*.

121. kisim A (syll. ki-si-im; KISIM_5: ki-si-im) "coagulated milk" Akk. *kisimmu*. Cf. *kasāmu* "to cut."

122. kisim B (DAG.KISIM_5×SI: ki-si-im) "sheepfold"; Akk. *tarbaṣu*.

123. kisim C (DAG.KISIM_5×Ú+GÍR: ki-si-im) "an insect"; Akk. *šīḫu*.

124. kišib (syll. ki-li-ib; DUB: ke-še-eb, ki-ši-ib) "seal, sealed document"; Akk. *kunukku*.

125. kešeg (syll. ke-še-eg; GÍR, Ú.GÍR: ki-ši) "a thorny plant" Akk. *ašāgu*, Arabic *šōk*.

126. kešer (syll. ke-še-er; GÌR.BAR) in ke-še-er nu-tuku "to have no limit" Arabic *kaṯara* "to be too much"; Akk. *kišda la išû*.

127. kezer (syll. ke-zé-er) in ke-zé-er—ak "to wear a chignon (or the like)"[24] Akk. *kezēru*, and cf. *kaṣāru* "to tie together, to knot," Heb. *qšr*, Aram. *qṭr*, Geʿez *q^{w}aṣara*.
128. libin (EZEN×LI: li-bi-in) "a disease of ovines"; Akk. *irdu*. See also laban and lubun.
129. libir (IGI.ŠÈ: li-bi-ir) "old" Akk. *labīru*.
130. libir; Emesal form of nimŋir, sukkal, etc.
131. libiš (ÁB.ŠÀ: li-biš; λεφεσ) "heart, courage"; Akk. *libbu*. The lex. attestations of this word are very late. Perhaps < *libbu* + *iš*.
132. lidim (AL×DÍM: li-dim) "?"; Akk. *rašû*. Probably a corrupt lex. entry (Aa VII/4:27).
133. ligim/n (IGI.TUR.TUR: li-gi-in, li-gi-ma) "offspring, offshoot" Akk. *ligimû*, also *ziqpu*, *niplu*, etc. The var. li-gi-ma and the Akk. form suggest a word with final vowel.
134. ligin (li-gi-in, li-gi$_4$-in) "a type of tablet" Akk. *liginnu*.
135. lilis (syll. li-li-is) "a musical instrument" Akk. *lilissu*. An onomatopoeic redupl. < *lis-lis.
136. nigin (U.UD.KID: ni-gi-in) (1) "fetus," (2) "inner room of a temple"; Akk. (1) *kūbu*, (2) *kummu*. There is no evidence for the nature of the middle consonant.
137. niŋin A (LAGAB, LAGAB.LAGAB: ni-mi-en, ni-me-in, ni-ge-en, ni-gi-in, ni-in-ni) "to encircle, to go around"; Akk. *lamû*, *paḫāru*, etc. Possibly a redupl. form.
138. niŋin B (LÁL×LAGAB: ni-mi-en, ni-gi-in, na-an-ga, na-ag-gi) "district" Akk. *nagû*. Derived from niŋin A, differs from it only graphically.
139. niŋir (GÍN-*gunû*: ni-mi-ir, ní-gi-ir, nim-gír, ne-gi-r(u$_{12}$- Ebla) "town crier, herald" Akk. *nāgiru*.
140. piriŋ (syll. ba-rí-g- Ebla; PIRIG: pi-ri-ig) "lion" (poetic); Akk. *labbu*, *nēšu*.
141. sikil A (syll. -s-ki-il, -š-ki-il; EL: si-ki-il, si-ke-el) "clean, pristine, virgin"; Akk. *ellu*, etc.
142. sikil B (as above) in sikil-dù-a "(acting) silly, stupid" Akk. *saklu* "simple person," Syr. *skl* "(to be) foolish." In Akk. lex. only, *magrû* "insulting."
143. silik A (GIŠGAL×IGI: si-li-ig, ši-li-ig; si-la-g- Ebla) "stopped, ended"(?); Akk. several translations, mostly unclear.
144. silik B (TAG×UD/GUD/KU: si-lig) "fist"; Akk. *upnu*.
145. silim (DI: si-li-im) "peace, good health" Akk. *šulmu*, Sem. *šlm*.

[24] One must consider *kezēru* a sort of doublet of *kaṣāru*. For the type of hairdo involved, see J. Börker-Klähn, "Haartrachten," *RLA* 4, pp. 1–12, and A. Spycket, "La coiffure féminine en Mésopotamie," *RA* 48 (1954): 131 ff., 161 ff.

146. simik. See samak.

147. šibir (U.EN×GÁN-*tenû*: si-bi-ir, ši-bir) "crooked staff" Akk. *šibirru*. The form with initial š- is better attested.

148. šidim (DÍM: ši-di-im, ši-te-em, ši-ti-im) "bricklayer"; Akk. *itinnu*. Perhaps a compound of something like *sig_4/$šeg_{12}$-dím.

149. šikin (syll. ši-kin; DUG, SÍG.LAM: ši-ki-in) "a type of clay pot" Akk. *šikinnu*.

150. šinik (GAD.NAGA: ši-ni-ig, še-ni-ig) "tamarisk"; Akk. *bīnu*.

151. tibir (syll. šu-búr; TAG, TAG×ŠU/UD/GUD/KU: ti-bi-ir; DUB.NAGAR: tibira; šibir) "fist"; Akk. *upnu* "fist," *šisītu* "wrist." Cf. perhaps Sem. *ṯbr* "to break."

152. tikil (syll. ti-ki-il, -t-ki-il) "to protrude(?)" (said of eyes, stomach); Akk. (*libbu*) *ebṭu*, *eddu*. Morph. igi-ti-ti-ki-il, šà-at-ki-il.

153. temen (TE: te-me-en) "perimeter, marked-off area" Akk. *temennu*, Gk. τέμενος.

154. zibin (DAG.$KISIM_5$×TAK_4, DAG.$KISIM_5$×Ú+GÍR: zi-bi-in) "caterpillar"; Akk. *nappillu*.

155. zeber (syll. giš.gud-zé-bé-er [M. Sigrist, *Tablettes du Princeton Theological Seminary* (Philadelphia, 1990), no. 248]) "a tool"; if this tool is the same as umbin-gud (despite the inversion of components), zeber could be a reflex of Akk. *ṣupru* "fingernail," Sem. **ṯupr* [*SED* no. 285].

CuCuC

156. buluŋ A (PAP.PAP: bu-lu-un, bu-lu-ug) "to grow, to raise (a child)"; Akk. *rabû*, *rubbû*.

157. buluŋ B (BALAG: bu-lu-un) (1) "a musical instrument" Akk. *balaggu*, var. of balaŋ; (2) "to boast, give oneself importance"; Akk. *kubburu*.

158. buluḫ (ḪAL: bu-lu-úḫ) "to vomit"; Akk. *arû* B "to vomit," also *ašû* "?," *ḫâšu* B "to worry." The latter equation indicates some confusion with puluḫ "to fear." Onomatopoeic.

159. burut (U: bu-ru, complemented -d) "hole, to pierce" Arabic *farata* (C. Brockelmann, *Lexicon Syriacum* [Edinburgh, 1895], p. 609).

160. d/tubul A (syll. du-bu-ul, var. du-gu-l-) "to mix ingredients" (soup, beer, river waters, dough, etc.) abstracted from šu-du-bu-ul (Akk. *šutābulu*, Sem. *wbl*), taken as šu+du-bu-ul.

161. dubul B (ŠU.BU: du-bu-ul) "to flourish, to be exuberant"; Akk. *elēpu*.

162. dubur (ḪI×U/ŠE: du-bu-ur) "the base of the sky" (mythical). Cf. Arabic *dub*(*u*)*r* "backside, buttocks," Akk. *išdu* "root" [*SED* no. 46].

163. dugud/t (syll. -d-gu-ud; DUGUD: du-gu-ud, du-ku-ud) "heavy"; Akk. *kabtu*.

164. durun (ŠU.LAGAB: du-ru-un) var. of šu-rin "oven."

165. guduk (syll. gú-du-g-; ḪI×NUN.ME: gu-du, complemented -g) "a religious occupation"; Akk. *pašīšu*.

166. gurud/t (NUN.KI: gu-ru-ud, gu-ru-da, ku-ru-ud; LÚ.KI: gu-ru-ud) "to drop"; Akk. *nadû*.

167. gurum (IGI.ERIM, IGI.GAR and vars.: bu-ru, gú-ru, [x]-ru-um, ku-rum) "inspection"; Akk. *piqittu*. Morph. gurúm-ak.

168. g/kurum (syll. gu-ru-um) "pile" Akk. *karāmu* B "to pile up."

169. gurun (GURUN and vars.: gu-ru-un) "fruit." See garan.

170. guruš (syll. gur_5-ru-uš; TAG: gu-ru-uš) "to tear to pieces" Akk. *qarāšu*, Arabic *qaraša*. Mostly in gur_5-ru-uš — búr "to bare the teeth, to bite" (said of wild animals); Akk. *gâʾu*. Morph. gur_5-ru-uš — dug_4/e, gú-gur_5-ru-uš (redupl.).

171. gušur (syll. gu-šu-r-) "to compensate" Akk. *kašāru* C. Morph. ḫa-mu-na-ab-gu-šu-re (Ur III).

172. ŋuruš (syll. mu-rí-š- Ebla; KAL: gu-ru-uš, mu-ru-uš, gi-ri-<x>; cf. ARAD×KUR: ki-ra-aš) "(able) man"; Akk. *eṭlu*. A compound < *ŋìr-uš or the like?

173. ḫubud (syll. ḫu-bu-us; KA.ŠU.GÁL: ḫu-bu-ud) "to present oneself to a deity" Sem. *ʿbd* "to serve" (often with religious overtones), Akk. *labān appi*, *šukênu*.[25]

174. ḫubur (NUNUZ.ÁB×BI: ḫu-bur) "a brewing vat" Akk. *ḫubūru*.

175. ḫubuš (syll. ḫu-bu-uš) (1) "to chop" (necks, limbs, malt) Akk. *ḫabāšu* "to chop up," Aram. *ḫbs*; (2) "to do something with rugs or felt" Arabic *ḥibs* "blanket," Heb. *ḥefeš* "material for saddles." Morph. al-ḫu-bu-uš, ba-ḫu-ḫu-bu-uš; periphrastic ḫu-bu-uš — dug_4.

176. ḫuduš (syll. ḫu-du-s- Ebla; TU: ḫu-du-uš) "leather armor"(?) Akk. *ḫuduššu*.

177. ḫuluḫ (syll. ḫu-luḫ) "to fear"; Akk. *galātu* and syn. Morph. bí-in-ḫu-luḫ, nam-bí-íb-ḫu-luḫ-e, etc. Perhaps related to Arabic *wahila* "to be frightened," *wahal* "terror," with metathesis.

178. ḫulum (DAG.$KISIM_5$×LUM/ḪA: ḫu-lum) "fishnet"(?); Akk. unknown.

179. ḫumuḫ (LAGAB×U+A: ḫu-mu-úḫ) "swamp, flooded land"; Akk. *miḫṣu*. The vars. /umaḫ/, /amaḫ/ are better attested, so that it is probably a compound *a-maḫ.

180. ḫutul A (syll. ḫu-tu-ul) "to shovel, to pile up" (clay, dirt, malt) Akk. *ḫutūlu* "piled up clay" and *ḫadālu* B(!) "to shovel."

---

[25] The gloss "ZI.UD" in Erimhuš V 170 (*CAD* B s.v. *balāṣu* lex. section) has to be read ḫu!-bu!-ud. Akk. *balāṣu* includes two verbs: *a*) "to present oneself to a deity," as above, and *b*) "to look at" (perhaps a by-form of *palāsu*). How the gloss ḫubud could be applied to the discontinuous lexeme KA.ŠU.GÁL is an interesting question.

181. ḫutul B (syll. ḫu-tu-ul) "to flare the nostrils" (said of a horse). Lit.: [an]še-kur-ra kir_4 ḫu-tu-ul-ḫu-tu-ul-e, i-bí gùn-nu-gùn-nu-e "a horse with flaring nostrils, with sparkling eyes" (CT 15 18:27 f.).

182. ḫutul C (syll. ḫu-tu-ul) "to wrap up, to bandage" Akk. *ḫadālu* A(!), Arabic *ḥatala*, Heb. *ḥtl*; Akk. also *ḫatû ša murṣi* "to bandage a wound/a diseased spot."

183. kurum (PAD: ku-ru-um) "share, portion" Akk. *kurummatu*.

184. kurun (DIN, DUG, etc.: ku-ru-un, ku-ru-um) "wine" Akk. *karānu, kurunnu*.

185. kurušt (KU_7: gu-ru-uš, ku-ru-uš, gu-ru-uš-da, gu-ru-uš-ta) "person in charge of fattening animals"; Akk. *mārû*.

186. kušlug (KI.NE: ku-uš-lu-ug) "?"; Akk. *netmertu*. Possibly a compound < *ki + s/šulug.

187. kušum A (U.PIRIG: ku-šu-um, ku-šu, ki-ši) "to advance creeping, or fearfully(?)" (said of an animal); Akk. *šâqu* A, *nâqu* B, *lâpu*, with unclear mngs.

188. kušum B (BI.LUL: ku-šu-um, ku-zu-um) "to tremble"(?); Akk. *nâqu* B, *šâqu* A. Also syn. of kušum A.

189. kušum C (ZUM: ku-šu-um) "?"; Akk. *marru* "bitter" (unclear).

190. lubun (EZEN×LU: lu-bu-un) "a disease of ovines"; Akk. *ḫinqu*. See also laban and libin.

191. lugut A (syll. -l-ku-d-; LAGAB: lu-gu-ud, lu-gú-ud, $lu-gu_4$-ud; LUM.GAR+LUM.GAR: lu-gu-ud) "short"; Akk. *katû, kurû*, etc. Perhaps /l(u)gud^r/ with short forms gur_4, gud_8, and kud_x.

192. lugut B (BAD.UD: lu-gu-ud) "(whitish) suppuration"; Akk. *šarku*.

193. lugut C (LAGAR×ŠE.SUM: lu-gu-ud) "threshing floor"; Akk. *raḫīṣu, maškanu*.

194. munsub A (SÍK.(LAM).SUḪUR: mu-un-su-ub, mu-un-šu-ub, mu-un-zu-ub) "hair" Mehri Harsusi *mensōb*, Soqoṭri *ménsub* "pubic hair"; Akk. *šārtu* [*SED* no. 239].

195. munsub B (syll. en-ša-b- Ebla; (PA).GÚ×NUN: mu-un-su-ub, mu-su-ub) "shepherd"; Akk. *rēʾû*.

196. munus (SAL: mu-nu-us, mu-nu-uš; Emesal nu-nus) "woman, female"; Akk. *sinništu*.

197. murub A (SAL.(LA), SAL.LAGAR: mu-ru-ub) "female sex organ"; Akk. *ūru* and related or metaphoric meanings: *amīltu* "woman," *šuḫḫu* "buttocks," *pû* "mouth," *kalû* "a priest." Also EN.ME.LAGAB: mu-ru-ub "a priestess"; Akk. *ēnu* of Nisaba.

198. murub B ($MURUB_4$: mu-ru-ub) "center part, waist"; Akk. *qablu*.

199. muru^{m}b (SAL.UŠ.DAM: mu-ru-ub; SAL.UD.EDIN: mu-rum) "brother-in-law"; Akk. *emu rabû*.

200. muruš (syll. mu-ru-uš) "buttocks"; Akk. *šuḫḫu, ilṣu*. Possibly scribal error for murub?

201. nuŋun (syll. nu-gú-n- Ebla, ni-gi-n-, níg-gi-n-; NUMUN: nu-mu-un) "seed"; Akk. *zēru*.

202. numdun (KA×NUN: nu-um-du-um, nun-du-un; Emesal šu-um-du-um) "lips"; Akk. *šaptu*.

203. numun (ZI+ZI.LAGAB and vars.: nu-mu-un; Emesal šu-mu-un) "a type of rush or sedge"; Akk. *elpetu*, etc.

204. puluḫ (syll. bu-lu-úḫ, bu-luḫ) "(to) fear" Akk. *pulḫu, palāḫu*, Sem. **frh*. Morph. i-im-bu-lu-úḫ, im-bul-lu-úḫ, in-bu-lu-ḫ(a), bu-bu-luḫ.[26]

205. puluk (syll. -b-lu-uk, bu-lu-k-; NAGAR: bu-lu-ug) (1) "chisel" Arabic *falaqa* "to split," (2) "boundary marker"; both Akk. *pulukku*.

206. pusuš (syll. pu-su-uš) "?" in pu-su-uš—ak Akk. *puššušu*.

207. putuk (syll. pu-du/tu-uk) "to destroy (the enemy)" Akk. *patāqu*, Arabic *fataqa*. In pu-du/tu-uk—ak/za "to destroy, to kill"; Akk. probably *ubbutu*.[27]

208. subur A (ŠUBUR: su-bur) "wagon." Cf. perhaps Arabic *safara* II, Geʿez "to travel," Akk. *šapāru* "to send on a journey." Perhaps Akk. *saparru* B, consistently written with *s*- and with a different logogram.

209. subur B (syll. su-bu-r-; ŠUBUR: su-bur, su-bar, su-bir$_4$, šu-bur) "servant" (derived from the gentilic "Subarian"). Form with š- only in the late source S^b.

210. s/šuḫur n. A (syll. šu-ḫu-r- Ebla, -š-ḫu-r-; SUḪUR: su-ḫu-ur, sú-mu-ur) (1) "hair" Akk. *šārtu* "hair," Sem. *s/šʿr*; (2) "crown of a tree" Arabic *šaǧar*, Soqoṭri *śohor* "tree"; (3) "tent" (made from goat hair) Akk. *ša/uḫūru* "a building" (originally "tent"); cf. *šārtu* "goat hair."

211. suḫur n. B (as in A) "carp"; Akk. *purādu*. Cf. perhaps Arabic *šuʿūr* "a saltwater fish."[28]

212. suḫur n. C (SUḪUR: su-ḫu-ur, etc.) "goadstick"; Akk. *mekkû, mēgigu*.

213. suḫur v. (SUḪUR: su-ḫu-ur) (1) "to trim or comb the hair," (2) "to make smaller" (Akk. *ṣuḫḫuru*), (3) "to goad, to scratch"; Akk. *qamāmu* (1), *nukkuru* (2), *ekēku* (3). See *z/suḫur* [254].

---

[26] Arabic *falaḥa* (*AHw*. 812) does not fit semantically.

[27] It would seem that in P. Michalowski, "An Old Babylonian Literary Fragment concerning the Kassites," *Annali dell'Istituto Orientale di Napoli* 41 (1981): 388:11–13, the gloss *ka-mar-šu-nu* to pu-tu-uk—ak in line 11 is misplaced: it would belong to tu$_{10}$-tu$_{10}$-bi—ak with gloss *da-ab-da-šu-nu* in line 13 and vice versa.

[28] *Letherinus nebulasis* according to C. Bailey, *A Culture of Desert Survival* (New Haven, 2004), p. 79.

214. suḫuš "root." See suruš.

215. sukuš (MÙŠ: su-ku-uš) "crest of a bird, head ornament"; Akk. *ṣipru*.

216. sukut (GALAM: su-ku-ud, šu-ku-ud) "tall, high"; Akk. *mēlû* "elevation."

217. s/zulug/k A (syll. su-lu-ug; -s-lu-ug; LUL: zu-lu-ug, za-la-ag) "(to be) brilliant, shiny"; Akk. *namāru*, *namru*. A syn. of zalag/k. Also in su-lu-ug-lá (var. LUL-lá) = *nappāḫu* "metalworker."

218. suluk B (LUL: su-lu-ug) "a clay pot"; Akk. *šakannu*.

219. sulun (syll. sú-lu-un) "to overwhelm"; perhaps, with metathesis, Akk. *raṣānu*, "to roar(?)," Arabic *raṣuna* "to be firm, strong." Morph. sú-sú-lu-un, sù-sù-lu-un Akk. *ruṣṣunu*. Cf. LUL su-lu-un = *le-x-u*.

220. sumuk A (syll. su-mu-ug, zu-mu-ug) (a) "to fear, to terrify," (b) "to be angry"; Akk. *adāru*, *palāḫu*; late mng. "eclipse" (for its psychological effects). Morph. su—mug-mug.

221. sumuk B (URUDA×U and vars.: su-mu-ug, šu-mu-ug) "a skin mark"; Akk. *šullu*. See samak.

222. sumun A (BAD: su-mu-un, šu-mu-un, su-un, su-gi-in) "old, worn out; old remainders" Akk. *sumkinnu*, also *labīru* "ancient."

223. sumun B (syll. su-me-n- Ebla, su-mu-n-; GUL: su-mu-un, sú-mu-un) "wild cow"; Akk. *rimtu*.

224. sumur (syll. su-mu-r-; SAG-*gunû*: su-mu-ur, su-ur, šu-ur) "angry"; Akk. *ezzu*.

225. suruš (DU-*gunû*: su-ḫu-uš, su-ru-uš) "root" Akk. Sem. *šuršu*; Akk. also *išdu*. See šuruš.

226. šubul (syll. šu-bu-ul) uncertain, in ga šu nu-bu-ul "milk that does not 'rise'"; Akk. *eldu*.

227. šubur (syll. šu-búr) "to break off" (a piece of bread) Akk. *šebēru* "to break" (pots, bones, etc.), Sem. *ṯbr*. Cf. šu-búr-búr with Akk. *qarāšu* "to carve, make bread into loaves." Morph. šu ḫé-im-da-an-búr-re.

228. šudul/n (syll. uš-ti-n- Ebla; ŠÚ.UR-*šeššig* and vars.: šu-du-un, šu-du-ul) "yoke";[29] Akk. *nīru*.

229. šugur A (syll. šu-gur_5) "a basket for fruits" Akk. *šug(u)rû* (note long final vowel) and var. (Landsberger *Date Palm*, pp. 37–38).

230. šugur B (syll. šu-gur) "bracelet"; Akk. *unqu*. Compound of šu + gur.

231. šuḫup (ŠÚ.MUL: šu-ḫu-ub) "shoe" Akk. *s/šuḫuppu*.

[29] The original meaning is "tool, utensil" in general, related to šu-du_7, $šita_4$, etc.; later specialized as "loom," "yoke," "tools for a trade," etc.

232. šuḫuz (syll. šu-ḫu-uz, šu-ḫuz, šu-ru-uš) "to set on fire," etc. Akk. *aḫāzu* Š, Sem. *ʾḥḏ*. Reanalyzed as šu + ḫu-uz: (izi) šu-ḫu-uz, šu-ḫuz—ak, abstracting a root: ḫu-uz. Morph. šu ḫu-uz-, šu-ḫu-za-ab, šu bí-in-ḫu-uz, šu mi-ni-ib-ḫu-uz, šu bí-in-ḫu-ḫu-uz.

233. šukur A (IGI.KAK: šu-ku-ur, šu-gur) "tip (of an arrow, etc.), stake, spear" Akk. *šukurru*.

234. šukur B (PAD: šu-ku-ur) "something made of reeds" (hut? fence?) Akk. *šukurû*.

235. šuluḫ (syll. šu-luḫ, šú-luḫ) "to dredge (canals), to clean (ritually)" Akk. *šuluḫḫu* (a religious rite).[30]

236. šurug A (syll. šu-ru-ug, šu-ru-ub) "water hole" Arabic *šarīʿa* "water hole," Ethiopic *śarg*. Lit. ^{giš}Ú.GÍR a-a šu-ru-(ug)-ga (var. šu-ru-ub) ^{giš}šukur a-a ub$_4$-ba "brambles inside the water holes, pointed stakes in the water of the wells," Dumuzi's Dream 120.

237. šurug B (syll. šu-ru-ug, šur-ru-ug) "a weaving of palm leaves" Arabic *šarīğa* "sack made of palm leaves," Ethiopic *sarga*, Mehri *śarawg* "to stitch up," Heb. *śrg*, Aram. Syr. *s^{e}rag* "tresser"; Akk. *zinû* in KA×BAD/ME-šur-ru-ug. Lit. ^{giš}KA×ME-šu-ru-ug-^{giš}KA×ME-šu-ru-ug-bi ^{giš}níg giš.nimbar-bi na-nam, Inana and Šukalletuda 79.

238. šurum (LAGAB×GUD/GUD+GUD: šu-ru-um, šu-ru-un, šu-ri-im) a) "bedding place for animals," b) "dung"; Akk. a) *rubṣu*, b) *piqqannu* and syns.

239. šuruš "root." See suruš.

240. šusub (syll. šu-su-ub) "to wipe, to polish, to scrape" Akk. *esēpu* Š, Sem. *ʾsp*; Akk. also *qatāpu* "to pick" (pomegranates). Reanalyzed as šu + su-ub, giving su-ub, written also sub$_6$. Morph. šu ḫé-eb-su-ub-be, šu u-me-ni-su-ub-su-ub. As a noun: (1) ^{túg}šu-su-ub Akk. *šusuppu* "wiping rag, towel," (2) šu-su-ub "scrapings"; Akk. *šukkultu*.

241. šušur (sign ŠL 365: šu-šur) "grate of a furnace(?)" Akk. *šuššuru*.

242. šutbul in šutubul (syll. šu-du-bu-ul, šu-tu-bu-úr) "to mix ingredients (at least one of them a liquid)" Akk. *šutābulu*, also *marāsu* "to stir into a liquid," *ṣe-e-ja-um* (mng. uncert.). Morph. šu im-tu-bu-ur (var. mi-ni-). See d/tubul.

243. šutuk (PAD: šu-tuk) "reed hut" Akk. *šutukku*.

244. šutum (GI.NA.AB.DU$_7$/TUM: šu-tu-um) "storehouse" Akk. *šutummu*.

245. šutur (syll. šu-du$_8$-ùr.túg Early Dynastic; MAḪ: šu-tur) "a garment" Akk. *šutūru*, Arabic *sutra* "tunic," *satara* "to cover."

---

[30] "Hand washing" is a popular etymology, already attested in Ebla (Conti, *Il sillabario*, p. 172, no. 626); originally the word had nothing to do with hand washing.

246. tugul (NAGAR.ZA-*tenû*: tu-gu-ul/gul) "hump, humpback"; Akk. *asqubbītu* "hump," *gilšu* "hip, flank."[31]

247. tukul (KU: tu-ku-ul) "mace, weapon" *zugullum* (/*sukullu*/) Ebla; Akk. *kakku*. Conti, *Il sillabario*, p. 142, no. 495, interprets *zugullum* as /*ṣukūrum*/ related to Arabic *ṣaqara* "battere col bastone."

248. tukun (ŠU.NÍG.TUR.LÁ: tu-ku-un) "moment, instant"; Akk. *surri*.

249. tukur A (KA×ŠE: tu-ku-ur) "to chew"; Akk. *kasāsu* A.

250. tukur B (LAGAB: tu-kur) "heavy, important"; Akk. *kabtu*.[32]

251. zub/gud (ḪA-*tenû*: zu-bu-d-, zu-gu-ud) (1) "a mace"; Akk. *patarru* (reading of logogram is uncert.), (2) "an animal" Akk. *zubuttu*. See also bandar.

252. zubur (sign ŠL 364: za-bar, zu-bur) (mng. uncert.) Akk. *zabaru*.

253. z/suḫul (syll. zu-ḫu-ul) "?" (said of face, neck, hands) Akk. *saḫālu* "to pierce" does not fit semantically, unless it has a figurative mng. Lex. igi zu-ḫu-ul = *pa-nu sà-aḫ-ru-*[*tum*], šu zu-ḫu-ul = *qá-tum sà-ḫi-il-t*[*um*]. Lit. [g]ú zu-ḫu-ul-a-ni-ta dù-dù-àm; šu-ni ab-zu-ḫu-ul ("a zuḫul hand cannot write well").[33]

254. z/suḫur (syll. zu/sú-ḫu-r-) "?"; see suḫur v. (2) [213]; (silver) ^{uruda}ḫu-bu-um zu-ḫu-re-dè (Ur III).

255. zukum (ZI+ZI.LAGAB: zu-ku-um) "to step on, to trample"; Akk. *kabāsu*.

256. zulug. See s/zulug/k.

257. zulu^{m}b (syll. zú-lum) "date" Akk. *suluppu*.

---

[31] No form *tuḫul seems to be attested; despite the discussion in *MSL* 9 20, all the forms there are clearly Middle Assyrian or Neo-Babylonian GUL-signs.

[32] Probably "full" form of g/kur$_4$.

[33] Arabic *ḏahala* "to be negligent" would fit the construction with šu "hand" but hardly with igi or gú.

PECUS NON OLET?
VISITING THE ROYAL STOCKYARDS OF DREHEM DURING THE FIRST MONTH OF AMARSU'ENA 2

Gertrud Farber, The University of Chicago

The smells emanating from the royal stockyards at Drehem must have been a familiar, and probably not very pleasant, daily experience for all the officials and personnel working there during the Ur III empire. Fortunately, they are not preserved on the administrative records that have survived into our times. The following article is meant to give a glimpse of the activities there, and I hope that its presentation in a *Festschrift* for Bob Biggs will not conjure up too much of a real-life atmosphere and will thus not interfere with the *erešu ṭābu* of cedar wood and incense more appropriate to a truly Mesopotamian celebration!

ÄS 1310[1] is a balanced ki-bi-gi$_4$-a account of the first month of Amarsu'ena 2 (AS 2), listing all livestock that was handled by the main administration of the stockyards in Drehem during that time. This text gives us the opportunity to compare a monthly summary with transactions recorded individually on single tablets during that month, thereby enabling us in a few cases to follow the tracks of a single animal from the time it entered the royal administration to its final distribution. By identifying day-by-day transactions with those recorded in the ki-bi-gi$_4$-a text, we can learn more about the officials handling the transactions, the origin of the animals, and the terminology for the different types of deliveries and expenditures.

Text ÄS 1310 has five sections (A.1–5) dealing with incoming livestock and seventeen sections (B.1–17) for expenditures. For the convenience of the reader, I have included a graphical analysis of the text below.

[1] A four-column tablet of the Staatliche Sammlung Ägyptischer Kunst, München (measurements 11.5 cm × 13.8 cm). My hand-copy was submitted in 2000, together with my article "One Bear for the Ensi, Fifteen Sheep for the Dogs," for publication in *Acta Sumerologica (Japan)* 21 (still in press). The copy is repeated here; see pp. 63–64. For the other texts of this small collection, see G. Farber (in collaboration with W. Farber), "Die Keilschrifttafeln der Staatlichen Sammlung Ägyptischer Kunst, München," *ZA* 91 (2001): 207–24.

TABLE 1. OUTLINE OF ÄS 1310 OBVERSE

<table>
<tr><th>i</th><th>ii</th><th>iii</th><th>iv</th></tr>
<tr><td rowspan="7">A: incoming livestock in 5 sections:

i 1–20: A.1:
2,794 animals
mu-DU lugal</td><td rowspan="2">i 29–ii 10: A.4:
166 animals
é-du$_6$-lá</td><td rowspan="3">end of šu-níg̃in</td><td>sag̃-níg̃-gur$_{11}$-ra-kam
šà-bi-ta</td></tr>
<tr><td rowspan="3">B: withdrawal of livestock in 17 sections:

iv 3–17: B.1:
773 animals
zi-ga lugal
ad$_6$-bi ur-ni$_9$-g̃ar
šu ba-ti
kuš-bi lugal-éren
šu ba-ti</td></tr>
<tr><td rowspan="3">ii 11–19: A.5:
920 animals
a-šà-ta</td></tr>
<tr><td rowspan="3">(blank)</td></tr>
<tr><td>iv 18–22: B.2:
5 animals
$^{\text{g̃iš}}$gu-za ^{d}šul-gi</td></tr>
<tr><td>end of deliveries</td><td rowspan="5">iv 23–29: B.3:
277 animals
níg̃-ba lugal</td></tr>
<tr><td rowspan="2">(blank)</td><td rowspan="7">beginning of kilib-ba

end of kilib-ba</td></tr>
<tr><td rowspan="2">i 22–24: A.2:
4 animals
[mu-DU ^{d}]šul-[g]i</td></tr>
<tr><td rowspan="5">beginning of šu-níg̃in</td></tr>
<tr><td rowspan="3">i 25–28: A.3:
14 animals
[ki ša]bra-ne-ta</td></tr>
<tr><td>iv 30–32: B.4:
30 animals
sá-du$_{11}$ ^{d}gu-la</td></tr>
<tr><td rowspan="2">iv 33–35: B.5:
6 animals
sá-du$_{11}$ inim-^{d}nanna</td></tr>
<tr><td></td></tr>
</table>

TABLE 1. OUTLINE OF ÄS 1310 REVERSE

<table>
<tr><th>viii</th><th>vii</th><th>vi</th><th>v</th></tr>
<tr><td>end of šu-níĝin</td><td rowspan="5">vii 1–9: **B.17**:
869 animals
⌜íb-tag$_{4}$⌝ a-šà-šè</td><td rowspan="2">v 29–vi 3: **B.11**:
515 animals
kišib ^{d}šul-gi-a-a-ĝu$_{10}$</td><td rowspan="3">v 1–5: **B.6**:
14 animals
mu ur-ra-šè *dan*-^{d}šul-gi
šu ba-ti</td></tr>
<tr><td rowspan="3">(blank)</td></tr>
<tr><td rowspan="4">vi 4–9: **B.12**:
12 animals
kišib lú-diĝir-ra
dumu ir$_{11}$-ḫùl-la</td></tr>
<tr><td rowspan="3">v 6–10: **B.7**:
30 animals:
ba-ug$_{7}$ mu ur-ra-šè
DINGIR-*ba-ni*
šu ba-ti</td></tr>
<tr><td rowspan="3">beginning of kilib-ba

end of kilib-ba</td></tr>
<tr><td>end of withdrawals</td></tr>
<tr><td>(blank)</td><td rowspan="3">vi 10–18: **B.13:**
1,051 animals
kišib na-lu$_{5}$</td><td>v 11–13: **B.8**:
1 animal: ba-úš
kišib ur-ni$_{9}$-ĝar</td></tr>
<tr><td>grand total: 3,898 animals</td><td rowspan="5">beginning of šu-níĝin</td><td>v 14–18: **B.9:**
4 animals
kišib énsi ù šabra-ne</td></tr>
<tr><td rowspan="3">(blank)</td><td rowspan="3">v 19–28: **B.10:**
137 animals
kišib lú-diĝir-ra dumu inim-^{d}šára</td></tr>
<tr><td>vi 19–22: **B.14:**
3 animals
kišib šu-ìr-ra</td></tr>
<tr><td>vi 23–27: **B.15:**
55 animals
kišib ur-šu-ga-lam-ma</td></tr>
<tr><td>ki-bi-gi$_{4}$-a
ab-ba-sa$_{6}$-ga
iti maš-dà-gu$_{7}$ mu ^{d}amar-^{d}su'en lugal-e ur-bí-lum^{ki} mu-ḫul</td><td>vi 28–34: **B.16:**
116 animals
šu$^{!}$(BA)-lá-a sila-a
sig$_{7}$-a
kišib *be-lí*-A.ZU</td><td></td></tr>
</table>

I have collected all documents pertaining to the first month of Amarsu'ena 2 that I could find[2] and have tried to match the animals from the individual documents with those of the monthly record.

TEXTS[3]

-/Ia = *PDT* 2 958 (-/I), mu-DU lugal ab-ba-sa$_6$-ga ì-dab$_5$

-/Ib = AUCT 1 230 (-/I), *be-lí*-A.ZU ì-dab$_5$

-/Ic = Or., s.p., 47–49 62 (-/I) and Genouillac *Trouvaille* 31 (-/I), lú-diĝir-ra šabra ì-dab$_5$

1/Ia = SAT 2 693 (1/I), ki ab-ba-sa$_6$-ga-ta ba-zi

1/Ib = 1/Ib+2/I+3/Ia+4/Ia = SAT 2 723 (1–4/I), ur-ni$_9$-ĝar šu ba-ti, ki ab-ba-sa$_6$-ga-ta ba-zi

1/Ic = *ROM* 1 119 (1/I), ki ^{d}šul-gi-a-a-ĝu$_{10}$-ta ur-ni$_9$-ĝar šu ba-ti

1/Id = NBC 10869 (1/I), ki ^{d}šul-gi-a-a-ĝu$_{10}$-ta ba-zi

2/I see 1/Ib

3/Ia see 1/Ib

3/Ib = Watson, *Birmingham* 7 (3/I), ki ^{d}šul-gi-a-a-ĝu$_{10}$-ta ur-ni$_9$-ĝar šu ba-ti

4/Ia see 1/Ib

4/Ib = *Acta Sumerologica (Japan)* 9 (1987): 266, no. 70 (4/I), ki ab-ba-sa$_6$-ga-ta ba-zi

4/Ic = Nesbit, *Sumerian Records* 13 (4/I), ki ^{d}šul-gi-a-a-ĝu$_{10}$-ta ur-ni$_9$-ĝar šu ba-ti

---

[2] I would like to thank W. Sallaberger, M. Molina, and M. Sigrist for their help in locating or checking publications that were not accessible to me. Special thanks go to N. Koslova and U. Kasten for giving me access to unpublished material and to W. W. Hallo for providing me with transliterations of five texts from the Yale Babylonian Collection.

[3] The sigla used to identify the texts from the first month of Amarsu'ena 2 (I/AS 2) correspond to the dates of the transactions documented in the texts; thus 1/Ia indicates the first (of four, in this case) document dated to day 1, month 1. Abbreviations for text publications not in the *CAD* are the following:

AICCAB J.-P. Grégoire, *Archives administratives et inscriptions cunéiformes de l'Ashmolean Museum et de la Bodleian collection d'Oxford*, Contribution à l'histoire sociale économique, politique et culturelle du Proche-Orient ancien (Paris, 1996–2001)

BAOM *Bulletin of the Ancient Orient Museum* (Tokyo)

DTBM J. Politi and L. Verderame, *The Drehem Texts in the British Museum (DTBM)*, NISABA 8 (Messina, 2005)

Nesbit, *Sumerian Records* W. M. Nesbit, *Sumerian Records from Drehem* (New York, 1914)

OIP 121 M. Hilgert, *Drehem Administrative Documents from the Reign of Amar-Suena, Cuneiform Texts from the Ur III Period in the Oriental Institute*, vol. 2, OIP 121 (Chicago, 2003)

PDT 2 F. Yıldız and T. Gomi, *Die Puzriš-Dagan-Texte der Istanbuler archäologischen Museen, Teil II: Nr. 726-1379*, Freiburger altorientalische Studien 16 (Stuttgart, 1988)

SANTAG 7 O. Tohru, *Keilschrifttexte aus japanischen Sammlungen*, SANTAG 7 (Wiesbaden, 2002)

SAT 2 M. Sigrist, *Texts from the Yale Babylonian Collections*, Part 1, Sumerian Archival Texts 2 (Bethesda, Maryland, 2000)

Sigrist, *Rochester* M. Sigrist, *Documents from Tablet Collections in Rochester, New York* (Bethesda, Maryland, 1991)

TAD S. Langdon, *Tablets from the Archives of Drehem* (Paris, 1911)

Torino I A. Archi and F. Pomponio, *Testi cuneiformi neo-sumerici da Drehem: N. 0001-0412*, Catalogo del Museo Egizio di Torino, serie seconda, collezioni, vol. 7 (Milan, 1990)

Watson, *Birmingham* P. J. Watson, *Neo-Sumerian Texts from Drehem*, Catalogue of Cuneiform Tablets in Birmingham City Museum, vol. 1 (Warminster, England, 1986)

4/Id = Torino I 175 (4/I), ù-tu-da, lú-diğir-ra ì-dab$_5$

6/I = *DTBM* 152 (6/I), ki ^{d}šul-gi-a-a-ğu$_{10}$-ta ur-ni$_9$-ğar šu ba-ti

7/I = MVN 15 374 (7/I), ki ^{d}šul-gi-a-a-ğu$_{10}$-ta ur-ni$_9$-ğar šu ba-ti

8/Ia = Fish *Catalogue* 248 (8/I), *šu-eš$_{18}$-tár* u$_4$-da-tuš ì-dab$_5$

8/Ib = 8/Ib+9/Ib+14/I = MVN 3 225 (8/9/14/I), ki ab-ba-sa$_6$-ga-ta ba-zi

9/Ia = MVN 13 442 (9/I), mu-DU ab-ba-sa$_6$-ga ì-dab$_5$

9/Ib see 8/Ib

10/Ia = BIN 3 304 (10/I), na-lu$_5$ ì-dab$_5$

10/Ib = OIP 121 117 (10/I), ur-šu-ga-lam-ma ì-dab$_5$

11/I = OIP 121 118 (11/I), na-lu$_5$ ì-dab$_5$

13/I = *TAD* 35 (= *AICCAB* I/3:Bod.A 71) (13/I), na-lu$_5$ ì-dab$_5$

14/I see 8/Ib

15/I = Boson *Tavolette* 344 (15/I), ki ^{d}šul-gi-a-a-ğu$_{10}$-ta ur-ni$_9$-ğar šu ba-ti

16/I = *Orient* 16 (1980): 45:22 (16/I), ki ^{d}šul-gi-a-a-ğu$_{10}$-ta ba-zi

17/Ia = NCBT 1644 (17/I), ki ab-ba-sa$_6$-ga-ta ba-zi

17/Ib = *DTBM* 193 (17/I), ki lú-diğir-ra-ta ur-ni$_9$-ğar šu ba-ti

18/Ia = *RA* 9 (1912): pl. I:SA 12 (18/I), ki ^{d}šul-gi-a-a-ğu$_{10}$-ta ba-zi

18/Ib = Fish *Catalogue* 249 (18/I), ki lú-diğir-ra-ta ur-ni$_9$-ğar šu ba-ti

20/Ia = MVN 13 94 (20/I), ù-tu-da, ^{d}šul-gi-a-a-ğu$_{10}$ ì-dab$_5$

20/Ib = *DTBM* 156 (20/I), ki ^{d}šul-gi-a-a-ğu$_{10}$-ta ba-zi

21/Ia = AUCT 1 643 (21/I), lú-diğir-ra ì-dab$_5$

21/Ib = YBC 14333 (21/I), na-lu$_5$ ì-dab$_5$

21/Ic = MVN 13 66 (21/I), ki lú-diğir-ra-ta ur-ni$_9$-ğar šu ba-ti

22/Ia = OIP 121 119 (22/I), lú-diğir-ra ì-dab$_5$

22/Ib = *TAD* 68 (= *AICCAB* I/1:Ash. 1910-761) (22/I), ki ab-ba-sa$_6$-ga-ta ba-zi

22/Ic = *PDT* 2 779 (22/I), na-lu$_5$ ì-dab$_5$

22/Id = Erm. 14807[4] (22/I), ù-tu-da, ^{d}šul-gi-a-a-ğu$_{10}$ ì-dab$_5$

22/Ie = *DTBM* 117 (22/I), ^{d}šul-gi-a-a-ğu$_{10}$ ì-dab$_5$

23/Ia = Nies *UDT* 158 (23/I), ki ab-ba-sa$_6$-ga-ta ba-zi

23/Ib = BIN 3 46 (23/I), ù-tu-da, ^{d}šul-gi-a-a-ğu$_{10}$ ì-dab$_5$

24/Ia = Conteneau *Contribution* 20 (24/I), ki ab-ba-sa$_6$-ga-ta ba-zi

24/Ib = *BAOM* 5 (1983): 31, no. 1 (= SANTAG 7, 69) (24/I), lú-diğir-ra ì-dab$_5$

25/Ia = BIN 3 302, ki ab-ba-sa$_6$-ga-ta ba-zi

25/Ib = 25I/b+28/Ia+30/Ia = CT 32 48 BM 103448 (now also *DTBM* 68) (25/28/30/I), ^{d}en-líl-lá ì-dab$_5$

25/Ic = Sigrist, *Rochester* 31 (25/I), na-lu$_5$ ì-dab$_5$

25/Id = Sigrist, *Rochester* 32 (25/I), *šu*-^{d}IDIM ì-dab$_5$

25/Ie = *DTBM* 326 (25/I), ù-tu-da, ^{d}šul-gi-a-a-ğu$_{10}$ ì-dab$_5$

27/Ia = MVN 8 116 (27/I), ki ab-ba-sa$_6$-ga-ta ba-zi

27/Ib = Fish *Catalogue* 472 (27/I), ki lú-diğir-ra-ta ur-ni$_9$-ğar šu ba-ti

28/Ia see 25/Ib

28/Ib = Nies *UDT* 135 (28/I), ^{d}šul-gi-a-a-ğu$_{10}$ ì-dab$_5$

29/Ia = BIN 3 300 (29/I), na-lu$_5$ ì-dab$_5$

29/Ib = *PDT* 2 799 (29/I), lú-diğir-ra ì-dab$_5$

29/Ic = MVN 15 339 (29/I), ki ^{d}šul-gi-a-a-ğu$_{10}$-ta ur-ni$_9$-ğar šu ba-ti

30/Ia see 25/Ib

30/Ib = *PDT* 2 1092 (30/I), ki ^{d}šul-gi-a-a-ğu$_{10}$-ta ba-zi

---

[4] To be published by N. Koslova.

In what follows I will discuss the ki-bi-gi_4-a document ÄS 1310 section by section and compare it with all individual transaction documents from I/AS 2.

A. Incoming Livestock

A.1. mu-DU lugal

The most important document to be matched with ÄS 1310 is *PDT* 2 958 (-/Ia), which records all mu-DU lugal deliveries of I/AS 2.[5] The number of animals is exactly the same as in the section ÄS 1310 A.1, but *PDT* 2 958 originally contained all information available about the deliveries to the Puzriš-Dagan organization: a more detailed description of the animals, the day they were delivered, and the names of the deliverers.[6]

Unfortunately, only *PDT* 2 958 cols. i–iii and vi?–viii? of what seemingly was a four-column tablet are preserved. We thus have detailed information on the delivery of only ca. 600 animals out of a total of 2,794. Surprisingly, the day-dates are only recorded for the first four days or for 45 animals. Since the tablet is complete to the end of col. iii, this could mean that all 565 remaining animals were delivered on the fifth day, which is, however, highly unlikely. I therefore assume that for some reason the recording scribe deemed it important to specify only the first four days of the month, and I have included all the information concerning those four days in table 2.[7]

Col. vi? of *PDT* 2 958 gives us the first summation, a šu-nígin of 31 different kinds of animals, sorted by species, several criteria of quality, sex, and age. Col. vii? contains a second summation, a šu-nígin of 18 different kinds of animals, this time indicating species, only fattened or unfattened quality, and sex. This is the same arrangement as seen in ÄS 1310 A.1. Finally, col. viii? contains the grand total, a kilib-ba of 12 entries, sorted by species and sex only.

With the help of *PDT* 2 958 vi? we can now identify 31, instead of 18, different types of animals in ÄS 1310 A.1.

Comparing A.1 with the deliveries A.2–5, we learn that in our text the following animals are delivered as mu-DU lugal only and do not come from other deliveries:

All fattened (niga) animals,[8] the anše-ZI.ZI, the $dara_4$, and the az.

---

[5] A similar text, recording the mu-DU lugal of a whole month, is YBC 3635 from the eleventh month of Amarsu'ena 2. See M. Sigrist, "Livraisons et dépenses royales durant la Troisième Dynastie d'Ur," in R. Chazan, W. W. Hallo, and L. H. Schiffman, eds., *Ki Baruch Hu: Ancient Near Eastern, Biblical, and Judaic Studies in Honor of Baruch A. Levine* (Winona Lake, Indiana, 1999), pp. 11–149, with an appendix by W. W. Hallo.

[6] For the names of the deliverers from *PDT* 2 958 and other documents from I/AS 2, see the appendix below.

[7] Information on the other animals and their deliverers is included in the appendix.

[8] Note, however, that in the ki-bi-gi_4-a documents, PIOL 19 345 (H. Sauren, *Les tablettes cunéiformes de l'époque d'Ur des collections de la New York Public Library*, Publications de l'Institut orientaliste de Louvain 19 [Louvain-la-Neuve, 1978]) and Hilgert, OIP 121, no. 248, fattened animals are also delivered from é-du_6-la.

All amar maš-dà recorded on individual delivery documents must also be part of the mu-DU lugal. The three coming from the fields would not be categorized as a delivery.

All animals classified as mu-DU are considered part of the mu-DU lugal[9] and are therefore entered in table 2 below.

Summary

Of the 2,794 animals of the mu-DU lugal, only 234 (or 233) animals can be documented in 24 (or 23)[10] individual transaction documents:

55 gu_4-niga, 71 gu_4, 8 áb, 1 $šeg_9$-bar munus(?), 2 anše-ZI.ZI munus, 45 udu-niga, 2 ud_5-niga, 22 udu, 7 máš, 1 $dara_4$ níta, 19 maš-dà, 1 az

The texts are: -/Ia, -/Ib, 1/Ia, 4/Ib, 8/Ia, 8/9/14/I, 9/Ia, 10/Ia, 10/Ib, 13/I, 17/Ia, 21/Ia, 21/Ib, 22/Ia, 22/Ib, 22/Ie, 24/Ia, (24/Ib), 25/Ia, 25/28/30/I, 27/Ia, 28/Ia, 29/Ia, 29/Ib.

A.2. [mu-DU ^{d}]šul-gi

1 udu	no details known
[3] máš	no details known

One might expect the expenditures for Šulgi's throne (B.2) to have been drawn from the deliveries for Šulgi.[11] Those expenditures, however (3 udu-niga from mu-DU lugal, 1 udu, 1 máš), do not match the deliveries.

A.3. [ki ša]bra-ne-ta

For deliveries ki énsi ù šabra-e-ne-ta, here šabra-ne only, see Maeda, "Bringing," pp. 81 ff.[12]

[9 anše]-kúnga níta	transferred to *dan*-^{d}šul-gi (B.6) and fed to the dogs, no individual document preserved
[5 anše]-kúnga munus	transferred to *dan*-^{d}šul-gi (B.6) and fed to the dogs, no individual document preserved

[9] See W. Sallaberger, *Der kultische Kalender der Ur III-Zeit*, Untersuchungen zur Assyriologie und vorderasiatischen Archäologie 7/1 and 7/2 (Berlin, 1993), pp. 27 f.

[10] There are a total of two $šeg_9$-bar munus delivered in ÄS 1310, one as mu-DU lugal, one as é-du_6-la. The animal transferred to lú-diğir-ra in text 24/Ib (1 $šeg_9$-bar munus ga) could come from either source.

[11] See Sallaberger, *Kalender*, pp. 28 f.

[12] T. Maeda, "Bringing (mu-túm) Livestock and the Puzurish-Dagan Organization in the Ur III Dynasty, *Acta Sumerologica (Japan)* 11 (1989): 69–111.

For transferrals to šabra and énsi, see B.9 below.

TABLE 2. mu-DU lugal (A.1)

ANIMALS IN ÄS 1310		DETAILED SPECIES *PDT* 2 958 VI		ANIMALS ATTESTED IN INDIVIDUAL DOCUMENTS			TOTAL OF INDIVIDUALLY ATTESTED ANIMALS		FINAL DISBURSAL OF ANIMALS IN ÄS 1310 DELIVERED AS mu-DU lugal
Amount	Species	Species	Amount	mu-DU (delivered by and processed)	ba-zi (disbursed by ab-ba-sa$_6$-ga)	ì-dab$_5$ (transferred to)	Subtotal	Total	
147	gu$_4$-niga	gu$_4$-niga	147	—	—	13 (-/Ib) to *be-lí*-A.ZU (B.16) 3 (10/Ib) to ur-šu-ga-lam-ma (B.15) 5 (22/Ia) to lú-diĝir-ra (B.10) 5 (22/Ie) to ^{d}šul-gi-a-a-ĝu$_{10}$ (B.11) 28 (25/Ia) to lú-diĝir-ra (B.10) 1 (28/Ib) to ^{d}šul-gi-a-a-ĝu$_{10}$ (B.11)		55	4 zi-ga lugal 9 níĝ-ba lugal 33 lú-diĝir-ra dumu inim-^{d}šára 35 ^{d}šul-gi-a-a-ĝu$_{10}$ 53 ur-šu-ga-lam-ma 13 *be-lí*-A.ZU
1	áb-niga	áb-niga	1	—	—	—		—	1 ur-šu-ga-lam-ma
99	gu$_4$	gu$_4$-gùn-a	1	—	—	—	—	71	71 of 73 transferred a-šà-šè
		gu$_4$	98	13 mu-DU (25/Ib) 4+54 mu-DU lugal (28/Ia, 30/Ia) (= 25/28/30/I)	— —	the same 71 to ^{d}en-líl-lá (B.17) (25/28/30/I)	71		
11	áb	áb-gùn-a	1	1 (9/Ia) by *ṣa-al-ma-nu-um* mar-tu	the same cow disbursed (9/Ib = 8/9/14/I)	the same cow transferred (9/Ib) to lú-^{d}nanna šabra ^{d}nanna (B.9)	1	8	2 of 11 transferred to énsi ù šabra-ne 6 of 14 transferred a-šà-šè (see B.17)
		áb-mu-2 (-gùn-a)	1	1 (9/Ia) by *ṣa-al-ma-nu-um* mar-tu	the same cow disbursed (9/Ib = 8/9/14/I)	the same cow transferred to lú-^{d}nanna šabra ^{d}nanna (B.9) (9/Ib)	1		
		áb-amar-ga	1	—	—	—	—		
		áb	8	6 mu-DU lugal (30/Ia = 25/28/30/I)	—	the same 6 to ^{d}en-líl-lá (B.17)(30/Ia = 25/28/30/I)	6		

TABLE 2. mu-DU lugal (A.1) (*cont.*)

ANIMALS IN ÄS 1310		DETAILED SPECIES *PDT* 2 958 VI		ANIMALS ATTESTED IN INDIVIDUAL DOCUMENTS			TOTAL OF INDIVIDUALLY ATTESTED ANIMALS		FINAL DISBURSAL OF ANIMALS IN ÄS 1310 DELIVERED AS mu-DU lugal
Amount	Species	Species	Amount	mu-DU (delivered by and processed)	ba-zi (disbursed by ab-ba-sa$_6$-ga)	ì-dab$_5$ (transferred to)	Subtotal	Total	
1	šeg$_9$-bar munus	šeg$_9$-bar munus	1	—	—	1 amar šeg$_9$-bar munus ga (24/Ib) to lú-diĝir-ra (B.12); this might also be the šeg$_9$-bar delivered as é-du$_6$-la (A.4)		(1)	1 of 2 transferred to lú-diĝir-ra dumu ir$_{11}$-ḫùl-la
1	anše-ZI.ZI níta	anše-ZI.ZI níta	1	—	—	—		—	1 lú-diĝir-ra dumu ir$_{11}$-ḫùl-la
2	anše-ZI.ZI munus	anše-ZI.ZI munus	2	—	—	2 (21/Ia) to lú-diĝir-ra (B.12)		2	2 lú-diĝir-ra dumu ir$_{11}$-ḫùl-la
255	udu-niga	udu-niga-sig$_5$	61	1 by KA.X (-/Ia: u$_4$-2)	—	4 (-/Ib) to *be-lí*-A.ZU (B.16)	5	45	2 zi-ga lugal 3 ^{giš}gu-za-^{d}šul-gi 5 níĝ-ba lugal 3 lú-diĝir-ra dumu inim-^{d}šára 7 ^{d}šul-gi-a-a-ĝu$_{10}$ 231 na-lu$_5$ 4 *be-lí*-A.ZU
		udu-niga	178	4 by ir$_{11}$-ĝu$_{10}$ (1/Ia = -/Ia i 5) 3 (-/Ia: u$_4$-1) by ur-^{d}lugal-bàn-da	the same 4 disbursed (1/Ia) as níĝ-ba lugal(?) (B.3) —	20 (10/Ia) to na-lu$_5$ (B.13) 2 (13/I) to na-lu$_5$ 3 (29/Ib) to lú-diĝir-ra (B.10)	32		
		sila$_4$-niga	16	1 by ir$_{11}$-ĝu$_{10}$ (1/Ia = -/Ia i 6) 1 by lú-^{d}nin-[ ] (9/Ia) 1 by lú-^{d}nanna šabra (-/Ia: u$_4$-4)	the same 1 (1/Ia) disbursed as níĝ-ba lugal(?) (B.3) — —	3 (10/Ia) to na-lu$_5$ (B.13) 1 (13/I) to na-lu$_5$ 1 (21/Ib) to na-lu$_5$	8		
4	u$_8$-niga	u$_8$-niga-sig$_5$	1	—	—	—		—	4 na-lu$_5$
		u$_8$-niga	2	—	—	—			
		kir$_{11}$-niga	1	—	—	—			
4	máš-niga	máš-gal-niga	4	—	—	—		—	4 na-lu$_5$

TABLE 2. mu-DU lugal (A.1) (*cont.*)

ANIMALS IN ÄS 1310		DETAILED SPECIES *PDT* 2 958 VI		ANIMALS ATTESTED IN INDIVIDUAL DOCUMENTS			TOTAL OF INDIVIDUALLY ATTESTED ANIMALS		FINAL DISBURSAL OF ANIMALS IN ÄS 1310 DELIVERED AS mu-DU lugal
Amount	Species	Species	Amount	mu-DU (delivered by and processed)	ba-zi (disbursed by ab-ba-sa$_6$-ga)	ì-dab$_5$ (transferred to)	Subtotal	Total	
5	ud$_5$-niga	^{munus}áš-gàr-niga	5	1 (22/Ib)by zé-na-na 1 (-/Ia: u$_4$-4) by ur-^{d}nin-gal	the same disbursed (22/Ib) —	1 (29/Ia) to na-lu$_5$ (B.13) —		3	1 zi-ga lugal 1 ^{d}šul-gi-a-a-g̃u$_{10}$ 3 na-lu$_5$
1,442	udu	udu	1,166	1 (22/Ib) by šu-^{d}EN.ZU di-ku$_5$	the same disbursed (22/Ib) as níg̃-ba lugal(?) (B.3)	—	1	22	3 zi-ga lugal 1 níg̃-ba lugal (?) no details known about the remainder
		udu-a-lum	3	—	—	—	—		
		gukkal	62	1 (-/Ia: u$_4$-2) by [...]-ni lú-má ninda dir-ra (?)	—	—	1		
		gukkal g̃iš-dù	3	—	—	—	—		
		sila$_4$	208	1 (9/Ia) by énsi 1 (17/Ia) by en ^{d}inanna 1 (22/Ib) by en ^{d}inanna 1 (24/Ia) by the zabar-dab$_5$ 9 (-/Ia: u$_4$-1) by *á-pi$_5$-lí-a*, ur-ni$_9$-g̃ar, ur-é-an-na, ur-^{d}lugal-bàn-da, lú-^{d}asar-lú-ḫi, NE.NI.NE-a, gù-dé-a, *za-ni-a*, ur-^{d}nin-a-zu 5 (-/Ia: u$_4$-2) by ZU.TI.X, ba-za-x, *šar-ru-um-ba-ni*, g̃á-a-kam 2 (-/Ia: u$_4$-4) by du$_{11}$-ga-zi-da, *pù-zur$_8$-eš$_{18}$-tár*	— the same disbursed (17/Ia) the same disbursed (22/Ib) the same disbursed (24/Ia) — — —	—	20		

TABLE 2. mu-DU lugal (A.1) (*cont.*)

ANIMALS IN ÄS 1310		DETAILED SPECIES *PDT* 2 958 VI		ANIMALS ATTESTED IN INDIVIDUAL DOCUMENTS			TOTAL OF INDIVIDUALLY ATTESTED ANIMALS		FINAL DISBURSAL OF ANIMALS IN ÄS 1310 DELIVERED AS mu-DU lugal
Amount	Species	Species	Amount	mu-DU (delivered by and processed)	ba-zi (disbursed by ab-ba-sa$_6$-ga)	ì-dab$_5$ (transferred to)	Subtotal	Total	
21	u$_8$	u$_8$-gukkal	21	—	—	—		—	no details known
746	máš	máš-gal	2	—	—	—	—	7	1 zi-ga lugal no details known about the remainder
		máš	744	1 (22/Ib) by en ^{d}inanna 3 (-/Ia: u$_4$-1) by lú-^{d}šára, ur-^{d}en-líl-lá 1 (-/Ia: u$_4$-2) by níĝ-gu-du 2 (-/Ia: u$_4$-4) by *á-pi$_5$-la-núm* nu-bànda, en-šà-kù-ge	the same 1 disbursed (22/Ib) — — —	—	7		
1	ud$_5$	ud$_5$	1	—	—	—		—	no details known
1	dara$_4$ níta	dara$_4$ níta	1	—	1 (14/I = 8/9/14/I)	the same transferred to lú-^{d}nanna šabra ^{d}nanna (B.9) (14/I)		1	1 énsi ù šabra-ne
52	maš-dà	amar maš-dà	52	4 by šeš-kal-la (1/Ia = -/Ia i 20) 1 by dam ur-^{d}en-líl-lá (-/Ia: u$_4$-2) 2 by ku-ù and 1 by *ḫa-ab-ru-še-er* (4/Ib = -/Ia ii 6 and 10) 4 (22/Ib): 2 by ur-tilla$_5$ saĝa, 2 dead 6 (24/Ia): 1 by *ir$_{11}$-ra-nu-id*, 3 by SUḪUŠ-*ki-in*, 1 by ^{d}šul-gi-*na-da*, 1 dead by *a-ḫu-um* dumu lugal 1 (27/Ia) by ur-tilla$_5$ saĝa	the same 4 disbursed (1/Ia) — the same 3 disbursed (4/Ib) the same 4 disbursed (22/Ib) the same 6 disbursed (24/Ia) the same 1 disbursed (27/Ia)	—		19	21 zi-ga lugal, of which 3 might have come a-šà-ta no details known about the remainder

TABLE 2. mu-DU lugal (A.1.) (*cont.*)

Animals in ÄS 1310		Detailed Species *PDT* 2 958 vi		Animals Attested in Individual Documents			Total of Individually Attested Animals		Final Disbursal of Animals in ÄS 1310 Delivered as mu-DU lugal
Amount	Species	Species	Amount	mu-DU (delivered by and processed)	ba-zi (disbursed by ab-ba-sa$_6$-ga)	ì-dab$_5$ (transferred to)	Subtotal	Total	
1	az	amar az	1	—	1 (8/Ib = 8/9/14/I)	the same transferred to *šu-eš$_{18}$-tár* u$_4$-da-tuš (8/Ia, 8/Ib), then to lú-^{d}nanna šabra ^{d}nanna (B.9) (8/Ib = 8/9/14/I)		1	1 énsi ù šabra-ne

A.4. é-du$_6$-la

4 gu$_4$	2 from níg̃-gur$_{11}$ PN (25/Ib = 25/28/30/I), transferred to ^{d}en-líl-lá a-šà-šè (B.17) (25/28/30/I)
12 áb	8 from níg̃-gur$_{11}$ PN (25/Ib and 30/Ia = 25/28/30/I), transferred to ^{d}en-líl-lá a-šà-šè (B.17) (25/28/30/I)
7 šeg$_9$-bar níta	all transferred to lú-dig̃ir-ra dumu ir$_{11}$-ḫùl-la (B.12); no individual documents preserved
1 šeg$_9$-bar munus	transferred to lú-dig̃ir-ra dumu ir$_{11}$-ḫùl-la (B.12)
	1 amar šeg$_9$-bar munus known from a transferral document (24/Ib); this could also be the šeg$_9$-bar munus from the mu-DU lugal (A.1)
2 dúsu níta, 1 dúsu munus	transferred (25/Id) to *šu*-^{d}IDIM, the father of *šu-ir-ra*, who sealed the receipt of these animals (see B.14)
32 udu	no details known
23 u$_8$	no details known
37 máš	no details known
47 ud$_5$	no details known

All gu$_4$ and áb (except those coming from the "fields") are delivered as mu-DU lugal or é-du$_6$-la.[13] Of the 73 gu$_4$ and 14 áb of CT 32 48 BM 103448 (25/28/30/I), 71 gu$_4$ and 6 áb were delivered as mu-DU lugal (A.1). The rest are 2 gu$_4$ and 7 áb níg̃-gur$_{11}$ in-na-ti (25/Ib) and 1 áb níg̃-gur$_{11}$ mar-tu-ne (30/Ia). Since 8 of 11 cows of the mu-DU lugal could be individually documented, the 8 cows from níg̃-gur$_{11}$ must come from other sources, in this case the é-du$_6$-la, a term closely related to níg̃-gur$_{11}$, which is some kind of semiprivate property.[14] The 2 gu$_4$ from níg̃-gur$_{11}$ most probably come from é-du$_6$-la as well.

---

[13] Sallaberger states (*Kalender*, pp. 27 f.) that the term mu-DU lugal combines all mu-DU deliveries, including é-du$_6$-la and níg̃-GA entries, which in ÄS 1310, however, are listed separately.

[14] See K. Maekawa, "Confiscation of Private Properties in the Ur III Period: A Study of é-dul-la and níg̃-GA," *Acta Sumerologica (Japan)* 18 (1996): 103–68.

A.5. a-šà-ta

17 gu$_4$	number identical with those being disbursed as zi-ga lugal (B.1) 8 gu$_4$ (-/Ic) transferred as bala *ar-ši-aḫ* énsi KÁ.DINGIR^{ki}[15] to lú-diğir-ra šabra via uš-ğu$_{10}$, the fattener; disbursed as zi-ga lugal (B.1); this lú-diğir-ra šabra not identical with lú-diğir-ra dumu inim-^{d}šára (B.10), nor one of the énsi ù šabra-ne (B.9) [16]
1 áb	no details known
347 udu	no details known
12 ⌜u$_8$⌝	number identical with those being disbursed as zi-ga lugal (B.1)
356 [má]š	45 máš (-/Ic) transferred as bala *ar-ši-aḫ* énsi KÁ.DINGIR^{ki} to lú-diğir-ra šabra via uš-ğu$_{10}$, the fattener (see gu$_4$ above and n. 16); disbursed as zi-ga lugal (B.1)
184 [u]d$_5$	number identical with those being disbursed as zi-ga lugal (B.1)
3 maš-dà	no details known

[15] Animals from the bala-fund were transferred by an official of the main administration into the care and responsibility of a representative of a province and eventually disbursed as zi-ga lugal. Assuming that it is not a coincidence that the number of gu$_4$ from the sections a-šà-ta and zi-ga lugal are identical, these 8 gu$_4$ were kept in the "fields" before final distribution.

For bala énsi GN, see P. Steinkeller, "The Administrative and Economic Organization of the Ur III State: The Core and the Periphery," in M. Gibson and R. D. Biggs, eds., *The Organization of Power: Aspects of Bureaucracy in the Ancient Near East*, 2d ed., SAOC 46 (Chicago, 1991), pp. 15–33; Maeda, "Bal-énsi in the Drehem Texts," *Acta Sumerologica (Japan)* 16 (1994): 115–64; Sallaberger, *Kalender*, pp. 23, 32 ff.; T. Sharlach, "Bala: Economic Exchange between Center and Provinces in the Ur III State" (Ph.D. diss., Harvard University, 1999 = University Microfilms International [UMI] no. 9949724, Ann Arbor, Michigan, 1999), pp. 99 ff. and, for uš-ğu$_{10}$, pp. 89 f.

[16] All gu$_4$ and 11 of the 18 máš that lú-diğir-ra dumu inim-^{d}šára (B.10) receives from ab-ba-sa$_6$-ga during this month are attested in individual transferral documents. Therefore these 8 gu$_4$ and 45 máš must have been transferred to a different lú-diğir-ra functioning as a bala-official. In Jones-Snyder, no. 137 (AS 4), a badly damaged text, a lú-diğir-ra šabra is attested performing a ğìri-function.

B. OUTGOING LIVESTOCK

B.1. zi-ga lugal

All animals appear to have been slaughtered. Their bodies are given (šu ba-ti) to ur-^{d}ni$_9$-g̃ar (see B.8); their skins go to lugal-éren.

Some documents tell us the purpose of the deliveries or the final destination of the animals. I assume that all animals that were meant for deities, for the kitchen, the é-uz-ga, and the é-kišib-ba were royal expenditures (zi-ga lugal).[17]

4 gu$_4$-niga	from mu-DU lugal (A.1)
17 gu$_4$	number identical with those coming a-šà-ta (A.5)
	8 gu$_4$ (-/Ic) transferred as bala *ar-ši-ah̬* énsi KÁ.DINGIR^{ki} to lú-dig̃ir-ra šabra via uš-g̃u$_{10}$, the fattener. See section A.5 and n. 16 above.
2 udu-niga	from mu-DU lugal (A.1)
1 ud$_5$-niga	from mu-DU lugal (A.1)
	1 ^{munus}áš-gàr-niga (22/Ib) for ^{d}en-líl
242 udu	9 sila$_4$ for deities: 4 for ^{d}*an-nu-ni-tum*, 3 for ^{d}*na-na-a* (1/Ia); 1 for ^{d}utu (22/Ib; see A.1); 1 for ^{d}nanna (24/Ia; see A.1)
	34 udu for é-muh̬aldim: 1 (1/Ia); 3 šu-gíd (1–4/I); 30 šu-gíd (17/Ia)
	18 sila$_4$ for é-muh̬aldim: 17 šu-gíd (1–4/I); 1 šu-gíd (4/Ib)
	1 sila$_4$ for é-uz-ga (17/Ia; see A.1)
	1 dead sila$_4$ for é-kišib-ba (23/I)
12 u$_8$	number identical with those coming a-šà-ta (A.5)
	2 šu-gíd for é-muh̬aldim (1–4/I)
261 máš	1 for ^{d}inanna (22/Ib; see A.1)
	50 máš šu-gíd for é-muh̬aldim: 1 (1/Ia); 21 (1–4/I); 28 (17/Ia)
	45 máš (-/Ic) transferred as bala *ar-ši-ah̬* énsi KÁ.DINGIR^{ki} to lú-dig̃ir-ra šabra via uš-g̃u$_{10}$, the fattener. They probably came a-šà-ta; see section A.5. and n. 16 above.
184 ud$_5$	number identical with those coming a-šà-ta (A.5)

[17] See Maeda, "Bringing," p. 83, and idem, "Bal-énsi," pp. 133 ff.

	151 ud$_5$ for é-muḫaldim: 147 ud$_5$ šu-gíd, 4 ^{munus}áš-gàr šu-gíd (1–4/I)
	1 ud$_5$ máš ná-a (17/Ia; see A.1) for é-uz-ga
50 maš-dà	from mu-DU lugal (A.1); 3 might have come a-šà-ta (A.5)
	6 amar maš-dà for deities: 1 for ^{d}en-líl, 1 for ^{d}nin-líl, 2 for ^{d}nanna (1/Ia; see A.1); 2 for ^{d}nanna (4/Ib; see A.1)
	11 amar maš-dà for é-uz-ga: 1 (4/Ib; see A.1); 2 (17/Ia); 2 (22/Ib; see A.1); 5 (24/Ia; see A.1); 1 (27/I; see A.1)
	4 amar maš-dà for é-kišib-ba, all dead: 1 (17/Ia); 2 (22/Ib; see A.1); 1 (24/Ia; see A.1)

B.2. ^{giš}gu-za ^{d}šul-gi

3 udu-niga	from mu-DU lugal (A.1)
1 udu	no details known
1 máš	no details known

The animals withdrawn for ^{giš}gu-za ^{d}šul-gi are not the same as the ones delivered as mu-DU ^{d}šul-gi; see A.2 above.

B.3. níĝ-ba lugal

9 gu$_4$-niga	from mu-DU lugal (A.1)
5 udu-niga	from mu-DU lugal (A.1)
	4 udu-niga and 1 sila$_4$-niga (1/Ia) withdrawn for da-da gala[18]
161 udu	1 udu from mu-DU lugal (A.1) withdrawn for *i-šar-kur-ba-aš* rá-gab (22/Ib)
101 máš	no details known
1 maš-dà	from mu-DU-lugal (A.1) or a-šà-ta (A.5)

B.4. and B.5 sá-du$_{11}$ ^{d}gu-la[19] and sá-du$_{11}$ inim-^{d}nanna

30 udu sá-du$_{11}$ ^{d}gu-la	no details known
6 udu sá-du$_{11}$ inim-^{d}nanna	no details known

The same amount, 30 udu for sá-du$_{11}$ ^{d}gu-la and 6 udu for sá-du$_{11}$ inim-^{d}nanna, is recorded in the ki-bi-gi$_4$-a document PIOL 19 345 iv 31–v 1 (V/AS 2); also in SAT 2

[18] For da-da gala, see idem, "Bal-énsi," p. 135.

[19] See Sallaberger, *Kalender*, p. 29 and no. 122.

724 ix 35–38; xi 9–12 (expenditures of ab-ba-sa$_6$-ga in XI/AS 2); and in MVN 11 184, 31, 34 (expenditures of ur-kù-nun-na in III/AS 3). In these texts inim-^{d}nanna is identified as dumu lugal. He is well attested as the son of Amarsu'ena; see D. R. Frayne, *Ur III Period* (2112–2004 B.C.), RIME 3/2 (Toronto, 1997), p. 268, and Sigrist, *Drehem*, p. 361, n. 41.[20]

For sá-du$_{11}$ ^{d}gu-la, see also Or., s.p., 47–49 67, a document for the first six months of AS 2[21] from the bureau of lú-sa$_6$-ga[22]: 90 udu, 90 máš sá-du$_{11}$ ^{d}gu-la ... ur-kù-nun-na ì-dab$_5$, and MVN 13 512 ii 43 (I–XII/Š 46): 25 udu, 25 máš sá-du$_{11}$ ^{d}gu-la delivered during the eleventh month.

B.6. mu ur-ra-šè *dan*-^{d}šul-gi[23] šu ba-ti

9 anše-kúnga níta	ki šabra-ne-ta (A.3), no individual document preserved
5 anše-kúnga munus	ki šabra-ne-ta (A.3), no individual document preserved

It does not seem very likely that the kúnga were raised to be fed to dogs, so perhaps their death was accidental. We also have attestations of dúsu being fed to dogs; see PIOL 19 345 iv 14–19 or Hilgert, OIP 121, nos. 498 and 499. For carcass removal by dogs, see W. Heimpel, "Hund," *RLA* 4, p. 495, § 4.2.

B.7. mu ur-ra-šè DINGIR-*ba-ni*[24] šu ba-ti

15 udu	no details known
15 máš	no details known

B.8. kišib ur-ni$_9$-g̃ar

For ur-ni$_9$-g̃ar, see Jones-Snyder, p. 223 and figure 4 on p. 224. This section lists only one animal for which ur-ni$_9$-g̃ar issued a sealed tablet (kišib). All the other animals whose carcasses are given to ur-ni$_9$-g̃ar and which are withdrawn as zi-ga lugal (see B.1) do not belong in this section.

1 áb (ba-úš)	1 of 7 cows (30/Ia = 25/28/30/I) transferred to ^{d}en-líl-lá (B.17), received as mu-DU lugal (A.1) or from é-du$_6$-la (A.4)

[20] M. Sigrist, *Drehem* (Bethesda, Maryland, 1992).

[21] Not from Š 45 because the total number of animals is noted on the left edge of the tablet, a practice starting in the fifth month of AS 1; see Hilgert, OIP 121, p. 18.

[22] See Sallaberger, *Kalender*, p. 33; Maeda, "Bal-énsi," pp. 122 f. and 148, where lú-sa$_6$-ga is not listed before AS 6.

[23] The recipients (šu ba-ti) of dead animals for dogs normally were herdsmen in charge of the dogs.

[24] See B.6. and n. 23 above.

This cow is not recorded in an individual document as dead or as transferred to ur-ni$_9$-g̃ar. If this, however, had been the cow's fate, the one missing cow in 25/28/30/I could be explained as follows.

In section B.17, 13 áb are returned to the fields. In the transferral document CT 32 48 BM 103448 (25/28/30/I), however, 14 cows are taken over by ^{d}en-líl-lá, the official who manages cattle in the fields (see B.17). Both documents, ÄS 1310 and BM 103448, were written on or after the 30th of the month. If one of the 7 cows taken over by ^{d}en-líl-lá on the 30th died after the three-day document was written but before the records for the whole month were compiled, that one dead cow could in the meantime have become the responsibility of ur-ni$_9$-g̃ar, who is known for handling carcasses. No text documenting the demise of this one cow is preserved.

EXCURSUS

We have only one individual document from I/AS 2 in which ur-ni$_9$-g̃ar "accepts" (šu ba-ti) animals from the central bureau of ab-ba-sa$_6$-ga: SAT 2 723 (1–4/I). Both ur-ni$_9$-g̃ar and his successor ^{d}šul-gi-iri-g̃u$_{10}$ receive dead animals from all units of the livestock-managing administration in Puzriš-Dagan and other cities, but the central bureau is very rarely explicitly mentioned.[25] This fact, however, does not necessarily mean that he did not handle carcasses coming from the main bureau. References such as ÄS 1310 iv 13 ff. demonstrate that most likely all animals for the zi-ga lugal that had been or were to be slaughtered, for instance, for the kitchen,[26] were handled by ur-ni$_9$-g̃ar (šu ba-ti).

The above-mentioned SAT 2 723 records 194 šu-gíd-animals destined (as zi-ga lugal; see B.1) for the kitchen.[27] This is one of the rare texts that record the "accep-

[25] See Hilgert, OIP 121, pp. 14 f. Other texts in which ur-ni$_9$-g̃ar receives dead animals from the central bureau are: Or., s.p., 47–49 131 (VII/AS 2); SAT 2 724 ix 32 f. and x 6 f. (IX/AS 2); Hilgert, OIP 121, no. 132 (XI/AS 2) and all its duplicates (see M. Hilgert, "Notes and Observations on Ur III Tablets from the Oriental Institute," *JCS* 49 [1997]: 46). Compare also a receipt for dead animals in *PDT* 1 585 (XII/AS 1) by *nu-úr*-^{d}EN.ZU, who seems better known for dealing with wool and hides; see Hilgert, OIP 121, p. 70.

[26] The texts normally do not specify the destination "kitchen" for animals "accepted" by ur-ni$_9$-g̃ar. Some other references in which ur-ni$_9$-g̃ar is mentioned in connection with the kitchen are MVN 15 36 (VIII/Š 47), MVN 13 530 (IX/Š 47), and Torino I 213 (X/AS 4).

[27] šu-gíd é muḫaldim-šè, é *pù-zur$_8$-iš-^{d}da-gan*^{ki}-ta, uri$_5$^{ki}-šè, má zi-kum-ma-ke$_4$ íb-DU, ur-ni$_9$-g̃ar šu ba-ti, ki ab-ba-sa$_6$-ga-ta ba-zi.

For má zi-kum-ma, see W. Heimpel, "Towards an Understanding of the Term siKKum," *RA* 88 (1994): 5–31, especially 24 f. and 29. This seems to be a boat used by the royal messengers for crossing a river. It seems surprising that such a boat would have been used to transport animals that were probably still alive to Ur. So far, no references for zi-kum/gúm are known from Drehem. The only other text recording a ziKKum-boat is *UTI* 3, no. 1678 (F. Yıldız and T. Gomi, *Die Umma-Texte aus den archäologischen Museen zu Istanbul*, Band 3 [Nr. 1601–2300] [Bethesda, Maryland, 1993]), which records mats (kid) má zi-ku-ma-šè.

The verbal form íb-gub "they were placed (on the boat)" seems to be another example

tance" (šu ba-ti) of dead or to-be-slaughtered animals by ur-ni$_9$-g̃ar or his successor as well as the withdrawal (ba-zi or zi-ga) of animals from one of the administration bureaus.[28]

ur-ni$_9$-g̃ar is recorded as handling many more dead animals during I/AS 2. They come from the bureaus of lú-dig̃ir-ra dumu inim-^{d}šára (B.10) and ^{d}šul-gi-a-a-g̃u$_{10}$ (B.11).

From lú-dig̃ir-ra dumu inim-^{d}šára:

17/Ib:	1 ud$_5$ a-dara$_4$, 1 máš a-dara$_4$, 1 sila$_4$-ga a-udu ḫur-sag̃, 1 máš-ga a-dara$_4$
18/Ib:	1 ^{munus}áš-gàr, 1 kir$_{11}$-ga
21/Ic:	2 máš-ga a-dara$_4$, 1 ^{munus}áš-gàr-ga a-dara$_4$, 1 amar maš-dà
27/Ib:	1 amar peš-ga, 1 gukkal-niga sig$_5$-ús, 1 u$_8$-niga sig$_5$-ús, 1 u$_8$, 1 gukkal, 1 ^{munus}áš-gàr, 2 sila$_4$-ga, 2 kir$_{11}$-ga, 2 ^{munus}áš-gàr-ga

From ^{d}šul-gi-a-a-g̃u$_{10}$:

1/Ic:	3 udu, 3 u$_8$, 5 sila$_4$, 1 máš-gal, 3 sila$_4$-ga, 1 kir$_{11}$-ga, 2 máš-ga
3/Ib:	1 amar peš-a-am-ga, 2 udu, 3 máš-gal, 6 sila$_4$, 1 kir$_{11}$, 1 máš, 2 sila$_4$-ga, 2 kir$_{11}$-ga, 2 máš-ga
4/Ic:	1 ^{munus}áš-gàr babbar, 1 áb, 5 udu, 1 ⸢gukkal⸣, 1 ud$_5$, 5 sila$_4$, 1 kir$_{11}$, 1 sila$_4$-ga, 1 kir$_{11}$-ga
6/I:	1 amar peš-ga gùn-a, 2 udu aslum$_x$(A.LUM)-niga sig$_5$-ús, 1 u$_8$-niga, 1 más-gal-niga, 2 udu, 2 kir$_{11}$, 1 máš, 2 kir$_{11}$-ga, 1 ^{munus}áš-gàr-ga
7/I:	1 gukkal-niga, 2 udu, 1 u$_8$, 2 máš-gal, 1 ud$_5$, 8 sila$_4$, 3 kir$_{11}$, 3 máš, 1 kir$_{11}$-ga, 1 máš-ga
15/I:	1 máš-gal sig$_5$, 1 máš-ga babbar, 2 udu-niga, 1 gukkal, 1 ud$_5$, 1 sila$_4$, 1 kir$_{11}$-gukkal, 1 máš, 1 máš-ga
29/Ic:	1 máš-gal-niga, 1 udu, 1 u$_8$, 1 sila$_4$, 1 kir$_{11}$, 1 sila$_4$-ga, 1 kir$_{11}$-ga, 2 máš-ga

---

for intransitive *ḫamṭu* forms with preradical -b-. For these forms and -b- as a dimensional element, see C. Wilcke, "Anmerkungen zum 'Konjugationspräfix' /i/- und zur These vom 'silbischen Charakter der sumerischen Morpheme' anhand neusumerischer Verbalformen beginnend mit ì-íb-, ì-im- und ì-in-," *ZA* 78 (1988): 1–49, esp. 15–23 and 37–42.

[28] Other examples for occurrences of šu ba-ti and ba-zi / zi-ga in the same text are MVN 15 36 (VIII/Š 47), MVN 13 530 (IX/Š 47), *PDT* 1 623 (I/ŠS 5), all withdrawals by the main withdrawing official, MVN 13 422 (II/ŠS 7, with no name of withdrawing official), MVN 13 830 (III/ŠS 2), and MVN 13 810 (VIII/ŠS 2), both withdrawals of na-lu$_5$. Similar documents are *PDT* 1 467 (VIII/Š 47), *PDT* 1 467 (III/AS 5), and MVN 13 89 (XII/ŠS 8) in which the keepers of the dogs receive dead animals withdrawn by officials of the main bureau.

B.9. kišib énsi ù šabra-ne[29]

2 áb	from mu-DU lugal (A.1)
	1 áb gùn-a, 1 áb-mu-2 gùn-a delivered by *ṣa-al-ma-nu-um* mar-tu (9/Ia); transferred together with the dara$_4$ and the az to lú-^{d}nanna šabra ^{d}nanna[30] (9/Ib = 8/9/14/I)
1 dara$_4$ níta	from mu-DU lugal (A.1)
	1 dara$_4$ níta transferred together with the 2 áb and the az to lú-^{d}nanna šabra ^{d}nanna (14/I = 8/9/14/I)
1 az	from mu-DU lugal (A.1)
	1 amar az transferred to *šu-eš$_{18}$-tár* u$_4$-da-tuš[31] (8/Ia), then together with the 2 áb and the dara$_4$ to lú-^{d}nanna šabra ^{d}nanna (8/Ib = 8/9/14/I)

B.10. kišib lú-diĝir-ra dumu inim-^{d}šára

For lú-diĝir-ra dumu inim-^{d}šára, see Maeda, "Bringing," pp. 90f., and Sigrist, *Drehem*, pp. 324f. He shared the responsibility for "normal" animals, such as cows, sheep, and goats, with ^{d}šul-gi-a-a-ĝu$_{10}$ (B.11) in the Nagabtum. For lú-diĝir-ra dumu ir$_{11}$-ḫùl-la, see B.12; for the bala-official lú-diĝir-ra šabra, see section A.5 (a-šà-ta) and n. 16 above.

33 gu$_4$-niga	from mu-DU lugal (A.1)
	33 gu$_4$-niga: 5 (22/Ia), 28 (25/Ia) transferred to lú-diĝir-ra
15 gu$_4$	2 gu$_4$-mu-2 (22/Ia) and 13 gu$_4$ (25/Ia) transferred to lú-diĝir-ra
7 áb	2 áb and 3 áb-mu-2 (22/Ia) transferred to lú-diĝir-ra
3 udu-niga	from mu-DU lugal (A.1)
	3 udu-niga (29/Ib) transferred to lú-diĝir-ra
38 udu	11 udu, 4 gukkal, 3 sila$_4$ (22/Ia) transferred to lú-diĝir-ra
15 u$_8$	6 u$_8$ (22/Ia) transferred to lú-diĝir-ra
18 máš	7 máš, 4 máš-ga (22/Ia) transferred to lú-diĝir-ra
8 ud$_5$	7 ud$_5$ (22/Ia) transferred to lú-diĝir-ra

---

[29] For deliveries by énsi and šabra, see A.3.

[30] Is this the same lú-^{d}nanna šabra as the bala-official? See Maeda, "Bal-énsi," p. 148. We also know a lú-^{d}nanna šabra delivering sila$_4$-niga from *PDT* 2 958 ii 8 (-/Ia) and Hilgert, OIP 121, no. 73 (III/AS 1).

[31] For the entertainer *šu-eš$_{18}$-tár*, see Sigrist, *Drehem*, pp. 221 and 284. Did he stay with the bear cub when it was handed over to the šabra? For u$_4$-da-tuš, see also W. H. Ph. Römer, "Der Spaßmacher im alten Zweistromland," *Persica* 7 (1975–78): 43–68, esp. 51.

lú-diĝir-ra dumu inim-^{d}šára is also known for being in charge of newborn animals for which we have one document during I/AS 2:

4/Id: 1 amar anše-ZI.ZI-munus-ga, 4 máš a-a-dara$_{4}$, 7 ^{munus}áš-gàr-ga a-dara$_{4}$ ù-tu-da šà na-gab-tum-ma

It is surprising that he deals with an equid here. Those are normally the responsibility of lú-diĝir-ra dumu ir$_{11}$-ḫùl-la (B.12), who, however, was not connected with the Nagabtum.

For the transferral of dead animals by lú-diĝir-ra to ur-ni$_{9}$-ĝar, see B.8.

B.11. kišib ^{d}šul-gi-a-a-ĝu$_{10}$

For ^{d}šul-gi-a-a-ĝu$_{10}$, see Maeda, "Bringing," pp. 89 f., and Sigrist, *Drehem*, pp. 332 ff. He was responsible, together with lú-diĝir-ra dumu inim-^{d}šára (B.10), for livestock in the Nagabtum.

35 gu$_{4}$-niga	from mu-DU lugal (A.1)
	5 gu$_{4}$-niga (22/Ie) transferred to ^{d}šul-gi-a-a-ĝu$_{10}$
	1 gu$_{4}$-niga (28/Ib) transferred to ^{d}šul-gi-a-a-ĝu$_{10}$
14 gu$_{4}$	no details known
1 áb	no details known
7 udu-niga	from mu-DU lugal (A.1)
1 ud$_{5}$-⸢niga⸣	from mu-DU lugal (A.1)
257 udu	8 gukkal (28/Ib) transferred to ^{d}šul-gi-a-a-ĝu$_{10}$
11 u$_{8}$	1 U$_{8}$.ḪÚL (28/Ib) transferred to ^{d}šul-gi-a-a-ĝu$_{10}$
189 máš	4 máš (28/Ib) transferred to ^{d}šul-gi-a-a-ĝu$_{10}$

^{d}šul-gi-a-a-ĝu$_{10}$ is also known for being in charge of newborn animals:

20/Ia: 2 sila$_{4}$-ga, 1 kir$_{11}$-ga, 1 máš-ga, 1 ^{munus}áš-gàr-ga ù-tu-da

22/Id: 2 amar gu$_{4}$-ga, 5 sila$_{4}$-ga, 4 kir$_{11}$-ga ù-tu-da

23/Ib: 4 sila$_{4}$-ga, 3 kir$_{11}$-ga, 2 máš-ga, 4 ^{munus}áš-gàr-ga ù-tu-da

25/Ie: 3 sila$_{4}$-ga, 2 kir$_{11}$-ga, 2 máš-ga, 1 ^{munus}áš-gàr-ga ù-tu-da

We also have five disbursal documents (ba-zi) from ^{d}šul-gi-a-a-ĝu$_{10}$'s own bureau during I/AS 2:

1/Id: 30 udu-niga sá-du$_{11}$ *a-bí-sí-im-ti*, *nu-ḫi*-DINGIR sukkal maškim[32]

[32] Cf. the exact number of udu-niga being disbursed for Queen Abisimti by the same official one year later: Hilgert, OIP 121, no. 11 (II/AS 3).

16/I: 1 udu-niga, 1 máš-gal-niga for *bu-ša-am* of Simanum, g̃ìri *ḫu-zi-ri* sukkal, ir$_{11}$-g̃u$_{10}$ maškim

18/Ia: 2 udu-niga for ME-^{d}šul-gi[33] dumu-munus lugal, 1 udu-niga, 1 máš-gal-niga for *bù-ša-am* of Simanum, g̃ìri *ḫu-zi-ri* sukkal, ir$_{11}$-g̃u$_{10}$ maškim

20/Ib: 2 udu-niga for *bu-ša-am* of Simanum, g̃ìri *ḫu-zi-ri* sukkal, ir$_{11}$-g̃u$_{10}$ maškim$^{!}$(KAŠ$_{4}$)

30/Ib: 2 udu-niga for *bu-ša-am* of Simanum, g̃ìri *ḫu-zi-ri* sukkal, ir$_{11}$-g̃u$_{10}$ maškim

For the transferral of dead animals by ^{d}šul-gi-a-a-g̃u$_{10}$ to ur-ni$_{9}$-g̃ar, see B.8.

B.12. kišib lú-dig̃ir-ra dumu ir$_{11}$-ḫùl-la

For lú-dig̃ir-ra dumu ir$_{11}$-ḫùl-la, see Maeda, "Bringing," p. 90, and Sigrist, *Drehem*, pp. 324 f. He was responsible for equids and "odd" animals such as bears, deer, ibexes, etc. For lú-dig̃ir-ra dumu inim-^{d}šára, see B.10; for lú-dig̃ir-ra šabra, see section A.5 and n. 16 above.

7 šeg$_{9}$-bar níta	from é-du$_{6}$-la (A.4)
2 šeg$_{9}$-bar munus	1 šeg$_{9}$-bar munus from mu-DU lugal (A.1), 1 from é-du$_{6}$-la (A.4)
	1 amar šeg$_{9}$-bar munus ga (24/Ib) transferred to lú-dig̃ir-ra
1 anše-ZI.ZI níta	from mu-DU lugal (A.1)
2 anše-ZI.ZI munus	from mu-DU lugal (A.1)
	2 anše-ZI.ZI munus (21/Ia) transferred to lú-dig̃ir-ra

B.13. kišib na-lu$_{5}$

Most of the "fattened" (niga) animals from the mu-DU lugal (A.1) were transferred to na-lu$_{5}$.

231 udu-niga	from mu-DU lugal (A.1, from a total of 255)
	27 udu-niga known from transferral documents:
	20 udu-niga, 3 sila$_{4}$-niga (10/Ia); 2 udu-niga, 1 sila$_{4}$-niga (13/I); 1 sila$_{4}$-niga (21/Ib)
4 u$_{8}$-niga	from mu-DU lugal (A.1, from a total of 4)
4 máš-niga	from mu-DU lugal (A.1, from a total of 4)

[33] For ME-^{d}šul-gi, one of Šulgi's daughters, see Sigrist, *Drehem*, p. 363.

3 ud_5-niga	from mu-DU lugal (A.1, from a total of 5)
451 udu	341 udu known from transferral documents:
	5 gukkal, 1 gukkal-g̃iš-dù (11/I); 1 $sila_4$ (21/Ib); 90 udu (22/Ic); 242 udu (25/Ic); 2 $sila_4$ (29/Ia)
1 u_8	1 U_8.ḪÚL (11/I) transferred to na-lu_5
357 máš	323 máš known from transferral documents:
	1 máš (11/I); 60 máš (22/Ic); 262 máš (25/Ic)

B.14. kišib *šu-ìr-ra*

For *šu-ìr-ra*, see K. van Lerberghe, "Une tablette de Drehem et le fonctionnaire Šu-Irra," OLP 10, pp. 109–23; Sigrist, *Drehem*, p. 284; Hilgert, OIP 121, p. 70; and Maeda, "Bringing," pp. 85 f.[34] Maeda and Sigrist list him as one of the fatteners ($kuš_7$) of *small* livestock, but in a number of texts he seems to be in charge of equids; see Hilgert, OIP 121, nos. 120, 220, 222, 306, 319, 498, 499, 500, 501; PIOL 19 345 v 31; and our text. For his father *šu*-^{d}IDIM, see Sigrist, *Drehem*, p. 331, and van Lerberghe, "Une tablette de Drehem," pp. 116 f. and 122. At the time Sigrist's book was published, *šu*-^{d}IDIM was known to us only during AS 1 and only in connection with the handling of asses. ÄS 1310, however, shows him still doing this in I/AS 2, and Hilgert, OIP 121, no. 115 (IX/AS 1) tells us that he worked with *small* livestock as well.

2 dúsu níta, 1 dúsu munus	from é-du_6-la (A.4)
	all 3 transferred (25/Id) to *šu*-^{d}IDIM, the father of *šu-ìr-ra*, who sealed receipt of these animals

B.15. kišib ur-šu-ga-lam-ma

53 gu_4-niga	from mu-DU lugal (A.1)
	3 gu_4-niga (10/Ib) transferred to ur-šu-ga-lam-ma
1 áb-niga	from mu-DU lugal (A.1)
1 gu_4	no details known

ÄS 1310 and 10/Ib show that ur-šu-ga-lam-ma already worked at the beginning of AS 2, not starting as late as AS 3 as assumed by Sigrist, *Drehem*, p. 335.

[34] Maeda, "Bringing," pp. 83 f., states that *be-lí*-A.ZU and *šu-ìr-ra* (B.14) received livestock from fields but never from mu-DU lugal. In our text, however, they receive animals both from é-du_6-la and mu-DU lugal.

B.16. kišib *be-lí*-A.ZU for šu!(BA)-lá-a sila-a sig$_7$-a

For *be-lí*-A.ZU, who was in charge of breeding animals, see Maeda, "Bringing," pp. 83 ff.,[35] and Sigrist, *Drehem*, pp. 116 f. and 320. He would also temporarily take care of animals that had not yet reached their final destination and were held in reserve (sila-a sig$_7$-a; see Sigrist, *Drehem*, pp. 112 f.).

13 gu$_4$-niga	from mu-DU lugal (A.1)	all of these animals transferred to *be-lí*-A.ZU (-/Ib) by ab-ba-sa$_6$-ga as šu-lá-a
4 udu-niga	from mu-DU lugal (A.1)	
99 udu		

B.17. íb-tag$_4$ a-šà-šè

The official in charge of breeding and managing cattle in the "fields" was ^{d}en-líl-lá; see Maeda, "Bringing," p. 84. We have one text recording the transferral of not-yet-distributed large cattle from ab-ba-sa$_6$-ga to ^{d}en-líl-lá (CT 32 48 BM 103448 = 25/Ib+28/Ia+30Ia = 25/28/30/I) but no documentation for small livestock. The official taking those animals back to the "fields" would have been ur-kù-nun-na.

73 gu$_4$	71 gu$_4$ (25/28/30/I) from mu-DU lugal (A.1)
	2 gu$_4$ níg̃-gur$_{11}$ in-na-ti (25/Ib) from é-du$_6$-la (A.4)
	all 73 transferred to ^{d}en-líl-lá (25/28/30/I)
13 áb	6 áb (30/Ia) from mu-DU lugal (A.1)
	8 áb from é-du$_6$-la (A.4): 7 níg̃-gur$_{11}$ in-na-ti (25/Ib), 1 níg̃-gur$_{11}$ mar-tu-ne (30/Ia)
	all 14 transferred to ^{d}en-líl-lá (25/28/30/I)
	according to ÄS 1310, only 13 of these 14 áb transferred a-šà-šè; 1 áb probably died and was transferred to ur-ni$_9$-g̃ar (see B.8)
522 udu	no details known
17 u$_8$	no details known
200 máš	no details known
40 ud$_5$	no details known
4 maš-dà	from mu-DU lugal (A.1) or a-šà-ta (A.5)

[35] See n. 34 above.

TABLE 3. ANIMALS RECORDED IN ÄS 1310 AND ANIMALS KNOWN FROM INDIVIDUAL TRANSACTION DOCUMENTS

SECTION IN ÄS 1310	ÄS 1310 NUMBER OF ANIMALS	NUMBER OF ANIMALS RECORDED IN INDIVIDUAL DOCUMENTS	NUMBER OF INDIVIDUAL DOCUMENTS PRESERVED AND TEXT SIGLA
A.1. mu-DU lugal	2,794	234 (maybe 233) (see note 10)	**23 (maybe 24)** -/Ia, -/Ib, 1/Ia, 4/Ib, 8/Ia, 8/9/14/I, 9/Ia, 10/Ia, 10/Ib, 13/I, 17/Ia, 21/Ia, 21/Ib, 22/Ia, 22/Ib, 22/Ie, 24/Ia, (24/Ib), 25/Ia, 25/28/30/I, 27/Ia, 28/Ia, 29/Ia, 29/Ib
A.2. mu-DU ^{d}šul-gi	4	—	—
A.3. ki šabra-ne-ta	14	—	—
A.4. é-du$_6$-la	166	13 (maybe 14) (see note 10)	**2 (maybe 3)** (24/Ib), 25/Id, 25/28/30/I
A.5. a-šà-ta	920	53	**1** -/Ic
B.1. zi-ga lugal	773	343	**9** -/Ic, 1/Ia, 1-4/I, 4/Ib, 17/Ia, 22/Ib, 23/I, 24/Ia, 27/I
B.2. ^{giš}gu-za ^{d}šul-gi	5	—	—
B.3. níĝ-ba lugal	277	6	**2** 1/Ia, 22/Ib
B.4. sá-du$_{11}$ ^{d}gu-la	30	—	—
B.5. sá-du$_{11}$ inim-^{d}nanna	6	—	—
B.6. *dan*-^{d}šul-gi	14	—	—
B.7. DINGIR-*ba-ni*	30	—	—
B.8. ur-ni$_9$-ĝar	1	(—)	(—)(see B.17)
B.9. énsi ù šabra-ne	4	4	**3** 8/Ib, 9/Ia, 8/9/14/I
B.10. lú-diĝir-ra dumu inim-^{d}šára	137	98	**3** 22/Ia, 25/Ia, 29/Ib
B.11. ^{d}šul-gi-a-a-ĝu$_{10}$	515	14	**1** 28/Ib
B.12. lú-diĝir-ra dumu ir$_{11}$-ḫùl-la	12	3	**2** 21/Ia, 24/Ib
B.13. na-lu$_5$	1,051	692	**7** 10/Ia, 11/I, 13/I, 21/Ib, 22/Ic, 25/Ic, 29/Ia
B.14. *šu-ìr-ra*	3	3	**1** 25/Id
B.15. ur-šu-ga-lam-ma	55	3	**1** 10/Ib
B.16. *be-lí*-A.ZU	116	116	**1** -/Ib
B.17. a-šà-šè	869	86 (+ 1 dead)	**1** 25/28/30/I

APPENDIX

I. DELIVERERS OF ANIMALS IN I/AS 2

a-a-g̃u$_{10}$	gu$_4$-niga, udu-niga, udu **-/Ia**
a-bu-ni	gu$_4$-niga, udu-niga, udu, máš **-/Ia**
a-ḫu-um dumu lugal	amar maš-dà **24/Ia**
a-mur-é-a	áb-[…], udu-niga-sig$_5$, udu-[…], máš, sila$_4$-[…] **-/Ia**
á-pi$_5$*-la-núm* nu-bànda	máš **-/Ia**
á-pi$_5$*-lí-a*	sila$_4$ **-/Ia**
ba-za-X	sila$_4$$^{?}$ **-/Ia**
du$^{?}$-ú-du	gu$_4$-niga, udu-niga-sig$_5$, udu-niga, sila$_4$-[…], udu **-/Ia**
du$_{11}$-ga-zi-da	sila$_4$ **-/Ia**
en ^{d}inanna (not name but title)	sila$_4$ **17/Ia**; sila$_4$, máš **22/Ib**
en-šà-kù-ge	máš **-/Ia**
énsi (no place name given)	sila$_4$ **9/Ia**
gù-dé-a	sila$_4$ **-/Ia**
g̃á-a-kam	sila$_4$ **-/Ia**
ḫa-ab-ru-še-er	amar maš-dà **-/Ia; 4/Ib**
ḫu-ba-a	gu$_4$-niga, udu-niga-sig$_5$, udu-niga, udu, máš, sila$_4$ **-/Ia**
ḫu-un-ḫa-ab-ur	gu$_4$-niga, udu, máš **-/Ia**
in-na-ti (níg̃-gur$_{11}$)	gu$_4$, áb **25/28/30/I**
in-ta-è-a	[…].X **-/Ia**
ir$_{11}$-g̃u$_{10}$	gu$_4$-niga, udu-niga-sig$_5$, udu-niga, sila$_4$-niga, udu, máš **-/Ia**; udu-niga, sila$_4$-niga **1/Ia**
ir$_{11}$*-ra-nu-id*	amar maš-dà **24/Ia**
iš-du-ki-in	gu$_4$-niga, udu-niga-sig$_5$, udu, máš, sila$_4$ **-/Ia**; see also SUḪUŠ-*ki-in*
KA.X	udu-niga-sig$_5$ **-/Ia**
ku-ù	amar maš-dà **-/Ia; 4/Ib;** […] **9/Ia**
lú-^{d}asar-lú-ḫi	udu-niga, sila$_4$ **-/Ia**
lú-^{d}nanna	[…] **-/Ia**
lú-^{d}nanna šabra	sila$_4$-niga **-/Ia**

lú-^{d}nin-šubur	gu$_4$-niga, udu-niga-sig$_5$, udu-niga, sila$_4$-niga, udu, máš **-/Ia**
lú-^{d}šára	máš **-/Ia**
lú-^{d}[...]	sila$_4$-niga **9/Ia**
lugal-má-gur$_8$-re	gu$_4$-niga, udu-niga-sig$_5$, sila$_4$-niga, udu **-/Ia**
na-ra-am-ì-lí	máš, sila$_4$ **-/Ia**
NE.NI.NE-a	sila$_4$ **-/Ia**
níĝ-gu-du	máš **-/Ia**
pù-zur$_8$-eš$_{18}$-tár	sila$_4$ **-/Ia**
SUḪUŠ-*ki-in*	amar maš-dà **24/Ia**; see also *iš-du-ki-in* or *šu-ru-uš-ki-in*
ṣa-al-ma-nu-um mar-tu	áb-gùn-a, áb-mu-2 **9/Ia**
šar-ru-um-ba-ni	sila$_4$ **-/Ia**; udu-niga-sig$_5$, udu-niga, udu, máš, SILA$_4$?. ḪÚL **-/Ia**
šeš-kal-la	amar maš-dà **-/Ia**; **1/Ia**
šu-^{d}EN.ZU di-ku$_5$	udu **22/Ib**
šu-ru-uš-ki-in	gu$_4$-niga, udu-niga-[...], [...], máš, sila$_4$ **-/Ia**; see also SUḪUŠ-*ki-in*
^{d}šul-gi-*na-da*	amar maš-dà **24/Ia**
ur-é-an-na	sila$_4$ **-/Ia**
ur-^{d}en-líl-lá (dam)	amar maš-dà **-/Ia**
ur-^{d}en-líl-lá	máš **-/Ia**
ur-^{d}lugal-bàn-da	sila$_4$ **-/Ia**
ur-ni$_9$-ĝar	gu$_4$-niga, udu-niga, udu, sila$_4$ **-/Ia**
ur-^{d}nin-a-zu	sila$_4$ **-/Ia**
ur-^{d}nin-gal	^{munus}áš-gàr-niga **-/Ia**
ur-^{d}nin-gublaga	[...] **-/Ia**
ur-tilla$_5$(AN.GE$_{23}$.AN) saĝa	amar maš-dà **22/Ib; 27/Ia**
za-ni-a	sila$_4$ **-/Ia**
zabar-dab$_5$ (not name but title)	gu$_4$-niga, udu-niga-sig$_5$,udu-niga, udu, máš, sila$_4$ **-/Ia**; sila$_4$ **24/Ia**
zé-na-na	gu$_4$-niga, udu, máš **-/Ia**; ^{munus}áš-gàr-niga **22/Ib**
ZU.TI.X	sila$_4$ **-/Ia**
[...].NI lú-má-ninda dir-ra	gukkal? **-/Ia**

II. Other Personal Names, Not Including the Administration Officials

a-a-kal-la (maškim) **17/Ia; 22/Ib**

a-bí-sí-im-ti **1/Ia** (g̃iri); **1/Id**

ar-ši-aḫ énsi KÁ.DINGIR^{ki} **-/Ic**

bu/bù-ša-am lú ši-ma-ni-um^{ki} **16/I; 18/Ia** (*bù-*); **20/Ib; 30/Ib**

da-da gala **1/Ia**

ḫu-zi-ri sukkal (g̃ìri) **16/I; 18/Ia; 20/Ib; 30/Ib**

i-šar-kur-ba-aš rá-gab **22/Ib**

i-ti-šu$^{!}$-[*lum*] (g̃ìri) **-/Ia**

ir$_{11}$-g̃u$_{10}$ (maškim) **1/Ia; 16/I; 18/Ia; 20/Ib; 22/Ib; 30/Ib**

lú-dig̃ir-ra šabra (ì-dab$_5$) **-/Ic**

lú-^{d}nanna šabra ^{d}nanna **8/9/14/I**

ME-^{d}šul-gi dumu-munus lugal **18/Ia**

^{d}nanše-ul$_4$-gal (maškim) **1/Ia; 4/Ib; 22/Ib; 24/Ia**

nu-ḫi-DINGIR sukkal (maškim) **1/Id**

šu-eš$_{18}$-tár u$_4$-da-tuš **8/Ia; 8/9/14/I**

ur-^{d}ba-ba$_6$ (maškim) **4/Ib; 24/Ia; 27/Ia**

uš-g̃u$_{10}$ kurušda (g̃ìri) **-/Ic**

zabar-dab$_5$ (not name but title; maškim) **1/Ia**

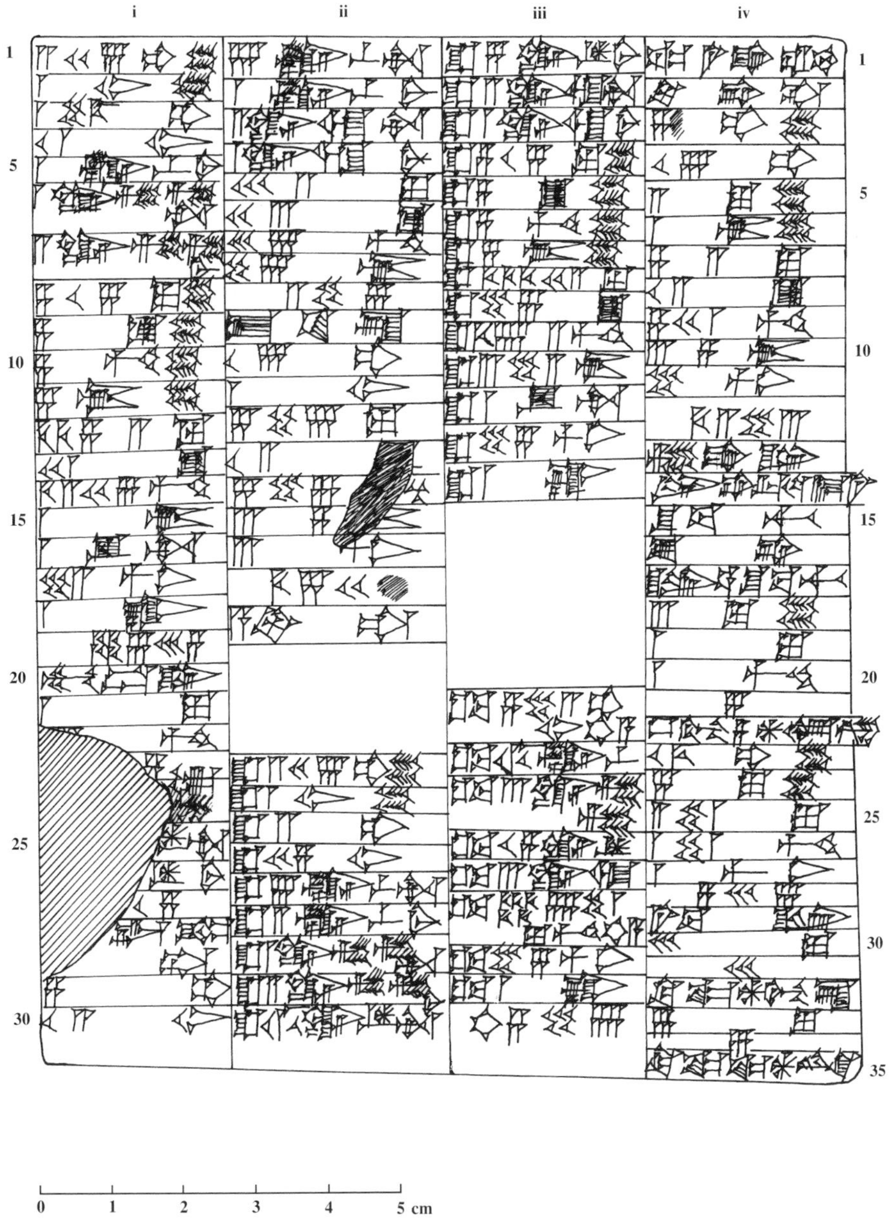

ÄS 1310, Obverse

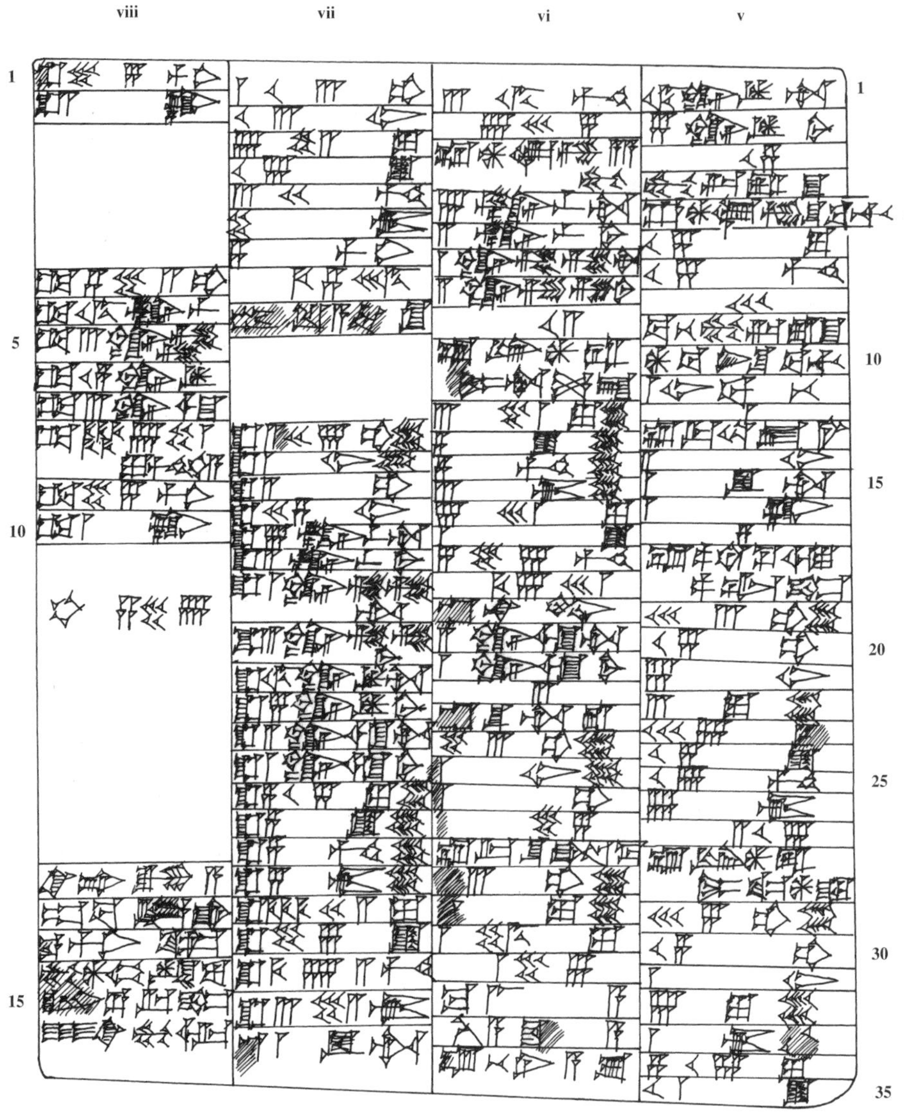

ÄS 1310, Reverse

IMGUR-SÎN UND SEINE BEIDEN SÖHNE: EINE (NICHT GANZ) NEUE ALTBABYLONISCHE ERBTEILUNGSURKUNDE AUS UR, GEFUNDEN WAHRSCHEINLICH IN LARSA

Walter Farber, The University of Chicago

Vor fast 50 Jahren hat W. F. Leemans[1] ein kleines Dossier altbabylonischer Urkunden zusammengestellt, das den Grundbesitz einer Familie zuerst in Ur, später in Ur und Larsa über drei Generationen hinweg dokumentiert. Er hat dabei überzeugend argumentiert, daß zumindest der Leittext dieses Dossiers in Ur geschrieben (wenn auch wohl nicht dort gefunden) wurde.[2] Dieser Text, damals nur erhalten in Form zweier Fragmente der Tafelhülle einer Erbteilung zwischen Sîn-muballiṭ und Enlil-issu, den Söhnen des Imgur-Sîn, wurde von V. Scheil noch lange vor Beginn der offiziellen Ausgrabungen in Ur auszugsweise publiziert[3] und von Leemans[4] paraphrasiert. Der Aufbewahrungsort der Bruchstücke war Leemans unbekannt, eine vollständigere Bearbeitung damit ausgeschlossen. Ein Datum war auf Scheils Fragmenten ebenfalls nicht erhalten.

Auch für die chronologisch auf diesen Leittext folgende Urkunde (Vindikation eines den beiden Brüdern gemeinsam gehörigen Hauses in Ur, datiert Rīm-Sîn 35)[5] ist mit Leemans sehr wahrscheinlich anzunehmen, daß sie noch in Ur geschrieben wurde.[6] Die verbleibenden beiden Urkunden des Dossiers, zuerst die Erbteilung zwischen Ilī-amtaḫar, Ilī-awīlī und Enlil-gāmil, den Söhnen des Sîn-muballiṭ (datiert Rīm-Sîn 51)[7], und danach noch die Vindikation eines Hauses in Ur, das Ilī-amtaḫar von Sîn-muballiṭ geerbt hatte (Datum aus der unvollständigen Publikation[8] nicht zu ersehen), sind dagegen wahrscheinlich nach dem Umzug des Sîn-muballiṭ nach Larsa zu datieren und

[1] W. F. Leemans, "The Old-Babylonian Business Documents from Ur" (Rez.-Artikel zu UET 5), *BiOr* 12 (1955): 112–22, bes. 119 ff. Appendix.

[2] Etwas anders Charpin *Archives familiales*, S. 60, der weiterhin mit einer aus Raubgrabungen in Ur stammenden Tafel zu rechnen scheint.

[3] V. Scheil, "L'expression NU-ḪA-SA-ṢI", *RA* 15 (1918): 80 f.

[4] Leemans, "Business Documents", S. 119.

[5] V. Scheil, "Le terme *put bîti ullulu* en Droit babylonien", *RA* 12 (1915): 115 f.

[6] Vgl. auch zu diesem Text Charpin *Archives familiales*, S. 60, und Leemans, "Business Documents", S. 119ff.

[7] C.-F. Jean, *Šumer et Akkad* (Paris, 1923), Nr. CLXXV–CLXXVII:166.

[8] V. Scheil, "L'expression *Qatam nasâḫu* 'retirer le main'", *RA* 14 (1917): 95 f.

dann dort geschrieben worden. Dennoch sind wohl auch die beiden in Ur abgefaßten Tafeln zusammen mit den letzteren in Larsa gefunden worden, und die vier Texte haben erst danach ihre separaten Wege in verschiedene Tafelsammlungen angetreten.[9] Leemans' gedankenreiche Ausführungen machen diese Gruppe von Urkunden auch heute noch zu einem Schulbeispiel dafür, daß textinterne Kriterien (hier die Namen der Protagonisten, sowie zwei ortstypische Klauseln) nur begrenzte Beweiskraft für den tatsächlichen Fundort von Tafeln aus unkontrollierten Grabungen haben können.

Vor Jahren spielte mir nun der Zufall die noch unpublizierte Innentafel zu den von Scheil bekanntgemachten Hüllenfragmenten des Leittextes in die Hände. Der damit rekonstruierbare volle Wortlaut der Erbteilung vermag zwar zu Leemans' archivalisch orientierter Argumentation nichts Wichtiges hinzuzufügen, erweitert aber trotzdem unsere Kenntnis des Zusammenhangs beträchtlich. Möge die Veröffentlichung dieser Tafel in einem Florilegium für Bob Biggs zur Buntheit des Gratulations-Straußes aus dem *CAD*-Garten beitragen!

Die Tafel A 13120 (Abb. 1–3) befindet sich heute im Übersee-Museum Bremen. Wann und wie sie dorthin gelangt ist, ist mir unbekannt.[10] Den ersten Hinweis auf sie erhielt ich 1978 von C. B. F. Walker. Kopieren konnte ich den Text dann anläßlich eines kurzen Aufenthaltes in Bremen im Jahre 1981.[11] Nach meiner Rückkehr nach Chicago stellte ich, angeregt durch einen Hinweis von M. Stol, fest, daß die Textauszüge bei Scheil[12] eine Passage dieser Tafel duplizierten. Kurz danach veröffentlichte J.-M. Durand eine vollständige Neukopie dieser inzwischen in der Sammlung der École Pratique des Hautes Études wiedergefundenen Hüllenfragmente.[13] D. Charpin machte mir später seine eigenen Kollationen und Notizen zu diesen zugänglich und überprüfte einige Details nochmals für mich, wofür ihm auch hier herzlich gedankt sei. Mit seiner Hilfe konnte auch mit Sicherheit geklärt werden, daß die Hüllenbruchstücke wirklich zu A 13120 gehören: Tafel und Hülle tragen Abdrücke desselben burgul-Siegels[14] (Abb. 1), und

[9] Vgl. dazu auch noch unten Anm. 10.

[10] Hinzuweisen ist in diesem Zusammenhang vielleicht noch auf die Tatsache, daß ein zweiter Text, der offenbar zusammen mit unserer Urkunde in das Übersee-Museum Bremen gelangt ist (A 13122; s. W. Farber, "Dr. med. Apil-ilišu, *Mārat-Anim*-Straße [am Ebabbar-Tempel], Larsa", in *Renger AV*, S. 135–50), sicherlich aus Larsa stammt. Was für ein Objekt sich hinter der dazwischenliegenden Museumsnummer A 13121 verbirgt, entzieht sich meiner Kenntnis – jedenfalls kein weiterer Keilschrifttext. Ein dritter solcher im Bremer Museum trägt die Nummer A 15225 und ist "Massenware": ein variantenloses Duplikat-Täfelchen der wohlbekannten Sîn-kāšid-Inschrift D. Frayne, *Old Babylonian Period (2003–1595 BC)*, RIME 4 (Toronto, 1990), S. 448–50, Nr. E4.4.1.4.

[11] An dieser Stelle sei dem damaligen Direktor des Übersee-Museums, Herrn Dr. H. Ganslmayer, sehr herzlich für die freundliche Genehmigung zur Publikation dieser Urkunde gedankt.

[12] S. Scheil, "Le terme *put bîti ullulu*", S. 115 f.

[13] Durand *Catalogue EPHE*, Taf. 68 Nr. 316+317.

[14] Bei Durand nur in Umschrift auf S. 75 als "no. 52" wiedergegeben. Kollation Charpin: Am Ende von Z. 2 ist nichts mehr zu sehen, so daß eine Lesung *šeš.[a] anstelle von Durands še[š.ni] durchaus möglich ist (Scheils Umschrift šeš-a-ni war wohl frei ergänzt); in Z. 3 ist auch nach den Hüllenfragmenten eine Lesung *dumu.*me[š] problemlos.

die beiden Fragmente zeigen auf der Innenseite sogar noch lesbare Teile des Negativ-Abklatsches der Originaltafel[15], die exakt der Textanordnung auf der Tafel entsprechen. Wie üblich stand dabei der Text der Hülle gegenüber der Innentafel Kopf, beginnend über dem Ende der Rückseite und endend über Z.1 der Vorderseite. Die folgende Partitur richtet sich in der Zeilenzählung nach dem Text der Innentafel; "H" bezeichnet die Hüllenfragmente nach der Kopie Durands (kollationiert von Charpin), und "N" die Reste des Negativabdrucks nach Umschrift von Charpin.

Bremen A 13120 (Innentafel) // Durand *Catalogue EPHE*, Taf. 68 Nr. 316+317 (Hülle)

Umschrift

1	2 sar 10 gín é.dù.a é e.sír dagal.la
2	da é DINGIR-*šu-na-ṣi-ir ù* da e.sír – –
H$^{1'-2'}$	[-*n*]*a-ṣi-ir* [ ] e.sír *na-an-ni*
3	1 ìr ^{d}EN.ZU-*ga-mi-el* mu.ni
H$^{3'}$	[ ] ^{d}EN.ZU-*ga-mi-il* mu.ni
4	1 ìr *šum-ma*-DINGIR mu.ni
H$^{4'}$	[ ] *šum-ma*-DINGIR mu.ni
5	1 ìr *ì-lí-ma-a-ḫi* mu.ni
H$^{5'}$	[-*l*]*í-ma-a-ḫi* mu.ni
6	2 ^{urudu}šèr.šèr 1 ^{urudu}kin.^{giš}kiri$_6$ ki.lá.bi? x[x]
H$^{6'}$	[.šè]r 1 ^{urudu}kin.^{giš}kiri$_6$ – –
7	1 naga$_3$.esir$_2$.è 1 ^{giš}ig.é!.gal!
H$^{7'}$	– – [?]
8	1 ^{giš}ig.ká!.bar.ra 1 ^{giš}banšur.zà.gu.la
H$^{7'-8'}$	[^{gi}]^{š}ig.ká.bar.ra [.l]a
9	1 ^{giš}ná – – 4 ^{giš}gu.za.sìr.da 1 ^{giš}bugin
H $^{8'-9'}$	1 ^{giš}ná 1 ^{giš}bugin [ ] – –
10	1 ^{giš}níg.baneš 1 ^{giš}níg.bán <<x?>>
H$^{9'}$	[^{g}]^{iš}níg.baneš 1 ^{giš}[ ]
11	ḫa.la ^{d}EN.ZU-*mu-ba-lí-iṭ* šeš.gu.la
H$^{10'}$	[ ]-*lí-iṭ* šeš.g[u.]
12	3 sar é.dù.a <<1>> da é ÌR-^{d}EN.ZU lu[mgi?]
13	*ù* da é *a-ḫi-mar-ši* nagar

[15] Vgl. dazu bereits Scheil, "L'expression NU-ḪA-SA-ṢI", S. 80; bei Durand sind diese Spuren weder erwähnt noch kopiert.

14	2 sar é.šub.ba da <é$^{?}$> *mi-su-ú-um*
15	*ù* da é *a-al*-$^{d?}$UTU$^{?}$
16	1 ìr *na-aḫ-lu*-WA-AN mu.ni
17	1 ìr *ì-lí*-TAB.BA-*e* mu.ni
N$^{1'}$	[ ] *ì-lí*-[ ]
18	1 ìr *ṣí-lí*-^{d}UTU mu.ni
N$^{2'}$	(unleserlich)
19	2 ^{urudu}šèr.šèr 1 ^{urudu}kin.^{giš}kiri$_{6}$
N$^{3'}$	(unleserlich)
20	1 naga$_{3}$.esir$_{2}$$^{!}$.è 1 ^{giš}ig.^{giš}gišimmar
N$^{4'}$	(unleserlich)
21	1 ^{giš}banšur 1 ^{giš}ná 4 ^{giš}gu.za.sír.da
N$^{5'}$	(unleserlich)
22	1 ^{giš}bugin 1 ^{giš}níg.baneš 1 ^{giš}níg.bán
N$^{6'}$	(unleserlich)
23	$\frac{1}{2}$ ma.na 5 gín kù.babbar ki.ta é e.sír dagal.la
N$^{7'}$	$\frac{1}{2}$ ma.na 5 gín kù.babbar [ ]
H$^{1''}$	[-l]a$^{?}$
24	ḫa.la ^{d}EN.LÍL-*is-su* šeš.tu[r]
N$^{8'}$	(unleserlich)
H$^{1''}$	[ḫ]a.la [ ]
25	ḫa.la ì.ba.e.ne
N$^{9'}$	ḫa.la ì.ba.[ ]
H$^{2''}$	[ḫa].la ì.ba$^{!}$.ẹ.n[e]
26	^{giš} šub.ba ì.šub.bu.e.ne
N$^{10'}$	^{giš}[šub.b]a ì.šub.bu.[ ]
(H)	– – –
27	u$_{4}$.kúr.šè dam.gàr ^{d}EN.ZU-*mu-ba-lí-iṭ*
N$^{11'}$	u$_{4}$.kúr.šè dam.gàr ^{d}EN.ZU-*mu*-[ ]
H$^{3''}$	– – [d]am.gàr ^{d}EN.ZU-*mu-ba-lí-iṭ*
28	^{d}EN.LÍL-*is-su* nu-ḫa-sa-zé-e-en
N$^{12'}$	^{d}EN.LÍL-*is-su* nu-ḫa-sa-[ ]
H$^{4''}$	^{Id}EN.LÍL-*is-su* nu-ḫa-sa-zé –
29	dam.gàr ^{d}EN.LÍL-*is-su*
N$^{13'}$	dam.gàr ^{d}EN.LÍL-*is-su*
H$^{5''}$	dam.gàr ^{d}EN.LÍL-*is-su*

30	^{d}EN.ZU-*mu-ba-lí-iṭ* nu-ḫa-sa-zé-e-en
N$^{14'}$	^{d}EN.ZU-*mu-ba-lí-iṭ* nu-[ ]
H$^{5''-6''}$	^{Id}EN.ZU-*mu-ba-lí-iṭ* nu-ḫa-sa-zé-e-en
(–)	– – –
(N)	– – –
H$^{7''}$	u$_{4}$.kúr lú.ulu$_{3}$ lú.ulu$_{3}$.ra
(–)	– – –
(N)	– – –
H$^{8''}$	[nu].mu.un.gi$_{4}$.gi$_{4}$.dè
31	mu.lugal.bi in.pàd.e.eš
N$^{15'}$	mu.lugal.[ ]
H$^{9''}$	[.lu]gal.bi in.pàd –
32	igi ur-^{d}nanše dumu *ši-ma-a-a*
(H)	– – –
33	^{Id}nanna-ma.an.sum dumu *ṣí-su-na-aw-ra-at*
H$^{10''}$	[-m]a.an.sum dumu$^{?!}$(ḪI) *ṣí-su-na-aw-ra-a*[*t*]
34	^{I}*ip-qú-ša* dumu *s*[*u*]$^{?}$*-ma-a*
35	^{I}*mi-il-ki*-^{d}EN.LÍL dumu ^{d}EN.ZU-APIN
36	^{I}*an-da-ku-ul-lum* dumu DU$_{10}$-*ṣí-lí*-URI$_{2}^{ki}$
37	^{I}é-*ga-mi-el* dumu PÙ.ŠA-*ìr*$^{!}$*-ra*
38	^{Id}IM-*ba-ni* dumu WA-*Za-a*
39	^{Id}EN.ZU-*ma-gir*$_{14}$(ḪA) d[um]u ^{d}EN.ZU-*ga-mil*
40	^{I}*e-te-el*-<KA>-^{d}EN.ZU dumu *da-da-a*
41	^{Id}IM-*ra-bi* dumu ^{d}EN.ZU-*ni-a*
42	^{I}*be-lí-i* dumu *im-gur*-^{d}EN.ZU
43	^{I}*na-bi-ì-lí-šu* dumu ^{d}EN.ZU-*i-di*[*n*$^{?}$*-na*]*m*$^{?}$
44	^{Id}EN.ZU-*re-me-ni* dub.sar <<1>>
45	lú.inim.ma.bi.meš
46	[i]ti.bára.zag.gar
47	mu.ús.sa íd.lagaša zag.a.ab.ba gá.ba.al

Burgul-Siegel (auf Tafel und Hülle)[16]: ^{d}EN.ZU-*mu-ba-lí-iṭ*
ù ^{d}EN.LÍL-*is-su* šes.a.<ni>
dumu.meš *im-gur*-^{d}EN.ZU

[16] Vgl. oben, Anm. 14.

Übersetzung

2 Sar 10 Gin Wohnhaus, Haus (an) der Hauptstraße,
angrenzend an das Haus des Ilšu-nāṣir und angrenzend an die Straße[17],
1 Sklave namens Sîn-gāmil,
1 Sklave namens Šumma-ilum,
1 Sklave namens Ilīma-aḫī,
2 Kupfer-Ketten, 1 kupferne Garten-Sichel von x[x] Gewicht[18],
1 Mörser für Trockenasphalt[19], 1 Tür für den Empfangsraum,
1 Tür für das äußere Tor, 1 Opfertisch,
1 Bett, 4 Trage-Stühle, 1 Trog,[20]
1 3-Ban-Maß, 1 1-Ban-Maß:
Anteil des Sîn-muballiṭ, des ältesten Bruders.
3 Sar Wohnhaus, angrenzend an das Haus des Bra[uers?] Warad-Sîn
und angrenzend an das Haus des Tischlers Aḫimarši,
2 Sar unbebautes Grundstück angrenzend an <das Haus des> Misûm?
und angrenzend an das Haus des Al-Šamaš?,
1 Sklave namens NaḫluWAN,
1 Sklave namens Ilī-tappê,
1 Sklave namens Ṣilli-Šamaš,
2 Kupfer-Ketten, 1 kupferne Garten-Sichel,
1 Mörser für Trockenasphalt, 1 Palmholz-Tür,
1 Tisch, 1 Bett, 4 Trage-Stühle,
1 Trog, 1 3-Ban-Maß, 1 1-Ban-Maß,
$\frac{1}{2}$ Mine 5 Sekel Silber, Ausgleichszahlung für das Haus (an) der Hauptstraße[21]:
Anteil des Enlil-issu, des jüngeren Bruders.
Sie haben! die Teilung durchgeführt,
haben! das Los geworfen.[22]
In Zukunft[23] wird ein Gläubiger des Sîn-muballiṭ
sich nicht an Enlil-issu halten können,
ein Gläubiger des Enlil-issu
sich nicht an Sîn-muballiṭ halten können.
(Hülle fügt ein:
In Zukunft wird einer auf den anderen nicht zurückkommen.)
Das haben sie beim König geschworen.

---

[17] Hülle: "Nanni-Straße"; cf. Kommentar zur Zeile.

[18] Hülle: "von x[x] Gewicht" ausgelassen.

[19] Auf der Hülle erst in Z. 9 genannt.

[20] Die Hülle nennt dieselben Gegenstände, aber in anderer Reihenfolge.

[21] Hülle: "Ausgleichszahlung ..." ausgelassen.

[22] Zeile auf der Hülle ausgelassen.

[23] Hülle: "In Zukunft" hier ausgelassen (s. jedoch nach Z. 30!).

32–43 Vor PN_{1-12} (= 12 Zeugen),
44 (und) Sîn-rēmēni, dem Schreiber,
45 den Zeugen dafür.
46–47 Datum (Nisan, Rīm-Sîn 10)

Kommentar

Z. 2: Nanni ist als PN in Ur mehrfach belegt (s. UET 5, Index S. 51b). Für Straßennamen des Typs *sūq* PN oder *sūqum ša* PN vgl. *CAD* S s.v. *sūqu* Bed. 1b-1′. Die Innentafel verzichtet auf eine Benennung der Straße.

Z. 6 und 19: Ein ^{urudu}šèr.šèr = *šeršerretum* ist als Wertgegenstand auch in UET 5 402:1 genannt; die nunmehr zwei Belege aus Ur sind in *CAD* Š/2 s.v. *šeršerratu* dem bisher recht spärlichen aB Material hinzuzufügen.

^{urudu}kin.^{giš}kiri$_6$ kann ich sonst nicht belegen; eine "Garten-Sichel" paßt jedoch gut zu der aus YOS 13 71:3 bekannten "Sichel für das Feld/die Feldarbeit" (^{urudu}šu.kin *ša* a.šà, s. *CAD* N/2 s.v. *niggallu* Bed. 1a).

Z. 7 (und 20): Für $^{(giš)}$naga$_3$.esir$_2$.è = *esittum ša kuprim* "Mörser für Trocken-Bitumen" vgl. *CAD* K s.v. *kupru* Bed. a zu ARM 7 263 iv 6. P. Steinkeller[24] argumentiert überzeugend für eine Übersetzung "Mörser" (und nicht "Stößel") für *esittum* (naga$_3$) und *madakkum* (^{giš}naga$_3$.zíd.gaz).

^{giš}ig.é.gal ist häufig in aB Erbteilungsurkunden erwähnt. Zur Deutung von *ekallum* als dem neben dem Hof gelegenen großen Repräsentativ-Raum eines altbabylonischen Wohnhauses s. zuletzt G. Kalla, "Wohnhaus"[25], S. 252.

Z. 8: ^{giš}ig.ká.bar.ra ist nach der Hülle eindeutig so zu lesen. Kalla[26] nimmt an, daß das gleichfalls in Erbteilungen aus Ur zu findende Lemma ^{giš}ig.é.bar.ra damit identisch sei, und beide Schreibungen in Ur akkadischem *dalat barakkim* entsprächen.[27] In der Tat ist es oft schwierig, die richtige Lesung des mittleren Zeichens zu eruieren, da die Schreiber hier offenbar gelegentlich geradezu "Mischzeichen" zwischen é und ká produziert haben (vgl. z.B. UET 5 100:6, 106:4, 115:2[28]). Als ein solches ist wohl auch die fast wie e$_1$ aussehende Unform auf unserer Tafel (ebenso UET 5 119:6), die Elemente von é mit dem gebrochenen Senkrechten von ká verbindet, zu deuten.

---

[24] P. Steinkeller, *Sale Documents of the Ur III Period*, Freiburger altorientalische Studien 17 (Stuttgart, 1989), S. 36–38.

[25] G. Kalla, "Das altbabylonische Wohnhaus und seine Struktur nach philologischen Quellen", in K. R. Veenhof, Hrsg., *Houses and Households in Ancient Mesopotamia*, Uitgaven van het Nederlands Instituut voor het Nabije Oosten te Leiden, *voorheen* Publications de l'Institut historique-archéologique néerlandais de Stamboul 78 (Istanbul und Leiden, 1996).

[26] Ibid.

[27] Zu der andernorts zumindest für ká.bar.ra einzusetzenden Lesung *bābum kamûm* vgl. zuletzt *PSD* B 98b und B. Lion, "Un contrat de vente de maison daté du règne d'Enlil-bâni d'Isin", *RA* 88 (1994): 131.

[28] Dieses Zeichen wurde von K. Butz, "Zwei Urkunden aus dem altbabylonischen Ur, Niessbrauch betreffend", *Oriens Antiquus* 19 (1980): 104 kommentarlos als KÁ gelesen.

Z. 9 und 21: Zu ${}^{\text{giš}}$gu.za.sìr.da = *kussi sirdê* s. *CAD* S s.v. *sirdû* A, sowie M. Van De Mieroop, *Crafts*[29]; unser Beleg, im Zusammenhang mit unten Z. 21 gesehen, legt auch für das bisher ${}^{\text{giš}}$gu.za.gíd.da gelesene Möbelstück (z. B. UET 5 109:10 und vgl. G. Kalla, "Nachlaß"[30], S. 41b) eine Lesung sír.da nahe, obwohl natürlich die Vererbung zweier verschiedener, zufällig fast homographischer Stuhltypen (Tragstuhl/Sänfte und Langstuhl/Sofa?) auch nicht ganz ausgeschlossen werden kann.

Z. 10 und 22: Die sumerischen und akkadischen Bezeichnungen für die zwei hier genannten Maßgefäße sind nicht ganz gesichert. Die Wiedergabe des Zeichens GAR als níg/nì folgt Kalla, "Nachlaß", S. 41b. Das darauf folgende 1(BÁN) ist nach der mehrfach belegten Variantenschreibung ba-an sicher einfach als bán zu lesen, woraus sich dann für das ${}^{\text{giš}}$níg.3(BÁN) als Lesung ${}^{\text{giš}}$níg.baneš nahelegt. Ein endgültiger Beweis hierfür steht meines Wissens noch aus. Daß die bekannten akkadischen Entsprechungen ${}^{\text{giš}}$bán = *sūtum* und ${}^{\text{giš}}$baneš = *ṣimdum* auch für ${}^{\text{giš}}$níg.bán/baneš zutreffen, ist zwar wahrscheinlich, aber ebenfalls meines Wissens bisher nicht beweisbar; die speziell aus Ur bekannten Schreibungen sind in keinem der beiden Wörterbücher gebucht.

Z. 13: Die Variante *a-ḫi-mar-ši* für grammatisch zu erwartendes *Aḫam-arši* ist auch sonst in Ur belegt, s. UET 5, Index S. 29a.

Z. 14: mi-su-ú-um ist offenbar über ein radiertes Zeichen, möglicherweise é, geschrieben, was die Deutung als PN in Frage stellt. Die unflektierte Endung legt trotzdem einen solchen nahe, doch ist mir ein zur Schreibung passender Name nicht geläufig. Oder ist vielleicht trotz der Nominativform an die Bezeichnung einer Straße zu denken und auf die bisher ganz unklare Gleichung sila.tur = *mi-su-u* (Izi D ii 13) zu verweisen?

Z. 15: Meine besonders beim dritten Zeichen (DINGIR?) unsichere Lesung des PN basiert auf Sollberger, *RA* 74[31], S. 54:20, wo derselbe Name vorzuliegen scheint (Hinweis M. Stol). Zur gelegentlich vorkommenden Schreibung *al-* statt aB geläufigerem *a-li/lí-* vgl. z. B. PBS 7 37:3: *a-lí-ta-li-mi* mit Var. aus Siegel Z. 2: *al-ta-li-m*[*i*] (= BE 6/1 32, wo allerdings das Siegel nicht kopiert ist; Hinweis Stol) und CT 2 49:13: *al-ba-nu-šu.*

Z. 16: Den (zweifellos nicht akkadischen) Sklavennamen NaḫluWAN kann ich bisher sprachlich nicht sicher einordnen. Hurrisch und Elamisch sind als Herkunftssprachen nicht sehr wahrscheinlich, trotz des Lemmas **naḫlia* in einer althurrischen

[29] M. Van De Mieroop, *Crafts in the Early Isin Period*, OLA 24 (Leuven, 1987), S. 140, Index.

[30] G. Kalla, "Nachlaß B. Altbabylonisch", *RLA* 7, S. 36–42.

[31] E. Sollberger, "The Cuneiform Tablets in the Chester Beatty Library, Dublin", *RA* 74 (1980): 43–59.

Beschwörung aus altbabylonischer Zeit.[32] Im Amurritischen existiert möglicherweise eine Verbalwurzel **nḫl*[33], doch ist diese bisher in PNN nicht sicher belegt.[34] Außerdem bleibt mir dabei das Ende des Namens morphologisch unklar. Auch eine Lesung *na-aḫ-lu-pi*-DINGIR wäre denkbar, zumal möglicherweise auch in Z. 38 das Zeichen WA mit der Lesung *pi* vorliegt.

Z. 20: BUGIN statt $ESIR_2$ offenbar Schreibfehler, vgl. die korrekte Schreibung weiter oben in Z. 7.

Z. 23: Die Formulierung "x kù.babbar ki.ta é e.sír dagal.la" gesellt sich zu den von F. R. Kraus, "Neue Rechtsurkunden"[35], S. 128 besprochenen und auch bei Kalla, "Nachlaß", S. 38b erwähnten Klauseln über Ausgleichszahlungen.[36] Sie ist noch kürzer als die bisher bekannten Vermerke und ist wohl einfach als "x *kaspum tappīlāt bīt sūqim rapšim*" aufzufassen.[37] Eine exakt parallele Klausel findet sich dreimal in der Erbteilungsurkunde TLB 1 23 (Tafel: 14′; Hülle: 21 und Rs. 11): x Silber *tap-pí-la-at bi-tim*. Weitere ähnliche Belege für *tappīlātum* sind den Wörterbüchern zu entnehmen. Weniger wahrscheinlich ist dagegen eine Lesung ki.ta = *šapiltum* "Rest".[38]

Zu *Z. 27–30* vgl. unten Exkurs: Die Gläubiger-Klausel in Z. 27–30.

Z. 34: Zum PN *Sumâ* vgl. UET 5 803:2 (^{d}EN.ZU-*ma-gir* DUMU *su-ma-a*). Auch eine Lesung *š*[*a*]-*ma-a* ist nicht ganz ausgeschlossen.

Z. 36: Zum PN *Andakullum* vgl. M. Stol, *AfO* 27[39], S. 163b und Charpin *Archives familiales*, Index S. 302f. Den Namen seines Vaters *Ṭāb-ṣilli-Uri* (überaus passend für einen "Ur-Einwohner"!) kann ich sonst nicht belegen.

---

[32] S. zum Text (YOS 11 64 // 28) jetzt D. Prechel und T. Richter, "Abrakadabra oder Althurritisch", in T. Richer, D. Prechel und J. Klinger, Hrsg., *Kulturgeschichten: Volkert Haas zum 65. Geburtstag* (Saarbrücken, 2001), S. 339 (*na-ah-li-a* in Z. A2//B8).

[33] S. dazu zuletzt M. Streck, *Das amurritische Onomastikon der altbabylonischen Zeit*, AOAT 271/1 (Münster, 2000), S. 106f.

[34] Vgl. höchstens *na-aḫ-li-lum* in I. J. Gelb, *Computer-Aided Analysis of Amorite*, AS 21 (Chicago, 1980), S. 328.

[35] F. R. Kraus, "Neue Rechtsurkunden der altbabylonischen Zeit", *WO* 2 (1955): 120–36.

[36] Zu den dort bereits behandelten Passagen aus UET 5 100, 112, 117 und 119 ist noch UET 5 109:9 nachzutragen. Ist hier evtl. ki.ta.ki.NE. àm! (Text: A.GIŠ) na_4 zu lesen und dann auch in 119:9 und 28 am Zeilenende entsprechend zu emendieren?

[37] Vgl. bereits Kraus, "Neue Rechtsurkunden", S. 128, der als erster die ausführlichere Formulierung ki.ta.ki.a/àm sicherlich zu Recht mit *tappīlātum* "Ausgleichszahlung" in Verbindung brachte und danach Ai.VI iv 1 (MSL 1 86:1) als [... ki.t]a. ki.a = *kunuk tappīlāti* ergänzte. Warum dieser Vorschlag trotz der überzeugenden Parallelen weder im *AHw.* noch im *CAD* Beachtung fand, bleibt mir unklar.

[38] Diese Möglichkeit wurde für die in UET 5 belegten Formen ki.ta.a und ki.ta.àm(.bi) ebenfalls schon von Kraus, "Neue Rechtsurkunden", S. 128 angesprochen, jedoch meines Erachtens zu Recht verworfen, da die entsprechenden Belege kaum von denen mit ki.ta.ki.àm getrennt werden können.

[39] M. Stol, Besprechung von B. Kienast, *Die altbabylonischen Briefe und Urkunden aus Kisurra*, Freiburger altorientalische Studien 2 (Wiesbaden, 1978), in *AfO* 27 (1980): 161–64.

Z. 38: **Waṣâ* könnte ein Hypokoristikon sein; ich kenne jedoch keine aB Personennamen, die mit **waṣi-* o. ä. beginnen. Stattdessen ist daher vielleicht eher *pe-ṣa-a* zu lesen (zu einer möglichen Verwendung von WA = *pi/e* in unserem Text vgl. bereits oben zu Z. 16); vgl. damit den PN *Peṣûm* (Stamm, *Namengebung*[40], S. 267) und vielleicht auch die in Ur belegten Namen *pa-(aZ-)Za-a* und PI-*sa-a* (UET 5, Index S. 53 f.)?

Z. 39: Zu der nicht ganz seltenen Schreibung des PN Sîn-māgir mit dem Zeichen ḪA=gir_{14} vgl. W. von Soden und W. Röllig, *AS*[41], S. 63 Nr. 317, sowie R. Borger, *Mesopotamisches Zeichenlexikon*[42], S. 441 Nr. 856, jeweils mit Literatur. Einen weiteren Beleg notiere ich in CT 47 57:3.

Exkurs: Die Gläubiger-Klausel in Z. 27–30

Diese Gläubiger-Klausel bildete den Ausgangspunkt von Leemans' Vermutung, unser Text sei in Ur geschrieben worden, da sie bisher nur in sicher oder zumindest möglicherweise in Ur gefundenen Texten vorkommt.[43] Auch Kraus hat ihr Vorkommen in den Texten aus UET 5 ausführlicher besprochen.[44] Die letzte Behandlung fand sie meines Wissens bei Charpin *Archives familiales*, S. 45 zu Jean, *Tell Sifr* 14 13–14. Alle drei Autoren nehmen von einer Übersetzung bzw. wörtlichen Wiedergabe Abstand und beschränken sich auf die kontextbezogene Deutung als Garantieklausel gegen spätere Ansprüche. Kraus weist darüber hinaus auf mehrere wichtige Varianten hin, wobei zweimal (UET 5 116:17–19; 114:8–11; s. unten, Belege *i* und *j*) das Verbum /ḫas/ durch dib bzw. *ṣabātum* ersetzt wird und einmal (Beleg *j*) statt dam.gàr "Kaufmann = Gläubiger" um.mi.a "Geldgeber, Prinzipal" steht. Sein Vorschlag, das Verbum der Klausel mit Antagal A 40: ḫa.za = MIN (*kullu*) *ša ṣabāti* zu verbinden, hat seither den Weg zumindest in das *CAD* gefunden, wo Belege für die Klausel s.v. *ṣabātu* und *tamkāru* gebucht wurden, während ich im *AHw*. vergeblich nach ihnen suchte.

Wohl wissend, daß ich damit nur ein altbekanntes Problem wieder einmal in Erinnerung rufe, ohne selbst zu einer neuen Lösung zu kommen, seien hier die bisher zehn (wohl alle in Ur geschriebenen) Belege[45] für die Gläubiger-Klausel in Erbteilungsurkunden nochmals in abkürzender Transliteration zusammengestellt:

---

[40] J. J. Stamm, *Die akkadische Namengebung*, MVAG 44 (Leipzig, 1939).

[41] W. von Soden und W. Röllig, *Das akkadische Syllabar*, 4. Auflage, AnOr 42 (Rom, 1991).

[42] R. Borger, *Mesopotamisches Zeichenlexikon*, AOAT 305 (Münster, 2003).

[43] Leemans, "Business Documents", S. 114.

[44] Kraus, "Neue Rechtsurkunden", S. 127 f.

[45] Ich danke G. Kalla für die Überlassung seiner Zusammenstellung aller altbabylonischen Erbteilungsurkunden, die mir bestätigte, daß ich offenbar keinen einschlägigen Text übersehen hatte. Auch die Diskussionen mit meiner Studentin T. Ponsford, die sich in Ihrer Magisterarbeit mit den aB Erbteilungsurkunden aus Ur befaßt hat, jedoch für diese Klausel ebenfalls keine endgültige Erklärung fand, seien hier dankend erwähnt.

a) Jean, *Šumer et Akkad*, Nr. CLXXVIII:165, 7–9 (vgl. Leemans, "Business Documents", S. 114b; zur wahrscheinlichen Herkunft aus Ur s. Charpin *Archives familiales*, S. 58); schlecht erhalten, wohl Teilung zwischen zwei Brüdern:

dam.gàr PN_1 / [P]N_2 nu.ḫa.ba(zu$^{!?}$).ab.ze.en

b) Jean, *Tell Sifr* 14 13 f. (aus Ur, s. Charpin *Archives familiales*, S. 45 f. und 209, und vgl. Kraus, "Neue Rechtsurkunden", S. 127; Klausel nur auf der Tafel, Hülle anders); Teilzettel mit Inventar des Erbteils eines Bruders (von zweien?):

dam.gàr šeš šeš.ra / nu.ḫa.sa.ab.ze.en

c) UET 5 109:31–37 (vgl. Leemans, "Business Documents", S. 114 und Kraus, "Neue Rechtsurkunden", S. 128); Teilung zwischen drei Brüdern:

u_4.kúr.šè dam.gàr PN_1 / PN_2 ù PN_3 / nu.ḫa.sa.ab.zé.en / dam.gàr PN_2 / ù^{sic} PN_3 PN_1 / nu.ḫa.sa.ab.zé.en / dam.gàr PN_3 PN_1 / ù PN_2 nu.ḫa.sa.ab.zé.en

d) UET 5 110:24–26 (vgl. Kraus, "Neue Rechtsurkunden", S. 128); Teilung zwischen drei Brüdern:

dam.gàr PN_1 / PN_2 ù PN_3 / nu.ḫa.sa.ab.[x]

e) UET 5 119:45–49 (vgl. Kraus, "Neue Rechtsurkunden", S. 27); Teilung zwischen zwei Brüdern:

dam.gàr PN_1 / PN_2 / nu.ḫa.sa.ab.zé.e$^?$.[en$^?$] / dam.gàr PN_2 / PN_1 nu.ḫa.s[a. ...]

f) YOS 8 98:63–67 (aus Ur, vgl. Leemans, "Business Documents", S. 114; K. Butz, "Konzentrationen wirtschaftlicher Macht im Königreich Larsa: Der Nanna-Ningal-Tempelkomplex in Ur", *WZKM* 65–66 [1973–74]: 1, Anm. 1; und Charpin *Archives familiales*, S. 56); Teilung in zwei Erbteile, wobei PN_1 mit PN_2 zusammen einen Teil erhält (Z. 35). Auch der zweite Teil wurde offenbar von zwei Personen geerbt, deren Namen jedoch an der zu erwartenden Stelle (Z. 62) nicht genannt und nur aus der Gläubiger-Klausel als PN_3 und PN_4 zu erschließen sind:

dam.gàr PN_1 / PN_3 ù P[N_4 n]u.ḫa.sa.ab.ze / dam.gàr PN_3 / PN_1 ù [$PN_2$$^?$] / nu.ḫa.sa.ab.zé$^{!?}$-e[n$^?$][46]

g) TIM 5 15:12–15 (aus Ur, vgl. Kalla, "Nachlaß", S. 41; bei Charpin *Archives familiales*, S. 56 noch nicht aufgeführt); Teilung zwischen drei Brüdern:

dam.gàr PN_1 / ù PN_2 / PN_3 / nu.ḫa.za.an.zé

---

[46] Da PN_2 (Z. 35: *Annum-pī-šu* oder AN.DÙL-[U.D]AR zu lesen?) nicht wie PN_4 (Z. 64) mit dem Zeichen A beginnt, ist Identität von PN_2 und PN_4 auszuschließen. PN_2 und PN_4 sind möglicherweise abhängige Familienmitglieder (Söhne?) der Haupterben PN_1 und PN_3.

h) A 13120: 27–30 // Durand *Catalogue EPHE*, Taf. 68 Nr. 316+317 rev. 3′–6′ (aus Ur oder zumindest in Ur geschrieben, vgl. Leemans, "Business Documents", S. 114 und Charpin *Archives familiales*, S. 60 zu *RA* 15 80f.); Teilung zwischen zwei Brüdern:

u_4.kúr. šè dam.gàr PN_1 / PN_2 nu.ḫa.sa.zé.e.en / dam.gàr PN_2 / PN_1 nu.ḫa.sa.zé.e.en

// dam.gàr PN_1 / PN_2 nu.ḫa.sa.zé / dam.gàr PN_2 PN_1 / nu.ḫa.sa.zé.e.en

i) UET 5 116:17–19 (vgl. Kraus, "Neue Rechtsurkunden", S. 128); Anerkennung des Erbteils eines Bruders durch den anderen:

dam.gàr PN_1 / PN_2 / nu.un.ne.dib.bé

j) UET 5 114:8–11 (vgl. Kraus, "Neue Rechtsurkunden", S. 128); Teilung zwischen zwei Brüdern:

um.mi.<a> PN_1 / PN_2 *ú-la i-ṣa-ba-at* / um.mi.a PN_2 / PN_1 *ú-la i-ṣa-ba-at*

Während die in *j*) vorliegende akkadische Klausel unmittelbar verständlich ist, legt in deren sumerischer Parallele *i*) das unerwartete Plural-Infix /ne/ eine Verschleppung der sonst ebenfalls leicht verständlichen Form aus einem pluralischen Kontext mit mehreren Subjekten nahe. Morphologie, Syntax und wörtliche Bedeutung der von der meines Wissens noch nicht eingehend untersuchten Verbalwurzel /ḫas/ bzw. /ḫaz(a)/ "festhalten, greifen" gebildeten Formen bleiben dagegen nach wie vor unklar. Es handelt sich offenbar um Imperative des Plurals, die hier aber entgegen allen grammatischen Regeln mit dem Negativ-Präformativ /nu/ verbunden sind. Ein negierter Imp. Pl., wenn es ihn also doch vielleicht gegeben hat,[47] ergibt jedoch in dem vorliegenden Kontext auch keinen Sinn, es sei denn, man wollte an eine zum Kürzel erstarrte Form einer Anrede an die Gläubiger "Ihr dürft nicht packen!" ohne Erwähnung des Vorgangs oder des Sprechers denken.

Schließlich sei noch ein nicht aus Ur stammender Text (Mananâ-Archiv) erwähnt, der – allerdings nicht im Kontext einer Erbteilung! – eine ähnliche Klausel enthält: Charpin, "Nouveaux textes de la 'Dynastie de Mananâ' II", *RA* 74 (1980): 116ff., Nr. 64/64a:1–9. Hier erklären drei Personen aus heute unklaren Gründen ihren Verzicht auf jegliche Ansprüche gegenüber PN_4. Die Formulierung lautet:

PN_1 / PN_2 / *ù* PN_3 / *e-li* PN_4 / *mi-ma ú-la i-šu-ú* /

dam.gàr.meš / PN_1 / PN_4 / *ú-la i-ṣa-ba-at*

[47] Vgl. zur Nichtexistenz dieser Form im Sumerischen zuletzt D. O. Edzard, *Sumerian Grammar*, Handbuch der Orientalistik 71 (Leiden, 2003), S. 130; da das Akkadische ebenfalls keinen negierten Imperativ kennt, ist auch die Annahme einer Lehnübersetzung ausgeschlossen.

Sowohl Charpin, als auch *CAD* T nehmen dabei an, daß trotz des fehlenden *ù* und der Nicht-Kongruenz zum singularischen Verbum *iṣabbat* das pluralische Nomen dam. gàr.meš hier für PN_2+PN_3 stehen müsse. Im Lichte der oben genannten Belege glaube ich jedoch eher, daß auch hier die Grammatik der starren Klausel nur flüchtig und ungenau dem Sachverhalt angepaßt wurde, und daß entsprechend alle etwaigen Gläubiger von PN_1, PN_2 und PN_3 (daher der Plural des Subjekts dam.gàr.meš) in den Verzicht, individuell zu klagen (daher der Singular der Verbalform *iṣabbat*) einbezogen wurden. Zu vergleichen sind hierbei vor allem die ebenfalls stark abgekürzten Beispiele oben *a*), *d*) und *g*), wo auch nicht alle theoretisch denkbaren Möglichkeiten durchgespielt werden, sowie vielleicht die mit dem Sachverhalt nicht harmonierende Numerus-Konstruktion in Beleg *i*).

KOPIEN

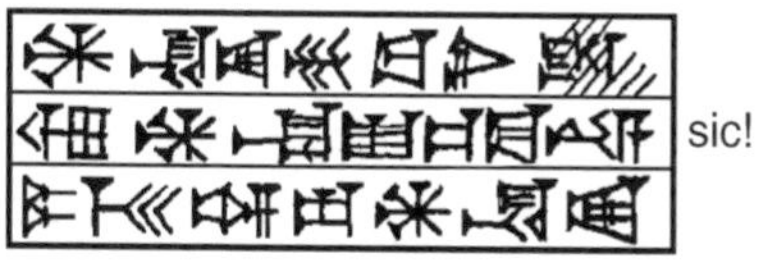

Abbildung 1. Burgul-Siegel auf Tafel Bremen A 13120

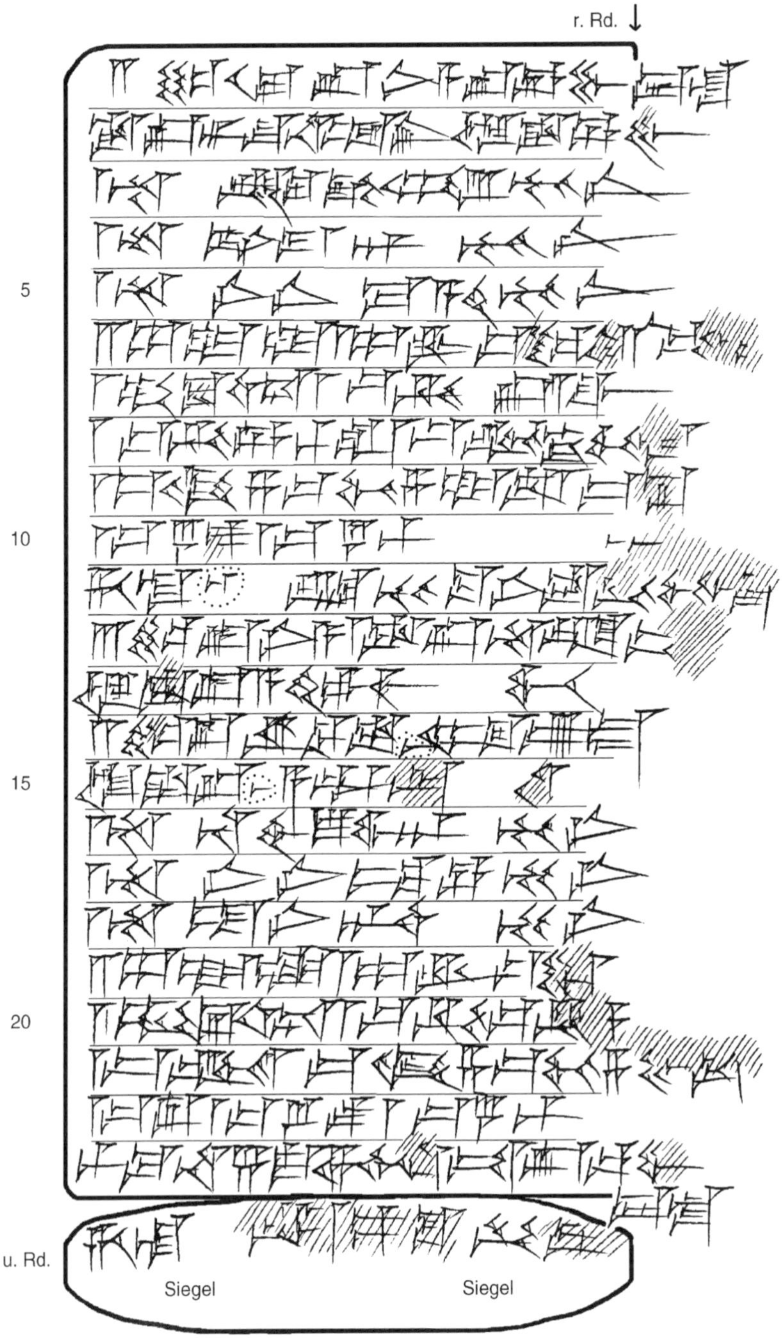

Abbildung 2. Tafel Bremen A 13120, Vorderseite

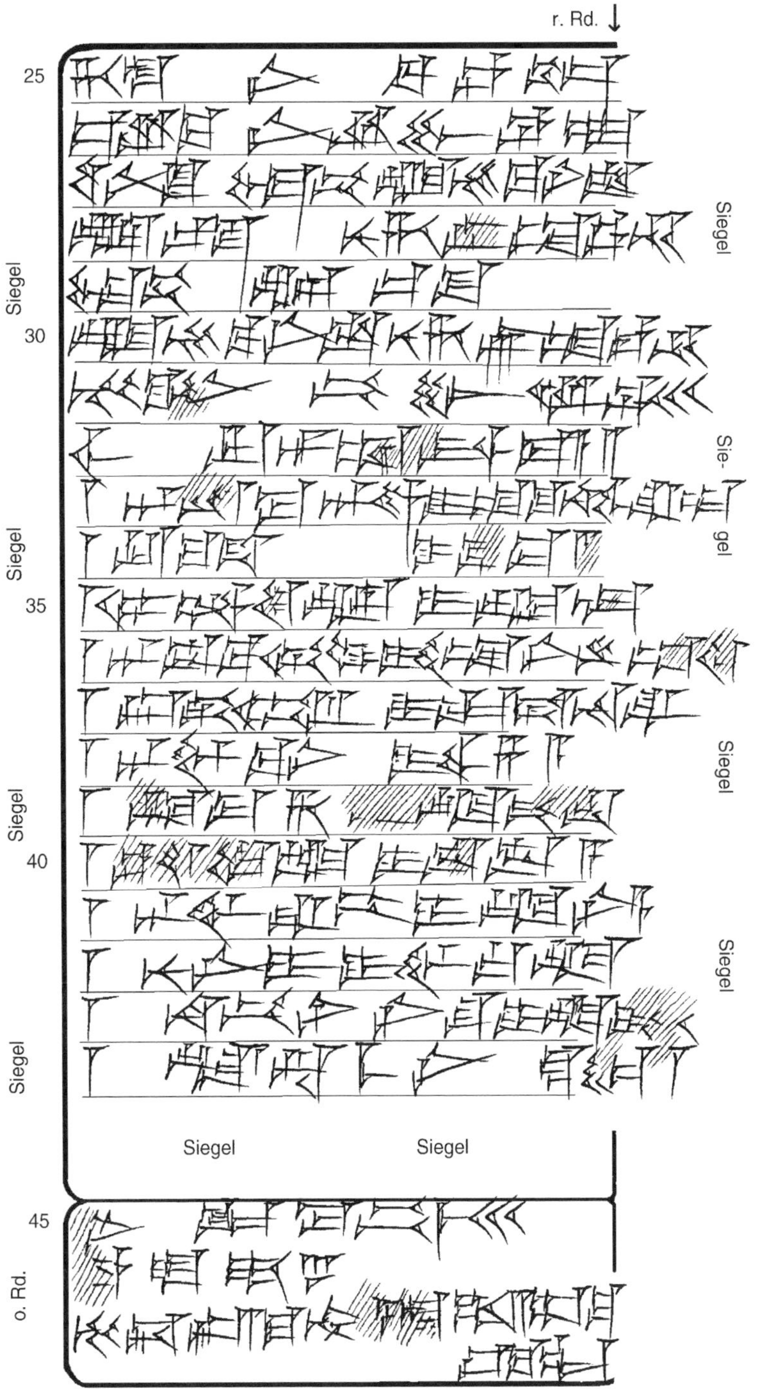

Abbildung 3. Tafel Bremen A 13120, Rückseite

A "GALLEON" AT NIPPUR

McGuire Gibson, The University of Chicago

Bob Biggs is famous at Nippur for having found a hoard of Islamic coins in 1963 by stubbing his toe on it. Thus it is appropriate to honor him with a numismatic article.

In 1964/65 Bob was the epigrapher not only for the ninth season of excavations at Nippur, but also for the second season of soundings at Abu Salabikh, which was being conducted for the Oriental Institute by Donald Hansen. The season at Nippur was a long one (November to June), and for me it was even longer, since I had arrived in Baghdad in late September, thinking that the rest of the team would arrive in a couple of weeks. I had already spent several months in Europe and Turkey, taking advantage of a Ryerson Traveling Fellowship to visit museums and see sites. My early arrival in Baghdad meant that I had a wonderful opportunity to get to know the city and the nearby archaeological sites in a way that most new members of field teams never do.

Much of the Nippur season was devoted to the construction of the expedition house, which engaged the time and effort of the director, James Knudstad. From November through late January, while the major construction of the walls and roof was under way, we lived in houses that were usually occupied by the Sherqati excavators or used for storage of the railroad and other equipment. In January, Bob, Donald Hansen, Diane Taylor (another Chicago graduate student), and Selma al-Radi, an Iraqi Antiquities Department representative, came to collect equipment and then go on to begin work at Abu Salabikh.

The archaeological goal of the season at Nippur was to expose as much as possible of the Parthian Fortress that was built around and above the ancient ziggurat complex É-Kur, the shrine of Enlil. The expedition intended to reexcavate the entire Fortress, which had been dug and mapped by the old University of Pennsylvania expedition in the 1890s. Once the Fortress was completely planned, and those plans had been compared to the ones presented by the Pennsylvania Expedition,[1] the entire structure was to be demolished in order to examine in a number of seasons the early levels of the ziggurat complex. The importance of É-Kur, as the shrine of the chief god of the pantheon, was thought justification enough to demolish the massive Parthian remains.

---

[1] H. Hilprecht, *Explorations in Bible Lands during the 19th Century* (Edinburgh, 1907), p. 559.

The first task of the season was the removal of a large dump that the Pennsylvania Expedition had deposited on the south corner of the Parthian Fortress. Even though I was new to excavation in the Near East, it was thought that I could be trusted to direct the seventy workmen who were to remove the dump, which we began to do in November.[2]

Even with the large workforce and a hand-pushed railroad, it still took more than two months to remove the dump. Consequently, the normal recording procedures were barely in operation during that time, except for the cataloguing, photographing, and drawing of the few objects coming from the dump or found on the surface of the mound. Many of those surface finds were made by Abdullah Sultan, the overseer of the dig house, who had been a fixture on Chicago expeditions since the 1930s. Although probably already seventy years old, Abdullah had remarkable eyesight, and on his occasional solitary afternoon walks over the mounds, he would spot objects that most people would have missed. Many evenings he returned with a handful of corroded, green coins.

In previous seasons, a few coins had been excavated and tripped over, and they had been catalogued, but we had little knowledge of the range of numismatic evidence at Nippur. Coins are a prime source for dating, and the sample from the surface would give some indication of the international connections of the city during the late periods and would furnish a rough date for the last occupation of the site. This season, having the time to do so, I decided to treat the surface coins as a sample collection, and I began to "clean" them using the methods then prescribed by standard field conservation manuals.

Throughout the season, I cleaned and catalogued about two hundred coins, identifying them as best I could, using the limited resources in our small dig library.[3] When the actual digging began in February, and I became fully engaged in the cataloguing and photography, I had much less time to spend on coins.

After the Abu Salabikh dig ended its three-week soundings in late January of 1965, Bob returned to Nippur, along with Diane Taylor and Selma al-Radi, who was to replace Tariq al-Janabi as government representative at Nippur. They brought with them the unbaked Early Dynastic tablets, some of unusually large size, which had been found in a stack, many stuck together.[4] By this time, the new expedition house had its

---

[2] I owe much to Carl Haines, who had been director at Nippur until the previous season. He and Thorkild Jacobsen were with us for the first month of the dig, and the days and evenings were rich in advice, as well as stories, of the early days of Oriental Institute expeditions across the Near East. I owe a great debt of gratitude to Tariq al-Janabi, our Antiquities Department representative for the first two months, and to Khalaf Jasim, the foreman, and the other Sherqatis as well as the local Nippur men from whom I also learned much, including basic Arabic.

[3] The coins are to be published by Edward J. Keall in his projected Oriental Institute volume on the Parthian Fortress.

[4] The returnees also included Siraj ad-Din, one of the great cooks that expeditions could have in those years. Having arrived with the British Indian Army in 1918, he, like many others, had chosen to stay in Iraq, where they worked for English

roof, windows, and doors, making it habitable although far from finished. We took up residence in its raw mud-brick rooms, using pressure lamps and kerosene lanterns to work by. The bathrooms and toilets were not yet finished, although we had cold running water in parts of the house, so we had the usual reed-mat-walled facilities outside the building. It was not until the next season, 1965/66, that Knudstad returned to finish the house, plastering the interior walls, laying tiles, installing the plumbing fixtures, the electrical systems, and so on. While doing that, he also made a new topographic map of the site. During 1966/67 he returned again to resume work on the Parthian Fortress. After the work was finished, the Directorate General of Antiquities found the ruins so impressive that it was decided that the Fortress had to remain standing as a tourist attraction, so the demolition never took place. The lower levels of the É-Kur complex were to remain unexplored.

Having brought the Abu Salabikh tablets back to Nippur, Bob and Selma began the laborious task of separating, baking, gluing, solidifying, and photographing them as well as making latex molds that we could take back to Chicago in order to make plaster casts. Until March 1965, when the actual digging at Nippur came to an end, I remained an observer of the labor on the tablets whenever I was at the expedition house. The tablets were mainly the task of Bob and Selma, since Diane was also working on the excavation and, at night, still completing the catalogue of other finds from Abu Salabikh. From seven in the morning until nine at night, they bent over the tablets, catching the best light from windows or from pressure lamps. Working through the winter with a kerosene heater on either side of him, bundled in a sweater, Bob would hunch over fragments. But before he could get to that stage, he had to bake the tablets in a specially built kiln, following the design of Delougaz.[5] The baking was a painstaking process that showed the care and precision with which Bob worked. Every two or three days, he prepared another set of fragments, placing them initially in earthenware bowls filled with sand that would protect the tablets from overfiring. Because of the number and size of the Abu Salabikh tablets, however, the bowls soon proved to be unsuited to the task. He had a smith create two large and deep steel containers, without tops, which he could fill with many more and larger fragments, thus speeding up the pace at which the tablets were baked. Until they were baked, the tablets could not be treated, and there were months of painstaking work before all would be processed.

officers, officials, and later for embassies and companies. Officially retired by the time we met him, Siraj was a gray-haired, pudgy gentleman with a mild manner and a repertoire of recipes that seemed endless. Rounding out the household was Jabbar Nasr, the driver, a local man from Afak, who was an expert on the desert tracks that linked the two rivers. He drove Bob Adams on most of his surveys in southern Iraq, and he served the Nippur Expedition until the 1980s. He was a mixed blessing, but his resourcefulness made him almost indispensable. He helped Bob Biggs set up and run a small sandblasting device from a spark plug of the Land Rover, allowing a gentle, controlled cleaning of the faces of tablets once they were baked.

[5] P. Delougaz, *I. Plano-convex Bricks and the Methods of their Employment, II. The Treatment of Clay Tablets in the Field*, SAOC 7 (Chicago, 1933).

Bob had made a careful record, using Polaroid photos and drawings, as he excavated the stack of tablets. Now, with each tablet or set of related fragments that he laid in the sand-filled steel containers, he would include a potsherd, into which he had scratched in the tablet's identifying number. A sherd would survive the firing, and no other material would. After the baking, that sherd would stay with the tablet throughout the cleaning, consolidation, and gluing process and would be discarded only when the tablet had been numbered with India ink. This procedure resulted in his knowing at all times exactly where each fragment had been found. The system, still in use at Nippur and on our other operations not only for tablets but also for ancient seal impressions, avoids the loss of provenience information, which was all too common an occurrence on older digs.

Bob was able to fit two of the steel containers into the upper chamber of the oven. He would then seal the entrance of that chamber with baked bricks and mud mortar, leaving a small space in which to insert a fragment of tempered glass, usually from a broken pressure lamp. This glass "window" was all-important in the process because it would give the signal that the firing had reached 800 degrees centigrade, meaning that after a well-calculated period of additional firing, the heat would approach 1,600 degrees centigrade, the optimum temperature for good tablet baking. The firing chamber, situated below the upper chamber, was equipped with a steel plate onto which crude oil would be dripped in a regulated way through a tube from a barrel on one side of the kiln. Another tube led down from a barrel of water on the other side.

Once the upper chamber was sealed, Bob would turn a spigot, and fuel would drip onto the plate at a very slow rate, a drop at a time. The fuel would be lit, and a tiny amount of water would be allowed to fall in slow drops onto the pan, creating a flashy, sustained, though low, heat. The process started with a very low fire in order to allow the heat to build gradually and penetrate slowly into the tablets, driving out any moisture so that the tablets would not explode. After several hours, the number of drops of oil and water would be increased, following a very strict schedule. Almost immediately upon firing, the glass window in the upper chamber would go black with carbon. At the height of the baking, sometime after dark, the fire would be roaring, and Bob would check the glass window from time to time. Finally, usually at about 9 P.M., the carbon on the inside of the window would burn off, indicating that the required temperature had been reached, ensuring a good baking. Usually he would wait for a half hour or so to make sure that the firing was sufficient; then he would cut off the oil and water, and he and Abdullah Sultan would seal up the firing chamber entry with baked bricks and mud. Overnight and during the following day, the oven would gradually cool. Then the chambers would be opened and the tablet containers removed. Throughout many firings over several months, Bob took notes and made adjustments in the fuel/water ratio, time sequence, and so forth. During seasons in which he could not join us, those notes were still used at Nippur. Of course, we preferred having him with us because he was an ideal team member, never complaining, always patient and cheerful, ready to help with anything, and not afraid of getting dirty in the trenches.

Once the tablets and tablet fragments had been fired, they would be very carefully removed from their beds of sand, joined and cleaned of surface salts, and then glued. After the actual digging was finished in March, I joined Bob and Selma in the cleaning and gluing of tablets and especially in the making of latex molds.[6] By now, it was hot and insects were numerous, so we tried to position ourselves near doorways to catch the light and any breeze as we worked.[7] At night, the pressure lamps gave great light, but they were sources of heat, even in the relative coolness of the evenings.

In between sessions of tablet work, I would check the progress of the coins, which I was still cleaning. From the sample of cleaned coins, we found out that Nippur had issues from as early as the Achaemenid period and as late as the early Abbasid. Some of the oldest coins were very early examples of Athenian owls and a variety of early Greek city issues from Caria, Ionia, and other locations in Anatolia. Also present in the sample of surface finds were Seleucid, Roman, Parthian, Characenian, Byzantine, Sasanian, and early Islamic coins. We had no issues later than shortly after A.D. 800. Coin finds in subsequent seasons confirmed that date as the terminal occupation of the city.

One small coin among my sample defied classification. As it emerged from the outer green corrosion layer and then from below the red layer, it became obvious that the coin was copper or bronze, but it had an unusual design. I could make out Latin letters. At first, I thought the inscription might be on an odd Byzantine issue. But as the design was exposed further, it became clear that the main motif was a European sailing ship such as a galleon, heading away from the viewer, toward the left. On the reverse was a rising sun with stars and a crescent moon.

I stopped the chemical treatment and put the coin in a distilled water bath in a small dish. I had not yet had time to photograph it, but I had made some rough sketches (fig. 1). I also had made some notes: "Bronze, 1.8 cm. Dm, Obv. Sailing ship (European?) with Latin(?) words in upper field. Rev. Rising sun, with rays, under 5 stars and a crescent, Inscription unclear and partial. There is a clear I. I. H." The edge of the coin

[6] We left Nippur in June, and the rest of the crew went back to Chicago, leaving me to spend another month in the old Ottoman house that was then the headquarters of the British School of Archaeology in Baghdad. I owe a debt of gratitude to David Oates for allowing me to reside there. Even after the departure of the British, I was allowed to stay and finish the photographing of the tablets, and I went to the Iraq Museum every day and took the shots with a 4″ × 5″ camera. Back at the British School, in the late afternoon and night, when the temperature had dropped to only about 90 degrees Fahrenheit, I would try to develop the film, but I had no way to control the temperature of the water, given the struggle that refrigerators have in that climate. Added to the difficulty was the presence in the darkroom of scorpions that skittered across the floor in the dark. Because of the warmth of the water, the negatives could not develop their full detail. Bob has always been very forgiving of the poor quality of the photographs that he had to use in his book on the texts. They deserved better than I could produce.

[7] Bob's response to the heat was to wear shorts. He suffered a sand-fly bite, which resulted in the development of a Baghdad boil on his thigh. When he arrived back in Chicago, he became a favorite show-and-tell object for the tropical medicine specialists at the University Hospital. Characteristically, he took all this with patience and forbearance.

was broken away in places. The coin was sitting on a table in its dish when we had a visit by a group of diplomats from at least ten of the embassies in Baghdad. After they left, I went to get the coin for photography, and it was not in the dish. I searched the floor, thinking it had been jostled by the crowd of visitors and had fallen. It was never found.

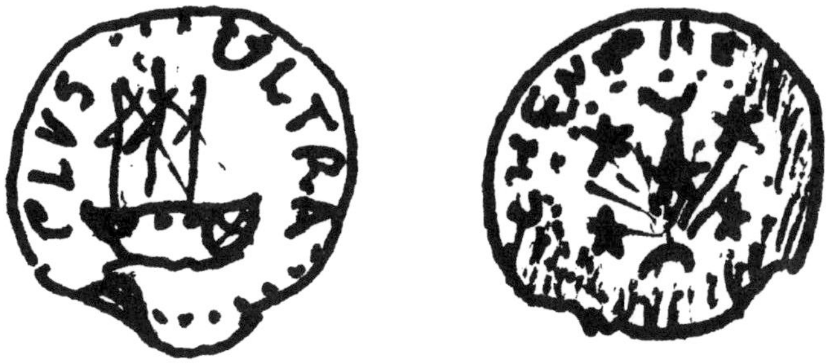

Obv. Rev.

Figure 1. Rough Sketch of Coin (1941.180.110). Scale 2:1

Figure 2. Obv. Scale 2:1

Figure 3. Rev. Scale 2:1

In 1966, I received a fellowship to attend the Summer Seminar at the American Numismatic Society, where I worked on a hoard of Sasanian coins. While there I described the mystery coin to some of the curators and showed my sketches. One of them said it did not appear to be a coin but, rather, a casting-counter (*jeton*, *Rechenpfennig*). He advised me to look at the Numismatic Society's counters, and there I found our "galleon" among the *Rechenpfennigs* struck in Nuremberg (figs. 2–3).

Casting-counters, or *jetons* (sometimes called "calculi"), were used in a system of accounting that is similar to the abacus, but they are laid down on lined boards or cloths. They were first given the form of coins in thirteenth-century France, although discs of stone, bone, wood, or horn had been used on lined or grooved boards or printed cloth in Classical antiquity. It is thought that the counting boards and calculi were developed to deal with "cumbersome Roman numerals."[8] But the use of calculi or tokens with a variety of shapes as part of a different kind of accounting system has been projected back to the Uruk period and even earlier times in Mesopotamia.[9] Throughout ancient Mesopotamian history the mathematical system, which was based on sixty, also would have been cumbersome. Counters for mathematics began to go out of use in Europe in the seventeenth century, and the introduction of the decimal system in Revolutionary France seems to have been the final blow.[10] But they continued to be produced as gaming pieces. Even though they were out of fashion for accounting in Europe, they continued in their original use far later in other parts of the world. The longevity of the idea behind the system is shown by the continued use of the abacus in Asia, despite the fact that most or all electronic calculators are now being manufactured there.

The system of counters and counting boards was widely used throughout Medieval and Renaissance Europe, initially being closely connected with royal establishments, and their manufacture was closely controlled. Counters were sold as sets, usually of a hundred. Metals used included gold, silver, and lead, but the most common material was copper and its various alloys. The size and weight of counters could vary widely, since there was not the necessity to maintain a fixed value, as with coins.

Functioning in a similar manner to an abacus, counters would be laid down on or between lines drawn on paper or parchment, or incised into a board or table, each line or space being given a certain numerical value. Addition, subtraction, multiplication, and division could be performed rapidly.[11] The counters had a wide circulation in Europe and the Mediterranean, and through foreign trade spread to many other parts of the world, where they sometimes took on the role of coins, either used fraudulently (gilding copper counters to pass them off as coins)[12] or used as petty change,[13] and, like real coins, transformed into jewelry.[14] Counters were sometimes also used as souvenirs of specific events and thrown out to crowds by kings or officials.

---

[8] F. P. Barnard, *The Casting-Counter and the Counting Board: A Chapter in the History of Numismatics and Early Arithmetic* (Oxford, 1916).

[9] D. Schmandt-Besserat, *Before Writing* (Austin, Texas, 1992), p. 26.

[10] Barnard, *Casting-Counter*, pp. 87–88.

[11] Barnard, *Casting-Counter*, is still a good treatment of the subject and is generally available in university libraries. D. E. Smith's, *Computing Jetons*, Numismatic Notes and Monographs 9 (New York, 1921) is concerned with the function of counters rather than with types. C. F. Gebert, "Die Nürnberger Rechenpfennigschläger," *Mitteilungen der Bayerischen Numismatischen Gesellschaft* 35 (1917): 1–138, and P. Eklund, "The Counters of Nuremberg," *The Numismatist* 39 (1926): 114–16, 164–69, 216–20, 266–69, 389–91, 478–79, present types of casting-counters. Recent and more comprehensive sources for Nuremberg counters are M. Mitchiner, *Jetons, Medalets and Tokens*, vol. 1, *The Medieval Period and Nuremberg* (London, 1988), and A. Koenig, *Rechenpfennige*, Band 1, *Nürnberg, signierte und zuweisbare Gepräge*, Staatliche Münzsammlung München, Kataloge der Staatlichen Münzsammlung (Munich, 1989). Although I was able to borrow the Mitchiner volume through Interlibrary Loan, I was unable to consult Koenig for this article.

[12] Barnard, *Casting-Counter*, p. 78.

[13] Ibid., p. 80.

[14] Ibid., pl. 27, 2 and 6 for pierced examples.

A great proportion of counters were struck in Nuremberg, apparently because they were cheaper than other counters, being light in weight.

> The old saying "Nuremberg's hand is in every land," which dates from the days before the overland trade-route from the East was replaced by the sea-route after the rounding of the Cape at the end of the 15th century, and when Nuremberg was perhaps the most important center of distribution in Europe, is peculiarly applicable to it as a source from which emanated immense numbers of cheap casting-pieces. The Nuremberg *jettons*, however do not seem to go farther back than about 1500, but their descendants, the *spielmarken*, or counters for play, outlived the casting-counter and survive to our own times.[15]

Nuremberg counters tended to become much smaller and lighter in the early nineteenth century, and it was in this time that the Nippur counter was most probably struck.

The Nippur counter was thin and small, measuring only 1.8 cm in diameter. On the obverse was a three-masted sailing ship, facing left and shown in three-quarter view. Around the edge, from the left, was the legend "PLUS UL[TRA]." The reverse had a rising sun with rays upon which were interspersed five stars under a crescent. Around the edge, from the lower left, could be seen a part of an inscription that I can now reconstruct as "RECHENPFENNIG." The initials I. I. H. indicate that the maker was Iohann Iacob Habelt, who died in 1867.[16] Counters of this type, with the ship and rising sun, were struck as early as the late eighteenth century by a number of men,[17] but the initials indicate that it was produced by Habelt. He and others were still striking counters of this type during the earlier half of the nineteenth century, giving us a rough date for the origin of the Nippur counter.

The appearance of a Nuremberg casting-counter at Nippur raises two questions. How did it get to Nippur and when? As far as I can determine, there was no sizable village near Nippur in the earlier half of the nineteenth century. The city of Nippur had been deserted since shortly after A.D. 800, according to the coin evidence. The entire area around Nippur appears to have been in great decline even before the Mongol invasion of 1258, and we assumed that the land around the site had remained uncultivated from that date until the early twentieth century. But in the late 1980s, a Nippur Expedition member, Margaret Brandt, discovered not more than 200 meters east of the ziggurat a small, crooked canal and a village site, which could be dated by the pottery and coins to the Ilkhanid period (fourteenth–fifteenth centuries A.D.). We had not seen the village before that because a giant dune belt, stretching to the north, east, and southeast, had covered that site and about half of Nippur during most of the period of

---

15 Ibid., pp. 65–66.

16 Mitchiner, *Jetons*, no. 2040.

17 See, for example, Gebert, "Die Nürnberger Rechenpfennigschläger," p. 40: Wolfgang Magnus Anert, who became a master in 1778; Mitchiner, *Jetons*, nos. 1989–90: Iohann Iacob Lauer, retired 1852; no. 2039: Iobst Carl Gerner, died 1854; nos. 2050–51, Ludwig Christian Lauer, died 1873; nos. 2175–77: Iohan Christian Reich, who died in 1814, struck similar counters that were significantly different in detail.

modern digging (1948 onward). Only in the 1980s did the belt begin to diminish and retreat from the area. We cannot find evidence of any villages of the Ottoman period in the immediate Nippur vicinity, and visitors in the mid-ninteenth century characterize the area to the north as desert, with areas of dunes, that was used by shepherds for grazing.[18] The mound of Nippur itself was at the northern edge of the extensive Afak marsh,[19] the original formation of which we cannot determine. In 1889, when the University of Pennsylvania Expedition arrived to begin its excavations,[20] the site still was approached by boat, and the village of Afak was little different than it was when Layard saw it. But by 1900, the marsh had dried up because of the breaking of the Hindiya Barrage north of Hilla, depriving the eastern branches of the Euphrates of water.

The marsh, in the mid-nineteenth century, stretched for many kilometers from at least as far west as present-day Dagharah toward the east, where it surrounded Bismaya, or ancient Adab.[21] It was estimated that the population of the marsh in 1850 was 3,000 families.[22] Loftus's description makes it clear that the inhabitants of the marsh were living on the products of the water buffalo and on rice cultivation, but we must assume that, like all marsh-dwellers, they also fished and hunted and sold items made from reeds. Layard gives some detail on the main village in the marsh, Suq al-Afak,[23] which consisted of reed houses and a small market around one mud-brick structure—the watchtower of the local *shaykh*. He describes the bazaar as consisting of a few reed buildings with merchants selling a variety of goods, including imported cloth from England, spices, and items from across the Middle East. There were, as well, Christian metalworkers making jewelry. The implication of this description is that even though there were no large towns and almost no masonry buildings in the vicinity, there was commerce in the area of Nippur.

In addition to the marsh-dwellers, there were other inhabitants of the region. Layard, Loftus, and Peters all describe the tent camps of "Arab herders" in the desert to the

---

[18] From W. K. Loftus, *Travels and Researches in Chaldaea and Susiana* ... (London, 1857), and A. H. Layard, *Discoveries in the Ruins of Nineveh and Babylon* ... (London, 1853), it is apparent that the great dune belt had already engulfed much of the area, including irrigated fields and villages directly east and southeast of Babylon and Kish and that villages southeast of Hilla were being overwhelmed by dunes at that time. Layard indicates that dunes were also forming in the area of Shomeli, which is just north of Dagharah, only 25 kilometers or so northeast of Nippur. The enveloping of the Nippur area took place some time after 1920 and before 1948. There is no evidence of dunes on the site in photographs taken by a University of Chicago group in 1920 (The Oriental Institute Archives), but most of the mounds were covered by 1948, when Chicago began work there.

[19] Loftus, *Travels and Researches in Chaldaea and Susiana*, pp. 101–2.

[20] J. P. Peters, *Nippur, or Explorations and Adventures on the Euphrates: The Narrative of the University of Pennsylvania Expedition to Babylon in the Years 1888–1890* (London, 1897), vol. 1, pp. 229 ff.; see also Hilprecht, *Explorations in Bible Lands*.

[21] Loftus, *Travels and Researches in Chaldaea and Susiana*, pp. 90–104.

[22] Ibid., p. 91.

[23] Layard, *Discoveries in the Ruins of Nineveh and Babylon*, pp. 544–55.

north.[24] We can also assume that the great camel-herding tribes of Arabia had already for centuries been making their yearly visit to the Nippur area, just as they were still doing each spring in the 1970s. Their annual round took them from Arabia through Iraq and into Syria before they turned back south through Jordan. One morning in 1975, we awoke to find the plain around Nippur dotted with hundreds of camels. Bedu tents were pitched next to villages across the plain. On the mound of Nippur itself was the tent of the nomadic *shaykh*. He had chosen this position for his tent because the tell was owned by the Department of Antiquities and was thus neutral territory for the tribal segments that farmed in the area. There was, therefore, no obligation on the part of the local people to extend continuous hospitality to him and his retinue, which would have been a great burden. Of course, the local *shaykh*s invited the nomadic leader to their houses, and he reciprocated. For the few days that they remained around Nippur, the nomads traded with the local people and in the town of Afak. Some marriages were arranged, resulting in the introduction of a few more women to the local population. I do not know if it happened on this occasion, but sometimes men and entire nuclear families remained behind, using real or fictive ties of kinship to ease their way into the local society.

The Nippur casting-counter may have arrived on the site any time after its manufacture in the first half of the nineteenth century. Perhaps it came as part of a piece of jewelry, dropped by a woman walking across the mound. Some of the counters in museum collections are pierced for suspension, and the Nippur example also may have been, since there is a bit missing on one edge. But it is equally probable that the counter was still in use as small change in the 1890s, and one of Pennsylvania's workmen might have lost it.

It is reasonable to assume that a casting-counter would first have been used in Iraq as a mathematical device even after it had gone out of its primary use in Europe. The Near East would have been familiar with such counters. There were merchants of the East India Company in Basra from the seventeenth century onward, as there had been Portuguese and Dutch traders even earlier. But it is likely that if the item came to Iraq as a counter, it was for the use of Turkish and Arab merchants, who probably still used the system in the early nineteenth century. Counters spread with trade, and trade was international and even intercontinental long before the striking of the counter.[25]

At any rate, I like to think that this little bit of copper, dropped by some unknown person on a site in the alluvial desert of southern Iraq, adds a small piece to the picture of international commerce, even if it last saw service as a dangling ornament in a woman's hair.

---

[24] Ibid., pp. 228 ff.; Loftus, *Travels and Researches in Chaldaea and Susiana*, pp. 84 ff.; and Peters, *Nippur, or Explorations and Adventures on the Euphrates*, pp. 288 ff.

[25] At Nippur, in a hoard of seventy-eight Islamic coins (M. L. Bates, "A Horde of Dirhams Found at Nippur," in M. Gibson et al., *Excavations at Nippur, Twelfth Season*, OIC 23 [Chicago, 1978], pp. 26–38), there were several that had been minted in North Africa, which is just as far from Nippur as Nuremberg is.

LIEBES- UND HUNDEBESCHWÖRUNGEN IM KONTEXT

Brigitte Groneberg, Universität Göttingen

ana bi-iṣ-ṣu-ri-ka šá tak-la-a-tú kalba(UR-GU$_7$) *ú-še-reb bāba*(KÁ) *a-rak-kás*[1]
Var: *a-na* [*bi-iṣ*]-*ṣu-ri-ki šá tak-la-te kal-bi ú-še-er-re-eb bāba*(KÁ) *a-rak-kas*[2]

In deine Vagina, der du vertraust, lasse ich den Hund eintreten, das Tor binde ich zu!

So heißt es am 5.(?) Tag des "Divine Love Lyrics"-Rituals. Wie so oft in diesem Ritual wird nicht ausdrücklich gesagt, wer gemeint ist oder wer die Beschwörung, um die es sich handelt, spricht. Nach einer Beschwörungssequenz von 5 Zeilen (Z. 7–11), die jeweils litaneiartig mit *biṣṣuru* "Vagina" beginnt, verläßt der *kurgarrû* das Stadttor und kauert sich gegenüber von Hursagkalamma hin, um Flehgebete zu sprechen und Seufzergesänge anzustimmen.[3] Deshalb ist es wahrscheinlich, daß dieser Kultdiener der Ištargestalten die *biṣṣuru*-Beschwörungssequenz auf dem Weg "vom Akītu-Haus bis zum Tor des Uraš" (Z. 6) ausführt.

Die Frage muß gestellt werden, welche Wirkung dem Akt des in der Vagina fest eingeschnürten Hunds zugeschrieben wird, und ausgehend vom Gegenstand der Beschwörung, *biṣṣuru*, wessen Vagina beschworen sein könnte.[4]

[1] Lambert Love Lyrics III 7; George, "Four Temple Rituals from Babylon," in *Lambert AV*, S. 270 verweist in Anm. 19 auf die Joins BM 40090+41005+41107 und erwähnt, daß noch viele andere unveröffentlichte Texte dieses Rituals in London und Istanbul liegen. S. 270–80 veröffentlicht er einen Text aus der parthisch-seleukidischen Epoche, der eine ganze Reihe von Berührungspunkten mit den "Divine Love Lyrics" aufweist.

[2] Die teilweise parallelen Zeilen in Lambert Love Lyrics, S. 122 "group IV": *LKA* 92: 11, 8, 4 entsprechen Sp. III 7, 8, 10. Nach den Z. 11, 8, 4 werden jeweils einige weiterführende Zeilen eingefügt, außerdem ist die Zitierung in *LKA* 92 rückläufig, d. h. *LKA* 92: 11 = Sp. III 7 usw.

[3] George, "Four Temple Rituals", S. 271, Anm. 23, auch zu Edzard, "Zur Ritualtafel der sog. 'Love Lyrics' ", in AOS 67, S. 57 ff. George lehnt Edzards Interpretationen zu den Kultdienern der Ištar zu Recht ab.

[4] Trotz des Suffixes der 2. P. mask. *-ka* in dem spätbabylonischen Exemplar ist die Trägerin der Vagina entweder als Wesen oder Ersatzfigurine gemeint. Das scheint die Variante aus Assur (*LKA* 92) zu bestätigen.

Man kann ausschließen, daß diese respektlose Beschwörungssequenz eine Gottheit anreden könnte, selbst wenn es sich um Göttinen wie Nanāya oder Šarrat-Nippuri handeln würde, die erotische Aspekte vertreten.[5] Höchst wahrscheinlich ist die Vagina einer Hündin gemeint, in die das Geschlechtsteil eines Rüden eingebunden wird, wie aus der Isin-"Liebesbeschwörung" und verwandten Texten hervorgeht[6]:

16 *uk-ta-as-sí-i-ka i-na* KA-*ja ša ša-ra-a-tim*
17 *i-na ú-ri-ja ša ši-i-na-tim ...*
20 *a i-li-ik na-ak-ra-tum i-na ṣe-ri-i-ka*

16 Ich habe Dich gebunden mit meinem Haar-Mund,
17 mit meiner Urin-Scham ...
20 die *Feindin*[7] soll nicht zu Dir gehen!

Das evozierte Bild meint unzweifelhaft die Eigenart des Hundes, nach der Kopulation einige Zeit mit der Hündin verbunden zu bleiben, eine Fähigkeit, die in beiden Beschwörungen, die über tausend Jahre auseinanderliegen, angesprochen ist. Diesem Akt kann man eine bannende Funktion zusprechen, aber auch eine erotisierende, Fruchtbarkeit anregende Wirkung, da die Bedeutung eines jeden Symbols jeweils kontextgebunden und im Einklang mit der Zielrichtung des gesamten Vorgangs gedeutet werden muß. In den "Divine Love Lyrics" geht aus dem Kontext nicht klar hervor, ob die Beschwörung Zauberei abwenden oder Zauberei bewirken soll. Dennoch möchte ich eine exorzistische Funktion annehmen, weil die Kultpriester mit Klagen befaßt sind und auch sonst als positive Helfer bei offiziellen wie privaten Ritualen auftreten.[8] Nur deshalb ist es wahrscheinlich, daß das Symbol "Hund" in diesem Text Übel abweisend evoziert wird und der Akt für eine negative Kraft verwendet wird, die eine Gefährdung bannen soll. In der oben zitierten Isin-"Liebesbeschwörung" wird, anders als in den "Divine Love Lyrics", die Gefährdung genannt: Es ist die *nakratum* "Feindin". Ein anonymes "Ich" will eine männliche Person mithilfe des Symbols "Hund" bannen und binden, um sie durch diesen Bann von der "Feindin" fernzuhalten.

Der Symbolwert des Hundes ist komplexer, als oft angenommen wird, denn sein Ansehen bewegt sich zwischen Extremen: Einerseits ist er das Begleittier der Heilgöttin Gula und verwandter Gottheiten, andererseits ist er ein schmutziges, verachtetes Tier.

---

[5] Der teilweise parallele Textzeuge *LKA* 92 spricht in dem fortführenden Teil (Z. 18–22), der auf die *biṣṣuru*-Passagen folgt, Ištar als "Mutter Babylons" an. Im Haupttext Sp. III 7 ff. hält die Prozession in Z. 5 vor dem Akītu-Haus der Šarrat-Nippuri.

[6] Wilcke, "Liebesbeschwörungen aus Isin", *ZA* 75 (1985): 198.

[7] *nakratum*: gemeint ist eine Feindin, von der aus dem Kontext der Beschwörungen hervorgeht, daß von ihr Zauberei vermutet wird.

[8] B. Groneberg, "Die sumerisch-akkadische Inanna/Istar: Hermaphroditos?", *WO* 17 (1986): 33–39.

Wie differenziert die Wahrnehmung des Tieres ist, soll im Folgenden dargestellt und gedeutet werden, soweit nicht schon früher geschehen.[9] Auch soll seine Rolle im Umfeld von "Liebeszauber", mit dem sich der Jubilar beschäftigte, erhellt werden.

Die negative Seite des Hundes wird in der altbabylonischen Hundebeschwörung VAS 17 8[10] beschrieben:

3	*[ṣi]-il*$_5$*-li du-ri-im mu-uz-za-zu-ú-šu*	Im Schatten der Mauer ist sein Aufenthaltsplatz,
4	*as-ku-pa-tum na-ar-ba-ṣú-šu*	die Schwelle ist sein Liegeplatz,
5	*i-na pi-i-šu na-ši-i ni-il-šu*	in seinem Maul trägt er seinen Samen.
6	*a-šar iš-šu-ku ma-ra-šu i-zi-ib …*	Wo er beißt, läßt er sein Kind zurück …
Rd.:	KA-inim-ma ur-gi$_7$ ti-la-kam	Es ist eine Beschwörung des lebenden Hundes.[11]

An diesen Plätzen liegt er, hungert, dürstet und wird schließlich vernichtet, z. B. in der Beschwörung OECT 11 4:

1	*ú-ug-gu-ur ši-pi-i[n]*	Schnellfüßig,[12]
2	*a-ru-úh la-sà-ma-am*	schnell rennend,
3	*bu-bu-ta-am ma-ad*	reichlich hungrig,
4	*it-ni-i[š] a-ka-la-am*	geschwächt durch (mangelndes) Essen,
5	*i-na as-[k]u-pa-tim*	ist er ständig auf der Schwelle
6	*ir-ta-na-bi-iṣ*	gelagert.
7	*e-ma iš-šu-k[u m]e-ra-nam i-zi-ib*	Wo er beißt, hinterläßt er ein Junges!
8	*ú-su-úh ša-ar-k[a]-am*	Reiße aus den Eiter
9	*ša pa-ni-š[u]*	[sei]nes Gesichtes
10	*ù pu-ul-hi-ta-am*	und den Schrecken

[9] B. Groneberg, "Tiere als Symbole von Göttern in den frühen geschichtlichen Epochen Mesopotamiens. Von der altsumerischen Zeit bis zum Ende der altbabylonischen Zeit", in J. Andreau et al., *Les animaux et les hommes dans le monde syro-mésopotamien aux époques historiques*, TOPOI, Orient-Occident, Suppl. 2 (Lyon, 2000), S. 302 f.

[10] M. Sigrist, "On the Bite of a Dog", in R. M. Good und J. H. Marks, Hrsg., *Love and Death in the Ancient Near East: Essays in Honor of Marvin H. Pope* (Winona Lake, Indiana, 1987), S. 86, und W. Farber, "Eine altbabylonische Formel gegen den Hundebiß", in W. Farber, H. M. Kümmel und W. H. Ph. Römer, *Rituale und Beschwörungen I*, Texte aus der Umwelt des Alten Testaments, Band II, Lfg. 2 (Gütersloh, 1987), S. 256.

[11] In Anlehnung an van Dijk (VAS 17 10 ad 8) übersetzt Sigrist ("On the Bite of a Dog", S. 86) ur-gi$_7$-ti-la-kam mit "for resurrecting a thorough-bred dog".

[12] O. R. Gurney, OECT 11, S. 22 f., führt aus, daß man wegen der Parallele LB 2001:2 einen Schreibfehler für *urruk* "lang (an Fuß) = schnell" annehmen solle.

11 *ša ša-ap-ti-šu*	seiner Lippen!
12 *ka-al-bu-um li-m*[*u-ut*]	Der Hund soll ste[rben] (und)
13 [*a*⌉-*we-lum li-ib-l*[*u-uṭ*]	der Mensch soll le[ben]!

(4 Zeilen zerstört)

Unterschrift: KA-inim-ma x x x

Von den älteren akkadischen Beschwörungen bis zum Ende der altbabylonischen Zeit sind eine ganze Anzahl gegen Hunde oder Teilaspekte des Hundes gerichtet.[13] Schon der Blick des schwarzen Hundes gilt als ein bedrohliches Zeichen, wie in einer altassyrischen Beschwörung, die offenbar zum Schutz der Karawanen vor den Gefährdungen in der freien Natur (Steppe) durch den schwarzen Hund verwendet wird[14]:

da-mu-um da-ma-mu-um	Blut, ja Blut(?).
kà-al-bu-um	Der schwarze Hund
ṣa-al-mu-um	
i-tí-li-im / *ra-bi*$_4$-*iṣ*	ist auf einem Hügel hingelagert
ú-qá-a illat-*tám*	(und) wartet auf die isolierte Karawane,
pá-ri-is-tám eṭ-lam$_x$	den braven Mann
dam-qám / *i-ta-na-áp-l*[*i-sà*]	belauern seine Augen!
e-na-šu	

Es folgen Ritualanweisungen, die in den Textfluß integriert sind: "14 Töchter Eas"[15] werden aufgefordert, ihre Töpfe aus Karneol und anderen kostbaren Steinen mit

[13] Die Beschwörungen wurden von mir nicht systematisch gesammelt, s. aber W. Farber, "Zur älteren akkadischen Beschwörungsliteratur", *ZA* 71 (1981): 57 zu C 31. Folgende Beschwörungen evozieren Hunde oder Emanationen des Hundes aus den älteren Epochen (bis zum Ende der altbabylonischen Zeit):

Owen, *NATN* 917 (s. G. Cunningham, *"Deliver Me from Evil": Mesopotamian Incantations 2500–1500 BC*, Studia Pohl, Series Maior 17 [Rome, 1997]), S. 97 Text 72 (nach S. 65 die einzige akkadische Beschwörung aus der Ur-III-Zeit; anders *CAD* K s.v. *kalbu* Bed. 1c: "OAkk. inc.").

TIM 9 72 (s. R. Whiting, "An Old Babylonian Incantation from Tell Asmar", *ZA* 75 (1985): S. 180f.).

TIM 9 73 Vs. (s. Farber, "Beschwörungsliteratur", S. 55: C 18).

Greengus *Ishchali* No. 302 (s. Farber "Beschwörungsliteratur", S. 57: C 31).

UET 6/2 399 (= Finkel bei Whiting, "Old Babylonian Incantation", S. 184).

Whiting, "Old Babylonian Incantation", S. 184: TA 1930-T117.

F. M. Th. de Liagre Böhl, "Zwei altbabylonische Beschwörungstexte: LB 2001 und 1001", *BiOr* 11 (1954) S. 82: LB 2001.

OECT 11 4.

Sigrist "On the Bite of a Dog", S. 85f. (AUAM 73 2416).

VAS 17 8.

Zu jüngeren Hundebeschwörungen s. *CAD* K s.v. *kalbu* Bed. 1h–2′.

[14] K. R. Veenhof, "An Old Assyrian Incantation against a Black Dog", in *Hirsch AV*, S. 425–33 (vgl. Farber, "Beschwörungsliteratur", S. 53: Ba).

[15] Es könnten 2 × 7 Geburtshelfergöttinnen gemeint sein. Der Ausgang der Beschwörung läßt ein abgeschlossenes Reinigungsritual vermuten: *ṣí-i eṭ-lúm* / [*a-n*]*a iš-ri-kà* [*t*]*ù-ur*: "gehe hinaus, Mann, zu deinem Ort kehre zurück!"

reinem Wasser zu füllen, jedoch erlaubt der dann zerstörte Text keine weitere funktionale Zuordnung des Rituals.

Die Anwendung der Hundebeschwörungen in den ganz unterschiedlichen Situationen ist ein Hinweis darauf, daß sie sich gegen das Phänomen des schwarzen Hundes an sich richteten und nicht gegen einen spezifischen schwarzen Hund.[16] Der schwarze Hund war bekanntlich mit der Dämonin Lamaštu assoziiert[17] und damit in der Tat ein lebendes Übel, das exorziert werden mußte.

Für eine auch positive Rezeption der Rolle des Hundes spricht seine Zuordnung zur Heilgöttin Gula (und verwandten Gottheiten).[18] Das offizielle Kultsymbol der Göttin Gula, das ^{d}*kalbum* genannt wird und als giš.tukul = *kakkum* "Signum" die Göttin vertritt, ist in der altbabylonischen Zeit ein Hund.[19]

Die Hundeart scheint für das Symbol der Gula nicht ausschlaggebend zu sein. Im sogenannten Hundefriedhof auf der Rampe in der Nähe des Heiligtums der Gula in Isin wurde sowohl ein bulliger, mastiffartiger Hund als auch eine halbgroße, zierlichere Rasse gefunden, die auch auf Rollsiegeln abgebildet werden.[20] Es ist daher zu vermuten, daß das Symbol nicht auf eine bestimmte Hunderasse, sondern auf den Begriff "Hund" an sich definiert wird.

Wie schon an anderer Stelle ausgeführt, können Symbole einen oder mehrere Aspekte ihrer Bezugsfigur widerspiegeln.[21] In diesem Fall vermute ich, daß das Hundesymbol mit dem Heilaspekt der Heilgöttin Gula (und ihrer Hypostasen bzw. verwandter Heilgöttinnen) zusammenhängt.[22]

---

[16] Contra Veenhof, "Against a Black Dog", S. 431.

[17] Ausführlich F. Wiggermann, "Lamashtu, Daughter of Anu: A Profile", in M. Stol, Hrsg., *Birth in Babylonia and the Bible: Its Mediterranean Setting*, Cuneiform Monographs 14 (Groningen, 2000), S. 234.

[18] Ausführlich Groneberg, "Tiere als Symbole", mit Literatur.

[19] Ibid., S. 293 f.

[20] B. Hrouda, Hrsg., *Isin, Išān Baḫrīyāṭ I. Die Ergebnisse der Ausgrabungen 1973–1974*, Bayerische Akademie der Wissenschaften, phil.-hist. Kl., Abhandlungen, n. F., Heft 79 (München, 1977), S. 17–20; J. Boessneck, "Die Hundeskelette von Išān Baḫrīyāṭ (Isin) aus der Zeit v. Chr.", ibid., S. 97–109; M. Haussperger, "Die Rolle des Hundes auf Rollsiegeln", in P. Calmeyer et al., Hrsg., *Beiträge zur altorientalischen Archäologie und Altertumskunde. Festschrift für Barthel Hrouda zum 65. Geburtstag* (Wiesbaden, 1994), S. 103–10; Groneberg, "Tiere als Symbole", S. 301 f.

[21] Groneberg, "Tiere als Symbole", S. 283–320.

[22] Ich gehe davon aus, daß Ninisina und Ninkarak ebenso wie Gula spätestens in der Ur-III-Zeit einen einzigen Heilgöttinnentyp verkörpern, der allerdings lokale Gestalten und funktionale Schwerpunkte zeigen kann. M. Such-Gutiérrez, "Beiträge zum Pantheon von Nippur im 3. Jahrtausend, Teil 1 und 2", in MVN 9, S. 246 f., trennt neuerdings eine Göttin Gú-lá von Gu-la, "deren Gleichsetzung in der altbabylonischen Zeit jedoch schon abgeschlossen war". Die Aufzählung der Gottheiten an verschiedenen Stellen in den Götterlisten, ebenso wie ihre Einbettung in unterschiedliche Beziehungen ist für ihre Trennung eigentlich kein Indiz. Lexikalische Listen führen häufig verschiedene Traditionen nebeneinander an und/oder verweben nur Teile miteinander. Zu Gula s. R. Frankena, "Gula", *RLA* 3, S. 695–97, zu Ninisina s. D. O. Edzard, "Nin-isina", *RLA* 9, S. 387 f.

In Mesopotamien spielte die Heilgöttin als Ärztin im konkreten medizinischen Heilungsprozess eine große Rolle, worauf schon ihr Titel *azugallatu* "große Ärztin" verweist.[23] Die Göttin trägt Kräuter, legt Verbände an und heilt auch die blutigen und eitrigen Wunden.[24] Die Erwähnung des Skalpells der Gula (*karṣillu*/*karzillu*, *naglabu*), das sie sorgfältig schärft,[25] gibt Grund zur Annahme, daß es in der Tat zu ihren Aufgaben gehörte, an Kranken Operationen auszuführen. Sie handelt auch als Hebamme.[26] Ihr "Sohn" und Helfer ist Damu,[27] dessen Name assoziativ zu *damu* "Blut" gebildet sein könnte.[28]

Ob allerdings konkrete Heilprozeduren in den Tempeln der Heilgöttinnen, z. B. im Tempel in Isin, ausgeführt wurden, ist bisher ungeklärt. Ex voto, deren Stiftung man als Dank (oder Bitte) des Gesundeten (oder Verletzten) stellvertretend für das erkrankte Körperteil erwarten würde, scheinen nicht bezeugt zu sein, denn im Tempelbereich der Göttin in Isin wurden keine Nachbildungen von Gliedmaßen gefunden,[29] wobei sich aber diese Fragestellung den Ausgräbern vermutlich nicht stellte. Bei chirurgischen Eingriffen und Kräuterbehandlungen ist daher bisher nicht auszumachen, wo welches Kultpersonal die Hantierungen in ihrem Namen konkret vornahm. Vielleicht hantierten auch an den Orten ihrer Heilkulte die *asû* – oder aber diese gelehrten Ärzte waren nur im Profanen für konkrete medizinische Verrichtungen zuständig, während im Kultverfahren nur Priester agierten.

---

[23] *CAD* A/2 s.v. Der *asû* war nach CH § 215 an chirurgischen Operationen beteiligt.

[24] W. H. Ph. Römer, *Hymnen und Klagelieder in sumerischer Sprache*, AOAT 276 (Münster, 2001), S. 111, Z. 17–23; W. G. Lambert, "The Gula Hymn of Bulluṭsa-rabi", *Or.*, n.s., 36 (1967) S. 120f., Z. 80–85.

[25] Römer, *Hymnen*, S. 111, Z. 11.

[26] Ibid., S. 113//118, Z. B 12–B 17 (und Textvarianten). Auffallend sind die Terrakottafiguren aus dem Tempelareal der Gula in Isin, die Gebärende darzustellen scheinen, s. B. Hrouda, Hrsg., *Isin, Išān Baḫrīyāt IV. Die Ergebnisse der Ausgrabungen 1986–1989*, Bayerische Akademie der Wissenschaften, phil.-hist. Kl., Abhandlungen, n. F., Heft 105 (München, 1992), S. 51f., Taf. 40–41. Sie wurden allerdings in der Ninurta-Cella gefunden.

[27] Zu Damu s. M. M. Fritz, *'... und weinten um Tammuz'. Die Götter Dumuzi-Ama'uschumgal'anna und Damu*, AOAT 307 (Münster, 2003), S. 177–94 und 249–68.

[28] Zur Deutung des Elements *damu* "Blut" und in übertragener Bedeutung in Ebla "Sippe" vgl. die Quellenangaben bei Fritz, *Die Götter*, S. 213f. Als Helfer der Heilgöttin scheint mir die wörtliche Bedeutung "Blut" für den Botengott der Heilgöttin wahrscheinlicher. Der Gott Damu ist erst ab der altakkadischen Zeit als Namenselement bezeugt; Belege enden in der Kassitenzeit (ibid., S. 220 mit Anm. 836). Identität zwischen Damu und Dumuzi ist m. E. nicht anzunehmen, wie auch ibid., S. 249–68 vermutet. Die phonetische oder philologische Umdeutung von Dumu-zi zu Damu (oder schon von Dumu zu Damu) kann ich nicht nachvollziehen. Dennoch kann eine semantische Nähe zwischen den Göttern bestehen, die sich über ihre Beziehungen zu den Heilgöttinnen einerseits (Damu) und Ištar andererseits (Dumuzi) erklären läßt, da beide Göttinnen in funktionaler Verbindung mit der Unterwelt stehen.

[29] Hrouda, Hrsg., *Isin, Išān Baḫrīyāt I*, S. 39ff. und Taf. 8–9. Die Fragmente der Füße und Beine werden als Teile von Stelen gedeutet. In der Tat fällt auf, daß nur diese Körperteile vorzukommen scheinen, aber z. B. keine Arme oder Hände.

Ein weiterer Titel der Göttin ist šim-mu$_2$/*āšiptu* "Beschwörungspriesterin".[30] Für die Heilgottheiten gehörte beides, Beschwörungen wie konkrete medizinische Versorgung, zweifellos immer zum Heilungsprozess, selbst wenn *asû* und *āšipu* eine andere Ausbildung durchlaufen, wie I. Finkel an unterschiedlichen Textgenres belegen will.[31] M. Geller wies jedoch zurecht darauf hin,[32] daß die Grenze zwischen Magie und Medizin zumindest immer dann aufgehoben war, wenn man sich den Verursacher und den Ablauf der Krankheit nicht erklären konnte. Das ist z. B. der Fall bei Epilepsie, der Toxoplasmose oder gar Tollwut, die erst Monate nach dem Biß ausbrechen kann.

Die Aufgaben der Heilgöttin zeigen, daß zwischen dem praktischen Anrühren und Verabreichen von Salben und Verbänden, den Verrichtungen am Körper des Patienten und dem Beschwören der unheilvollen Kräfte nicht zu trennen ist.

Der Hund wird in der Rolle als "Hund der/für Gula" sicherlich als positives Element wahrgenommen, das beiden dient, Göttin wie Mensch. Die positive Assoziation baut wahrscheinlich auf der Analogie: "Hund = Attribut-Tier der Heilgöttin" auf, ohne dem Tier selbst eigenständige Mächte zuzuschreiben. Diese Wahrnehmung dürfte Hintergrund für eine ganze Reihe von Hund-und-Mensch- oder Nur-Hund-Abbildungen sein, die in Isin gefunden wurden.[33] Vermutlich als Geschenk an die Göttin sollen sie die Göttin, der sie durch hündisches Gehabe, Schwanzwedeln und Zähneblecken dienen, an ihre Schenker erinnern. Dieses Ziel jedenfalls wird in dem sumerischen Text "A Dog for Nintinuga" formuliert, den ich als Weihgabe interpretiere.[34]

---

[30] Lambert, "Gula Hymn", S. 128 f., Z. 183.

[31] I. L. Finkel, "On Late Babylonian Medical Training", in *Lambert AV*, S. 146; auch J. A. Scurlock, "Was There a 'Love-hungry' Entu-Priestess Named Eṭirtum?", *AfO* 36–37 (1989–90): 69–79.

[32] M. J. Geller, "West Meets East: Early Greek and Babylonian Diagnosis", *AfO* 48–49 (2001–2002): 58–75.

[33] M. Haussperger, B. Hrouda und E. Strommenger, "Gula-Tempel 1975–1978 (4.–6. Kampagne)", in B. Hrouda, Hrsg., *Isin, Išān Baḫrīyāṭ II. Die Ergebnisse der Ausgrabungen 1975–1978*, Bayerische Akademie der Wissenschaften, phil.-hist. Kl., Abhandlungen, n. F., Heft 87 (München, 1981), S. 18 f., zum Hortfund von Hundeterrakotten im Gula-Tempel. Hund-und-Mensch-Darstellungen s. bei Hrouda, Hrsg., *Isin, Išān Baḫrīyāṭ I*, Taf. 12.25; einen Hund mit Leine(?) s. bei idem, *Isin, Išān Baḫrīyāṭ III. Die Ergebnisse der Ausgrabungen 1983–1984*, Bayerische Akademie der Wissenschaften, phil.-hist. Kl., Abhandlungen, n. F., Heft 94 (München, 1987), Taf. 21 [den Hund IB 1428 bezeichnet A. Spycket, ibid., S. 55, als "le dieu de Gula"]; zu Hundeterrakotten und Hundeamuletten s. Hrouda, Hrsg., *Isin, Išān Baḫrīyāṭ II*, Taf. 27.

[34] Ich danke J. Black und G. Cunningham, die mich auf diesen Text hinwiesen: [1]lugal-murub$_4$-e dumu zu-zu um-mi-ia nibru^{ki}-ke$_4$ [2]tu$_6$-ni-lu$_2$-sag$_9$ ur kig$_2$-gi$_4$-a-ka-ni ^{d}nin-tin-ug$_5$-ga-ra mu-na-an-dim$_2$ [3]nam-bi-še$_3$ ur-e nin-a-ni-ir kun mu-na-ab-gun$_3$-gun$_3$ zu$_2$ mu-na-ab-⸢ra?-ah?⸣ … [10]nin-g̃u$_{10}$ mu-un-dim$_2$-en-na [11]tu$_6$-ni-lu$_2$-sag$_9$ mu-še$_3$ mu-un-sa$_4$ [12][xx]an-sag$_9$-ga mu-še$_3$ mu-sa$_4$ [13][x]-ga-DI zi-pa-ag̃$_2$ u$_3$-mu-ni [xx] a$_2$-⸢sag$_3$⸣ zi ba-an-⸢da⸣-[x]: "Lugalmurube, Sohn des Zuzu, Gelehrter von Nippur, hat für die Göttin Nintinugga den Botenhund Tuni-lu-sag angefertigt. Das geschieht, damit der Hund seinen Schwanz wedelt oder seine Zähne bleckt für seine Herrin …!" (Es folgen lobende Epitheta der Nintinugga, Z. 4–9.) "Meine Herrin, ich habe ihn (= den Hund) angefertigt und mit dem Namen Tuni-lu-sag benannt … Er wird … durch die Kehle? und der Asag-Dämon wird sich beruhigen …", s. ECTSL composite: c.5.7.2. und translation: t.5.7.2 "A Dog for Nintinuga" mit weiteren Literaturangaben (http://etcsl.orinst.ox.ac.uk/cgi-bin/etcsl.cgi?=c.5.7.2).

Weihgaben dieser Art sind "Stellvertretergaben".[35] Mit ihnen soll einerseits die Aufmerksamkeit der Göttin auf den gefährdeten Spender gelenkt und andererseits das Böse gebannt werden. Es liegt nahe anzunehmen, daß die Hunde im "Hundefriedhof" in Isin semantisch in die gleiche Kategorie gehören und wie Stellvertreter-"Figuren" für Menschen, die durch Krankheit befallen oder in Todesnähe geraten sind, behandelt werden – mit allen Konsequenzen für ihre Gesundheit und ihr Leben.

Mehrfach, z. B. von I. Fuhr,[36] H. Avalos[37] und D. O. Edzard,[38] wurde die Hypothese geäußert, der Hund sei wegen seines "heilenden Speichels" in konkreter Therapie eingesetzt worden und gehöre deshalb attributiv zur Heilgöttin. Es fällt schwer zu glauben, daß der Speichel des Hundes als medizinisch wertvoll angesehen war, weil der Hund in der Regel als unrein galt.[39] Auch kenne ich keinen Beleg für die heilende Wirkung des Hundespeichels, sondern nur Gegenargumente, die sich in Beschwörungen gegen seinen Biß und seinen Speichel äußern. Der Speichel wird als "sein Samen" bezeichnet, der sich unkontrolliert vermehrt. War dieses der Fall, dann wünschte man den sofortigen Tod des Tieres, um in sympathetischer Magie das Unheil mit dem Tier zu begraben und den Menschen zu retten.

Gegen diesen kranken oder doch zumindest als gefährlich eingestuften Hund richtet sich die Beschwörung AUAM 73 2416[40]:

3	*ka-al-bu-um a-wi-lam iš-šu-uk*	Ein Hund biß einen Mann!
4	*a-nu-um-ma a-na ša-ri-im*	Nunmehr sagt zum wehenden
5	*a-li-ki-im qí-bi-a-ma*	Wind:
6	*ni-ši-ik ka-al-bi-im*	"Der Biß des Hundes
7	*me-ra-né-e a-i-ib-ni*	soll nicht junge Hunde erschaffen!"
8	*šu-ri-ba ka-al-ba-am*	Steckt den Hund ins Gefängnis!
9	*a-na ṣí-bi-it-ti-im*	

[35] Dazu könnten die folgenden Gegenstände gezählt werden, die über einer Rampe und seitlich davon gefunden wurden: Darstellungen von Hunden auf Bronzeplättchen mit Löchern zum Aufhängen, die Bronzestatue eines knieenden Beters mit Hund, das Fragment eines Tonhundes mit einem Gebet an Gula und ein goldenes Amulett in Gestalt eines sitzenden Hundes. Die Rampe wird in das ausgehende 2. Jt. vor Chr., in die Zeit des mittelbabylonischen Herrschers Adad-apla-iddina (1068–1047) datiert, s. Hrouda, Hrsg., *Isin, Išān Baḥrīyāt I*, S. 17–20.

[36] I. Fuhr, ibid., S. 135–46.

[37] H. Avalos, *Illness and Health Care in the Ancient Near East: The Role of the Temple in Greece, Mesopotamia, and Israel*, HSM 54 (Atlanta, 1995), S. 60f.

[38] Edzard, "Nin-isina", S. 388.

[39] Belege bei Groneberg, "Tiere als Symbole", S. 302. In vielen Kulturen Asiens und Indiens meidet man in der Regel den engen Kontakt mit diesen Tieren, die den Kot und das Aas fressen. Allerdings ist es andererseits auch nicht zu verstehen, warum das Haar eines schwarzen Hundes, das in Verbindung mit anderen ekelerregenden Ingredienzien als Medizin zum Einreiben oder Schlucken verwendet wurde, nicht durch empirische Fakten als Behandlungsfehler erkannt und verbannt wurde, s. z. B. das Rezept bei Finkel, "Medical Training", S. 172 und öfter; zu anderen Quellen über die Verwendung von Hundeingredienzien s. *CAD* K s.v. *kalbu*, Bed. 1g.

[40] S. die ausführliche Bearbeitung bei Sigrist, "On the Bite of a Dog", S. 85–88.

10	*ka-al-bu-um li-mu-ut-ma*	Der Hund soll sterben, und
11	*a-wi-lum li-ib-lu-uṭ* «*ma*»	der Mensch soll leben!

In erster Instanz soll der Wind den Fluch hinwegtragen und damit die Katharsis bewirken, in zweiter Instanz ist das Einsperren und sogar der Tod des Hundes nötig, um den Menschen gesunden zu lassen. Damit wird ein Ersatzritual impliziert, nicht aber die Anwendung beschrieben oder angeordnet. Die Frage bleibt stehen, ob die rituelle Sequenz der verbalen Beschwörung ausreichte, das Böse hinwegtragen zu lassen, oder ob die Tötung des Hundes so obligatorisch war, daß sie nicht einmal beschrieben wurde.

Eine ähnliche Aussage enthält die Beschwörung LB 2001[41]:

5	*i-na ši-in-ni-šu*	in seinen Zähnen
6	*e-hi-il ni-il-šu*	hängt sein Samen
7	*a-šar iš-šu-ku*	wo er biß,
8	*ma-ra-šu*	ließ er seinen Sohn
9	*i-zi-ib*	zurück!

Im altbabylonischen Brief AbB 11 57 bemühte man sich, den Biß eines Hundes durch Ölverbände zu heilen.[42] Hier zeigt sich eine interessante Differenzierung im Umgang mit dem Hund. Man behandelte den Hundebiß ganz normal und ohne Panik, gegen den kranken oder vernachlässigten Hund ging man jedoch mit einer Beschwörung vor.[43] Durch den krankmachenden Biß ist der Hund ebenso wie Skorpion und Schlange anderen Tieren in negativer Weise überlegen. Es fällt auch auf, daß von den Sekreten des Hundes selbst das Übel ausgeht und nicht von anonymen Dämonen oder einer "Hand" einer "Gottheit". Dadurch erweckt der Hund den Eindruck eines an sich potentiell sehr negativen Elements. Die Charakterisierung des verunreinigten Speichels dieses Hundes als "sein Sohn" oder "sein Junges" stilisiert diese Emanationen wiederum wie belebte Elemente.

In einigen Beschwörungsritualen kommt dem Hund eine tragende Rolle als Medium bei der Bannung und Vernichtung des Bösen zu. Diese Rituale sind im Umfeld des "Liebeszaubers" einzuordnen und wollen entweder das Einwirken eines unheilvollen Anti-Liebes-Zaubers abwehren oder zur Liebe veranlassen.

"Liebeszauber"-Texte stellte der Jubilar kurz im *Reallexikon der Assyriologie* vor.[44]Als deren Ziel gab er an: "to gain the affection of a woman or to gain her aquiescence in lovemaking"[45] und trennte sie deshalb von den šà-zi-ga-(Potenz-)Beschwörungen der jüngeren Zeit, die ausschließlich der Erweckung oder Versicherung der männlichen Potenz gewidmet seien.[46] Die Zielrichtung der

[41] de Liagre Böhl, "Zwei altbabylonische Beschwörungstexte", S. 82 (s. auch Whiting, "Old Babylonian Incantation", S. 182).

[42] Vgl. schon Sigrist, "On the Bite of a Dog", S. 85, Anm. 3.

[43] Groneberg, "Tiere als Symbole", S. 303.

[44] R. D. Biggs, "Liebeszauber", *RLA* 7, S. 17 f.

[45] Ibid., S. 17, linke Sp., Ende 1. Abschnitt.

[46] Idem, *Šaziga*.

Liebeszaubertexte ist allerdings bei den älteren Beschwörungen, die er aus der altakkadischen,[47] altassyrischen und altbabylonischen[48] Zeit anführt, schwierig zu erschließen. Die jüngeren Liebeszaubertexte scheinen Beschwörungsrituale zum Erlangen der Zuneigung (?) einer Frau zu sein.[49]

G. Cunningham verbuchte unter den "love related incantations" einige der Liebeszaubertexte, die schon Biggs anführte,[50] und verwies zusätzlich auf die Beschwörung CT 58 10 und die verschiedenen Beschwörungssequenzen der Isin-Liebesbeschwörung, Wilcke, "Liebesbeschwörungen", S. 198–209.[51]

Diese altbabylonische Liebesbeschwörung ist in vielerlei Hinsicht bemerkenswert. Sie enthält nicht das sonst übliche Musterritual, das als Vorlage für einen Beschwörungspriester gelten dürfte, sondern ein ganz konkretes Ritual, das mit namentlich genannten Teilnehmern[52] stattgefunden hat und schriftlich fixiert wurde. Unklar bleibt, ob die Verschriftung einer Beschwörung auch sonst häufiger üblich war, um das magische Verfahren noch zu intensivieren, oder ob es sich um einen Ausnahmeakt handelte,

---

[47] MAD 5 8, s. zuletzt Groneberg, "Die Liebesbeschwörung MAD V 8 und ihr literarischer Kontext", *RA* 95 (2001): 97–113 mit weiterführender Literatur.

[48] YOS 11 87 evoziert ebenso wie MAD 5 8 das *irēmu* der Ištar und ist wie dieser Text auch wohl in der Tat eine Liebesbeschwörung, auch wenn letztlich unklar bleibt, für wen oder gegen wen sich die Beschwörung tatsächlich wendet, ebenso die Beschwörung A. Falkenstein, "Sumerische religiöse Texte", *ZA* 56 (1964): 113–29. Alle drei sind literarische Kunstwerke und bedürfen weiterer formaler Untersuchungen. Davon zu trennen ist VAS 17 23(!), s. Farber, "Beschwörungsliteratur", S. 56, C 25, das m. E. in das Umfeld der *Ardat-Lilî/Lamaštu*-Beschwörungen gehören könnte. — Zu TIM 9 73 s. J. Cooper, "Magic and M(is)use: Poetic Promiscuity", in H. L. J. Vanstiphout und M. E. Vogelzang, Hrsg., *Mesopotamian Poetic Language: Sumerian and Akkadian* (Groningen, 1996), S. 50: Beschwörungen vom Typ "Selbstbefruchtung"; die Vorderseite erwähnt einen Hund und ^{d}Ea. — Zu dem einzigen von Biggs genannten "old Ass. text" vgl. oben S. 92 mit Anm. 14; diese Beschwörung wendet sich gegen den schwarzen Hund.

[49] Zu den Texten KAR 61 und 69 s. die Bearbeitung bei Biggs, *Šaziga*, S. 70–78 und idem, "Liebeszauber", S. 17, lk. Spalte 1. Absatz; sie gehören nach Biggs zu einem Genre *sinništu ana alāku* "for a woman to come (to a man)" und sind Beschwörungen, die auf eine Frau einwirken sollen. Der Text V. Scheil, "Catalogue de la Collection Eugène Tisserant", *RA* 18 (1921) S. 21 ff. Nr. 17 mit Duplikat STT 257 (Biggs, "Liebeszauber", S. 17, lk. Spalte unten) weicht von den anderen spätbabylonischen "Liebesbeschwörungen" ab, da er die Liebe eines erzürnten Mannes beschwört (Z. 20), die Frau will geliebt werden (Z. 6). Alle Liebesbeschwörungen scheinen inhaltlich und formal so unterschiedlich zu sein, daß sie genauer in Hinblick auf ihre Zielrichtung untersucht werden sollten.

[50] Cunningham, *"Deliver Me from Evil"*, S. 111 zu Nr. 150 (= Falkenstein, "Sumerische religiöse Texte", 113 ff.) und Nr. 405 (= YOS 11 87).

[51] Cunningham, ibid. zu Nr. 312 (CT 58 10; vgl. dazu B. Alster im Vorwort zu CT 58, S. 11). Nr. 137, 138, 139, 315, 316, 317 und 319 sind Isin-Liebesbeschwörungen, die mit Ausnahme des sumerischen Beginns (Z. 1–7 = Nr. 137) alle in akkadischer Sprache gehalten sind (contra Cunningham, a. a. O.).

[52] Z. 30: Herr Erra-bānī in der "Beschwörung des Liebens": Er ist wohl das Objekt der ganzen Beschwörung, der verhexte Mann, auf den ein Gegenzauber einwirken soll, s. auch Z. 117 und 120. Z. 61: "Piṭirtum" ist m. W. nicht als Eigenname bezeugt und Scurlock, "'Love-hungry' Entu-Priestess", S. 108, hat sicherlich recht, wenn sie diesen Terminus als "Löseakt" oder ähnlich versteht. Z. 100 wird zusätzlich jemand namens Iddin-Damu in der "Beschwörung des/eines Salzklumpens" genannt.

der diesen einen verhandelten Fall besonders wirkungsmächtig absichern wollte. Die Beschwörungstafel mit sehr unterschiedlich titulierten Beschwörungsteilen,[53] die aber dennoch nach meiner Meinung zu einem einzigen Beschwörungsvorgang gehören,[54] wurde anschließend zerbrochen und in einem verschlossenen Topf begraben. Das geschah vermutlich, um die Tafel unschädlich zu machen, damit kein dem magischen Akt widerläufiger Gegenzauber ausgeführt werden konnte.

Diesem Liebeszaubertext ist es zu verdanken, daß bisher nur einzeln tradierte Beschwörungssequenzen im Zusammenhang gesehen werden können.

Die Isin-Beschwörung verzeichnet als zweite Beschwörungssequenz nach einer mir weitgehend unverständlichen Passage auf Sumerisch (Z. 1–8) eine Hundebeschwörung, in der eine mit Urin besudelte Hundescham und ein mit Speichel bedecktes Hundemaul eine männliche Person/Sache binden. Diese Beschwörungssequenz tritt auch schon in der altakkadischen Liebesbeschwörung MAD 5 8: 12–16 (Abschnitt C) auf. In der Isin-Beschwörung richtet sich dieser Abschnitt gegen die *nakratum* "Feindin", s. Wilcke, "Liebesbeschwörungen", S. 198:

9 *e-el-li-a-at ka-al-bi-im ṣú-mi-im*? *em-ṣú-tim*
10 *me-hi-iṣ pa-ni-in*! *ši-pi-ir tu-ú*[*r*?]*-ti i-ni-im*
11 *am-ta-ha-aṣ mu-úh-ha-ka uš-ta-an-ni ṭe-e-em-ka*
12 *šu-uk-nam ṭe-e-em-ka a-na ṭe-e-mi-ja*
13 *šu-uk-nam mi-li-ik-ka a-na mi-il-ki-ja*
14 *a-ka-al-la-ka ki-ma* ^{d}*Ištár ik-lu-ú* ^{d}DUMU-ZI

[53] Beschwörungsuntertitel sind: Für Abschnitt Z. 1–8: KA-inim-ma-ki-ág-gá-kam "Beschwörung des Liebens" = Liebesbeschwörung?, ebenso für Abschnitt 9(?)–36; Abschnitt Z. 38–40: KA-inim-ma *ša* ki-ág-gá-kam "Beschwörung der/des des Liebens" (?); Abschnitt 42–51: KA-inim-ma-ki-ág-gá-kam "Beschwörung des Liebens"; Abschnitt 53–60: KA-inim-ma *piṭirtum* "Beschwörung: *piṭirtum*-(Akt?)"; Abschnitt 62–71: KA-ini[m-ma-ki-ág-g]á-[kam] "Beschwörung des Liebens". Es folgen 3 Beschwörungen des Typs "*uzzum*" in Z. 78–98, der dazugehörige Beschwörunguntertitel ist KA-inim-ma lag-mun-kam "Beschwörung des/eines Salzklumpens", ebenso für Z. 100–102. Der letzte Beschwörungstitel am linken unteren Rand (nach der Zeilenzahl "120" und dem Titel an-mul ki-mul-mul / an-mul an-mul-mul) lautet KA-inim-ma-šika-e-sír-ka-límmu "Beschwörung: Scherbe von der Straßenkreuzung".

[54] Scurlock, "'Love-hungry' Entu-Priestess", S. 109 rechts unten, ist der Ansicht, daß es sich um eine Sammlung von verwandten Beschwörungen handelt, die alle ökonomische Kontrolle über ein Gegenüber zu erlangen suchen. Gegen den Sammlungscharakter spricht der Akt der Zerstörung und Begrabung der Tafel und die Nennung konkreter Personen. Aufgrund der hohen Stellung der *ēntu*-Priesterin halte ich es für wenig wahrscheinlich, daß sie aktiv an diesem Ritual als Ausführende oder als Auftraggeberin beteiligt ist, ein Sachverhalt, auf den auch schon Scurlock (ibid., S. 110) hinwies. Ihr Vergleich (ibid., S. 108 f.) des Abschnitts der Isin-Beschwörung, Z. 53–60 (Unterschrift: *pi-ṭi-ir-tum*) mit den KA-inim-ma šu-du$_8$-a-kam-Beschwörungen aus dem 1. Jahrtausend dürfte den Sinn dieses Abschnitts, das Erlangen der Kontrolle (über Hexer und Hexerinnen?) treffen. Das würde auch die Wechselrede an Mann und Frau erklären, nicht aber den sehr individuellen Wortlaut dieses Beschwörungsteils, der die *aššatu* "Ehefrau" als Verursacherin der Schwierigkeiten des Klienten und damit Veranlasserin der Verhexung hinstellt.

15 *Ze-e-ra-aš ú-ka-as-sú-ú ša-a-ti-ša*
16 *uk-ta-as-sí-i-ka i-na* KA*-ja ša ša-ra-a-tim*
17 *i-na ú-ri-ja ša ši-i-na-tim*
18 *i-na* KA*-ja ša ru-ha-tim*
19 *i-na ú-ri-ja ša ši-i-na-tim*
20 *a i-li-ik na-ak-ra-tum i-na ṣe-ri-i-ka*
21 *ra-bi-iṣ ka-al-bu-um ra-bi-iṣ ša-hi-ú-um*
22 *at-ta ri-ta-bi-iṣ i-na hal-li-ja*

9 Speichel des Hundes, des Durstes (?), des Hungers!
10 Mit der Niederlage (?), dem Werk des Augenwendens (?)
11 habe ich deinen Schädel geschlagen und deinen Verstand verwirrt!
12 Richte deine Entscheidung nach meiner Entscheidung,
13 Folge meinem Rat!
14 Ich werde dich halten wie Ištar Dumuzi gehalten hat,
15 (wie) Zeraš (die Biergottheit) ihren Trinker gebunden hat!
16 Ich habe Dich gebunden mit meinem Haar-Mund
17 mit meiner Urin-Scham
18 mit meinem Speichel-Mund
19 mit meiner Urin-Scham!
20 die *Feindin* soll nicht zu Dir gehen!
21 Hingelagert ist der Rüde, gelagert ist der Eber:
22 Du lagere dich (auch) ständig auf meine Oberschenkel!

Die Wirkung dieser Beschwörung ist auf eine männliche Person gerichtet, wie die meisten Teile der Isin-Beschwörung. Angeredet wird wohl ein männliches Substitut,[55] das in der Tiervagina magisch gebannt werden soll. Dadurch steht es in den folgenden Prozeduren (stellvertretend für den zu Beschwörenden) zur Verfügung und dieser ist gleichzeitig gebannt. Es redet die/der Ausführende der Beschwörung in den Zeilen 16–19 für das Medium "Hund".

[55] Der Fisch könnte das Substitut sein. Die erste Beschwörungssequenz wird begleitet von der rituellen Handlung (Z. 23): *ša ina muḫḫi nūnim warqim ana šamnim inandi ippaššaš*: "Was sich auf(?)/im Schädel(?) dem/des grünen Fisches befindet, wirft sie/er ins Öl und salbt sich (damit)". Dann spricht sie/er eine weitere Beschwörung (Z. 24–28) mit einem weiteren Salbungsvorgang, der aber nicht ganz erhalten ist (Z. 29). Sehr schwierig ist die Erwähnung des Iddin-Damu im Beschwörungsabschnitt Z. 100–107, für die ich nur dann eine Erklärung habe, wenn sie sich auf den Fisch bezieht. Er wird mit einem dummen ("mit umwickelten Ohren": kontrastiv zu dem Begriff für klug = "offene Ohren" zu deuten) Fisch verglichen, der schon zu Anfang als Teil des manuellen Rituals behandelt wird. Wird vermutet, daß ein realer Iddin-Damu schon einen Zauber auslöste und ist dieses Ritual schon der Gegenzauber dagegen?

Beschwörungen dieser Art sind entweder exorzistisch oder bezwecken eine Attraktion, die Erzwingung der Zuneigung. Sie dienen der Abwendung des Liebeszaubers einer anderen Person oder der Attraktion eines geliebten Menschen. J. A. Scurlock[56] und J. Cooper[57] erkannten die enge Beziehung der Hundebeschwörungen zu den Beschwörungen gegen *uzzum* "rage" und verwiesen beide auf einen dritten Beschwörungstyp, einen sogenanten "Selbstbefruchtungstyp". Cooper führte aus, daß dieser einen Fluch provoziere und dadurch den eigenen Sprecher – in Abkapselung gegen das äußere Böse – beschützen solle.

Beide, sowohl die *uzzum*-Beschwörungen als auch der "Selbstbefruchtungstyp", kommen in der Isin-Beschwörung vor. Die Passage über die Selbstbefruchtung findet sich in den letzten Zeilen von Wilcke, "Liebesbeschwörungen", S. 198 f.:112–16, und schließt damit den Beschwörungsteil ab:

112 *ù šu*$^{?}$*-mu-um i-na-ši pa-la ra-ma-ni-šu*
113 *ù al-pu-um i-na-ši pa-la ra-ma-ni-šu*
114 ⌈*ki*⌉*-ma na-ru-um ir-hu-ú ki-ib-ri-i-ša*
115 [*a*]*-ra-ah-hi ra-ma-ni-ma*
116 *a-ra-ah-hi pa-ag-ri*

112 Aber der Lauch hebt für sich selbst hoch den Stengel!
113 Und das Rind hebt für sich selbst hoch die Stange!
114 Wie der Fluß seine Ufer befruchtete,
115 So werde ich mich selbst befruchten,
116 werde ich meinen Körper befruchten!

Die Beschwörung von *uzzum* ist in mindestens drei Beschwörungssequenzen in den Zeilen 78–84, 85–94, 95–98 bezeugt.[58]

95 *uz-zu-um* [?] *uz-zu-um*
96 *ki-ma as-*[*k*]*u-u*[*p-p*]*a-t*[*i*]*m lu-ka-bi-is-k*[*a*]
97 *ki-ma qá-aq-*⌈*qá-ri-i*⌉*m lu-te-et-ti-iq-ka*
98 *še-hi-iṭ* [*uz-*]*zu-um ša* ^{d}*Na-na-a*

[56] Scurlock, "'Love-hungry' Entu-Priestess", S. 109 ff.

[57] Cooper, "Magic and M(is)use", S. 47 ff.

[58] Die drei Beschwörungen enden mit: *šehiṭ uzzum ša* ^{d}*Nanāya* "springe an, Raserei der Nanāya". Sie enthalten jeweils Überschreitungsriten, die sich auch in den Hundebeschwörungen aus Ešnunna, Ur und Tell Harmal finden. So findet sich das Motiv "Überschreiten der Brücke" in der Isin-Beschwörung, Z. 92 und in UET 6/2 399:13 f., und ebenso das Überschreiten des Tigris in der Isin-Beschwörung, Z. 93 und in UET 6/2 399:15 f.; das "Überschreiten der Schwelle" in der Isin-Beschwörung, Z. 96, in Whiting, "Old Babylonian Incantation", S. 180 (TA 1930-T117): 1, sowie in TIM 9 72: 8 f.

Andere parallele Zeilen haben Tiervergleiche: Mit Z. 82 vgl. Whiting, "Old Babylonian Incantation", S. 180: 4′f.; mit Z. 83 vgl. Whiting, "Old Babylonian Incantation", S. 181, Z. 6′f.; mit Z. 86–89 vgl. TIM 9 72:1–7 und UET 6/2 399:1–7.

95 Raserei, Raserei!
96 wie eine Schwelle will ich dich niedertreten,
97 wie einen Erdboden will ich dich immer wieder überschreiten!
98 Springe an, Raserei der Nanāya!

Als Unterschrift wird verbucht (vermutlich die Nennung einer *materia magica*):

99 KA-inim-ma-lag-mun-kam
99 Beschwörung (mithilfe/des) Salzklumpens.

Hier wird *uzzum* als Raserei (der Liebesgöttin) Nanāya bezeichnet.[59] Gemeint ist wörtlich die "rage", vielleicht nur die "(sexuelle) Erregung" oder aber auch ein "Vor-Liebe-in-Raserei-Versetzen", das auf den Verursacher des Übels gerichtet sein soll. Aus anderen *uzzum*-Beschwörungen geht hervor, daß *uzzum* etwas Negatives ist, das den Kontrahenten entmachtet. Das zeigen Überschreitungsriten, mit denen man die (Liebes-)Kraft des Gegners bezwingt, wobei gemeint ist, daß der Gegner in konkretem oder übertragenem Sinn impotent werden soll. Die *uzzum*-Beschwörung TIM 9 72 macht das in den Zeilen 15–18 deutlich:

15 *ki-ma šu-mu-nim*
16 *lu-ne-ʾ ki-bi-ís-ka*
17 *lu-še-ṣí i-ša-tam*
18 *ša li-ib-bi-ka*

15 Ebenso wie das 'Halteseil'
16 will ich deinen Schritt verändern,
17 ich will herausgehen lassen das Feuer,
18 das, was in deinem Inneren (haust)![60]

Nutznießerin der Isin-Beschwörung ist ein anonymes "Ich". Die Liebesbeschwörung der Zeilen 42–46 richtet sich an eine männliche Person und ist so individuell gestaltet, daß sie im Wortlaut nach meinem Wissen ohne Parallelen ist:

42 *na-ra-mu-um na-ra-mu-um*
43 *ša iš-ku-nu-ka é-a ù* ^{d}EN-LÍL
44 *ki-ma* ^{d}*Ištár i-na pa-ra-ak-ki-im wa-aš-ba-at*
45 *ki-ma* ^{d}*Na-na-a i-na šu-tu-mi-im wa-aš-ba-at*
46 *a-la-mi-ka e-né-e-tum ma-aq-li-a-am e-ra-am-ma*
47 *aš-ša-a-tum mu-te-ši-na i-ze-er-ra*

[59] Damit kann *uzzum* schwerlich die Tollwut meinen, wie ich "Tiere als Symbole", S. 302 f., annahm.

[60] Whiting, "Old Babylonian Incantation", S. 181.

48 *bu-ut-qá-am ap-pa-ša ša-qá-a-am*
49 *šu-uk-na-am ap-pa-ša ša-pa-al še-pí-ja*
50 *ki-ma ra-am-ša iš-qù-ú e-li-ja*
51 *ra-mi li-iš-qá-a-am e-li ra-am-ša*

42 Oh Geliebter, Geliebter!
43 Dich, den Ea und Enlil einsetzten,[61]
44 so wie Ištar im Heiligtum wohnt,
45 (und) wie Nanāya im Schatzhaus wohnt,
46 dich werde ich einkreisen! Die *ēntum*-Priesterinnen lieben *Maqlû*!
47 Die Ehefrauen hassen ihre Ehemänner!
48 Schneide ihre (Sg.) erhabene Nase ab!
49 Setze ihre (Sg.) Nase unter meinen Fuß!
50 Wie sich ihre (Sg.) Liebe über mich erhob,
51 So soll sich meine Liebe über ihre (Sg.) Liebe erheben!

Für den angeredeten "Geliebten" könnte die Person Errabānī stehen, der in Zeilen 117 und 120 nochmals beschworen wird:

117 *up-te-et-ti-ku-um se-bé-et ba-bi-ja* ^{I}*èr-ra-ba-ni* ...
120 *[i$^{?}$-t]a-ku-ul li-ib-bi-ka šu-ta-aq-ti-a-am i-na ṣe-ri-ja*
117 Ich öffnete dir immer meine sieben Tore, Errabani! ...
120 [Das immer wieder Ver]letztwerden deines Herzens beende in Bezug auf mich![62]

Trotz der Unklarheiten der dazwischen liegenden Zeilen geht aus dieser Bitte hervor, daß das redende "Ich" sich um Errabānī bemüht: Auch dieses sind Zeilen mit individuellen Redewendungen, die einen konkreten Sachverhalt anzusprechen scheinen.

Von der *ēntu* wird in Zeile 46 gesagt, daß sie *Maqlû* liebt. Entweder ist diese *ēntu* hier mit *Maqlû* befaßt und begleitet diese Beschwörungen – oder gibt sie selbst in Auftrag. Ob diese Aktionen in Verbindung mit einer Hohen Priesterin *ēntu* eher ungewöhnlich sind, läßt sich nicht entscheiden, weil über ihre Aufgaben ohnehin kaum etwas bekannt ist. Es könnte sich auch um ein weiteres Zitat bei der Anrufung kultischer Mächte handeln, denn die Bilder, die den Geliebten wie "Ištar im Heiligtum" und "Nanāya im Schatzhaus" festhalten wollen, sind als Stilfiguren aufzufassen, und auch die Anrufung der obersten Priesterin könnte dieser Versicherung der Hilfsmächte dienen.

---

[61] Gemeint ist, daß der Geliebte auch nach Wunsch der Götter im Herzen fest verankert ist.

[62] Was mit den "sieben Toren" gemeint ist, wird nicht näher ausgeführt. Zu der Bedeutung von *akālum* N-Stamm "to hurt" im Passiv, s. *CAD* A/1 s.v. *akālu* Bed. 12. Der hier angenommene Infinitiv Ntn **itākulum* ist allerdings bisher sonst nicht belegt.

Tatsächlich kommen die beiden zitierten Beschwörungstypen der Isin-Beschwörung, "*uzzum*" und der "Selbstbefruchtungstyp", in der Beschwörungsserie *Maqlû* vor, die erst im 1. Jt. kanonisiert wurde.[63] Sie richten sich in *Maqlû*, wie alle Beschwörungen und Handlungen, gegen Emanationen von Hexern oder Hexerinnen, womit sowohl lebende Menschen gemeint sein können, die Zauberei verwenden, als auch Dämonen und diffuse Mächte. Das Vorkommen dieser beiden für *Maqlû* typischen Beschwörungsformeln und die Erwähnung von *Maqlû* selbst weist Teile der Isin-Beschwörung als Prototyp von *Maqlû* aus, das in dieser, noch individuellen Form im Isin der altbabylonischen Zeit praktiziert worden wäre.

... und der Hund?

Die Ritualtafel von *Maqlû* gibt an, daß das Übel – die Hexe – als Figürchen aus Teig gebacken wird und schließlich einem Hund zum Fraß vorgeworfen wird, der sie endgültig entsorgen wird.[64] Der Hund als Entsorger des Übels ist, soweit ich sehen konnte, in den jüngeren Ritualen außer in *Lamaštu*-Ritualen nur noch in *Maqlû*-Ritualen üblich.[65]

Es könnte also sehr gut sein, daß lebende Hunde im Kult der Heilgöttin von Isin bei Exorzismen und Ritualen vom Typ Maqlû als endgültige Vernichter von Übel galten, mutiliert wurden und ihr Leben ließen.[66] Der Liebeszauber, der in der Isin-Beschwörung angewendet wird, versucht, das Einwirken der "Feindin" zu beenden, wie die überwiegend paradigmatischen Beschwörungsteile (Hundebeschwörung, piṭirtum, uzzum-Beschwörung und "Selbstbefruchtungstyp") deutlich machen. Sie bannen die Zauberin, trennen die Kontrahenten, machen die Übeltäter unfruchtbar und beschwören die Fähigkeit des Beschworenen, seine eigene Potenz erhalten zu können.[67] Ein klei-

[63] T. Abusch, "Maqlû", *RLA* 7, S. 346–51; Scurlock, "'Love-hungry' Entu-Priestess," erkannte schon deutliche phraseologische Parallelen zu *Maqlû*.

[64] T. Abusch, "The Socio-Religious Framework of the Babylonian Witchcraft Ceremony *Maqlû*: Some Observations on the Introductory Section of the Text, Part 1", in *Jacobsen Mem. Vol.*, S. 13–15. Auch die Hexerin kann Figurinen ihrer Kontrahenten anfertigen und sie von Hunden fressen lassen, s. W. G. Lambert, "An Incantation of the Maqlû Type", *AfO* 18 (1957–58), S. 292: 25.

[65] *Maqlû* bietet ausser der Verbrennung noch die Vernichtung durch Zerstreuen im Wind oder durch Auffressen, alles Aktionen, die Abusch zufolge dem Übel auch noch die Anwesenheit in der Unterwelt versagen wollen, s. Abusch, "Socio-Religious Framework", S. 7–8.

[66] Aus den Skelettuntersuchungen der Tiere im Hundefriedhof von Isin ging hervor, daß es sich um eine domestizierte Art von Hunden handelte. Die Knochenbefunde ergaben, daß fast alle dort begrabenen Tiere an Verletzungen litten, davon die Mehrzahl mit sofortigem tödlichem Ausgang. Auch eine Hundetotgeburt wurde beigesetzt. Auffallend bei dieser Fundlage war der Umstand, daß die Hunde zu Grabe gelegt wurden, allerdings außerhalb des unmittelbaren Tempelbereiches der Göttin. Hrouda, *Isin, Išān Baḫrīyāṭ I*, deutete den Befund als kultische Versiegelung des Heiligtums, bevor man darauf profane Gebäude errichtete. Dieser Weihvorgang mit lebenden Tieren ist allerdings sonst nicht bekannt.

[67] Diese Deutung scheint mir beim "Selbst-befruchtungstyp" angebracht zu sein, wenn man den Wortlaut wortgetreu deutet. Das impliziert die eigene Absperrung gegenüber den Zaubereien eines Anderen.

nerer Teil des Liebeszaubers beschwört direkt den Erhalt der Liebe des Beschworenen. Denn während sich die Zeilen 33–36[68] und 38–40 an eine Frau, wahrscheinlich an die Feindin, wenden, gibt es auch Ansprachen an einen Beschworenen, vielleicht schon in den Zeilen 24–28 und 30–32,[69] sicher in den Zeilen 42–51. Einerseits will man die einwirkende Hexerin (vermutlich ist die Ehefrau unter Verdacht) entmachten, andererseits versichert man sich magisch auch der Potenz des Beschworenen und seiner Liebe. Ihm soll nicht geschadet werden. Das macht die Interpretation der Beschwörungen auch so ambivalent, da Beschwörungsteile eigene Zielrichtungen enthalten,[70] die aber nicht der gesamten Zielrichtung des Rituals entsprechen. Wie bei der Interpretation von Symbolen, die nur kontextgebunden verstanden werden können, sind auch Beschwörungen in ihrer Semantik keineswegs eindimensional.

---

[68] "Deine inneren Teile sollen sich freuen, fröhlich sein sollen deine Leberteile! Ich will dick sein wie ein Rüde! Wie ein Halteseil ist es stark geschwollen für dich, verschütte es mir nicht!" – *šu-mu-un-ni-im* ist wohl Variante zu *šummannum* "Halteseil", wie schon Wilke, "Liebesbeschwörungen", S. 201 und 207, sowie Whiting, "Old Babylonian Incantation", S. 186 zu B:15, vorschlugen. *ḫu-bu-ú-ša-ki* fasse ich als ungewöhnliche Schreibung des Stativ 3.m.s. + Ventiv + Dat. 2.f.s. (*ḫubbušakki*) zu *ḫabāšum* D "hart schwellen lassen" (*AHw. ḫabāšum* I, S. 303) auf.

[69] "Es sollen deine Schenkel laufen, Erra-bānī, deine Hüften sollen sich in Bewegung setzen, (und) deine Sehnen sollen folgen", s. Wilcke, "Liebesbeschwörungen", S. 200 f.

[70] Scurlock, "'Love-hungry' Entu-Priestess", S. 111 f.

EINE VERBALFORM ZUM NACHDENKEN

Hans Hirsch, Universität Wien

Der recht dramatische Brief, den Iddin-Ištar vor Jahrhunderten, ja Jahrtausenden an Aššur-nādā geschrieben hat, ist uns seit Jahrzehnten bekannt.[1]

In diesem Beitrag möchte ich hauptsächlich über die Verbalform in der Aussage in den Zeilen 14f. sprechen: (14) *Aššur-ma ú i-il*$_5$*-kà* (15) *a-wi-lam i-tí-dí-ma*....

Die Fortsetzung dazu, die mit einer Verbalform+*ma* schließt, sei kurz erwähnt: (16) *ú* :[2] KÙ.BABBAR *a-qá-tí-a ma-qí-*/[3]*it-ma* (17) *a-dí u*$_4$*-mì-im* (18) *a-nim šu-ta-bu-a-tí*.

Dazu die Zeilen 14–18 in der Übersetzung von Larsen: "While Aššur himself and your own god have rejected the man, still silver has fallen into my hands and until this day you have been fully satisfied."

Vor gut fünfundzwanzig Jahren hat das *CAD* N/1 s.v. *nadû* v. Bed. 1c–6′, an BIN 6 39:19: DN *u* DN$_2$ *ilka li-dí-a-ni* "may Aššur and your personal god, DN$_2$, reject me", und BIN 6 97:22: cf. DN *u* DN$_2$ ... *li-dí-a-ni* diese Stelle mit "also" angeschlossen und übersetzt: "Aššur himself and your god have rejected the man."

Während man in der Übersetzung "may... reject me" nicht genau erkennen kann, wie man *li-dí-a-ni* analysiert hat, ist bei unserer Stelle klar, daß die deutliche 3. Person Sg. *i-tí-dí-ma* frei als Plural (genau genommen als Dual, den man aber nicht ausdrücken kann) übersetzt wird; das ist dem Sinn nach richtig, aber warum im Altassyrischen die 3. Sg.?

Aššur mit, sagen wir kurz, betonendem *-ma*,[4] gefolgt von der Kopula *u*: "und dein Gott ..." – dann die Verbalform.

Man soll sicherlich noch einmal darauf hinweisen, daß auch nach der Verbalform *i-tí-dí* ein *-ma* steht und die weiteren Mitteilungen wieder mit der Kopula *u* angeschlossen werden.

---

[1] Seit 1925: Sidney Smith, CCT 3 16b. Vor einiger Zeit bearbeitet von Mogens Trolle Larsen, *The Aššur-nādā Archive*, Old Assyrian Archives, 1 (Leiden, 2002), Nr. 116, S. 160ff. Zu diesem Buch und zu diesem Brief möge man auch meine Rezension in *AfO* 50 (2003/2004): 366–72, besonders 371f. einsehen.

[2] Bezeichnet den Worttrenner.

[3] Vom Ende der nächsten Zeile.

[4] Vgl. E. Cohen, "Akkadian *-ma* in Diachronic Perspective", *ZA* 90 (2000): 207–26, besonders 214–17, und E. Cohen, "Focus Marking in Old Babylonian", *WZKM* 91 (2001): 85–104, besonders 89–91.

Wir wollen ferner hier schon bemerken, daß wir in dieser in einer *t*-Form im Grundstamm formulierten Aussage gewissermaßen einen auf eine andere Person bezogenen Vollzug der vorher zitierten Selbstverfluchung ... *li-dí-a-ni* sehen können.

Kurz zu dieser Form: nach dem eben zu *i-tí-dí-ma* Gesagten soll man darin vermutlich eine 3. Sg. +-*anni* sehen, nicht etwa einen Dual +-*ni*.

Dafür spricht auch die im *CAD* als letztes altassyrisches Zitat gebrachte ganz eindeutige Stelle Kienast *ATHE* 65:29: "and note *Aššur i-ta-ad-a-ni-ma*", in der wieder eine klare 3. Sg. vorliegt, die hier auf das einzige Subjekt, Aššur, bezogen ist. Wie haben Schreiber und Leser die vorher zitierten Aussagen verstanden? Sollen wir von dieser Stelle ausgehen und annehmen, daß diese Vorstellung so stark war, daß man das am Ende stehende Verbum auf jeden Fall auf Aššur bezogen – Aššur mit *-ma* betont – und dazu angefügt hat, daß auch "dein Gott" sich dem angeschlossen hat? Oder die Verbalform auf das unmittelbar davor stehende *ilka* beziehen, eine Aussage, durch die das am Satzbeginn stehende *Aššur*(*-ma*) erklärt wird?

Der Sinn ist offensichtlich, daß beiden Göttern diese Handlung zugeschrieben wird, aber – und darauf soll man in einer Analyse schon Wert legen – eben nicht in einer Verbalform im Dual, in der beide Götter gewissermaßen gleichberechtigt enthalten sind – wie in der "*liṭṭulā*-Formel", um nur dies zu nennen.

Davor steht im *CAD* nur mehr das mit "cf." an unsere Stelle CCT 3 16b: 15 angeschlossene Zitat *JCS* 14 8 No. 4:35: *Aššur u ilka i-ta-ad-a-ni-ma* – ohne Übersetzung, wo man in der Verbalform sicherlich ebenso eine 3. Sg. sehen soll: "Aššur und dein Gott hat mich ...", also hier auf den Sprecher bezogen.

Wir sehen, daß in allen diesen sehr ernsten negativen, offensichtlich in der Religion gegründeten Aussagen, genauer, in dem Wirken der Götter in den Bereich des Menschen hinein, Verbalformen mit infigiertem *-t-* stehen.

Das *CAD* meint diese und andere solche Formen, wenn es S. 69 rechts im *heading* heißt: I, I/2, ..., während das *AHw.*, S. 705 ff., nur ein G und Gtn ... kennt.

Dort wird auf diese Stellen kurz S. 706 unter G 12) b) "jmd. preisgeben, verwerfen. β) v Göttern: aA ..." hingewiesen.

Das heißt, daß diese Verbalformen als "Perfekta" verstanden werden – eine Bezeichnung und Unterscheidung, die das *CAD* bekanntlich nicht angenommen hat.[5]

Um diese Verbalform besser verstehen zu können, habe ich aus der Literatur, die nach *CAD* N erschienen ist, sehr flüchtig – wenn ich auch kürzere Zitate aus unveröffentlichten Kt-Nummern mitrechne – etwas mehr als 6 200 Texte überflogen, vor allem altassyrische und altbabylonische; um diese Perioden geht es auch im wesentlichen in den folgenden Bemerkungen.

---

[5] Vgl. Michael P. Streck, *Die akkadischen Verbalstämme mit ta-Infix*, AOAT 303 (Münster, 2003). S. dazu meinen Rezensionsartikel "Eine höchst interessante Erscheinung der akkadischen Grammatik: Die Verbalstämme mit *ta*-Infix", *AfO* 50 (2003/2004): 81–94. In AOAT 303 wird für *nadûm*, um dies hier kurz zu erwähnen, kein Gt genannt, vgl. den Index, S. 153, sondern nur ein $Št_1$; ein $*Št_2$ wird eliminiert.

Dabei habe ich nicht nur entsprechende Formen von *nadûm* gesucht, sondern auch andere Verben kurz angesehen; weil *t*-Formen bekanntlich auch mit der "Ventivendung" erscheinen, habe ich auch manche Verbalformen mit dieser Endung notiert.[6]

Vollständigkeit war dabei in keiner Weise beabsichtigt, auch deshalb nicht, weil ich es mir erspart habe, in der National- oder Universitätsbibliothek zu arbeiten, sondern nur die Bücher und Zeitschriften angesehen habe, die ich selbst besitze; ebenso folgte die Auswahl der Verben keinerlei bestimmten Regeln, es wurden aber vorwiegend Formen notiert, die nicht in einer Sequenz Prt. – *t*-Form stehen; aber solche Formen werden sehr wohl besprochen und analysiert.

Ähnlich ging es bei den Verben mit einer "Ventivendung" eher um Formen, die nicht deutlich "her zu (mir)" u. ä. zeigen – um absichtlich hier so vage zu formulieren.

Die Belegsammlung aller dieser Verben kann hier nicht vorgeführt werden, sie wird hoffentlich an anderer Stelle erscheinen; deshalb muß ich auch auf allgemeine Bemerkungen verzichten, ich darf aber auf meine eben in den Anmerkungen genannten Arbeiten verweisen.

Ausgehend von der Form *i-tí-dí-ma* bleiben wir hier also beim Verbum *nadûm*, wobei wir zunächst noch einmal auf das *CAD* zurückblicken, dieses also in gewisser Hinsicht auch als Forschungsobjekt betrachten.

Dort werden I/2-Formen verstreut, in verschiedenen Abschnitten zitiert; uns interessiert neben dem Altassyrischen, das wir in den eben zitierten Formen gefunden haben, und dem Altbabylonischen vor allem auch die jüngere literarische Sprache.

Alle diese Formen sind lang bekannt, aber doch einige Worte wert: Da findet sich ganz nebenbei sogleich im ersten Abschnitt zu *lu ana mê lu ana išāti* ŠUB-*ú* *BBSt.* No. 4 iii 3, cf. MDP 2 113 ii 16: "also, wr. *it-ta-di*" MDP 2 pl. 22 v 51 *CAD* N/1 s.v. *nadû* v. Bed. 1a–1′) – und das ist es dort. Dann kommen schon literarische Belege aus der jüngeren Literatursprache, STT 38:131 (Poor Man of Nippur, Bed. 1a–1′c′) und Gilgamesch (Bed. 1a–1′d′), in I ii 34 ... *iktariṣ ittadi* ...; Gilg. noch öfters: *it-ta-di quliptu* XI 289 (Bed. 1c–1′), III iv 21 *indi it-ta-di* ... (Bed. 2a–9′), VI 158 *it-ta-di a-ru-ru-ta* (Bed. 6 s.v. *arūrūtu*) oder XI 217. 227 ... *it-ta-di* (Bed. 6 s.v. *šību*).

Ebendort wird unter *ṣerretu* En. el. IV 117 zitiert: *it-ta-di* (var. *it-ta-ad-di*) ... . Das ist in den jüngeren Texten bekanntlich nicht überraschend, so daß man manchmal auch an defektive Schreibungen einerseits oder eher neue Deutungen alter Formen andererseits denken könnte. Deshalb sind die altassyrischen Formen so kostbar, weil es dort keinen Zweifel gibt: *i-tí-dí* ist I/2, das so häufige *i-ta-dí* u. ä. ist Prt. I/3. Weitere Formen aus jüngeren literarischen Texten müssen wir nicht erschöpfend nennen, aber doch betonen, daß sie häufig sind, auch, nochmals, in Verbindungen wie ... *attapaḫ attadi* ... Šurpu V–VI 174 (*CAD* N/1 s.v. *nadû* v. Bed. 1b–2′); und vielleicht sollte man

[6] Zum "Ventiv" darf ich hinweisen auf meine Arbeit *Gilgamesch-Epos und Erra-Lied. Zu einem Aspekt des Verbalsystems*, AfO Beiheft 29 (Wien, 2002) und N. J. C. Kouwenberg, "Ventive, Dative and Allative in Old Babylonian", *ZA* 92 (2002): 200–40.

hinweisen auf: "wr. UZU.ME-*šu ur-qá it-ta-du-ú* Labat *TDP* 218: 5"; " ..., and note, wr. *ur-qá it-ta-du-ni* ibid. 20", nach "cf. *šerānušu* SIG$_7$ ŠUB-*ú* ibid. 154 r. 19" (*CAD* N/1 s.v. *nadû* v. Bed. 3b–3′), und schließlich *marṣa tuk-ka-ka ta-at-ta-di eli*[*ja*] "you (my god) have directed your harsh proclamation against me", *JNES* 33 286 Section III 9 – wieder eine Aussage über das Eingreifen eines Gottes in das Leben eines Menschen (*CAD* N/1 s.v. *nadû* v. Bed. 6 s.v. *tukku* b).

Sehen wir uns aber altbabylonische Stellen im Zusammenhang dieser Bemerkungen noch einmal etwas genauer an, beginnend mit Kraus AbB 1 63:6, das im selben Abschnitt steht wie die altassyrischen Zitate – es paßt auch dazu (*CAD* N/1 s.v. *nadû* v. Bed. 1c–6′): Ein ganz kurzer Brief, nach der Segensformel ^{d}utu *li-ba-al-l*[*i*]-*iṭ-ki*, von Kraus mit "Šamaš möge dich gesund erhalten!" übersetzt, sogleich das im *CAD* gebrachte Zitat: *a-wi-lum it-ta-di-na-ti* "der Herr hat uns fallen lassen", gefolgt von der Aufforderung "komm und hole uns!" (*al-ki-im-ma tu-ri-na-ti*). Nach zwei unklaren Zeilen der Schluß, wieder ein Imperativ und ein Prekativ: "Geh (*al-ki-ma* ...) zu Bellānum, dem Obmann der Opferschauer, ‹‹und›› er soll *für dich/dir austauschen*!" (*li-iš-te-ni-ki*).[7]

Man wird zugeben, daß dies eine sehr wichtige Stelle ist – die *t*-Form am Beginn, Trägerin der wichtigen, dramatischen Mitteilung, von der alles Folgende abhängt.

Anschließend daran vielleicht wieder in der Reihenfolge des *CAD* selbst:

Dem kurzen Zitat *it-ta-di-a-aš-šu* OECT 3 41:9 (*CAD* N/1 s.v. *nadû* v. Bed. 1c–3′) kann man nicht entnehmen, daß diese Verbalform in einer -*ma*-Verbindung steht, aber nicht in einer Sequenz Prt.-*ma* – *t*-Form.

In der Bearbeitung von Kraus, AbB 4 119:(5)–13:

> (Betreffs des Feldes des Apil-Šamaš von der Ortschaft Aḫa-nuta, *welches beansprucht wird*: er kann *aus dem Hause der Festung* nicht "hinuntergehen" (*wa-ra-da-am ú-ul i-le-ḫi-ma*) und hat es (deshalb) aufgegeben (*it-ta-di-a-aš-šu*). Als Ersatz des Feldes, das er aufgegeben hat (*ša id-di-a-aš-šu*), stelle ihm ([*š*]*u-ku-un-šu*) nach seiner Wahl ein Feld gleicher Art (zur Verfügung)![8]

Man beachte das "(deshalb)" der Übersetzung und wohl auch das zweimalige -*a-aš-šu*.

Auf ARM 2 10:6 *ana* GN *alākam ta-at-ta-di* "you have neglected going to GN" (*CAD* N/1 s.v. *nadû* v. Bed. 1c–4′) wird mit "note" hingewiesen.

---

7 Ich zitiere absichtlich meist in dieser Form; darüber mehr in der geplanten oben erwähnten größeren Arbeit.

8 Mit der Anmerkung "Wörtlich: 'wie das Feld' ". Im Text (12): a.šà-*lam ki-ma* a.šà-*lim*. Das ist eher eine allgemeine Aussage, ein Zitat, eine Verfahrensvorschrift, "Feld um Feld" – das ist nicht ganz dasselbe.

Das ist so nicht ganz richtig, aber die Stelle ist aus anderen Gründen interessant. Das Verbum steht in einem *šumma*-Satz. Durand nimmt in *Documents de Mari*, Nr. 470, für Zeile 4 einen alten Vorschlag von W. von Soden an[9] und übersetzt überzeugend: "Si après réflexion, en fonction de ma tablette précédente que je t'ai envoyée, tu as abandonné (le projet) d'aller à Heššum ...".

Das erste Verbum ist sicher richtig ergänzt, wir haben dann zwei *t*-Formen verschiedener Funktion nebeneinander.

Die Stelle VAS 16 200:9 (*CAD* N/1 s.v. *nadû* v. Bed. 2c–1′b′) wird mit gutem Grund ohne Übersetzung nur als "cf. [...] x *kaspam it-ta-di-i*" zitiert, wobei man den Akkusativ *kaspam* bemerkt.

Die Stelle ist schwierig, weil sie in großteils zerstörtem Zusammenhang steht. In der Bearbeitung von Frankena, AbB 6 200: 8 ff.: " ..., aber das Haus ist ruiniert.[10] Drei ... ein Sekel Silber ist soeben herausgeworfen worden." Man bemerkt "soeben", auch, daß *-i* in der Übersetzung ignoriert ist; "herausgeworfen" steht vielleicht für "hinausgeworfen", was ganz etwas anderes bedeutet; "herausgeworfen" ergibt für mich in diesem Zusammenhang keinen Sinn. Der Brief ist alles andere als lustig: Von "kämpfen um das Haus" ist die Rede, ein "Mann wird vernichtet werden", Schuldhaft und dergleichen mehr (12 ff.).

Zwei Stellen sollen noch zitiert werden; in der ersten, CT 4 19a:22, kann man aus dem Zitat im *CAD* (N/1 s.v. *nadû* v. Bed. 2e) wieder nicht erkennen, daß das Verbum nicht isoliert steht, sondern diesmal in einer Prt.-*ma* – *t*-Form-Sequenz. Sie ist aber trotzdem interessant: *eqlam ... u kakkarātim ana mudasî at-ta-di* "I put down the field and the (uncultivated) plots on the list."

Dazu etwas ausführlicher die Bearbeitung von Frankena, AbB 2 90:10 ff.:

> Mein Herr möge den Qīšti-Nabû befragen (*li-iš-ta-al*). Sein Sinn ist darauf gerichtet, die Felder der *rēdû* zu vernichten. Ich habe den Herrn "Leutevater" unterrichtet. Man hat den Nanna-mansi, den Obmann ... zitiert (*is-sú-šu-ma*), und daß er ein *ausgewähltes* Feld den *rēdû* gegeben hat (*id-di-n*[*u* o], hat er zugegeben (*a-an-na i-ta-pa-al* [o]) (und) man hat die Tafel der Ausgabe (der Felder)[11] der Verstorbenen mir gebracht (*ub-lu-nim-ma*), und (die Stellen), wo die *rēdû* ein Feld besitzen (*ṣa-ab-tu*), und die Grundstücke habe ich auf eine Liste eingetragen (*a-na ... at-ta-di*) und die Liste habe ich in ... hineingebracht (*uš-te-ri-ib*) ... .

---

[9] "Neue Bände der Archives Royales de Mari," *Or.*, n.s., 22 (1953): 195: ... *šum-ma t*[*a-aš-ta-a*]*l-ma*.

[10] Mit der Anmerkung, daß in *ḫu-ul-lu-uq* das Zeichen UG ganz unsicher sei.

[11] *ṭup-pí tam-li-tim ša mi-tu-t*[*im*]. Deutsche Übersetzung schwer verständlich; wird aber hier nicht diskutiert.

Aber die folgende, letzte Stelle paßt wieder sehr gut zu unseren Überlegungen: UCP 9 341 Nr. 16: 9 (*CAD* N/1 s.v. *nadû* v. Bed. 6 s.v. *tuššu*) *awīlum tu-ša-am elija it-ta-di* "the man has accused me wrongly", in Stol, AbB 11, die Nummer 180. Ein kurzer Brief – die Vorderseite nach Resten in Zeile 11 abgebrochen, die Rückseite war nicht beschrieben – der hauptsächlich aus dieser Mitteilung besteht.

Nach Anrede und Segensformel in Zeilen 6ff.: "Concerning the letter*s* (*un-ne-du-uk-ki*) that you sent to me (*ša tu-ša-bi-lam*), the man has uttered slander against me. I want to come (*lu-ul-li-kam-ma*), and that ... (remainder lost)."

Der Eindruck, den wir beim Durchgehen der Bearbeitung von *nadû* im *CAD* gewonnen haben, hat sich bei der Durchsicht der neueren Literatur, von der ich oben gesprochen habe, durchaus bestätigt. Das war nicht anders zu erwarten, ist aber doch willkommen, als weitere Bestätigung dafür, daß man das *CAD* sehr wohl als statistisch hinreichende Quelle verwenden kann. Auch soll man dieses Verbum, um darauf nochmals hinzuweisen, zusammen mit allen anderen betrachten, die anderswo besprochen werden sollen: Die Ergebnisse passen gut zusammen.

Kienast *ATHE* 61: 25 wurde schon von Hecker in *Grammatik* § 97c zusammen mit den anderen hier besprochenen Stellen genannt und die *t*-Formen wurden als Perfekt notiert. Es heißt in *ATHE* 61 nach der Kopie: (23) ... *i-lá-qé* (24) *i-na na* x̣x̣ *a-na-ku-ma* (25) *i-na ra-mì-*⌈*ni-a*⌉ : *a-tí-dí* (26) *um-ma a-na-ku-ma* .... Also *anākūma* ... *a-tí-dí*, und zwar *i-na ra-mì-*⌈*ni-a*⌉, und dann die Erklärung *umma anākūma* ... .

Damit mag man die nüchterne Formulierung in KTS 2 40:17 vergleichen: "(Du hast mir geschrieben: '1 1/3 Mi[ne Silber]) habe ich auf eigene Kosten d[em Kārum-Haus] hingelegt' " (*i-ra-mì-ni-a* ... *a-dí-i*). Und in Z. 11 und 15 der Imperativ *i-dí-*(*i-*)*ma*, in 12 ... *l*[*i-d*]*í-ú*, in KTS 2 19:11′ *lá a-ta-na-dí* und in KTS 2 34:8 der Imperativ Gtn (Zinn) *r*[*a*]*-bu-ma i-ta-dí-šu-ma* "... 'deponiere es regelmäßig unauffällig ...' " – aber von diesen Formen, die sich auch in den anderen Textgruppen finden, aus denen wir zitieren werden, müssen wir nicht besonders sprechen.

Es sei bei dieser Gelegenheit aber gestattet, doch kurz auf einige religiöse Aussagen einzugehen, weil wir ja von einem solchen Kontext ausgegangen sind.

In KTS 2 45:28 finden wir eine interessante, sehr logische Variante der *liṭṭulā*-Formel, nämlich (28) ... ᵈ*A-šur ù* DINGIR.ḪI.A*ᵃ*-*ni* (29) *li-ṭù-lu* ... "Aššur und unsere Götter mögen Zeugen sein (, daß sich niemand auch nur einem S(ekel) von deinem Silber nähert!)".

Es geht wieder einmal um viel Gold in diesem Brief der Gläubiger (*umme'ānū*) an Idī-Ištar, um eine Urkunde des Fürsten, die es schon gibt, und eine andere, die man ausstellen lassen könnte ... .

Also "unsere Götter" – die nicht namentlich genannt werden – zusammen mit, nach Aššur genannt, so daß es also völlig unmöglich ist, Aššur in einer Zusammenfassung "unsere Götter" zu subsumieren. Daß in der Verbalform der korrekte Plural steht, sei nur am Rande erwähnt.

Da ist aber der an Innā'a gerichtete Brief von Šumma-libb-Aššur,[12] KTS 2 52. Der Brief weist mehrere Fehler auf und ist nicht gut verständlich – das sei sogleich eingangs betont.

Wir geben zuerst die Umschrift und Übersetzung der Zeilen 8b–18 nach KTS 2:

> (8) ... *ma-tí-ma* (9) *i-na re-ší-kà* (10) *lá a-zi-iz* /[13]*ma a-na-ku* (11) *šu-um-kà i-na* (12) *lá i-dim a-za-kà-*[*ar*] (13) ‹‹*a-za-kà-ar*›› *A-š*[*ùr*] *il*$_5$-*kà* (14) *ù* MAR.TU (15) *il*$_5$-*kà* KI *li it ku-ni* (16) *e-zi-ib šu-mì-kà lá* (17) *za-kà-ri-im šu-mì* ÌR-^{dí}-[*kà*] (18) *za-kà-ra-am lá a-le-*[*e*]
>
> Stand ich jemals dir nicht (hilfreich) zu Häupten, und nenne ich etwa grundlos deinen Namen? Dein Gott Aššur und dein Gott Amurru *mögen Zeugen sein*: Abgesehen davon, daß ich deinen Namen nicht nenne, kann ich auch den Namen deines Sklaven nicht nennen.

Cécile Michel hat diesen Text bearbeitet. Ihre Umschrift und Übersetzung folgen hier:[14]

> (8) ... *ma-tí-ma* (9) *i-na re-ší-kà* (10) *lá a-zi-iz-/ma a-na-/*[15]*ku* (11) *šu-um-kà i-na* (12) *lá i-dim a-za-kà-/*[*ar*] (13) ‹‹*a-za-kà-ar*›› *A-š*[*ùr*] / *il*$_5$-*kà* (14) *ù* MAR.TU (15) *il*$_5$-*kà* KI *li-id-gu*$_5$-*/lá* (16) *e-zi-ib šu-mì-kà* (17) *za-kà-ri-im šu-mì* ÌR^{dí}-/*kà* (18) *za-kà-ra-am lá a-le-/*[*e*]
>
> N'ai-je pas toujours été à ton service, et moi-même prononcerai-je ton nom sans raison? Qu'Aššur, ton dieu, et Amurrum, ton dieu, considèrent, indépendamment de ton nom que (je ne peux) citer, je ne peux pas citer (non plus) le nom de ton serviteur.

In dieser Umschrift, die zweifellos einen Fortschritt bringt, ist ganz wichtig, daß angemerkt wird, welche Zeichen aus einer folgenden Zeile herausgehoben wurden – wir kommen sofort darauf zurück. Es ist aber auch klar, daß das deutliche NI am Ende von Zeile 16, das in der Umschrift in KTS 2 am Ende von Zeile 15 steht, fehlt!

Fragen wir zuerst nach dem Sinn der Aussage "Aššur, dein Gott" und "Amurrum, dein Gott". Sie ist, um zunächst so zu formulieren, völlig unerwartet – und gänzlich unlogisch. Ist es nicht die Idee hinter der Vorstellung von einem persönlichen Gott, daß – jedenfalls in einer gegebenen Situation – ein Gott sich einer Person oder einer Gruppe annimmt? Und wenn zwei oder mehrere Götter einer Gruppe oder Person zugeordnet werden, dann würden wir eine Formulierung der Art, wie wir sie eben gesehen haben, erwarten: A und B, deine beiden Götter – nicht eine Formulierung, die im Grunde genommen eine Konkurrenz bezeichnet – A, dein Gott, B, (auch?) dein Gott.

---

[12] Schreibung der Personennamen nach den jeweiligen Autoren.

[13] Bezeichnet den Worttrenner.

[14] Michel *Innāja*, Band 2, S. 93 f., Nr. 65.

[15] Bezeichnet den Worttrenner (hier in Z. 10 vor *ma*!) oder weist darauf hin, daß das oder die folgenden Zeichen am Ende der nächsten Zeile stehen.

Wir haben am Beginn dieser Ausführungen die Übersetzung "... Aššur himself and your own god" zitiert, gewiß zustimmend, weil wir es so erwarten, und eben auf die Formulierung "Aššur und unsere Götter" hingewiesen: Die vorgeschlagene Umschrift und Übersetzung müßte völlig zweifelsfrei sein, wenn man sich ernsthaft damit auseinandersetzen sollte. Das ist sicher nicht der Fall. Aber vielleicht war der Wunsch der Vater des Gedankens.

Jeder, der nüchtern und vorurteilsfrei den Text ansieht, merkt sofort, daß am Ende von Zeile 12 *a-za-⌈kà⌉-* steht; schräg darunter ahnt man Spuren von [*ar*]. In 13 dann sehr deutlich, groß, weit auseinandergezogen nochmals *a-za-kà-ar*, das in den Umschriften als Wiederholung getilgt wird. Oder war es absichtlich nochmals geschrieben, zur Betonung, damit es ganz klar ist? *A-⌈šùr⌉* am Ende von Zeile 13 ist zweifelsfrei, *ù* MAR.TU *il₅-kà* in Zeile 14 auch, dann am Beginn von Zeile 15 noch einmal *il₅-kà*, das man doch am besten ebenso als Wiederholung betrachten sollte wie *a-za-kà-ar* – Unaufmerksamkeit oder Absicht.

Für die Fortsetzung halte ich *li-id-gu₅-/lá* von Michel für beachtenswert, aber statt KI *li-id-gu₅-/lá* NI so zu lassen, möchte man vielleicht doch in KI die Subjunktion *kī* sehen und in NI die Subjunktivendung *-ni*. Ungewöhnlich, aber nicht unmöglich, daß gemeint war: "Aššur und Amurrum, dein Gott, dein Gott – daß sie 'schauen' mögen!"[16]

In Matouš *Prag* möchte ich auf zwei Texte hinweisen, zuerst I 479: 5 ff.: ("Wenn du mein Bruder bist, schicke mir den (Wert) meiner Stoffe, des früheren und von diesem, zusammen!") (9) ... DINGIR^{lu-um} (10) ⌊*lu i*⌋*-dí-a-‹ni›-ma* (11) ⌈*ke-na*⌉*-tù-ni* "Der Gott soll mich verwerfen, (wenn) es (nicht) wahr ist: (4 Stoffe gab ich dir vor ...)."

Wir kommen auf diesen Text noch zurück, aber vorher kurz zu Matouš *Prag* I 711. Dort heißt es: (8) *ù ni-im-ta-lik-ma* (9) *a-wa-tí-ni a-mì-ša-am* (10) *ni-na-dí-am* "Dann können wir beraten, ob wir unseren Rechtsstreit dorthin verlegen" und (18) *lu-ba-tí-qá-ma ší-it-a-al* (19) *a-wa-tí-ni a-mì-ša-am* (20) *lu ni-dí-a-am* "(Wenn du willst, dann soll Anina dort ...) beenden. Dann berate dich (mit ihm), ob wir unseren Rechtsstreit dorthin verlegen (und dann möge dein Bescheid zu mir kommen ...)."

Und Michel und Garelli *Kültepe* 1 47:[17] 17 f. mit der bekannten Phrase (17) ... *A-šùr* (18) *ù* ^{d}NIN.ŠUBUR *lu i-/dí-a*. Sollen wir demnach doch versuchen, in Matouš *Prag* I 479: 10 ohne Emendation auszukommen?

---

[16] Ich lasse diese Überlegungen so stehen: Im nachhinein habe ich Rezensionen zu KTS 2 angesehen; seinerzeit habe ich mir keine Notizen daraus gemacht, ich kann mich auch nicht erinnern, sie (aufmerksam) gelesen zu haben. Das Ergebnis finde ich sehr erfreulich: Kh. Nashef, *WO* 24 (1993): 171 f., sagt ausdrücklich, daß "*A-šur il-kà* (von der nächsten Zeile)" – er weist also darauf hin! – "*ù* MAR.TU *il₅-kà* kaum möglich ist" – nicht zwei persönliche Götter des Innaja; *il₅-kà* von Z. 15 sei als Wiederholung zu tilgen. Also nicht "Aššur, dein Gott". J. G. Dercksen spricht in seiner sehr ausführlichen Rezension in *BiOr* 48 (1991): Sp. 182 – wie die anderen Rezensenten, deren Rezensionen ich eingesehen habe (W. Farber, Gwaltney, Oelsner) – darüber nicht, aber er schlägt als einziger eine Umschrift *ki li-id-gu₅-/lá-ni* mit der Übersetzung "(the gods) may look with indifference at me (if that were true)" vor; *ki* als "modal particle".

[17] Vgl. zu diesem Text J. G. Dercksen, Rezension, Michel und Garelli *Kültepe*, *AfO* 44–45 (1997–98): 336.

Wir wollen das Altassyrische nicht verlassen ohne einen Hinweis auf Biggs, *WZKM* 86 (1996): 47: 6: *it-ta-ni-a-ma*, eine Verbalform, die der Jubilar auf S. 49 kommentiert hat. Wie immer im einzelnen, besonders betont?

Zum Altbabylonischen am Beginn mit sicherem Griff ein sehr schwieriger, interessanter Brief, ARMT 10 60.

Wir begnügen uns hier damit, auf Durand *Documents de Mari*, Nr. 1091, hinzuweisen, wo auf S. 275 zur Übersetzung "Maintenant, de l'audace!" in der Anm. 14 zu den Zeilen 9–14 die Lesung [*la-a i*]*t-ta-di*, ... gegeben wird, womit ARMT 10 60: 8 f. [*i-na-a*]*n-na a-aḫ-ka*, [*ta*$^{?}$*-a*]*t*$^{?}$*-ta-di* verbessert wird.

Aus Mari nur kurz noch Lackenbacher, ARMT 26 480:17–21: "Si des troupes ne se hâtent pas vers moi (*la i-ha-mu-ṭá*/*-am*), j'évacuerai (*a-na-di-a-am-ma at-ta-la*$^{!}$*-kam*) la place de Mulhân et le district de mon seigneur devra être évacué (*in-na-ad-*⸢*di*⸣)" und Kupper, ARMT 28 113:10–11: "(Les Anciens du Yapṭur et Ibâl-Addu (et) Asqur-Addu) sont descendus à Urkiš (*a-na* ... [*u*]*r*-[*d*]*u*-[*n*]*im*) et ils ont tenu une assemblée (⸢*ù*⸣ *i*[*t-t*]*a-du-ma pu-uḫ!-ra-am*) (, disant ...)".

Gehen wir nochmals zum *CAD*, Band Ḫ s.v. *ḫuptu* A Bed. b in Elam.[18] Das erste Zitat: "field and garden PN has given as a gift (*iddiššin u iqīssi*) to PN_2 his wife, he has set it aside as a *ḫ*.-holding (*a-na ḫu-up-ti ittadi* [*i-ta-di*]) (she may give it to an heir)", MDP 24 378:8.

Noch ein Blick in AbB:

Cagni, AbB 8 100:5–6 erinnert an unseren Ausgangspunkt: (Zu ... sprich: also (sagt) das Mädchen:) "Seit dem Tag, an dem du mich preisgegeben hast und weggegangen bist" (*iš-tu* ... *ša ta-di-a-an-ni-ma*, *t*[*a*]*-al-li-ḳu*) (, als Gegenleistung für (geschuldete) 10 Sekel Silber ...).

Doch wenigstens eine Š-Form: Stol, AbB 11 33:9, in einem Satz, der nach der Anrede und Segensformel beginnt: "I myself have hindered Gimil-Gula, ... , from even approaching the head of the district" ((7) *a-na ša-pí-ir ma-tim* (8) *a-na sa-na-qí-im-ma* (9) *a-na-ku uš-ta-ad-di-šu*) ...".

Eine *-am*-Form in van Soldt, AbB 13 6:27: "We poured five kor of barley into one boat (... *ni-it-bu-uk-ma*), but it (began to) take in water and would have sunk (*me-e id-di-a-am-ma iṭ-ṭe-bu-ú-ma-an*)."

Ein trauriger Beleg zum Abschluß – der aber auch zum Beginn paßt:

van Soldt, AbB 13 85:21: "They have treated Iluni harshly (*a-na* ... *qá-ta-ạm ud-da-an-ni-nu*) (and) they have *put him in fetters* (*ma-an-da-a it-ta-du-šu*). In accordance with his high status let my father negotiate his release ..." – um doch mit einer positiven Wendung zu schließen.

---

[18] Lies in N/1 s.v. *nadû* v. Bed. 2h *ḫuptu* A statt C.

A BRIEF COMMENTARY ON THE HITTITE ILLUYANKA MYTH (CTH 321)

Harry A. Hoffner, Jr., The University of Chicago

Although Bob Biggs is not a Hittitologist, he has contributed significantly to the understanding of Akkadian literary texts, including myths. Since the Illuyanka Myth is one of the most important myths in the Hittite repertoire,[1] and is widely known in translation far beyond the field of Hittitology, it seems appropriate to me to dedicate to him this brief commentary on the myth. In the notations of the lines that follow I have used the sigla of the editions of the text, but I have engaged as many of the various published translations and commentaries as possible.

In the form we have it today the Illuyanka Myth consists of two stories recounted on a single tablet. Each story is followed by a ritual. The main cuneiform text is KBo 3.7 with seven duplicates.[2] The text has been often translated[3] and studied.[4]

---

[1] E. Laroche, *Catalogue des textes hittites* (Paris, 1971), no. 321 (hereafter *CTH*).

[2] For a listing, see either of the two editions: G. M. Beckman, "The Anatolian Myth of Illuyanka," *ANES* 14 (1982) and J. V. García Trabazo, *Textos religiosos hititas: mitos, plegares y rituales*, Biblioteca de Ciencias Bíblicas y Orientales 6 (Madrid, 2002), pp. 75–103.

[3] A. Goetze in J. B. Pritchard, ed., *Ancient Near Eastern Texts Relating to the Old Testament*, 2d ed. (Princeton, 1955), pp. 125–26 (hereafter *ANET*²); T. H. Gaster, *Thespis: Ritual, Myth, and Drama in the Ancient Near East*, 2d ed. (Garden City, New York, 1961), pp. 245–67; H. G. Güterbock, "Hittite Mythology," in S. N. Kramer, ed., *Mythologies of the Ancient World* (Garden City, New York, 1961), pp. 139–79; H. G. Güterbock, "Hethitische Literatur," in W. Röllig et al., *Altorientalische Literaturen*, Neues Handbuch der Literaturwissenschaft, Band 1 (Wiesbaden, 1978), pp. 246–48; C. Kühne, "Hittite Texts," in W. Beyerlin, ed., *Near Eastern Religious Texts Relating to the Old Testament*, The Old Testament Library (Philadelphia, 1978), pp. 155–59; B. DeVries, "The Style of Hittite Epic and Mythology" (Ph.D. diss., Brandeis University, 1967), pp. 16–19, 64–66; A. Bernabé, *Textos literarios hetitas* (Madrid, 1987), pp. 29–37; H. A. Hoffner, Jr., *Hittite Myths*, Writings from the Ancient World 2 (Atlanta, 1990), pp. 10–14 (hereafter *HM*¹); F. Pecchioli Daddi and A. M. Polvani, *La mitologia ittita*, Testi del Vicino Oriente antico 4/1 (Brescia, 1990), pp. 39–55 (hereafter *LMI*); V. Haas, *Geschichte der hethitischen Religion*, Handbuch der Orientalistik, 1. Abteilung, Band 15 (Leiden, 1994), pp. 703–7 (hereafter *GhR*); A. Ünal, "Hethitische Mythen und Epen," in O. Kaiser, ed., *Mythen und Epen*, Texte aus der Umwelt des Alten Testaments III/4 (Gütersloh, 1994), pp. 802–65; G. M. Beckman, "The Storm-god and the Serpent (Illuyanka)," in W. W. Hallo and K. L. Younger, eds., *The Context of Scripture*, vol. 1, *Canonical Compositions from the Biblical World* (Leiden, 1997) (hereafter *CoS* 1); and H. A. Hoffner, Jr., *Hittite Myths*, 2d ed., rev., Writings from the Ancient World 2 (Atlanta, 1998), pp. 9–14 (hereafter *HM*²).

[4] A. H. Sayce, "Hittite Legend of the War with the Great Serpent," *JRAS*, 1922, pp. 177–90; A. Goetze, *Kleinasien*, 2d ed., rev., Handbuch der

I. THE DATING OF THE COMPOSITION

Although all extant manuscripts of the Illuyanka text are copies made after the Old Hittite period,[5] the original form of the composition derives from Old Hittite. One can see this from sporadic linguistic archaisms.[6] Pecchioli Daddi and Polvani note the following linguistic archaisms:[7] the enclitic pronoun *-e* in § 10 B i 12′, 13′, *-apa* in *an-da-ma-pa* § 4 A i 13 and *am-mu-ug-ga-za-pa* § 26 A iii 29, and the use of the allative in *gi-im-ra* § 13 C i 18. It may be that Stefanini's *mān* with final force (§ 1 A i 3), if he is right in his analysis, is also an archaism.[8] To these examples we may also add: Old Hittite *ma-a-wa* (§ 8 A i 25, § 13 C i 18, 21) for later *ma-a-an-wa*, *kat-ti-ti* (§ 8 A i 25) for later *-ta katta(n)*, the writing *-z* for the reflexive particle in ^{d}*Inarašš=a=z* (§ 9 B i 4), and *andan* É-[(*ri*)] (§ 13 C i 16) instead of later É-*ri anda*. The Old Hittite nongeminating *-a* for change of topic (often rendered "but") is also attested in *a-pa-a-ša* § 14 C i 23 (beginning apodosis after a *mān* clause), *mān=aš pa-a-i-ta* "but when he went" § 24 A iii 13, ^{d}*Za-li-nu-i-ša* in § 29 D iv 6, *ku-i-ta* § 33 A iv 18, and erroneously for the geminating *-a* in *ša-ku-wa-aš-še-<et->ta* "*and* his eyes" § 24 A iii 18. Archaic elements having to do with the *contents* of the stories are amply discussed in *LMI*, p. 39, n. 4.

It would be interesting to determine if the archaic elements are equally distributed between the *narrative* and *ritual* portions of the two accounts. If they are, this would indicate that the rituals as well as the narratives stem from the Old Hittite period. If not, we may be permitted to look to religious-political influences from the thirteenth century on the rituals. As for archaic linguistic elements in the ritual portion of Account 1 (§§ 18–19: A ii 21–30), there is nothing linguistically distinctive of Old Hittite versus

---

Altertumswissenschaft, Kulturgeschichte des Alten Orients (Munich, 1957), pp. 139–40; V. Haas, "Jasons Raub des goldenen Vliesses im Lichte hethitischer Quellen," *UF* 7 (1975): 227–33; C. Mora, "Sulla mitologia ittita di origine anatolica," in O. Carruba, ed., *Studia Mediterranea Piero Meriggi dicata*, Studia Mediterranea 2 (Pavia, 1979), pp. 380–83; H. Gonnet, "Institution d'un culte chez les hittites," *Anatolica* 14 (1987): 89–100; F. Pecchioli Daddi, "Aspects du culte de la divinité hattie Teteshapi," *Hethitica* 8 (1987): 361–80; C. Watkins, "How to Kill a Dragon in Indo-European," in C. Watkins, ed., *Studies in Memory of Warren Cowgill (1929–1985)* (Berlin, 1987); V. Haas, "Betrachtungen zur Rekonstruktion des hethitischen Frühjahrsfestes (EZEN *purulliyas*)," *ZA* 78 (1988): 284–98; E. Neu, "Der alte Orient: Mythen der Hethiter," in G. Binder and B. Effe, eds., *Erzählende Weltdeutung im Spannungsfeld von Ritual, Geschichte und Rationalität*, Bochumer Altertumswissenschaftliches Colloquium 2 (Trier, 1990), pp. 101–3; C. Watkins, "Le dragon hittite Illuyankas et le géant grec Typhôeus," *CRAI*, avril–juin (1992): 319–30; and M. Popko, *Religions of Asia Minor* (Warsaw, 1995), pp. 121–23.

5 So, for example, García Trabazo, *Textos religiosos hititas*, p. 78, and compare the on-line concordance of S. Košak at http://www.orient.uni-wuerzburg.de/hetkonk/hetkonk_abfrage.php. García Trabazo dates them all to the fourteenth century B.C., while Košak dates KBo 12.83 ("F") to the thirteenth ("sjh.").

6 A. Kammenhuber, "Die Sprachstufen des Hethitischen," *Zeitschrift für vergleichende Sprachforschung* 83 (1969): 259.

7 *LMI*, p. 39, n. 3.

8 R. Stefanini, "Alcuni problemi ittiti, lessicali e sintattici," in F. Imparati, ed., *Studi di storia e di filologia anatolica dedicati a Giovanni Pugliese Carratelli*, Eothen 1 (Florence, 1988), p. 255.

later periods.[9] But in the ritual of Account 2 (§§ 27–35) there are a few possible linguistic archaisms: *pa-i-u-wa-ni* § 30 D iv 9 (and *pa-a-i-wa-ni* in A and C) with its Old Hittite/Middle Hittite *-wani* ending, the older *e-šu-wa-aš-ta* of § 30 D iv 10 (contrasted with its duplicate A iv 7, which modernized as *e-šu-wa-aš-ta-ti*), the construction of middle *eš-* "sit down" with *-šan* but no *-za*, the Old Hittite spelling *ša-al-li-iš* (A iv 17) versus post-Old Hittite *šal-li-iš*.

This is scant evidence, but it is enough to suggest an Old Hittite archetype for the ritual in Account 2. On the other hand, New Hittite spellings (which arguably could be due to the scribe rather than the original) abound in the ritual portions. If these New Hittite spellings belong to the original form of the rituals, one could suppose that the old narratives were joined to newly created rituals.

Kellerman mentions several elements of the contents of the two rituals to argue that the second is more recent and more appropriate to the late empire period (Tudḫaliya IV) than the first.[10] In the first ritual the name of the god Zaliyanu is written with the mountain determinative, $^{\text{ḪUR.SAG}}$Zali(ya)nu, while in the second it is written with the DINGIR determinative ^{d}Zali(ya)nu. In the second ritual he has both a wife and a concubine and is therefore portrayed as fully anthropomorphic. But is this evidence compelling? If the transfer from mountain to anthropomorphic deity could be conclusively shown to be a widespread and virtually exceptionless trend in Hittite cult, this would be a significant indication of a later date for the second ritual. Kellerman quotes Laroche[11] for the elements of Tudḫaliya IV's religious reforms, which include the replacement of ancient theriomorphic images, stelae, and different objects thought to be divine incarnations by anthropomorphic statues. But a mountain deity is not theriomorphic, and there is no way to show a mountain-god in art other than in the traditional style with human heads but sloping rocky flanks, i.e., half and half.

With respect to the content of the text, one can see its original Old Hittite setting in the following five features, already noted by *LMI*: (1) the role played by the city of Nerik, which was lost to the Hittites from the late Old Kingdom until the reign of Ḫattušili III, (2) the use of the matrimonial institution of the ^{LÚ}*antiyanza*, known to us only in the Old Hittite laws, (3) the fact that the myth furnishes an etiology for the Old Hittite festival of *purulli*, (4) the mention (in the second account) of the ^{LÚ}GUDU$_{12}$ Taḫpurili (see below in § 29), who is mentioned in an Old Hittite Script text, and (5) the names of the deities, all of which belong to the pre-Hittite Hattian sphere.

---

[9] Unless one wishes to exaggerate the importance of the mildly temporal use of *mān* in line 22. But since it is likely that in *ḫi-ni-ik-ta* we have a "dynamic" (i.e., deponent) middle form, present tense (correctly in *LMI*, p. 52, "avrà distribuito"), there is nothing unusual in New Hittite about a temporal use *mān* with a pres.-future ("whenever"). Its clause establishes a contingency for the action of *pīdāi* in line 24.

[10] G. Kellerman, "Towards the Further Interpretation of the *purulli*-Festival," *Slavica Hierosolymitana* 5/6 (1981): 36.

[11] E. Laroche, "La réforme religieuse du roi Tudhaliya IV et sa signification politique," in *Les syncrétismes dans les religions de l'antiquité* (Leiden, 1975), pp. 92–93.

II. TRANSMISSION

LMI, p. 40, argues against oral transmission from the Old Hittite period to the first written form in New Hittite for the following reasons. (1) The linguistic archaisms in the text are grammatical, not just lexical, and would not have survived oral transmission for centuries in a nonmetrical form. (2) The name of the text's author, Kella, is only attested in the pre-imperial period.[12] A copy attested in one small fragment appears to show Middle Hittite script. But the vast majority of the extant copies are New Hittite and were probably made during a period of reinterest in the north, such as in Ḫattušili III's reign, and were copied from Kella's Old Hittite exemplar, which has never been recovered. But if the extant copies are only one copying away from an Old Hittite archetype, I am surprised at how few archaisms remain. *LMI*'s assessment of the age of the Kella name militates against the view of Kellerman,[13] who assumes that Kella is not the ancient author of the stories, but a New Hittite GUDU$_{12}$-priest contemporary with the copy, that is, during the reigns of Ḫattušili III and the cult reformer Tudḫaliya IV.

III. INTERPRETATION

Purulli was an Old Hittite festival, which continued to be celebrated in the early empire before the revival of contact with Nerik in the north under Ḫattušili III. We know this because in his annals Muršili II wrote: "I celebrated the *purulli* festival, the great festival, for the Storm-god of Ḫatti and the Storm-god of Zippalanda."[14] Some scholars claim that the *purulli* festival was the Hattic festival of the New Year,[15] although this can only be an inference, since it is never called such in the texts.

While each has a subplot, both stories focus on a conflict between the chief Storm-god of the Hittites, the Storm-god of Heaven, and a huge and powerful reptile, Sum. MUŠ, Hitt. *illuyanka-* or *elliyanka-*. In English translations this reptile is sometimes called a "dragon" (*LMI*, "il drago"). But one should not prejudice the conception of this huge being by a word associated with a particular mythological creature that figures in Western fairy tales.

The word *illuyanka-*, also written *elliyanka-*, is thought by Puhvel to be an "autochthonous term," that is, non-Indo-European.[16] But in a recent article Katz has proposed

---

[12] The name occurs in Old Assyrian Kültepe texts, in the Telepinu Proclamation, and in an Old Hittite land-grant text (according to *LMI*).

[13] Kellerman, "Towards the Further Interpretation of the *purulli*-Festival," pp. 36–37.

[14] *nu* EZEN$_4$ *pu-ru-ul-li-ya-aš ku-it* GAL-*in* [EZEN$_4$-*an*] *A-NA* [d]U [URU]*Ḫa-at-ti U A-NA* [d]U [URU]*Zi-ip-pa-*[*la-an-da*] *i-ya-nu-un*, KBo 2.5+ iii 44–46, edited by A. Goetze, *Die Annalen des Muršiliš*, MVAG 38 (Leipzig, 1933), p. 188.

[15] For example, García Trabazo, *Textos religiosos hititas*, pp. 77–78, 83 with n. 16.

[16] J. Puhvel, *Hittite Etymological Dictionary*, vols. 1–2, *A, E, I*, Trends in Linguistics, Documentation 1 (Berlin, New York, and Amsterdam, 1984), vol. 2 (E/I), pp. 358–59 (hereafter *HED*); cf. also *LMI*, p. 40, n. 11.

an Indo-European etymology for the word.[17] What is certain is that it is a noun, not a proper name, and should be translated—failing any more specific evidence—with as general a term as possible, "serpent" or "reptile."

Most interpreters would agree today that there is more to these stories than literature. One can read the Kumarbi Epic without reference to Hittite concepts of ritual and kingship, for whatever theological and ritual concepts are embedded in those stories are most probably Hurrian or Mesopotamian but not necessarily Hittite. This is not the case with Old Hittite myths such as this one and the so-called Telepinu Myth.

Where interpreters are *not* in agreement is in the details of the interpretation of the symbolism. It is inevitable in literary works employing symbolism that only some details of the story are intended to be understood symbolically. Many elements are merely details essential to the plot of the narrative and to lend verisimilitude. It is difficult for interpreters to know which details are intended to be taken symbolically. Which of the following elements of the first Illuyanka story, for example, should one consider as having a symbolic meaning?

1. The Storm-god and serpent fight, and the Storm-god is defeated.
2. The fight takes place in Kiškilušša.
3. The Storm-god appeals to the other gods for help (§ 4 A I 13).
4. Inara prepares a feast with the emphasis on beverage types.
5. Inara finds Ḫupašiya in Zikkaratta and proposes that he assist her.
6. Ḫupašiya agrees on condition that he may sleep with her, and she concurs.
7. Inara hides Ḫupašiya.
8. Inara ornaments herself and calls the serpent up (*šarā kallišta*) out of his hole/cave.
9. The serpent and his children come up, eat and drink to excess.
10. They are unable to go back down into their hole.
11. Ḫupašiya ties (*kalēliet*) the serpent up with a cord (or with cords).
12. The Storm-god kills the serpent, and the other gods side with him once again.
13. Inara builds a house/temple for herself on a rock/cliff in Tarukka.
14. She installs Ḫupašiya in the house.
15. She warns him against looking out the window at other mortals while she is away.
16. After 20 days of obedience, he looks outside and sees his wife and children.
17. When she returns, he begs to be able to return to his family.

---

[17] J. T. Katz, "How to Be a Dragon in Indo-European: Hittite *illuyankaš* and Its Linguistic and Cultural Congeners in Latin, Greek, and Germanic," in J. Jasanoff, H. C. Melchert, and L. Olivier, eds., *Mír Curad: Studies in Honor of Calvert Watkins*, Innsbrucker Beiträge zur Sprachwissenschaft, Band 92 (Innsbruck, 1998), pp. 317–34.

Most interpreters would consider numbers 1, 12, and 13 as theologically and ritually significant, but the rest of the details are folkloristic and are present only in order to fill out a plausible story. Yet one wonders if there is a theological or ritual significance to some of the other details, such as the locus of the original fight in Kiškilušša (no. 2), the choice of Zikkaratta as Ḫupašiya's hometown (no. 5), and the entire set of events involving Ḫupašiya, who seems to have been the unsuccessful prototype of the Hittite king in his relationship to Inara, the daughter of the Storm-god. Certainly the specification of 20 days as the duration of Inara's absence from Ḫupašiya (§ 14 C I 23) serves no obvious part of the narrative plot itself and raises the suspicion that there is some obscure allusion here to the duration of a festival of Inara celebrated in the open country (Hittite *gimra-*). An official at Tapikka bore the Akkadian name ᴵ*mār-ešrē*, also written in Sumerian as DUMU.UD.20.KAM "son (born on) the 20th day." Which 20th day does this name refer to, if indeed there was not a particular 20th day of a festival that was particularly auspicious for the birth of children? Admittedly, this Babylonian personal name already existed in Mesopotamia, and the day referred to was the 20th day of the month on which a joyful festival was celebrated in honor of the Sun-god Šamaš.[18] But an official in Maşat-Tapikka would hardly have taken a name referring to his own date of birth, if that was to refer to a festival for Šamaš that did not exist in Hatti. Most likely, therefore, the name was reinterpreted in terms of a known Anatolian festival.

It is widely believed, perhaps correctly, that the conflict between the serpent and the Storm-god is over the control of the waters, so necessary for agriculture and life.[19] The Storm-god would presumably be lord of the rainfall, while the serpent controlled the subterranean water sources. By defeating the Storm-god, the serpent thwarts the rainfall and continues by himself to control the subterranean springs, which he can cut off at will. But there are unanswered questions regarding the theory that it was only the Storm-god who controlled the rains. Strange as it seems, where the Illuyanka Myth itself mentions a divine being who is asked to give rain (§ 19), it is not a storm-god, but Mt. Zaliyanu, a deified mountain near the city of Nerik. Why is the Storm-god not asked? Furthermore, the triad of deities who in their priests or emblems remain to preside over the cult location at Tanipiya, include in the persons of the Mountain-god Zaliyanu and the goddesses Za(š)ḫapuna and Tazzuwašši (perhaps deified springs[20]) precisely these two sources of water. Indeed, Haas claims that both of these goddesses were "Tochtergöttinnen" and "Quellnymphen."[21] But his further claim that Tazzuwašši[22] has the variant name Tašimi or Tešimi is unsupported by his evidence.[23]

---

[18] See *CAD* E s.v. *ešrā* usage b-2′ and *ešrūa* for the name *Mār-ešrē* in Akkadian texts.

[19] For example, García Trabazo, *Textos religiosos hititas*, p. 78 ("por el control de las aguas").

[20] As mountain deities are always male in Hittite, so springs are female. And the spring name ᵀᵁᴸTauttawazi (KUB 38.6 obv. 31) is tantalizingly close to Tazzuwašši.

[21] *GhR*, p. 446.

[22] Ibid., p. 446, n. 39.

[23] Ibid., pp. 598–99.

All that is known is that Tešimi is the beloved of the Storm-god of Nerik, and in some texts dZaḫapuna is also associated with him as a consort. Tazzuwašši, on the other hand, is called the concubine (*šašanza*) of the Mountain-god Zaliyanu, whose wife (DAM) is Za(š)ḫapuna. The picture offered by the two narratives and their two ritual sections is not uniform theologically.

The two accounts exhibit other important differences: (1) The first contains several geographical references that permit localization in the north near Nerik, while the second has no such references and involves only an anonymous "sea," which could be the Black Sea, the Mediterranean, the Tuz Gölü (Salt Lake), or (according to *LMI*) it refers simply to the mythical "sea," the locus of the marine enemies of ancient Near Eastern storm-gods. (2) The serpent of Account 1 lives in a cave or hole in the ground and is terrestrial, while that of Account 2 is marine. The serpentine opponent of the Storm-god in both Illuyanka and the Kumarbi cycle of stories is stereotypical: powerful and gluttonous. *LMI* maintains that he is also portrayed as stupid. But it can be argued that he is merely outwitted by the more crafty and clever Inara and her father. Certainly the point of the stories is the superior wisdom of the Storm-god. If his opponent were portrayed as a dunce, it would reduce his triumph to mere "child's play." In both the Illuyanka and Ḫedammu (*CTH*, no. 348)[24] stories the protagonist, or one of his allies, defeats the serpent by trickery. The trick in the second Illuyanka story is so complex (involving an understanding of the *antiyanza* marriage customs[25]) and works only over such a lengthy period of time (during which the child born to the Daughter of a Poor Man grows to adulthood), that one would be hard-pressed to say that the serpent was stupid not to have detected it. Since nothing in the account suggests that the true parentage of the son of the Daughter of a Poor Man was known in advance by the serpent, he could not have suspected the trap. *LMI* is right in pointing out that we have no clue as to what the serpent thought he would derive from the marriage other than a son-in-law. No dowry (Hittite *iwaru*) paid by the boy's mother is mentioned.

---

[24] The Ḫedammu Myth was edited by J. Siegelová, *Appu-Märchen und Ḫedammu-Mythus*, Studien zu den Boğazköy-Texten 14 (Wiesbaden, 1971), translated in *LMI*, pp. 131–41 and *HM*², pp. 48–52.

[25] On the *antiyanza* marriage, see K. Balkan, "Eti hukukunda içgveylik," *Ankara Üniversitesi Dil ve Tarih-Coğrafya Fakültesi Dergisi* 6 (1948): 147–52; J. Friedrich, *Hethitisches Wörterbuch: Kurzgefaßte kritische Sammlung der Deutungen hethitischer Wörter*, 1st ed. (Heidelberg, 1952), p. 23 (hereafter *HW*); H. A. Hoffner, Jr., review of J. Friedrich and A. Kammenhuber, *Hethitisches Wörterbuch*, 2d ed., rev., Lieferungen 2–3 *(annaz - arahza)* (Heidelberg, 1979–80) in *BiOr* 37 (1980): 198–202; F. Imparati, "Il trasferimento di beni nell'ambito del matrimonio privato ittita," *Geo-archeologia*, no. 2 (1984): 109–21; and T. R. Bryce, *Life and Society in the Hittite World* (Oxford, 2002), pp. 123–24; 279, n. 9. The first scholar to interpret the actions of the second version of the Illuyanka Myth in terms of the *antiyanza* marriage was Güterbock, in "Hittite Mythology," p. 152. García Trabazo, *Textos religiosos hititas*, p. 79 with n. 8, adopts this view without, however, citing Güterbock, or any of the translations of the laws that have followed this view previously.

Both *LMI*, p. 42, and Haas consider the goddess Inara to be the real protagonist of Account 1. She shows similarities to ^{d}*IŠTAR* in the Hurrian myths, who in those stories aids her brother, the Storm-god (^{d}U), uses her feminine charms to seduce opponents, and remains faithful to the powerless Storm-god when the other deities have deserted him. But unlike *IŠTAR*, Inara is also a protectress of kingship.[26] Whether she was the *only* divine protectress of Hittite kingship depends on whether one considers Ḫalmaššuit in the originally Old Hittite ritual for building a new palace (KUB 29.1 and duplicates) to be the embodiment of Hittite kingship. And as *LMI* correctly notes, since we lack the original Old Hittite version and detailed knowledge of Hattic theology, we do not know if Inara's *IŠTAR* traits are Old Hittite or added by the New Hittite scribes. Judging from Inara's role of providing abundant wine, ordinary beer, and *walhi* beer (§ 5), she may have also been associated with the growth of vines and cereal crops necessary to produce these fermented beverages. The coda to Account 1 (§§ 13–16) suggests that she was a deity of the wild, open spaces (*gimra-*), where she lived alone, isolated from human life in the cities and villages. In another myth about Inara there is mention of a horn, perhaps a hunting horn, by which cult officials could produce a sound called ^{d}*Inaraš ḫaluga-* "the message of Inara." See *CHD* P s.v. *palwatalla-*.

LMI, p. 43, offers two reasons why Ḫupašiya was chosen to assist Inara in rescuing the Storm-god: courage (binding the serpent) and initiative (asks to sleep with Inara). It is true that these are only displayed after she has made him the initial offer, but they are intended to reveal innate qualities that he possessed before she selected him.

As for why he was prohibited from looking out the window at fellow mortals, Gaster suggested it was to prevent him from having sex with his wife and thereby weakening himself and transmitting to her some of the special powers now transmitted to him by his sexual union with Inara.[27] Mora prefers to think that it was a matter of preserving Ḫupašiya's purity, which would be violated by even looking at his wife.[28] Beckman attributes Ḫupašiya's death to *hybris* in first connecting with a goddess and then renouncing her.[29] Pecchioli Daddi and Polvani (in *LMI*) compare Ḫupašiya's role with that of the Old Hittite kings in their relationship to the gods and propose that in respect to his sacred royal duties—heroic (i.e., military) and sacral—he failed in the sacral and having become impure was no longer worthy of the preeminence accorded him. The explanation offered by Gaster, Gurney, and Beckman need not have any reference to Hittite kingship. But those of Mora, Pecchioli Daddi, Polvani, and García Trabazo do. Once again, we must decide if even such a prominent part of the story needs to be taken symbolically. If so, we must follow those four scholars. I am inclined to do so. My published remark (cited in *LMI*, p. 43, n. 22) that the mention of the lo-

[26] García Trabazo, *Textos religiosos hititas*, p. 79, agrees with this conception.

[27] Gaster, *Thespis*, p. 246.

[28] Mora, "Sulla mitologia ittita di origine anatolica," pp. 373–85.

[29] Beckman, "The Anatolian Myth of Illuyanka," p. 25.

cality (Tarukka) of Inara's house might have had an etiological motive, to explain a prominent ruin in the area, was predicated on the common view that the house on the rock was destroyed by Inara and sown with cress so as never again to be inhabited. Even if that house was not destroyed, its survival in that area could still have motivated the mention of Tarukka. My remark never intended to deny that the entire episode concerning the house on the rock might have a function other than etiology as well.

The "house" (or temple) built on the rock does indeed—as *LMI* correctly notes[30]—remind one of the palace of the Labarna, which in a famous Old Hittite liturgical song (KUB 36.110:13–16) is said to be built on a rock, where it endures, in contrast to the house of the traitor (*appaliyalla-*)[31] whose house built in the path of the flood is washed away. But, contrary to *LMI*, p. 43, Inara builds the house "for herself" (§ 13 C I 14 *nu=z=(š)an* ᵈ*Inaraš* É-*er wetet* "Inara built a house for herself (-*za*))—note the reflexive particle -*za*. The house "for herself" must be a temple, not a palace for Ḫupašiya as king. It is true that Ḫupašiya would also live in this house/temple but as her lover and consort, which symbolically might correspond to her priest.

There seems to be some misunderstanding of the nature of Ḫupašiya's offence. It is true, as others have pointed out, that he disobeys the goddess. But his action is more than merely becoming impure and unworthy. When he pleads to return to his home (§ 15 C i 27), he is not simply asking for a short leave to enjoy family life and return to Inara. Rather, he is renouncing the special relationship that had been established between the two of them involving the permanent renunciation of his former earthly ties. This has to be taken into consideration before symbolic allusions to Hittite kingship are drawn from the story. We know from the Instructions for Priests[32] that ordinary priests could go home to eat their main meal at dusk and even have sexual intercourse with their wives, but they had to return to the temple in the evening to spend the night there.[33] And before returning to duty they had to bathe and report in the temple that they had slept with a woman. But the purity demands on the king were more stringent and of a different order from those imposed on priests. The king was the "holy priest" (*šuppiš šankunniš*) above all others. Yet even Hittite kings occasionally became temporarily impure. If there is a symbolic allusion to the duties of kingship here, I would think that

[30] Followed by García Trabazo, *Textos religiosos hititas*, p. 79.

[31] Various attempts have been made to interpret the word *appaliyalla-* ("trapper," etc.). I myself once suggested that it meant "deceived one, fool." But since it is in a *political* aspect that Labarna's house is contrasted with that of the *appaliyalla-*, and since in Hittite treaties it is traitors who perform the action *appāli da-* "to betray (the king)," I think it best to translate *appaliyalla-* as "traitor."

[32] Edited by A. Süel, *Hitit kaynaklarında tapınak görevlileri ile ilgili bir direktif metni*, Ankara Üniversitesi Dil ve Tarih-Coğrafya Fakültesi Yayınları 350 (Ankara, 1985), translations by A. Goetze, "Hittite Instructions," in J. B. Pritchard, ed., *Ancient Near Eastern Texts Relating to the Old Testament*, 3d ed. (Princeton, 1969), pp. 207–10 (hereafter *ANET*^{3}); Kühne, "Hittite Texts," pp. 180–84; and by J. G. McMahon in *CoS* 1, pp. 217–21.

[33] KUB 13.4 ii 75–iii 1. See also iii 15, 68, and 74.

instead of sexual impurity it might lie in putting the interests of his human subjects above those of the gods who have chosen and installed him: a species of "spiritual unfaithfulness" rather than a physical one. There was always the danger that pressure from his subjects would dissuade a king from actions for which divine guidance had been given by oracular means. It is for this reason that in the Political Testament of Ḫattušili I[34] the king instructs his council (*pankuš*) regarding his successor: "Let not the elders continually speak to him ... Let not the elders of Ḫatti continually speak to you, (my son)" (KUB 1.16 ii 58–60).

It appears that recent interpreters who have expressed themselves on the issue assume that Inara killed Ḫupašiya.[35] If his sin was *hybris*, as Beckman proposed,[36] there is ample reason to expect such a harsh punishment. But we should be clear that nothing in the preserved parts of the relevant lines remotely suggests that he was killed.[37] *LMI* even says that Inara destroyed "the house." And since only one "house" is mentioned in the story, this would mean that she destroyed the temple/house that she had built on the rock. Yet only a few lines later we read that she placed in the hands of the Hittite king "her *house* and the subterranean waters." The reader must be expected to understand by "her house" precisely that house in which she had kept Ḫupašiya. The Hittite king was expected to be Ḫupašiya's successor in this house, even if not in the literal sense of Inara's consort. It seems more likely to me that Ḫupašiya was rejected as Inara's consort and sent home, although it is likely that once he was rejected by Inara, the narrator Kella would not bother to dwell upon details of his later life in this text.

If, despite the doubts I have just raised, the missing part of the tablet did tell of the death of Ḫupašiya, since it would have been Inara who killed him as punishment, it is difficult to follow Gaster, Haas, and García Trabazo in seeing his death as symbolizing the death of plant life with the arrival of another winter.[38] Why would Inara, the daughter of the Storm-god and protectress of kingship, be the appropriate one to put an end to the fertile season, symbolically initiating another cycle of infertility and the renewed

---

[34] Edited by F. Sommer and A. Falkenstein in *Die hethitisch-akkadische Bilingue des Hattusili I. (Labarna II.)*, Abhandlungen der Bayerischen Akademie der Wissenschaften, phil.-hist. Abt. n.F. 16 (Munich, 1938) (hereafter *HAB*); I. Klock-Fontanille, "Le testament politique de Ḫattušili Ier ou les conditions d'exercise de la royauté dans l'ancien royaume hittite," *Anatolia Antiqua* 4 (1996): 33–66. Translation by G. M. Beckman, "Bilingual Edict of Ḫattušili I," in W. W. Hallo and K. L. Younger, eds., *The Context of Scripture*, vol. 2, *Monumental Inscriptions from the Biblical World* (Leiden, 2000). pp. 79–81 (hereafter *CoS* 2).

[35] Güterbock, "Hittite Mythology," p. 151 ("we may assume that he was killed"); A. Goetze, "Hittite Myths, Epics, and Legends," in *ANET*[3], p. 126 ("she [killed him] in the quarrel"); Mora, "Sulla mitologia ittita di origine anatolica," pp. 373–85; Beckman, "The Anatolian Myth of Illuyanka," p. 19 ("[... killed?] him"); *LMI*, p. 51 ("l'uccisione di Hupasiya"); *GhR*, p. 104; Beckman, "The Storm-god and the Serpent (Illuyanka)," p. 150 ("[... killed?] him"); and García Trabazo, *Textos religiosos hititas*, p. 91 ("le [llegó] un pen[oso final]").

[36] Beckman, "The Anatolian Myth of Illuyanka," p. 25.

[37] See the remark in *HM*[1], p. 38, n. 1.

[38] See García Trabazo, *Textos religiosos hititas*, p. 79 and n. 7.

reign of the serpent? If it turns out that Inara killed Ḫupašiya, I would be more inclined to see this as a punishment for his *hybris*, as Beckman claimed.

LMI, pp. 47 f., propounds a theory to explain why, although the chief male deity of the two accounts is just called ᵈU or ᵈIŠKUR, the ritual at the end exalts ᵈZaliyanu (a mountain-god, not a storm-god) as the rain-giver. *LMI* thinks that the ritual pertains to the situation at the beginning of both myths, when the Storm-god was disabled, and *purulli* is performed to replace his functionality with Zaliyanu. The account of the Storm-god's recovery is merely an appendix. This theory is at first glance plausible, but I find it ultimately improbable, since the Storm-god's recovery is the main point of both stories and is not placed at the end as an appendix. No mention is made of ill effects on the land from his defeat or disablement. Unlike in the so-called Disappearing Deity Myths, the text does not elaborate the natural catastrophes that must have followed from the Storm-god's disablement. Furthermore, the text says that the occasion for celebrating the *purulli* festival was Inara's gift of her house and the subterranean waters to the king (§ 17 A ii 18–19), and this was impossible until *after* the killing of the serpent and his kin, which also resulted in the gods' aligning themselves with the Storm-god again. In terms of the narrative, then, *purulli* could be celebrated only after the Storm-god recovered his old position. *Purulli* then ensured a fruitful spring and harvest but not by surrogates of the Storm-god.

The existence of the two versions is explained as depending on when (first or second *purulli*) and where (Nerik, Kaštama, Tanipiya) it was performed in connection with the *purulli* (*LMI*, p. 48).

Gonnet proposes the theory that in the second account the son of the Storm-god represents ᵈU ᵁᴿᵁ*Nerik*, and the serpent represents the Kaškaeans who had overrun Nerik.[39] Certainly the epithet "snake" was hurled at enemies, as is clearly seen in the Political Testament of Ḫattušili I: *nu annaš=šaš* MUŠ[*-aš kuit uttar nu apāt daškit*] "he always took the word of his mother, (that) snake" (KUB 1.16 ii 10).[40] If Gonnet is right in this assumption, it shows that the characteristics associated in Hittite myths with serpents—malevolence and greed and possibly stupidity[41]—were also attributed by them to the Kaška people. Other examples of such unfavorable epithets used for the Kaška are "swineherds."[42]

---

[39] Gonnet, "Institution d'un culte chez les hittites," pp. 93–95, and cf. *LMI*, p. 45, n. 33.

[40] Edited in *HAB*; Klock-Fontanille, "Le testament politique de Ḫattušili Iᵉʳ ou les conditions d'exercise de la royauté dans l'ancien royaume hittite," with translations by Beckman in *CoS* 2, pp. 79–81, and A. Bernabé and J. A. Álvarez-Pedrosa, *Historia y leyes de los hititas: textos del imperio antiguo, el código* (Madrid, 2000), pp. 114–15.

[41] But see my doubts expressed above on the supposed stupidity of the serpent.

[42] On this point, see H. A. Hoffner, Jr., review of E. von Schuler, *Die Kaškäer* (Berlin, 1965), in *JAOS* 87 (1967): 179–85. For a general discussion of Hittite attitudes toward foreign and outsider groups, see J. Klinger, "Fremde und Außenseiter in Hatti," in V. Haas, ed., *Außenseiter und Randgruppen: Beiträge zu einer Sozialgeschichte des Alten Orients*, Xenia: Konstanzer althistorische Vorträge und Forschungen, Heft 32 (Konstanz, 1992), pp. 187–212.

Finally, I would agree with *LMI*, pp. 41–42, that the presence of what appear to be folkloristic motifs in the stories—especially the alleged "stupidity" of the serpent—are not evidence of the naiveté (*LMI*'s word is "ingenuità") of these tales. Many of the same motifs can be found not only in the Hittite myths of Hurrian origin (Ḫedammu, Ullikummi), but also in other myths and epics from the ancient Near East, such as the Egyptian tales of Horus and Seth, the Doomed Prince, and the Babylonian Gilgamesh. As *LMI* correctly notes, since the serpent tales were part of a cult legend, they had to be mere outlines, very schematic, in order to fit within the parameters of the *purulli* festival.

Line-by-Line Comments (§ Numbers from Beckman's Edition)

The Serpent Story: Account 1

§1 A i 1 The restoration [^{LÚ}GUDU$_{12}$] depends on A iv 30. In the northern Anatolian cult centers, as depicted in the cult inventories,[43] each temple had three major cult officials: a ^{LÚ}GUDU$_{12}$, a ^{LÚ}SANGA (*šankunni-*), and an ^{f}AMA-DINGIR-*LIM* (i.e., *šiwanzanni-*). The syllabic reading of ^{LÚ}GUDU$_{12}$ was not *tazzeli-*, as is still anachronistically maintained by Haas and García Trabazo.[44] The correct reading, which we know from phonetic complements was an a-stem, was probably *kumra-*, borrowed from *kumru*, which was the Old Assyrian reading of ^{LÚ}GUDU$_{12}$.[45]

A i 2 Güterbock wished to read: [*U*]*M-MA* ^{m}*Ki-il-l*[*a ŠA*] ^{d}U ^{URU}*Ne-ri-ik* (2) *ne-pí-ša-aš* ^{d}I[M-*aš* DUMU-]*aš*!? (3) *pu-ru-ul-li-ia-aš ut-tar* and render: "Thus says Killa: the words of the *purulli* festival of the Storm-god of Nerik, [the son of] the Storm-god of heaven (are as follows)."[46] If this reading were accepted, Killa would not be given here, as he is in the colophon of copy A, the title ^{LÚ}GUDU$_{12}$. Otten's collation of the line yielded different traces,[47] which were followed by *LMI*, namely, *ne-pí-ša-aš* ^{d}I[M-*ḫ*]*u-*[*n*]*a* (i.e., Tarḫuna).

A i 3 Despite a certain similarity of sound, there is no etymological connection between *purulli* and the word for the lots, *pul*, cast in the ritual at the end of one of the versions. Rather, *purulli* is a Hattic word, probably derived from *w/pur*

---

[43] Edited by C. W. Carter, "Hittite Cult Inventories" (Ph.D. diss., University of Chicago, 1962).

[44] García Trabazo, *Textos religiosos hititas*, p. 83 with n. 14.

[45] See H. A. Hoffner, Jr., "Hittite Equivalents of Old Assyrian *kumrum* and *epattum*," *WZKM* 86 (1996): 151–56, where I proposed *kumra-* as the Hittite reading of ^{LÚ}GUDU$_{12}$. H. Otten, "Erwägungen zur Kontinuität altanatolischer Kulte," in *Uluslararası 1: Hititoloji Kongresi Bilderileri (19–21 Temmuz 1990)* (Çorum, Turkey, 1990), pp. 34–42, had already correctly derived this Hittite *kumra-* from Old Assyrian *kumru*(*m*) but did not suggest that it was the syllabic equivalent of the logogram ^{LÚ}GUDU$_{12}$. For a brief discussion of Anatolian deities served by *kumru*-priests in Old Assyrian texts, see Popko, *Religions of Asia Minor*, pp. 24–25.

[46] Güterbock, "Hethitische Literatur," p. 246.

[47] H. Otten, *Or.*, n.s., 20 (1951): 331, n. 1.

"land."[48] It may have been a spring festival designed to ensure abundant crops in the coming harvests (in *LMI* "probabilmente in primavera"). The festival was originally performed in Nerik but after the loss of Nerik transferred to Hakmiš and Utruna.

LMI, p. 50, n. 7, and García Trabazo[49] quite correctly exclude Goetze and Kellermann's reading *nu-ma-a-an* "no longer," but neither notes that *nūman* does not even mean "no longer" but "does not want to" (see § 11 B i 14 below).[50]

§ 2 A i 6 Stefanini argues for a "final" force for *mān* "so that," comparing Latin *ut* and Greek *hōs*.[51] This suggestion was followed by *LMI*, p. 50, n. 8 ("[proprio] perché"), and García Trabazo[52] but not by others.[53] No "final" sense of *mān* was indicated in the *CHD* article on the word, which appeared a year after Stefanini's article.

§ 3 A i 10 Contrary to the claim in *LMI*, p. 50, n. 10, Kiškilušša is not "unattested elsewhere": it is found as Ga[š]kiluššа in KUB 19.33 + 34 i 34 (DŠ frag. 34[54]), where—as in this myth—it is also associated with URUTarukka. This fact was noted already by Gonnet[55] and was registered by del Monte.[56] One of the features that distinguishes the first Serpent Story (Account 1) from the second (Account 2) is the presence in the first of toponyms, several of which are known from other texts, and all of which establish the locale of the action in north-central Asia Minor (on this see *LMI*, p. 41).

---

48 See V. Haas, *Der Kult von Nerik*, Studia Pohl, Dissertationes Scientificae de Rebus Orientis Antiqui, 4 (Rome, 1970), p. 252 (hereafter *KN*); O. R. Gurney, *Some Aspects of Hittite Religion* (London, 1977), pp. 38–39; G. F. del Monte, "Utruna e la festa *purulli*," *Oriens Antiquus* 17 (1978): 179–92; Kellerman, "Towards the Further Interpretation of the *purulli*-Festival," pp. 35–46; *GhR*, pp. 699–747; and S. de Martino, review of V. Haas, *Geschichte der hethitischen Religion* (Leiden, 1994), in *BiOr* 54 (1997): 411–16.

49 García Trabazo, *Textos religiosos hititas*, p. 85, n. 25.

50 See H. A. Hoffner, Jr., "Hittite *mān* and *nūman*," in E. Neu, ed., *Investigationes Philologicae et Comparativae: Gedenkschrift für Heinz Kronasser* (Wiesbaden, 1982), pp. 38–45, and the concurrence of A. Morpurgo Davies, review of E. Neu, ed., *Investigationes Philologicae et Comparativae*, in *Kratylos* 28 (1983): 95–102.

51 Stefanini, "Alcuni problemi ittiti, lessicali e sintattici," p. 255.

52 García Trabazo, *Textos religiosos hititas*, p. 85, n. 26.

53 Compare *HM*[1], pp. 10–14; *GhR*, p. 704; or Beckman, "The Storm-god and the Serpent (Illuyanka)," pp. 150–51, who follow the pre-Stefanini understanding reflected in Goetze, in *ANET*[2], p. 125; Beckman, "The Anatolian Myth of Illuyanka," pp. 11–25; and Gonnet, "Institution d'un culte chez les hittites," p. 89.

54 Translated in *CoS* 1, p. 191, rt. col.

55 Gonnet, "Institution d'un culte chez les hittites," p. 100 with nn. 51 and 54.

56 G. F. del Monte, *Répertoire géographique des textes cunéiformes*, Band 6/2, *Die Orts- und Gewässernamen der hethitischen Texte, Supplement*, Beihefte zum Tübinger Atlas des Vorderen Orients, Reihe B, no. 7/6 (Wiesbaden, 1992), p. 80.

§4 A i 13 As pointed out in *CHD* s.v. *-mu*, *an-da-ma-pa* is to be analyzed as *anda=m(u)=apa*; so that Beckman's translation "Come in!" (in *CoS* 1) is excluded, and the word "mio" in Pecchioli Daddi and Polvani's translation "Accorrete (in mio aiuto)" (*LMI*) and the "mí" in García Trabazo's "¡Venid a (mí)!" should be removed from inside the parentheses, since the pronoun *-mu* is actually present in the form *-ma-pa* from **-mu* + *-apa*.

A i 14 Beckman (*CoS* 1) includes line 14 in the Storm-god's quoted invitation, probably because of the paragraph line after it. But that leaves the immediately following sentence in line 15 without an explicit subject. I prefer *LMI*'s interpretation as a statement. That *anda=m(u)=apa tiyatten* means to come to someone's aid or join his side rather than assemble for a party or festival seems clear from the evil invitation to treachery quoted in KUB 21.42 + 26.12+ iii 10 *nu=wa=kan eḫu tamedani anda tiyaweni* "Come, let's join someone else's side"; compare also KUB 26.32+ iii 10–15. Furthermore, Beckman's interpretation ignores the *nu* in line 15, which continues the statement of line 14.

§5 A i 15–18 *mekki ḫandait* and *iyāda iet* make the same statement: a lot of drink was prepared. Accordingly, Beckman (*CoS* 1) is right to translate *palḫi* as plural "vessels" (contra *LMI* "*un* vaso di vino, *uno* di ..." and García Trabazo "una *marmita* de vino, una ...").[57] In fact, the form is probably a collective in *-i*, not a neuter pl. Stefanini seems to think the three beverages are drawn from a single large vessel.[58] But that would not fit with the three mentions of *palḫi*. The beverages *marnuwan* and *walḫi* are varieties of beer.[59] The New Hittite Script copy's *i-ia-a-"šu"* is explained by the "stepped" form of DA in Old Hittite Script, which makes confusion with ŠU possible for a New Hittite copyist. For the loss of final *r* in Hittite, see Neu and Melchert.[60] For another (Middle Hittite in New Script) example of *iyata tameta*, see KBo 12.42:4–5 *uwaweni nu=wa iyata tameta* / *pe harweni*. See also Puhvel, *HED* s.v. *iyata(r)*.

A i 20 I prefer "found" (*HM*[2] 12) rather than "encountered" (*LMI*, *CoS* 1, García Trabazo) for *wemi(e)t*, since it seems unlikely that Inara's meeting with him was by chance: I think she intentionally went in search of a particular man and made her offer to him, just as the bee in the Telepinu Myth searches for and eventually finds the god who will restore fertility and plenty.

---

57 García Trabazo, *Textos religiosos hititas*, p. 87.

58 Stefanini, "Alcuni problemi ittiti, lessicali e sintattici," pp. 255–56.

59 Correctly García Trabazo, *Textos religiosos hititas*, p. 87.

60 E. Neu, "Hethitisch /r/ im Wortauslaut," in J. Tischler, ed., *Serta Indogermanica: Festschrift für Günter Neumann zum 60. Geburtstag*, Innsbrucker Beiträge zur Sprachwissenschaft 40 (Innsbruck, 1982), pp. 205–26; H. C. Melchert, "Word-final *r* in Hittite," in Y. L. Arbeitman, ed., *A Linguistic Happening in Memory of Ben Schwarz: Studies in Anatolian, Italic, and Other Indo-European Languages* (Louvain-la-Neuve, 1988), pp. 215–34; and H. C. Melchert, "A New Anatolian 'Law of Finals'," *Journal of Ancient Civilizations* 8 (1993): 105–13.

§7 A i 21 Instead of a dative-locative form ᵐ*Ḫupašiya* might be a vocative here: "Thus spoke Inar: 'O Ḫupašiya, I am about to…'."

A i 23 For the use of *ḫarp-* (mid.) for divorce (and remarriage?), see Laws §31 (with *-kan*) and for livestock wandering from one corral or fold to another in Laws §66 (without local particle). This double emphasis of separation from association and joining another is particularly appropriate here, where in order to become Inara's partner, Ḫupašiya must first leave his wife and family. Inara needs the assistance of a mortal to accomplish her task, much as there was a necessary collaboration between divine and human participants in the rituals to recover the "Disappearing Deity" in the Old Hittite Telepinu-type myths (cf. Beckman's observation quoted in *LMI*, p. 43, n. 22). To his observation may be added that even in the building rituals it is always stressed in the ritual dedicatory prayers that the mortal king who authorized its building was not acting alone as a human but in concert with all the gods: "This temple which we have just built for you, O god—and here he calls by name the deity for whom they were building it—it was not we who built it: all the gods built it."[61]

§8 A i 24–26 Ḫupašiya consents on the condition that he be permitted to sleep with the goddess. His motive here is clearly not mere lust, but precisely what is it? Is he expressing a belief (shared also by the narrator of this story) that sexual intercourse with the goddess will confer upon him the necessary courage and skill to succeed in her commission? If the latter is the case, then his precondition both ensures his success in the near future and obligates him in the long run to abandon his family permanently. This is an important question in view of *LMI*'s theory about the reasons why Inara chose Ḫupašiya (*LMI*, p. 43, top). In Hittite belief, as expressed in the Paškuwatti ritual, sleeping with a goddess in her temple (Lat. *incubatio*[62]) conferred sexual potency on a previously impotent man.[63]

§9 B i 4′–5′ There is a certain (perhaps deliberate) ambiguity in *munnāit* "hid": Inara hid Ḫupašiya from his own family (wife and children), and she hid him from the invited serpent. Although the text does not state it explicitly, the Storm-god himself is in hiding until the serpent has been tied up. There is a sexual motive in the words *-z unuttat* "adorned herself" (line 5′). The serpent is attracted to the feast not just by the lavish food but by the sexual charms of Inara. Compare the actions of *IŠTAR* in the Kumarbi Cycle, where she seeks to disable

[61] *kāša kē kue* É.DINGIR-*LIM tuk ANA* DINGIR-*LIM wetummen* DINGIR-*LIM=ya=kan* / *ŠUM=ŠU ḫalzai wedanzi=ya=at kuedani nu=war=at UL* / *anzaš wetummen* DINGIR.MEŠ=*war=at ḫūmanteš weter*, KBo 4.1 i 28–30 (*CTH*, no. 413).

[62] Goetze, *Kleinasien*, p. 148.

[63] See the edition of the Paškuwatti ritual by H. A. Hoffner, Jr., "Paškuwatti's Ritual against Sexual Impotence (*CTH* 406)," *Aula Orientalis* 5 (1987): 271–87 and the discussion there of the Hittite concept of *incubatio*.

or distract the Storm-god's reptilian foes twice, successfully in Ḫedammu[64] and unsuccessfully in Ullikummi (*HM*², p. 61 § 36), by displaying her naked charms and singing.[65]

§ 10 B i 9–10 (cf. B i 17–18) Although the serpent's offspring are not mentioned in B i 17–18, it is clear that they are present at the banquet because it is necessary to kill the entire family to ensure that no other member of the brood can later rise against the Storm-god and regain control of the subterranean waters. Compare Kumarbi's emasculation of Anu to prevent any descendant from taking revenge (*HM*², pp. 41–43).

B i 11 *LMI*, *HM*², and Beckman (*CoS* 1) translate ᴰᵁᴳ*palḫan ḫūmandan* as "every vessel" and García Trabazo as plural accusative "todas las *marmitas*."[66] But Melchert has correctly observed that there is no evidence other than this passage for an a-stem variant of ⁽ᴰᵁᴳ⁾*palḫi-*.[67] He interprets the two-word phrase as the Old Hittite genitive plural in *-an*: "they drank (some) of all the vessels," a partitive genitive, which makes better sense.

§ 11 B i 14 *nūman* can mean either "not want to" or "be unable to."[68] Contrary to earlier claims, it never means "no longer."[69] In *HM*² I rendered this line as "not want to," while *LMI* and García Trabazo chose "be unable to" ("non furono ... in grado di," "no pueden bajar"). It could be either.

B i 16 The verb *kalel(i)ye-* is archaic (not noticed in *HED* K 22): all datable texts or fragments in which it appears have an Old Hittite archetype. It tends to be replaced by other words for "bind, tie" in later Hittite.[70] There is a noun *kaliliulli-* derived from this verb root in KUB 7.1 + KBo 3.8 ii 40 (Old Hittite in New Hittite Script).

§ 12 B i 17–18 Although the Storm-god needs a mortal's help to trap and disarm the serpent, the execution must be carried out by the Storm-god himself. For line 18, see *LMI*, p. 51, n. 14, where the views of Gonnet and *LMI* are contrasted. The gods fall in behind whichever party wins. Although they were all invited to the $EZEN_4$, they waited until after the serpent's death to take the side of the Storm-god.[71]

---

[64] Edited in Siegelová, *Appu-Märchen*, pp. 54–55, translated in *HM*², p. 54.

[65] For the importance of these two seduction attempts in determining the sequence of the myths in the Kumarbi Cycle, see *HM*², p. 42 (introduction).

[66] García Trabazo, *Textos religiosos hititas*, p. 89.

[67] H. C. Melchert, review of D. Yoshida, *Die Syntax des althethitischen substantivischen Genitivs* (Heidelberg, 1987), in *Kratylos* 34 (1989): 182.

[68] As demonstrated in Hoffner, "Hittite *mān* and *nūman*," pp. 38–45.

[69] García Trabazo, *Textos religiosos hititas*, p. 89: "ya no pueden" should have been rendered "(ya) no pueden," since there is no Hittite term for "(no) longer" in the text.

[70] Suggested already in H. A. Hoffner, Jr., review of Ph. H. J. Houwink ten Cate, *Records of the Early Hittite Empire (C. 1450–1380 B.C.)* (Istanbul, 1970), in *JNES* 31 (1972): 29–35.

[71] A point recognized also by García Trabazo, *Textos religiosos hititas*, p. 89, n. 53.

§13 C i 14–15 *-za-an* stands for *-z(a)* + *-šan*. The duplicates equate ^{d}Inaraš here with ^{d}LAMMA-*aš*. But since the copies are late, how early does this equation go back?[72] The "house" on a rock is obviously a temple. On the significance of *-za* here, see the discussion above.

C i 17 *ašaš-/ašeš-* "to settle (someone)" implies that she established his *permanent* residence with her.[73] Quite likely Ḫupašiya has been made Inara's priest not just her lover. And since, if as a special kind of celibate, live-in priest, he sleeps every night in the cella, he thus sleeps *with* Inara. It is not possible to assume that the Hittite ^{LÚ}GUDU$_{12}$ was celibate, since the "wife of the G.," DAM ^{LÚ}GUDU$_{12}$, is mentioned in IBoT 3.1 23, 26, but perhaps an earlier Hattian equivalent was celibate and was conceived as the bedfellow of the goddess. Hittite priests did not sleep in the cella.

C i 17–22 The text suggests that Inara's house was so close to Ḫupašiya's home that looking out the window would cause him to see his family. What is the significance of keeping Ḫupašiya from seeing his family? Possibly it is that he has agreed to become a celibate priest and voluntarily cuts himself off from wife and family. In a similar way the "son of the Storm-god" in Account 2 severs his familial ties in order to join the family of the serpent, as an *antiyanza*.[74] Looking through windows, especially temple or cella windows, was potentially dangerous. In one oracle inquiry it was determined that the deity was angry because someone outside the cella had looked through a window and seen the divine statue.[75] In this case, however, we have the opposite: a lover-priest of the goddess looking *out* a temple window and seeing a woman whom he was supposed to have renounced. Temple windows marked the boundary between sacred and profane. For this reason offerings made to holy places in the temple always include the windows.[76]

§14 C i 25 Ḫupašiya's plea here is to be released from his vows (as a priest?) to Inara.

[72] For a discussion, see J. G. McMahon, *The Hittite State Cult of the Tutelary Deities*, AS 25 (Chicago, 1991), pp. 24–25.

[73] Cf. García Trabazo, *Textos religiosos hititas*, p. 89, "estableció a Ḫupašiya."

[74] For the significance of *-z(a)* in 22 ("your *own* wife and children"), see H. A. Hoffner, Jr., "Studies of the Hittite Particles, I," review of O. Carruba, *Die satzeinleitenden Partikeln in den indogermanischen Sprachen Anatoliens* (Rome, 1969), in *JAOS* 93 (1973): 524, on its use with the synonymous *šakuwai-*.

[75] The relevant passage reads: "Because it was determined by oracle that the god's anger was because of sacrilege (*maršaštarri-*), we questioned the temple servants. (One of them,) Tila, said: 'People aren't supposed to look at (the statue of) the Stormgod. Yet a woman looked in through a window'" (D. J. Wiseman, *The Alalakh Texts*, Occasional Papers of the British Institute of Archaeology in Ankara, no. 2 [London, 1953], p. 454 ii 7–10).

[76] See Goetze, *Kleinasien*, p. 162.

§16 A ii 9–12 *LMI* assumes the broken section contains three important events: "la descrizione dell'ira di Inara, la distruzione della casa - sulle cui rovine sembra che il dio della tempesta semini erba - e l'uccisione di Ḫupašiya." None of these assumed events, however, is supported by the traces that remain. It is true that the mortal who collaborates with the Storm-god in the second account dies at the end. But this is the only reason to assume that Inara kills Ḫupašiya. His disobedience in looking out the window and his plea to return home very likely resulted in his dismissal from Inara's house (temple) and from the priesthood.

A ii 13 Goetze (*ANET*²) arrived at his translation "sowed cress/weeds over the ruins" by reading Ú[ZÀ.A]Ḫ.LI = Akk. *saḫlû*, Hitt. *zaḫḫeli*. He was followed by *LMI*, p. 51 ("sembra che ... semini erba") but not by Beckman (edition and *CoS* 1) or by me (*HM*²).[77] The gesture is, of course, perfectly appropriate to condemning a site never to be inhabited again. But the reading of the traces raises objections. In the copy there is insufficient space to restore ZAG. Furthermore, in attested examples of ZÀ.AḪ.LI in Hittite texts it either has no determinative or it has the postposed determinative SAR. It never has the preposed determinative Ú. In addition, a new text from Ortaköy (Or 95/3)[78] gives the correct "Hittite" reading of ZÀ.AḪ.LI(.SAR), namely, *marašḫanḫaš*. I used quotation marks on "Hittite" because this could be either a real Hittite word or a Hattic loanword. The previously known reading *zaḫḫeli*, if it is not a misreading, appears on its face to be a Sumero-Akkadian loanword into Hittite. With regard to the possibility of reading ZÀ.AḪ.LI here in Illuyanka, we learn from the immediately following context that Inara went to Kiškilušša and placed her house/temple and the subterranean waters in the lands of the (Hittite) king (see discussion above). She could hardly do this if she had sown its ruins with cress/weeds.

§17 A ii 15–20 Stefanini prefers to translate: "And since (*kuit*) we are (re-)performing the first *purulli*—(that is) how (*mān*) Inara ... in Kiskilussa set her house and the river of the watery abyss into the hands of the king—the hand of the king [will hold] the house of Inara and the watery abyss."[79] But one could render this: "And (this is) why (*kuit*) we celebrate the first *purulli*." The *purulli* celebration was motivated by Inara's gift to the king of the subterranean waters, which she obtained by killing the serpent. This would agree with what *LMI*, p. 41, writes: "Inara affida al re ...; in ricordo di tale avvenimento viene istituita la prima festa del *purulli*." And since Inara makes this grant only *after* the defeat of the serpent, causing the gods to realign with the Storm-god, it

[77] García Trabazo, *Textos religiosos hititas*, pp. 90–91, line 13′, printed Beckman's transliteration but translated using Goetze's older reading instead: "El dios de la Temptestad [*sembró*] ma[lez]a [*sobre las ruinas de la casa*]."

[78] Published by A. Süel and O. Soysal, "A Practical Vocabulary from Ortaköy," in G. M. Beckman, R. H. Beal, and J. G. McMahon, eds., *Hittite Studies in Honor of Harry A. Hoffner, Jr. on the Occasion of His 65th Birthday* (Winona Lake, Indiana, 2003), pp. 349–65.

[79] Stefanini, "Alcuni problemi ittiti, lessicali e sintattici," p. 256.

would be an objection to the later assertion in *LMI*, p. 48 ("Nel momento di debolezza del dio della tempesta l'ordine di importanza degli dei viene modificato e la festa del *purulli* viene celebrata proprio per assicurare che il paese di Hatti prosperi anche senza la momentanea protezione della sua divinità principale"). The granting of her house/temple to the Hittite king further shows that the king has inherited what Ḫupašiya had forfeited, namely, the priesthood of Inara and the control of the subterranean water sources.

§ 18 A ii 21 Although ḪUR.SAGZali(ya)nu (also written dZali(ya)nu) is worshiped in various festival texts, ironically he does not appear in the Tetešḫawi festival, the very one Pecchioli Daddi thinks might be *purulli*.

A ii 22–23 *LMI* takes *ḫeuš* as nom. sg., *ḫinikta* as pres. middle(!), and the thought is a pres.-future passive. It renders *ḫeuš* ... *ḫinikta* as "dopo che avrà distribuito la pioggia" "after the rain will have been distributed." My earlier translation in HM^2 is wrong on this point and should be corrected accordingly.

A ii 24 Although this in itself does not prove Pecchioli Daddi's theory that the Tetešḫawi festival is the *purulli*, it is interesting that the LÚ GIŠGIDRU participates in the Festival of dTetešḫawi (*CTH*, no. 738), as (judging from this line) he also does in $EZEN_4$ *purulli*, and other festival texts mention the "staffs of Zaliyanu" (GIŠGIDRU.ḪI.A dZaliyanu, KUB 20.80 iii 17).

The Serpent Story: Account 2

§ 21 D iii 1–5 In the broken context we are not told the circumstances of the original defeat of the Storm-god. But here he is not only defeated. Although, contrary to nature, the injured Storm-god can continue to live even without a heart, he is clearly disabled. What is the significance of the choice of "heart and eyes" among all other body parts (ears, nose, head, brain, etc.) that could be taken from him? There are rituals that refer to parts of the Storm-god's body. In KUB 17.29 ii 6–19 the violating of a neighbor's boundary line is said to be tantamount to violating or injuring the Storm-god's knees, and violating a roadway (which also served as an even more conspicuous boundary) was violating the Storm-god's chest (UZUGABA). Do the eyes and heart refer to his "intelligence and courage"? Perhaps, but without a commentary like the one just cited from KUB 17.29 we really cannot be certain. In the Late Egyptian story of the Contendings of Horus and Seth, the evil god Seth removes from the sleeping Horus his two eyes and buries them. Later, Hathor, the Mistress of the Southern Sycamore, miraculously restores Horus's eyes. Here there is much native Egyptian symbolism involving the "Eye of Horus."[80]

---

[80] Translated in $ANET^2$, pp. 14–17, and W. K. Simpson, ed., *The Literature of Ancient Egypt* (New Haven and London, 1973), p. 119.

§ 22 A iii 4 *LMI* has pointed out that a DUMU.MUNUS ^{LÚ}MAŠ.EN.KAK "daughter of a poor man" appears in a festival text for ^{d}Tetešḫabi (*CTH*, no. 738: KBo 25.48 iii 6′), which may be another name for ^{d}Inara. The context mentions a NIN.DINGIR, a LÚ ^{GIŠ}GIDRU, and DUMU.MEŠ É.GAL. She may also appear without the ^{LÚ}MAŠ.EN.KAK in another EZEN$_4$ ^{d}*Tetešḫabi* fragment in the sequence NIN.DINGIR [DU]MU.MUNUS AMA.DINGIR-*LIM=ya* (KUB 11.32 + 20.17+ ii 8, 25). In all of these contexts there are many Hattic words and phrases (*illuwaya illuwaya*, and *awazza awazzanga* and *hakanteš kantišma mayamauma*) called out by the participants. Since this DUMU.MUNUS ^{LÚ}MAŠ.EN.KAK in the Tetešḫabi festival always occurs as a kind of priestess, it is possible that she represented a class of girls given to the cult of Tetešḫabi by poorer parents who could not afford a dowry to obtain husbands for them. If so, then perhaps in the second version of the Illuyanka Myth the Storm-god actually takes an unmarried temple-girl as his wife. Against this interpretation is the grouping of the DUMU.MUNUS between NIN.DINGIR and AMA.DINGIR-*LIM* in KUB 11.32 + ii 8, since she is flanked by relatively high-ranking women in the cult, a position not to be expected of a poor girl donated to a temple. Her prominence in the festival suggests an important position. Perhaps she is the priestess who plays the role of the wife of the Storm-god in the Serpent Story as a cult drama.

A iii 10 ff. The É DAM-*KA* constitutes more than just her father. Note the -*šmaš* dative forms in 11, 13, 15 and the plural verbs *pier* in 14, 16. The decision on the nature of the "dowry" to this *antiyanza* was apparently made by her father and at least one other person, perhaps his wife. Compare Laws §§ 28–28. Of course the marriage customs and laws reflected in the original Serpent Story were not Hittite but Hattian. Nevertheless, in the present Hittite adaptation they probably reflect Hittite family law as well.

A iii 22 *LMI*, p. 53 does not seem to translate the *namma*, which I take as "again" (he fought the serpent there before). If the sea is a historical one, *LMI* prefers the Black Sea to the Mediterranean, since the *antiyanza* marriage custom reflected in Account 2 is thought to be Hattian and therefore "northern."

A iii 23 The -*ši* is anticipatory for the serpent mentioned in line 24. The apparent acc. sg. ^{MUŠ}*illuyanka*[*n*] shows that *namma* cannot mean "again" here but "at last" (*HM*^{2}, p. 13). See the discussion in *CHD* s.v. *namma*. Here, too, *LMI*, p. 53, chose not to render the *namma* explicitly.

A iii 25 I would personally include among the linguistic archaisms of this text the use of a supinum on a perfective stem: *tarḫ*(*u*)*wan*, instead of imperfective *tarḫiškiwan*, and the genitive + postposition (*illuyankaš katta*).

§ 26 A iii 29 First clause: not "seize me" (*LMI*) but "include me" (*HM*^{2}, p. 13). This is the meaning of -*za* + *apa* … *anda ep*-. For a different view, see E. Rieken, in *Die Indogermanistik und ihre Anrainer* (Innsbruck, 2004), p. 255.

A iii 30 This clause is asyndetic, indicating that it is essentially describing the action of iii 29 more fully. "Including" the son means having no pity upon him.

A iii 31 The referrent in -*ŠU* is (perhaps intentionally?) vague: is the young man here styled as the natural son of the Storm-god (*LMI*, p. 53, "il suo proprio figlio"; *GhR*, p. 705, "seinen [eigenen] Sohn") or the legal son (*antiyant-*) of the serpent? Perhaps the lack of a -*za* to identify the -*ŠU* with the subject of the sentence points to the second alternative: he is now the legal son of the serpent, and it is as such that he is killed (*kuenta*).

§ 28 D iv 1′–4′ Beckman and *LMI* agree on the translation. But what does this mean? Notice that the verbs are preterites: the action is not prescriptive but a record of something once done. *LMI*, pp. 47–48, gives a plausible explanation: with the disablement of the Storm-god at the beginning of the story, it is necessary to find a new deity to provide the water to sustain the land. This means that the Storm-god, who was once the "foremost" god (*ḫantezziyaš*) has been made "last" (*appezziyaš*), and a subordinate deity (*appezziyaš*), in this case the Mountain-god Zaliyanu, has been elevated or promoted to assume the role of the "foremost" deity (*ḫantezziyaš*). The specific method of choosing a subordinate to fill this role as "foremost" is the casting of the lot (§ 31 C iv 13). The reason for the use of the plural *ḫantezziuš* and *appezziuš* is that this is a general statement, one that does not refer specifically to the incident of the replacement of the Storm-god by Zaliyanu but to the reversal of roles in times of emergency.

§ 29 D iv 5′–7′ ᵈZalinuiša appears to be a Hattic stem form.[81] Haas renders this sentence: "(Deshalb) ist Zali(ya)nu, nämlich seine Gemahlin Za(š)ḫapuna, größer als der Wettergott von Nerik."[82] My translation in *HM*² should be amended to "Zalinuwa's wife, Zašḫapuna, is greater than the Storm-god of Nerik." ᵈZalinu(iša), being a mountain-god, is certainly a male, which means ᵈZa(š)ḫapuna is female.

Exemplar D reads ᴸᵁ́*taḫpurili*, while the other manuscripts, A and C, have ᵐTaḫpurili.[83] This Hattic personal name may be built upon a variant spelling of the DN ᵈTaḫ(a)puna. This name was mistakenly read as ᵐ*Taḫ-pu-tal-li* by Laroche.[84]

§ 30 D iv 10 *eš-* (mid.) with -*šan* but without -*za* could be an archaic feature surviving from the original Old Hittite version. And if so, it would be a rare piece of evidence for an Old Hittite origin of the *ritual* portion of the text. But then again it might just be an affectation, that is, an archaizing feature. *paiwani ešuwašta*

---

[81] According to B. H. L. van Gessel, in *Onomasticon of the Hittite Pantheon*, Parts 1–3, Handbuch der Orientalistik, 1. Abteilung, Band 33:1–3 (Leiden, 1998–2001), pp. 572–73.

[82] *GhR*, p. 706.

[83] Cf. *LMI*, p. 53, n. 23.

[84] E. Laroche, *Les noms des Hittites* (Paris, 1966), p. 169, no. 1204.

occurs in an Old Hittite Script passage (KUB 31.143 ii 36), which might suggest that D's *kuwapi ešuwašta* is closer to the Old Hittite version than A's *kuwapit ešuwaštati*.

§ 31 D iv 12 Manuscript D has the post-Old Hittite nonassimilated form *ma-a-an-wa*, versus A and C with the Old Hittite form *ma-a-wa*.
D iv 15 Beckman, *LMI*, and Haas all render ^{NA_4}ŠU.U as "diorite," although there is reason to translate it as "basalt."[85] The precise identification of this stone type in Hittite must for the time being remain open. As for the translation of lines D iv 14–16 and duplicates, see the long note in *LMI*, p. 54, n. 26. *LMI* and Polvani[86] understand that the $GUDU_{12}$-priest who holds Zaliyanu sits on the throne above the spring, while Haas paraphrases ("setzt ... (ihn) auf den Dioritstuhl nieder") in order to make the text say that the $GUDU_{12}$ seats Zaliyanu on the throne above the spring.[87] The $^{LÚ}GUDU_{12}$'s holding Zaliyanu is probably the same thing as his holding the staff (^{GIŠ}GIDRU) of Zaliyanu, mentioned in Bo 3649 iii 4′.[88] The ^{GIŠ}GIDRU "staff" is a visible symbol of the Mountain-god Zaliyanu. And if this is the case, then it rules out Haas's idea that the god's statue is "seated," since one cannot "seat" (*ašeš-*) a staff.

§ 32 A iv 14 ff. A iv 17 preserves an archaic writing of *ša-al-li-iš*, for which D iv 19 has *šal-li-iš*.

§ 33 The text reads "these three LÚ.MEŠ remain in Tanipiya," *perhaps* using the logogram LÚ.MEŠ (literally "men") to refer to the god Zaliyanu and two goddesses Zašḫapuna and Tazzuwašši. Kellerman is wrong when she writes that the expression LÚ.MEŠ (§ 33 A iv 19) is "usually found in cult inventories as designating statues."[89] The collocation DINGIR.MEŠ LÚ.MEŠ in all Hittite text genres denotes male deities and in the cult inventories ALAM LÚ designates the statue of a male (deity). But LÚ.MEŠ alone does not designate statues of deities, either in the cult inventories or anywhere else in Hittite texts. So unless it refers to three male priests of these three deities, the use of LÚ.MEŠ in § 33 remains an unsolved problem.

---

[85] Cf. A. M. Polvani, *La terminologia dei minerali nei testi ittiti, Parte prima*, Eothen 3 (Florence, 1988), pp. 38–46, and add now *CAD* Š/3 161 f. s.v. *šû* s.

[86] Ibid., pp. 160–61.

[87] *GhR*, p. 706.

[88] Haas, *KN*, p. 80, n. 4.

[89] Kellerman, "Towards the Further Interpretation of the *purulli*-Festival," p. 36.

HOW TO MAKE THE GODS SPEAK: A LATE BABYLONIAN TABLET RELATED TO THE MICROZODIAC

Hermann Hunger, Universität Wien

I

The tablet BM 33535[1] (fig. 1) belongs to a small group of texts based on the so-called microzodiac and was used in connection with medical treatment. In view of Bob Biggs's long-standing work on medical texts, this little tablet may be of interest to him. He may also be able to solve the problems that I could not.

BM 33535 (= Rm 4, 91)

Obv.

1 MÚL.MAŠ.MAŠ *šá* MÚL.PA Lagaš(ŠIR.BUR.LA)^{ki} ⸢x x⸣ [x$^?$]

2 *kiškanû*(GIŠ.KÍN) *peṣû*(BABBAR) *kiškanû*(GIŠ.KÍN) *ṣalmu*(MI) *kiškanû*(GIŠ.KÍN) *sāmu*(SA$_5$) Ú.NI[R]$^?$

3 *amīlānu*(Ú.LÚ-*an*) *engisû*(NA$_4$.EN.GI.SA$_6$) *anzaḫḫu*(NA$_4$.AN.NE)

4 *šá 2-i eṣ-pu* NA$_4$ ḫe-e$^?$-en-zu // SA.A

---

5 MÚL.MAŠ.MAŠ *šá* MÚL.PA *ūm*(UD) *il āli*(URU) *ma-a-šú* ^{d}*Sin Šamaš*(^{d}UTU)

6 ^{d}U.GUR *isinni*(EZEN) *Ninurta*(^{d}MAŠ)

---

7 DIŠ *ina Simāni*(ITI.SIG$_4$) *ištu*(TA) UD-1-KAM *adi*(EN) UD-30-KAM

8 *amīlu*(LÚ) *lim-ta-*[*a*]*s*$^?$*-su šaman*(Ì) *šimeššalî*(ŠIM.ŠEŠ) *lippašiš*(ḪÉ.ŠÉŠ)

9 *taktīma*(TÚG.AN.TA.DUL) *liltabiš*(MU$_4$.MU$_4$) *šēna*(KUŠ.E.SÍR) *liškun*(ḪÉ.GAR)

10 *akla*(NINDA) *šá arsuppi*(ŠE.EŠTUB) *līkul*(KÚ) KAŠ.ŠE.GA$^?$ *lišti*(NAG)

11 *li-pi-ir ina ūri*(ÙR) *linīl*(ḪÉ.NÁ)

12 AN KUN NU MU$_4$.MU$_4$ *ilū*(DINGIR.MEŠ) *mu-ši-ti*

13 *itti*(KI)*-šú i-dab-bu-bu*

---

[1] I thank the Trustees of the British Museum for granting me permission to publish this tablet.

14 *ina mašak*(KUŠ) *imēri*(ANŠE) *ina šer'ān*(SA) *imēri*(ANŠE) *ina ṭurri*(DUR) *takilti*(SÍG. ZA.GÌN.NA)

15 *tál-pap ina kišādi*(GÚ)*-šú tašakkan*(GAR)

16 MÚL.MAŠ.MAŠ GIŠ.ḫa-lu-úb MUŠEN$^?$ ab$^?$ si$^?$ ki$^?$

Rev.

1 MÚL.ALLA *šá* MÚL.PA *Mu-ta-ba*[*l*^{ki}]

2 GIŠ.ḫa-lu-úb *šaššūgu*(GIŠ.MES.GÀM) Ú [x]

3 *zēr*(NUMUN) *urṭî*(URI) NA$_4$.AN.BAR NA$_4$.URUDU NA$_4$.*mu-ṣa*

4 GIŠ$^?$ SA.A

5 MÚL.ALLA *šá* PA *ūm*(UD) *ìl āli*(URU) *Šamaš*(^{d}UTU) *dajjān*(DI.KUD) *māti*(KUR)

6 *u* ^{d}Šul-pa-è-a *pīt*(BAD) *bābi*(KÁ)

7 DIŠ *ina Du'ūzi*(ITI.ŠU) *ištu*(TA) UD-1-KAM *adi*(EN) UD-30-KAM

8 *amīlu*(LÚ) *lim-tas-sa šaman*(Ì.GIŠ) sa ba li za ma$^?$ li

9 *lippašiš*(ḪÉ.ŠÉŠ) *li-tar-ri-šú šēna*(KUŠ.E.SÍR) *ṣeḫerta*(TUR$^?$.RA) *liškun*(GAR-*un*)

10 *ḫallūra*(GÚ.GAL) *līkul*(ḪÉ.KÚ) *kakkâ*(GÚ.TUR) *līkul*(ḪÉ.KÚ)

11 *erša*(GIŠ.NÁ) *li-is-kùp-ma linīl*(ḪÉ.NÁ)

12 *ištar*(^{d}15)*-šú itti*(KI)*-šú idabbub*(KA-*ub*)

13 *ina mašak*(KUŠ) *sisî*(ANŠE.KUR.RA) *ina šer'ān*(SA) *sisî*(ANŠE.KUR.RA)

14 *ina ṭurri*(DUR) *šipāti*(SÍG) *sāmāti*(SA$_5$) *tál-pap ina kišādi*(GÚ)*-šú tašakkan*(GAR-*an*)

15 MÚL.ALLA MUŠEN *qa-qu-ú* GIŠ.ḪAŠḪUR$^?$

Translation

Obv.

1 (Subsection) Gemini of Sagittarius. Lagaš, ...;

2 white *kiškanû*-tree, black *kiškanû*-tree, red *kiškanû*-tree, ...,

3 *amīlānu*-plant, *engisû*-stone, *anzaḫḫu*-glass

4 which is multiplied by$^?$ two, ...-stone. SA.A

5 (Subsection) Gemini of Sagittarius: (feast)day of the city god. The twins$^?$ Sin and Šamaš.

6 Nergal. Feast of Ninurta.

---

7 In Simanu, from the 1st to the 30th day,
8 let the man wash himself, let him anoint himself with the oil of the *šimeššalû*-plant,
9 let him be clothed with a blanket, let him put on a sandal,
10 let him eat bread (made) from *arsuppu*-barley, let him drink beer (made) from *arsuppu*-barley,
11 let him put on a headdress?, let him sleep on the roof,
12 let him not be clothed ..., (and) the gods of the night
13 will talk with him.

---

14 You wrap (a medication) in a (piece of) hide of a donkey, with a sinew of a donkey, with a thread of red wool,
15 you place (it) on his neck.

---

16 Gemini: ḫalub-tree, ...-bird.

Rev.

1 (Subsection) Cancer of Sagittarius. Mutabal.
2 ḫalub-tree, *šaššūgu*-tree, [...]-plant,
3 seed of *urṭû*-plant, iron ore, copper ore, *muṣu*-stone.
4 ... SA.A

---

5 (Subsection) Cancer of Sagittarius: (feast)day of the city god, Šamaš, judge of the land,
6 and Šulpaʾe. Opening of the gate.

---

7 In month Duʾuzu, from the 1st to the 30th day,
8 let the man wash himself, let him anoint himself with oil of ...,
9 let him ..., let him put on a small? sandal,
10 let him eat chickpeas, let him eat lentils,
11 let him lie still (on) a bed and sleep,
12 his goddess will talk with him.

---

13 You wrap (a medication) in a (piece of) hide of a horse, with a sinew of a horse,
14 with a thread of red wool, (and) place (it) on his neck.

---

15 Cancer: bird *qaqû*, apple? tree.

Commentary

Obv.

1 The traces at the end of the line could be taken for GIŠ.KÍN, as in the following line, but there is little space in the break at the end to add a color. The usual sequence of colors is white, black, red, and green; the first three of them follow in line 2, so the missing green would have to be restored at the end of line 1. Since colors are usually enumerated beginning with white, the color green in line 1 would be out of sequence.

4 In view of the number 2-*i*, I take *eṣ-pu* to be from *eṣēpu* "to double." It should be noted, though, that usually *eṣēpu* is construed with *ana*; even the reading of the following stone name is unclear to me; the signs SA.A are preceded by a separation sign. Their meaning is obscure. They occur again at the end of the first paragraph of the reverse.

5 f. Cf. Weidner *Gestirn-Darstellungen*, p. 25 "Gemini" (read probably EZEN ^{d}MAŠ there too).

8 There is little space for [*a*]*s*, but in view of rev. 8 this is the most likely restoration.

10 ŠE.GA is probably an error for ŠE.EŠTUB, which looks similar; I could not find a suitable reading for KAŠ ŠE.GA.

11 The interpretation of *li-pi-ir* as a precative of *apāru* is uncertain because it is not said what the headdress should be.

12 If an emendation of AN KUN to GIŠ.KUN is accepted, one could understand this sentence as *rapašta la ulabbaš* "let him leave his loin without clothing."

16 On the basis of the parallel line at the end of the reverse, I expect the name of a bird here too but cannot read it.

Rev.

9 I could not find a satisfactory explanation for *li-tar-ri-šú*. Neither (*w*)*arāšu* nor *erēšu* makes much sense.

11 One would expect *ina erši*.

II

The astrological concept of a microzodiac was first detected in cuneiform material by A. Sachs.[2] Each sign of the zodiac is subdivided into twelve parts; these parts have the usual names of the zodiacal signs, beginning with the name of the sign that is subdivided. In this way, the first part of the first sign, Aries, is called Aries of Aries, the

[2] A. J. Sachs, "Babylonian Horoscopes," *JCS* 6 (1952): 71f.

second Taurus of Aries, and so on. Since each sign has a length of 30 degrees, each part has a length of $2\frac{1}{2}$ degrees. A celestial body, such as the moon or a planet, can then by its position in the zodiac be associated not just with the main signs, but also with their parts. Thereby the possible astrological associations are multiplied.

Since Sachs's discovery, more texts that in some way made use of a microzodiac were published, notably by E. Weidner.[3] The following related materials are known to me at present.

From Uruk

[1]	VAT 7851	(Weidner *Gestirn-Darstellungen*, pp. 12 ff.)
[2]	VAT 7847 + AO 6448	(TCL 6 12; Weidner *Gestirn-Darstellungen*, pp. 15 ff.)
[3]	W 22554/7a	(von Weiher *Uruk* 167)
[4]	A 3427	(J. Schaumberger, "Anaphora und Aufgangskalender in neuen Ziqpu-Texten," *ZA* 51 [1955]: 238 f.)[4]

From Babylon

[5]	BM 34572	(*LBAT* 1580)
[6]	BM 34664	(*LBAT* 1503)
[7]	BM 34713	(*LBAT* 1499)
[8]	BM 33535	(published here)
[9]	BM 35784	(*LBAT* 1578)
[10]	BM 36292	(unpublished)
[11]	BM 41583	(*LBAT* 1579)
[12]	BM 56605	(N. Heeßel, *Babylonisch-assyrische Diagnostik*, AOAT 43 [Münster, 2000], pp. 112 ff.)

There is no common format to these tablets, and not all of them use the microzodiac for the same purpose. Three ([4], [6], [7]) give a scheme for the rising times of sections of the ecliptic and are not immediately concerned with astrology. One ([12]) is not really understood. Of the remaining seven, five were dealt with by Weidner; an additional tablet parallel to them ([10]) is found in the British Museum.[5] There is one

[3] Weidner *Gestirn-Darstellungen*.

[4] This and the tablets BM 34664 and 34713 below have been dealt with by F. Rochberg in "A Babylonian Rising-Times Scheme in Non-Tabular Astronomical Texts," in C. Burnett et al., eds., *Studies in the History of the Exact Sciences in Honour of David Pingree* (Leiden and Boston, 2004), pp. 56–94.

[5] I intend to publish this elsewhere.

more fragment from Uruk ([3]).[6] The tablets have been well described by Weidner, and I repeat just what can be said about the microzodiac.

The table for the microzodiac (in nos. [1], [2], and [5], for example) has twelve columns, each of which is labeled with the name of a microsign, as explained above. In the first row of boxes, the following items are listed for each microsign: a place-name (city or temple) and one or two names of trees, plants, and stones. The computations that follow the first row are obscure to me; they are not connected with the signs of the microzodiac. The next row of twelve boxes contains elements of predictions of the kind occurring in the apodoses of omens; they are said to depend on the brightness of the planets. After this there is another row of boxes mentioning cultic events and another one with prescriptions for actions to be taken or avoided, in the style of hemerologies.

III

The present text deals with the two subsections Gemini (MÚL.MAŠ.MAŠ) and Cancer (MÚL.ALLA) of the sign Sagittarius (MÚL.PA), which are the seventh and eighth subsections of this sign according to the description given above. Unfortunately, these subsections are not preserved in the other tablets dealing with microzodiacs so that a comparison is not possible. In general, the text belongs to the field of medical astrology.[7] Obverse and reverse have five paragraphs each that are separated by rulings.

The first paragraph begins with the heading, the microzodiacal sign. Then a place-name and the names of trees, plants, and stones are listed. This is also the case in texts [2], [5], [9], [10], [11], and [12] in the list above; nothing of the preserved parts of these texts is exactly the same as in our text. Such an enumeration of trees, plants, and stones need not in itself have anything to do with medicine. Several similar texts exist, however, that clearly show that medicine is involved. First, some of the so-called *Kalendertexte* can be mentioned.[8]

---

[6] As recognized by von Weiher, the layout of this fragment is parallel to the tablets treated by Weidner *Gestirn-Darstellungen*. Since the sections labeled "Row B" always have the same text for a given microzodiacal sign (ibid., p. 26), it is possible to identify the signs. The microzodiacal signs on the obverse are Aries, Taurus, and Gemini; on the reverse they are Pisces, Aries, and Taurus. This shows that the signs subdivided here are Cancer and Gemini: if the rows of microzodiacal signs end with Gemini and Taurus, they must have begun with Cancer and Gemini respectively; and the subdivisions always begin with the microzodiacal sign of the same name as the sign subdivided. It follows that obverse and reverse are to be interchanged. The double ruling in the lower part of the obverse makes it likely that the text ended here and was followed by a colophon. This tablet from Uruk therefore was concerned with the same part of the zodiac as *LBAT* 1580, from Babylon ("Text 3" in Weidner *Gestirn-Darstellungen*; E. Reiner told me that the fragment BM 78831 joins the right edge). This makes improved readings (if not understanding) of von Weiher's tablet possible; see the appendix below.

[7] This topic was explored by E. Reiner in her *Astral Magic in Babylonia* (Philadelphia, 1995).

[8] For a complete listing, see the article by L. Brack-Bernsen and J. M. Steele, "Babylonian Mathemagics," in Burnett et al., eds., *Studies in the History of the Exact Sciences*, pp. 95–125.

[13]	VAT 7815	(Weidner *Gestirn-Darstellungen*, pp. 41 ff.)
[14]	VAT 7816	(Weidner *Gestirn-Darstellungen*, pp. 41 ff.)
[15]	W 20030/127	(*Bagh. Mitt.* Beiheft 2, no. 79)
[16]	W 20030/133	(unpublished)
[17]	W 22619/9+	(von Weiher *Uruk* 105)
[18]	W 22704	(von Weiher *Uruk* 104)

Each entry in such a *Kalendertext* begins with two pairs of integer numbers, which do not concern us here.[9] The names of one or more trees, stones, and plants are listed, as are sometimes also place- or temple-names. Then prescriptions as they are found in hemerologies follow: which ceremonies are to be performed on that day and in which activities it is propitious to engage. Texts [17] and [18], however, assign to each calendar date an ointment the ingredients of which are related to the zodiacal sign in question by an association, either linguistic or just orthographic, based on the name of the sign. Not all of these associations are clear to a modern reader, but it is evident that they are based on the creatures forming the zodiac as it was in use in Hellenistic times.

There are more texts of a similar kind. One was published by I. L. Finkel;[10] I quote his description: "Twelve sections, one for each month of the year, prescribe in turn two or three of the following elements: a certain stone in an oil to apply to part of the body; a certain plant to be drunk in a certain liquid; and a certain colour wool to be tied on as an amulet at a certain body part." In this text it is clear how the stone, plant, and wool are to be used, but it is not stated for which purpose the treatment is intended. This example, too, makes it likely that those of the texts mentioned above that just enumerate stones, plants, and trees also imply their use in medications.

The second paragraph of our text is exactly the same as that found in Weidner's *Gestirn-Darstellungen* listing cultic events and called by him "Row B."[11]

The third paragraph gives instructions about what a man should eat, drink, put on, etc., and where he should sleep so that the "gods of the night" (or, on the reverse, "his goddess") will talk to him. This paragraph (like the corresponding one on the reverse) is similar to the last part of the *Kalendertexte* listed above as [13] and [14].[12] Unfortunately, they are fragmentary and seem not to have the same purpose as our text.[13]

---

[9] Their mathematical structure has been explained by Brack-Bernsen and Steele (ibid., pp. 105–15).

[10] I. L. Finkel, "On Late Babylonian Medical Training," in A. R. George and I. L. Finkel, eds., *Wisdom, Gods and Literature* (Winona Lake, Indiana, 2000), pp. 212–17.

[11] Weidner *Gestirn-Darstellungen*, p. 24.

[12] Read the beginning of rev. 17 of the first text in Weidner's book: DIŠ *ina* 1 ..., and the beginning of rev. 9 of the second: [DIŠ] ⌈*ina* 9⌉ ..., where the numbers 1 and 9 represent the months Nisannu and Kislimu.

[13] In [13], the result of the procedure is: *bēl nukurtišu ana* KI GAR [...].

The important point is that the instructions of this paragraph prepare for a dream incubation: the gods of the night, or the personal goddess, are to speak to the one who is sleeping. Such incubation has been assumed with good reason for Mari,[14] Assyria, Babylonia,[15] and other regions of the Near East, but specific procedures have so far been rare in cuneiform sources.[16] Most examples adduced for incubation are uncertain. Some rites attested in texts of the first millennium B.C.[17] that are to be performed in order that one may receive a "decision" (EŠ.BAR) while sleeping could be seen as concerning incubation. They include, for example, the cleaning of the place of offerings and reciting incantations to the Big Dipper. The procedures in our text are quite different: they consist of preparations applied to the person who wishes to have the gods speak.

In the fourth paragraph, some ingredients are to be wrapped in animal hide, tied together with wool, and put on a person's neck. Whether this person is the same as the one in the preceding lines cannot be said. The procedure seems, rather, to be therapeutic. I can see no connection between the animal whose hide was used (donkey, horse) and the zodiac.

The fifth paragraph is just one line long. The name of the microzodiacal sign is repeated, and the name of a tree and a bird appear. Nothing is said about their meaning in this context.

The purpose of this text is unclear to me. It draws together material that is attested elsewhere, and it presupposes the invention of the microzodiac. It also seems to be only a small part of a larger ensemble; considering that two microzodiacal signs make up only 5 degrees of the zodiac, one could assume the existence of seventy-one more tablets of this type. I tend to doubt this, however; there is much diversity in tablets dealing with medical astrology. Rarely do two tablets have exactly the same layout and contents. Rather, selections from previously existing material mixed with new ideas are arranged according to the interests or needs of the authors of new texts.

---

[14] J.-M. Durand, ARMT 26/1, p. 461.

[15] A. L. Oppenheim, *The Interpretation of Dreams in the Ancient Near East* (Philadelphia, 1956), p. 188.

[16] S. A. L. Butler, *Mesopotamian Conceptions of Dreams and Dream Rituals* (Münster, 1998), pp. 221 ff.

[17] Ibid., pp. 355 ff.

APPENDIX

von Weiher *Uruk* 167

Obv.

A x+1	[	] 2 30 8 18 U.MEŠ x [		]
				30? ⸢x x⸣
	(Aquarius)	(Pisces)	(Aries)	(Taurus)
B 1	[ ]	[u_4-*um* ^{d}*i*]*š-tar*	u_4-*um* BAD KÁ	// u_4-*um ìl* URU x[18]
2	[ ]	[*bēlet*] KUR.KUR *u*	EN GAL-*u* ^{d}AMAR.UD	GAL-*u* ^{d}MAŠ
3	[ ]⸢x⸣	^{d}AMAR.UD LUGAL	*u* UR.SAG ^{d}*Nin-urta*	// BAD KÁ
C 1	[ ]⸢x⸣ //	*ana di-nim* GIN-*ma* //	*šá*? *di-nim* NU	*ṣal-tum la i-ṣa-al*
2	[ ]	[ ] ⸢x x⸣	ŠE.GA *ana* ^{d}UTU	
3	[ ]	[ ]	[*l*]*i*?-*iš-ken* MUŠ	*la i-tam-mu*
4	[ ]	[ ]	⸢NU IGI⸣	
D	[1,54?]	[1,53?]	[1,52?]	⸢1,51⸣(?)

(remainder broken)

Rev.

A x+1	[	] ⸢URU.MEŠ⸣ *an-nu-ti* [	]
x+2	[MUL].ALLA! KI! ISKIM!	KUR.SU.BIR$_4$^{ki} EŠ.BAR-*šú-nu*	M[E-*a* GAR]
	(Aries)	(Taurus)	(Gemini)
B 1	u_4-*um* BAD KÁ	u_4-*um ìl* URU	u_4-*um ìl* URU
2	EN GAL-*u* ^{d}AMAR.UD	UR.SAG GAL-*u*	BAD KÁ *ma-a-tú*?[19]
3	*u* UR.SAG ^{d}*Nin-urta*	^{d}MAŠ // BAD KÁ	^{d}XXX ^{d}XX
4			*u* ^{d}U.GUR EZEN? ^{d}MAŠ?
C 1	[ ] EŠ *u* NUMUN GAR-*un*	*ṣal-tum la*	SAG.ÌR NA.AN.⸢ŠÁM?⸣
2	[ ] x ta? me	*i-ṣa-al*	^{d}*Šamaš* DAB-*su*
3	[ ]	*ana* DI ⸢*là*⸣ È	
D	[1,41]	1,40	1,39
E 1	[ ]	[-*r*]*e-e* //	ZALAG a a za? ⸢x⸣ [ ]
2	[ ]	[GA]R-*an*	ZI-*iḫ* [ ]
3	[ ]	[ ]	[ ]⸢x⸣-te?

(remainder broken)

[18] The parallels in rev. B 3 and in text [2] (TCL 6 12 x 8′, see Weidner *Gestirn-Darstellungen*, p. 25) have UR.SAG.

[19] The parallel in text [2] (TCL 6 12 xi 8′) has *ma-a-šú*.

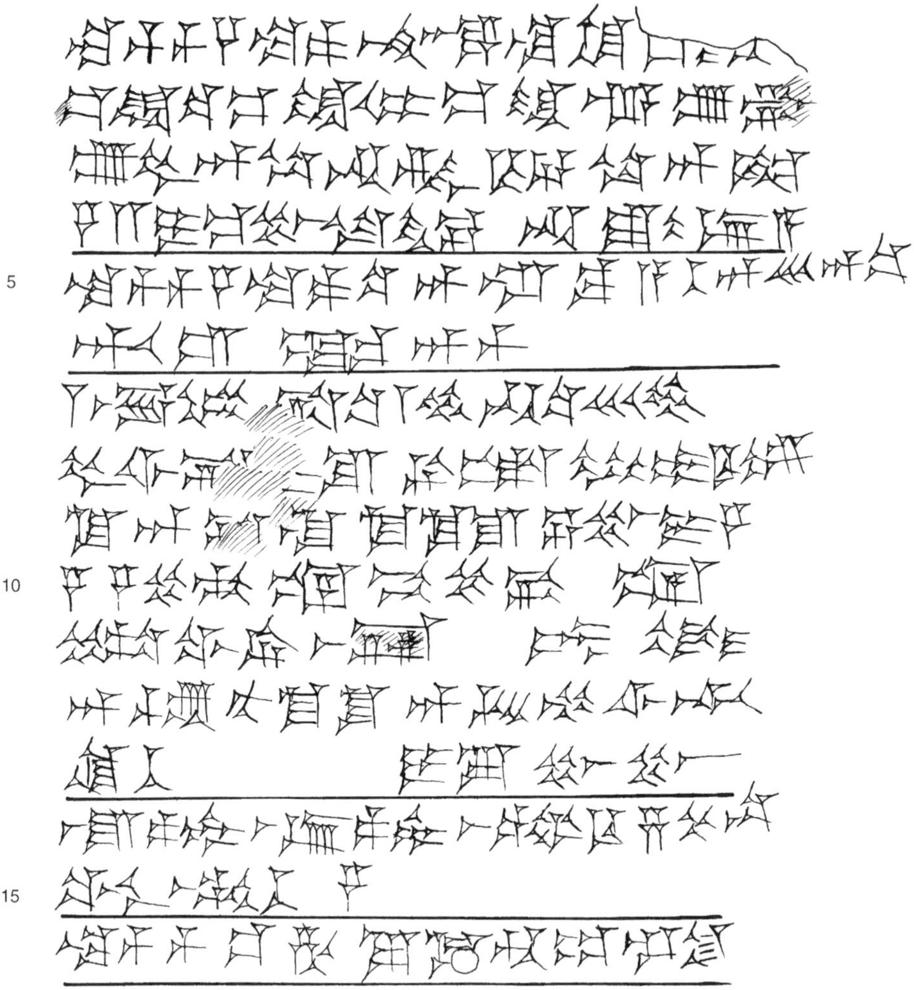

Figure 1a. BM 33535, Obverse

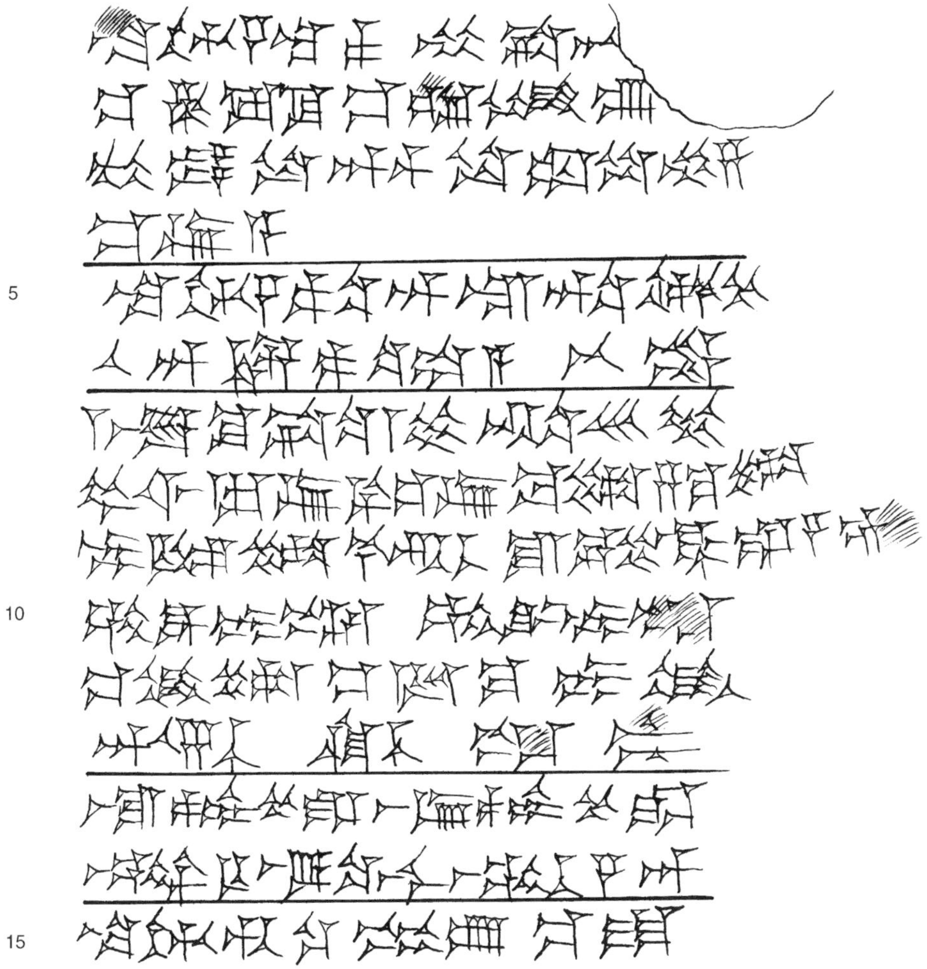

Figure 1b. BM 33535, Reverse

ZUM IMPERATIV DES SEMITISCHEN

Burkhart Kienast, Universität Freiburg i. Br.

1.1. Der Imperativ wird in allen semitischen Sprachen einheitlich gebildet und scheint von daher keine Probleme zu bieten. Doch bei näherem Hinsehen zeigt sich, daß eine Reihe von Fragen einer Beantwortung harren. Bevor wir uns dem eigentlichen Thema zuwenden, scheint es aber geboten, die **Entwicklung der semitischen Tempora** aus unserer Sicht kurz darzustellen. Vgl. im einzelnen die entsprechenden Kapitel in B. Kienast, *HSSp*.[1]

1.2. Das altsemitische "Tempussystem" beruht auf der Aspektopposition imperfektiv : perfektiv (wie akkadisch *iparras* : *iprus*). Die beiden Präfixkonjugationen sind aus nominalen Syntagmen hervorgegangen, die aus einem proklitischen Personalelement als Subjekt und einem nominalen Prädikat bestehen. Letzteres bildet die verbale Basis, wobei die einfache Grundform (*paras-*, *paris-* und *parus-*) entsprechend ihrer Funktion für das perfektive "Präteritum" (*iprus*), die einfache Steigerungsform (*parras*, *parris* und *parrus*) für das imperfektive "Präsens" (*iparras*) steht. Und da der semitische Nominalsatz wegen des Fehlens einer Kopula sowohl indikativische wie modale Funktion haben kann, sind auch die aus dem Nominalsatz abgeleiteten "Tempora" grundsätzlich modusneutral, d. h. sie können indikativisch wie modal gebraucht werden (vgl. *HSSp* § 178–80).

1.3. Demnach haben die beiden Präfixkonjugationen des Altsemitischen neben unterschiedlichen indikativischen Gebrauchsweisen beide auch jussivische Funktion (vgl. *HSSp* § 227). Eine deutliche Abgrenzung der Modi erfolgt nur ungenügend und besonders im Gebrauch unterschiedlicher Negationen bei Verneinung. Vgl. die babylonischen Beispiele:

Präteritum:	*iddin* "er hat gegeben"
Prekativ:	*liddin* "er möge geben"
Vetitiv:	*aj iddin* "er soll nicht geben"
Präsens:	*ul inaddin* "er wird nicht geben"
Prohibitiv:	*lā inaddin* "er soll nicht geben"

[1] B. Kienast, *Historische semitische Sprachwissenschaft*, mit Beiträgen von E. Graefe und G. B. Gragg (Wiesbaden, 2001).

1.4. Im Frühjungsemitischen steht die Kurzform **jaqtul* > $j^{e}qt^{e}l$ (Prohibitiv *ʾī* $j^{e}qt^{e}l$) zwar noch neben dem alten Präsens **jaqattal* > $j^{e}qatt^{e}l$, aber beide Formen sind nun modal differenziert: $j^{e}qatt^{e}l$ wird nur noch indikativisch verwendet, die jussivischen Funktionen beider Präfixkonjugationen sind in $j^{e}qt^{e}l$ konzentriert, dessen präteritaler Gebrauch ganz auf das neue Perfekt *qatala* verlagert worden ist (vgl. *HSSp* § 228.)

1.5. Im Spätjungsemitischen gehört der Jussiv *jaqtul* (Prohibitiv *lā jaqtul*) in das Modalsystem des Imperfektes *jaqtulu*, das in Opposition zum Perfekt *qatala* steht.

1.6. Anders als die eng verwandten hamitischen Sprachen kennt das Semitische Verbalstämme mit Verdoppelung des mittleren Radikals dreikonsonantiger Wurzeln. Dieses Merkmal des sog. D-Stammes stellt kein besonderes, stammbildendes Charakteristikum dar, wie die zum G-Stamm gehörenden Steigerungsformen des Nomens (z. B. *parras* und *parrās*) und das "Präsens" G *iparras* zeigen. Hinzu kommt die deutliche Anlehnung an die Formenbildung des Kausativ, sodaß der D-Stamm vermutlich als eine Neubildung anzusehen ist, die freilich in historischer Zeit schon fest im System verankert war (vgl. *HSSp* § 197.5–7 und unten 4.1.)

2.1. Der Imperativ wird in allen semitischen Sprachen einheitlich von der 2. Person der Präfixkonjugation (z. B. akkadisch Präteritum *taprus*, arabisch Jussiv *taqtul*) durch Weglassen der Personalpräfixe abgeleitet. Die dadurch entstehende Doppelkonsonanz im Anlaut ist lautgesetzlich nicht vertretbar; sie wird daher zumeist (wie im Akkadischen, Äthiopischen, Kanaʿanäischen oder Aramäischen) durch einen anaptyktischen Vokal aufgesprengt (vgl. akkadisch *taprus* > **prus* > *purus*) oder (wie nur im Arabischen) durch einen prosthetischen Vokal erweitert (*taqtul* > **qtul* > *ʾuqtul*). Eine früher oft erwogene nominale Ableitung des Imperativs ist nicht nur wegen der unterschiedlichen Behandlung der anlautenden Doppelkonsonanz, sondern auch deshalb ausgeschlossen, weil es keine gemeinsemitische, zweisilbige Nominalform mit einem anderen Vokal als *a* in der ersten Stammsilbe gibt (vgl. *HSSp* § 94.3e).

2.2. Allen semitischen Sprachen gemeinsam ist auch ein besonderes Phänomen: Der Imperativ lässt sich grundsätzlich nicht mit einer Negation verbinden; negierte Befehle müssen daher auf andere Weise dargestellt werden: Im Akkadischen stehen dafür der Prohibitiv (*lā*+Präsens) und der Vetitiv (*aj/ē*+Präteritum) zur Verfügung, in allen anderen semitischen Sprachen nur der Prohibitiv, der hier durch *lā* oder *ʾal* mit dem Jussiv gebildet wird. Vgl. die folgenden Beispiele:

a) **Akkadisch** (von Soden *GAG* § 84a [Imperativ], § 84h–i [Prohibitiv und Vetitiv]):

positiver Befehl:	*kaspam ana* PN *idin* "gib das Silber dem PN"
negiert Prohibitiv:	*kaspam ana* PN *lā tanaddin* "du sollst das Silber nicht dem PN geben" = "gib das Silber nicht dem PN"
negiert Vetitiv:	*kaspam ana* PN *ē taddin* "du sollst das Silber nicht dem PN geben" = "gib das Silber nicht dem PN"

b) **G^{eʿe}z** (Dillmann, *EG* § 190 [Imperativ], § 197a [Prohibitiv]):[2]
positiver Befehl: *q^{e}t^{e}l nafsō* "töte ihn"
negiert Prohibitiv: *ʾī t^{e}qt^{e}l nafsō* "du sollst ihn nicht töten" = "töte ihn nicht"

c) **Ugaritisch** (Verreet, *Modi Ugaritici* § 10 [Imperativ], § 9.5 [Prohibitiv]):[3]
positiver Befehl: *bhtm l bn* = **bahātī-ma lū bini* "baue doch Häuser" (V 120)
negiert Prohibitiv: *ʾl tbkn* = * *ʾal tabki-nī* "du sollst mich nicht beweinen" = "beweine mich nicht" (V 117)

d) **Arabisch** (Wright und de Goeje, *GAL*, Bd. 1 § 98 [Imperativ], Band 2 § 17b [Imperativ] und § 30 [Prohibitiv]):[4]
positiver Befehl: *ʾuktub* "schreib"
negiert Prohibitiv: *lā taḥzan ʾinna-llāha maʿa-nā* "du sollst nicht traurig sein, denn Gott ist mit uns" = "sei nicht traurig, denn Gott ist mit uns"

3.1. Im **Jungsemitischen** ist der Jussiv mit dem davon abgeleiteten Imperativ voll in das jeweilige imperfektive Modalsystem integriert und bietet so auf den ersten Blick keinerlei Probleme (hier G^{eʿe}z, für Ugaritisch und Arabisch vgl. oben 2.2c–d): *q^{e}t^{e}l nafsō* "töte ihn" und *t^{e}qt^{e}l nafsō* "du sollst ihn töten" sind beides imperfektive Aufforderungen, deren Negierung jederzeit in gleicher Weise möglich sein sollte. Aber man kann nur sagen *ʾī t^{e}qt^{e}l nafsō* "du sollst ihn nicht töten", nicht aber * *ʾī q^{e}t^{e}l nafsō* "töte ihn nicht", denn letzterem steht das genannte Gesetz von der Nichtnegierbarkeit des Imperativs entgegen, ohne daß es dafür eine plausible Begründung gibt.

3.2. Im **Altsemitischen** liegen die Dinge komplizierter, weil hier dem positiven Imperativ negiert zwei Modi, der Prohibitiv und der Vetitiv, gegenüberstehen und eine klare Abgrenzung der beiden Modi in den Grammatiken bisher nicht zu finden war. Vgl.: "Die Form des entschiedenen Verbots ist der Prohibitiv" (von Soden *GAG* § 81h) und "Der Vetitiv bezeichnet einen negativen Wunsch oft sehr dringender Art, der Höher- und Gleichgestellten gegenüber geäußert wird, aber wohl kein formales Verbot" (von Soden *GAG* § 81i). Es mag immerhin von Interesse sein, daß der Vetitiv im ersten Jahrtausend nur noch in literarischen Texten vorkommt, sonst aber vom Prohibitiv abgelöst wird.

---

[2] A. Dillmann, *Ethiopic Grammar* (London, 1907) (Übersetzung von: *Grammatik der äthiopischen Sprache* [Leipzig, 1857]).

[3] E. Verreet, *Modi Ugaritici: Eine morpho-syntaktische Abhandlung über das Modalsystem im Ugaritischen*, OLA 27 (Leuven, 1988).

[4] C. P. Caspari, *A Grammar of the Arabic Language*, übersetzt und erw. von W. Wright, 2 Bände, 3. Auflage, erw. von W. R. Smith und M. J. de Goeje (Cambridge, 1896–98; Neudruck, Cambridge, 1951).

3.3. Eine deutliche Abgrenzung der beiden Modi ist aber sehr wohl möglich und fügt sich, wenigstens primär, in das allgemeine Spektrum der Tempora Präsens und Präteritum ohne Schwierigkeiten ein (vgl. *HSSp* § 254):

a) Der Prohibitiv ist entsprechend der Verbindung der Negation mit dem Präsens imperfektiv; vgl. etwa:

Altakkadisch: *adī ēnēja lā tāmuru akalam šikaram lā talaʾʾamu* "(du seist beschworen:) Bevor du meine Augen (= mich) nicht gesehen hast, sollst du weder Speis' noch Trank zu dir nehmen."

Altbabylonisch: *kaspam ana* PN *lā tanaddin* "du sollst das Silber nicht dem PN geben" = "gib das Silber nicht dem PN." Hier liegt ein Verbot vor, dem PN das Silber jetzt oder später auszuhändigen.

b) Der Vetitiv aber besteht aus der Verbindung der Negation mit dem Präteritum und muß daher, zumindest von Hause aus, perfektiver Natur sein. Dafür gibt es auch eindeutige Beispiele:

Eine altakkadische Fluchformel besagt: *aplam a ulid šumam a irši* "einen Erben soll er nicht zeugen, einen Namen(sträger) nicht bekommen." Das Zitat ist nicht ganz genau übersetzt, denn es ist ja nicht nur gemeint, daß der Übeltäter hinfort keine Nachkommen mehr zeugen soll – dafür müßte der Prohibitiv stehen – , sondern vor allem auch, daß seine in der Vergangenheit bereits gezeugten Erben ausgelöscht werden sollen, als hätten sie nie existiert. Wir müssen also korrekt übersetzen: "Einen Erben soll er nicht gezeugt, einen Namen(sträger) nicht bekommen haben."

In einer jungbabylonischen Beschwörung heißt es, gerichtet an einen Krankheitsdämonen: *ana marṣi ē taṭḫi* "dem Kranken sollst du dich nicht nähern." Da die Beschwörung exorzistischen Charakter hat, der Kranke also bereits von dem Dämonen besessen ist und dieser zum Verlassen seines Opfers aufgefordert werden soll, müssen wir übersetzen: "Dem Kranken sollst du dich nicht genähert haben."

c) In den vorstehenden Beispielen bezieht sich die Verbotsform aber nur formal ausschließlich auf die Vergangenheit, sachlich ist natürlich auch die Zukunft mit eingeschlossen. Und es bedarf nur einer geringfügigen Aspektverschiebung, um den Vetitiv inhaltlich dem Prohibitiv anzunähern: Vgl. etwa Altassyrisch: *assurri mamman ē taqīp-ma ina warkītim libbaka ē imraṣ* "irgendjemandem sollst du nicht vertrauen, (damit) später dein Herz sich nicht betrübe."

Dieser Prozeß der funktionalen Annäherung des Vetitivs an den Prohibitiv hat letztlich zu seiner völligen Verdrängung geführt. Und man darf die Vermutung äußern, daß die Entwicklungen beim Imperativ wenigstens indirekt diesen Prozeß beeinflußt haben.

4.1. Der **Imperativ** nun ist auf Grund seiner Ableitung von der perfektiven Präfixkonjugation in jussivischer Verwendung naturgemäß ebenfalls primär perfektiv. In dem Befehl akkadisch *dūk-šu* "habe ihn getötet" = "töte ihn" wird dann aus Sicht des Auftraggebers der Vollzug der Order bereits antizipiert. Auch hier ist eine allmähliche Veränderung des Aspektes hin zu einem imperfektiven Gebrauch des primär perfektiven Imperativs anzunehmen. Ausschlaggebend mag aber ein anderer Grund gewesen sein: Die Ausbildung des D-Stammes geschah in Anlehnung an den Š-Stamm und unter Einbeziehung des imperfektiven Imperativs, eine Entwicklung, die sich aus folgender Übersicht der einschlägigen Formen leicht nachvollziehen läßt (vgl. oben 1.6):

	Präsens	Präteritum	Imperativ	Partizip	Verbaladjektiv
G:	*iparras*		(**parrVs*)		*parrVsum*
D:	*uparras*	*uparris*	*purris*/parris	*muparrisum*	*purrusum*/parrusum
Š:	*ušapras*	*ušapris*	*šupris*/šapris	*mušaprisum*	*šuprusum*/šaprusum

Damit wurde es notwendig, die Funktionen des alten, imperfektiven Imperativs des G-Stammes auf den perfektiven Imperativ zu übertragen, was dann auch auf die Entwicklung beim Vetitiv Wirkungen gezeigt haben mag. So heißt es in der Briefeinleitungsformel: *ana* PN *qibi-ma* "Zu PN sprich", was keineswegs perfektiv verstanden werden kann.

4.2. Die ursprünglich perfektive Funktion des Imperativs mag einen Hinweis darauf geben, warum eine Verbindung mit einer Negation ausgeschlossen ist. Zwei Beispiele: Man kann imperfektiv sagen "gehe weg" und "gehe nicht weg". Die positive perfektive Variante "sei gegangen" impliziert die unmittelbare Ausführung der Anweisung in dem Sinne "sei schon weg". "Sei nicht gegangen" als Aufforderung an einen Anwesenden zu bleiben, kann nicht in der gleichen Weise interpretiert werden, weil die Formulierung allenfalls eine punktuelle Befolgung des Befehls beinhaltet, nicht aber zu längerem Verweilen anhält.

Bei der Suche nach einem Verbrecher ist imperfektiv die Anweisung "töte ihn" genauso gut möglich wie der Befehl "töte ihn nicht", weil ein zukünftiges Handeln verlangt wird. Das gleiche gilt aber nicht bei einem perfektiv formulierten Auftrag: Wenn der Verbrecher gefaßt ist, kann man zwar positiv anordnen: "Habe ihn getötet", indem damit die Ausführung des Befehls antizipiert wird. Negativ aber ist die Order "habe ihn nicht getötet" unsinnig, wenn der Verbrecher bereits getötet wurde, und ansonsten natürlich ebenso punktuell wie in unserem ersten Beispiel.

4.3. Wie wir gesehen haben, ist der Vetitiv noch gelegentlich in seiner primären perfektiven Funktion zu belegen, aber er hat sich in vielen Fällen dem Prohibitiv angenähert und ist schließlich von diesem verdrängt worden. In ähnlicher Weise ist die Negierung des primär perfektiven Imperativs schon in vorhistorischer Zeit aufgegeben und durch den imperfekten Prohibitiv ersetzt worden. Das Gesetz, daß der Imperativ nicht negiert werden darf, hat sich aber im Altsemitischen immer erhalten, selbst nachdem der Imperativ imperfektive Funktionen übernommen hat. Und dieses Gesetz gilt sogar noch in allen jungsemitischen Sprachen, in denen der Imperativ zum imperfektiven Modalsystem gehört, sodaß seine Negierung durchaus möglich geworden war.

4.4. Die hier angesprochenen Fragen sind, soweit mir bekannt, bisher weder in der Altorientalistik noch in der Semitistik sonst behandelt worden, und es scheint, daß erst die historische Betrachtung unsere Untersuchungen ermöglicht hat. In jedem Fall sind weitere, einzelsprachliche Detailuntersuchungen zum Gebrauch der Modi wünschenswert, um unsere Vorstellungen einer Überprüfung zu unterziehen.

5.1. Auch andere Sprachen mit einem imperfektiven und einem perfektiven Imperativ können nur die imperfektive Form negieren, während die perfektive Variante einer modalen Umschreibung bedarf. Herr Oberstudienrat N. Kilwing, Freiburg, weist für das Griechische auf die Grammatik von Menge, Thierfelder und Wiesner, *Repetitorium der griechischen Syntax*,[5] hin; dort heißt es § 138.2. (S. 188 f.):

> Der **Imperativ**, der Modus des Befehls und der Aufforderung (...), kommt nur in der 2. und 3. Person vor.
>
> Der **Imperat. Präsens** bezeichnet einen dauernden, für die Folge berechneten Befehl oder ein allgemeingültiges Gebot: Τοὺς θεοὺς φοβοῦ (= *die Götter fürchte*). [...]
>
> Der **Imperat. Aorist** bezeichnet einen besonderen, auf unmittelbare Verwirklichung berechneten Befehl: Δός μοι τὸ βιβλίον" (= *gib mir das Buch*). [...]
>
> Ein an die zweite Person gerichtetes Verbot wird mit gleichem Bedeutungsunterschied entweder durch den **Imperat. Präs.** oder durch den **Konj. Aor.** mit μή, nicht durch den Imperat. Aor. mit μή ausgedrückt: Μηδένα τῶν πονηρῶν φίλον ποιοῦ (= *mache dir keinen Tunichtgut zum Freunde!*). Μὴ ἀθυμήσητε ἐπὶ τοῖς πεπραγμενοῖς (= *verliert nicht den Mut in Anbetracht der Geschehnisse!*).

[5] H. Menge, A. Thierfelder und J. Wiesner, *Repetitorium der griechischen Syntax*, 10. erw. Auflage (1878; Darmstadt, 1999).

OF BABIES, BOATS, AND ARKS*

Anne Draffkorn Kilmer, University of California, Berkeley

I. INTRODUCTION

I would like to start this contribution with an apology: neither of the two types of texts that I discuss in this paper, the Hebrew Book of Genesis, on the one hand, and the Sumerian and Akkadian birth incantations, on the other, are texts in which I have done any original work, nor do I claim to be a biblical scholar. Nevertheless, I hope that my observations will be of interest.

This article presents another means of understanding the time frame of the biblical flood story as it is described in Genesis 7–8. The impetus for this approach originated during the course of the oral portion of Father Emmerich Vogt's doctoral qualifying examinations in 1985, in which I participated. Father Vogt was at that time a student in the Joint Doctoral Degree Program sponsored by the Graduate Theological Union of Berkeley and the Department of Near Eastern Studies. He, in connection with examination questions on the Book of Genesis, had calculated the time span for the Noachic flood as follows:

150 days (Gen. 7:24) = 5 months (including the 40 days), calculated as 1 January to 1 June of Noah's 600th year.

121 days = 4 months (Gen. 8:5) when the flood waters receded, calculated as 1 June to 1 October.

Total number of days = 271. If we add the 7 days (Gen. 8:12) after which the dove landed for good, the total is 278 days.

At the time of the oral examination, I asked those biblical scholars present whether anyone had noticed that the number of days, 270–80, is *exactly* the length of time for human gestation and that, as a result, one might suggest that the biblical ark be considered a uterine symbol. My query was met with surprise and received no answer. In the intervening years I have had very useful discussions with Francis I. Andersen, David Noel Freedman, Isaac Kikawada, and, more recently, with Sheldon Greaves and Mary

---

* This article was originally presented as a paper at the American Oriental Society's annual meeting in Toronto in March 2001.

Frances Wogec. I thank all of them for their advice and their cautionary comments.[1] Though warned that the Flood "calendar" was a "sticky wicket," I decided to rethink my question and to try to discover whether the topic, viz., the comparison between the length of Noah's Flood and the length of human gestation, had been discussed in the scholarly literature. Thus far I have not been able to find this specific suggestion anywhere, even though comparisons between the first creation of Genesis 1 and the Flood narrative have been made. I hope that what follows here will add a new perspective to the biblical narrative and to the Mesopotamian materials I adduce as comparanda as well.

II. Noah and the Ark

Duration of Stay in the Ark

Noah and the animals were enclosed (perhaps "enwombed" or even "entombed" might be said) from 17 February (Gen. 7:11) to 1 October (Gen. 8:5), plus 40 days (Gen. 8:6), plus 14 days (Gen. 8:10–12). (The initial 7-day grace period of Gen. 7:4 and 10 are not counted because the rains had not yet started.) For the classical/antique traditional folkloric rationale behind not counting the first 7 days of pregnancy and the reasons that the significant subsequent 40 days are counted separately from the remainder of the gestation period (it concerns the physical substance of the fetal material), see the materials collected by M. Stol.[2] All together, the stay in the ark was 278 days, or 9 months and 1 week, which is the normal length of human gestation. Gen. 7:16 tells us that YHWH "shut Noah in" (the ark), using the verb *sgr*, which is also used in 1 Sam. 1:5 and 6 of the womb of Hannah.[3] We might also note that the verb *yṣ'* "to come out," used by YHWH in Gen. 8:16 in his command to Noah to leave the ark, is also used elsewhere in the Old Testament of babies emerging at birth, as *waṣû* is used in the cuneiform materials.

It appears, then, that Genesis offers us a rebirth or a re-creation of earth's living creatures by means of their new gestation in the ark.

---

[1] Our former University of California, Berkeley, doctoral student, Sheldon Greaves, has been kind enough to supply me with a table (see table 1 below) of the biblical flood chronology taken from his article "Interpretation of the Biblical Ark and Chronology of the Flood," in which he presents the many discussions in the secondary literature of the symbolism of the ark and the patterns of the flood chronology. The flood "calendar," as it is often referred to, has been calculated in many different and confusing ways. Greaves' article is an informative summary of the arguments among biblical scholars. I have relied on it very much. It has been published at Berkeley in the *Journal of Associated Graduates in Near Eastern Studies* 11 (2005): 43–50.

[2] M. Stol, *Birth in Babylonia and the Bible*, Cuneiform Monographs 14 (Groningen, 2000), p. 18.

[3] I thank F. I. Andersen for this reference.

The same period of 278 days is that in which YHWH's *mayim* overpowered *ʾereṣ* to which we may compare Adad's *abūbu*, which conquered earth's creatures in the Atrahasis Epic. Essentially, earth is being re-created or reborn at the same time that the ark's creatures are being saved or reborn. Note that just as the *ruaḥ Elohim* in Gen. 1:2 played a role in the first creation of earth, YHWH's *ruaḥ* once again causes the waters to begin to disappear so that earth can reemerge (Gen. 8:5). This parallel and others (such as key vocabulary, the loading of animals) between the first Creation of Genesis 1 and the second Creation of Genesis 7–8 have been discussed by biblical scholars.[4] Note also that Otto Rank,[5] already in 1909, considered Moses' ark/basket as a uterine symbol; furthermore, G. S. Kirk[6] discusses, in passing, Freudian interpretations of "enclosure motifs" as uterine symbols. He alludes to Noah's ark but makes no specific point.

The Significance of the 150 Days

The meaning of Gen. 7:24 and 8:3 must be that the flood waters reached their height and stayed at that level, covering even the highest mountains before they began to recede.

In human pregnancy, 150 days, or 20–22 weeks, is a highly significant time, for it is then that the fundus of the uterus reaches the umbilicus; this is measured by palpation and permits the midwife or obstetrician to determine whether the size of the fetus and progression of the uterus are adequate and "healthy." The umbilicus is the fixed reference point by which one can measure the height of the fundus and is used as a benchmark by which to estimate the day of birth.[7]

Thus when Gen. 7:18 tells us that "the water swelled and increased greatly," it seems to be reporting that all was well "with mother and baby" at close to the halfway point in a normal pregnancy. I might also point out[8] that the period of 150 days here is mentioned twice, once in Gen. 7:24 and again in 8:4, near the midpoint of the 278 days and at the halfway point of the 46 verses that comprise the Flood narrative of Genesis 7 and 8. Moreover, the fifth month is the middle month of nine. I consider this placement in the center as a sign of its significance in the story-telling pattern.[9]

---

[4] See especially G. Rendsburg, *The Redaction of Genesis* (Winona Lake, Indiana, 1986), pp. 9–13.

[5] O. Rank, *The Myth of the Birth of the Hero: A Psychological Interpretation of Mythology*, trans. F. Robbins and S. E. Jelliffe (New York, 1964), p. 73.

[6] G. S. Kirk, *Myth: Its Meaning and Function* (Berkeley, 1970), pp. 200 f.

[7] See, for example, P. Ladewig, M. London, and S. Olds, *Essentials of Maternal Newborn Nursing* (Redwood City, California, 1990), pp. 193 f.

[8] See A. D. Kilmer, "Visualizing Texts: Schematic Patterns in Akkadian Poetry," in A. Guinan et al., eds., *If a Man Builds a Joyful House: Essays in Honor of Erle Verdun Leichty* (Leiden and Boston, 2006), pp. 209–19, in which I discuss the importance of repetitions at "half-time" in the tablet design of Akkadian poetic texts.

[9] Cf. the analysis of G. Wenham, "The Coherence of the Flood Narrative," *VT* 28 (1987): 336–48.

The Significance of the Seventh Month, Seventeenth Day

Likewise, the text of Gen. 8:4 seems to assure us that the ark and the creatures within had reached the time of certain viability; the ark had come to a secure rest on the mountain and was therefore safe.

Human fetuses (before incubators, etc.) are generally considered viable outside the womb after 7 months. Delivery may occur relatively safely for a 7-month or older fetus. As for the mountain tops that were seen in Gen. 8:5, perhaps they may be seen to symbolize the top of a baby's head that appears at the start of birth; in this case, one thinks of the earth's reemergence/rebirth.

The Safe Delivery of God's Creatures from the Ark

On 1 January, Noah's 601st year, Noah (who functions in some sense both as midwife and baby) is careful not to "deliver" his cargo too soon lest it come to harm. The 40-day wait (8:6) and the 14 days of trial flights of birds delay the "birth" until exactly the right time, 278 days.

In Gen. 8:13 we are told that, after an additional 36 days, "the earth was dry." I would suggest that this could well refer to the normal period of postpartum menstruation, which, maximally, is considered to end at six weeks, or 42 days, after which the new mother may resume all normal activities.

As to the final count in Gen. 8:14, is it 10 days more than a lunar-solar year, or should it be corrected to one year exactly? If one should emend the reading *b*^{e}*šib ʿāh w*^{e} *ʿeśrīm* to *b*^{e}*šib ʿāh- ʿāśār yôm*, then the biblical flood lasted from 17 February of Noah's 600th year to 17 February of his 601st year. I find Hendel's arguments about a textual error convincing.[10]

Selected Parallels with the Story of Adam and Eve

Reflections of the events in the garden may be seen in the following passages in Genesis:

(1) 6:19: the loading of the ark "two by two, male and female"; cf. 1:27: "male and female created he them."

(2) 8:17: God gives instructions to Noah and family regarding their responsibilities to nature; cf. 1:28 f.

(3) 9:3–4: instructions as to what they can and cannot eat; cf. 2:16–17.

(4) 9:20–21: the wine of the vine that leads to Noah's shame; cf. 3:10–13: the fruit of the tree that leads to Adam's shame.

---

[10] See R. Hendel, "4Q252 and The Flood Chronology of Genesis 7–8: A Text-Critical Solution," *Dead Sea Discoveries* 2 (1995): 72–79.

(5) 9:21–23: covering Noah's nakedness; cf. 2:25 and 3:7 and 21: clothing for Adam and Eve.

(6) 9:25: the curse against Canaan as agent of the shame; cf. 3:14: the curse against the serpent as agent of Adam's shame.

III. The Cuneiform Texts

If it is indeed convincing to think of Noah's ark as the dark womb (and perhaps also as a tomb) as well as the baby, which must survive the watery journey, then certain Sumerian and Akkadian parallels may be brought to bear on the question.[11]

Boats and Neonates

Cuneiform birth rituals and incantations regularly refer to the fetus as a boat that must find its way through dark waters and/or that must be untied from its mooring. J. Scurlock puts it this way: "The Mesopotamian woman was understood as the steerswoman of a boat formed inside her by the man's semen. It was her [dangerous] duty to float this boat on her amniotic fluid."[12]

I have counted eight, possibly nine, passages in the birth incantations that give us our information about the fetus being visualized or conceptualized as a boat loaded with the cargo that will determine its sex and that, I think, ensures that the baby has all its parts. The following examples should suffice for our purposes here.[13]

KAR 196 = Köcher *BAM* 248 ii 49–56: one text describes a difficult birth where the baby is "stuck"; it says "May her massive mooring rope be loosened, and may her locked gate be opened ... may (the baby) come out promptly and see the light of the sun."[14] In another passage of the same text (Köcher *BAM* 248 ii 47 f.) we find "May the boat [here meaning the baby] come in safely from [the waters?], may the vessel proceed directly" (*lišlima eleppu lištēšera makurru*).

[11] In the cuneiform flood accounts the duration was 7 days and 7 nights. Note the contribution by V. Emelianov on the calendar of the flood, its relation to the cultic calendar and royal ideology, and the probable timing as being the end of the year, thus January through February ("The Calendar Date of the Flood in Cuneiform Texts," *NABU* 1999/41–45).

[12] J. Scurlock, "The Status of Women in Ancient Mesopotamia," in P. Cannistraro and J. Reich, eds., *The Western Perspective: A History of Civilization in the West* (Belmont, California, 1999), pp. 62–64.

[13] I thank our Berkeley student Mary Frances Wogec, who is currently finishing her doctoral dissertation on cuneiform childbirth incantations (under the supervision of Wolfgang Heimpel), for supplying me with pertinent references.

[14] See J. Scurlock, "Baby-snatching Demons, Restless Souls and the Dangers of Childbirth: Medico-Magical Means of Dealing with Some of the Perils of Motherhood in Ancient Mesopotamia," *Incognita* 2 (1991): 137–85.

Note that the words used for the boats are *makurru* "cargo boat" and *eleppu* "boat"; both these Akkadian words are used of the arks in the cuneiform flood stories (in a late version of the Atrahasis Epic it is named the *nāṣir napištim*, the "lifesaver"). Comparable to the loading of Noah's ark, these baby-arks in the cuneiform birth incantations are loaded with a variety of things, notably with carnelian (for girls?) and lapis (for boys?); the texts also say that the mother does not know what is loaded with respect to these two items, which probably means that she does not know whether the baby yet to be born will be a girl or a boy.

In a Middle Assyrian medical text[15] "the boat (i.e., the baby) is held at the quay of death; the vessel is held at the quay of distress" (*ina kār mūti kalât eleppu, ina kār dannati kalât makurru*).[16] W. G. Lambert's remark (p. 37) that this metaphor of a boat as a baby is "curious" (because "quays on the Tigris and Euphrates can rarely have been dangerous ... to boats") may be explained by the basic knowledge that in rising or sinking waters (whether slow or fast) a boat will come to harm unless the lines are loosened (i.e., lengthened) adequately before they break or unless the boat is cut loose to allow it to float safely and not be damaged against the docks. It may be germane to compare this to Old Babylonian Atrahasis III ii 55, where, as the storm becomes savage, the mooring rope is cut, thus releasing the boat.[17] For a similar imagery of the baby as a shipwrecked sailor (as opposed to a boat), note the passage in Lucretius, *On the Nature of the Universe*: "Then again, an infant, like a shipwrecked sailor, cast up by the cruel sea, lies naked on the ground, speechless and helpless, when Nature first has thrown him forth with painful birth from his mother's womb to the sunlit world...."[18]

Loading and Unloading the Ark

It may also be mentioned that the cuneiform flood hero, Utnapishtim (Gilg. XI 83), loaded into the ark "all the seed of living creatures," thus the loading might be understood as being the equivalent of implanting seed in a uterine chamber.

Other small points of comparison exist between Mesopotamian language about human birth and Flood narratives that contrast the darkness of the womb with the light at its opening. For example, in Old Babylonian Atrahasis I 282 f., at the birth of the baby, "the destined time opened the womb; light (*namru*) and joy were on her (the midwife's) face."[19] In the birth incantation Köcher *BAM* 248 ii 56: "Let it (the baby) come out and see the light." Cf. Gilg. XI: the flood hero recounts that at the end of the flood

[15] W. G. Lambert, "A Middle Assyrian Medical Text," *Iraq* 31 (1969): 28–39. This text is in a private collection in Venice.

[16] Ibid., p. 36.

[17] Lambert-Millard *Atra-hasīs*, pp. 92 f., line 55.

[18] I thank Denise Greaves for this reference.

[19] A. D. Kilmer, "Fugal Features of Atrahasis: The Birth Theme," in M. E. Vogelzang and H. L. J. Vanstiphout, eds., *Mesopotamian Poetic Language: Sumerian and Akkadian*, Cuneiform Monographs 6 (Groningen, 1996), pp. 128, 132.

when the ark was on the mountain, "I opened the *nappašu* 'airhole' and daylight (*urru*) fell upon my face (literally 'on the side of my nose')." I note the cognate relationship of *nappašu* with *npš*, the "baby's first breath," and with *napištu*, "life," all of which surely includes wordplay. There is, in fact, quite a bit of wordplay in the birth incantations.[20] Note, moreover, from an incantation to soothe a baby: "Oh little one who lived in the house of darkness, you have indeed come out (and) seen the light of day."[21]

Thus the flood hero may, as mentioned above, be seen as both midwife and as one of the "newborns" or "reborns."

IV. Conclusion

The associative evidence would seem to favor an interpretation of Noah's ark as a uterine symbol, the vessel that contained—for rebirth—representatives of all of earth's creatures. The time frame can thus be explained in terms of human gestation. Putting it differently, the accounting of the passage of time in Genesis 7 and 8 should perhaps be seen as a "biological" and not solely "calendrical" reckoning, whether lunar or solar.

I conclude by quoting from an article by N. Lemche on the chronology of the Flood: "I have no intention of reviewing the various theses on the chronological system in the flood story. Nobody has achieved a coherent review and for very good reason, since most of the debate has been highly speculative and, strictly speaking, not very useful"[22]—I hope that the "biological" approach suggested here, however, will, at the very least, be considered a "useful" one.

---

[20] Scurlock, "Baby-snatching Demons," passim.

[21] G. Cunningham, *"Deliver Me from Evil": Mesopotamian Incantations 2500–1500 B.C.*, Studia Pohl, Series Maior 17 (Rome, 1997), p. 109.

[22] N. Lemche, "The Chronology in the Story of the Flood," *Journal for the Study of the Old Testament* 18 (1980): 52–62.

TABLE 1. SCHEMA OF THE FLOOD CHRONOLOGY

DATES	EVENT	INTERVAL	FLOOD: TOTAL NO. OF DAYS	YEAR: TOTAL NO. OF DAYS	COMMENTS	REFERENCE IN GENESIS
1 January 600	600th year of Noah's life	na	0	47	–	–
17 February	Flood begins	40	40	87	–	7:11–12
n.d.	"Waters 150 days"	150	150	197	Stated twice	7:24
17 July	Ark "rests" on Ararat, waters abate	–	150	197	Waters begin to decline. This is the end of the "high-water mark"	8:4
1 October	Tops of mountains visible	74	224	271	–	8:5
n.d.	Noah waits 40 days; sends out raven and dove	40	264	311	Estimated date is 11 November	8:6
n.d.	Noah sends dove again; it brings back an olive leaf	7	271	318	Estimated date is 17 November Noah knows flood is over	8:10–11
n.d.	Noah sends dove again; it does not return	7	278	325	Estimated date is 24 November	8:12
1 January 601	Earth was dry	36	314	361	–	8:13
27 February 601	Earth was dry	57	371	418	Added to bring the length of the Flood to one solar year?	8:14

AN EXOTIC BABYLONIAN GOD-LIST

W. G. Lambert, University of Birmingham, England

VAT 10608 is a small fragment of a cuneiform tablet from Assur in the Vorderasiatisches Museum, Berlin, given in copy by E. Ebeling as *KAR* 339a, not previously edited. It has been recopied by the present writer courtesy of the then Director, L. Jakob-Rost, and is published here by kind permission of the present curators, B. Salje and J. Marzahn.

This fragment is literary and Middle Assyrian, though it is not mentioned in E. Weidner's article on the supposed library of Tiglath-pileser I ("Die Bibliothek Tiglat-pilesers I," *AfO* 16 [1952–53]: 197–215), nor in the two volumes of O. Pedersén, *Archives and Libraries in the City of Assur*, Acta Universitatis Upsaliensis, Studia Semitica Upsaliensia, 6 (Uppsala, 1985–86). Ebeling entitled it "Rel. Fragment" and avoided committing himself on which side was obverse and which side reverse by labeling the side with the lower left corner "1. Seite" and the side with the upper left corner "2. Seite." No line is completely preserved, only the beginnings of each line. Ebeling's "1. Seite" is in fact the flat side, his "2. Seite" is more convex, but nevertheless the present writer takes the convex side as the obverse because of the content. The text is part of a list of gods, one in each short section as divided by rulings and arranged according to a ranking of the gods in the Babylonian pantheon. It was a small tablet when complete and possibly gives only the earlier parts of a longer list. If so, it is an extract tablet. For convenience we have numbered the text by sections, not by lines:

VAT 10608

Obv.

1	^{d}*lugal-du*$_{6}$*-kù-g[a …* *za/ṣa-x-ri ki-ma* x […	Lugal-dukuga [… … like […
2	^{d}*ḫa-mur-ni* ^{d}*a-nu* [… *ra-šu-ba-te* […	Ḫamurni: Anu [… terror […
3	^{d}*ḫa-*⌈*ia*⌉*-šu* ^{d}*enlil*(idim) [… *a-na* […] […	Ḫayašu: Enlil [… to […

4	^{d}*ti-la* x [... x-*li*[*l*...	Tila . [... .. [...
5	^{d}*nun/ú*?-x-x [... x x [...	... [... .. [...
6	^{d}[...	. [...
	(remainder of obverse lost)	
Rev.	(beginning lost)	
1	^{d}[... *a*-[	
2	^{d}*ší-mu-*[*ut* ^{d}*nerigal* ... *ki-ma* x [...	Šimu[t: Nerigal ... like [...
3	^{d}*ḫi-li-be* ^{d}[... *ša* ^{d}*enlil*(idim) *qar*-[...	Ḫilibe [... of Enlil, war[rior ...
4	^{d}*za-na-ru* ^{d}*ištar*(U+DA[R)[... *i+na qab*[*li*](MUR[UB$_4$] *ù tāḫazi* (KA×ÉRIN)[...	Zanaru: Ištar [... in battle and warfare [...
5	^{d}[x (x)]x^{meš} N[E ... x [x] x *l*[*i* ... [x x] x *li* [...	
	(end of tablet)	

Notes

Only three sections are sufficiently preserved to give an indication of the general pattern: obv. 2, 3, and rev. 4. Each begins with the name of a rare or foreign deity, and this is immediately followed by the normal Babylonian name of that deity. Descriptive epithets follow the names. Rev. 2 can be restored with some confidence to follow the same pattern.

Obv. 1 Elsewhere this god is either father or grandfather of Enlil, or a name of Ea; see *RLA* 7, pp. 133–34. His paternity of Enlil, however, appears comparatively late in our documentation. The Enki-Ninki pairs as ancestors of Enlil-Ninlil appear already in Early Dynastic Sumerian lists from Fara and Ṣalābīkh (see P. Mander, *Il Pantheon di Abu-Ṣalābīkh* [Naples, 1986], p. 29: 273–88 and p. 109: 1–14) without any Lugal-dukuga. He first appears with such listings in An = Anum II 137, but after Enmešarra and Ninmešarra (themselves an addition to the older list) and their seven children; see CT 24 4–5:26–37. In contrast, the pair En-dukuga–Nin-dukuga already occurs in the Old Babylonian forerunner to An = Anum (TCL 15 10:1–24), in its listing of the Enkis and Ninkis. As a name of Ea, Lugal-dukuga's influence spread to Marduk theology; for example, Dumuduku is one of the fifty names of Marduk in En. el. VII 99–100. In our list Lugal-dukuga appears as a prime mover, and probably he had this status in some small place in Babylonia, and scholars of bigger and more important places in due course incorporated him in their own theologies.

Obv. 2–3 The Marduk Prophecy begins: ^{d}*ḫa-mur-nim* ^{d}*ḫa-a-a-šum*, immediately followed by Anu, Enlil, and Ea (R. Borger, "Gott Marduk und Gott-König Šulgi als Propheten: Zwei prophetische Texte," *BiOr* 28 [1971]: 5:1 = p. 13:15′, where obverse 2–3 of VAT 10608 was compared). But the reading of the first name was uncertain, and Borger wisely read ^{d}*ḫa-ḪAR-num*. The present writer discovered in an unpublished Late Babylonian copy of Tablet I of the god-list Anšar = Anum, line 6: ^{d}*ḫa-mu-ur-ni* = MIN (^{d}*a-nu-um*) and so identified the pair with the Hurrian terms *ḫawurni* and *eše*, "heaven" and "earth," though as a cosmic pair they occur in the opposite order: *eše ḫawurni* (E. Laroche, *Glossaire de la langue Hourrite* [= *RHA* 34–35 (1976–77): 83–84 and 99]; G. Wilhelm, *Grundzüge der Geschichte und Kultur der Hurriter* [Darmstadt, 1982], p. 80). This reverse order formerly resulted in giving the wrong translation to each word, but from both Hurrian-Hittite and Babylonian material just given, the correct meanings are now clear. The Babylonian material was presented in a paper by the present writer to the 34ème Rencontre Assyriologique Internationale, 1987, in Istanbul, but was not published. The spelling Ḫay(y)ašu raises big questions about Hurrian phonetics and etymology (is a development *ḫayya-* to *e-* normal in Hurrian?), for which there is simply no evidence so far. Ḫamurni also occurs in the Theogony of Dunnu, CT 46 43 obv. 38: [...] *ṣi-ḫi-ir* ^{d}*ḫa-mur-ni* [...]. The context is too damaged to be explicable, but so far as can be judged, the creation of heaven has not been previously told in this story.

Obv. 4 One could read ^{d}*ti-la* ^{d}[...], making Tila a foreign god like Ḫamurni and Ḫayašu, identified with a native Babylonian god. After Anu and Enlil one might think of Ea, provided he is not meant by Lugal-dukuga in obv. 1, but no god Tila or Tila... so far known suits Ea. As a foreign god the Hurrian Tilla could be compared. Mostly he is one of the bulls that pulled Teššup's chariot, but at Nuzi he was of similar status to Teššup, and at Ulamme he was head of the pantheon; see V. Haas, *Geschichte der hethitischen Religion*, Handbuch der Orientalistik I/15 (Leiden, 1994), pp. 318, 545. If this is correct, our text should be restored: ^{d}*ti-la* ^{d}[*adad*...].

Rev. 2 ^{d}*ší-mu-ut* was an Elamite god; see W. Hinz and H. Koch, *Elamisches Wörterbuch* (Berlin, 1987), pp. 1084–86, 1166–67. He is called "the strong herald of the gods," if *berir* is correctly rendered "herald," but his character is little known. In Akkadian he occurs in the Weidner God-List (A. Cavigneaux, *Textes scolaires du temple de Nabû ša harê*, vol. 1 [Baghdad, 1981], pp. 90–91), line 118, taken there as a name of Nerigal, which is stated explicitly in the explanatory column of the two-column edition: ^{d}*ší-mu-ut* = ^{d}U+GUR (*KAV* 63 iii 20; 148+165 obv. 16). Nerigal is appropriate to this position in the list.

Rev. 3 One could read ^{d}*ḫi-li-bat*, etc., but with a foreign name the simpler and more common value is to be expected. No god Ḫilibe is so far known, but in lists the common noun "god" is seen in this or in a homophone:

qa-ad-mu	=	*i-*[*lum*]
di-gi-ru-ú	=	MIN
ḫi-li-bu-ú	=	<MIN>
e-ne	=	MIN SU^{ki}
nap	=	MIN *elam*^{ki}

CT 25 18 rev. ii 9–11

$^{ḫi-li-bu}$E.NUN E.NUN	=	*ilu*

CT 19 19 iv 28 = MSL 17, p. 228: 283

The final long vowel in CT 25 18 could be explained from the preceding *digirû*: an Akkadianization of Ḫilibe. A particular deity could bear as a name a common noun; cf. West Semitic El and ancient Mesopotamian Inanna/Aštar/Ištar. If one dares to frame a hypothesis on such a narrow basis, one will conclude that Ḫilibe was a foreign god of this kind, equated with a Sumero-Babylonian of the same theological type. The context and what remains of these lines suggests as a possible restoration:

^{d}*ḫi-li-be* ^{d}[*ninurta māru ašarīdu*]
ša ^{d}*enlil*(idim) *qar-*[*ra-du rabû*]

Ninurta would fit very nicely between Nergal and Ištar, but this is only speculation.

Rev. 4 For Zanaru as a name of Ištar, see W. G. Lambert in *Kraus AV*, p. 213, note on III 67–68. It is rare in texts, more common in lists glossing ^{d}MÙŠ or ^{d}ZA.MÙŠ. The present writer hesitated there to accept the common identification of this name of Ištar with the Sumero-Akkadian musical instrument *zannaru* (see *CAD* s.v.) and the Proto-Hattic *zinar* (for the Hittite evidence, see S. de Martino, "Il lessico musicale ittita II. GIŠ ^{d}INANNA=cetra," *Oriens Antiqvvs* 26 [1987]: 171–85). It now seems likely that the two words are in origin unrelated. The instrument, in Akkadian and Sumerian, can be written with one *-n-* but is rightly normalized with two, but there seems to be no single example of the name of the goddess with a doubled *-nn-*. The lack of any known association of the goddess with the instrument is a serious problem, and another source is more probable. There is an Elamite noun written *za-na* "lady," used as a divine name and written ^{d}*za-na* (W. Hinz and H. Koch, *Wörterbuch*, p. 1282). Elamite nouns occurring in Akkadian contexts bear the delocutive ending; note *sú-uk-ki-ir* in Akkadian texts from Susa of Old Babylonian times (passages in *CAD* S s.v. *sukkir*) and *ki-ri-ir* in a Late Assyrian copy of a god-list (CT 25 18 rev. ii 17), for *sukki/sunki* "king" and *kiri* "goddess." Thus the word could have been loaned as *Zanar*, to which the Akkadian case ending was added. The sign KA×ÉRIN, for the normal AG×ÉRIN, seems to be specifically Assyrian.

Rev. 5 A restoration ^{d}[*bēlet-ilā*]*ni*^{meš} N[E... is possible, and if correct then a good Mesopotamian name is offered, not followed by any other name. It is also possible to read ^{d}[*bēlet-il*]*āne*$^{\text{meš}.n}$[^{e}..., which allows for another following divine name, now lost.

CONCLUSIONS

Despite its exiguous remains, this tablet strongly gives the impression of being a variety of triple-column god-list, for which see *RLA* 3, pp. 473–79, "Götterlisten," though the text is not set out on the tablet as a list. Each section begins with a rare name of the deity, follows that with the ordinary name, and concludes with descriptive phrases. The longest and best-known example of such a list is drawn on in En. el. VIb and VII, though the literary format required the omission of the main name to avoid repetition. Parallels to VAT 10608 are scattered throughout K.4339 (CT 25 9–14) from which we cite a few lines as examples:

^{d}en-bàn-da	^{d}*nin-urta*	*ṣa-bit purussî*(eš.bar) *ilāni*(dingir)^{meš}
^{d}ḫal-ḫal-la	^{d}*nin-urta*	*nāṣir*(ùru) *purussî*(eš.bar) *a-bi* ^{d}*en-líl*
^{d}me-maḫ	^{d}*nin-urta*	*ḫa-mi-im parṣi*(garza)^{meš} *ṣīrūti*(maḫ)^{meš}
^{d}zú-lum-ma	^{d}*nin-urta*	*a-ni-ku a-ni-ḫu*
^{d}usu-maḫ	^{d}*nin-urta*	*bēl*(en) *e-mu-qí*
		CT 25 11 ii 17–24

En-banda	Ninurta	who holds the decree of the gods
Ḫalḫalla	Ninurta	who guards the decree of father Enlil
Memaḫ	Ninurta	who controls the exalted ordinances
Zulumma	Ninurta	... he who strives(?)
Usumaḫ	Ninurta	master of strength

Most triple-column god-lists deal with one god only, or one god at a time in detail, but VAT 10608 apparently took an existing short god-list covering the whole pantheon and expanded that with some extremely exotic material, but not giving more than one section to each deity. As for date of origin, the parallel of Ḫamurni and Ḫayašu with the Marduk Prophecy, from the reign of Nebuchadnezzar I, strongly suggests a Middle Babylonian origin.

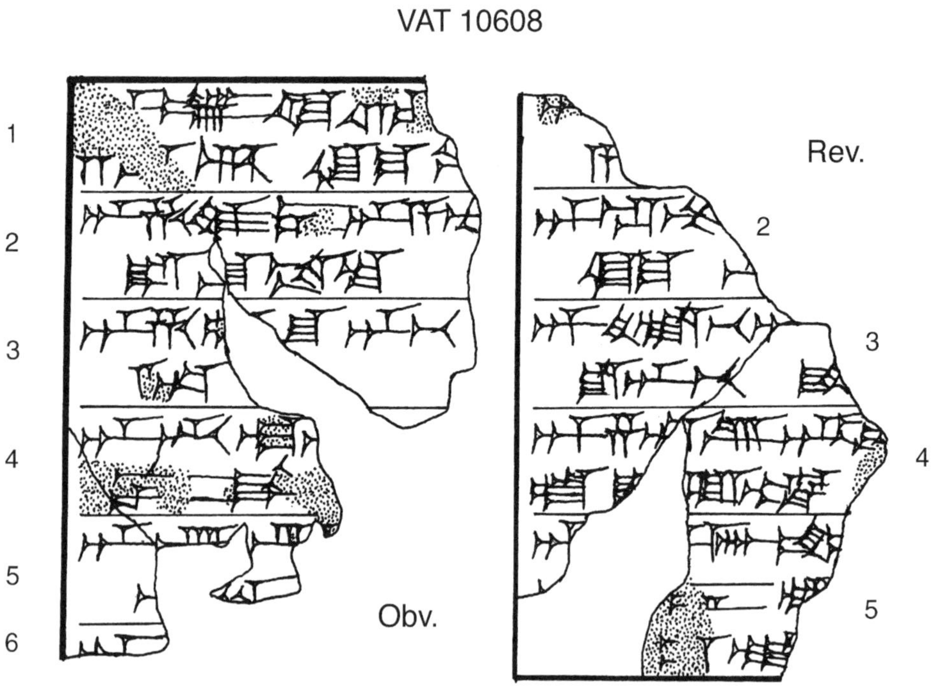

Figure 1. VAT 10608

GOING TO THE RIVER

Mogens Trolle Larsen, Københavns Universitet

I. THE LEGAL DOCUMENT KT 94/K 1153

In a document recording a discussion between representatives of the Assyrian community and the king and queen of an Anatolian principality we hear for the first time of the Anatolian judicial custom of the river ordeal, "going to the river."[1] An Assyrian trader named Aššur-taklāku is accused of working for the king of neighboring Tawinia, an enemy of the rulers of Kanesh, and he has been thrown in jail. The Assyrian negotiators turn up at the palace and try to secure the release of their countryman; if the rulers simply refuse to set him free, he should be allowed either to swear an oath on the sword of Assur or "like a citizen of your city" to submit to the river ordeal in order to clear himself: *lizziz <mahar> paṭrim ša Aššur litma ul kīma mera ālika ana Id lillik*. These two possible courses of action clearly represent the Assyrian and the Anatolian practices.

To date, this is the only text we know of to mention this special legal procedure, but the legal document kt 94/k 1153 published here provides us with an interesting parallel. It is an unopened envelope that stems from an archive discovered at Kültepe in 1994.[2]

Text

Obv.

Ša-lim-A-šùr DUMU *I-sú*-SUD$_x$[3] *ù A-šu-wa-an-zi*
DUMU *Ha-ar-ša ša dí-nam ru-ba-um*
ù GAL *sí-ki-tim dí-nam i-dí-nu-ni-ma*
ṣú-ha-ra-am ša Šál-ma-A-šùr a-na i-id

[1] C. Günbattı, "The River Ordeal in Ancient Anatolia," in *Veenhof AV*, pp. 151–60. The question of where this discussion took place was discussed by C. Michel and P. Garelli, "Heurts avec une principauté anatolienne," *WZKM* 86 (1996): 277–90, and by Günbattı, "River Ordeal," pp. 158–59; Garelli and Michel thought it was Durhumit, a view rejected by Günbattı. Kanesh seems the most likely place.

[2] I thank Tahsin Özgüç for his permission to let me publish the texts from that year.

[3] The sign is MUŠ, which in Old Assyrian texts appears to have been conflated with SUD, *arāku*.

i-dí-nu-ni Ša-lim-A-šùr ù A-šu-wa-an
i-mì-ig-ru-ma ni-iš A-na ni-iš ^{d}*A-šùr*
ni-iš ru-ba-im ni-iš GAL *sí-ki-tim*
Wa-li-iš-ra ù ni-iš e-ba!(RA)*-ru-tim*
ša a-wa-tí-šu-nu ig-mu-ru-ni
it-mu-ú-ma
1 *ma-na* KÙ.BABBAR *ù* 1 TÚG *ku-ta-nam*
lo. e. *Ša-lim-A-šur a-na A-šu-wa-an*
i-dí-in-ma A-šu-wa-an ù a-hu-šu me-er-ú Ha-ar-ša-a

Rev.

a-na Ša-lim-A-šùr me-er-e-šu
ù me-er-e I-dí-a-bi-im a-na mì-ma
šu-um-šu ù-lá i-tù-ru
šu-ma
i-tù-ru lá-am-nu-ut A-na : *A-šùr*
ru-ba-im ù GAL *sí-ki-tim* KIŠIB *Ku-ra-áš-mì-iš*
DUMU GAL *na-pá-hi-im* KIŠIB *Bu-li-na*
u. e. DUMU *ra-*bi_4 *ša-qí-im* KIŠIB *Šé-ṣú-ur*
DUMU *Kà-zu-ba*
KIŠIB *A-šu-wa-an* DUMU *Ha-ar-ša*
KIŠIB *A-zu* DUMU *Kà-zu* (over erasure)
l. e. KIŠIB *Ú-ra-a* KIŠIB ^{d}MAR.TU*-ba-ni me-er-ú Ma-na-na*
KIŠIB *Zu-ba* DUMU *Ištar-pá-li-*il_5 KIŠIB *A-*de_8*-lá-at*
DUMU ^{d}IM*-ba-ni*

seal A: *A-mur-A-šur* / DUMU *Šu-li*[4]
seal B: *A-šùr-ba-ni* / DUMU *Ma-na-na*[5]

[4] The seal is no. 264 in B. Teissier, *Sealing and Seals from Kültepe Karum Level 2* (Istanbul, 1994) and probably used by Zuba.

[5] The seal is no. 646 (ibid.), used by Uraya son of Manana; see M. T. Larsen and E. Møller, "Five Old Assyrian Texts," in *Mélanges Garelli*, p. 228.

Translation

Šalim-Aššur son of Issu-rik and Ašuwanzi son of Harša, for whom the king and the *rabi sikkitim* had given a verdict stating that they would hand over a servant of Šalim-Aššur to the river (ordeal)—Šalim-Aššur and Ašuwan came to an agreement, and they swore an oath by Anna, Aššur, the king, the *rabi sikkitim* Wališra, and by the colleagues who had resolved their dispute, and Šalim-Aššur gave 1 mina of silver and 1 *kutānu*-textile to Ašuwan, and Ašuwan and his brothers, sons of Harša, will raise no claim whatsoever against Šalim-Aššur, his sons, and the sons of Iddin-abum. If they do raise a claim, it will be a crime against Anna, Aššur, the king, and the *rabi sikkitim*.

Sealed by Kurašmiš son of the overseer of smiths, Bulina son of the chief cup-bearer, Šeṣur son of Kazuba, Ašuwan son of Harša, Azu son of Kazu, Uraya (and) Amurrum-bani sons of Manana, Zuba son of Ištar-pālil, Adad-ellat son of Adad-bani.

Summary

An Assyrian, Šalim-Aššur, and an Anatolian, Ašuwan(zi), have appealed to the king (of Kanesh) and his chief officer, who have handed down a verdict. This involved sending a servant of the Assyrian merchant to the river ordeal, but rather than carrying out this verdict, the two men submitted their case to the mediation of a group of "colleagues," who instead imposed a solution whereby the Assyrian paid 1 mina of silver and 1 textile to his adversary. He, in turn, relinquished the right to raise any further claims. The two men then swore an oath to uphold this agreement, swearing by the gods Anna and Aššur, by the king and by his chief officer, and, finally, by the men who had mediated the agreement. If this settlement should be violated, it would then constitute an "evil" to the gods, the king, and his officer.

Nine people have witnessed this agreement, four Anatolians and four Assyrians as well as Ašuwan(zi), the Anatolian litigant.

THE PLAYERS

The texts found at Kültepe in 1994 came from two houses that were some 60 meters apart. The text under consideration here belongs to the second archive found that year, consisting of the texts numbered 569 to 1,789, a substantial archive that documents the activities of the family of Šalim-Aššur son of Issu-rik. The latter appears as a living person only in a few texts, and we know that he moved to Assur; since, however, there are no letters from him sent from Assur, we must assume he died soon after his move. He had three sons, Aššur-bēl-awātim, Iddin-abum, and Šalim-Aššur; the first one held an official position in Assur as *laputtā'um*,[6] a member of the city

[6] For the office, see J. G. Dercksen, *Old Assyrian Institutions*, Uitgaven van het Nederlands Instituut voor het Nabije Oosten te Leiden, *voorheen* Publications de l'Institut historique-archéologique néerlandais de Stamboul 98 (Leiden, 2004), pp. 65–72.

administration, and, as far as we know, he did not take an active part in the overland trade. The archive of Iddin-abum and his sons must be in another building at Kültepe, but these persons figure quite prominently in the 1994 archive as well. Šalim-Aššur had two sons, Ennam-Aššur and Alāhum, and he is known to have died in his house in Durhumit in the year KEL 104.[7]

The conflict with Ašuwan(zi) is not mentioned in any other text in the archive. Some of the Anatolians, however, are known from other contexts. Ašuwan(zi)[8] appears in four other texts: Jankowska *KTK* 86:2, where he has a debt of 2 minas 10 shekels of silver to an Assyrian called Sahri-ilī; in a text from level 1b, kt 89/k 383:1, where he is said to be a priest of the local god Higiša;[9] and in two unpublished texts, kt h/t 330:17, a witness, and kt 73/k 14:12, a list of personal names. The name of his father, Harša, appears in kt g/t 36:2, the well-known list of palace personnel under Turupani, the *rabi simmiltim*, probably the local crown prince;[10] here Harša is one of eight persons who are described as *urki Halkiaššu rabi huršātim* "under Halki-aššu the chief of the storehouses," but he cannot be identical with our man, Harša the father of Ašuwan(zi), since the text is from the 1b period. Written either Harša or Harši, the name appears in CCT 6 37b:2, ICK 1 30:18, and ICK 2 1:11 (in both cases as a witness) and in the unpublished text kt n/k 67:11, where Harša is involved in an affair concerning *amūtum*.

We are informed in our text that the name of the high official *rabi sikkitim* was Wališra;[11] persons with this name are found in *JCS* 14 12:3, 7, in TCL 4 87:13 as debtors, and in Matouš *KK* 38:10 in an unrevealing context; in a text from level 1b, kt n/k 31:7, a man with this name is a witness and said to be the priest of Adad, and in another text, kt 89/k 379:1, he is said to be the chief of the heralds.[12]

One of the names of the Anatolian witnesses, Bulina, recurs a number of times, twice referring to members of the local elite: in kt a/k 1263:9 Bulina is a member of the retinue (*upatinnum*) of the *rabi sikkitim*, and in kt n/k 32:12, another level 1b text, a man with this name is the head of the staff of Inar, the priest of Bēl-qablim. The name Azu is used by both Assyrians and Anatolians, and no Azu son of Kazu is otherwise attested; however, the father's name appears once in *JCS* 14 12, where he and Wališra are both debtors, and this may provide a link with our text. At least it clearly shows that the witness is an Anatolian.

---

[7] KEL (Kültepe Eponym List); see K. R. Veenhof, *The Old Assyrian List of Year Eponyms from Karum Kanish and Its Chronological Implications*, Türk Tarih KurumuYayınları VI/64, (Ankara, 2003).

[8] Only once in the present text is he called Ašuwanzi, and this may be a mistake, for all other occurrences give the form Ašuwan.

[9] Published by V. Donbaz, "Some Remarkable Contracts of 1-b Period-Kültepe Tablets II," in *N. Özgüç AV*, pp. 131–54.

[10] E. Bilgiç, "Three Tablets from the City Mound of Kültepe," *Anatolia* 8 (1964): 145–63.

[11] See G. Kryszat, "Herrscher, Herrschaft und Kulttradition in Anatolien nach den Quellen aus den altassyrischen Handelskolonien," *AoF* 31 (2004): 15–45, for a thorough discussion of the term *sikkātum* and the title in question.

[12] Donbaz, "Some Remarkable Contracts II," p. 137.

THE PROCEDURE

It can be assumed that the eight witnesses are identical with the "colleagues who resolved their dispute," persons who are otherwise often referred to as *gāmer awātim*. These men were drawn into the affair, since the litigants wanted a compromise settlement instead of implementing the verdict of the king. Such a verdict could accordingly be disregarded or treated more as a suggested solution than as a binding decision if the parties to the conflict could agree on a different procedure.

The fact that the matter was originally brought before the king of Kanesh rather than the Assyrian authorities needs to be explained, for it is highly unusual for the Anatolian authorities to become involved in strictly legal decisions. Among the few examples, one may point to the last text mentioned above, kt n/k 32, which involves the dissolution of some kind of partnership between two Anatolian brothers, Tamurya and Šalkuata, and an Assyrian called Eddin-Aššur; the matter concerned the two kings Hurmeli and Inar of Kanesh, and although it deals with matters in both Kanesh and Mamma, it was concluded in Kanesh, where seven negotiators, three Anatolians and four Assyrians, "divided" their joint assets.

This text, from the level 1b period, belongs to the *iqqāti* genre, where Anatolian kings (sometimes the *rabi simmiltim*) notarize a document with a legal decision or agreement. Such documents otherwise deal with matters of family law, mostly divorce cases, and they concern only Anatolians.[13] These texts are accordingly a reflection of local Anatolian legal customs, despite the fact that they are written in Assyrian.

In cases where merchandise disappeared, stolen by brigands, the king was responsible in accordance with the treaties set up, and he had to recompense the firm, and if murder was involved in such a situation, the case would have to be dealt with by the king. One of Šalim-Aššur's sons, Ennam-Aššur, was in fact murdered in the district of Tamnia; text kt 94/k 937, a draft of a letter that is unfortunately badly written and poorly preserved, informs us that the surviving son, Alāhum, went to Tamnia together with the envoys of the Kanesh colony to discuss this with the king, asking him to "search for the blood money for the man together with us."[14] Both Alāhum and the Tamnia colony insist that Ennam-Aššur was murdered because of a presumably large sum of money the king had paid him for a delivery of meteoric iron.[15]

---

[13] For a selection of such texts, including kt n/k 32, see V. Donbaz, "Some Remarkable Contracts of 1-b Period Kültepe Tablets," in *T. Özgüç AV*, pp. 75–98; see also n. 8 above.

[14] (1) *iš-tí ší-ip-ri-ku-nu* (2) *a-na da-me-e ša a-hi-a* (3) *šé-[a]-im a-ta-lá-ak iš-tí* (4) *ru-ba-im Ta-am-ni-a-i-im* (5) *[ni]-na-me-er-ma um-ma š[í-i]p-ru* (6) *x ni i-na ib-ri ša x* (7) *x a-hu-šu a-ba-ú-kà . iš-t[í-ni]* (8) *[da-m]e-e ša a-wi-lim . šé-e* "I left together with your envoys to claim the blood money for my brother. We met with the King of Tamnia, and the envoys said: '…among the friends of … his brother … your fathers … search for the blood money for the man together with us!'"

[15] (16) *a-hi-i a-šu-<mì> a-mu-tí-kà* (17) *[x] x* KÙ.BABBAR *ša šu-mì Lá-qé-ep* (18 l.e.) *[i]t-bu-lu* (erasure) KÙ.BABBAR (19 rev.) *[a]-mu-tim sú-re-e . ša ta-dí-/nu-šu-ni* (20) *dí-ik a-li-ik-ma* (21) *da-me-e ša a-hi-a . šé-e* (22) *kà-ru-um iš-al-šu-ma* (23) *um-ma kà-ru-ma a-wi-*IL$_5$ *a-šu-mì* (24) *a-mu-tí-kà . dí-ik a-li-ik-ma* (25) *da-me-e ša a-*

Our text does not inform us about the background of the litigation, only that Šalim-Aššur had to accept a settlement that meant he had to pay 1 mina of silver and 1 piece of a textile. This is not a very large obligation for a very wealthy businessman, but the size of the payment itself does not tell us what the problem may have been.

THE OATH

The special oath that refers to both gods and to the Anatolian king and his chief officer appears once more in the available evidence, in Matouš *Prag* I 651. Apart from that, we have one document, ICK 1 32, where we find an oath by the gods Aššur and Anna and by the king; finally, in kt 91/k 282:19–21 an oath is sworn by "Anna, the king, and the queen";[16] only Anatolians appear in that text, which is concerned with a division, perhaps of an inheritance.

Dercksen has suggested that we are in fact dealing with an oath by the Assyrian king in the first two cases,[17] but that is clearly excluded in our text. Both the other two texts deal with divorce proceedings. The first, ICK 1 32, states that the Assyrian Pilah-Ištar has divorced his "maid" Walawala;[18] although this name is Anatolian, her family members who appear on her behalf at the proceedings have Assyrian names: her two brothers are called Nunu and Amur-Aššur, and her mother's name is Šāt-Ištar.[19]

The second text is Matouš *Prag* I 651, a badly broken divorce settlement involving a man called Pūšu-kēn and his wife, whose name is partly broken away but that may be Lamassī.[20] The text itself is in fact unusual, since it seems to begin with the statement that the two divorcees swore an oath; the editors have suggested that it was an oath by the City, that is, Assur, but other explanations are equally possible. We are told

---

wi-lim šé-e "my brother has been killed because of your iron ... the silver that he took away in Laqīp's name, the iron that you indeed gave to him. Go and search for the blood money for my brother! The colony interrogated him, saying: 'The man has been killed because of your iron. Go and search for the blood money for that man!'"

16 *CAD* R s.v. *rubātu* usage a.

17 Dercksen, *Old Assyrian Institutions*, p. 71, n. 232.

18 For the status of an *amtu*-wife, see C. Michel, *La correspondance des marchands de Kaniš au début du IIe millénaire av. J.-C.*, Littératures anciennes du Proche-Orient 19 (Paris, 2001), p. 424, and M. T. Larsen, *The Aššur-nādā Archive*, Uitgaven van het Nederlands Instituut voor het Nabije Oosten te Leiden, *voorheen* Publications de l'Institut historique-archéologique néerlandais de Stamboul 96, Old Assyrian Archives, vol. 1 (Leiden, 2002), p. xxv.

19 We may be dealing with an Anatolian family that was closely associated with the Assyrian milieu that adopted Assyrian names.

20 The well-known Assyrian trader called Pūšu-kēn, whose extensive archive was dug up by the villagers at Kültepe before 1948, was in fact married to a woman called Lamassī, but there are very good reasons to think that she could not be meant in this text; for one thing, we know that she died in Assur as Pūšu-kēn's wife (see TCL 4 30), and it seems clear that she never set foot in Anatolia. Dercksen has therefore suggested (*AfO* 48–49 [2001–2]: 191) that the text in question is concerned with the divorce of Pūšu-kēn II, the grandson of the famous man, and that seems reasonable. It is difficult, however, to believe that he too was married to a woman called Lamassī — however popular that name may have been. Since the name is only partially preserved, we should withhold an identification for the time being.

that the lady in question has received her divorce payment and therefore cannot raise further claims against Pūšu-kēn, his sons and daughters, or his donkey packers, but, confusingly, she cannot do so together with her husband. The two are then said to have sworn an oath by Aššur, Anna, the king, and the *rabi sikkitim*.[21]

It seems likely to me that both cases refer to divorces involving an Assyrian man and an Anatolian woman, and that could explain why the Anatolian authorities became involved in the oath ceremony. Dercksen's objection that "after all, divorce of Assyrians in Kanesh will have fallen under Assyrian jurisdiction"[22] is invalid if we assume that the women involved were Anatolians. There are many indications that the status of women differed significantly in the two societies, and intermarriage must under all circumstances have been a complex affair in which the two social and legal systems had to be brought into harmony with each other.

The king referred to must, accordingly, be the local one, and in line with the symmetrical structure of the negotiation process I suggest that the two gods mentioned, Aššur and Anna, represented the two groups involved, so that Anna is understood to be the main god of Kanesh.[23]

II. "GOING TO THE RIVER"

The river ordeal may well have been a fairly common procedure in Anatolian legal practice. Among the texts found in 1994, there is one other reference in a text that records a conflict between the sons of Šalim-Aššur and an Anatolian called Haršumnuman: kt 94/k 1397 (and duplicate kt 94/k 1399).

> Anu-pīya acting for the sons of Šalim-Aššur seized us (as witnesses) in the case against Galgalya and Haršu(mnu)man, and they heard the tablet concerning their debt of 10 minas of silver.
>
> Anu-pīya said: "Is this the tablet with your seal?"
>
> Galgalya answered: "It is my seal; however, it is Haršumnuman who paid the silver."
>
> Anu-pīya said: "We appear as inheritors. Bring evidence as to whether you paid the silver either to Šalim-Aššur or to the sons of Šalim-Aššur."

---

[21] Cf. discussion in Dercksen, *Old Assyrian Institutions*, p. 71, n. 232.

[22] Ibid.

[23] This is not the place to pursue this idea. The god(dess) Anna occurs in quite a few purely Assyrian names, such as Puzur-Anna or Anna-ilī (written *A-na-li/lí*), and the deity was clearly adopted by the Assyrians. There was, however, a festival in Kanesh for the god, mentioned in loan documents as the time for repayment. If the name is to be seen as Hittite in origin, it was probably a designation for a mother goddess (cf. *annaš*). See M. T. Larsen, *The Old Assyrian City-State and Its Colonies*, Mesopotamia 4 (Copenhagen, 1976), p. 46, n. 69.

Haršumnuman answered: "I personally paid the silver of our tablet in full to Šalim-Aššur. I will let myself be put to the river ordeal for you."

The Kanesh colony gave us (as witnesses) to these proceedings, and we delivered our testimony before Aššur's dagger.

Witnessed by Kura son of Ulaya; by Ennam-Aššur son of Hurāṣi.[24]

This text belongs to the time after the death of Šalim-Aššur, when his two sons were engaged in collecting old debts outstanding to their father; they are said to appear as *mer'u mētim* "sons of the dead man," a phrase that indicates their status as heirs with special rights to question people. The substantial loan to the two Anatolians was recorded on a tablet found in Šalim-Aššur's archive, and they have asked another person to find out whether the money has been paid. Under normal circumstances the original deed would have been handed over to the debtor once the loan was repaid, so the presence of the tablet in the archive would, of course, indicate that the money was still outstanding. One of the debtors, however, claims that he personally paid Šalim-Aššur, and he declares himself willing to submit to the river ordeal to prove this assertion.

The case is tried in accordance with Assyrian legal practices, using a standard textual format, and the declaration by Haršumnuman is therefore unusual and may indicate that in special cases such conflicts could be put before the local king, who would surely have been the one to authorize the river ordeal.

III. Anatolian or Assyrian Courts

In almost all disputes between Anatolians and Assyrians involving loans, debts of various kinds, and other commercial issues, the Assyrian legal institutions are directly involved in the decision-making process.[25] Such matters are therefore only in special instances brought before the Anatolian king. No doubt the kings and queens had the right to intervene in cases where the Assyrians acted in contravention of the treaties and regulations governing the relationship between the two groups. For instance, people caught smuggling, thus avoiding paying taxes to the local palaces, could simply be thrown in jail.

---

[24] *A-nu-pí-a ki-ma me-er-e* (2) *Šál-ma-A-šur a-na* (3) *Ga-al-ga-li-a* (4) *ù Ha-ar-šu-ma-an* (5) *iṣ-ba-at-ni-a-tí-ma ṭup-pá-am* (6) *ša* 10 *ma-na* KÙ.BABBAR *ša hu-bu-li-/šu-nu* (7) *iš-me-ú um-ma A-nu-pí-a-/ma* (8) *ṭup-pu-um ša ku-nu-ku-kà-a* (9) *um-ma Ga-al-ga-li-a-ma* (10) *ku-nu-ku-a : a-ma Ha-ar-šu-um-nu-/ma-an* (11) *ša-qí-il*$_5$ KÙ.BABBAR-*pì-im* (12) *um-ma A-nu-pí-a-ma me-er-ú* (13) *me-tim né-nu* (14 l.e.) *lu a-na Šál-ma-A-šur* (15) KÙ.BABBAR *ta-áš-qú-ul* (16 rev.) *lu a-na me-er-e* (17) *Šál-ma-A-šur : ta-áš-qú-ul* (18) *a-na a-ni-e-ma ru-a-am* (19) *um-ma Ha-ar-šu-um-nu-ma-an-/ma* (20) KÙ.BABBAR *a-na-ku ša ṭup-pì-ni* (21) *Šál-ma-A-šur ú-ša-bi*$_4$*-i* (22) *a-na i-id : a-ša-kà-na-/ku-nu-tí* (23) *a-na a-wa-tim* (24) *a-ni-a-tim kà-ru-um* (25) *Kà-né-eš i-dí-ni-a-tí-ma* (26) IGI GÍR *ša A-šur* (27) *ší-bu-tí-ni : ni-dí-in* (28) IGI *Ku-ra-a* DUMU *Ú-lá-a* (29 u.e.) IGI *En-um-A-šur* (30 l.e.) DUMU *Hu-ra-ṣí*.

[25] See K. R. Veenhof, "Old Assyrian Period," in R. Westbrook, ed., *A History of Ancient Near Eastern Law* (Leiden, 2003), pp. 431–83.

The examples collected here indicate that matters of family law involving mixed marriages could become the concern of the local palace, and the Šalim-Aššur case could perhaps therefore be explained as having its background in a dispute involving family matters in which both Assyrians and Anatolians had a stake. It would, however, be expected that other texts in this large archive would give hints of such a relationship.

Another obvious possibility is that the rank of the Anatolians involved in a conflict with one or more Assyrians played a role. The merchants apparently had limited powers in their relations with local officials as shown by a verdict of the Kanesh colony in which Assyrians are prohibited from having dealings with the *rabi simmiltim*, perhaps the crown prince, until he has paid what he owes to an Assyrian called Ikūnum.[26] Obviously, there was no way in which Ikūnum could force the Anatolian official to appear before the colony, and he may not have been interested in having his case dealt with by the local palace.

Haršumnuman, the man who declared his willingness to undergo the river ordeal, is known from another text in the archive, kt 94/k 1756, in which he is said to be the priest of the sun-god.[27] He was accordingly a member of the absolute elite in Kanesh, like Ašuwan(zi) in the first text, and this raises the possibility that in cases involving high-ranking Anatolians, the Assyrians at least sometimes would have to accept that legal disputes were brought before the local king.

In general we are poorly informed about Anatolian legal procedures during the level 2 period. The material available from level 1b reflects a situation in which the king and his highest officials, the *rabi simmiltim* and the *rabi sikkitim*, functioned as judges, and the conflicts brought before them were almost exclusively related to family law. It would not be surprising if the Assyrians became increasingly dominated by the Anatolian system during the later period, and although there is little concrete evidence of this, one of the level 1b treaties published recently by Günbattı does refer directly to Assyrians involved in lawsuits brought before the king. The treaty with the ruler of Hahhum contains the following passage (col. ii, 1–10):

> You (plural) shall not take a decision concerning any citizen of Assur or anyone from *kārum* Hahhum (based on) [the testi]mony of your followers, your slave-girls, your slaves, or any citizen of Hahhum. You shall not pass a verdict based on decrees, but you shall pass a verdict truthfully, in accordance with the law of Hahhum. The verdict of any citizen of Assur, a slave-girl, or anyone from the *kārum* Hahhum you shall pass truthfully.[28]

[26] G. Eisser and J. Lewy, *Die altassyrischen Rechtsurkunden von Kültepe*, MVAG 33 and 35/3 (Leipzig, 1930 and 1935), p. 306, no. 273.

[27] 5 *ma-na* (28) KÙ.BABBAR *i-ṣé-er Ga-al-ga-li-a* (29) *A-lu* DUMU *A-x x ù Ha-ar-šu-nu-ma-an* (30) *ku-um-ri-im ša* ^{d}UTU [*ú-mu-šu-nu*] (31) *ma-al-ú ù* KÙ.BABBAR *i-n*[*a*] (32) *qá-qá-ad šál-mì-šu-nu ra-k*[*i-is*].

[28] C. Günbattı, "Two Treaty Texts Found at Kültepe," in J. G. Dercksen, ed., *Assyria and Beyond: Studies Presented to Mogens Trolle Larsen*, Uitgaven van het Nederlands Instituut voor het Nabije Oosten te Leiden, *voorheen* Publications de l'Institut historique-archéologique néerlandais de Stamboul 100 (Leiden, 2004), pp. 249–68.

Figure 1. kt 94/k 1153, Upper Edge

Figure 2. kt 94/k 1153, Obverse

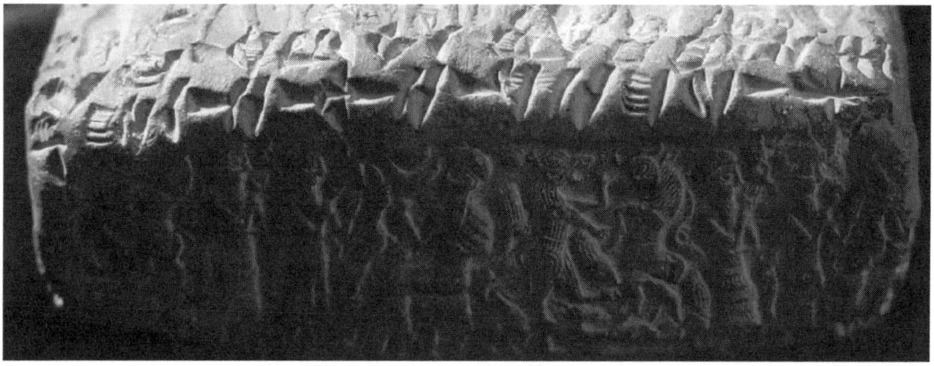

Figure 3. kt 94/k 1153, Lower Edge

Figure 4. kt 94/k 1153, Reverse

Figure 5. kt 94/k 1153, Upper Edge

Figure 6. kt 94/k 1153, Left Edge (1)

Figure 7. kt 94/k 1153, Left Edge (2)

Figure 8. kt 94/k 1153, Right Edge

ESARHADDON'S EXILE: SOME SPECULATIVE HISTORY

Erle V. Leichty, University of Pennsylvania

One of the minor mysteries of Neo-Assyrian history is the location of Esarhaddon's place of refuge when he fled the menacing threat posed by his brothers. I would like to offer a possible solution to this problem based on circumstantial evidence and what I hope is informed speculation.

In the institution of Assyrian kingship there were no formal rules of succession. While still on the throne, each king designated his own successor.[1] Normally the successor whom the sitting monarch named was one of his own sons, but this was not hard and fast. Since the Neo-Assyrian kings had harems and large numbers of children with their numerous wives and concubines, the designation of a successor must have been the subject of intense infighting within the royal family.

Esarhaddon (680–669 B.C.) was the youngest son of Sennacherib (704–681 B.C.) and, in all probability, the sole son of Naqiya. While he was growing up, his father, Sennacherib, was deeply involved with his "Babylonian problem." The Chaldean, Merodach-baladan, and his successors and their Elamite allies were continually stirring up rebellions in Babylonia, and Sennacherib struggled for a solution to the problem. In 700 B.C. Sennacherib seized Babylon and installed Assur-nadin-šumi, his eldest son and designated successor, as king of Babylon, but six years later Assur-nadin-šumi was captured and killed in an Elamite raid on Babylonia, leaving Sennacherib with no designated successor. Seven years later, in 683 B.C., Sennacherib named Esarhaddon, his youngest son, as successor and installed him in the *bīt redûti* "the house of succession."

Faced with this fait accompli, Esarhaddon's elder brothers plotted a coup. Esarhaddon somehow received warning of the plot, probably from his mother, who heard of it in the harem.[2] He promptly sought refuge in a safe place in the west. This prompted

[1] An interesting modern analogy is the recent succession in Jordan. King Hussein was critically ill at the Mayo Clinic in America, and there were rumblings of a coup in Amman. He flew home and designated a successor from among his sons.

[2] In her recent book on Naqiya, *The Role of Naqia/Zakutu in Sargonid Politics*, SAAS 9 (Helsinki, 1999), S. C. Melville plays down the power and position of Naqiya vis-à-vis the Neo-Assyrian monarch because she had not attained "first wife status." I do not believe that such a thing as "first wife status" existed but, rather, that any ranking within the harem was informal and cannot be revealed by titles. I follow the more traditional view that Naqiya was a major power behind the throne, citing the fact that her son Esarhaddon, the youngest of Sennacherib's sons, was named as successor, and that she remained prominent throughout the reign of Esarhaddon and well into the reign of Assurbanipal.

his brothers to assassinate their father, Sennacherib, and Esarhaddon had to march on Nineveh and seize the throne to which he was entitled. Over the years there has been extensive speculation as to where Esarhaddon took refuge, but the exact location of his exile has remained unknown. Here I will argue, albeit on inconclusive evidence, that this place of exile was Harran.[3]

The Sargonid dynasty was almost certainly West Semitic. I believe that Sargon and his successors were Arameans who took Akkadian throne names. The rapid and wide geographical spread of the use of Aramaic in this period is well attested,[4] and I would also note that the Neo-Assyrian kings took West Semitic wives.[5] There is no evidence that this was for diplomatic or political advantage.

Neo-Assyrian society was organized in groups of patriarchal extended families, and in such societies marriage was normally between cousins or between members of closely related family groups. Consequently, the Neo-Assyrian kings and their queens, in our case Sennacherib and Naqiya, probably came from the same geographical area. When Esarhaddon sought refuge, it must have been with his mother's family. That would have been the only haven that was guaranteed, or nearly guaranteed, to be safe. Because Esarhaddon was only one of many children of Sennacherib, his father's relatives would almost certainly have had divided loyalties and could not be trusted to protect him in such a situation.

My suspicion that Harran was the ancestoral home of Naqiya, and perhaps of the whole of the Sargonid dynasty, was raised when I recently served as outside examiner for the excellent dissertation of Jamie R. Novotny.[6] Novotny convincingly demonstrates that the major Assyrian building activity in Harran began in the last years of Esarhaddon's reign and that the various temples were finished in the first part of Assurbanipal's reign. I would like to suggest that this building activity was a thank-you gift from Esarhaddon to his relatives in Harran who had sheltered him. In the early part of his reign Esarhaddon was preoccupied with securing his throne and rebuilding Babylon, which his father had destroyed. The reconstruction of Babylon was a significant component of Esarhaddon's policy to pacify the south of Mesopotamia. Any major

[3] There have been several attempts to identify Naqiya's place of birth or Esarhaddon's place of exile. H. Lewy argued that Naqiya came from Lahiru in Babylonia (see "Nitokris-Naqê'a," *JNES* 11 [1952]: 273–74), but her thesis did not receive general acceptance. On the basis of *ABL* 1216 rev. 14, Schmidtke (*AOTU* 1/2, p. 107) identified Zaqqap as the village where Esarhaddon took refuge, but Labat ("Asarhaddon et la ville de Zaqqap," *RA* 53 [1959]: 113–18) discredited this reading of the text. Nougayrol and Parrot suggested that Naqiya came from Harran. They based their argument on an art motif on Naqiya's Louvre bronze implying that she came from the west but not specifically from Harran.

[4] See, for example, H. Tadmor, CRRA 25, pp. 449 ff.

[5] M. S. B. Damerji, *Gräber assyrischer Königinnen aus Nimrud* (Mainz, 1999), with bibliography, p. 11.

[6] J. R. Novotny, "Ehulhul, Emelamana, and Sin's Akitu-House: A Study of Assyrian Building Activities at Harran" (Ph.D. diss., University of Toronto, 2003).

construction in a backwater such as Harran would, of necessity, have come toward the end of his rule when the vital concerns of his reign had been seen to.

When Esarhaddon left his place of exile to claim his throne, he tells us: "I followed the road to Nineveh with difficulty and haste and before my (arrival) in the land (of) Hanigalbat all of their crack troops blocked my advance."[7] Hanigalbat is on the road between Harran and Nineveh.

Another small tie to Harran lies in the Neo-Assyrian references to the moon-god, Sin. Three of the eight Sargonid kings use the theophoric element Sin in their throne names: Sennacherib, Sin-shumu-lisher, and Sin-shar-ishkun. This is unusual, as only four other Assyrian kings in the Assyrian king-list use this theophoric element, and all four lived in much earlier periods. The god Sin also figures prominently in Esarhaddon's royal inscriptions. In lists of gods evoked by Esarhaddon, Sin is frequently listed immediately after Assur. Furthermore, one Esarhaddon prophecy states: "When your mother gave birth to you, sixty great gods stood with me and protected you. Sin was at your right side, Shamash at your left."[8]

Finally, it is probably not a coincidence that after the fall of Nineveh in 612 B.C., the last of the Sargonid kings made his final stand at Harran.

The historical hints listed above do not offer proof of anything, but taken all together they suggest that it is indeed possible that Harran was the home of the Sargonid kings and the place of refuge for Esarhaddon.

---

7 Thompson *Esarh.* 12 i 69–70.

8 S. Parpola, *Assyrian Prophecies*, SAA 9 (Helsinki, 1997), p. 6.

ŠAMAŠ OF SIPPAR AND THE FIRST DYNASTY OF BABYLON *

Jennie Myers, The University of Chicago

In the prologue to his famous collection of laws, Hammurapi describes himself as called by Anu and Enlil to "rise like Šamaš over the blackheaded ones, to illuminate the land,"[1] and as "the sun of Babylon, who spreads light over the lands of Sumer and Akkad."[2] In addition, like the god Šamaš, Hammurapi is *šar mīšarim*, "the king of justice,"[3] begotten by the god Sîn.[4] It is, of course, not surprising that Hammurapi would invoke Šamaš, the god of justice, on the stela that proclaims his just laws and whose relief depicts him receiving the emblems of kingship from the sun-god. The language Hammurapi uses, however, reveals that the image he wished to portray of himself was not simply that of the prototypical just king. Rather, Hammurapi casts himself in the role of human counterpart to the god Šamaš, who is, along with Marduk, the divine patron of his kingship.

The privileged position that Hammurapi accords to Šamaš on his stela represents the culmination of a special relationship that existed between the kings of the First Dynasty of Babylon and the patron deity of Sippar. Prior to this dynasty, kings had consistently legitimated their rule over Sumer and Akkad by claiming control over Nippur, the religious capital of southern Babylonia and the seat of Enlil, chief god of the Babylonian pantheon. While Hammurapi gives due nod to the supremacy of Enlil in his prologue by mentioning him first among the deities whose temples he has patronized and by claiming that he was selected by Enlil as shepherd, his inscriptions and year-names, as well as those of his predecessors and successors, in addition to evidence from legal and economic texts all suggest that these kings based their legitimacy primarily on Šamaš and his city Sippar rather than on Enlil and Nippur.

---

* This article was first presented at the 213th Meeting of the American Oriental Society, Nashville, Tennessee, in April 2003, as "The Importance of Sippar as a Religious and Cultural Center for the First Dynasty of Babylon." Much of the material herein stems from my doctoral dissertation, "The Sippar Pantheon: A Diachronic Study" (Ph.D. diss., Harvard University, 2002).

[1] LH i 40–49: *kīma Šamaš ana ṣalmāt qaqqadim waṣêmma mātim nuwwurim*, in Roth *Law Collections*, pp. 76 f.

[2] LH v 4–9: *šamšu Bābilim mušēṣi nūrim ana māt Šumerim u Akkadîm*, in Roth *Law Collections*, p. 80.

[3] LH xlvii 79; xlviii 96; xlix 13.

[4] LH ii 14–15 (prologue); l 41–42 (epilogue).

It is indeed well known that one of the goals of the kings of this dynasty was to establish the city of Babylon as the capital of a unified Babylonia and to promote their city-god Marduk to an exalted position within the national pantheon. One of their main obstacles from the outset was the fact that the city of Babylon was quite insignificant politically, religiously, and culturally, its patron deity being but a minor player on the religious scene. In order to gain legitimacy for their cause, it was necessary for them to align themselves with a cult center whose importance was unquestioned. Their choice was the city of Sippar with its patron deity Šamaš.

While it could be argued that it was impossible for the kings of Babylon to align themselves with Nippur until Hammurapi had gained control of the south, there are strong arguments to suggest that their focus on Sippar was a deliberate choice that fit their political as well as religious agenda. It could also be argued that Sippar was a natural choice, since it was a northern Semitic city with a large Amorite population, situated on lucrative trade routes. These facts may indeed be true; however, there appear to have been other, more dominant, motivations leading to their choice of Sippar. I submit that the main motivating factor in the choice of the kings of Babylon to align themselves with Sippar was its reputation as the old religious "capital"[5] of northern Babylonia—indeed, of the entire north, from Ebla in the west to the Diyala region in the east.[6]

The great antiquity of Sippar is in no doubt; archaeological excavations reveal its existence as early as the Uruk period.[7] According to the Sumerian King List, Sippar was the fourth antediluvian city to receive kingship, testifying to its reputation as *āl ṣiātim*—the ancient or eternal city—a designation for Sippar first attested in the reign of Hammurapi.[8] Of the antediluvian cities, Sippar was the only one to retain its prominence throughout the history of Babylonia, serving as a religious and cultural center. We know that the sun-god UTU-Šamaš was the patron deity of Sippar by at least the mid-third millennium, as the earliest extant Semitic literary text—known from copies discovered at Abu Salabikh (R. D. Biggs, *Inscriptions from Tell Abū Ṣalābīkh*, OIP 99 [Chicago, 1974], 326+342) and Ebla (*ARET* 5 6)[9]—concerns this god and his city Sippar.

---

[5] I enclose the word capital in quotation marks, as this term carries ramifications that may not apply to Sippar.

[6] I am grateful to P. Steinkeller for first pointing out to me the similarities between Sippar and Nippur and for encouraging me to investigate the importance of Sippar as an early religious center in the north.

[7] See H. Gasche, "Tell ed-Dēr et Abu Ḫabbah: deux villes situées à la croisée des chemins nord-sud, est-ouest," *MARI* 4 (1985): 580.

[8] D. Frayne, RIME 4, p. 335 (Ḫammu-rāpi 2): 56 ff. (Sum.), 58 f. (Akk.).

[9] For a composite transliteration and translation of *ARET* 5 6 and OIP 99 326+342, see M. Krebernik, "Mesopotamian Myths at Ebla: *ARET* 5, 6 and *ARET* 5, 7," *Quaderni di Semitistica* 18 (1992): 72–86. See also W. G. Lambert, "Notes on a Work of the Most Ancient Semitic Literature," *JCS* 41 (1989): 1–33. For a discussion of Šamaš's role in this text, see Myers, "The Sippar Pantheon," pp. 15 ff.

The widespread importance of Sippar as a northern religious center during the Early Dynastic period has not been duly recognized. The earliest known Semitic literary text (see above)—a hymn with mythological elements—attests to the worship of Šamaš of Sippar as far as Ebla in the northwest. Šamaš also appears as the recipient of offerings in the third-millennium royal archives of Ebla.[10] And, in one scene from this literary text, Šamaš is described as meeting with, among other gods, Ištaran, the patron deity of Dēr—a city located in the far eastern reaches of Babylonia. In addition, according to Steinkeller, the majority of third-millennium seals with mythological scenes found in northern Mesopotamia—from Mari in the west to the Diyala region in the east—portray myths involving the god Šamaš.[11] Finally, an Early Dynastic votive statue dedicated to Šamaš for the life of Ikūn-Šamagan, king of Mari, which was excavated at Sippar,[12] demonstrates the active worship of Šamaš at Sippar by the Early Dynastic kings of Mari. All of this evidence points not only to the widespread popularity of the god Šamaš in northern Mesopotamia during this period, but also to the importance of Sippar as his cult center.

But the evidence does not end there. Significant similarities can be seen between Sippar and Nippur, the undisputed religious capital of southern Babylonia. Like Nippur, Sippar was never the seat of political power in historical periods. Further, Sippar was the only northern city whose main temple, the Ebabbar—like the Ekur at Nippur—served as a repository for royal inscriptions and monuments, legal documents, kudurrus, and literary texts. And, like Nippur, Sippar was an intellectual center, whose great scribal activity produced its own literary traditions. These similarities, in combination with the evidence from the Early Dynastic period, suggest that Sippar played a role in the north roughly parallel to that of Nippur in the south. Naturally, Sippar was not an exact duplicate of Nippur, for Šamaš was never proclaimed the chief deity of a "northern" pantheon. If, however, one accepts Steinkeller's arguments for the existence of a sharp distinction between northern and southern Babylonia during the Early Dynastic period, in terms of political leadership and the organization of the pantheon,[13] it is possible that the north had its own religious center—that is, Sippar—with its own distinctly northern character. Thus the sun-god, who was not particularly prominent in the south, appears to have played a supreme role in this northern tradition, and his city seems to have enjoyed the status of religious capital for the entire region of northern

[10] See F. Pomponio and P. Xella, *Les dieux d'Ebla: étude analytique des divinités éblaïtes à l'époque des archives royales du IIIe millénaire*, AOAT 245 (Münster, 1997), pp. 335 ff.

[11] P. Steinkeller, "Early Semitic Literature and Third Millennium Seals with Mythological Motifs," *Quaderni di Semitistica* 18 (1992): 256.

[12] See Gelb-Kienast *Königsinschriften*, p. 9.

[13] P. Steinkeller, "Mesopotamia, History of (Third Millennium)," in D. N. Freedman, ed., *Anchor Bible Dictionary*, vol. 4 (New York, 1992), pp. 724–32.

Mesopotamia. The prominence of Šamaš in the inscriptions of the Sargonic kings and their enthusiastic patronage of his cult at Sippar also lend credence to this idea.

Later traditions may, in addition, contain a memory of Sippar as the religious capital of the north. In one of his inscriptions, Nebuchadnezzar I claims to be descended from Enmeduranki, the antediluvian ruler of Sippar, who, according to tradition, had learned the secrets of divination from the gods Šamaš and Adad and had taught them to the men of Sippar, Babylon, and Nippur.[14] As Lambert points out, the grouping of these three together as cities with special status is found in additional texts from the first millennium.[15] The literary piece Advice to a Prince concerns the protection of the special privileges of Sippar, Babylon, and Nippur and warns of divine retribution should the king revoke any of them.[16] Neo-Babylonian kings, as well as Neo-Assyrian rulers who assumed the Babylonian throne, continued the tradition of grouping these three cities together in their inscriptions.[17] Thus if Sippar can be accepted as having been the religious capital of the north, the motivation behind the grouping of Babylon, Sippar, and Nippur together as privileged cities by later Babylonian kings becomes clear: the three cities represent, respectively, the contemporary political capital, Babylon, and the two traditional religious capitals of Babylonia: Sippar in the north and Nippur in the south.

Returning to the Old Babylonian period, it is clear that the First Dynasty kings recognized the importance of a close relationship between Babylon and Sippar and used it to their advantage. It is likely that the ties between these two cities predate this period; indeed, Lambert has suggested that Babylon was probably "drawn into the cultural orbit" of the more important city of Sippar during the Early Dynastic period.[18] Therefore it would not only be natural for the rulers of Babylon, whose own god, Marduk, was not important enough alone to grant them kingship over all of Babylonia, to turn to Šamaš of Sippar in this regard, but by aligning themselves with the religious capital of the north, they could draw upon its great importance and antiquity in order to legitimate their rule.

---

[14] W. G. Lambert, "Enmeduranki and Related Matters," *JCS* 21 (1967): 127 ff.; see also idem, "The Qualifications of Babylonian Diviners," in *Borger AV*, p. 148: 3–14.

[15] Idem, "Enmeduranki," p. 127.

[16] Ibid. and Lambert *BWL*, pp. 110–15.

[17] Nabopolassar (VAB 4, p. 58, Npl. 4:25) and Nebuchadnezzar II (VAB 4, p. 88, Nbk. 9 i 3); cited in idem, "Enmeduranki," p. 127; for Sargon II, see Winckler Sar. 164–165:2–3, 80 f.:3, 174 f. i 9–12, cited in G. Frame and A. K. Grayson, "An Inscription of Ashurbanipal Mentioning the *Kidinnu* of Sippar," *SAA Bulletin* 8 (1994): 7; for Esarhaddon, see Borger *Esarh*. 81:41, cited in Frame *Babylonia*, p. 75 and n. 53. It is interesting to note that Assyrian kings add Borsippa to the list of privileged cities; this is most likely due to the fact that Nabû was even more popular in Assyria than in Babylonia at this time. See F. Pomponio, *Nabû: il culto e la figura di un dio del pantheon babilonese ed assiro*, Studi semitici 51 (Rome, 1978), pp. 241–42. Notably, Sennacherib did not follow this tradition in his inscriptions; see Frame *Babylonia*, p. 35.

[18] W. G. Lambert, "The Historical Development of the Mesopotamian Pantheon: A Study in Sophisticated Polytheism," in H. Goedicke and J. J. M. Roberts, eds., *Unity and Diversity: Essays in the History, Literature, and Religion of the Ancient Near East* (Baltimore, 1975), p. 194.

In addition to this motivating factor, there was every reason for these kings to focus their attention on Šamaš and Sippar rather than on Enlil and Nippur. Since, as noted earlier, one of their goals was to promote Marduk to an exalted position within the national pantheon—perhaps even at this early date to "king of the gods"[19]—Enlil would naturally have been in competition with this agenda. Šamaš, on the other hand, posed no such threat.[20]

Direct involvement by the kings of Babylon in the affairs of Sippar began early on in the Old Babylonian period. Sumu-abum is invoked along with Šamaš in the oath formula of a Sippar tablet, which also contains one of his year-names.[21] In addition, several early Old Babylonian texts from Sippar invoke both the local ruler of Sippar and the contemporaneous king of Babylon, Sumu-la-el, in the oath formulas, possibly indicating co-rule of Sippar by the First Dynasty of Babylon at the beginning of this period.[22] By at least the 29th year of Sumu-la-el, however, Sippar was under the full control of Babylon, as the name of this year commemorates his building of the wall of Sippar,[23] and local rulers no longer appear in the oath formulas after this time. In a possibly political move, Sumu-la-el dedicated his daughter as a *nadītu* of Šamaš, a tradition that was followed by at least two later kings of this dynasty.[24]

More direct influence by the crown on the cultic affairs of Sippar can be detected in the reign of Ṣabium,[25] namely, in the creation of a second *šangû* of Šamaš, referred to by R. Harris as "junior" *šangû*, based on the order in which the two *šangû*s are listed as witnesses in the texts.[26] While E. Woestenburg has shown that the position of "senior" *šangû* was held by the same Sipparian family from the period of local rule of Sippar

[19] Of course, Marduk did not achieve this status until, most likely, during the reign of Nebuchadnezzar I, but it is possible that the Babylon I kings envisioned this development.

[20] Given the etymology of Marduk as amar-utu-(a)k—whether this represents a folk etymology or the actual meaning—a connection between the god of Babylon and Šamaš is confirmed from early on in Babylonian history; see W. G. Lambert, "Studies in Marduk," *BSOAS* 47 (1984): 7f.

[21] VAS 8 1 (tablet) / 2 (case): l.e., cited in Harris *Sippar*, p. 5 and n. 18.

[22] Sumu-la-el and Immerum: CT 4 50a and BM 82437, cited in Harris *Sippar*, pp. 3, n. 9; 133, n. 76; and Dekiere *OB Real Estate* 12:19–20; Sumu-la-el and Buntaḫtun-ila: Waterman *Bus. Doc.* 31, cited in Harris *Sippar*, p. 4, n. 13. F. Al-Rawi and S. Dalley suggest, citing M. T. Larsen's scenario for the Old Assyrian period, that "the presence of different 'kings' in oaths, year formulae and seals is due to economic cooperation and is not related to political and military circumstances"; al-Rawi and Dalley *OB Sippir*, p. 25, citing Larsen, *The Old Assyrian City-State and Its Colonies*, Mesopotamia 4 (Copenhagen, 1976), pp. 228–36, 242–43.

[23] See A. Ungnad, "Datenlisten," *RLA* 2, p. 176; see also Harris *Sippar*, p. 5.

[24] For Ayalatum, daughter of Sumu-la-el, see R. Harris, "*Nadītu* Woman," in *Studies Oppenheim*, p. 123. For Iltani, daughter of Sîn-muballiṭ, and a second Iltani, daughter of either Samsuiluna or Abī-ešuh, both attested at Sippar as *nadītus* of Šamaš (ibid. and idem, "Biographical Notes on the *Nadītu* Women of Sippar," *JCS* 16 [1962]: 6–8).

[25] For Ṣabium rather than Sabium, see M. Streck, *Das amurritische Onomastikon der altbabylonischen Zeit*, AOAT 271/1 (Münster, 2000), pp. 156f.

[26] Harris *Sippar*, pp. 155ff.

down to the reign of Ammī-ṣaduqa,[27] the "junior" *šangû*s appear to have been natives of Babylon, for several had names formed with the theophoric element Marduk or Nabû and referred to themselves in their seals as "servant of Marduk/Nabû."[28] Thus these individuals were most likely appointed to this position by the king and sent to Sippar to promote the interests of the crown in the affairs of the Ebabbar Temple.[29] Ṣabium was also, as far as we know, the first king of Babylon to have rebuilt the Ebabbar.[30]

Patronage as well as direct interference in the temple administration of Sippar continued and increased during the reigns of subsequent kings of the First Dynasty of Babylon, culminating, of course, in the reign of Hammurapi. Harris has shown that Hammurapi effected a change within the administration of the Ebabbar, transferring power over temple business from local temple administrators to city officials who represented the interests of the crown.[31] The Ebabbar Temple appears to have grown extremely wealthy in the years leading up to the reign of Hammurapi, owing most probably to its involvement, through the *gagûm*, or "cloister," in lucrative mercantile activity with the Assyrian colony Kanesh-Kültepe as well as with its own trade networks in Ešnunna and Susa, as suggested by Al-Rawi and Dalley.[32] Naturally, control of this wealthy institution would be beneficial to the king and his administration. Thus, a close connection with Sippar and its patron deity had the double advantage of lending cultural legitimacy to Babylon and of providing a regular income to the crown. While earlier kings of this dynasty appear to have recognized these advantages, it was Hammurapi who capitalized on them.

It is clear from his inscriptions and year-names that Hammurapi spent a great deal of energy on building-projects in Sippar and on patronizing the Ebabbar Temple there. But even more telling of his special relationship with Šamaš is the language he employs in the inscriptions commemorating his activities in Sippar in comparison to those concerning projects in other cities. In the latter, Hammurapi follows the traditional royal ideology in claiming to have been chosen by Anu and Enlil to rule Sumer and Akkad. In contrast, his inscriptions concerning Šamaš and Sippar mention only Šamaš and Marduk as his divine patrons. Significant, in this regard, is that Hammurapi's inscription commemorating his restoration of the Ebabbar of Šamaš in Larsa[33] follows

---

[27] E. Woestenburg, review of Dekiere *OB Real Estate* in *AfO* 44–45 (1997–98): 356, see also pp. 358 f., table 1.

[28] Šalim-pālih-Marduk, "servant of Marduk" in his seal (TCL 1 69); and Etel-pī-Nabium, "servant of Nabium" in his seal (Dekiere *OB Real Estate*, pp. 132, 158); see again Woestenburg's *AfO* review of Dekiere, pp. 356 ff.

[29] See Myers, "The Sippar Pantheon," chap. 3, sec. 3.1.

[30] Ṣabium years 8a and b: Ungnad, "Datenlisten," p. 176.

[31] R. Harris, "Some Aspects of the Centralization of the Realm under Hammurapi and His Successors," *JAOS* 88 (1968): 727 ff., and idem, "On the Process of Secularization under Hammurapi," *JCS* 15 (1961): 117 ff.

[32] Al-Rawi and Dalley *OB Sippir*, pp. 16 ff.

[33] Frayne, RIME 4, p. 351 (Ḫammu-rāpi 14). There is also a stamped brick inscription commemorating this event: ibid., p. 350 (Ḫammu-rāpi 13); naturally, only the fact of the restoration is included.

the standard southern theology, naming An and Enlil first in his list of epithets; in addition, the language lacks the enthusiasm and intimacy with which Hammurapi speaks of Šamaš of Sippar.[34] It appears that Hammurapi was well aware that once he had control of the south, it was incumbent upon him, as king of all of Sumer and Akkad, to adhere, at least in word if not in spirit, to the traditional theology, whereas he had felt no such restriction in the north.

It is also significant that Sippar was the only city, as far as we know, for which Hammurapi canceled corvée duty. In the inscription commemorating his reconstruction of the wall of Sippar, he claims, "In my gracious reign, which the god Šamaš called, I canceled corvée duty for the men of Sippar, the eternal city of the god Šamaš."[35] As noted above, the notion of Sippar as a special city recurs in the inscriptions of later Babylonian kings, where it is grouped with the two other cities of privileged status, whose citizens were also exempt from corvée duty, namely, Babylon, the political capital, and Nippur, the religious capital of the south.

Thus while Sippar aided the kings of the First Dynasty of Babylon in their struggle to make their city the capital of a unified nation and to promote their god Marduk within the Babylonian pantheon, the close relationship that subsequent Babylonian kings maintained with Sippar and its patron deity helped to ensure its continued importance throughout the history of Babylonia. Indeed, Sippar's reputation as the eternal city may have survived even beyond this history, as it appears still to have been associated with the Flood by the local population when Rassam rediscovered the city at the end of the nineteenth century.[36]

---

[34] Ibid., esp. pp. 334 ff. (Ḫammu-rāpi 2).

[35] Ibid., p. 335: 53 ff. (Sum.), 56 ff. (Akk.).

[36] As reported by H. V. Hilprecht (*Explorations in Bible Lands during the 19th Century* [Philadelphia, 1903], p. 268) and W. H. Ward (*The Seal Cylinders of Western Asia* [Washington, D.C., 1910], pp. 101 f.) in their anecdotal accounts of the discovery of Sippar by Rassam, quoted in C. Woods, "The Sun-God Tablet of Nabû-apla-iddina Revisited," *JCS* 56 (2004): 23–103.

ANOTHER HARBINGER OF THE GOLDEN AGE

Erica Reiner†, The University of Chicago

What is the hallmark of a golden age? For the Babylonians, it was a time when the gods gave reliable answers to the query of the diviner. Conversely, inauspicious times were those when the gods refused to answer the diviner's query.

We know this from the description of the "blessed times," or golden age, found in various details in a few omen apodoses, and of their opposite, the harsh and inauspicious times, attested, so far, more rarely in similar texts. It is fitting that a brief characterization of this golden age be offered in honor of Bob Biggs in whose work omen texts have played such a pivotal role.

The blessed times predicted in omen texts are bestowed by the gods as a mark of their favor toward the king; they are signaled by a significant celestial event. It is especially the heliacal rising of the two brightest planets, Venus and Jupiter, that is associated with these apodoses and that is a harbinger of the coming golden age.

In a few texts the apodoses that herald the golden age are preceded by those that predict times of hardship. Thus both K.10189 and Sm. 1234 (the latter included in the edition of Enūma Anu Enlil [EAE] Tablets 64–65) begin with two sections of opposite predictions. In the first six lines of Sm. 1234, three apparently unconnected, unfavorable omens predicted by the behavior of Jupiter are cited; then, after a ruling, comes the description of the golden age, predicted by the rising of Jupiter. The first section corresponds to Hunger, SAA 8 369:1–5[1] sent by Nabû-šumu-iškun; the author of the report comments only on the name of the constellation MUL.IN.DUB.AN.NA.

In the description of the golden age in K.10189, preceded by four lines that describe evil times (for which see below), the formulation is as follows:

8′ [¶ MUL *Ni-bi-ru* SAR-*ma* DINGIR.MEŠ SILIM].MA TUK.MEŠ *me-šìr-tum* GÁL [*e-šá-a-ti i-nam-mi-ra*]

9′ [*dalhāti izakkâ* ŠÈG] *u* A.KAL TU.MEŠ-*ni di-iš* EBUR [*ana* EN.TE.NA *di-iš* EN.TE.NA]

10′ [*ana* EBUR *uštabarri* KUR] KI.TUŠ *ne-eh-tú* [TUŠ.MEŠ DINGIR.MEŠ SIZKUR *mah-ru*]

11′ [*tas-li-ti še-mu*]-⌈*ú*⌉ UZU.HAR.MEŠ LÚ.H[AL *i-ta-nap-pal*]

[1] H. Hunger, *Astrological Reports to Assyrian Kings*, SAA 8 (Helsinki, 1992).

> If Jupiter rises, the gods will show favor, there will be abundance, what is blurred will become bright, what is troubled will clear up, rain and flood will come (on time), the harvest-time grass will last until winter, the winter grass until harvest time, all lands will live in peaceful dwellings, the gods are accepting sacrifices, listening to prayers, they will always answer the diviner's queries.

Restorations are from Sm. 1234 and its parallels.

Sm. 1234

7′ [¶ MUL *Né-bi*]-*ru* SAR-*ha-ma* DINGIR.MEŠ SILIM.MA [TUK.MEŠ]

8′ [...-*h*]*a*? *e-šá-a-tu i-na*[*m-mi-ra*]

9′ [*dalhātu i*]-*zak-ka-a* ŠÈG *u* A.KAL TU.[MEŠ]

10′ [*dīš* EN.TE.NA *ana*] EBUR *di-iš* EBUR *ana* EN.TE.[NA *uštabarra*]

11′ [KUR].KUR KI.TUŠ *ne-eh-tú* TUŠ.[MEŠ]

12′ [DINGIR.MEŠ SIZKUR *mahru tas-l*]*i-tú še-*[*mu-ú*]

King Esarhaddon cites such a propitious rising of Jupiter when he describes, as favorable signs from the gods for the rebuilding of Babylon (Borger *Esarh.* p. 17 Ep. 13 A: 34–39), the omen given by the brilliant appearance of Jupiter in the month of Simānu: it predicted that the gods that had been angry with Babylonia will become reconciled, that there will be copious rains and regular high water in Babylonia. He quotes, as we now know, the omen preserved on K.2341+, a tablet that is one of the sources of EAE 64, which lists, after omens about Jupiter as ^{d}SAG.ME.GAR, two omens designating Jupiter as the Marduk Star (MUL ^{d}AMAR.UD), the first of which depicts the golden age and the second the opposite.

K.2341+

12′ ¶ MUL ^{d}AMAR.UD *ina* ITI.SIG$_4$ *ú-qar-*⸢*rib*⸣*-ma a-šar* ^{d}UTU *ul-tap-pa-a* DU-*iz*

13′ *ba-ìl zi-mu-šú* SA$_5$ SAR-*šú* GIM SA[R ^{d}UTU]-*ši ga-mir* DINGIR.MEŠ *zi-nu-tum* KI KUR URI.KI SILIM.MEŠ

14′ ŠÈG.MEŠ *ṭah-du-tum u* A.KAL.MEŠ *si-i*[*d-ru-t*]*u ina* KUR URI.KI GÁL.ME ŠE *u* ŠE.GIŠ.Ì *ina* KUR *i-mad*

15′ KI.LAM 1 SÌLA *ana* 1 GUR SUM-*in* DINGIR.MEŠ [*ina* AN-*e ina*] *man-zal-ti-šú-nu* DU.MEŠ BÁRA.MEŠ-*šu-*⸢*nu*⸣ ⸢*ṭuh-du*⸣[2] IGI.MEŠ

This omen is also cited in Hunger, SAA 8 115:1–10 and 170:1–13.

---

[2] Reading after ibid. 170:13. Line, bottom of tablet. Omen cited in 115:1–10.

The next omen, K.2341+ rev. 1–3, predicts evil times but in a less-detailed manner than the previously cited ones.

A similar golden age is predicted by the rising of Jupiter — under the name Nēbiru — in Hunger, SAA 8 323 and 254:

> If Nēbiru rises: the gods will be reconciled, there will be abundance, confused things will become bright, blurred things will clear up, rain and high water will come, the summer grass will last until winter, the winter grass until summer, all the lands will dwell in peaceful settlements, the gods, accepting the sacrifices (and) listening to the prayers, will keep answering the diviner's queries (Hunger, SAA 8 323:7–rev. 4).

The prediction in Report 254 rev. 2–10 differs only in replacing the participles "accepting (and) listening" (*mahru*, *šemû*) by the finite verb forms *imahharu* "they will accept" and *išemmû* "they will listen." While it is not so specified in the protasis, the omen refers to the heliacal rising of Jupiter.

Not only Jupiter but also Venus can herald a golden age by her rising. If Venus rises in month VI and has a beard,

> *ešâtu ušteššera* (written SI.SÁ) *dalhātu izakkâ arni māti ippaṭṭar libbi māti iṭâb ešēr ebūri napāš Nisaba*
>
> What is confused will become straight, what is blurred will become clear, the sin of the land will be loosed, the land's mood will be happy, the harvest will thrive, the grain will be plentiful (Labat *Calendrier* § 85:19–22).

This corresponds to the Venus omen *ešâtu* SI.SÁ *dalhātu izakkâ arni māti ippaṭṭar mātu ṭūb libbi immar ešēr ebūri napāš Nisaba* (K.137 rev. 19′ff., in *BPO* 3 151 rev. 6).

In contradistinction to these and similar propitious predictions, which are couched in general terms, and which, by the way, are also echoed in the so-called prophecy texts,[3] a genre to which Bob Biggs has made valuable contributions over the years,[4] there is a small group of texts that include more specific descriptions of the golden age. Two of the texts have been available in copy; a third one, an unpublished duplicate, is published here with the permission of the Trustees of the British Museum.

---

[3] A. K. Grayson and W. G. Lambert, "Akkadian Prophecies," *JCS* 18 (1964): 7 ff.; R. Borger, "Gott Marduk und Gott-König Šulgi als Propheten: Zwei prophetische Texte," *BiOr* 28 (1971): 11 iii 8′–12′. The latter includes, following upon the predictions of economic prosperity, both *lemnūtu* (HUL.MEŠ-*tu*) *ušteššera* (iii 11) and *lemnūtu* (HUL.MEŠ) *inammira* (ZALÁG.MEŠ).

[4] "More Babylonian 'Prophecies'," *Iraq* 29 (1967): 117–32; "Babylonian Prophecies, Astrology, and a New Source for 'Prophecy Text B'," in AOS 67 1 ff.; "The Babylonian Prophecies and the Astrological Traditions of Mesopotamia," *JCS* 37 (1985): 86–90.

Of the three texts, source C, ND 5497/16, no. 22 in Wiseman and Black *Literary Texts*, pl. 19, contains the essential part of the description of the golden age in lines 13′–16′; the preceding lines 5′–12′ describe the locations of the planets Venus, Jupiter, Saturn, Mars, and Mercury, in that order. These lines 5′–16′ are preceded by two ruled sections, of which the first is almost completely destroyed, and the second mentions the series EAE and a *ṣâtu*-commentary.

The second text, source B, *LBAT* 1556, duplicates ND 5497/16 over four lines, beginning with the location of Saturn; from lines 5′ to 9′ it duplicates the description of the golden age.

The third text, the so-far unpublished K.6444 (source A), begins, in line 2′, with a fragmentary subscript to the preceding section; lines 3′–11′ contain the descriptions of the planets and their locations and lines 12′–15′ the description of the golden age.

A 12′ [...D]I.KUD *ina* KUR *id-da-an* DINGIR.MEŠ KUR GALGA x
B 5′ [DI].KUD *ina* KUR *id-da-nu* DINGIR.MEŠ *ana* KUR ARHUŠ TUK.MEŠ
C 13′ DINGIR.MEŠ *ana* KUR ARHUŠ TUK.MEŠ

A 13′ [*kit*]-*tum u mi-šá-ru ina* KUR GAR.MEŠ-*ma* AD *u* [DUMU *kit-tú i-ta-mu-ú*]
B 6′ [...] KÚ *kit-tu u mi-šá-ri ina* KUR GAR-*an* 7′ AD *u* [DUMU *kit-tú i-ta-mu-ú*]
C 14′ *ina* KUR GAR-*an* AD *u* DUMU [*kit*]-*tú i*-[*ta-mu-ú*]

A 14′ [*taš-mu-ú u*] SILIM.MU *ina* KUR GÁL-*ši* LÚ.ENGAR EGIR [GIŠ.APIN-*šú* DU-*ak*]
B 8′ *taš-mu-ú u* SILIM.MA [*ina* KUR GÁL-*ši* LÚ.ENGA]R EGIR GIŠ.APIN-*šú* DU-*ak*
C 15′ *taš-mu-ú u* SILIM.MU *ina* KUR GÁL-[*ši*] LÚ.ENGAR EGIR [GIŠ.APIN-*šú* DU-*ak*]

A 15′ [ ]-*ma* UZU.HAR.MEŠ LÚ.HAL.MEŠ *i*-[*tap-pal*]
B 9′ [-*m*]*a* UZU.HAR.BAD.MEŠ LÚ.HAL *i-tap-pal*
C 16′ [ ] x.MEŠ UZU.HAR.MEŠ LÚ.HAL ⌈*i*⌉-[*tap-pal*]

[...] judgment will be given in the land,[5] the gods will have pity on the land,
there will be justice and redress in the land, father and son will speak truthfully,
there will be hearing (of prayers) and peace in the land, the farmer will walk behind his plow,
[there will be ...], they? will give an answer to the diviner's query.

Note that lines 4′–13′ of A (K.6444) and lines 1′–9′ of its parallel B (*LBAT* 1556) are duplicated by the very fragmentary K.12216.

[5] A lexical novum in this omen is the passive (N-stem) of the verb *dânu* "to judge."

An exception among the descriptions of the blessed times is the specific reference to tilling the fields, which is made possible by peace reigning in the land; in contrast, abandoning agriculture is a sign of troubled times, as in omen 95 of VAT 10218, in *BPO* 3, p. 48: *errēšu arki epinnišu ul illak* "the farmer will not walk behind his plow."

The times of hardship and loss of divine favor that in some of the exemplars cited precede the description of the golden age are signaled by the late sighting of Jupiter. Jupiter's lateness is expressed with the verb *šadādu*; see *CAD* Š/1 s.v. *šadādu* v. mng. 6a. The latest edition of the text there cited, K.1551, is by Simo Parpola, SAA 10 362 (previous editions, cited in *CAD* Š/1, are *ACh* Supp. 2 Ištar 62 [copy], *ZA* 47 92 f., and Parpola *LAS* 289). The last of the Jupiter omens adduced in this letter runs:

> *šumma Nēbiru išdudma ilū izennû mešer<tu> ibbašši namrāti iššâ zakâti iddallaha ilū ṣul[ê] ul <i>šemmû taslīti ul ima[hharu] têrēte bārî ul īt[anappalu]*
>
> If Jupiter is late, the gods will become angry, there will be a *miširtu*-plague,[6] what is bright will become confused, what is clear will become troubled, the gods will not heed prayers, will not accept supplications, will not answer the queries of the diviner.

At a time[7] when both Venus and Jupiter shine brightly even among the city lights, it is indeed a propitious time to wish Bob Biggs many happy years of research in his busy retirement.

---

[6] For *miširtu* signifying both a beneficial event and a calamity, see *CAD* s.v. At the time of Parpola's commentary in *LAS* this omen was not known from any other source; it is likely that it occurs as the first partially preserved omen of K.3111+, edited in *BPO* 3, pp. 90 f.

[7] May 2004.

ON AMPUTATION, BEATING, AND ILLEGAL SEIZURE

Martha T. Roth, The University of Chicago

I

A Neo-Babylonian document published more than a century ago, *ZA* 3 (1898): 224 f., no. 2,[1] records the receipt of silver to settle an extraordinary debt. Two compensations are referred to in the text: *a*) 140 shekels of silver paid in lieu of amputating the hand (*ša ana kūm batāqu ša ritti*, lines 2 and 7) of Marduk-rēmanni / Bēl-uballiṭ / Iqīša // Ṣāhit-ginê, and *b*) 60 shekels of silver as compensation for the illegal seizure of property belonging to Itti-Nusku-īnāja / Nusku-ajalu (*kūm ṣibtēti*, line 5).[2] The entire sum of 200 shekels of silver is paid by Marduk-rēmanni to Itti-Nusku-īnāja. The unusual circumstances can now be elaborated by two more documents involving the same individuals and case.

ZA 3 (1898): 224 f., no. 2 (Text A in this article) has received remarkably little attention in the literature and that attention all only within the last few years.[3] One of the principals, Marduk-rēmanni, is, however, well known. He is attested in documents for at least twenty-five years prior to this event.[4] He was a member of a prominent family, known from both his involvements in private business affairs and with the economy of

[1] J. N. Strassmaier, in E. A. Wallis Budge, "On Some Recently Acquired Babylonian Tablets," *ZA* 3 (1898): 211–30, at pp. 216 f., copy pp. 224f., no. 2. The tablet (Bu. 1888-5-12,27 = BM 78192) was collated by me in July 2003, with the permission of C. B. F. Walker and the Trustees of the British Museum. It dates to the reign of Darius I (8/XII/25 = 16 March 496 B.C.) and was written in Babylon.

[2] The term *ṣibtētu* (*ZA* 3 [1898]: 224, no. 2) has been understood by those commenting on the text (see following note) and by *CAD* Ṣ s.v. *ṣibtētu* as "imprisonment," "restraints." Following an insight communicated to me by M. W. Stolper, however, I hold that it means "stolen goods," possibly a plural of *ṣibtu*; see *CAD* Ṣ s.v. *ṣibtu* B mng. 5, and note the Old Babylonian pl. *ṣibtātu*, and cf. *qāt ṣibitti* "stolen property (found in the thief's possession)" in *CAD* Ṣ s.v. *ṣibittu* mng. 4.

[3] See S. Zawadski, "Zazannu and Šušan in the Babylonian Texts from the Archive of the *Ṣāhit ginê* Family," in R. Dittmann et al., eds., *Variatio Delectat: Iran und der Westen: Gedenkschrift für Peter Calmeyer*, AOAT 272 (Münster, 2000), pp. 723–44 at pp. 728f., 740f., no. 9. C. Waerzeggers included it, along with a duplicate (1882-9-18, 4171+ = BM 64196+), in her dissertation "Het archief van Marduk-rēmanni" (Ph.D. diss., Ghent University, 2001), vol. 2, pp. 162–64, no. 124a. I thank Waerzeggers for providing me with her dissertation, the texts from which she will be publishing with new copies in a forthcoming volume. B. Wells, "Neo-Babylonian Period," in R. Westbrook, ed., *A History of Ancient Near Eastern Law* (Leiden and Boston, 2003), p. 966 at 8.10.1 and 8.10.2, referred to the text briefly.

[4] Zawadski, "Zazannu and Šušan," p. 725 with n. 14.

the Ebabbar temple in Sippar. His temple-related activities included responsibility for herds of sheep and cattle and the obligations of the butcher's prebend, and he bore the title *ṭupšar Ebabbar*.[5] Itti-Nusku-īnāja / Nusku-ajalu, however, is otherwise unknown to me outside of the texts discussed here.

II

Text A does not indicate why Marduk-rēmanni's hand was in danger of being amputated, nor why the sum of 140 shekels of silver was an acceptable amount for him to pay to avoid that amputation. It does not indicate what property of Itti-Nusku-īnāja's was illegally seized, nor why the sum of 60 shekels of silver was an appropriate compensation for that seizure. As it happens, however, Text A is one of three extant documents dealing with the same, or an overlapping, set of circumstances.

The second text, Text B (AH 1882-9-18, 252a = BM 74529),[6] has long been known to the editors of the *CAD*.[7] The text (15/XII/25 Darius I = 23 March 496 B.C.) is dated only seven days later than Text A and makes reference to three sets of compensation and punishment. There is again mention of a payment to avoid amputating Marduk-rēmanni's hand (*ša kūm la batāqu ritti*, lines 1, 2 f., 7 f., 20),[8] although this time the sum specified is seven-fold greater than the amount in Text A: 980 shekels of silver. The new punishment mentioned is a flogging or beating of 21 strokes (21 *mihṣū*, later simply *ṭirûtu* "a beating"), to avoid which (*ša kūm*, line 2) Marduk-rēmanni must pay 63 shekels of silver. The total for these compensations is 1,043 shekels. As of the writing of Text B, Itti-Nusku-īnāja has received 149 shekels, as well as another compensation of 60 shekels to compensate for (*kūm*, line 6) goods stolen from his brother, Baʾ-Ilteri-ahattu. Thus according to Text B, Itti-Nusku-īnāja has received for himself and his brother a total of 209 shekels of silver from Marduk-rēmanni "for not amputating the hand, (for) the beating, and (for) the stolen property" (*kūm la batāqu rittu ṭirûtu u ṣibtēti*).[9]

---

[5] Ibid., pp. 725–28, passim.

[6] Collated by me in July 2003; published by Waerzeggers, "Het archief van Marduk-rēmanni," vol. 2, pp. 166–68, no. 125.

[7] Cited as 1882-9-18, 252a from notes made by A. Leo Oppenheim in the 1960s as well as from a Bertin copy (pls. 2561 f.) in *CAD* M/2 s.v. *miḫṣu* mng. 2 and in *CAD* R s.v. *rittu* A mng. 1a-3′.

[8] Note the presence or absence of the negation *la* in these clauses: Text A omits it (silver *ša ana kūm batāqu ša rittum*, etc.), while Text B adds it (silver *ša kūm la batāqu rittum*, etc.). Similar variation occurs with guarantee clauses such as *pūt* (*la*) *našû*, etc., passim; for a discussion, see M. W. Stolper, "Fifth Century Nippur: Texts of the Murašûs and from Their Surroundings," *JCS* 53 (2001): 83–132, esp. pp. 121 f. with n. 45.

[9] It is clear now that the preposition *kūm* is used differently with various payments: the amounts of silver paid to Itti-Nusku-īnāja by Marduk-rēmanni are (1) *ša* (*ana*) *kūm* threatened bodily harms (the amputation of Marduk-rēmanni's hand, a beating inflicted on Marduk-rēmanni, thus (*ša*) *kūm* signifies "in place of"), and (2) *kūm* losses suffered (the improper seizure of animals belonging to Itti-Nusku-īnāja and his brother; thus *kūm* signifies "in consideration for"). Note two or all three compensations or punishments in one summary clause, as in Text A: 7 f., *ša ana kūm batāqa ša rittu … u ṣibtēti*; Text B: 2 f., *ša kūm la batāqu rittu u* 21 *mihṣū*; 7 f. and 20 f., *ša kūm la batāqu rittu ṭirûtu u ṣibtēti*.

A third text, now published in Waerzeggers's study, provides more information. The date of Text C (Bu. 1882-9-18, 4183 = BM 64208)[10] is only partially preserved, but it was written in Babylon in the 25th year of Darius I. From the contents, it is certain that it was composed within days of Texts A and B and probably in the intervening days. Text C allows a deferral of that payment imposed upon Marduk-rēmanni of the 140 shekels in lieu of the amputation ([*kūm* (*la*)] *batāqa ša ritti*)—the payment we saw imposed in Text A and identified as paid in Text B—until the end of the first month of the following year, that is, for a matter of only a few weeks; if my sequencing of the texts is correct, Marduk-rēmanni did not take all the time allowed him. Furthermore, Text C indicates that Marduk-rēmanni has already made yet another payment, of an unspecified amount, to compensate Itti-Nusku-īnāja for stolen goods (*ṣibtēti*). The crucial new information in Text C concerns this last compensation (lines 8 ff.): *kaspu šīm ṣēnu ša ṣibtē*[*ti ša*] *Itti-Nusku-īnāja Itti-Nusku-īnāja* [*ina qātē*] *Marduk-rēmanni e*[*ṭir*] "Itti-Nusku-īnāja has been paid by Marduk-rēmanni the silver, the equivalent of the herds that are Itti-Nusku-īnāja's stolen property."

Now, finally, with the mention of the herds in Text C, there is a clue to the nature of the events and circumstances. First, comparison of the amounts indicated for avoiding the amputation in Text A (140 shekels) and Text B (980 shekels), and the specification of 21 strokes in Text B, suggest that the penalties and payments in Text B were totaled with seven persons in mind. That is, the brothers Nusku-īnāja and Baʾ-Ilteri-ahattu and five other persons (perhaps all kinsmen) held claims against Marduk-rēmanni. Second, the mention of silver paid as the equivalent of stolen animals suggests that at least part of Marduk-rēmanni's offense involved his misappropriation of animals properly belonging to Nusku-īnāja and Baʾ-Ilteri-ahattu (and probably to the other five persons as well). The seven persons were therefore entitled to inflict specific and limited physical mutilations upon his person: each was entitled to cut off his hand, each was entitled to deliver three blows, and two (and possibly all seven) were entitled to payment for the seized animals. Obviously, Marduk-rēmanni had only two hands to lose, making any literal execution of the mutilations problematic. But in any event the physical punishments were commuted to monetary ones: each person was awarded (or accepted) 140 shekels instead of exercising the right to amputate a hand and 9 shekels instead of inflicting three stripes; the compensation for the seized animals was set at 60 shekels.

We are not given any indication of what Marduk-rēmanni did to warrant these extraordinary physical punishments. For the misappropriated animals he paid an amount of silver; 60 shekels (1 mina) is a considerable amount indeed.[11] But that misappro-

---

[10] Waerzeggers, "Het archief van Marduk-rēmanni," vol. 2, p. 169, no. 126.

[11] Compare the penalties imposed upon Gimillu / Innin-šum-ibni, who collected animals from the chief herder and the shepherds of the Lady-of-Uruk but then failed to turn the animals over to the Eanna temple (YOS 7 7 [–/–/1 Cyrus (538 B.C.), Uruk]); for animals, the authorities ordered a thirty-fold compensation in kind; for a *siriam* garment, 10 shekels. See further Wells, "Neo-Babylonian Period," pp. 962 ff. at 8.4–8.9 for various offenses and remedies, almost always simple or multiple compensation or fines.

priation could not have been his only offense against these seven persons; there had to be something more that led to the threat of amputation and beating.

The amputation and beating here were almost certainly punishments imposed by a court authority; note the reference in Text C to judges (albeit in a fragmentary clause). I know of no other instances in the Neo-Babylonian period in which there was a physical punishment (short of death[12]) imposed by a court. In a few contractual agreements, however, we do find the threat of physical punishment.[13] *Cyr.* 307 (3/IV/8 Cyrus [531 B.C.], Sippar) and *Cyr.* 312 (11/V/8 Cyrus [531 B.C.], Babylon) both include threats of slave-marking for the young women who continue prohibited relationships with their paramours,[14] and three contracts from the Murašû archives call for beatings, imprisonments, and/or fines for failure to perform contracted services.[15] The first, Stolper, *Entrepreneurs*, no. 91 (28/–/5 Darius II [419/418 B.C.], Til-Gabbara), concerns arable land for which two men are responsible for completing the ground-breaking work by the first day of the first month of the following year. The relevant passage (lines 5–10) is:[16]

> If they have not completed the ground-breaking work by the first of Nisannu, they will be beaten 100 blows, (their) beards and heads will be plucked, and they will be imprisoned in the prison of Rībat / Bēl-erība, the servant of Rīmūt-Ninurta.

Stolper, *Entrepreneurs*, no. 90 (12/VIII/39 Artaxerxes I [426 B.C.], Nippur) and Donbaz and Stolper, *Istanbul Murašû Texts*, no. 98 (–/VI(?)/39 Artaxerxes I [426 B.C.], Nippur) are both contracts in which Enlil-šum-iddin arranged for a contractor to deliver 500 pairs of split wood; for failure to meet this commitment, 1 ME *immahhiṣ u* 10 MA.NA KU$_3$.BABBAR *inamdin* "he (the contractor) will be beaten 100 (strokes), and he will pay ten minas of silver."

In these few contracts cited, the physical punishments are merely threatened; we do not know if there was ever an attempt to enforce them. But the amputations and beatings faced by Marduk-rēmanni were most likely real, imposed penalties, which were

[12] See E. Weidner, "Hochverrat gegen Nebukadnezar II., ein Großwürdenträger vor dem Königsgericht," *AfO* 17 (1954–56): 1–5; see F. Joannès, in *Rendre la justice en Mésopotamie* (Saint-Denis, 2000), pp. 203 f., no. 147 (slitting the throat for treason); note also LNB § 7 (death for witchcraft).

[13] And note the threat of death in the contractual clauses in marriage agreements, for which see M. T. Roth, "'She Will Die by the Iron Dagger': Adultery and Neo-Babylonian Marriage," *JESHO* 31 (1988): 186–206, and Roth *Marriage Agreements*, p. 15 (death by iron dagger for female adulterer).

[14] Idem, "Marriage, Divorce, and the Prostitute in Ancient Mesopotamia," in C. Faraone and L. McClure, eds., *Prostitution in the Ancient World* (Madison, Wisconsin, 2006), pp. 21–39.

[15] M. W. Stolper, *Entrepreneurs and Empire* (Leiden, 1985), nos. 90 and 91, and V. Donbaz and M. W. Stolper, *Istanbul Murašû Texts* (Leiden, 1997), no. 98.

[16] See M. Heltzer, "The Flogging and Plucking of Beards in the Achaemenid Empire and the Chronology of Nehemiah," *AMI* 28 (1995–96): 305–7; M. W. Stolper, "Flogging and Plucking," *Topoi* Supplément 1 (1997): 347–50.

commuted, perhaps by negotiation, to monetary payments. Nonetheless, the threatened punishments in contracts and the imposed punishments by courts would have all had deterrent and punitive effects. And these should not be confused with physical abuse construed as a wrong to be remedied.[17]

The two punishments in the texts under discussion—amputating the hand and beating—are not unique punishments. Amputation of the hand (like that of the tongue) is often a sympathetic punishment: the offending member is targeted.[18] Thus, for example, the offending hand is cut off for the child who strikes a parent (LH § 195),[19] the unsuccessful surgeon (LH § 218), the barber who removes the *abbuttu* slave-mark (LH § 226), the farmhand who pilfers grain or seed (LH § 253), and the thief (Wiseman *Alalakh* 2). Commonly, too, amputation of the hand and tongue figures in the standard penalty clause in Susa for one who violates a contract (passim in MDP 22, 23, 24, and 28).[20]

---

[17] For example, BIN 1 94; see M. W. Stolper, "Thrashing and Plucking," *NABU* 1998/110, and references cited *CAD* M/1 s.v. *mahāṣu* mngs. 1a, 1b, 7b; *CAD* Ṭ s.v. *ṭerû* B v.; see also C. Wunsch, "Die Jugendsünden eines Babyloniers aus gutem Hause," *AoF* 24 (1997): 231–41, and C. Wunsch, "Du hast meinen Sohn geschlagen!" in *Walker AV*, pp. 355–64 (with further references cited on p. 355, n. 2).

A difficult case is that in YOS 7 184, which records the receipt into the Eanna treasury of 10 shekels of silver *kūm ṭirûtu ša* PN ... *iṭṭerû* "in compensation for a beating that PN inflicted" (it is also possible that *iṭṭerû* in line 7 is an N-stem, thus "the beating that was inflicted," but see further below). The relevant portion of YOS 7 184 reads: (1) 10 GIN_2 KU_3.BABBAR *ku-um ṭi-ru-tu* (2) *šá* [Id]IM-LUGAL-ŠEŠ A-*šú šá* [Id]*na-na-a*-MU (3)[I]*ri-mut u* [I]*ba-ri-ki*-DINGIR LU_2.HUN.GA_2.ME (4) *šá* [I]*šu-la-a* A-*šú šá* [I]*gi-mil-lu a-na* (5) [I]ARAD-*ia* A-*šú šá* [Id]EN-ŠEŠ.MEŠ-*su* (6) LU_2 *na-qid šá ṣi-e-nu šá* [d]INNIN UNUG[ki] (7) *iṭ-ṭi-ru-ú i-na ri-e-hu* (8) *šá ṣi-e-nu šá ina* UGU-*hi* (9) [I]ARAD-*ia* [Id]IM-LUGAL-ŠEŠ (10) *a-na* NIG_2.GA E_2.AN.NA *ma-hi-ir* "(1) Ten shekels of silver (9–10) are received by Adad-šar-uṣur into the treasury of Eanna (7–9)—(the silver is) part of the outstanding balance for flocks that is owed by Ardia—(1–2) in compensation for (*kūm*) the beating that Adad-šar-uṣur / Nana-iddin (7) inflicted (3–4) upon Rīmūt and Bariki-ili, the laborers of Šulā, son of Gimillu (4–6) because of (*ana*) Ardia, son of Bēl-ahhe-erība, the herder of the flocks of (the temple of) Ištar of Uruk." Because *ṭerû* takes a direct object, "to beat someone (d.o.)," we cannot understand *ana Ardia* in lines 4–5 to indicate that Ardia was the recipient of the beating; it is the two named laborers (lines 3–4) who are the direct objects. The precise circumstances remain unclear to me, but the connection of herding responsibilities to the beatings inflicted is reminiscent of the Marduk-rēmanni case. (YOS 7 184 is included in M. Kozuh, "The Sacrificial Economy: On the Management of Sacrificial Sheep and Goats at the Neo-Babylonian/Achaemenid Eanna Temple of Uruk" [Ph.D. diss., University of Chicago, 2006].)

[18] See *CAD* R s.v. *rittu* A mng. 1a-3′ for other, nonsympathetic, punishments involving cutting off the hand. Citations below from the law collections are from Roth *Law Collections*.

[19] See M. T. Roth, "Elder Abuse," in A. Guinan et al., eds., *If a Man Builds a Joyful House: Essays in Honor of Erle Verdun Leichty* (Leiden and Boston, 2006), pp. 349–56.

[20] For a discussion of the sympathetic element in punishments, see S. Franke, "'Magische Praktiken' im Codex Hammurapi," *Zeitschrift für altorientalische und biblische Rechtsgeschichte* 6 (2000): 1–15. For cutting off of other body parts (ear, nose, tongue, lip, breast, foot), see *CAD* B s.v. *batāqu* mngs. 1a, 8a, 9; *CAD* N/1 s.v. *nakāsu* mngs. 2b-1′ and 6b; and the entries under *uznu*, *appu*, *lišānu*, etc. Such "punishments" can serve ulterior motives as well, as in ARM 14 78, *īnīšunu lilputuma i*[*na nepārim*] *liṭēnu uluma lišānāšunu* [*linnaksa*] *awassunu la uṣṣi* "they should blind them and have them grind in the workhouse, or

"Beating" (*mihṣu*, *ṭirûtu* in our texts) is a vague term that could include many forms of physical torture. The law collections include the penalties of flogging (*naṭû*, LH § 127, MAL A §§ 44, 59) and beating with an instrument (x *ina haṭṭāte imahhuṣušil šu* "they shall beat her/him x blows with rods," MAL A §§ 7, 18, 19, 21, 40; B §§ 7–10, 14, 15, 18; C §§ 2, 3, 8, 11; E § 1; F § 1; N § 1; MAPD §§ 17, 18, 21).

III

In conclusion, returning to the three texts involving Marduk-rēmanni, we have a better understanding of the case but remain ignorant about at least one essential point: the precise or complete scope of Marduk-rēmanni's offense. But the limiting of the harms here is noteworthy. In these texts, there is a calculated correlation between compensation and harm: 140 shekels to avoid the amputation of one hand, 3 shekels for each stripe or blow, 60 shekels for misappropriated animals. These amounts are those agreed to by the parties, and there is no reason to expect that the same amounts of silver per amputation, stripe, or particular number of animals might apply to other cases. The commutation of the physical harms into monetary sums solves the logical absurdity of carrying out multiple claims—Marduk-rēmanni having seven hands amputated or seven persons participating in a single amputation—but more importantly offers the wronged parties tangible redress rather than solely emotional satisfaction. While we might have suspected that corporal punishments were commutable by mutual agreement or by court order before, the commutation of corporal punishments into monetary payments has never been so clearly demonstrated.

APPENDIX

Text A: BM 78192 (*ZA* 3 [1898]: 224 f., no. 2) and duplicate BM 64196+

1 $2\frac{1}{3}$ MA.NA KU$_3$.BABBAR UD-*ú šá ina* 1 GIN$_2$ *bit-qa nu-uh-hu-tu*
2 *šá a-na ku-um ba-ta-qa*(dupl. *-qu*) *šá rit-tum šá* ^{Id}AMAR+UD-*re-e-man-ni*
3 DUMU *šá* ^{Id}EN-TIN-*iṭ* A LU$_2$.I$_2$.ŠUR-*gi-ni-e a-na ma-la*
4 HA.LA *šá* ^{I}KI-^{d}NUSKU-IGI-*ia* DUMU *šá* ^{Id}NUSKU-*a-a-lu*
5 *ù* 1 MA.NA KU$_3$.BABBAR UD-*ú ku-um ṣib-te-e-ti šá* ^{I}KI-^{d}NUSKU-IGI-*ia*
6 PAP $3\frac{1}{3}$ MA.NA KU$_3$.BABBAR UD-*ú šá ina* 1 GIN$_2$ *bit-qa nu-uh-hu-tu*
7 *šá a-na ku-um ba-ta-qa šá rit-tum šá* ^{Id}AMAR+UD-*re-e-man-ni*
8 *ù ṣib-te-e-ti šá* ^{I}KI-^{d}NUSKU-IGI-*ia* ^{I}KI-^{d}NUSKU-IGI-*ia*

---

else their tongues should be cut out so that their secret does not get out"; see K. van der Toorn, "ARM XIV 78 (= TCM I 78)," *RA* 79 (1985): 189–90. According to C. Zaccagnini, "Nuzi," in Westbrook, *History of Ancient Near Eastern Law*, p. 611: "Death and corporal punishment are attested [in Nuzi], but not as punishments for criminal offences. Mutilation is sometimes mentioned as a special sanction for breach of contract or other misconduct, but always related to the sphere of civil law."

9 DUMU *šá* ^{Id}NUSKU-*a-a-lu ina* ŠU^{II} ^{Id}AMAR+UD-*re-e-man-ni*
10 DUMU *šá* ^{Id}EN-TIN-*iṭ* A LU$_2$.I$_2$.ŠUR-*gi-ni-e ma-hi-ir*
11 *e-ṭi-ir* ^{I}KI-^{d}NUSKU-IGI-*ia*$_5$ *a-hi-iš-tum* KI ^{Id}AMAR+UD-*re-man-ni*
12 *ana* UGU-*hi ba-ta-qa šá rit-tum šá* ^{Id}AMAR+UD-*re-e-man-ni*
13 *u ṣib-te-e-ti šá* ^{I}KI-^{d}NUSKU-IGI-*ia*$_5$ ‹‹^{I}KI-^{d}NUSKU-IGI-*ia*$_5$
14 *it-ti* ^{Id}AMAR+UD-*re-e-man-ni*›› *i-te-pu-uš*
15 *dib-ba šá* ^{I}KI-^{d}NUSKU-IGI-*ia*$_5$ *ana* UGU *ba-ta-qa*
16 *šá rit-tum šá* ^{Id}AMAR+UD-*re-e-man-ni ù*
17 *ṣib-te-e-ti šá* ^{I}KI-^{d}NUSKU-IGI-*ia*$_5$ *it-ti*
18 ^{Id}AMAR+UD-*re-e-man-ni ia-a-nu dib-bi-šú-nu* KI *a-ha-meš*
19 *qa-tu-ú a-na* UGU *a-ha-meš ul i-tu-ru-nu*
20 LU$_2$ *mu-kin-nu* ^{I}*bul-ṭa-a* DUMU *šá* ^{I}*ri-mut*-^{d}EN A ^{I}ZALAG$_2$-^{d}ŠU$_2$ ^{Id}AMAR+UD-SU
21 DUMU *šá* ^{I}*li-nu-uh*-ŠA$_3$-DINGIR ^{Id}IM-*še-zib* DUMU *šá* ^{I}*ri-ba-a-tú*
22 ^{I}*ni-din-tum* DUMU *šá* ^{I}*e-til-lu* A LU$_2$.SANGA-^{d}UTU
23 ^{I}*i-qu-pu* A-*šú šá* ^{Id}EN-MU A ^{Id}BE-‹DINGIR›-*ta*-DU$_3$ ^{Id}EN-*ri-man-ni*
24 DUMU *šá* ^{Id}EN-MU A LU$_2$.GAL.DU$_3$ ^{Id}EN-TIN-*iṭ* DUMU *šá* ^{Id}UTU-MU A LU$_2$.I$_3$.ŠUR-*gi-ni-e*
25 ^{Id}EN-*it-tan-nu* DUMU *šá* ^{Id}AMAR+UD-LUGAL-URU$_3$ ^{Id}EN-*ik-‹ṣur›* (dupl.: ^{Id}EN-*ik-ṣur*) DUMU *šá* ^{Id}AG-TIN-*su*-E
26 ^{Id}EN-*it-tan-nu* DUMU *šá* ^{I}*ni-din-tum* ^{I}*ni-din-tum* DUMU *šá* ^{Id}30-DINGIR A ^{Id}EN-*e-ṭè-ru*
27 ^{I}*gi-mil-lu* DUMU *šá* ^{I}*ri-mut*-^{d}EN A LU$_2$.SANGA-^{d}UTU ^{Id}AG-ŠEŠ.MEŠ-*bul-liṭ*
28 DUMU *šá* ^{Id}EN-MU A LU$_2$.BAHAR$_2$ ^{Id}UTU-MU DUMU *šá* ^{I}*ki-rib-tu* A LU$_2$.ŠU.HA
29 ^{I}SUM-*na*-^{d}AG DUMU *šá* ^{I}*lib-luṭ* A ^{I}*ši-gu-ú-a* ^{I}*ú-bar* DUMU *šá* ^{I}*ṣil-la-a*
30 A ^{I}DU$_3$-*eš*-DINGIR ^{Id}EN-MU DUMU *šá* ^{Id}30-DINGIR A ^{I}*aš-kan-nu* ^{Id}EN-GI DUMU *šá*
31 ^{I}*ni-qu-du* DUMU ^{I}A$_2$.GAL$_2$-*e-a* ^{Id}AG-GI DUMU *šá* ^{Id}AG-DU-A A ^{I}DINGIR-*ia*
32 ^{I}*mi-nu-ú-a*(dupl. omits -*a*)-*na*-^{d}EN-*da-a-nu* DUB.SAR DUMU *šá* ^{I}KAR-^{d}AMAR+UD
33 DUMU ^{I}*im-bu*-IGI-*ia* E.KI ITU.ŠE UD 8.KAM$_2$ MU 25.KAM$_2$
34 ^{I}*da-ri-ia-muš* LUGAL E.KI LUGAL KUR.KUR.MEŠ

Translation

(1–4) $2\frac{1}{3}$ minas of white silver, with one-eighth alloy per shekel, of *nuhhutu*-quality, which is in lieu of the cutting off of the hand of Marduk-rēmanni, son of Bēl-uballiṭ, descendant of Ṣāhit-ginê, for the portion (of the total agreed compensation) owed to[21] Itti-Nusku-īnāja, son of Nusku-ajalu, (5) and also 1 mina of white silver as compensation for Itti-Nusku-īnāja's stolen property—(6) a total of $3\frac{1}{3}$ minas of white silver, with one-eighth alloy per shekel, of *nuhhutu*-quality, (7–8) which is in lieu of cutting off of the hand of Marduk-rēmanni and (as compensation for) Itti-Nusku-īnāja's stolen property—(8–11)

[21] *ana mala zitti ša* PN (Text A: 3–4; Text B: 4–5, 8–9, 18, 21; Text C: 7) must refer to that portion of the total compensation for the seven wronged individuals that is owed to the one individual named.

Itti-Nusku-īnāja, son of Nusku-ajalu, has received from Marduk-rēmanni, son of Bēl-uballiṭ, descendant of Ṣāhit-ginê; he is paid.

(11–14) Itti-Nusku-īnāja has made final settlement with Marduk-rēmanni in regard to the cutting off of Marduk-rēmanni's hand and Itti-Nusku-īnāja's stolen property. (15–18) There is no cause for suit on the part of Itti-Nusku-īnāja against Marduk-rēmanni in regard to the cutting off of Marduk-rēmanni's hand or Itti-Nusku-īnāja's stolen property. (18–19) Their suit is settled by mutual agreement. They shall not return (with suits) against each other.

(20–31) Witnesses: Bulṭaja, son of Rīmut-Bēl, descendant of Nūr-Marduk; Marduk-erība, son of Linūh-libbi-ili; Adad-šēzib, son of Rībātu; Nidintu, son of Etillu, descendant of Šangû-Šamaš; Iqūpu, son of Bēl-iddin, descendant of Ea-ilūta-bani; Bēl-rēmanni, son of Bēl-iddin, descendant of Rab-banî; Bēl-uballiṭ, son of Šamaš-iddin, descendant of Ṣāhit-ginê; Bēl-ittannu, son of Marduk-šar-uṣur; Bēl-ikṣur, son of Nabû-balāssu-iqbi; Bēl-ittannu, son of Nidintu; Nidintu, son of Sîn-ili, descendant of Bēl-ēṭir; Gimillu, son of Rīmūt-Bēl, descendant of Šangû-Šamaš; Nabû-ahhē-bulliṭ, son of Bēl-iddin, descendant of Pahhāru; Šamaš-iddin, son of Kiribtu, descendant of Bāʾiru; Iddin-Nabû, son of Libluṭ, descendant of Šigûa; Ubaru, son of Ṣillā, descendant of Eppēš-ili; Bēl-iddin, son of Sîn-ilī, descendant of Aškannu; Bēl-ušallim, son of Niqūdu, descendant of Lēʾea; Nabû-ušallim, son of Nabû-mukīn-apli, descendant of Ilija; (32–33) Minû-ana-Bēl-dānu, the scribe, son of Mušēzib-Marduk, descendant of Imbu-īnija.

(33–34) Babylon, month XII, day 8, year 25 of Darius, King of Babylon, King of the Lands.

Text B: BM 74529

1 $16\frac{1}{3}$ (text: $16\frac{5}{6}$) MA.NA KU$_3$.BABBAR *šá ku-um la ba-ta-qu rit-tum ù* 1 MA.NA 3 (text: 2) GIN$_2$ KU$_3$.BABBAR

2 *šá ku-um* 21 *mi-ih-ṣu* PAP $17\frac{1}{3}$ MA.NA 3 (text: 2) GIN$_2$ *šá ku-um la ba-ta-qu*

3 *rit-tum ù* 21 *mi-ih-ṣu šá ina* UGU ^{Id}AMAR+UD-*re-man-ni* DUMU-*šú šá* ^{Id}EN-TIN-*iṭ*

4 DUMU LU$_2$.I$_3$.ŠUR-*gi-ni-e šak-nu ina* ŠA$_3$-*bi* $2\frac{1}{3}$ MA.NA 9 GIN$_2$ KU$_3$.BABBAR *a-na ma-la*

5 *zi-it-ti šá* ^{I}*ba-ʾ-ìl-te-ri-a-ha-at-ta* DUMU-*šú šá* ^{Id}NUSKU-*a-a-lu*

6 ŠEŠ *šá* ^{Id}NUSKU-IGI^{II}-*ia ù* 1 MA.NA KU$_3$.BABBAR *ku-um ṣib-te-e-ti šá*

7 ^{I}*ba-ʾ- ìl-te-ri-a-hat-tum* PAP $3\frac{1}{3}$ MA.NA *ù* 9 GIN$_2$ KU$_3$.BABBAR *šá ku-um*

8 *la ba-ta-qu ri-it-tum ṭi-ru-ú-tu u ṣib-te-e-ti a-na*

9 *ma-la* HA.LA *šá* ^{I}*ba-ʾ-ìl-*⸢*te*⸣*-ri-a-ha-at-tum* DUMU-*šú šá* ^{Id}NUSKU-*a-a-lu*

10 ^{Id}NUSKU-IGI-*ia* (text, in error: ^{Id}NUSKU-*a-a-lu*) ŠEŠ *šá* ^{I}*ba-ʾ-ìl-te-ri-a-ha-at-tum ina* ŠU^{II} ^{Id}AMAR+UD-*ri-man-an-ni*

11 DUMU-*šú šá* ^{Id}EN-TIN-*iṭ* DUMU LU$_2$.I$_3$.SUR-*gi-ni-e ma-hi-ir e-ṭir* KU$_3$.BABBAR *aʾ*

12 $3\frac{1}{3}$ MA.NA *ù* 9 GIN$_2$ ^{Id}NUSKU-IGI-*ma it-ti* ^{I}*ba-ʾ-ìl-te-ri-a-ha-at-tum*

13 ŠEŠ-*šú ú-šá-az-zi-iz-ma a-na* ^{Id}AMAR+UD-*ri-man-an-ni i-nam-din pu-ut*

14 *la* (text: KU) *da-ba-bu di-i-ni šá* ^{I}*ba-ʾ-ìl-te-ri-a-ha-at-tum* ŠEŠ-*šú ana* UGU *ba-ta-qu*

15 *ri-it-tum ṭi-ru-tum ù ṣi-ib-te-e-tum* ^{Id}NUSKU-IGI^{II}-*ia* ŠEŠ

16 *šá* ^{I}*ba-ʾ-ìl-te-ri-a-ha-at-ta na-ši a-ha-ra-ti* ^{Id}NUSKU-IGI^{II}-*ia*

17 *ana* ⌜UGU⌝ *ba-ta-qu ri-it-tum ṭi-ru-ú-tu ù ṣib-te-e-ti*

18 ⌜*a-na ma-la zi-it-ti šá*⌝ ^{I}*ba-ʾ-ìl-te-ri-a-ha-at-ta* ⌜ŠEŠ-*šú*⌝

19 ⌜*it-ti*⌝ ^{I}AMAR+UD-*ri-man-an-ni i-te-pu-uš e-lat* ⌜*šá*⌝-*ṭa-ru mah-ru-ú*

20 ⌜*šá*⌝ [$3\frac{1}{3}$] MA.NA KU$_3$.BABBAR *šá ku-um la ba-ta-qu ri-it-tum ṭi-ru-ú-tu*

21 [*ù ṣib-te*]-*e-tum šá a-na* ⌜*ma*⌝-*la* HA.LA *šá* ^{Id}NUSKU-IGI^{II}-*a ina* ŠU^{II}

22 ⌜^{Id}⌝[AMAR+UD]-*ri-man-an*-⌜*ni*⌝ *in-ni-iṭ-ru ù* 9 (text: 8) GIN$_2$ KU$_3$.BABBAR *šá ina šá-ṭa-ru*

23 ⌜*mah*⌝-[*ru*]-*ú i-te-ṭir*$_5$-ʾ ^{Id}NUSKU-IGI^{II}-*ia ba-ab-tu* $3\frac{1}{3}$ MA.NA 9 GIN$_2$

24 KU$_3$.BABBAR ⌜*a*ʾ⌝ [*ina* ŠU^{II}] ^{Id}AMAR+UD-*ri-man-ni* DUMU-*šú šá* ^{Id}EN-TIN-*iṭ* DUMU *šá* LU$_2$.I$_3$.ŠUR-*gi-ni-e ma-hi-ir e-ṭir*

25 LU$_2$ *mu*-⌜*kin*$_7$⌝ ^{I}*li-ib-lu-ṭi*(copy: *-ba-ṭi*?) DUMU-*šú šá* ^{I}URU-*ba*-^{I}AMAR+UD DUMU ^{I}ARAD-^{d}BE ^{I}SUM.NA-*a*

26 DUMU-*šú šá* ^{I}⌜*ka*⌝-*ṣir* DUMU LU$_2$.SIMUG ^{I}*ni-din-tum*-^{d}EN DUMU-*šú šá* ^{Id}30-DINGIR-*šú* DUMU ^{Id}EN-*e-ṭè-ru*

27 ^{I}*si-lim-mu* DUMU-*šú šá* ^{I}*ba-ni-ia* DUMU ^{I}*ši-gu-ú-a* ^{Id}EN-TIN-*iṭ* DUMU-*šú šá* ^{Id}EN-*i-ri-ba*

28 DUMU ^{I}*e-gi*$_7$-*bi* ^{I}*ze-ri-iá* DUMU-*šú šá* ^{I}M[U-X]-MU-KI DUMU ^{Id}ILLAT-I

29 ^{Id}EN-URU-*ba* DUMU-*šú* ^{I}*im-bi*-^{d}30 ^{I}*bul*-[*ṭa*]-*a* DUMU-*šú šá* ^{I}*ri-e-mut*-^{d}EN

30 DUMU ^{I}⌜ZALAG$_2$-^{d}ŠÚ ^{Id}AG-MU-DU DUMU-*šú šá* ^{I}⌜^{d}⌝[x]-SUM-*na* DUMU *šá* ^{I}*šá-na-bi-ši-šú*

31 ^{Id}EN-KAR-*ir* DUMU-*šú šá* ^{I}*ṣil-la-a* DUMU ^{I}*mu*-[…] ^{I}*šá*-^{d}EN-*at-ta* DUMU *šá* ^{Id}EN-*ka-ṣir*

32 DUMU LU$_2$.BAHAR$_2$ ^{Id}EN-MU DUMU-*šú šá* ^{I}[…] DUMU ^{I}*da-bi-bi* ^{I}*mu-ṣe-zib*-^{d}AMAR+UD

33 DUMU-*šú šá* ^{Id}EN-TIN-*iṭ* […] x DUMU-*šú šá* ^{Id}AG-DU-MU DUMU ^{I}*šá-na-bi-ši-šú*

34 ^{I}*šá*-^{d}EN-*at-ta* DUMU *šá* [^{I}SUM]-*na*-^{d}AG DUMU E$_2$.BAR-^{d}UTU ^{Id}EN-SUM-*na* DUMU-*šú šá* ^{I}*ṣil-la-a*

35 DUMU *ba-bu-tu* ^{I}*gu-za-nu* DUMU-*šú šá* ^{Id}AG-MU-MU DUMU LU$_2$.BAHAR$_2$ ^{Id}EN-*it-tan-nu*

36 DUMU-*šú šá* ^{I}*ni-din-tú* ^{Id}EN-A-MU DUMU-*šú šá* ^{I}*šad-din-nu* DUMU ^{I}ZALAG$_2$-^{d}30 ^{Id}EN-*it-tan-nu*

37 DUMU-*šú šá* ^{Id}EN-TIN-*iṭ* [^{I}*ni-din*]-*tú* DUMU-*šú šá* ^{I}ARAD-^{d}*gu-la* DUMU ^{I}ZALAG$_2$-^{d}30 ^{I}*ni-din-tú*

38 DUMU-*šú šá* ^{I}*kal-ba-a* ^{I}*ha-ba-ru-ṣu* (for *habaṣīru*?) DUMU-*šú šá* ^{I}*a-na*-^{d}AG-APIN-*eš* ^{I}*ú-bar* DUMU-*šú šá*

39 ^{Id}AG-ŠEŠ.MEŠ-GI DUMU LU$_2$.BAHAR$_2$ ^{I}*haš-da-a-a* DUMU *šá* ^{Id}U+GUR-TIN-*iṭ*

40 ^{Id}U+GUR-MU DUMU *šá* ^{I}*ri-mut* DUMU LU$_2$.SIPA-ANŠE.KUR.RA LU$_2$.UMBISAG ^{Id}EN-ŠEŠ.MEŠ-MU

41 DUMU-*šú šá* ^{Id}AG-x-*ú-ṣur* DUMU LU$_2$.E$_2$.BAR-^{d}UTU TIN.TIR^{ki} ITU.ŠE

42 UD 15.KAM$_2$ MU 25.KAM$_2$ ^{I}*da-ri-ʾ-muš* LUGAL E^{ki} *u* KUR.KUR.MEŠ

Translation

(1–2) (Concerning) 16⅓ minas of silver, which is in lieu of not cutting off the hand, and 1 mina and 3 shekels of silver, which is in lieu of the 21 blows, (2–4) a total of 17 minas and 23 shekels, which is in lieu of both not cutting off the hand and the 21 blows that are imposed upon Marduk-rēmanni, son of Bēl-uballiṭ, descendant of Ṣāhit-ginê:

(10–11) Nusku-īnāja, brother of Baʾ-Ilteri-ahattu, received from and is paid by Marduk-rēmanni, son of Bēl-uballiṭ, descendant of Ṣāhit-ginê: (4–7) 2 minas and 29 shekels of silver for the portion (of the total agreed compensation) owed to Baʾ-Ilteri-ahattu, son of Nusku-ajalu, brother of Nusku-īnāja, and 1 mina of silver in compensation for Baʾ-Ilteri-ahattu's stolen property—(7–9) a total of 3 minas and 29 shekels of silver, in lieu of not cutting off the hand, the beating, and the stolen property, for the portion (of the total agreed compensation) owed to Baʾ-Ilteri-ahattu, son of Nusku-ajalu.

(11–13) That silver, 3 minas and 29 shekels, Nusku-īnāja entered into the ledger of his brother Baʾ-Ilteri-ahattu to the credit of Marduk-rēmanni.[22] (13–16) Nusku-īnāja, the brother of Baʾ-Ilteri-ahattu, bears responsibility that there be no complaint or suit on behalf of his brother Baʾ-Ilteri-ahattu in regard to the cutting off of the hand, the beating, or the stolen property. (16–19) Nusku-īnāja has made final settlement with Marduk-rēmanni for the portion (of the total agreed compensation) owed to Baʾ-Ilteri-ahattu in regard to the cutting off the hand, the beating, and the stolen property.

(19–22) (This transaction is) apart from (that recorded in) a prior document for [3⅓] minas of silver, which was in lieu of not cutting off the hand, the beatings, and the stolen property, which has been paid by Marduk-rēmanni for the portion (of the total agreed compensation) owed to Nusku-īnāja. (22–23) And the 9 shekels of silver that were in a prior document were (also) paid. (23–25) Nusku-īnāja has received from Marduk-rēmanni, son of Bēl-uballiṭ, descendant of Ṣāhit-ginê, the amount due, the aforementioned 3 minas and 29 shekels of silver; he is paid.

(25–40) Witnesses: Libluṭ, son of Erība-Marduk, descendant of Arad-Ea; Iddinaja, son of Kāṣir, descendant of Nappāhu; Nidintu, son of Sîn-ilišu, descendant of Bēl-ēṭir; Silimmu, son of Banija, descendant of Šigûa; Bēl-uballiṭ, son of Bēl-erību, descendant of Egibi; Zērija, son of ..., descendant of Balīhu/Illatu; Bēl-erība, son of Imbi-Sîn; Bulṭaja, son of Rīmūt-Bēl, descendant of Nūr-Marduk; Nabû-šum-ukīn, son of ...-iddina, descendant of Ša-nāšišu (text: -nabišišu); Bēl-ēṭir, son of Šillaja, descendant of MU-[...]; Ša-Bēl-atta, son of Bēl-kāṣir, descendant of Pahhāru; Bēl-iddin, son of ..., descendant of Dābibi; Mušēzib-Marduk, son of Bēl-uballiṭ; ..., son of Nabû-mukīn-šumi, descendant of Ša-nāšišu (text:

[22] For a review of the discussions of the Neo-Babylonian expression *šuzzuzu-ma nadānu*, see M. Weszeli, "Eseleien, II," *WZKM* 87 (1997): 233–36, and see Stolper, "Fifth Century Nippur," p. 120, who reiterates his contention that the clause "is to assure that the transaction *is* final from the point of view of the principals"—certainly the correct interpretation here, given the subsequent clauses in lines 13–19 stressing that Nusku-īnāja is responsible for any question about the payments. (Note *ušazzizma* instead of the expected present form *ušazzazma*.)

-nabišišu); Ša-Bēl-atta, son of Iddin-Nabû, descendant of Šangû-Šamaš; Bēl-iddina, son of Šillaja, descendant of Babūtu; Guzānu, son of Nabû-šum-iddin, descendant of Pahhāru; Bēl-ittannu, son of Nidintu; Bēl-apla-iddin, son of Šaddinnu, descendant of Nūr-Sîn; Bēl-ittannu, son of Bēl-uballiṭ; Nidintu, son of Arad-Gula, descendant of Nūr-Sîn; Nidintu, son of Kalbaja; Habaṣīru, son of Ana-Nabû-ēreš; Ubār, son of Nabû-ahhē-šullim, descendant of Pahhāru; Hašdaja, son of Nergal-uballiṭ; Nergal-iddin, son of Rīmūt, descendant of Rē'i-sisê. (40–41) Scribe: Bēl-ahhē-iddin, son of Nabû-x-uṣur, descendant of Šangû-Šamaš.

(41–42) Babylon, month XII, day 15, year 25 of Darius, King of Babylon and the Lands.

Text C: BM 64208

1 [2$\frac{1}{3}$] MA.NA KU$_3$.BABBAR UD-*ú šá ina* 1 GIN$_2$ *bit-q*[*a nu-uh-hu-tu*]
2 [*šá* ^{I}]KI-^{d}NUSKU-IGI-*ia* DUMU *šá* ^{Id}NUSKU-*a-a-*[*lu*]
3 [*ina*] UGU-*hi* ^{Id}AMAR+UD-*ri-e-man-ni* DUMU *šá* ^{I}⸢^{d}EN⸣-[TIN-*iṭ*]
4 A LU$_2$.I$_3$.SUR-*gi-ni-e ina* ITI.BARA$_2$ *ina* SAG.[DU-*šú*]
5 *i-na-ad-di-in* KU$_3$.BABBAR *a$_4$* 2$\frac{1}{3}$ MA.NA *šá* [*ku-um* (*la*)]
6 *ba-ta-qa šá rit-tum šá* ^{Id}AMAR+UD-*ri-e-man-ni*
7 *a-na ma-la* HA.LA *šá* ^{I}KI-^{d}NUSKU-[IGI-*ia*]
8 KU$_3$.BABBAR ŠAM$_2$ *ṣe-e-nu šá ṣib-te-e-*[*ti šá*]
9 [^{I}]KI-^{d}NUSKU-IGI-*ia* ^{I}KI-^{d}NUSKU-IGI-[*ia*]
10 [*ina* ŠU^{II}] ^{Id}AMAR+UD-*ri-e-man-ni e-*[*ṭi-ir*]
11 [x x x x LU$_2$].DI.KUD.MEŠ *a-na* x [...]
12 [^{I}KI-^{d}NUSKU]-IGI-*iá* ^{Id}AMAR+UD-[*ri-e-man-ni*]
13 [*i-na-áš-šá*]-*am-ma a-na* ^{I}[KI-^{d}NUSKU-IGI-*ia*]
14 [DUMU *šá* ^{Id}NUSKU-*a-a-lu i*]-⸢*na*⸣-*ad-din*
15 [LU$_2$ *mu-kin*]-*nu* ^{Id}AMAR+UD-MU-[x DUMU *šá* ^{I}...]
16 ^{I}*ni-din-tum* DUMU *šá* ^{I}NUMUN-*tú* [...]
17 ^{Id}EN-DIB-‹UD.DA› DUMU *šá* ^{I}[... ^{I}...]
18 DUMU *šá* ^{I}*la-ba-ši* [...]
19 ^{I}*šu-lum*-[TIN].TIR^{ki} DUMU [*šá* ^{I}...]
20 ^{Id}EN-*ri-e-man-ni* [DUMU *šá* ^{I}...]
21 ^{I}*ba-si-iá* DUB.SAR DUMU *šá* [... DUMU]
22 ^{Id}EN-*e-ṭe-ru* TIN.TIR[^{ki} ITU.x UD x.KAM$_2$]
23 MU 25.KAM$_2$ ^{I}*da-ri-iá-muš* [LUGAL E.KI LUGAL KUR.KUR.MEŠ]

Translation

(1–4) (Concerning) 2 minas 20 shekels of white silver, with one-eighth alloy per shekel, of *nuhhutu*-quality, owed to Itti-Nusku-īnāja, son of Nusku-ajalu, by Marduk-rēmanni, son of Bēl-uballiṭ, descendant of Ṣāhit-ginê—(4–5) he (Marduk-rēmanni) will pay in month I, without interest. (5–7) The aforementioned 2 minas 20 shekels of silver, which is in lieu of (not) cutting off the hand of Marduk-rēmanni, is for the portion (of the total agreed compensation) owed to Itti-Nusku-īnāja. (8–10) Itti-Nusku-īnāja has been paid by Marduk-rēmanni (another sum of) silver, the equivalent of the herds that are Itti-Nusku-īnāja's stolen property. (11–14) [...] the judges to [... of] Itti-Nusku-īnāja—Marduk-rēmanni will fetch and deliver to [Itti-Nusku-īnāja, son of Nusku-ajalu].

(15–20) Witnesses: Marduk-mu-[..., son of ...]; Nidintu, son of Zērūtu, [descendant of ...]; Bēl-mušētiq-uddi, son of [...; ...], son of Lābāši, [descendant of ...]; Šulum-Bābili, son of [...]; Bēl-rēmanni, [son of ...]; (21–22) Basija, the scribe, son of [..., descendant of] Bēl-ēṭir.

(22–23) Babylon, month x, day x, year 25 of Darius, King of Babylon, King of the Lands.

ON SAND DUNES, MOUNTAIN RANGES, AND MOUNTAIN PEAKS*

Piotr Steinkeller, Harvard University

I. SAND DUNES

MVN 4 1, an Ur III text of unknown origin, lists field-allotments of the military organization settled in the town or village Al-Šu-Šuen-reʾi-nišišu.[1] Some of the fields listed there include plots described as du_6-mun, while others have small lots of land designated as IŠ. The first designation, meaning "saline hummock," is otherwise documented,[2] but, to the best of my knowledge, the other term appears as a qualification of arable land/soil only here. Of the two readings of IŠ that are possible in this context—sahar and iš(i)—the first may safely be excluded, since sahar means "dust, loose earth, soil, debris" (Akk. *eperu*). This leaves us with iš(i), whose Akkadian equivalents are: (1) *bāṣu* (later *baṣṣu*) "sand"; (2) *issû* (a loanword from iš(i)) "excavated sand"; and (3)—at first sight inexplicably—"mountain" (Akk. *šadû*).[3] But

* I am very happy to be able to contribute to this volume, which honors the scholarly achievement of Robert D. Biggs, my teacher, colleague, and friend. Bob's generosity in sharing his knowledge with me and his proverbial kindness count among the highlights of my Oriental Institute days. It would please me to think that this little lexicographic offering shows at least some signs of his intellectual influence.

I am deeply grateful to Gianni Marchesi and Christopher E. Woods, who read earlier versions of this article and offered valuable suggestions and criticisms.

Citations of Sumerian compositions generally follow the Electronic Text Corpus of Sumerian Literature, Oxford University: http://www-etcsl.orient.ox.ac.uk.

[1] A detailed discussion of this text will be offered by me elsewhere.

[2] UET 3 1357:9, 1367 ii 2. Closely related (if not identical) soil designations are (ki-)mun "saline ground" (*DP* 573, 577; Nikolski 1 31; Contenau *Contribution* 100 i 5, ii 8, and passim in this text) and mun-mun "saline" (*DP* 575 i 2; UET 3 1372:4). When used alone as a soil designation (as in Contenau *Contribution* 100 i 4, v 18′), du_6 describes various small elevations in a field, such as hillocks, mounds, and the remains of ancient habitations. [N.B.: du_6 "mound" is actually $dudr_x$, as shown by Ebla Syllabary 23: du_6 = [d]u-tum, and spellings such as du_6-du_6-da (Lamentation over Sumer and Ur 346, Temple Hymns 530, etc.), du_6-du_6-dam (Inana's Descent 34), du_6-dè (Ninmešara 35), du_6-du_6-rá (Šulgi X 136), and du_6-du_6-ra (Uruk Lament 4.25, RIME 4 149 Nur-Adad 7:80).]

[3] See iš IŠ = *šá-du-u*, iš IŠ = *ba-aṣ-ṣu* (Ea IV 82, 89, in MSL 14 358); i-ši IŠ = *ba-*[*aṣ-ṣu*], i-ši IŠ = *i-s*[*u-ú*] (MSL 12 105:48–49); IŠ = *ba-ṣú* (Proto-Izi I 289, in MSL 13 27); i-ši IŠ = *šá-du-u* (S^b II 120); i-iš IŠ = *ša-d*[*u-u*] (A IV/2); iš IŠ = *ša-du-u* (Ea IV 82). As is shown by the fact that the basic Sumerian correspondents of *issû* are pú and túl, when corresponding to *issû*, iš(i) means literally "sand from a pit." In that sense iš(i) also corresponds to the Akk. *šatpum* "pit, excavation,"

since the basic Sumerian term for "mountain" is kur,[4] iš(i), whose attestations with this particular meaning are quite rare (see below), must describe some type of a mountain-like natural formation. That formation, as is strongly indicated by the context of MVN 4 1, is almost certainly "sand dune."[5]

This conclusion is confirmed by the fact that *bāṣu*, one of the correspondents of iš(i), in many instances specifically means "sand dune."[6] Furthermore, notice the following passages from literary sources where the sense "sand dune" of iš(i) is quite evident:

(1) iš(i) ì-zi-zi iš(i) ì-gá-gá = *ba-aṣ-ṣu i-na-as-sa-aḫ tam-la-a ú-mál-li*

(The storm) raises sand, it sets up dunes.

(Lugale 84)

In this example, iš(i) is additionally equated with Akk. *tamlû*, which describes various types of earth-fills and embankments.[7] Significantly, *tamlû* is in turn a lexical correspondent of iš(i)/sahar ... gá-gá "to pile up sand/earth,"[8] thus confirming that iš(i) is an accumulated, or piled-up, mass of sand.

---

which is usually equated with pú, túl, and búr. See iš(i) ba-ni-íb-dub-dub sahar ba-ni-íb-šú-šú = *ša-at-pu it-ta-at-ba-ak ša-pí-ku it-ta-aš-pa-ak* (*KAR* 375 iii 51–52).

[4] See in detail section II of this article below.

[5] For dune fields as one of the dominant landforms of Iraq's central floodplain, see R. McC. Adams, *Heartland of Cities: Surveys of Ancient Settlement and Land Use on the Central Floodplain of the Euphrates* (Chicago, 1981), pp. 22, 30–32. Note, especially, ibid., p. 22: "Shown in stippling on the base map are areas of dunes. In large part these lie outside the cultivation perimeter, although in places farmers have sought to stabilize some of the looser, less actively moving dune groups and to extend field canals and cultivation into their midst. There has been no systematic study of dune formations in this area, but the dune fields whose outlines have been traced from the air photographs generally consist of symmetrical, lunate forms of *barchans*, sometimes closely grouped into oscillating, wavelike ridges with alternating barchanoid and linguoid elements. In this region individual dunes are generally small, though some can cover a hectare or more and rise to a height of 7 or 8 meters. It is not the individual, isolated dune that furnishes the principal obstacle to archaeological survey, but rather the much larger, dense grouping that may extend almost impenetrably over several square kilometers ... Low hummocks or *nebkhas* that have formed around desert shrubs also occur over vast areas, continuing a very rough microtopography within a contour interval of 50 centimeters or less even after the surface vegetation has disappeared and the roots have been reduced to a brittle skeleton lacing the sand together." Further, see J. A. Armstrong and M. C. Brandt, "Ancient Dunes at Nippur," in H. Gasche et al., eds., *Cinquante-deux reflexions sur le Proche-Orient ancien offertes en hommage à Léon De Meyer*, Mesopotamian History and Environment, Occasional Publications 2 (Leuven, 1994), pp. 255–63, who offer a detailed description of the mechanics of dune formation, emphasizing the point that "the unusual large dune fields found in the southern alluvial plain of Iraq are a distinctive feature that seems to relate directly to the practice of irrigation agriculture" (p. 258).

[6] This is true of many of the examples listed in *CAD* B s.v. *baṣṣu*, esp. usage a. Cf. also the GN Bāṣum (*Rép. géogr.* 3, p. 39), which evidently means "sand-dune."

[7] See *AHw.*, p. 1316a.

[8] See sahar-gá-gá = *tam-[lu-ú]* (MSL 12 105:50).

(2) maš-gán á-dam-bi mu-⌈un-gul⌉-gul-lu-uš du$_6$-du$_6$-ra mi-ni-in-si-ig-eš Ki-en-gi sag-e iš(i)-gim mu-un-dub-bu-uš

They (i.e., the enemies) destroyed its villages and hamlets; they turned them into tells; (the land of) Sumer they heaped up high like sand dunes.

(Uruk Lament 4.25–26)

(3) erim$_6$-ma-mu iš(i) ba-da-dub-dub sahar ba-da-šú-šú erim$_6$-ma-mu sahar-gar íd-da-ke$_4$ šu àm-ši-nigin

In my storehouse sand dunes have formed, it has been covered with dust; in my storehouse river silt[9] has accumulated.

(Krecher *Kultlyrik* 55 ii 39–40)

(4) É-an-na iš(i) ba-da-dub-dub [sahar ba-da]-šú-šú É-an-na sahar-gar íd-da-ke$_4$ [šu àm-ši]-nigin

(Cohen *Eršemma* 32:47–48)

The fact that iš(i) is "sand dune" elucidates the question of the mysterious toponym iš(i) Za-bu$^{(ki)}$, which is documented in three literary sources:[10]

(5) ^{d}I-bí-^{d}Suen kur Elam^{ki}-ma-šè ^{giš}búr-ra túm-mu-dè iš(i) Za-bu$^{(ki)}$ gaba a-ab-ba-ka-ta (var.: gaba hur-sag-gá-ta) zag An-ša$_4$-an^{ki}-šè

That Ibbi-Suen will be taken to the land Elam in fetters from the sand dunes of Zabu on the coast of the Sea (var.: on the border of the mountain ranges[11]) to the border of Anšan.

(Lamentation over Sumer and Ur 35–36)

(6) ^{d}Lugal-bànda^{da} kur ki sud-rá / su-ùd-da gá-la ba-ni-in-dag iš(i) Za-bu^{ki}-a nir ba-ni-in-gál / iš(i) Sa-a-bu-a n[ir ...] = ^{d}MIN *ana šadî*(KUR)^{i} *a-šar ru-ú-qi* [...] *ina šadî*(KUR)^{i} *Sa-a-bi* [...]

Lugalbanda ran off to the faraway mountain, he trusted his lot to the sand dunes of Zabum.

(Lugalbanda Epic I 1–2)

---

[9] For sahar-gar íd-a(k), Akk. *šapīk nāri* "heaped-up / accumulated river silt" (*CAD* Š/1 s.v. *šapīku*), see sahar-gar = *šá-pi-*[*ik* ÍD] (Igituh I 287); sahar-gar íd-da (Proto-Izi I 298, in MSL 13 27); ^{gi}pisan ninda èrim-ma kalam-ma-ka ^{d}Nanše-er sahar-gar íd-da-gim ki mu(-un)-na-ab-ús / mu-un-ši-íb-ús "in the storehouses of the Land baskets with food have been set up (lit.: densely packed) for Nanše like the heaped-up river silt" (Nanše Hymn 15–16); sahar-gar íd-da-gim = *ki-ma ša-pi-ik na-a-ri* (*AfO* 23 [1970]: 44 Section III 16–17). For ki ... ús, see n. 19 below.

[10] See Wilcke *Lugalbanda*, pp. 33–35; P. Michalowski, *The Lamentation over the Destruction of Sumer and Ur* (Winona Lake, Indiana, 1989), p. 74.

[11] For hur-sag = "mountain range," see in detail section II below.

(7) umbin-bi-ta iš(i) Za-bu-e ka-bi-ta SUR gál-tag-e

With the claws (like) the sand dunes of Zabu, with the mouth (like) the open....
(Lugalbanda Epic II 189–90)[12]

In both examples 5 and 6 the "sand dunes of Zabu" mark the starting point of a journey to the Iranian plateau when departing from the southernmost section of Babylonia: Ur in the case of Ibbi-Suen, Uruk in the case of Lugalbanda. Significantly, in example 5 that point is located specifically "on the coast of the sea," i.e., on the Persian Gulf. Since sand dunes are a ubiquitous feature of the coastal landscape of the Gulf, iš(i) Za-bu$^{(ki)}$ could theoretically be found at any place along the northern section of the Gulf; a location to the east of the present-day Iraqi-Iranian border seems to be favored by the context of both examples 5 and 6. There is reason to think, however, that the "sand dunes of Zabu" are a very specific topographical point. In his discussion of the southern margins of the Tigris-Euphrates floodplain,[13] H. T. Wright notes the presence in that area of a long belt of large sand dunes, probably dating to the Pleistocene era, which extends for almost three hundred kilometers along the southern edge of the alluvium. The belt is over ten kilometers wide, with some dunes reaching over fifty meters in height.[14] One may be certain that this impressive "mountain" chain was well known to the ancients. If, as appears likely, Ibbi-Suen was transported to Anšan via the sea route (which one would expect would begin on the coast to the south of Eridu), those dunes may have been the last glimpse of his homeland he carried with him, never to return there again.

---

[12] Another likely attestation of iši with the meaning "sand dune" is found in an Ur III incantation: muš kur-ta zi gìr iš(i)-ta ì-zi "the snake rose from the mountain, the scorpion rose from the sand dune" (see J. J. A. van Dijk and M. J. Geller, *Ur III Incantations from the Frau Professor Hilprecht-Collection, Jena*, TuM 6 [Wiesbaden, 2003], p. 110, no. 2 ii 14–15).

[13] *The Administration of Rural Production in an Early Mesopotamian Town*, Museum of Anthropology, University of Michigan, Anthropological Papers 38 (Ann Arbor, 1969), pp. 10–11; Wright, "Appendix, The Southern Margins of Sumer: Archaeological Survey of the Area of Eridu and Ur," in Adams, *Heartland of Cities*, p. 300.

[14] Cf. also *Iraq and the Persian Gulf*, Geographical Handbook Series, Naval Intelligence Division (London, 1944), p. 118: "Along the northern border of the Dibdibba and Hajara regions is a belt of sand varying in width from 5 to 15 miles and lying parallel to the Euphrates. As a continuous belt of undulating sand it begins about 10 miles south-west of Shinafiya and reaches south-eastwards almost to the Batin until held up by the ridges of Makhazuma and Matiyaha. North-west of Shinafiya it breaks up into low isolated dunes separated by hard ground; before reaching Makhazuma it changes in character and becomes a level area of soft sand which banks up against every bush to form numerous small tufted hillocks."

II. MOUNTAIN RANGES AND MOUNTAIN PEAKS: THE MEANINGS OF HUR-SAG AND KUR

Throughout his long Sumerological career, Thorkild Jacobsen insisted that the topographical term hur-sag means "foothills" or "piedmont." The last—and also the most extensive—elaboration of this position is found in his *Harps*: "*Hur-sag̃*, literally 'head of the valleys', denotes the near mountains, the foothills, and contrasts with the more daunting, less accessible high mountains farther in, the 'highland' (*kur*)."[15] While it is true that hur-sag and kur are opposing terms, the contrast between them does not rest on the "nearer/lower" and "farther/higher" distinction. Instead, the underlying contrast is between "multiple/continuous" and "single/punctual," meaning that hur-sag denotes "mountain range/chain,"[16] whereas kur means "(single) mountain, mountain peak" (and "mountains, mountain peaks" in the plural). This is shown most emphatically in the contexts describing the traversing of mountains, in which the noun used is invariably hur-sag and never kur. Here note especially the following example, where both terms are employed:

> kur-úr-ra kur-bàd-da ma-du-um-e zag An-ša$_4$-na-ta sag An-ša$_4$-an^{ki}-na-šè
> hur-sag 5 hur-sag 6 hur-sag 7 im-me-re-bala-bala
>
> By mountain low (lit.: the base of the mountain), by mountain high, (and) over the plain he crossed five, six, seven mountain ranges, from the border of Anšan to the top of Anšan.
>
> (Lugalbanda Epic I 343–44)

And see also these occurrences:

> hur-sag 5 hur-sag 6 hur-sag 7-e im-me-ri-bala
>
> Five, six, seven mountain ranges he crossed.
>
> (Enmerkar and the Lord of Aratta 170, 509)

> hur-sag 1-e in-ti-in-bala ... hur-sag 7-kam-ma bala-e-da-ni
>
> He crossed the first mountain range ... as he crossed the seventh mountain range.
>
> (Gilgameš and Huwawa Version B 60–61)

---

15 Th. Jacobsen, *The Harps That Once ... Sumerian Poetry in Translation* (New Haven, 1987), p. 254, n. 27.

16 To be sure, I am not the only person to understand hur-sag in this way. See, for example, D. O. Edzard, "Deep-Rooted Skyscrapers and Bricks: Ancient Mesopotamian Architecture and Its Imagery," in M. J. Geller et al., eds., *Figurative Language in the Near East* (London, 1987), p. 14, who translated it "mountains," "mountain range," "mountain chain."

Further evidence that hur-sag denotes "mountain range" is provided by the passages in which hur-sag is said to be "wide" and to have "plateaus" and "meadows":

kur Gú-bí-na-šè igi na-ni-íl hur-sag dagal téš-bi nam-ta-an-si-ig

He (i.e., Enlil) looked as far as the land of Gubin; he scoured all of the wide mountain ranges.

(Curse of Akkade 152–53)

am gal-gim temen-na hur-sag-gá-ka ú sikil mu-un-kú-e $šag_4$-túm-$šag_4$-túm hur-sag-gá-ka gú mu-un-peš-peš-e

She (i.e., Ninhursag) made them (i.e., Summer and Winter) eat like wild bulls fresh grass on the mountain plateaus, she reared them on the mountain meadows.

(Summer and Winter 17–18)

Equally characteristically, hur-sag frequently serves as a simile for city walls, as in the following examples:

bàd-bi hur-sag-gim an-né an-ús

Its city wall touched the sky like a mountain range.

(Curse of Akkade 42)

ur_5-ta kalam gi-né sig nim GAM-e-dè bàd gal za-pa-ág-ba šu nu-ku_4-ku_4 hur-sag sig_7-ga-gim uru^{ki}-né im-mi-dab_6

In order to submit the lower and upper countries to the 'true' land, he installed at his city a great wall, which, like a verdant mountain range, cannot be penetrated when it roars (lit.: in its roaring).

(RIME 3/2, pp. 368–69 Ibbi-Sin 1:11–17)

bàd gal hur-sag íl-la-gim šu nu-ku_4-ku_4-dè ní-bi-šè è-a mu-na-dù

He erected for him a great wall, which like a mountain range raised high cannot be penetrated, which came forth by itself.

(RIME 4, pp. 237–38 Warad-Sin 19:13–16)

bàd $Sippar^{ki}$ hur-sag gal-gim mi-ni-íl

I raised the city wall of Sippar like a great mountain range.

(RIME 4, pp. 374–78 Samsuiluna 3:65–66 [Sumerian])

Lastly, note that in the royal Ur III correspondence the mountain ranges of Jebel Hamrin (ancient Ebih) are consistently referred to as hur-sag:

> bàd-bi 26 danna-àm dím-e-da-mu-dè dal-ba-na hur-sag min-a-bi-ka sá di-da-mu-dè dím-me-mu-šè MAR.TU hur-sag-gá-ka íb-tuš-a géštug mu-ši-in-ak Si-mu-ur$_4^{ki}$ nam-tab-ba-ni-šè im-ma-da-gin dal-ba-na hur-sag Ebih^{ki}-ke$_4$ ^{giš}tukul sìg-ge-dè im-ma-ši-gin
>
> As I was constructing this wall to the length of 26 danna, and reached the (plateau) between the two mountain ranges, I learned, as a result of my building activity, about the Amorites camping in the mountain ranges. The Simurreans had come to their assistance. Thus I went up (the plateau) between the mountain ranges of Ebih in order to smite (them).
>
> (Šarrumbani to Šusin 12–16)

Sumerian is not unique in sharply distinguishing between "mountain" and "mountain range." Various other languages make the same distinction, for example, Spanish, which uses separate words for each meaning: *montaña* as opposed to *sierra* and *cordillera*. On the other hand, Akkadian differs in this respect, since *šadû* means both "mountain" and "mountain range." Significantly, however, Akkadian also knows the loanword *ḫuršānu*, which is used strictly in the sense of "mountain range."[17] It seems certain that this borrowing had been motivated by the absence of an unequivocal term for "mountain range" in Akkadian.

That hur-sag and kur meant two distinctly different things to the Sumerians is best illustrated by the contrasting usage of both terms in a single literary composition. Here the prime case is Gudea's cylinders, where hur-sag and kur serve as similes of temples and related structures:

> kun na$_4$ é-a nú-a-bi hur-sag ul nun-né-éš nú-àm
>
> Its stone stairway set down in the temple is (like) a mountain range laid with princely flowers.[18]
>
> (A xxviii 19–20)

---

17 See *CAD* Ḫ s.v. *ḫuršānu* A, translating (slightly incorrectly) "mountain region"; *AHw.*, p. 360, translating (correctly) "Gebirge." A good illustration of the *šadû-ḫuršānu* contrast is provided by the recently published manuscript OB Schøyen$_2$ of the Gilgameš Epic: *i-li-ma* ^{d}G[I]Š *a-na ṣe-er šadîm*(KUR) *it-ta-na-ap-*⌈*la*⌉*-ás ka-li-šu-nu* ⌈*ḫur*⌉*-sa*-MI "Gilgameš climbed up to the top of the mountain, he looked around at all the mountain ranges" (A. R. George, *The Babylonian Gilgamesh Epic*, vol. 1 [Oxford, 2003], p. 234, lines 27–28).

18 Cf. hur-sag sukud-rá ul gùr-ru "high mountain range laden with flowers" (van Dijk *Götterlieder*, p. 57, line 6). For ul, "flower," see P. Steinkeller, "Stars and Stripes in Ancient Mesopotamia: A Note on Two Decorative Elements of Babylonian Doors," *Iranica Antiqua* 37 (2002): 361–65.

hur-sag za-gìn-na-gim mu-mú hur-sag gišnu$_x$(ŠIR) bar$_6$-bar$_6$-ra-gim u$_6$-di-dè ba-gub

He made (the temple) grow like a mountain range of lapis lazuli; he set it up to be admired like a mountain range of white alabaster.

(A xxiv 15–17)

é-e hur-sag-gim an ki-a sag an-šè mi-ni-íb-íl

The temple raised its top like a mountain range between heaven and earth.

(A xxi 23)

é hur-sag-gim im-mú-mú-ne

They make the temple grow like a mountain range.

(A xxi 19)

hur-sag sig$_7$-ga-gim hi-li gùr-a

(The temple is) like a verdant mountain range full of allure.

(A xxx 10–11)

hur-sag nisig-ga u$_6$-e gub-ba kur-kur-ta è-a é kur gal-àm

(The temple) is a green mountain range set up to be admired; it stands out above all the mountains; the temple is a great mountain indeed!

(B i 4–6)

kur gal-gim mu-mú

He made (the temple) grow like a great mountain.

(A xxii 10)

é ^{giš}gigir-ra-bi kur ki-a gub-ba

Its chariot house is a mountain standing on the earth.

(A xxviii 15–16)

é igi-bi kur gal ki ús-sa

The temple whose front is (like) a great mountain set up[19] on the earth.

(A xxvii 11)

---

[19] For ki ... ús, "to compact (earth), to pile up / accumulate (by wind), to pack densely, to set up, to trample," corresponding to Akk. *kabāsu*, see especially IŠ.DU$_6$.TAG$_4$-bi eden-na ki ba-ni-ús-ús "he set up burial mounds on the plain" (H. Steible, *Die altsumerischen Bau- und Weihinschriften*, Freiburger altorientalische Studien 5/1 [Wiesbaden, 1982], Ent. 28 i 30–31); bàd-gal An-

kur a-ta íl-la Nimin^{ki}

Nimin, a mountain rising from among the waters.

(A iii 19)

And note also Keš Hymn 15–17:

hur-sag-da mú-a an-da gú lá-a
É-kur-da mú-a kur-ra sag íl-bi
Abzu-gim gùn-a / ri-a hur-sag-gim sig_7-sig_7-ga

(The temple of Keš) grown together with the mountain ranges, embracing the sky,
grown together with the Ekur, lifting its top among the mountains,
multicolored / springing up like the Abzu, verdant like a mountain range.

My insistence on this terminological distinction is not just philological pedantry. The knowledge of what hur-sag and kur precisely mean is essential for the proper understanding of how the Sumerians visualized and conceptualized the natural landscape and of how they used that mental imagery to speak about and to relate emotionally to man-made structures. As shown in the passages just cited (and amply confirmed by other sources), in Sumerian literature "mountain range" takes precedence over "mountain" as a preferred figurative description of temples. From this, one might infer that the horizontal, curtainlike aspect of a mountain range was particularly pleasing visually to the Sumerians, possibly also influencing their architectural aesthetics and actual building practices. If so, the "ideal" Sumerian temple (by which I mean the entire temple complex) was meant to look more like a massive, cragged wall than an isolated, upward-thrusting structure (of the Tower of Babel type).

On a more basic level, an appreciation of the contrast between hur-sag and kur is absolutely essential for the understanding of temple topography and its (still extremely opaque) technical terminology. One of the most important parts of the temple of Ekur was the structure called Hur-sag-galam-ma, "stepped mountain range."[20] Although it

né ki ús-sa-a-ba "its great walls set up by An" (Gilgameš and Akka 33); kur gal-e $muru_9$(IM.DUGUD)-e ki hé-ús-sa-a-ba "in the great mountain which was set up by the sand storm" (Lugalbanda Epic II 82); ^{giš}lí-id-ga mah-a-ni ki ⌈ba⌉-[an]-ús (Enmerkar and the Lord of Aratta 324), é ùkur-ra sahar ki ús-sa-a-ba (Sheep and Grain 59).

[20] Written Hur-sag-ga-lam-ma in Ur III sources. For the Ur III attestations, see W. Sallaberger, *Der kultische Kalender der Ur III-Zeit* (Berlin, 1993), Teil 1, pp. 99, 112; Teil 2, p. 191. For the later attestations, see Sjöberg *Temple Hymns*, p. 50; George *Temples*, p. 100, nos. 480–81; Hymn to Ekur 9; Ur-Namma B 29.

Although George *Temples*, p. 100, translates galam in this name as "skillfully-built," it is certain that the word involved is galam "stair, step" (and thus not galam = *nakālu* "to be clever," *nikiltu* "skillful work," *naklu* "clever, skillful, ingenious"). This point was demonstrated long ago by Landsberger, in B. Landsberger and H. G. Güterbock, "Das Ideogramm für simmiltu ('Leiter, Treppe')," *AfO* 12 (1937–39): 55, based on the following evidence: (1) lexical entries that equate galam with *simmiltu* "ladder, staircase, stair, step": ^{giš}galam = *si-mil-tu*, "ladder" (Hh. VIIA 107 = MSL 6 92); ^{giš}galam-ma = MIN (= *sim-mil-tú*) *šu-pa-li* "ladder (leading to) cellar/

is thought by some Sumerologists that Hursag-galama is a poetic term for *ziqqurratu*, "temple tower,"[21] this term is hardly a generic one, since it is documented exclusively in connection with Ekur.[22] Moreover, since u$_6$-nir, the standard Sumerian word for "temple tower," does otherwise appear as the description of Ekur,[23] one can be confident that Hursag-galama did not signify Ekur's entire temple tower (which apparently was known as u$_6$-nir), but only a part of it. Speculating along those lines, A. R. George concluded that Hursag-galama was the cella on the top of Ekur's zikkurrat,[24] but, as far as I know, there is no evidence to support this view. In my opinion, the best explanation was provided by Jacobsen,[25] who described Hursag-galama as the stairway leading to Ekur's upper temple, which, according to him, bore the name of *gigunû*. For this interpretation, of particular importance is Ur-Namma B 29–30, where Hursag-galama and a *gigunû* building are mentioned side by side:

> Hur-sag-galam-ma gi-gun$_4$-na ki-tuš kug kur-gal-la-ra u$_{18}$-ru-gim [š]ag$_4$-bi-a
> ki àm-ma-ni-in-ús

basement" (Erimhuš II 275); galam = *sì-mi-il-tu* (M. Krebernik, "Wörter und Sprichwörter: Der zweisprachige Schultext HS 1461," *ZA* 94 [2004]: 240 i 19); galam-galam-ak-a = *su-um-mu-lu* "to provide with stairs, to form a stairway," ^{giš}kun$_4$ = *si-mil-tu* "ladder," galam = 2 *ša nak-ba-s*[*i*] "ladder/staircase with steps," [k]un-sag = ⸢3⸣ *ša gi-gu-né-e* "main staircase of the *gigunû*" (Nabnitu VII 284–87, in MSL 17 113). For *nakbasu*, see ^{giš}kun$_4$-tur = *maš-ḫa-*[*ṭu*] = [*na*]*k-ba-su* (Hg. I 38, in MSL 5 187). For kun-sag, see especially Enki and the World Order 151: kun-sag Eridug^{ki}-ga kar dùg-ga im-mi-íb-galam-e-ne "they put in place the main stairway of Eridu, the sweet quay"; (2) the fact that ga-lam means "step of a ladder" in Pre-Sargonic Lagaš sources: 104 ^{giš}ga-lam ^{giš}kun$_5$ "104 ladder steps" (Genouillac *TSA* 26 iv 1); 100 ^{giš}ga-lam ^{giš}TUR<.ŠÈ> (*DP* 436 iv 4); 40 ^{giš}ga-lam kun$_5$ (*DP* 446 i 6).

Cf. Th. Jacobsen, "Notes on Ekur," *Eretz-Israel* 21 (1990): 44 and n. 23, who translates Hur-sag-galam-ma as "the stairwise rising foothill," deriving it from galam "to rise in steps." Although it would seem that galam "stair" is a separate lexeme from galam = *nakālu*, *nikiltu*, *naklu*, this is by no means certain. Here note especially galam-ak-a = *na-ak-lu* (Nabnitu VII 166, in MSL 17 110), which seems to match galam-galam-ak-a = *su-um-mu-lu* (see above)! Is it possible, then, that the meaning "skillful, ingenious work" derives from "stair, staircase"? In this connection, note also the unclear Šu-ga-lam, the name of the main gate of Eninnu (W. Heimpel, "The Gates of the Eninnu," *JCS* 48 [1996]: 20–21, 25–28; cf. Ur III PNs Šu-ga-lam-zi-mu and Ur-šu-ga-lam-ma in Limet *Anthroponymie*, pp. 531, 561, and É-igi-šu-galam of Ninurta at Nippur [George *Temples*, p. 105, no. 524]). A. Falkenstein, *Die Inschriften Gudeas von Lagaš*, AnOr 30 (Rome, 1966), p. 140, assumed that Šu-ga-lam involves galam "stair" ("die sich erhebende 'Hand' "), but a connection with the other galam cannot be excluded ("skillful hand"?). So also Heimpel, "Gates of Eninnu," p. 21, who suggests the meaning "ingeniously fashioned hand."

21 Sjöberg *Temple Hymns*, p. 50: "A poetical expression for *ziqqurratu* is ḫur-sag-galam-ma 'storied tower'."

22 The only possible exception here is Ur-Namma EF 9, where Ekišnugal is qualified as hur-sag galam-ma "stepped (or here: 'skillfully made'?) mountain range." But this is almost certainly a free simile, rather than a proper name. Cf. E. Flückiger-Hawker, *Urnamma of Ur in Sumerian Literary Tradition*, Orbis Biblicus et Orientalis 166 (Fribourg and Göttingen, 1999), pp. 276–77. See also Gudea Fragments 8+3+5+4 iii′ 6′ (RIME 3/1, p. 102), where hur-sag ga-lam-ma is a simile of Eninnu: hur-sag ga-lam-ma-gim an ki-a bad-bad-e "it is like a stepped mountain range separating heaven from earth."

23 See Sjöberg *Temple Hymns*, p. 26.

24 George *Temples*, p. 100, no. 480 ("cella of Enlil on the ziqqurrat at Nippur").

25 Jacobsen, "Notes on Ekur," pp. 43–44.

> Like a huge whirlwind he (i.e., Ur-Namma) set up within it (i.e., the Ekur) the Hursag-galama (and) a *gigunû* as the holy dwelling of Great Mountain.[26]

Since it is conclusively known that the *gigunû* building customarily stood on the temple's upper level,[27] the most likely interpretation of the above passage is that Hursag-galama was the monumental stairway of Ekur's temple tower (u_6-nir), on top of which a *gigunû* with the cella of Enlil was situated. This solution agrees with the earlier-cited passage from Gudea Cylinder A xxviii 19–20, where the stone stairway of Eninnu is compared to a flowery "mountain range." It finds still further corroboration in the fact that the specialized meaning of Akkadian *ḫuršānu*, a loanword from hur-sag, is "siege ramp."[28]

Another illustration of the need to render hur-sag and kur precisely may be found in the passage describing the creation of Summer and Winter by Enlil in Summer and Winter 12: hur-sag gal-gal-la g̃ìš bí-in-dug_4 kur-re ha-la ba-an-sum. In H. L. J.

---

[26] Cf. Lugalbanda Epic II 82 cited in n. 19 above.

[27] Of particular significance here are the following examples, which identify the *gigunû* with the top of the temple tower or connect the two structures together: u_6-nir gi-gun_4-na mah-a-ni sag-bi an-gim íl-i-dè = U_6.NIR *gi-gu-na-šu ṣi-ra-am re-ši-ša ki-ma ša-me-e ul-la-a-am* "to raise as high as the sky the top of the temple tower, his lofty *gigunû*" (RIME 4, pp. 374–78 Samsuiluna 3:11–12 [Sumerian] = lines 13–16 [Akkadian]; cf. also ibid., lines 68–69 [Sumerian] = lines 83–87 [Akkadian]); u_6-nir gi-gun_4-na mah-a-ni sag-bi an-šè mi-ni-in-ús-sa (Samsuiluna 18, *RLA* 2, p. 183); é-gi-gun_4-na u_6-nir Nibru^{ki} "the *gigunû* building of the temple tower of Nippur" (Streck *Asb.*, p. 353, no. 4); *ša zi-qu-ra-ti gi-gu-[na]-šu re-e-ši-ša e-li ša pa-ni$_7$ ul-li-ma* "to raise higher than before the top of the temple tower, his *gigunû* building" (H. Schaudig, *Die Inschriften Nabonids von Babylon und Kyros' des Großen samt den in ihrem Umfeld entstandenen Tendenzschriften*, AOAT 256 [Münster, 2001], p. 401 Nabonid 2.11 ii 3–4). Further, note that kun-sag "main stairway" is explained lexically as *simmiltu ša gigunê* "main stairway of the *gigunû*" in Nabnitu VII 287 (see n. 20 above). For *gigunû* as the upper temple, see now the extensive discussion by H. Waetzoldt, "Tempelterrassen und Ziqqurrate," in Y. Sefati et al., eds., *"An Experienced Scribe Who Neglects Nothing": Ancient Near Eastern Studies in Honor of Jacob Klein* (Bethesda, Maryland, 2005), pp. 323–39. In the same study (pp. 329–34), Waetzoldt identifies u_6-nir as the "temple tower" but still thinks (following Sjöberg and others) that Hursag-galama is but an alternative term for the temple tower (*Stufenturm*).

[28] See *CAD* Ḫ s.v. *ḫuršānu* A usage b. A similar use of hur-sag to describe an oblong elevation is found in the Ur III field plan *RTC* 416 = *RA* 4 (1897): 13, 15, where hur-sag uniquely designates the quality of land. Since this designation is confined to five contiguous plots along the left edge of the field, with the hur-sag totaling 6.5 bùr or ca. 42.12 ha of land, it is clear that the field in question adjoined a massive ridge or a similar kind of longitudinal elevation. Referring to this text, J. Black, "The Sumerians in Their Landscape," in T. Abusch, ed., *Riches Hidden in Secret Places: Ancient Near Eastern Studies in Memory of Thorkild Jacobsen* (Winona Lake, Indiana, 2002), p. 46, wrote that "the [field] plans use *ḫursag̃* for the 'hilly' parts of the fields, which are difficult to cultivate (so that *ḫursag̃* can be translated as 'hill(s)'), and *dul* for areas of fields which are unproductive because they are tell-ground (that is, ground untillable because it is the site of ruined habitations)." This is largely incorrect, however, since: (1) *RTC* 416 is the only Ur III administrative source where hur-sag is employed in this manner; (2) the hilly sections of fields are consistently described by the term du_6 "hillock, hummock, mound" (see above n. 2).

Vanstiphout's translation this passage appears as: "With the great Hursag-hill he copulated, yes, gave that mountain her share."[29] A similar translation is offered in Oxford's Electronic Text Corpus: "He copulated with the great hills, he gave the mountain its share." But the "mountain" (kur) is of course Enlil! Apart from the grammar (the agentive case -e marking kur), this is confirmed by the fact that Ninhursag is never referred to as "mountain."[30] Accordingly, the passage should be translated: "With the great mountain ranges (= Ninhursag) he copulated, the Mountain allotted (his) share (to her)."

A similar confusion surrounds the meaning of hur-sag in the beginning lines of Sheep and Grain, which are of great interest for the Sumerian concepts of the creation of the universe: hur-sag an ki-bi-da-ke$_4$ An-né dingir-dingir ^{d}A-nun-na im-tu-dè-eš-a-ba. Some scholars translate hur-sag in this passage as "hill." Thus, for example, J. Black stated that "in *The Debate between Sheep and Grain* the landscape location where that creation occurred is described as 'the *hursağ* (hill) of Heaven-and-Earth'—neither a flat plain nor a mountain, but a hilly landscape."[31] Taking into account my earlier conclusions, however, the translation has to be: "After An had created the Anuna gods on the mountain range (between) heaven and earth," where hur-sag denotes a huge mountainous barrier separating the sky from the earth. This, in fact, is the proper (and expected) context of the creation of the gods, which, as other compositions tell us, occurred following the original separation of heaven and earth.[32] Quite possibly it is this cosmic hur-sag, which separates—but also links together—heaven and earth, that the Sumerian temple is meant to represent when it is compared to a "mountain range."

---

[29] W. W. Hallo, ed., *The Context of Scripture*, vol. 1, *Canonical Compositions from the Biblical World* (Leiden, 1997), p. 585.

[30] For Ninhursag = hur-sag, see especially ^{d}Nin-gí[r-su] a zi ^{d}En-l[íl-lá] hur-sag-e tu-da máš-lulim-e ga zi kú-a "Ning[irsu], the true seed of Enl[il], given birth by the mountain ranges, fed with genuine milk by the deer" (Gudea Fragments 8+3+5+4 iv′ 3′–4′), where "mountain ranges" and "deer" are images of Ninhursag. Cf. ù-tu-ud-da hur-sag-gá ù-mu-un-e É-ninnu in CT 15 11 line 3 = VAS 2 2 iii 25. Finally, note the etiology of Ninhursag's name in Lugale 393–94, 408 (Ninurta addressing Ninmah): gu-ru-um gar-ra-gá / gu-ru-un gar^{ga}-ra-mu [hur-s]ag mu-bi hé-em hur-sag-mu-bi hé-em za-e nin-bi hé-me-en = *ina gu-ru-un-ni ša ag-ru-nu* KUR-*ú* [*lu šu*]*m-šú at-ti lu be-let-su* ... munus-zi $^{(d)}$nin hur-sag ki-sikil "let the name of the burial mound I have heaped up be 'mountain range,' and be you its 'mistress'! ... faithful woman, the 'mistress of the mountain range,' the virgin place."

[31] J. Black, "Sumerians in Their Landscape," p. 45. Cf. also B. Alster and H. L. J. Vanstiphout, "Lahar and Ashnan: Presentation and Analysis of a Sumerian Disputation," *Acta Sumerologica (Japan)* 9 (1987): 15, who translate the passage in question: "Upon the Hill of Heaven and Earth / When An had spawned the divine Godlings."

[32] See Sjöberg, "In the Beginning," in Abusch, ed., *Riches Hidden in Secret Places*, pp. 234–36 and nn. 9–12. And note also Gudea Fragments 8+3+5+4 iii′ 6′: hur-sag ga-lam-ma-gim an ki-a bad-bad-e "(Eninnu) is like a stepped mountain range separating heaven from earth."

III. Conclusion

I close with some comments on kur. As has already emerged from the preceding discussion, kur, when referring to mountains, invariably signifies a single mountain or a mountain peak. More broadly, kur means "mountain land" or "highland," hence also "foreign land," because from the Sumerian geographical perspective foreign lands were predominantly mountainous regions. When used with that meaning, kur is the opposite of kalam, which means "native land," roughly identical with the alluvial plain of the Euphrates and the Tigris; kur's meaning of "foreign," also "strange, alien"—and hence "hostile"—is also evident in the word kúr, "strange, hostile, foreign(er), enemy" (Akk. *nakru*), which in all probability is a semantic disjunct of kur.[33]

Not only used in descriptions of foreign lands, kur is also one of the terms designating the netherworld. Such usage is not surprising since, on the one hand, it reflects the understanding of the netherworld as a place that is not only physically distant but also hostile and totally alien. This image of the netherworld is most eloquently expressed by the appellative kur-nu-gi_4, "land of no return." On the other hand, this usage palpably connects the netherworld with the mountains to the west and east of Babylon, where, according to the native beliefs, the gates to the netherworld were situated. Thus, although the Babylonian netherworld was located directly below the Land of the Living and, as a virtual copy of the latter, was devoid of mountainous character, the descent to the netherworld commenced in the western mountains (with the ascent taking place in the eastern mountains), which made a comparison with kur, "mountain," totally logical and convincing. In fact, it is this double meaning of kur—"foreign land" and "mountain"—that makes it such a rich and powerful metaphor of the netherworld.

In making these comments about the Babylonian netherworld, I stress the point that ancient ideas about it—whether Sumerian or Akkadian—consistently and unequivocally placed it beneath the Land of the Living. The recent study by Dina Katz—otherwise an exceptionally fine work—revives the unfortunate notion that the Sumerian concept of the netherworld differed radically from the Akkadian one in that the Sumerians considered the universe to be horizontal, believing that the netherworld was situated "beyond the mountains, outside the land of Sumer."[34] But as I have re-

[33] For this connection, note the use of kur in the sense of "foreigner, enemy," in Steible, *Altsumerischen Bau- und Weihinschriften*, Ent. 28 iii 1 = 29 iii 27: kur-kur e-ma-hun "he hired foreigners / foreign mercenaries." Very similar conclusions about the meaning of kur (and its relationship to kúr) have recently been reached by C. Wilcke, "Altmesopotamische Feindschaften," in M. Brehl and K. Platt, eds., *Feindschaft* (Munich, 2003), pp. 107–8: "Sumerisch ist der Feind lú kúr 'der oder die Andere'. Das darin enhaltene Wort [kur] 'anders', als Verbum 'anders sein' oder 'anders werden', ist homophon, vermutlich sogar identisch mit dem mit einem anderen Schriftzeichen (kur) geschriebenen Wort für 'Berg', 'Bergland', 'Fremdland', dem Gegensatz zu kalam 'eigenes Land', 'Heimatland'. kur ist auch Name der Unterwelt, verdeutlicht in ihrer Bezeichnung als kur nu-gi_4-a 'Fremdland ohne Wiederkehr'."

[34] D. Katz, *The Image of the Netherworld in the Sumerian Sources* (Bethesda, Maryland, 2003), pp. 43–61.

cently discussed elsewhere,[35] there is no evidence whatsoever to support such a view. Although statements about the netherworld are exceedingly rare among third-millennium documentation, enough evidence survives to indicate that the Sumerians also imagined the universe to be vertical.[36] As for the Sumerian sources that, according to Katz, allegedly attest to the horizontal perspective of the netherworld, they are without exception of Old Babylonian and later date and, as such, in no way permit extrapolations about the "pristine" Sumerian cosmological concepts of earlier times. In other words, how is one to distinguish between "Sumerian" and "Akkadian" ideas among this evidence? Moreover, all of the examples Katz cites in this connection are the descriptions of travel to the netherworld in which one "walks" or "rides" to get there. But, since the *route* to the netherworld began in horizontal space, such statements do not contradict the idea that the netherworld *itself* was subterranean. Even more important, one needs to make allowance for at least some imprecision in such matters. It is unrealistic and unfair to expect total exactness from the Sumerians in their statements about the netherworld, since we too are on occasion lax in this respect, as, for example, when we tell someone "to *go* to hell," even though we understand that "to descend" is meant. In fact, equally imprecise in their choice of words were the "vertical" Akkadians, who "went," and did not "descend," "to their fate" (*ana šīmti alāku*).

---

[35] "Of Stars and Men: The Conceptual and Mythological Setup of Babylonian Extispicy," in A. Gianto, ed., *Biblical and Oriental Essays in Memory of William L. Moran*, Biblica et Orientalia 48 (Rome, 2005), p. 19 and n. 18.

[36] See, in particular, Abu Salabikh Temple Hymns, lines 30–32 (= R. D. Biggs, *Inscriptions from Tell Abū Ṣalābīkh*, OIP 99 (Chicago, 1974), p. 47), which identify and physically connect the netherworld with the subterranean Abzu, the abode of Enki: Abzu kur ki-gal men nun an ki ^{d}En-nu-dim$_{x}$(TE)-mud, zà-mì "Abzu, the land of the netherworld, the crown of the Prince of Above and Below—Lord Nudimmud be praised."

REMARKS ON SOME SUMEROGRAMS AND AKKADIAN WORDS

Marten Stol, Vrije Universiteit, Amsterdam

Lexicographers love the study of words, and in their work they follow the order of the alphabet. In this contribution for Bob Biggs I will present some remarks on a few words, following that hallowed order, harking back to the abecedaries of Ugarit and visible in the Sumerogram for the scribe in Ugarit, A.BA, according to Simo Parpola the "ABC-man."

ālum "city"

Royal women are sometimes portrayed with headgear that looks like the crenellated wall of a city. This headdress is called a "Mauerkrone" in German (English "mural crown").[1] The Akkadian word for it is simply *ālum* "city." It is attested in a list of precious gifts, a dowry for the queen, after four pairs of golden *šuqallulu* (eardrops?): "One golden city (URU KÙ.GI), its weight (is) 215."[2] A second reference is found in a Hittite text, an URU-*lum* (= *ālum*) made of silver as a votive offering to the gods.[3] A third reference is found in a *namburbi* text: "That malformed birth, you put a golden city (URU KÙ.GI) on its head."[4] Can we explain the epithet of the goddess Tašmētum *ša dūri* "that of the city wall" as "she who wears the *Mauerkrone*"?[5]

---

[1] See P. Calmeyer, "Mauerkrone," *RLA* 7, pp. 595–96; M. L. Barré, *The God-List in the Treaty between Hannibal and Philip V of Macedonia: A Study in Light of the Ancient Near Eastern Treaty Traditions* (Baltimore and London, 1983), pp. 71–73; J. Börker-Klähn, "Mauerkronenträgerinnen," in H. Waetzoldt and H. Hauptmann, *Assyrien im Wandel der Zeiten* (Heidelberg, 1997), pp. 227–34; S. Dalley, in T. Abusch et al., eds., *Proceedings of the XLVe Rencontre Assyriologique Internationale: Historiography in the Cuneiform World*, vol. 1 (Bethesda, Maryland, 2001), p. 158; and T. Ornan, "The Mural Crown," in S. Parpola and R. M. Whiting, eds., *Sex and Gender in the Ancient Near East: Proceedings of the 47th Rencontre Assyriologique Internationale, Helsinki, July 2–6, 2001*, vol. 2 (Helsinki, 2002), pp. 474–77.

[2] J. Nougayrol, MRS 6, p. 182 RS 16.146+161:4.

[3] H. A. Hoffner, "The 'City of Gold' and the 'City of Silver'," *IEJ* 19 (1969): 178–80.

[4] S. M. Maul *Namburbi*, p. 338:11 (correct his AŠ GUR). The manuscripts are *LKA* 114:11 and *STT* 1 72:95. Note the problematical URU in an Amarna list EA 22 ii 36f.; Moran *Letters*, p. 59, n. 19.

[5] A. Livingstone, SAA 3, p. 35, no. 14:6. This is one of the suggestions in the edition of this hymn made by M. Nissinen, "Love Lyrics of Nabû and Tašmētu: An Assyrian Song of Songs," in M. Dietrich and I. Kottsieper, eds., *"Und Mose schrieb dieses Lied auf": Studien zum Alten Testament und zum Alten Orient: Festschrift für Oswald Loretz zur Vollendung seines 70. Lebensjahres...*, AOAT 250 (Münster, 1998), p. 603, n. 86.

ebīḫu "a big rope"

The dictionaries offer few references and give some more under *ibīḫu*. An update: the verb *ebēḫu* "to fasten, to gird" is associated with the rope *eblu*.[6] A letter from Mari speaks of bringing down by boats (*neqelpûm* Š) ropes (ÉŠ.ḪI.A, *eblū*) that bind together (*e-bi-ḫi*) siege towers and a battering ram.[7]

Sumerian ÉŠ.MAḪ is to be read ebih, as the variant EN.TI-gim for ÉŠ.MAḪ-gim in Inanna and Ebih, line 41, shows. This has been central in the discussion of whether *e-bi-iḫ dan-nu-um* in a royal inscription, a metaphor for a city wall, means the "belt-cord, cincture" (A. R. George), or Mt. Ebih (W. Farber), or both (H. L. J. Vanstiphout).[8] In the Sumerian context it is a big rope made mostly of goat hair.[9] Ropes made of wool or palm fibers (KA×SA) are also known.[10]

This Sumerogram is attested in two Old Babylonian texts from Nippur (éš.maḫ.šè al.sur.ru.e.dè); see below, under SUR.GIBIL, at the end of this article (n. 58).

In Middle Babylonian it is goat hair, 9 minas for normal ropes (*a-na eb-le-e*), 1 mina for big ropes (*a-na e-bi-ḫe-e*).[11] In Neo-Babylonian it belongs to the harness of a horse (silver *a-na eb-bi-ḫi šá* ANŠE.KUR.RA), and we read in a letter, "Do not be negligent about the *ṣi-ip-re-ti ù e-bi-ḫi*.MEŠ that I sent to my brother."[12] In the Neo-Assyrian

[6] W. Mayer, "Waffen und Stricke in einer altbabylonischen Urkunde," *Or.*, n.s., 72 (2003): 374, n. 9: éš = *eblu* "Schnur, Strick, Leine"; éš.maḫ = *ebīḫu* 'großer Strick', also "Seil, Tau." The copy of the lexical text Sultantepe 1951/53+ 106 v 10′ (= Hh. XXII), cited in *CAD* E s.v. *ebīḫu*, has been published by O. R. Gurney, "The Sultantepe Tablets: Addenda and Further Corrigenda," *AfO* 28 (1981–82): 112. What MSL 11 31 A v 11′ proposes is wrong.

[7] ARM 14 45:5. J.-M. Durand interprets *e-bé-ḫi* as an infinitive: ARMT 21, p. 349 ("cordes qui servent à attacher (ensemble) les 'tours' et le bélier"); Durand *Documents de Mari* 1, p. 284, no. 148 ("cordes (qui doivent) servir d'attaches aux tours et au bélier"); Ph. Talon, "Le matériel de siège," *MARI* 5 (1987): 672. *CAD* N/2 s.v. *neqelpû* would agree with Durand but offers a simpler solution by positing a participle: *ēbiḫī* "ropes to fasten the siege towers and battering rams."

[8] The reading ebiḫ has been pointed out by many scholars; Å. W. Sjöberg, "Contributions to the Sumerian Lexicon," *JCS* 21 (1967): 275, n. 3; B. L. Eichler, in T. Abusch, ed., *Lingering over Words: Studies in Near Eastern Literature in Honor of William L. Moran* (Atlanta, 1990), p. 166, n. 20. For discussion, see A. R. George, *NABU* 1991/101; W. Farber, *NABU* 1991/72; and H. L. J. Vanstiphout, *NABU* 1991/103.

[9] MVN 20 64, with comments by F. d'Agostino: "una funa assai spessa (del peso di ca. 1 kg.) per un baldacchino di carro o di nave"; T. Gomi, "Kollationen zu den von T. Fish in *Manchester Cuneiform Studies…*," *Orient* 17 (1981): 42, BM 105417 (length 15 ninda, 90 meters). Its weight is also indicated in Waetzoldt *Textilindustrie*, no. 50 and *ITT* 3 6228.

[10] B. Lafont, *Documents administratifs sumériens provenant du site de Tello et conservés au Musée du Louvre* (Paris, 1985), no. 363:5; G. A. Reisner, *Tempelurkunden aus Telloh* (Berlin, 1901), no. 121 III 14.

[11] Sassmannshausen *Beitr.*, p. 397, no. 343:2–3. Cf. B. I. Faist, *Der Fernhandel des assyrischen Reiches zwischen dem 14. und 11. Jh. v. Chr.* (Münster, 2001), p. 128.

[12] CT 57 186 ii 11 and J. MacGinnis, "Letters from the Neo-Babylonian Ebabbara," *Mesopotamia* 31 (1996): 110, no. 10:13 ("sashes and belts").

Nimrud letter NL 39 we read: "You will quickly bind (*rakāsu*) your rope (*e-bi-iḫ-ka*) on them" (H. W. F. Saggs).[13]

ḫarāsu

The dictionaries first assumed that this word is the infinitive of a verb.[14] Cognate words in Hebrew (*ḥèrès*) and Syriac (*ḥarsā, ḥ*ᵉ*rāsā*) suggest a skin disease, and this must be true in Akkadian too.[15] This word is poorly attested in the texts. It shares the Sumerogram GAN with *garābu*. It is a gloss on GÁN in a school exercise; it produces boils, etc., on the skin; I cite this text in full:[16]

> NE.SI.A, gloss: *bu-bu-uḫ-tum*; GIG.NI, gloss: *sí-ik-ka-tum*; GÁN, gloss: *ḫa-ra-su-um*; UD.DU, gloss: *ṣé-nu-um*.

In a later "group vocabulary" it follows *garābu*, but here both words have unusual Sumerograms: [x].gar.ra = *ga-ra-bu*, [x x] SAR = *ḫa-ra-su*.[17]

In the Diagnostic Handbook we read: "If the appearance of his wound (GIG, *simmu*) is black: *ḫa-ra-su* is its name. If the skin of a man is full of *birdu* marks, his flesh stings him, and redness (*rišûtu*) falls upon him: *ḫa-ra-su* is its name."[18]

Elsewhere, we find the disease together with *ekketu* "itch" and *rišûtu* "redness."[19]

---

[13] Parpola, SAA 1 1 rev. 50 ("you will 'snap your belt' on them"), *CAD* R s.v. *rakāsu* ("soon you will tie your belt on them"), H. W. F. Saggs, *The Nimrud Letters, 1952* (London, 2001), p. 191. W. von Soden, *AHw*., discovered [... *i-n*]*a e-bi-ḫi rak-su-ma* [...] in a Sennacherib inscription; R. C. Thompson, "A Selection from the Cuneiform Historical Texts from Nineveh (1927–32)," *Iraq* 7 (1940): 89, fig. 4 A 9; see now E. Frahm, *Einleitung in die Sanherib-Inschriften* (Vienna, 1997), p. 92 IV 29″.

[14] *CAD* Ḫ s.v. *ḫarāsu* "to itch," partly based on Sumerian sa.kú; s.v. *ḫarāšu* C. *AHw*., p. 323b "kratzen"; p. 1559a "Krätze" (substantive!). MSL 9 82: neither *ḫarāsu* nor *garābu* can be derived from verbs; cognates in Hebrew and Aramaic are given.

[15] In Syriac: literally *asper*; the disease is *scabies* (*palpebrarum*); the sufferer *ḥarsā* is *scabiosus*. F. Köcher, "Ein Text medizinischen Inhalts aus dem neubabylonischen Grab 405," in R. M. Boehmer, ed., *Uruk: Die Gräber*, Ausgrabungen in Uruk-Warka: Endberichte 10 (Mainz, 1995), p. 212a, on 21′ (= Köcher *BAM* 409:18): "eine schwere, bisher noch nicht identifizierte Infektionskrankheit. - Krätze (Skabies) ist nach den nun vorliegenden Symptomsbeschreibungen nicht mehr zu halten." See also M. Stol, review of B. Palmer, *Medicine and the Bible*, in *BiOr* 46 (1989): 130. Job, suffering from a skin disease, scratches his skin with a sherd, Hebrew *ḥèrès* (Job 2:8).

[16] UET 6/2 361, with Å. W. Sjöberg, "Beiträge zum sumerischen Wörterbuch," *Or*., n.s., 39 (1970): 95, on MSL 9 77 ff.: 35–36a ("Aussatz"). Also idem, review of UET VI/2, in *Or*., n.s., 37 (1968): 238, and B. Landsberger, MSL 9 82, line 50.

[17] K.4177+, 2R 44 no. 2 rev. iii 17–18.

[18] Von Weiher *Uruk* 152:20–21, with N. P. Heeßel, *Babylonisch-assyrische Diagnostik*, AOAT 43 (Münster, 2000), p. 354 XXXIII 20–21, dupl. Köcher *BAM* 409:18, 19–20; see Heeßel, *Diagnostik*, p. 368 (at top of page).

[19] CT 19 49 K. 26 rev. 4 = Antagal E IV 4–6, in MSL 17 212.

ḫīṭu "sin"

Tablet I of *Enūma Anu Enlil* has a mysterious apodosis that can be explained by its older version, attested in Emar. We begin with this earlier omen. "Two men will be seized (DIB.BA, *ṣabātu* N) in their sin (*ḫīṭu*); they will not be beaten (*maḫāṣu* N); they will be released (*wašāru* Dt)."[20] "Two men" is striking, and I believe that the "sin" of the two men refers to homosexual activities. The forecasts of omens are often unexpected, and one may assume that normally the two men were not left alone unharmed.[21] The later canonical version indeed reflects a severe judgment. Without an introduction it says: "The king will make the men go out (UD.DU, *waṣû* Š) for burning (*ana qalê*), and those men who have been summoned (*zakāru*) without being guilty (*ina la annišunu*) will be saved (KAR, *eṭēru* N)."[22] Death by being burnt alive (*qalû*; see *CAD* Q s.v. *qalû* mng. 2c) is a severe punishment meant for people who endanger society by, for example, breaking a taboo.[23]

Does the omen in the later canonical series still refer to homosexual men, or did the scribes no longer understand its original meaning? I think that the omen was still aware of its original intent; the "being burnt alive" is suggestive. It wished to reinterpret the unexpected release of the men in the older omen by stating that this happens to only the "innocent" men.

ḫunzû

In the first tablet of *Šumma ālu* the ominous significance of various types of weak or handicapped people seen in the city is given: "the lame" (*pessû*), "the idiots" (*lillû*), "the soft" (*rabbu*), "the wise men." They are followed by people with warts and pocks, the deaf, and the blind.[24] Why do we encounter here "wise men"? The text offers KÙ.ZU.MEŠ.[25] I would suggest that this is a writing for *ḫuzzû* "lame, limping" (*CAD* Ḫ),

---

[20] Arnaud *Emar* 6/4, p. 251, no. 650:10; copies: idem, *Emar* 6/1, p. 349, and idem, *Emar* 6/2, p. 478.

[21] Note the positive prophecies regarding homosexual behavior in CT 39 44:13, 32–33; 34 is negative. See V. Haas, *Babylonischer Liebesgarten: Erotik und Sexualität im Alten Orient* (Munich, 1999), p. 21. He writes: "In Babylonien galt Homosexualität nicht als strafwürdiges Vergehen. Nach den bereits zitierten Beischlafomina verheißt ein solcher Umgang sogar Glück und Erfolg" (p. 116). This interpretation of the omen predictions—shared by others—is naive. On homosexuality, see W. G. Lambert, in V. Haas, ed., *Außenseiter und Randgruppen: Beiträge zu einer Sozialgeschichte des Alten Orients* (Konstanz, 1992), pp. 145 ff.

[22] Virolleaud, *ACh Sîn* I 17; L. Verderame, *Le tavole I–VI della serie astrologica* Enūma Anu Enlil (Rome, 2002), pp. 9, 26 (score of manuscripts) § 5, 203 (quoted in commentary).

[23] M. San Nicolò, "Feuertod," in *RLA* 3/1, p. 59; M. Stol, *Epilepsy in Babylonia* (Groningen, 1993), p. 15 (a patient suffering from the epilepsy "Spawn of Šulpaea" is to be burned); F. Joannès, "Une chronique judiciaire d'époque hellénistique et le châtiment des sacrilèges à Babylone," *Assyriologica et Semitica: Festschrift für Joachim Oelsner* (Münster, 2000), pp. 206–9 ("Bûchers et sacrilèges").

[24] Freedman *Alu*, p. 32, Tablet I 85–89.

[25] CT 38 4:70 (copy); Freedman *Alu*, p. 32, line 90; manuscripts: ibid., p. 52:90.

ḫunzû "etwa lahm"? (W. von Soden, *AHw.*). This word has been hitherto attested only as a personal name. One commentary now equates a lame person, LÚ BA.AN.ZU, with *ḫu-zu-*[*u*].[26] In the Seleucid personal name KU-*zu-u* the sign KU stands for *ḫun*, and here again we have the name Ḫunzû.[27]

The Sumerogram KÙ.ZU stands for *emqu* "wise," according to the most modern sign list. On closer inspection, it is attested as such only in bilingual texts. In our passage, however, it must be a playful elaboration on KU-*zu-u*.

V. Haas has commented on our omen saying, "Mir nicht ganz verständlich ist die Nennung der Weisen (*emqūtu* [line] 70) an dieser Stelle; ist etwa an eine den antiken Wanderphilosophen vergleichbaren Gruppe zu denken?"[28]

maklalu (a garment)

A. R. Millard discovered the Akkadian word *dannu* "vessel" in corrupted form in the list of merchandise of Tyre given by the prophet Ezekiel by reading "the vessels of wine from Izalla" in Ezek. 27:19.[29] Another Babylonian item in the list is easier to identify, *maklūl* (Ezek. 27:24; there the plural is given). The standard Hebrew dictionary translates it "Prachtgewand (unbestimmter Art)" and is not aware of the Akkadian word *maklalu*.[30] The Practical Vocabulary Assur gives precisely this variant, TÚG *ma-ak-lul*. The Hebrew word settles the question of the quality of the *k* or *q* in the middle of the Akkadian word: *k* is best.

The Akkadian garment is listed among the precious gifts given by the royal house of Egypt to that of the Hittites. The Akkadian letters found in Ḫattuša qualify them as "royal clothing" (*lubulti* LUGAL), "good" (SIG_5) and "dyed" (*ṣapû*). Egyptian texts

[26] *STT* 403:2, commenting on Labat *TDP*, p. 4 I 38. See B. Alster, "Crippled or Dwarf," in M. Dietrich and O. Loretz, eds., *Vom Alten Orient zum Alten Testament: Festschrift für Wolfram Freiherrn von Soden zum 85. Geburtstag am 19. Juni 1993* (Münster, 1995), pp. 1–4. The reference for the verb *ḫuzzû* in Kraus *Texte* (*CAD* Ḫ s.v.) is now Böck *Morphoskopie*, p. 260:38, with n. 787.

[27] W. G. Lambert, "Ancestors, Authors, and Canonicity," *JCS* 11 (1957): 4, n. 13; *CAD* K s.v. ***kuzû*.

[28] Haas, *Außenseiter und Randgruppen*, p. 44; mentioned by R. Rollinger in his article "Altorientalische Motivik in der frühgriechischen Literatur am Beispiel der homerischen Epen: Elemente des Kampfes in der Ilias und in der altorientalischen Literatur (nebst Überlegungen zur Präsenz altorientalischer Wanderpriester im früharchäischen Griechenland)," in C. Ulf, ed., *Wege zur Genese griechischer Identität: Die Bedeutung der früharchäischen Zeit* (Berlin, 1996), pp. 156–210 (p. 207, n. 367). News travels fast!

[29] A. R. Millard, "Ezekiel XXVII:19: The Wine Trade of Damascus," *JSS* 7 (1962): 201–3. See H. R. Cohen, *Biblical Hapax Legomena in the Light of Akkadian and Ugaritic* (Missoula, Montana, 1978), pp. 135 f. For wine from A/Izalla, see K. Radner, *Ein neuassyrisches Privatarchiv der Tempelgoldschmiede von Assur*, Studien zu den Assur-Texten 1 (Saarbrücken, 1999), p. 158; *CAD* M/1 s.v. *madnanu* A, discussion.

[30] L. Koehler and W. Baumgartner, *Hebräisches und aramäisches Lexikon zum Alten Testament*, Lieferung 2 (Leiden, 1974), p. 549. See *CAD* M/1 s.v. *maklalu* (or *maqlalu*) (a garment).

offer instead of "royal clothing" the qualification "made of byssos" (*sšr-nsw*).[31] A letter from Egypt found in Ugarit indicates that the *ma-ak-la-lu* are made of linen ([GAD]A); they are "thin" (SIG.MEŠ) and "good" (SIG_5.MEŠ).[32]

A Middle Babylonian list of garments mentions [TÚG *ma-a*]*k-la-lu* BABBAR (?) *ta-kil-ta up-pu-us*. It is made of colored wool (*takiltu*).[33] The word TÚG *ma-ak-lu-lu* is attested in a Middle Assyrian list at the end of which we read "good clothing" (*lubultu da'iqtu*, line 12).[34]

Other Assyrian texts speak of *muk-lal*, *mu-uk-lal*, *muk-lul*, and *ma-ak-lil* garments.[35]

masdaru B "knife"

According to the dictionaries, this word is attested only in the lexical tradition. We now have references in context. In a fragmentary line of an incantation on the treatment of wounds: "[...] of healing, your scalpel (*karzillu*), your *masdaru* (written *mas-dàra*)"; "your" is feminine and refers to the goddess of medicine Gula.[36] In the hymn to Gula she says: "I am carrying the knife of healing (*našāku mas-da-ru ša šalāmu*)"[37] and "May the *mas-da-ra* not come near to you."[38] In the Tukulti-Ninurta Epic *mal-ṭa-rat a-su-ti né-peš na-aṣ-m*[*a-da-te* ...] is commonly translated as "medical texts, procedure for bandaging."[39] I admit that "scalpels of healing" is somewhat less probable.

[31] E. Edel, "GAD.TÚG *maklalu* gleich *jdg*, etwa "Mantel, Umhang," in *Sedat Alpa'a Armağan: Festschrift für Sedat Alp* (Ankara, 1992), pp. 127–35. Cf. G. Beckman, *Hittite Diplomatic Texts*, 2d ed. (Atlanta, 1999), p. 130, no. 22C § 6, "Two dyed cloaks of byssus, two dyed tunics of byssus" (KBo 28 44:15–16).

[32] S. Lackenbacher, in M. Yon and D. Arnaud, eds., *Études ougaritiques*, vol. 1, *Travaux (1985–1995)* (Paris, 2001), p. 240 RS 88.2158:39 ("mantaux de bon fil fin").

[33] PBS 2/2 135 i 23, as restored by Aro, *Kleidertexte*, pp. 27, 34; *AHw*., p. 1425 s.v. *uppusu*: etwa "(mit Wolle) säumen"?

[34] *MARV* 1 (= VAS 19) no. 24:7. I thank W. Farber for the following observation: "I think that the amounts and types of wool in this list might be materials and prefabricated parts for the 'good clothing', since *maklalu* is also part of a garment in *KAV* 99:16 and possibly in VAS 19 24:3" (personal communication). *KAV* 99:16, cited in *CAD*; see S. Jacob, *Mittelassyrische Verwaltung und Sozialstruktur: Untersuchungen* (Leiden, 2003), p. 427. For Neo-Assyrian, see 1 TÚG *muk-lul* GIBIL, in Radner, *Ein neuassyrisches Privatarchiv*, no. 39, with a copy in J. Jakob-Rost, K. Radner, and V. Donbaz, *Neuassyrische Rechtsurkunden II* (Saarbrücken, 2000), no. 39:1; this text is VAT 8659, quoted by K. Deller, in "Drei wiederentdeckte neuassyrische Rechtsurkunden aus Aššur," *Bagh. Mitt.* 15 (1984): 239 ff.

[35] Deller, "Drei wiederentdeckte neuassyrische Rechtsurkunden," p. 239; J. MacGinnis, "A Neo-Assyrian Text Describing a Royal Funeral," *SAA Bulletin* 1 (1987): 6, commenting on K.7856+ ii 11; Postgate *Palace Archive*, no. 152 152:2, 6.

[36] Wiseman and Black *Literary Texts*, 116 rev. 21, with M. J. Geller, "Fragments of Magic, Medicine, and Mythology from Nimrud," *BSOAS* 63 (2000): 337.

[37] W. G. Lambert, "The Gula Hymn of Bulluṭsa-rabi," *Or.*, n.s., 36 (1967): 120 82.

[38] K.6057+ ii 23, courtesy M. J. Geller; line 2 mentions the cautery, *nakmû*. For that word, see M. Stol, review of H. Avalos, *Illness and Health Care in the Ancient Near East* (Atlanta, 1995), in *BiOr* 54 (1997): 409.

[39] W. G. Lambert, *AfO* 18 (1957–58): 44 B rev. 8; I repeat here B. R. Foster, *Before the Muses: An Anthology of Akkadian Literature*, vol. 1 (Bethesda, Maryland, 1996), p. 228.

nannû "order, command"

According to the *CAD*, this word is attested only in En. el. VI 132 and in two other texts, one of them an Old Babylonian literary text. It refers to the word of a god. It is possible to see in this word an artificial loan from a Sumerian verbal form, attested in a Pre-Sargonic letter(?), na-na-e-a, meaning: "What NN says to him." In the address formulas in other letters, na-e-a "What NN says," which is less precise, is also known. In later Sumerian letters it is normally na-(ab-)bé-a.[40] I admit that the Pre-Sargonic "letter" is in fact a text of obscure contents, but E. Sollberger has pointed out that the address formula e-na-dug_4 follows some lines later.[41]

There is another argument in favor of my proposition. A similar loan from Sumerian, ù-na-dug_4 "say to him," is *unnedukkum* "letter" in Southern Old Babylonian.[42] This Sumerian word again is part of the standard address in Sumerian letters.

šinnu "ivory"

A dowry in Ugarit lists "three beds, overlaid with ivory (ZÚ.GUL GAR.RA), together with their footstools (*kilzappu*)."[43] The Sumerogram for ivory, ZÚ.GUL, is found here and in a list from Amarna.[44] Earlier in Assyriology the sign GUL was taken to be sún, *rīmtu* "wild cow." Thus ivory was understood as the tooth of an exotic animal by J. Nougayrol, H.-P. Adler, and W. von Soden (*AHw.*). The discussion section in *CAD* R s.v. *rīmtu* rejects this interpretation and says, "read ZÚ.GUL." I prefer this proposal.

I explain the element GUL as "worked" (i.e., "chiseled" or "carved"); the verb is *naqāru* in Akkadian. In most cases, the verb indicates work on stone, for example, "to recondition millstones" (M. Civil). In a year-name and an inscription of Abi-sare, na_4.nì.gul.da means "des pierres à tailler" (J.-M. Durand).[45] The verb gul is an element in the words bur.gul, *parkullu* "seal-cutter"; gul.me, *qulmû* (an ax) (used for hewing stone); nì.gul, *akkullu* (a hammerlike tool) (*CAD*). The lexical tradition (*naqāru ša erî* in Antagal III 199) and the Sumerian myth Inanna and Enki (urudu.gul.la) show that gul also refers to working copper. H. Waetzoldt understands it as follows: "gul bei

---

[40] Sollberger *Correspondence*, pp. 2f. (6.1.2, example a.2). For this address formula, see Kienast-Volk *SAB*, pp. 4ff.

[41] "Burrows UET II Supplement 25," in A. Alberti and F. Pomponio, *Pre-Sargonic and Sargonic Texts from Ur Edited in UET 2, Supplement*, Studia Pohl, Series Maior 13 (Rome, 1986), p. 73, no. 25 rev. i 8. See also Sollberger *Correspondence*, p. 3.

[42] M. Yoshikawa, "Four Sumerian Letter-Orders in Japanese Collections," *Acta Sumerologica (Japan)* 6 (1984): 122–23 (grammatical analysis). Note the Sumerian word ù-na-a-da in Old Babylonian Uruk; see D. Charpin, *NABU* 1998/71.

[43] J. Nougayrol, MRS 6, p. 184 RS 16.146+161:14.

[44] H.-P. Adler, *Das Akkadische des Königs Tušratta von Mitanni* (Kevelaer and Neukirchen-Vluyn, 1976), p. 357.

[45] M. Civil, "Daily Chores in Nippur," *JCS* 32 (1980): 232 with n. 5; J.-M. Durand, "Notes sur l'histoire de Larsa (I)," *RA* 71 (1977): 23, n. 2; cf. Stol *On Trees*, p. 90.

Metall-, Holz- und Steingegenständen heißt wohl '(roh) bearbeiten'."[46] I would add "bei Elfenbeingegenständen."

There is another zú.gul = *šinnu ḫasirtu* "chipped tooth."[47]

At the end of this discussion, I confess that I still like zú.sún "tooth of a wild cow." Here the hippopotamus could be meant. And in the case of GUL, do we not expect zú.gul.la?

šum ili šūlû

In one Middle Babylonian and in several Neo-Babylonian and Neo-Assyrian texts we find this expression for "to swear an oath." B. Landsberger established this meaning, literally, according to him, "den Namen Gottes (zum Himmel) emporsteigen lassen," and in this graphic rendering he was quickly followed by the standard work San Nicolò-Ungnad *NRV*, "Berichtigungen und Nachträge" and its glossary.[48] The expression must have been frozen because in cases where the verbal form is followed by a suffix, we have to translate "to make (him) swear."[49]

Everybody who is familiar with the Ten Commandments will now be reminded of the third commandment, the prohibition against using God's name in vain; in Hebrew, "to raise (*nāśā'*) the name of the Lord in vain" (*šāw'*) (Exod. 20:7). Landsberger saw this too and said, "Vgl. vielleicht hebr. נשׂא שׁם יהוה [*nś' šm jhwh*]":[50] "to raise" the name of God in Hebrew, "to make go up" in Akkadian. The Hebrew dictionaries do not point out this similarity.

The standard Hebrew dictionary assumes that the expression refers to swearing an oath.[51] This is in line with Jewish tradition (Targum and later). Oblique references to the Ten Commandments in the Bible itself explicitly speak of an oath (Lev. 19:12, Jer. 7:9).

The modern commentaries do not say much and even seem to avoid the interpretation "to swear an oath."[52] These remarks are useful in a modern commentary: "Es soll eine von ihrer Bedeutung durchdrungene feierliche Handlung sein, wie *das Erheben der Hand* zum Schwur. Daher das Wort *nś'* = den Namen mit gehobener Stimme aus-

---

[46] H. Waetzoldt, remarks on G. Farber-Flügge, *Der Mythos "Inanna und Enki" unter besonderer Berücksichtigung der Liste der me*, Studia Pohl 10 (Rome, 1973), p. 60, pl. 2 vi 44 (see his review in *BiOr* 32 [1975]: 383a).

[47] Kagal 246 Section 6:7; zú.gul.gul = *ḫussuru* follows.

[48] B. Landsberger, review of San-Nicolò-Ungnad *NRV*, in *ZA* 39 (1930): 289. See *CAD* E s.v. *elû* mng. 12; Š/3 s.v. *šumu* mng. 1c–1′; T. Abusch, *Babylonian Witchcraft Literature: Case Studies* (Atlanta, 1987), p. 103; another meaning is "to summon to court."

[49] M. P. Streck, review of Cole *Nippur* in *ZA* 89 (1999): 290, no. 2:8. Note the translation "swear to us/them" and the aberrant explanation "to elevate by the life (*nīšu*) of god" in *ABL* 502 by Fuchs and Parpola, in SAA 15 no. 162 rev. 3, 8, with note. *CAD* Š/3 s.v. *šumu* translates rev. 8: "I will make them take an oath."

[50] Landsberger, review of San-Nicolò-Ungnad *NRV*, p. 289, n. 2.

[51] Koehler and Baumgartner, *Hebräisches und aramäisches Lexikon*, Lieferung 3 (1983), p. 685a; Lieferung 4 (1990), p. 1324b, mentioning A. Jepsen, "Beiträge zur Auslegung und Geschichte des Dekalogs," *ZAW* 79 (1967): 291 f. (schwören).

[52] No mention of the oath in the *Theologisches Wörterbuch des Alten Testaments*, vol. 5 (1986), p. 641, vol. 8 (1995), pp. 170 f.

sprechen." One is still at a loss: should one raise the hand or the voice? But we can appreciate the two *Denkanstöße*.[53]

turu'u

This is attested only once: *AHw*., p. 1373 s.v.: "ein Ruf? jB. (in das kranke Ohr) *tu-ru-'a-a* [*iš*]*assi* (ruft er) AMT 36, 1, 8."

The passage has been recopied as Köcher *BAM* 503 iii 8. I would suggest that this word is identical with Hebrew *t*ᵉ*rūʿāh* "battle cry." A book has been written on it.[54]

SUR.GIBIL

This Sumerogram haunted Assyriology for a long time until I. F. Finkel was able to reconstruct its context: Esagil-kīn-apli's declaration on his editorial work of scattered diagnostic and physiognomic texts. They had "from old time not received an [authorised] edition" (*ultu ulla* SUR.G[IBIL] *la ṣabtu*), Finkel translates,[55] following W. G. Lambert. This word, here clearly a Sumerogram, is not mentioned in R. Borger's new *Mesopotamisches Zeichenlexikon*.[56] Let me attempt an explanation.

The Sumerian verb sur has the meaning "to spin." A telling passage is found in the bilingual series Sa.gig.ga: "Let a menopausal woman (*paristu*) spin (sur, *ṭamû*) with the right hand and twine (tab, *eṣēpu*) with the left hand."[57] It is also said of twisting a rope.[58] The word sur also has the general meaning "to weave."[59]

---

[53] Benno Jacob, *Das Buch Exodus* (Stuttgart, 1997), p. 566.

[54] Paul Humbert, *La 'terouʿa': analyse d'un rite biblique* (Neuchâtel, 1946).

[55] I. L. Finkel, "Adad-apla-iddina, Esagil-kin-apli, and the Series SA.GIG," in *Sachs Mem. Vol*., pp. 148 f., B obv. 18′; Lambert, "Ancestors, Authors, and Canonicity," pp. 6b, 13 f.

[56] R. Borger, *Mesopotamisches Zeichenlexikon*, AOAT 305 (Münster, 2004).

[57] Von Weiher *Uruk* 2 ii:75 f. The duplicate CT 17 20:75 offers kešda "to knot" instead of sur. But kešda, *kaṣāru*, is the next activity in lines 77 f.: "Knot seven knots, two times."

[58] "To twist a rope" (éš.maḫ, *ebēḫu*): Heimpel *Tierbilder*, p. 506 (for éš.maḫ.gim al.sur.ra, *kīma ibīḫi i-za-ár*, CT 17 25:24, dupl. Hunger *Uruk* 171:2 [R. Borger]; see now MSL 9 23); "Laḫar and Ašnan," line 100, in B. Alster and H. L. J. Vanstiphout, *Acta Sumerologica (Japan)* 9 (1987): 20. "A leash of spun wool" (éš.síg. sur.ra): Gordon *Sumerian Proverbs* 5.56, with B. Alster, "The Proverbs of Ancient Sumer: Updates," *NABU* 1999/88, C. "Twister of a whip" (lú.kuš.usàn.sur): BE 6/2 55:3. The lú.éš/túg. KA.sur.ra, *mupattilum*, is a "yarn twister" (*CAD* M/2). A problem is PBS 8/2 121:6, 123:3 (éš. maḫ.šè al.sur.ru.e.dè) (Old Babylonian); with T. Richter, *Untersuchungen zu den lokalen Panthea Süd- und Mittelbabyloniens in altbabylonischer Zeit*, AOAT 257 (Münster, 1999), p. 63, and ibid., 2d ed. (Münster, 2004), p. 74. The "rope" is meant for the god Anzû and one could think that túg.maḫ "splendid garment" is better (Richter). I prefer "rope" because large quantities of goat hair are used.

[59] B. L. Eichler, in T. Abusch, J. Huehnergard, and P. Steinkeller, *Lingering over Words: Studies in Ancient Near Eastern Literature in Honor of William L. Moran* (Atlanta, 1990), pp. 166–69. To Eichler the verb basically indicates a wringing or twirling motion. I will not examine the activity sur or sir_5 (NU) with the spindle; see Šurpu V/VI 150 and "Two Women" B 69; see *PSD* B, p. 64 and K. Volk, "Methoden altmesopotamischer Erziehung nach Quellen der altbabylonischen Zeit," *Saeculum* 47 (1996): 191, n. 77.

For us it is interesting that the Sumerian Kesh Hymn says that words are "spun like a net (sa)" (line 11). Its first editor, G. B. Gragg, remarked: "the verb seems to refer to the artful construction of Enlil's praise by comparing it to the intricate weaving of a net." Th. Jacobsen saw the same imagery in the preceding line (line 10); "Nidaba was its spinner (NU) of a single statement (NU inim.dili.bi.im)," and he translated the following line (line 12) as "it was written on its tablet and was being laid to hand." He concluded: "The recording of an oral poem or formal statement in writing seems thus here to imply (1) establishing of a single authoritative text (2) editing for poetic form — or perhaps even rendering it in poetic form — and (3) writing it down for ready reference."[60]

It now becomes obvious that SUR.GIBIL can mean "new text," whereby we have to understand the word "text" in its original meaning: Latin *textus* "woven," "textile." Lambert's translation "(authorised) edition" seems to reflect the same line of thought.[61]

[60] G. B. Gragg, "The Keš Temple Hymn," in Sjöberg *Temple Hymns*, p. 178b; Th. Jacobsen, "Oral to Written," in *Studies Diakonoff*, pp. 131 f.

[61] J. V. Kinnier Wilson, "Two Medical Texts from Nimrud," *Iraq* 18 (1956): 138, followed by others, suggested that SUR.GIBIL is equivalent to *za-ra-a* in an editorial remark on *Uruanna*, Hunger *Kolophone*, no. 321:3. For this obscure word attested in colophons, see *CAD* Z s.v. *zarû* B (mng. unkn.), *AHw*., p. 1514b *z/ṣarâ* "etwa 'in Abschnitte gegliedert,' ... Wz. SUR.N[E]." See further Heeßel, *Diagnostik*, p. 106, with M. J. Geller, "West Meets East: Early Greek and Babylonian Diagnosis," *AfO* 48–49 (2001–2002): 69b; for more references in context, see *Sachs Mem. Vol*., p. 11, no. 9a rev. 5 ([...] SUR.GIBIL *ṣab-tu*), and 14 no. 9d obv. 17.

KASR TEXTS: EXCAVATED—BUT NOT IN BERLIN*

Matthew W. Stolper, The University of Chicago

Time and events were not kind to the Babylonian legal documents that recorded acquisitions and activities of the Achaemenid governor Bēlšunu, son of Bēl-uṣuršu, and of his forebears, his son, his servants, and his associates. The texts had belonged to an archive, in the loose Assyriological sense of the word, and the archive had once been deposited near one of the centers of power of the Achaemenid Empire, the palaces on the Kasr mound of Babylon. But at some time in or after the early fourth century B.C. a severe fire damaged the tablets terribly, leaving many of them partially vitrified, some partially or wholly melted, and many shattered. Various later agencies, including burials in the Parthian period and brick quarries in the modern era, broke still more of the tablets and scattered the pieces widely over the Kasr and even to other mounds at Babylon. Visitors and collectors took some of them away, especially after Western

* My work on these and other late Achaemenid Babylonian texts was supported by a summer stipend from the National Endowment for the Humanities, a grant from the American Council of Learned Societies, and by a subsequent Fellowship from the National Endowment for the Humanities.

I am indebted to W. W. Hallo, Ulla Kasten, P.-A. Beaulieu, and F. Joannès for help with the texts in the Yale Collections; to Erle V. Leichty and Pamela Gerardi for help with the text in the Free Library of Philadelphia; to Cornelia Wunsch and Miguel Civil for help with the texts at Montserrat; to C. B. F. Walker, Julian Reade, and Irving Finkel for help with the Kasr texts from various sources in the British Museum; to John G. Pedley, Elaine Gazda, Pam Reister, and Robin Meador-Woodruff for help with texts in the Kelsey Museum, Ann Arbor; and to Liane Rost, Joachim Marzahn, Evelyn Klengel-Brandt, Beate Salje, and Olof Pedersén for help with texts in the Vorderasiatisches Museum, Berlin.

Babylon excavation numbers, cited with the prefix "Bab" (rather than "BE"), and Babylon photograph numbers are drawn from O. Pedersén, *Archive und Bibliotheken in Babylon: Die Tontafeln der Grabung Robert Koldeweys 1899–1917*, Ausgrabungen der Deutschen Orient-Gesellschaft 25 (Saarbrücken, 2005). Texts with known excavation numbers are arranged in order of those "Bab" numbers. Unless otherwise noted, comparanda cited in comments to the texts are from texts of the Kasr group, whether from the excavated N6 group or from other sources.

Dates are cited in this form: day (in arabic numerals) / month (in roman numerals) / regnal year (in arabic numerals) king's name. Conversions from Babylonian dates to Julian dates follow Richard A. Parker and Waldo H. Dubberstein, *Babylonian Chronology 626 B.C.–A.D. 75*, Brown University Studies 19 (Providence, Rhode Island, 1956). Personal names are sometimes cited in this form: name/patronym(//ancestor's name or family name).

The editions of these twenty-three texts and citations of other Kasr texts reflect repeated collations. Errors of substance, judgment, expression, and citation are my own responsibility.

attention to the remains of Mesopotamian antiquity grew in the late eighteenth century. The hundreds of tablets and fragments that the archaeologists of the Deutsche Orient-Gesellschaft (DOG) eventually found on the Kasr, beginning in the spring of 1913, among layers of trash disturbed by pits, were the sorry remains of this archive. But even the DOG's painstaking work of collecting and recording these remains did not put an end to the archive's travails, for the remains were disturbed and scattered yet again by the aftermath of World War I.[1]

Most of the DOG team left for the war soon after it broke out in August 1914, and some of them were already dead or wounded by the time Robert Koldewey recovered the last of the Kasr fragments in 1915.[2] Koldewey and Gottfried Buddensieg first withdrew ahead of the British advance to the Diyala, then returned to work at Babylon after the British had been besieged and defeated at Kut al-Amara by von der Goltz and the Ottoman army. By the time Koldewey and Buddensieg withdrew again to Aleppo ahead of the final British advance on Baghdad in March 1917, some 1,022 pieces from the Kasr N6 group had been recorded, and 957 of them had been photographed. They were put in storage with the other excavated collections in the sealed excavation house.[3]

In 1926, after negotiating a division of the excavated material under the terms of the new antiquities law, Walter Andrae came to Babylon with Julius Jordan to pack finds for shipment to the new Pergamon Museum in Berlin. They were dismayed by the condition of the stores. When Koldewey and Buddensieg had left the site in 1915, the household goods had been pillaged, but the stores of excavated material were untouched. Since 1917, however, the finds had also been raided and picked over. When the Germans and Mr. Cooke, the Honorary Director of Antiquities after Gertrude Bell's death, broke open the sealed door, they saw finds partially unpacked, scattered, and water-damaged, eliciting the feelings of archaeologists who had opened a tomb that seemed intact, only to find it already violated and plundered.[4]

---

[1] I have referred to these texts loosely as the Kasr texts or the Kasr Archive in various publications (cited below). Olof Pedersén first labeled the group "Babylon 8" (*Archives and Libraries in the Ancient Near East 1500–300 B.C.* [Bethesda, Maryland, 1998], p. 184) and now labels it more precisely "N6: Archiv des Statthalters Bēlšunu," to distinguish it from other texts that were also excavated on the Kasr (*Archive und Bibliotheken in Babylon*, pp. 144–84). I am indebted to Pedersén for making this comprehensive study of the excavation records, photographs, texts, and fragments in Berlin and elsewhere available to me for citation in advance of publication. The counts and descriptions of Kasr N6 texts given here rely primarily on Pedersén's work.

[2] See, for example, Anonymous, "Vereinsnachrichten," *MDOG* 55 (December 1914): 2–3.

[3] For an account of the site, the excavation house, and the excavators in spring 1916, see S. Hedin, *Bagdad, Babylon, Ninive* (Leipzig, 1918), pp. 211–83. W. Andrae, in *Babylon, die versunkene Weltstadt und ihr Ausgräber, Robert Koldewey* (Berlin, 1952), pp. 238 f., gives the impression that Buddensieg was drafted and captured after he went to Aleppo with Koldewey in 1915 and that Koldewey returned to Babylon alone, but Hedin's account and photographs show Buddensieg at the site in 1916, still in civilian dress.

[4] W. Andrae, "Reise nach Babylon zur Teilung der Babylon-Funde," *MDOG* 65 (April 1927): 12; *Lebenserinnerungen eines Ausgräbers* (Berlin, 1961), pp. 264 f. See the brief summary and chronology by E. Klengel-Brandt, "Babylon und das Vorderasiatische Museum," in J. M. Renger, ed., *Babylon: Focus mesopotamischer Geschichte,*

Writing specifically to rebut their expressions of dismay, H. R. Hall viewed the situation with a victor's condescending tolerance for disorder, expressed in terms that seem sad and ludicrous under today's postwar conditions. He had occupied rooms in the Babylon excavation house in January 1919, he said, and found the place "in better condition than might have been expected. It is not always that during such *interregna* in war-time, when the sense of *meum* and *tuum* is blunted, so little untoward happens." In 1923, he said, an examination of the house by Gertrude Bell and J. M. Wilson, and another by Sidney Smith, confirmed the orderly condition of the museum stores. Repeating that "it is an extraordinary thing that in lawless southern ʿIraq in war-time the contents of the 'Museum' [of the German excavation house] were preserved, more or less, intact from the day of Koldewey's flight to that of the first walling-up," he admitted that while the house was still open "some of the stupider and more ignorant type of British or Indian soldier ... may have pocketed an occasional small 'souvenir' from its shelves," but he rejected the idea of any major loss to looting.[5]

The Babylon finds that reached Berlin in 1927, at any rate, included only 701 pieces from the Kasr N6 archive. More than 300 went somewhere else. Only a few have been relocated for study.

Seventeen Kasr N6 pieces that appear on the excavation photos have been identified in other collections: eleven in the Yale Babylonian Collection, three in the collection of the Kelsey Museum of Ancient and Medieval Archaeology at the University of Michigan, and one each in collections at the Free Library of Philadelphia, the British Museum, and the Museu Biblíc of the monastery of Montserrat, Spain. The certainty that these pieces came from the DOG excavation creates a strong presumption that other pieces in the same collections that can be assigned to the Kasr group on the basis of their appearance and contents, if they do not have a known pre-World War I provenance, also stem from the DOG excavations, even though they cannot be identified among the excavation photographs: two more texts in the Yale Babylonian Collection, one in the Nies Babylonian Collection at Yale, one in the collection of the Kelsey Museum, and two in the Montserrat collection.

I present here terse editions of these twenty-three scattered texts and fragments. Hundreds of other excavated Kasr N6 texts remain unaccounted for, and it is likely that some will be recognized in other private and public collections.

These texts are, of course, a sample formed only by the vicissitudes of war, occupation, and the antiquities trade, without meaningful implication for the structure of the archive or the history behind it. Some of the fragments, preserving nothing more than partial lists of witnesses, have no intrinsic interest except as comparanda with other Kasr texts. Nevertheless, even as an accidental sample, this is a fair representation of

---

Wiege früher Gelehrsamkeit, Mythos in der Moderne, Colloquien der Deutschen Orient-Gesellschaft 2 (Saarbrücken, 1999), pp. 242f.

[5] H. R. Hall, *A Season's Work at Ur, al-ʿUbaid, Abu Shahrain (Eridu), and Elsewhere* (London, 1930), pp. 50–53. See comments to no. 19, below.

the general appearance, contents, and characteristics of the archive as a whole. Almost all show severe fire damage, especially on one face (nos. 15, 17, and 19 are exceptions). Most are contracts involving the governor Bēlšunu, his subordinates, or associates, mostly recording various transactions connected with agricultural contracting, and these are on tablets in "horizontal" format (that is, with larger horizontal dimension than vertical dimension). A few are fragments of large tablets, originally in "vertical" format (that is, with larger vertical dimension than horizontal dimension), of the kind usual for sales, divisions, and conveyances of real estate (e.g., nos. 13, 21), and these are older than the texts involving Bēlšunu, by a few years or by a generation. Some have seal impressions with Hellenic or Greco-Persian styles and motifs (nos. 6, 16), and several have Aramaic epigraphs (nos. 3, 7, 8, 12) in a ductus surprisingly different from that of the nearly contemporary Murašû texts from Nippur.

Yale Babylonian Collection

With Known Excavation Numbers

1. YBC 11555 (fig. 1) — Hurbat-Šīhu — 7/IX/5 Darius II
Bab 49388 — 25 November 419 B.C.
Bab. Photo 2995
Pedersén N6 13

(reverse 1′) LÚ *mu-kin-nu* ^{m}KI-^{d}AG-*nu-ru* (2′) DUMU *šá* ^{m}*Ku-ṣur-a* ^{m}ŠEŠ.MEŠ-MU (3′) DUMU *šá* ^{m}GI-*a* ^{md}AG-DIN-*su* (4′) DUMU *šá* ^{m}*Ni-din-tum*

(5′) ^{m}*Ba-la-ṭu* DUB.SAR DUMU *šá* ^{md}EN-*it-tan-nu* (6′) ⸢*Ḫur*⸣-*bat-Ši-i-ḫu* ITI.GAN UD <<UD>>.7.KÁM MU.5.KÁM (7′) ^{m}*Da-a-ri-ia-a-muš* LUGAL KUR KUR

The obverse is entirely vitrified.

2. YBC 11552 (fig. 2) — — —
Bab 54593
Bab. Photos 3101–2
Pedersén N6 86

(1) 20 MA.NA KÙ.BABBAR *qa-lu-ú ina* ŠÁM ŠE.NUMUN *šá ina* URU?[...] (2) *šá* ^{md}AMAR.UTU-NUMUN-DÙ DUMU *šá* ^{m}EN-*šú-nu* (3) *a-na* KÙ.[BABBAR] *a-na* ^{m}EN-*šú-nu* LÚ.NAM E.KI (4) DUMU *šá* ^{m}⸢^{d}EN⸣-ÙRU-⸢*šú*⸣ *id-din-nu* ^{md}AMAR.UTU-NUMUN-DÙ (5) DUMU *šá* ^{m}EN-*šú-nu i-na qa-at* (6) ^{m}EN-*šú-nu* LÚ.NAM E.KI DUMU *šá* (7) [^{md}E]N-ÙRU-[*šú ma-ḫi*]-*ir*

(obverse) NA_4.KIŠIB / ^{md}AMAR.UTU-NUMUN-DÙ (left edge) NA_4.KIŠIB / [...] (right edge) NA_4.⸢KIŠIB⸣ / ^{m}*x*-[...] / *x*-[...] (lower edge) [NA_4.KIŠIB] / [...]-MU.NA // [NA_4].KIŠIB / [...]-*x* / [...]-*x* (upper edge) NA_4.KIŠIB / ^{m}MU-MU // NA_4.KIŠIB / ^{md}AG-/DIN-*su*-E

(1–7) Marduk-zēr-ibni, son of Bēlšunu, has received from Bēlšunu, governor of Babylon, son of Bēl-uṣuršu, 20 minas of fine silver as part of the purchase price of arable land located in the town of [....], which Marduk-zēr-ibni, son of Bēlšunu, sold to Bēlšunu, governor of Babylon, son of Bēl-uṣuršu.

(obverse) Seal of Marduk-zēr-ibni. (left edge) Seal of [...]. (right edge) Seal of [...]. (lower edge) [Seal of ...]-ittanna. [Seal] of [...]. (upper edge) Seal of Šum-iddin. Seal of Nabû-balāssu-iqbi.

Notes

1 The line continues around the right edge. The end is lost on the vitrified reverse.

2 I see no reason to surmise (as Pedersén, *Archive und Bibliotheken in Babylon*, p. 147, appears to do) that Marduk-zēr-ibni/Bēlšunu, the seller of the field and recipient of the payment, was the son of Bēlšunu/Bēl-uṣuršu, the buyer and payer. This Marduk-zēr-ibni, however, was a witness to one of the texts in the Murašû archive (BE 9 84:12 and upper edge = TuM 2–3 202, drafted at Nippur, 4/I/41 Artaxerxes I = 25 April 424 B.C.). His distinctive seal impression on that tablet (TuM 2–3 pl. 100 no. LXXVIII; see L. Bregstein, "Seal Use in Fifth Century B.C. Nippur, Iraq: A Study of Seal Selection and Sealing Practices in the Murašû Archive" [Ph.D. diss., University of Pennsylvania, 1993], no. 208) was made by the same seal as the impression on this one (M. W. Stolper, "The *šaknu* of Nippur," *JCS* 40 (1988): 141, n. 32; "The Kasr Archive," in H. Sancisi Weerdenburg and A. Kuhrt, eds., *Centre and Periphery: Proceedings of the Groningen 1986 Achaemenid History Workshop*, Achaemenid History 4 [Leiden, 1990], p. 198).

The reverse is entirely vitrified.

3. YBC 11558 (fig. 3) Ālu ša Bēl 12/VIII/– Darius II
Bab 54693
Bab. Photos 3105–6
Pedersén N6 89

(obverse) (fragments of signs from the ends of two lines)

(reverse 1′) ⸢LÚ *mu-kin*⸣*-nu* ^{m}SILIM-E.KI A-*šú šá* (2′) ^{m}*Ka-ṣir* ^{m}*Ri-bat* DUMU *šá* (3′) ^{md}BE-MU ^{m}*Ri-bat* DUMU *šá* (4′) ^{md}EN-*ik-ṣur*

(5′) ^{m}MU-ÙRU LÚ.ŠID DUMU *šá* ^{m}SILIM-E.KI (6′) ⸢URU⸣ *šá* ^{d}EN ITI.APIN UD.12.KÁM (7′) [MU.x.K]ÁM ^{m}*Da-ri-muš* (8′) [LUGAL KUR.KUR]

(reverse) *š*⸢*ṭr*⸣ *krn* 2

Notes

FuB 14 13f. no. 3 was written at the same place by the same scribe and before at least one of the same witnesses (Rībat/Bēl-ikṣur [*sic*]) on 21/VIII/14 Darius II = 1 December 410 B.C.

The Aramaic docket is very lightly incised, although the strokes are broad. Judging from the docket, the document is a receipt for a payment of barley.

The obverse and edges are entirely vitrified.

4. YBC 11586 (fig. 4) — –/–/– Darius II
Bab 55388
Bab. Photos 3164–65
Pedersén N6 372

(1) 1 GUR 3 (PI) 2 (BÁN) ŠE.NUMUN *me-re-šu šá ina* URU É *Ap-la-a* (2) *ni-din-tú* LUGAL *šá a-na* ^{m}EN-*šú-nu na-din* (3) É GIŠ.BAR *šá* ^{md}*Uraš*-PAP A-*šú šá* ^{m}DÙ-*a* (4) ^{md}*Uraš*-PAP ŠE.NUMUN *a-na* GIŠ.BAR (5) *a-di* 5 MU.AN.NA.MEŠ *a-na* MU.AN.NA (6) 5 GUR ŠE.BAR *a-na* ^{md}EN-*ku-ṣur-šú* (7) A-*šú šá* ^{md}AG-EN-TUR *id-din šá* MU.AN.NA (8) *ina* ITI.SIG$_4$ ŠE.BAR *a*$_4$ 5 GUR GIŠ.BAR A.ŠÀ (9) *gam-mir-tum ina ma-ši-ḫu šá* ^{md}*Uraš*-PAP (10) *ina* ÍD *Eš-šú* ^{md}EN-*ku-ṣur-šú* (11) *a-na* ^{md}*Uraš*-PAP *i-nam-din* (lower edge 12) 1-*en* TA.ÀM *šá-ṭa-ri* TI-*ú*

(reverse 1′) [...].KÁM (2′) [...] ^{m}*Da-ri-iá-a-muš* (upper edge 3′) LUGAL KUR.KUR

(1–3) $1\frac{2}{3}$ gur of cultivated arable land that is located in Bīt Aplâ, a crown grant that was given to Bēlšunu, property leased to Uraš-nāṣir, son of Ibnâ–(4–7) Uraš-nāṣir leased the arable land to Bēl-kuṣuršu, son of Nabû-bēl-ṣeḫri, for five years, for 5 gur of barley yearly. (7–11) Each year in month III, Bēl-kuṣuršu will pay Uraš-nāṣir those 5 gur of barley, the full rent for the field, determined by the measure of Uraš-nāṣir, on the New Canal. (12) Each (party) has taken one copy of (this) document.

(reverse 2′–3′) [...] Darius, King of Lands.

Notes

1–7 Cf. Usko:1–7 = M. W. Stolper, "The Kasr Texts, the Rich Collection, the Bellino Copies and the Grotefend Nachlass," in J. G. Dercksen, ed., *Assyria and Beyond: Studies Presented to Mogens Trolle Larsen*, Uitgaven van het Nederlands Instituut voor het Nabije Oosten te Leiden, *voorheen* Publications de l'Institut historique-archéologique néerlandais de Stamboul 100 (Leiden, 2004), pp. 534 f. and 549. Uraš-nāṣir/Ibnâ is the most frequently named associate of Bēlšunu the governor.[6] He appears frequently as a tenant and/or sublessor (as here). He is never characterized as a "servant" of Bēlšunu, or with another title, but the inclusion of the texts in which he is the principal with the other Kasr texts implies that he was not merely a contractor but a member of the concern that operated Bēlšunu's interests. His relationship to Bēlšunu and his agents was perhaps comparable to the relationship of Rībat/Bēl-erība to the Murašûs (see G. Cardascia, *Les archives des Murašû: une famille d'hommes d'affaires babyloniens à l'époque Perse (455–403 av. J.-C.)* (Paris, 1951), p. 14; G. van Driel, "The Murašûs in Context," *JESHO* 32 [1989]: 222, 225).

The reverse is almost entirely vitrified.

5.	YBC 11557 (fig. 5)	Borsippa	5/IX/9 Darius II
	Bab 55409		8 December 415 B.C.
	Bab. Photo 3166		
	Pedersén N6 382		

(right edge 1′) [...]-⌈ÙRU?⌉-*šú*

(reverse 1″) LÚ *mu-kin-nu* ^{md}AG-DIN-*su*-E A-*šú* ^{md}EN-MU (2″) ^{md}EN-DUMU.UŠ-ÙRU A-*šú šá* ^{md}EN-MU (3″) ^{md}AG-MU A-*šú* ^{md}EN-GI (4″) ^{md}AG-ÙRU-*šú* A-*šú* ^{m}*Šá*-KA-UR.KU

(5″) ^{md}EN-ÙRU-*šú* LÚ.DUB.SAR A-*sú* ^{m}*Ba-la-ṭu* (6″) BÁR.SIPA.KI ITI.GAN UD.5.KÁM MU.9.KÁM (7″) ^{m}*Da-ri-ia-a-muš* LUGAL KUR.KUR

Notes

1′ Continued from obverse.

2″ Bertin 2312 rev. 3 (witness, year 14, Darius II, Dilbat).

The obverse and edges are entirely vitrified.

---

[6] See M. W. Stolper, "Late Achaemenid Texts from Dilbat," *Iraq* 54 (1992): 121; Pedersén, *Archive und Bibliotheken in Babylon*, p. 147.

6. YBC 11562 (fig. 6) Bīt Šākin-šumi 15/X/9 Darius II
Bab 55045 17 January 414 B.C.
Bab. Photos 3141–42
Pedersén N6 243

(1) 1 ME 50 GUR ⸢ZÚ⸣.LUM.MA GIŠ.BAR A.ŠÀ.MEŠ *šá* MU.7.KÁM MU.8.⸢KÁM⸣ *u* MU.⸢9⸣.[KÁM *šá*] ^{m}*Da-ra-ia-a-muš* LUGAL (2) *šá* ŠE.NUMUN *šá* ^{m}*Si-ri-*⸢*di*?⸣*-a-muš šá* AN.TA (3) URU GABA-*šá-x-x-*⸢*x ni-din-tú* LUGAL *šá a-na*⸣ (4) ^{m}*Is-si-pi-ta-am-ma* ⸢SUM.NA⸣ É GIŠ.BAR (5) *šá* ^{m}EN-*šú-nu* LÚ.NAM DIN.TIR.KI A-*šú šá* ^{md}EN-ÙRU-*šú* (6) ZÚ.LUM.MA a_4 1 ME GUR 50 GUR *gam-ru-*⸢*ú*⸣*-tu* (7) ^{m}*Pa-ad-di-ia* A-*šú šá* ^{m}*Ḫar*?*-ra*?*-ḫi-e-bi*? (8) LÚ.ARAD *šá* ^{m}*Is-si-pi-ta-am-ma ina* ŠU^{II} (9) ^{m}EN-*šú-nu* LÚ.NAM DIN.TIR.KI A-[*šú šá*] ^{md}EN-ÙRU-*šú ma-ḫi-ir* (10) *e-ṭir* (11) *a-di* ZÚ.LUM.MA ⸢MU⸣.7.KÁM MU.8.KÁM ⸢MU⸣.9.KÁM (12) *šá* ^{m}*Pa-ad-di-iá*

(reverse 13) ⸢LÚ⸣ *mu-kin-ni* ^{md}AG-MU.NU A-*šú šá* ^{md}A-É-KÁD (14) ^{md}AG-ŠEŠ.MEŠ-GI A-*šú šá* ^{md}AG-MU.NU (15) ^{m}*Ú-bal-liṭ-su-*^{d}EN A-*šú šá* ^{m}MU-DU (16) ^{md}UTU-⸢MU?⸣ A-*sú šá* ^{md}GAŠAN?-⸢*x-x*⸣ (17) ⸢^{m}*Ba-la*⸣*-ṭu* A-*šú šá* ^{md}EN-MU.NU

(18) ^{m}*Šul-lu-mu* LÚ.DUB.SAR A-*šú šá* ^{md}AG-ÙRU-*šú* (19) URU É GAR-MU ITI.AB UD.15.KÁM MU.9.⸢KÁM⸣ (20) ^{m}*Da-ra-ia-a-*⸢*muš* LUGAL KUR.KUR⸣

(lower edge) ‹‹[NA$_4$.KIŠIB ^{m}*Pa-ad*]*-di-ia* / A-*šú šá* ^{m}*Ḫar-*[*r*]*a-ḫi-e-bi*›› (all erased)
(upper edge) NA$_4$.KIŠIB / ^{m}*Pa-ad-di-iá*

(1–5) 150 gur of dates is the rent on fields for the years 7, 8, and 9 of King Darius, due on arable land of Siridiamuš?, located above the town of …, (land) given to Issipitamma as a crown grant, a property leased to Bēlšunu, governor of Babylon, son of Bēl-uṣuršu. (6–9) Paddija, son of Harrahēbi?, servant of Issipitamma, has received all those 150 gur of dates from Bēlšunu, governor of Babylon, son of Bēl-uṣuršu; he is paid in full. (11–12) (The payment) includes dates owed to Paddija (himself?) for years 7, 8, and 9.

(13–17) Witnesses: Nabû-ittannu, son of Mār-Bīti-kāṣir; Nabû-ahhē-ušallim, son of Nabû-ittannu; Uballissu-Bēl, son of Šum-ukīn; Šamaš-iddin?, son of Bēlet?-x; Balāṭu, son of Bēl-ittannu.

(18–20) Scribe: Šullumu, son of Nabû-uṣuršu. Bīt Šākin-šumi, month X, day 15, year 9, Darius, King of Lands.

(lower edge) ([Seal of P]addija, son of Harrahēbi?) (all erased). (upper edge) Seal of Paddija.

Notes

2 Siridiamuš (or: Sirikiamuš): presumably an Iranian name, perhaps compounded with *–va^{h}uš* "good" (like *Dārya-va^{h}uš*); conceivably compounded with **srī-* "beauty, pride." Tavernier (personal communication) suggests the possibility **Sṛdiya-vaush-* "challenging the good," with *sṛd-* "to challenge."

3 Perhaps URU É$^{!}$ GAR-MU$^{!}$, as in line 18.

4 Issipitamma = Iranian **Spita-ama-*; see Manfred Mayrhofer, *Die altiranischen Namen*, Iranisches Personennamenbuch I/1 (Vienna, 1979), p. 77, no. 291; W. Hinz, *Altiranisches Sprachgut der Nebenüberlieferungen*, Göttinger Orientforschung III/3 (Wiesbaden, 1975), pp. 226 f.; J. Tavernier, "Iranica in de Achaemenidische Periode (ca. 550–330 v. Chr.)" (Ph.D. diss., Katholieke Universiteit, Leuven 2002), p. 576.

7 ff. Paddija (Egyptian *pꜣ-dj*): see R. Zadok, "Some Egyptians in First-Millennium Mesopotamia," *Gött. Misz.* 26 (1977): 65. Harrahēbi, if correctly read, is presumably an Egyptian name.

The tablet is smoke-blackened. The reverse is partly vitrified.

7. YBC 11537 (fig. 7) — Halpattu — –/–/⸢4?⸣ Artaxerxes II
Bab 55760 — 401/400 B.C.
Bab. Photos 3175–76
Pedersén N6 506

(1) 16 GUR 2 (PI) 3 (BÁN) ZÚ.LUM.MA ZAG.LU EBUR A.ŠÀ (2) *šá* ŠE.NUMUN *šá* DUMU LÚ.GÍR.LAL *ù e-du-ú-tu* (3) *šá Ḫal-pat-tum*.MEŠ É GIŠ.BAR *šá* ^{md}*Uraš*-PAP (4) A ^{m}DÙ-*a ina muḫ-ḫi* ^{md}EN-ÙRU-*šú* A *šá* ^{md}EN-*ana-mi-ri-*[*iḫ-tum*] (5) *ina* ITI. APIN MU.4.KÁM ZÚ.LUM.MA *aʾ* 16 GUR 2 (PI) 3 (BÁN) (6) *gam-ru-tu* <*ina*> *Dil+bat*.KI *ina* GIŠ *ma-ši-ḫu* (7) *šá* ^{md}*Uraš*-PAP KI 1 GUR 1 (BÁN) 3 QA (8) *i-piš-tum lìb-lìb-bi man-ga-ga* (9) *ù bil-tum šá ḫu-ṣab ina-an-din*

(reverse 10) ⸢LÚ.MU.KIN$_{7}$⸣ […]-⸢^{d}EN⸣ (11) […] ⸢*na*?⸣ […] ⸢^{d}*x*⸣ […] (12) ^{m}[…] ⸢^{d}*x x x*⸣

(13) ^{m}⸢*x*⸣ […] (14) *Ḫal-*⸢*pat-tum*.KI⸣ […] ⸢MU.4?.KÁM⸣ (15) ^{m}*Ár-tak-šat-*⸢*su*⸣ LUGAL KUR.KUR

(upper edge) ⸢*š*⸣*ṭr tmrn krn* 26$^{!}$ / *zy*? *x k x zy br* …

(1–4) 16½ gur of dates (is) the rent assessed on the crop for the land of the "swordbearer(s)?" and the isolated palms of the people of (the town) Halpattu, (properties) held on lease by Uraš-nāṣir, son of Ibnâ, (rent that is) owed by Bēl-uṣuršu, son of Bēl-ana-mīriḫtu. (5–9) In month VIII, year 4, he will pay those 16 gur of dates, all of them, <in> Dilbat, using the measure of Uraš-nāṣir, (and) with each gur (he will also pay) a premium of $1\frac{1}{2}$ *sūtu*, palm fronds, fiber, and a load of pieces of wood.

(10–12) Witnesses: [...]-Bēl; [...].

(13–15) [Scribe: ...] Halpattu, [month x, day y], year 4?, Artaxerxes, King of Lands.

(upper edge) Document concerning 26 [*sic*] gur of dates, of? ..., son of? ...

Notes

2 DUMU LÚ.GÍR.LAL = *mār nāš paṭri* or *mār ṭābiḫi*? The translation of this ambiguous writing reflects these conjectures: that DUMU is not genealogical but classificatory; that the term is honorific rather than professional; that the noun-phrase is a collective; and that it refers to a land-holding group, like the *haṭru* of "swordbearers" found in Murašû texts (see M. W. Stolper, *Entrepreneurs and Empire: The Murašû Archive, the Murašû Firm, and Persian Rule in Babylonia*, Uitgaven van het Nederlands Instituut voor het Nabije Oosten te Leiden, *voorheen* Publications de l'Institut historique-archéologique néerlandais de Stamboul 54 [Leiden, 1985], pp. 54f. with n. 12). Moore Michigan Coll. 43:3 (no. 16 below) refers to "people of Halpattu" as members of a *haṭru*.

2 The ghost word *edūtu* should be stricken from the dictionaries; see Jursa *Landwirtschaft*, p. 38.

3 For the gentilic, see LÚ *Ḫal-pat-ú-a* Moore Michigan Coll. 43:3 (no. 16 below); for the place-name, see BM 40066:6 and VAT 15610:1.

6 For Dilbat in connection with Uraš-nāṣir, see Stolper, "Late Achaemenid Texts from Dilbat," pp. 120f.

8 *ipištu*: see Landsberger *Date Palm*, p. 44; Stolper, "Late Achaemenid Texts from Dilbat," pp. 130, 134; Jursa *Landwirtschaft*, p. 152. Since *gimru*, *elletu*, and *ipištu* appear in nearly identical phrases, and are identified by identical amounts, it is difficult to accept the disparity of meanings in the usual translations *gimru* = (transportation) expenses, *elletu* = upward adjustment (of the repayment measure), and *ipištu* = downward adjustment (of the measure).

Upper Edge The Aramaic docket is lightly incised. The number 26 (vs. $16\frac{1}{2}$ gur in the text) is clear.

The reverse is almost entirely vitrified.

8. YBC 11585 (fig. 8) Bāb Surru? 11/I/9 Darius II
Bab 57468 23 April 415 B.C.
Bab. Photo 3341
Pedersén N6 927

(reverse 1′) LÚ.MU.KIN$_7$ mdEN-*ana*-NE-*tum* A-*šú sá* m*Bu-na-nu* (2′) mdAG-SUR A-*šú šá* mdEN-MU (3′) mdEN-PAP A-*šú šá* m*Bul-ṭa-a* (4′) m*Bar-zip*.KI-*a-a* A-*šú šá* mdAG-GAR.NU

(5′) [m]dAG-DIN-*su*-E LÚ.ŠID A-*šú šá* m*Ri-bat* (6′) [URU KÁ] ⌈*Sur-ru*⌉ ITI.BÁR UD.11.KÁM MU.9.KÁM (7′) [...]-*x-x-muš* LUGAL KUR.KUR.MEŠ

(lower edge) [*šṭr*] *l bṭ x x x* / *x x t n* ⌈*š*⌉*nt* 9

Notes

Rev. 1′ Bēl-ana-mīriḫtum/Bunānu: *FuB* 14 12f. no. 2 rev. 2 (coll.), 24f. no. 15 rev. 3, 26f. no. 18 rev. 4; Bab. 55038 rev. 8 (Pedersén N6 236); Bab. 55761:15 (Pedersén N6 507).

Rev. 3′ Bēl-nāṣir / Bulṭā: *FuB* 14 28 no. 20 rev. 2.

Rev. 5′ The same scribe recurs in *FuB* 14 19 no. 8 (coll.), Dar. 78, VAT 15714 (Pedersén N6 252) (all at Bāb Surru), and Bab. 56340 (Pedersén N6 745) and 55767 (Pedersén N6 513).

The obverse is entirely vitrified, with a green crust, showing illegible traces of 4+x lines. The reverse is heavily burned and has a green surface. The upper left corner is melted, deformed, and broken. The Aramaic docket is lightly incised.

9. *Oelsner AV* 469 (fig. 9) — —
YBC 11560
Bab 57799
PhBab 3341
Pedersén N6 932

(1) MU.AN.NA 2 (PI) 3 (BÁN) SUM.SAR m⌈EN⌉-[*šú-nu*] (2) A-*šú šá* mŠEŠ-*ú-nu ku*-⌈*ú*⌉ *la e-pe*-⌈*šú*⌉ (3) *šá piš-ki-šú a-na* m*Uš-kar-ri* (4) LÚ.ARAD *šá* mEN-*šú-nu i-nam-din* (5) *pu-ut la e-pe-šú šá piš-ki šá*! (6) mEN-*šú-nu* A-*šú šá* mŠEŠ-*ú-nu* m*Uš-kar-ri* (7) *na-ši*

(reverse 8) LÚ *m*[*u-kin-nu* ...]

(1–7) Each year Bēlšunu, son of Ahūnu, will pay Uškarri, servant of Bēlšunu, ½ gur of onions in compensation for no unwarranted assessment being made against him (lit. no harm being done him). Uškarri guarantees that no unwarranted assessment will be made against Bēlšunu, son of Ahūnu.

(8) Witnesses: ....

Notes

See full edition and discussion in M. W. Stolper, “No Harm Done,” *Oelsner AV*, pp. 469–77.

The reverse (not copied) is vitrified. The obverse is an even medium gray with some incrustation in the signs. There is a green crust over the reverse and edges. On the upper edge are black marks, possibly traces of a faded or effaced Aramaic docket.

The excavation photographs of the Kasr N6 texts show another guarantee against *pišku* (Bab. 55156, Pedersén N6 280, present whereabouts unknown), only partially legible to me:

(1) MU.AN.NA 1-*en* TÚG *gu-la-nu* (2) *ana ku-ú pi-iš-ki-šú* ^{f}*Ḫi-x* (3) DUMU.SAL *šá* ^{md}AG-GAR.NU TA ŠU *x x x* (4) *a-na* ^{fd}*Ba-ni-tum* UŠ.BAR *x x* (5) *x šá* ^{m}SU-*a ta-nam-din* (6) ⌈*pu*?-*ut*?⌉ LÚ *x-tum šá* ^{fd}*Ba-ni-tum*? *x* (7) ⌈*pu*?-*ut*⌉ *pi-iš-ki šá* ^{f}*Ḫi-x* (8) ⌈^{fd}*Ba*⌉-*ni-tum* UŠ.BAR ŠU *x x x x* (reverse destroyed)

(1–5) (Each) year, Hi-..., daughter of Nabû-iškunu, ... will give Banītu, the weaver, ... of Erība, one outer garment. (6–8) Banītu, the weaver ..., (guarantees) against? (claims of x) against Banītu, (and) against unwarranted assessment (lit. harm) against Hi-x.

10. YBC 11554 (fig. 10) — –/XII/2 Artaxerxes II
Bab 58307 February/March 402 B.C.
Bab. Photos 3395–96
Pedersén N6 950

(1) *mim-ma dib-bi di-nim u ra-ga-mu šá* ^{m}*Ri-bat* (2) A-*šú šá* ^{m}*Ḫa-ri-ṣa-nu ana muḫ-ḫi* 3.TA GIŠ.BAN.MEŠ (3) *šá* LÚ *Ṭa*-⌈*ab*?⌉-*ba-še-e šá ina* URU É *Da-di-ia* (4) *šá ina* URU É GIŠ.GU.ZA *šá ina* URU *E-bu-ri-ia* (5) ⌈*šá ina* ŠU^{II} *šá*⌉ ^{m}SU-*a* LÚ.NAM DIN.TIR.KI *šá ana* GIŠ.BAR (6) [TA?] MU.1.KÁM ^{m}*Ar-tak-šat-su* LUGAL TA ŠU^{II} (7) [...]-NUMUN-SI.SÁ <KI?> ^{m}SU-*a ana* u_4-*mu ṣa-a-tim* (8) [*ia-a-nu* ...] MU.MEŠ ^{m}*Ri-bat i-na* IGI ^{m}SU-*a* (9) [...] x ⌈*šá-ṭar*⌉ *šá e-lat* $2\frac{1}{3}$ MA.NA KÙ.BABBAR (10) [...] x x

(reverse 11) [...]-x-*a* (12) [(...)] (13) [...]-*x* ^{md}EN-*da-nu* (14) [...] ^{m}*Ni-din-tum*-^{d}AG (15) [... ^{m}]^{d}BE-KÁD

(16) [...] A-*šú šá* ^{m}*Mu-šal-lim*-^{d}AMAR.UTU (17) [...] ⸢ITI.ŠE⸣ ⸢IGI-*ú*⸣ MU.2.KÁM
(18) ^{m}*Ar*-⸢*tak-šat*⸣-*su* LUGAL KUR.KUR

(upper edge) *un-qa* / ^{m}*Ri-bat* // NA$_4$.KIŠIB / ^{md}AG-MU.NU

(1–7) [There will be no] lawsuit, legal action, or complaint [brought] by Rībat, son of Hariṣānu, regarding three bow properties, which belong to the ... , which are located in the towns of Bīt Dādija, Bīt Kussê, and Bīt Ebūrija, which are in the possession of Erība, governor of Babylon, which were leased from ...-zēr-līšir as of? year 1 of King Artaxerxes—against Erība, ever. (8–10) Rībat [...] this [...] in the presence of Erība [...] document? that is aside from $2\frac{1}{3}$ minas of silver....

(11–15) [Witnesses: ...] Bēl-dānu; [... Ni]dintu-Nabû; [...] Ea-kāṣir.

(16–18) [Scribe: ...] son of Mušallim-Marduk. [...,] first month XII, year 2, Artaxerxes, King of Lands.

(upper edge) Ring of Rībat. Seal of Nabû-ittannu.

Notes

3 *Ṭabbašê* or *Dabbašê*: presumably a gentilic.

5 *Erība pīḫat Bābili* = ^{m}SU-*a* LÚ.NAM DIN.TIR.KI A-*šú šá* ^{m}EN-*šú-nu* Bab 55767:1 f. (Pedersén N6 513; date and place lost); ^{md}AMAR.UTU-SU LÚ.NAM E.KI VAT 15946:3 (Pedersén N6 123; date and place lost); ^{md}AMAR.UTU-SU [(...)] A-*šú šá* ^{m}EN-*šú-nu* LÚ *pa-ḫa-ti* DIN.T[IR.KI] *Aula Orientalis* 15 185 no. 36:3′f. (see no. 23 below, year 4, Darius II). In the last, the title "governor of Babylon" applies to the father, Bēlšunu. His son (Marduk)-erība succeeded as governor of Babylon when Bēlšunu became governor of Syria early in the reign of Artaxerxes II, 407 B.C. or earlier.

This succession may have been a stage in a long history of the family's service in Achaemenid provincial administration, if Pedersén is right to identify Aḫušunu/Lābāši, governor (LÚ.GAR.KU, *šākin ṭēmi*) of Borsippa, as the grandfather of Bēlšunu (*Archive und Bibliotheken in Babylon*, p. 146). For reasons to hesitate over this identification, however, see M. W. Stolper, "Achaemenid Legal Texts from the Kasr: Interim Observations," in Renger, ed., *Babylon: Focus*, p. 371.

17 Intercalary Addaru occurs in year 2 of all three Artaxerxeses. There is no space for the indication of a day between the month and the regnal year.

The left side and almost all of the reverse are vitrified.

11. YBC 11550 (fig. 11) — –/–/(2) Darius II
Bab 58594 (422/421 B.C.)
Bab. Photos 3398–99
Pedersén N6 961

(1) 2 (PI) 3 (BÁN) *saḫ-le-e šá* ^{m}EN-*šú-nu* (2) *pi-ḫat* E.KI A-*šú šá* ^{md}EN-ÙRU-*šú re-ḫi* GIŠ.BAR (3) *saḫ-le-e šá* MU.2.KÁM ^{m}*Da-ri-ia-muš* (4) *ina muḫ-ḫi* ^{md}AG-*i-di-šú* A-*šú šá* ^{md}EN-DIN-*iṭ* (5) *ina* ITI.SIG$_4$ MU.3.KÁM *saḫ-le-e a*$_4$ (6) 2 (PI) ⌈3⌉ (BÁN) *ina* GIŠ *ma-ši-ḫu šá* ^{m}EN-*šú-nu* (7) ^{md}A[G]-*i-di-šú a-na* ^{md}EN-MU.NU (8) LÚ.AR[AD] *šá* ^{m}EN-*sú-nu i-nam-din*

(reverse 1′) [...] (2′) [...]-⌈*ši*?⌉-*i-x-šú* LÚ.ARAD *šá* ^{m}EN-*šú-nu* (3′–5′) [... (vitrified)]

(1–4) ½ gur of cress-seed is owed to Bēlšunu, governor of Babylon, son of Bēl-uṣuršu, as the balance of the rent due in cress-seed for year 2 of Darius, by Nabû-idīšu, son of Bēl-uballiṭ. (5–8) In month III, year 3, Nabû-idīšu will pay that ½ gur of cress-seed, using the measure of Bēlšunu, to Bēl-ittannu, servant of Bēlšunu.

(9–17) [...] ... servant of Bēlšunu [...]

Notes

7f. Bēl-ittannu, servant of Bēlšunu: *FuB* 14 12f. no. 2:1; *Iraq* 4 17:2f.; K.8485:1f. (= Rich 109); Pedersén, *Archive und Bibliotheken in Babylon*, p. 147.
The reverse is entirely vitrified.

Without Known Excavation Numbers

12. YBC 11532 (fig. 12) Kār-Nabû 19/XII/16 Darius II
4 April 407 B.C.

(1) 1 GUR 1 PI ŠE.BAR *bab-ba-*⌈*ni-tum*⌉ (2) *šá* ^{md}URAŠ-*na-ṣir* A-*šú šá* ^{m}DÙ-*a* (3) *ina muḫ-ḫi* ^{md}EN-A×A-ÙRU (4) A-*šú šá* ^{md}AG-DIN-*su* ^{m}*Ri-bat* (5) A-*šú šá* ^{md}DUMU-É-MU (6) *ina* ITI.GUD MU.17.KÁM (7) ŠE.BAR *a*$_4$ 1 GUR 1 PI (8) *ina* GIŠ *ma-ši-ḫu šá* ^{md}*Uraš*-PAP (lower edge 9) *ina* URU *Kar-ri*-^{d}AG (10) *i-nam-din-nu-*ʾ (reverse 11) *pu-ut e-ṭè-ru šá* ŠE.BAR *a*$_4$ (12) 1 GUR 1 PI ^{m}*Ni-ḫiš-tum*-^{d}EN-*ṭa-bat* (13) A-*šú šá* ^{md}DUMU-É-MU *na-ši*

(14) LÚ *mu-kin-nu* ^{md}EN-DIN-*su* (15) A-*šú šá* ^{m}*Lib-luṭ* (16) ^{m}NU.UR A-*šú šá* ^{md}EN-MU.NU (17) ^{m}ARAD-^{d}EDIN-*ú-a* A ^{md}EN-MU.NU

(18) ^{md}EN-DÙ LÚ.ŠID A ^{md}AG-DIN-*su* (upper edge 19) URU *Kar-ri*-^{d}AG ITI.ŠE UD.⌈20 1-LAL⌉.KÁM (20) MU.16.KÁM ^{m}*Da-a-ri-ia-*⌈*muš*⌉ (21) LUGAL KUR.KUR

(left edge) *nḥystblṭbt* ⸢*šnt*?⸣ 16

(1–5) 1 gur, 1 *pānu* of fine barley is owed to Uraš-nāṣir, son of Ibnâ, by Bēl-apil-uṣur, son of Nabû-bullissu (and) Rībat, son of Mār-Bīti-iddin. (6–10) They will pay that 1 gur, 1 *pānu* of barley, using the measure of Uraš-nāṣir, at Kār-Nabû. (11–13) Niḫištu-Bēl-ṭābat, son of Mār-Bīti-iddin, assumes warranty for the repayment of that 1 gur, 1 *pānu* of barley.

(14–17) Witnesses: Bēl-bullissu, son of Liblut; Lābāši, son of Bēl-ittannu; Arad-Šerūa, son of Bēl-ittannu.

(18–21) Scribe: Bēl-ibni, son of Nabû-bullissu. Kār-Nabû, month XII, day 19, year 16, Darius, King of Lands.

(left edge) Niḫištu-Bēl-ṭābat, year 16.

Notes

Cf. Dar. 364 with the same creditor, written by the same scribe, at the same place, three days earlier.

16 Lābāši/Bēl-ittannu: TCL 13 186:16; Dar. 364:8.

The tablet is burned. The right side of the obverse is vitrified. The Aramaic docket was incised with an instrument that caused some strokes to appear as double strokes.

13. YBC 11600 (fig. 13) Borsippa 30/XI/27 Artaxerxes I
15 February 437 B.C.

(reverse 1′) [...]-*x* DUMU? ^{m}ŠEŠ-⸢*ia-tal-li*?⸣ (2′) [...]-*šal-lim* DUMU-*šú šá* ^{md}AG-MU-*ú-ṣur* DUMU ^{m}*x-x-x* (3′) [...]-DUMU.UŠ-MU DUMU-*šú šá* ^{md}AG-DÙ-ŠEŠ DUMU ^{m}*Ba-x*-[...] (4′) ^{m}*Ni-din-tum*-^{d}EN DUMU-*šú šá* ^{md}AG-ŠEŠ.MEŠ-MU DUMU ^{m}ZALÁG?-^{d}*x* (5′) ^{m}*Šá-maš-a-a* DUMU-*šú šá* ^{md}EN-SUM.NA DUMU LÚ.⸢SIMUG⸣ [...] (6′) ^{md}EN-*tab-ta-ni-bul-liṭ-su* DUMU-*šú šá* ^{md}AG-*bul-liṭ-su* DUMU ^{m}*Šá-la-la* (7′) ^{m}*Ni-din-tum*-^{d}AG DUMU-*šú šá* ^{md}AG-ÙRU-*šú* ^{md}AG-*eri*$_{4}$-*ba* DUMU-*šú šá* ^{md}EN-*it-tan-ni* (8′) ^{md}EN-*bul-liṭ-su* DUMU-*šú šá* ^{m}*Mu-ra-šu-ú* (9′) ^{md}EN-*bul-liṭ-su* DUMU-*šú šá* ^{m}KI-^{d}AG-DIN DUMU ^{m}*Ki-din*-^{d}30 (10′) ^{md}AG-EN-*šú-nu* DUMU-*šú šá* ^{m}ARAD-*É-sa-bad*

(11′) ^{md}A[G-DIN-*s*]*u*-E DUB.SAR DUMU-*šú šá* ^{md}EN-SUM.NA DUMU ^{m}*Ár-kát*-^{d}⸢SIG$_{5}$?⸣ (12′) BÁR.SIPA.KI ITI.ZÍZ UD.30.KÁM MU.27.KÁM ^{m}*Ar-tak-šat-su* LUGAL KUR.MEŠ

Notes

The obverse and the upper, left, and right edges are entirely vitrified. There are illegible traces of ten or more lines on the obverse. The lower edge and corners are deformed, the reverse cracked. The upper part and left side of the reverse are vitrified and deformed, the remainder of reverse burned black, red, or pale gray.

NIES BABYLONIAN COLLECTION

14. NBC 8394 (fig. 14) — [–/–/36–39 Artaxerxes I] (430–426 B.C.)

(1) 3 ME 30 GUR ŠE.BAR *šá* ^{m}EN-*šú-nu* A-*šú šá* ^{md}EN-ÙRU-*šú* (2) *ina muḫ-ḫi* ^{m}*Ri-bat* A-*šú šá* ^{md}AG-*di-i-ni-an-na* TA UD.1.KÁM (3) *šá* ITI.APIN *šá* MU.39.<KÁM> ŠE.BAR a_4 3 ME 30 GUR (4) *a-di* 3 MU.AN.NA.MEŠ *ina* SAG.DU-*šú* KI GIŠ.BAR *šá* (5) GIŠ.APIN *šá ina* IGI-*šú* ^{m}*Ri-bat a-na* ^{m}EN-*šú-nu* (6) *i-nam-din ki-i a-di* 3 MU.AN.NA.MEŠ ŠE.BAR a_4 (7) 3 ME 30 GUR ^{m}*Ri-bat a-na* ^{m}EN-*šú-nu* (8) *la it-ta-din lìb-bu-ú a-ra-na-tum šá* (9) ITI.APIN *šá* MU.39.KÁM *a-na ṭup*$^{!}$*-pu* 10 GUR ŠE.BAR (10) *a-na* 1 MA.NA KÙ.BABBAR ^{m}*Ri-bat a-na* ^{m}EN-*šú-nu* (11) *i-nam-din e-lat* GIŠ.APIN *šá* GIŠ.BAR *šá ina* IGI-*šú*

(1–2) 330 gur of barley is owed to Bēlšunu, son of Bēl-uṣuršu, by Rībat, son of Nabû-dīnianna. (2–6) Beginning day 1, month VIII, year 39, Rībat will pay Bēlšunu that 330 gur of barley in its full original amount, along with the rent for the plowing unit that is in his possession, over the course of$^{?}$ three years. (6–11) If Rībat has not paid that 330 gur of barley to Bēlšunu over the course of$^{?}$ three years, Rībat will pay Bēlšunu (in silver) at the rate of exchange prevailing in month VIII of year 39, paying 10 gur of barley per mina of silver for the extra time$^{?}$. (11) (This obligation) is over and above (the matter of) the plowing unit that he holds on lease.

Notes

5, 11 GIŠ.APIN refers to a rented package including land, plow, team, and workers; see Stolper, "The Kasr Texts, the Rich Collection, the Bellino Copies and the Grotefend Nachlass," p. 532 to Bellino Q 1.

8 See M. W. Stolper, "Tobits in Reverse," *Archaeologische Mitteilungen aus Iran* 23 (1990): 166f. to YBC 11607:8.

9 I know of no exactly comparable clauses, but *ṭuppu* in *ana ṭuppi* can only have the same sense as *ṭuppu* in *adi ṭuppišu* and *ina ṭuppišu* in clauses referring to extended terms of payment; see M. Rowton, "*Ṭuppu* and the Date of

Ḫammurabi," *JNES* 10 (1951): 188 f., and M. W. Stolper, "Texts of the Murašûs and from Their Surroundings," *JCS* 53 (2001): 107. Furthermore, compare G. van Driel, "The Rise of the House of Egibi: Nabû-aḫḫē-iddina," *JEOL* 29 (1985–86): 52 and n. 9 on the clauses *akî maḫīri ša* MN *ina* 1 GÍN x ŠE.BAR *inandin* Nbk. 112:6 f., Nbk. 82:4 f., OECT 10 70:10 f., VAS 4 22:5–7 and 28:8–10, and *ina* MN *akî maḫīri ša* GN *itti* 1 GÍN *kaspi* x *suluppē inandin* Cyr. 60:5 f. and M. Jursa, "Debts and Indebtedness in the Neo-Babylonian Period: Evidence from the Institutional Archives," in M. Hudson and M. Van De Mieroop, eds., *Debt and Economic Renewal in the Ancient Near East*, International Scholars Conference on Ancient Near Eastern Economies 3 (Bethesda, Maryland, 2002), p. 200 on the clause *akî* KI.LAM *ša* MN *ina* GN *ina* 1 GÍN 1 (BÁN) 3 QA *alla* KI.LAM *uḫinnu*! *inamdin* YOS 17 22:4–7, all referring to payments to be made at the specified rates of exchange along with supplementary payments (not to dramatically high commodity prices).

Formally, the text is a promissory note. The note must be a companion to a lease issued at about the same time. Bēlšunu leased to Rībat a property referred to simply as a plow, presumably for a term of three years. This note obligates Rībat either to pay a further 110 gur of barley per year along with the annual rent stipulated in that lease or else to pay a larger amount after the term of the lease has expired. In the latter case, he is to pay in silver, at the rate of equivalence that pertained at the beginning of the lease, and with a premium for the extension of the terms of payment. To calculate the premium, the 330 gur of barley are to be converted into silver at the specified exchange rate, then for each mina of silver that results, 10 more gur of barley are to be converted into silver at the same rate and added to the original amount. The premium of 10 gur per mina = 3 *qû* per shekel is well below the 12 *qû* per shekel found in Nbk. 82 and 112, VAS 4 22 and 28, and the 18 *qû* per shekel in OECT 10 70 (all from the reign of Nebuchadnezzar).

The reverse is entirely vitrified. The source from which the text was acquired is unknown; it was entered in the catalogue of the NBC in 1944.

KELSEY MUSEUM OF ANCIENT AND MEDIEVAL ARCHAEOLOGY, ANN ARBOR, MICHIGAN[7]

With Known Excavation Numbers

15. Moore Michigan Coll. 46 | Borsippa | 22/–/3 Artaxerxes II
KM 89396 | | 402/401 B.C.
Bab 55039
Bab. Photos 3141–42
Pedersén N6 237

(1) 1 GUR ŠE.NUMUN *bar-rat šá ina* ŠE.NUMUN *šá* ^{m}*Is-pa-ú*?*-du* A-*šú šá* [^{m}*A-te-ba-ga-*ʾ] (2) *šá ina* BARÁ *šá* ^{d}DUMU-É *šá* UŠ.SA.DU A.ŠÀ *šá* ^{md}EN-SUR ⸢A-*šú*⸣ [...] (3) *u* UŠ.SA.DU A.ŠÀ *šá* ^{m}*Ri-mut-*^{d}EN A-*šú šá* ^{m}MU-*a* [(...)] (4) ^{m}*Is-pa-ú*?*-du* A-*šú šá* ^{m}*A-te-ba-ga-*ʾ ŠE.NUMUN *a-na za-qí-*[*pa-nu-tu*] (5) *a-di* 20 MU.AN.NA.MEŠ *ana* ^{md}AG-DIN-*su* A-*šú šá* ^{md}AG-MU *i*[*d-din*] (6) *a-di qí-it* MU.AN.NA.MEŠ 20 *a*$_4$ *mi-nu-ú ki-i* (7) [^{m}]^{d}AG-DIN-*su* A-*šú šá* ^{md}AG-MU *i-zaq-qa-pu ina lìb-bi*! [(...)] (8) *ina* MU.AN.NA.MES 6 GÍN KÙ.BABBAR *ku-ú* EBUR *qaq-qa-*[*ru* (...)] (9) [^{m}]^{d}AG-DIN-*su ana* ^{m}*Is-pa-ú*?*-du* A-*šú šá* ^{m}*A-te-ba-ga-*ʾ [*i-nam-din*] (10) [TA IT]I.BÁR MU.4.⸢KÁM ^{m}*Ar*⸣-[*tak-šat-su* LUGAL] (11) [ŠE.NUMUN *ina* IGI ^{md}AG-DIN-*su* ...]

(reverse 1′) [...] *x* A *x* [...] (2′) [...]-ÙRU A ^{md}EN-DIN-*su*-E [...] (3′) [...]-^{d}*Uraš* A ^{m}ARAD-^{d}*Uraš* [...] (4′) [^{md}EN]-AD-ÙRU A ^{m}*Ḫaš*!*-da-a* ^{m}[...]

(5′) ^{md}AG-A×A-ÙRU DUB.SAR A ^{md}EN-*ib-ni* [(...)] (6′) BÁR.SIPA.KI ⸢ITI⸣.[x] UD.22.KÁM MU.3.KÁM (7′) ^{m}*Ar-tak-šat-su* LUGAL KUR.KUR

(reverse) *un-qu* ^{md}EN-*e-ṭe-*[*ru*] (upper edge) NA$_4$.KIŠIB ^{md}EN-AD-ÙRU

(1–3) 1 gur of undeveloped? arable land, which is part of the arable land belonging to Ispaʾudu, son of [Atebagā], located in (the district called) the Dais of Mār-Bīti, adjoining the field of Bēl-ēṭir, son of [...] and adjoining the field of Rīmūt-Bēl, son of Iddinâ—(4–5) Ispaʾudu, son of Atebagā, turned (that) property over to Nabû-bullissu, son of Nabû-iddin, for 20 years, for the planting of a date orchard. (6–9) Until the end of those 20 years, however much (of an orchard) Nabû-bullissu, son of Nabû-iddin, plants, every year Nabû-bullissu [will pay] Ispaʾudu, son of Atebagā, 6 shekels of silver in lieu of the crop from the property. (10–11) [The property is in the possession of Nabû-bullissu as of] month I, year 4 of King Artaxerxes.

---

[7] Digital images of the Kelsey tablets are available (as of December, 2006) at http://128.97.154.154/cdli/kelsey/km_browse.html.

(1′–4′) [Witnesses: ... ...]-uṣur, son of Bēl-balāssu-iqbi; [...]-Uraš, son of Arad-Uraš; [Bēl]-ab-uṣur, son of Hašdâ; [...].

(5′–7′) Scribe: Nabû-apil-uṣur, son of Bēl-ibni. Borsippa. Month x, day 22, year 3, Artaxerxes, King of Lands.

(reverse) Ring of Bēl-eṭēru. (upper edge) Seal of Bēl-ab-uṣur.

Notes

1 *bar-rat*: see Stolper, "Late Achaemenid Texts from Dilbat," pp. 132–34.

1, 4, 9 *Is-pa-ú?-du*: in all three places *-ú?-* looks unlike *-ú* in lines 6 (*mi-nu-ú*) and 8 (*ku-ú*). The same name appears in *FuB* 14 15 no. 4 lower edge (coll.), in the caption of a seal in Hellenic style, where the sign resembles LU more than Ú, but the clearly Iranian patronym argues against a name containing *-l-*. If correctly read, Ispaʾudu represents Iranian **Vispa-vada-* or **Vispa-vāda-* (R. Zadok, review of M. A. Dandamayev, *Iranians in Achaemenid Babylonia*, Columbia Lectures on Iranian Studies 6 [Costa Mesa, California, 1992], in *BSOAS* 58 [1995]: 158; Tavernier, "Iranica in de Achaemenidische Periode," p. 610).

Atebagā: Babylonian transcription of the name found in Achaemenid Elamite as Attebaka and Hatiyabaka; authorities agree on the Iranian origin, but not on the Iranian etymology: **Aθiya-baga* (R. Zadok, "On the Connections between Iran and Babylonia in the Sixth Century B.C.," *Iran* 14 [1976]: 77; idem, "Iranians and Individuals Bearing Iranian Names in Achaemenid Babylonia," *Israel Oriental Studies* 7 [1977]: 99); **Āθiyāpāka-* (Hinz, *Nebenüberlieferungen*, p. 50); **Haθyabaga* (Tavernier, "Iranica in de Achaemenidische Periode," p. 477 [with other references]).

5, 7 Nabû-bullissu/Nabû-iddin: *FuB* 14 15 no. 4 rev. 4 (scribe).

The tablet had no clear fire damage, beyond a faint orange discoloration on the upper part of the obverse and some incrustation on the reverse; prior to modern baking, the core was unfired.

16. Moore Michigan Coll. 43 — Babylon — 15/IV/14 Darius II
KM 89392 — 28 July 410 B.C.
Bab 55044
Bab. Photos 3141–42
Pedersén N6 242

(1) 3 MA.NA KÙ.BABBAR *a-na taš-li-in-du* (2) *šá* 14 MA.NA KÙ.BABBAR *ina il-ki* (3) *šá* LÚ *Ḫal-pat-ú-a šá* LÚ *ḫa-aṭ-ri* (4) *šá* LÚ *ú-ra-šú šá* É LÚ.IGI+DUB (5) *šá ina* ŠU^{II} ^{md}EN-SU LÚ *šak-nu šá* LÚ *<ú>-ra-šú* (6) *šá* É LÚ.IGI+DUB DUMU *šá* ^{md}EN-MU.NA (7) *šá* MU.14.KÁM ^{m}*Da-ri-ia-a-*⸢*muš* LUGAL⸣ (8) ^{m}*I-da-an-ni-*^{d}AG

LÚ *x* [...] (lower edge 9) DUMU *šá* ^{md}*Na-na-a*-MU *ù* [^{md}EN-*it-tan-nu*] (10) LÚ.ARAD *šá* ^{md}EN-SU *ina na-áš-*[*par-ti*] (11) *šá* ^{md}EN-SU [*ina* ŠU^{II} ^{md}*Uraš*-PAP DUMU *šá*] (reverse 12) ^{m}DÙ-*a maḫ-r*[*u šá* KÙ.BABBAR *a*ʾ 3 MA.NA] (13) KI ^{md}EN-SU *a-na* $^{m⌈d}$*Uraš*⌉-[PAP? *ú-šá-az-za-zu-ma*?] (14) *i-nam-din-nu-*ʾ LÚ *mu-kin-nu* [(...)] (15) ^{md}EN-KAM DUMU *šá* ^{m}*Ḫa-áš-da-a-a* (16) ^{md}EN-*lu-mur* DUMU *šá* ^{m}*I-qu-pu* (17) ^{m}SUM.NA-*a* DUMU *šá* ^{m}BA-*šá-a* (18) ^{m}KI-^{d}EN-*nu-uḫ-šú* DUMU *šá* ^{md}EN-SUR (19) ^{m}*Mi-nu-ú-ana*-^{d}EN-*da-nu* DUB.SAR DUMU *šá* ^{m}*Šu-zu-bu* (20) E.KI ITI.ŠU UD.15.KÁM MU.14.KÁM (upper edge 21) ^{m}*Da-ri-ia-a-muš* LUGAL KUR.KUR

(upper edge) NA_4.KIŠIB / ^{md}EN-*lu-mur* // NA_4.KIŠIB / ^{m}KI-^{d}EN-*nu-u*[*ḫ-šú*] (right edge) NA_4.KIŠIB / ^{m}MU-*a* (left edge) NA_4.KIŠIB / ^{md}EN-KÁM // NA_4.KIŠIB / ^{m}ZU-*an-ni*-^{d}AG // *ṣu-pur* ^{md}EN-*it-tan-nu*

(1–12) Idanni-Nabû, the [...], son of Nanâ-iddin, and [Bēl-ittannu], servant of Bēl-erība, acting on the instruction of Bēl-erība, have received [from Uraš-nāṣir, son of] Ibnâ, 3 minas of silver as the final installment on 14 minas of silver, for the taxes due from the people of Halpattu who belong to the *ḫaṭru*-association of *urāšu* workers of the *mašennu* official's estate, who are under the control of Bēl-erība, the overseer of the *urāšu* workers of the *mašennu* official's estate, son of Bēl-ittannu, (taxes due) for year 14 of King Darius. (12–14) They will [enter the receipt of the said 3 minas of silver] in the records of Bēl-erība and provide (confirmation of the entry) to Uraš-nāṣir.

(14–17) Witnesses: [(...)]; Bēl-ēreš, son of Hašdâ; Bēl-lūmur, son of Iqūpu; Iddinâ, son of Iqīšâ; Itti-Bēl-nuḫšu, son of Bēl-eṭir.

(19–20) Scribe: Mīnû-ana-Bēl-dānu, son of Šūzubu. Babylon, month IV, day 15, year 14, Darius, King of Lands.

(upper edge) Seal of Bēl-lūmur. Seal of Itti-Bēl-nuḫšu. (right edge) Seal of Iddinâ. (left edge) Seal of Idanni-Nabû. Fingernail mark of Bēl-ittannu.

Notes

3 See YBC 11537:3 and 14 (no. 7 above).

5 Bēl-erība/Bēl-ittanna: *FuB* 14 25 no. 16 rev. 3 (witness).

15 Bēl-ēreš/Ḫašdâ: *FuB* 14 11 no. 1 rev. 1, Moore Michigan Coll. 45:8 (see no. 17 below).

Upper Edge, Right Edge The seals of Itti-Bēl-nuḫšu and Iddinâ are both Hellenic in motif and style, both showing standing, naked male figures (fig. 15).

The tablet was burned but not vitrified. The upper edge, upper part of the obverse, and lower part of the reverse were deep red before modern baking, the lower part of the obverse, lower edge, and upper part of the reverse green and dark gray-green, the core dark red.

17. Moore Michigan Coll. 45 Bīt Gir$^{?}$-da$^{?}$ 23/III/15 Darius II
Kelsey 89395 25 June 409 B.C.
Bab 58069
Bab. Photos 3395–96,
Pedersén N6 946

(1) 8 GUR ŠE.BAR *šá* ⸢*uš*$^{??}$ *ṭu*$^{?}$⸣ *tum* (2) GIŠ.BAR A.ŠÀ *šá* ŠE.NUMUN É GIŠ.BAN *šá* TA$^{!}$ (text: GUD) MU.13.KÁM MU.14.KÁM MU.15.KÁM ⸢MU.16$^{!}$.KÁM⸣ (3) *šá* ^{m}*Na-za-zi-ú* DUMU *šá* ^{m}EN-*šú-nu* (4) *ina* <*na*>*-áš-par-tum* *šá* ^{md}*Uraš*-PAP DUMU *šá* ^{m}*Ib-na-a* (5) ^{m}*Na-za-zi-ú* DUMU *šá* ^{m}EN-*šú-nu* (6) *ina* ŠU^{II} ^{md}EN-*ina-É-sag-íl*-IGI (7) ⸢*u* ^{m}*x-x*⸣-^{d}EN$^{!}$-PAP *ma-ḫi-ir* (erasure)

(reverse 8) [LÚ.MU.KIN$_7$ ^{md}E]N-KÁM DUMU *šá* ^{m}*Ḫaš-da-a-a* (9) [...-*í*]*l* A-*šú* *šá* ^{m}ARAD-^{d}U.GUR (10) ⸢^{md}EN-*x*⸣ DUMU *šá* ^{md}BE-MU (11) ^{md}EN-DÙ DUMU *šá* ^{m}DIN (12) ^{md}EN-ŠE.NUMUN$^{?}$ DUMU *šá* ^{m}MU-^{d}EN

(13) ^{md}EN-*ina-É-sag-íl*-IGI LÚ.ŠID (14) A-*šú* *šá* ^{m}SILIM-E.KI URU É *Gir*$^{?}$*-da*$^{?}$ (upper edge 15) ITI.SIG$_4$ UD.23.KÁM MU.15.KÁM (16) ^{m}*Da-ri-ia-a-muš* LUGAL

(left edge) *un-qu* / [...]

(1–7) Nazaziu, son of Bēlšunu, acting on an authorization of Uraš-nāṣir, son of Ibnâ, has received from Bēl-ina-Esagil-lūmur and ...-Bēl-uṣur 8 gur of barley of ..., rent for fields, due on the arable land of a bow-tenancy, (rent) that is from$^{?}$ years 13, 14, 15, and 16, that is owed to Nazaziu, son of Bēlšunu.

(8–13) [Witnesses:] Bēl-ēreš, son of Ḫašdaja; [...]-il, son of Arad-Nergal; Bēl-x, son of Ea-iddin; Bēl-ibni, son of Balāṭu; Bēl-zēri, son of Iddin-Bēl.

(13–16) Bēl-ina-Esagil-lūmur, scribe, son of Šulum-Bābili. Bīt-Girda$^{?}$, month III, day 23, year 15, Darius, King.

(left edge) Ring [of Nazaziu$^{?}$].

Notes

1 Abraded; the signs are not as clear as in Moore's copy. Cf. *AHw*., p. 1253 and *CAD* Š/III s.v. *šīṭūtu*.

2 The line continues around the edge to the reverse, as in YBC 11562:1 (see no. 6 above). ⸢MU.16$^{!}$.KÁM⸣ (if correctly read) is on the right edge, below the level of line 2, partially obscured by the final *-a* of ^{m}*Ib-na-a*, line 4.

4 Authorizations termed *našpartu* (*našpaštu*) ordinarily come from the ultimate creditor, and the recipient acting on the authorization is a servant (*ardu*, *qallu*) or bailiff (*paqdu*) of the creditor. Here, therefore, Uraš-nāṣir is the ultimate creditor,

Nazaziu a tenant, and the payer a subtenant. Alternatively, the *našpartu* may be of a different sort, not an authorization from the creditor, but a letter-order from a tenant (Uraš-nāṣir) authorizing his agent (Bēl-ina-Esagil) to pay the creditor (Nazaziu) on his behalf. The choice depends in part on the correct reading of line 7, where collation does not support, for example, ⸢LÚ! *paq*!-*du*! *šá*!⸣ ^{md}URAŠ!-PAP.

8 Bēl-ēreš/Ḫašdâ: *FuB* 14 11 no. 1 rev. 1; Moore Michigan Coll. 43:15 (see no. 16 above).

11 Bēl-ibni/Balāṭu: *FuB* 14 25 no. 16 rev. 4 (coll.); VAT 15927:2.

14 *Gir*?-*da*?. Collation does not support KAR!-DA, suggested by Zadok *Rép. Géogr.* 8, p. 107, s.v. Bīt-Šūzuba-ileʾi.

Left Edge Impression of a ring, indistinct, half preserved.

The tablet was burned, but not vitrified, with (before modern baking) black and red discoloration across the obverse and a gray core.

Without Known Excavation Number

18. Moore Michigan Coll. 49 — –/–/– Darius II
KM 89401

(1) *a*-⸢*na*? UD⸣.3.KÁM *šá* ITI.[x MU.y.KÁM *šá*] (2) ^{m}*Da-ri-a-muš* [LUGAL (...) ^{md}EN-DÙ] (3) A-*šú šá* ^{md}EN-MU.NU ID-[... ^{md}*Uraš*-PAP] (4) A-*šú šá* ^{m}DÙ-*a a-na muḫ-ḫi* ŠE.NUMUN ⸢*zaq-pu*⸣ (5) *šá* GÚ ÍD ⸢^{d}*Taš*⸣-*me-tum* <<*ana*?>> ^{md}EN-DÙ *iq-bu*-⸢*ú*⸣ (6) *um-ma* ŠE.⸢NUMUN *at-ta-ú*⸣-*a šu-ú* (7) *ár-ki* ^{md}EN-DÙ *mu-kal-lim-tum iš-šá-am-ma* (8) *it-ti* ^{md}*Uraš*-PAP *la*? [(x)] *ir*? *šu*? *ú* (9) ŠE.NUMUN *šu-a-tim šá* ^{md}*Uraš*-PAP ⸢*šu-ú*⸣ (10) *mim*(text IM)-*ma di-i-ni u ra*!-*ga-m*[*u šá*] (lower edge 11) ^{md}EN-DÙ A-*šú šá* ^{md}EN-MU.[NU (...)] (12) *ina muḫ-ḫi* ŠE.NUMUN *zaq-pi šá* [GÚ] (reverse 13) ÍD ^{d}*Taš-me-tum it-ti* [(...)] (14) ^{md}*Uraš*-PAP A-*šú šá* ^{m}DÙ-*a a-na u*$_4$-*mu* (15) *ṣa-a-tum ia-a-nu*

(16) LÚ.MU.KIN$_7$ ^{md}EN-MU A-*šú šá* ^{md}AG-ŠEŠ-MU.NU (17) ^{md}[...]-MU-MU A-*šú šá* ^{m}*x-x-x*

(left edge) NA$_4$.KI[ŠIB] / ^{m}[...]

(reverse) *šṭr* [...]

(1–6) On? day 3 of month [x, year y of King] Darius [... Bēl-ibni], son of Bēl-ittannu, <lodged a complaint?> ag[ainst? Uraš-nāṣir,] son of Ibnâ, concerning arable land planted with date palms that is located on the bank of the Tašmētu Canal, (and) Bel-ibni said: "That property belongs to me"–(7–9) subsequently, Bēl-ibni produced a document to demonstrate (his claim), but ... not? ... with Uraš-nāṣir. (9–15) That property belongs to Uraš-nāṣir. Bēl-ibni, son of Bēl-ittannu, will have no complaint or legal claim against Uraš-nāṣir, son of Ibnâ, regarding the arable land planted with date palms that is on the [bank] of the Tašmētu Canal, ever.

(16-17) Witnesses: Bēl-iddin, son of Nabû-aḫ-ittannu; [...]-šum-iddin [...].

Notes

The issue and outcome are clear, but the terms in which the issue is introduced are not. I am unable to find convincing restorations of the phrasing of lines 1–4, or the apparent verb at the end of line 8.

1 *a*-⸢*na*?⸣: traces, like the published copy, allow *a*-⸢*di*⸣.

3 ID-[...]: restoring *id*-[*bu-ub-ma*] or another form of *dabābu*, puts the verb in an odd position that would make the phrase difficult to understand. Restoring *it*-[*ti* (...)], in addition to leaving a space unaccounted for in the middle of line 3, also leaves no place for an accompanying form of *dabābu* or another verb.

5 Before the *Personenkeil* of ^{md}EN-DÙ is another sign, perhaps *ana* (DIŠ), less likely *šá*. If it is *šá*, I see no plausible interpretation. If it is *ana*, it requires an unlikely change of subject from the apparent plaintiff, Bēl-ibni, to the respondent, Uraš-nāṣir: "[Bēl-ibni lodged a complaint] and Uraš-nāṣir said as follows about the field...."

6 *at-ta-ú-a* as in copy.

Reverse The traces of an Aramaic docket, not represented in the published copy, are lightly incised.

Left edge The impression of a circular stamp seal shows a standing bearded figure facing right, holding a standing winged lion by the throat with his left hand, stabbing it in the belly with a weapon in his right hand.

The lower half and right side of the reverse, the upper edge, and the upper part of the obverse are vitrified. The edges are burned green, and most of the obverse is burned red.

BRITISH MUSEUM

19. BM 116622 (fig. 16) Bīt Bārê 28/–/13 Darius II
1924-5-6,1 411/410 B.C.
Bab 55126
Bab. Photos 3146–47
Pedersén N6 267

(1) [...] (2) *x* [...] *x* (3) *šá x* [...]-*x*-^{d}AG (4) 2? *x x* [...] ÍD *Ri-bat* (5) É GIŠ.BAR *šá* ^{md}⸢*Uraš*-PAP A-*šú šá* ^{m}⸣DÙ-*a u* ^{m}*Gu-zi-ia* (6) ^{md}*Uraš*-PAP *u* ^{m}*Gu-zi-ia* ŠE.NUMUN.MEŠ *a*$_4$ *zaq-pi* (7) *u bar-rat-tum*.MEŠ NÍG.GA LUGAL *a-na* GIŠ.BAR *a-di-i* (8) 4.TA MU.AN.NA.MEŠ *a-na* MU.AN.NA 1 ME 50 GUR (9) [ZÚ.LUM.MA ...]-*x-ru-ni-mu a-na* (10) [...]-⸢LUGAL-DU⸣ *u* ^{md}EN-⸢SUM.NA⸣

(reverse 1′) *x* [...] (2′) *ina muḫ-ḫi* ÍD *Eš*-⸢*šú*⸣ [*i-nam*]-⸢*din-nu-*ʾ TA ITI.x *šá*⸣ (3′) MU.13.KÁM ŠE.NUMUN *ina* IGI-*šú-nu ina* MU.13.KÁM (4′) 1 ME 60 GUR ZÚ.LUM.MA *i-nam-din-nu-*ʾ 1-*en pu-ut* (5′) *šá-ni-e na-šu-ú šá qé-reb iṭ-ṭi-ir a-šar* (6′) ^{md}*Uraš*-PAP *u* ^{m}*Gu-zi-ia ṣe-bu-ú in-na*-<*ṭe*>-*ru-*ʾ

(7′) LÚ.MU.KIN$_7$ ^{m}*Ni-din-tú*-^{d}*Uraš* A-*šú šá* ^{m}ARAD-^{d}*Uraš* (8′) ^{md}EN-*lu-mur* A-*šú šá* ^{m}*Ni-din-tú* ^{md}EN-KAM? A-*šú šá* (9′) ⸢^{md}*x-x*⸣ ^{m}*Tab-tan-ni-e-a* A-*šú šá* ^{m}DIN

(10′) [... L]Ú.ŠID A-*šú šá* ^{md}EN-DIN-*iṭ* URU É LÚ.ḪAL.ME (11′) [ITI.x UD].28.KÁM MU.13.KÁM ^{m}*Dar-ia-a-muš* (12′) [LUGAL KUR.KUR]

(left edge) *ṣu-pur* / ^{md}EN-MU.NA

(1–5) [(Arable land) ... ... (located on)] the Canal of Rībat, held on lease by Uraš-nāṣir, son of Ibnâ, and Gūzija: (6–10) Uraš-nāṣir and Gūzija have [given] that arable land, planted with date palms and undeveloped? parcels, property of the king, [on lease] to x-šar-ukīn and Bēl-ittanna [...] for four years, for an annual (rent) of 150 gur [of dates] ...

(1′–3′) [They will pay (the annual rent) ...] on the New Canal. The land is at their disposal [as of month x,] year 13. (3′–4′) In year 13, they will pay 160 gur of dates. (4′–6′) Each assumes warranty for the other. Whoever is available will pay. Uraš-nāṣir and Gūzija will be paid wherever they wish.

(7′–9′) Witnesses: Nidintu-Uraš, son of Arad-Uraš; Bēl-lūmur, son of Nidintu; Bēl-ēreš?, son of ...; Tabtannēa, son of Balāṭu.

(10′–12′) Scribe: [...], son of Bēl-uballiṭ. Bīt Bārê, [month x], day 28, year 13, Darius, [King of Lands].

(left edge) Fingernail of Bēl-ittanna.

Notes

The text was obtained by Sir Arnold T. Wilson, Chief Civil Commissioner in Iraq in the period immediately after World War I. It was presented to the British Museum by C. L. Woolley.

6 Cf. *Gūzija ardu ša Bēlšunu* (= *Gwzy*) (tenant of date orchard) TCL 13 208:5 and reverse.

6′ For the spelling of the verb, cf., e.g., *ašar* PN *ṣebû in-na-ṭe-<ru>-ʾ* K.8485:8, *ašar* PN *ṣebû i-na-ṭir* Bab. 55387:14 (Pedersén N6 371). Here, as in, e.g., *FuB* 14 11 no. 1:10, the clause overrides the previous specification of the time and place at which the rent is to be paid.

10′ Bīt Bārê in Kasr texts, e.g., *FuB* 14 11 no. 1; OECT 10 140.

The tablet has no visible fire damage, apart from a faint red patch on the obverse.

FREE LIBRARY OF PHILADELPHIA

20. *JCS* 28 34 no. 20 — Bīt Surā? — 24/VIII/4 Artaxerxes II
FLP 1450 — 27 July 401 B.C.
Bab 55390
Bab. Photos 3164–65
Pedersén N6 374

(1) *ú-il-tim šá* ⸢5?⸣ GUR ŠE.BAR (2) *šá* ^{m}*Ḫu-ú-ru* A-*šú* ^{m}*Il-ta-gu-ba-ti* (3) *šá ina muḫ-ḫi* ^{md}EN-DIN-*su*-E A-*šú* (4) *šá* ^{md}EN-SUR-*ru ina lìb-bi* 1 GUR ŠE.BAR (5) ^{m}*Ḫaš-da-a-a* A-*šú* ^{md}EN-ÙRU-*šú* (6) *ina na-áš-par-tum šá* ^{m}*Ḫu-ú-ru* (7) *ina* ŠU^{II} ^{md}EN-DIN-*su*-E *ma-ḫi-ir*

(reverse 8) LÚ *mu-kin-nu* ^{md}AG-PAP A-*šú* ^{md}EN-DÙ (9) ^{m}*Mi-nu-ú-*^{d}EN-*da-nu* A-*šú* ^{md}AG-DIN-*su*-E (10) ^{md}EN-KI-*ia-si?-lim* LÚ.ARAD *šá* ^{m}SU-*a*

(11) ^{md}AG-DIN-*su*-E LÚ.ŠID A-*šú* ^{m}*Nu-uḫ-šá-nu* (12) URU É SUR-*a* ITI.APIN UD.24.KÁM

(13) MU.4.KÁM ^{m}*Ár-tak-šat-su* (14) LUGAL KUR.KUR.MEŠ

(left edge) *ṣu-pur* / ^{m}*Ḫaš-da-a-a*

(1–7) An obligation for 5 gur of barley owed to Hūru, son of Iltagubāti, by Bēl-balāssu-iqbi, son of Bēl-eṭēru: Hašdâ, son of Bēl-uṣuršu, acting on an authorization from Hūru, has received 1 gur of barley of it from Bēl-balāssu-iqbi.

(8–11) Witnesses: Nabû-nāṣir, son of Bēl-ibni; Mīnû-Bēl-dānu, son of Nabû-balāssu-iqbi; Bēl-ittija-silim?, servant of Erība.

(11–14) Scribe: Nabû-balāssu-iqbi, son of Nuḫšānu. Bīt Surā, month VIII, day 24, year 4, Artaxerxes, King of Lands.

(left edge) Fingernail of Hašdaja.

Notes

2 Hūru < Egyptian *ḥr(.w)*: R. Zadok, "On Some Egyptians in First-Millennium Mesopotamia," *Gött. Misz.* 26 (1977): 64; "On Some Foreign Population Groups in First Millennium Babylonia," *Tel Aviv* 6 (1979): 172; "On Some Egyptians in Babylonian Documents," *Gött. Misz.* 64 (1983): 73; and A. C. V. M. Bongenaar and B. J. J. Haring, "Egyptians in Neo-Babylonian Sippar," *JCS* 46 (1994): 68. The patronym, Iltagubāti, is West Semitic, formed on the root *śgb* "prevail, be exalted" (see R. Zadok, *On West Semites in Babylonia during the Chaldean and Achaemenian Periods: An Onomastic Study* [Jerusalem, 1978], pp. 81, 103, 109; review of Edward Lipiński, *Studies in Aramaic Inscriptions and Onomastics* I, OLA 57 (Leuven, 1975–94) in *BiOr* 33 [1976]: 230; and "Assyro-Babylonian Lexical and Onomastic Notes," *BiOr* 41 [1984]: 41).

10 Bēl-ittija-silim: *ZA* 79 93:7, 10, with note on p. 95.

12 *ZA* 79 93:22.

The tablet shows no sign of severe fire damage.

MUSEU BIBLÍC, MONTSERRAT[8]

With Known Excavation Number

21. *Aula Orientalis* 15 187 no. 38 — —
MM 893
Bab 50410
Bab Photos 2997–98
Pedersén N6 31

(1′) LÚ *mu-kin-ni* ^{m}EN-*ú-š*[*al-lim* A-*š*]*ú š*[*á*] ^{m}*Ba-la-ṭu* A ^{m}LÚ.SIPA GUD.MEŠ (2′) ^{md}AG-⸢x-x-DU⸣ A-*šú šá* ^{md}EN-MU ^{m}KI-^{d}EN-*nu-uḫ-šú* (3′) [...] ⸢ *x x x x x* ⸣

The obverse, edges, and most of the reverse are entirely vitrified, black and green.

Without Known Excavation Numbers

22. *Aula Orientalis* 15 186 no. 37 Bāb Surru 10+/XI/–
MM 1153

(1′) x x [...] (2′) [*ina* IT]I.SIG$_4$ [...] (3′) [*k*]*i-i* ITI.ŠU KÙ.[BABBAR *a*ʾ x] (4′) [*l*]*a it-tan-nu šá* ITI *ina m*[*uḫ-ḫi*] (5′) [1 *m*]*a-né-e* 1 GÍN KÙ.BABBAR ḪAR.R[A] (6′) *i-rab-bi* 1-*en pu-ut šá-ni-i* (7′) *na-šu-ú šá qé-reb iṭ-ṭi-ir*

(8′) LÚ *mu-kin-nu* ^{md}EN-[SU]R-*ru* (9′) A ^{md}EN-GAR-*nu* ^{md}EN-*u-ṣur-šú* (10′) A ^{m}*Pat-ti*?-*ri* ^{m}*Rab*?-*bi*? A ^{m}*Kal-ba-a* (upper edge 11′) ^{md}EN-DIN-*su* A ^{m}MU-^{d}EN

(12′) ^{md}AG-DIN-*su*-E LÚ.ŠID A ^{md}EN-*ú*-[...] (13′) ⸢URU⸣ KÁ *Sur-ru* ITI.ZÍZ UD.10[+x.KÁM] (14′) [...] *x x* [...] (left edge 15′) [...] ⸢KUR?⸣

(1′–7′) [They will repay the silver in month] III. If they have not paid the silver by month IV, on each mina one shekel of interest will accrue to (their) debit monthly. Each one assumes warranty for the other.

(8′–11′) Witnesses: Bēl-eṭēru, son of Bēl-iškunu; Bēl-uṣuršu, son of Pattiri?; Rabbi?, son of Kalbâ; Bēl-bullissu, son of Iddin-Bēl.

[8] Purchased by Father Bonaventura Ubach in 1922/1923, somewhere in the Near East; see Cornelia Wunsch, "Neu- und spätbabylonische Urkunden aus dem Museum von Montserrat," *Aula Orientalis* 15 (1997): 139f.

(12′–15′) Nabû-balāssu-iqbi, scribe, son of Bēl-u[...]. Bāb Surru. Month XI, day 10+x, [year x ..., King of Land]s.

The obverse and edges are vitrified, dark green to black.

23. *Aula Orientalis* 15 185 no. 36 — –/I/4 Darius II
MM 1145 420/419 B.C.

(1′) TA ITI.BÁR MU.4.KÁM ^{m}*Da-*[*ri-ia-a-muš* LUGAL] (2′) A?.ŠÀ? *ina*? IGI?-*šú*? *il-ki-šú ina* MU.AN.NA [...] (3′) 5 GÍN KÙ.BABBAR *a-na* ^{md}AMAR.UTU-SU [(...)] (4′) A-*šú šá* ^{m}EN-*šú-nu* LÚ *pa-ḫa-ti* DIN.T[IR.KI] (5′) *i-nam-din*

(1′–5′) Beginning in month I, year 4 of Darius [the King], the field? is in his possession?. He will pay to Marduk-erība, son of Bēlšunu, governor of Babylon, 5 shekels of silver per year for his *ilku* obligation.

2′ The reading of the first signs, over erasures, is uncertain. Also possible is ḪAR.?RA? *il-ki-šú*, hence "he will pay 5 shekels of silver as interest on? (money paid in lieu of) his *ilku* obligation."

3′f. See comments to YBC 11554:5 (see no. 10 above).

All preserved surfaces are black. The reverse and most edges were melted and cooled into a convex blob with rough, bubbled surface.

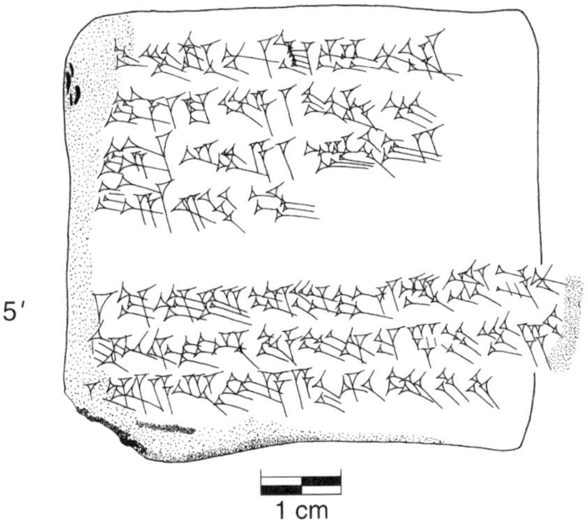

Figure 1. YBC 11555

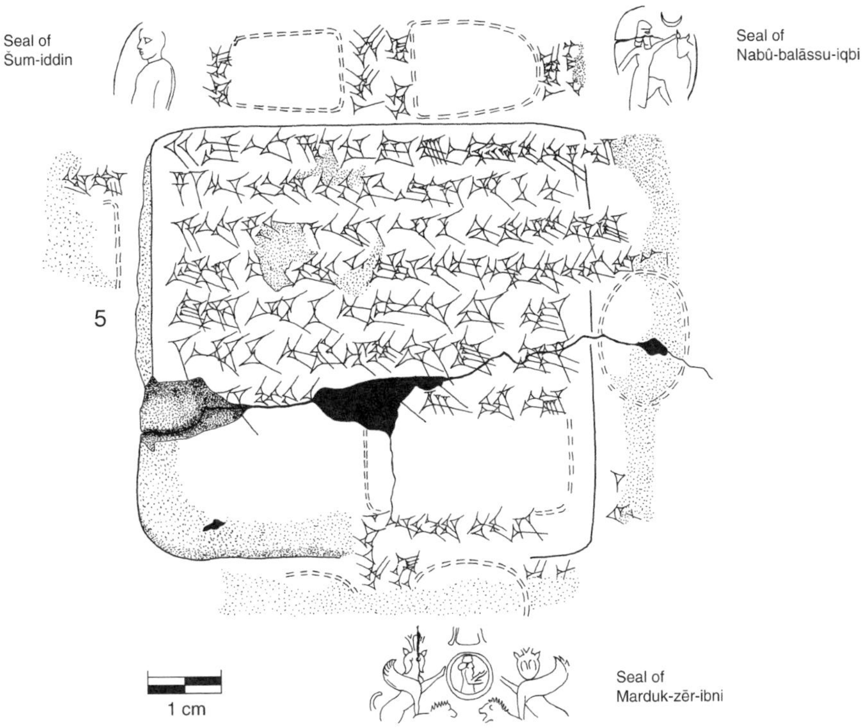

Figure 2. YBC 11552

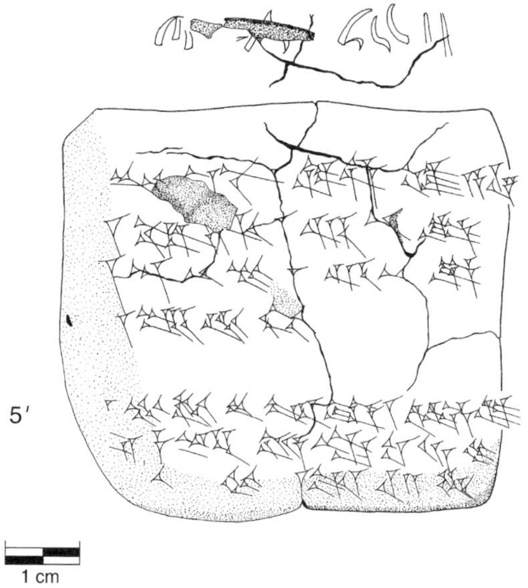

Figure 3. YBC 11558

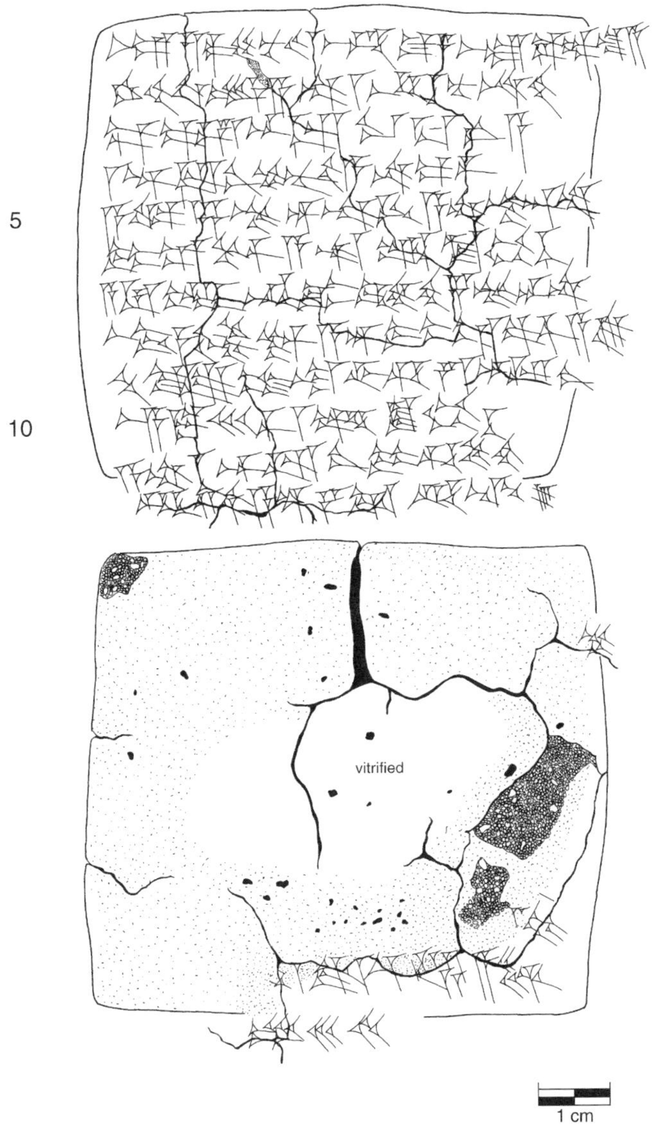

Figure 4. YBC 11586

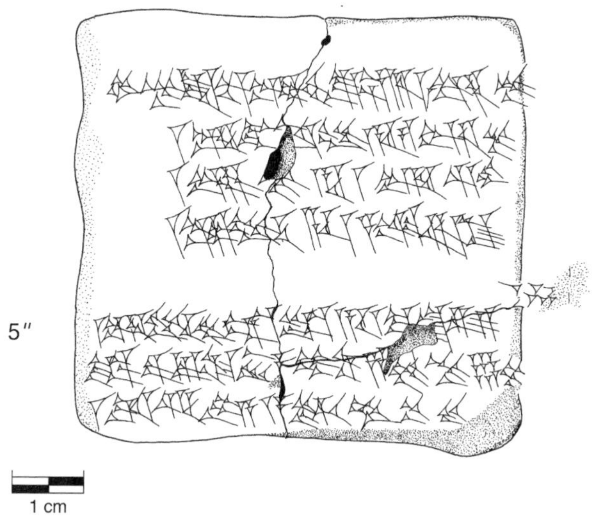

Figure 5. YBC 11557

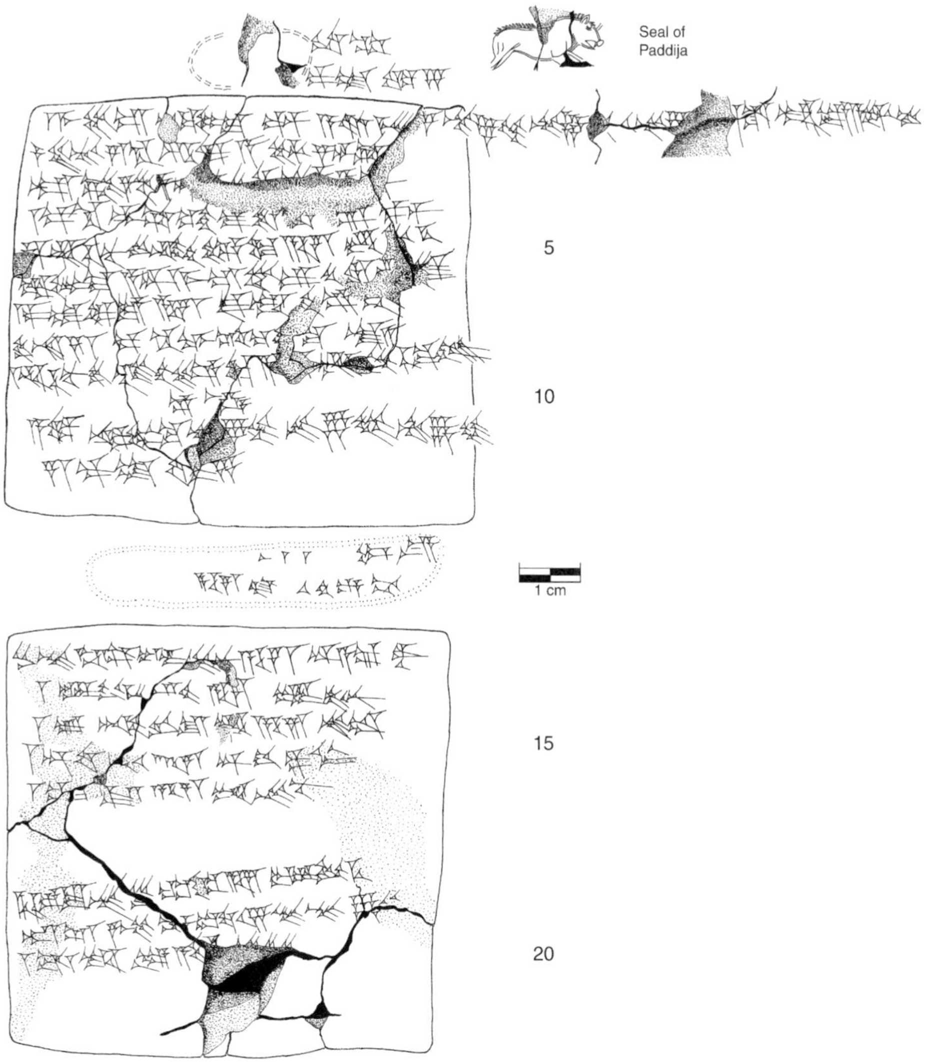

Figure 6. YBC 11562

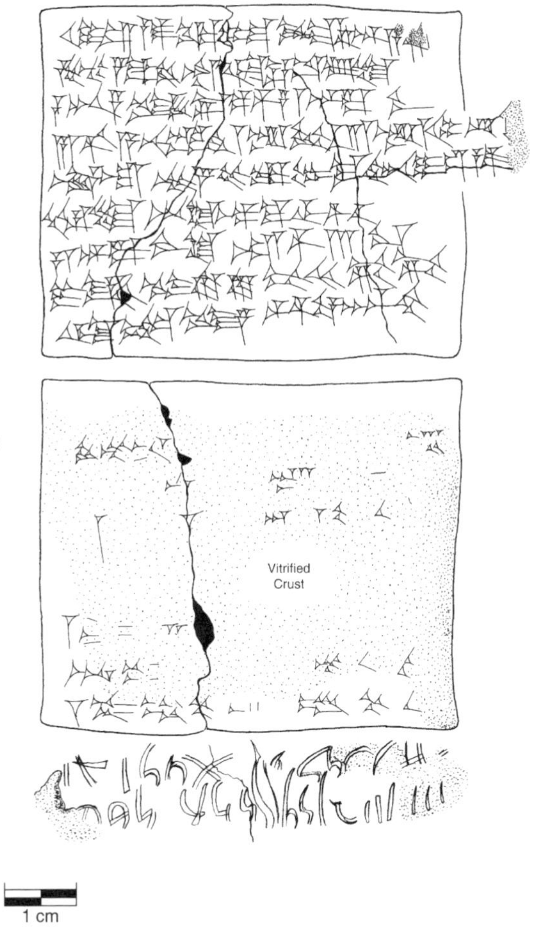

Figure 7. YBC 11537

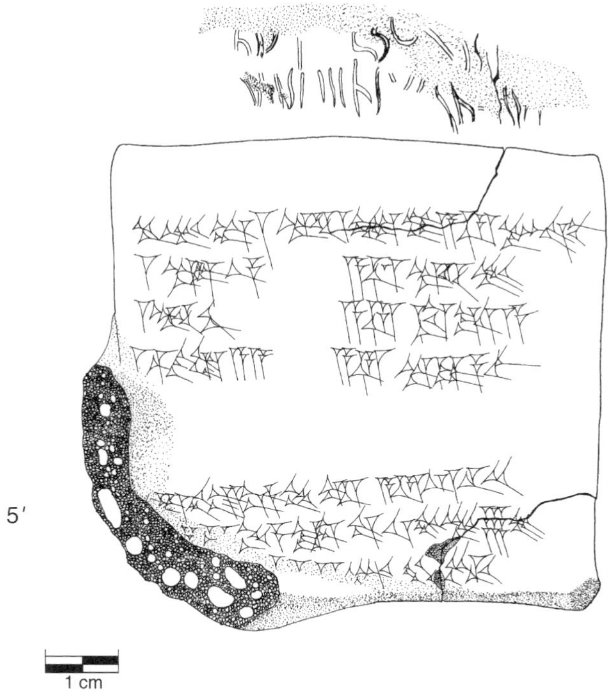

Figure 8. YBC 11585

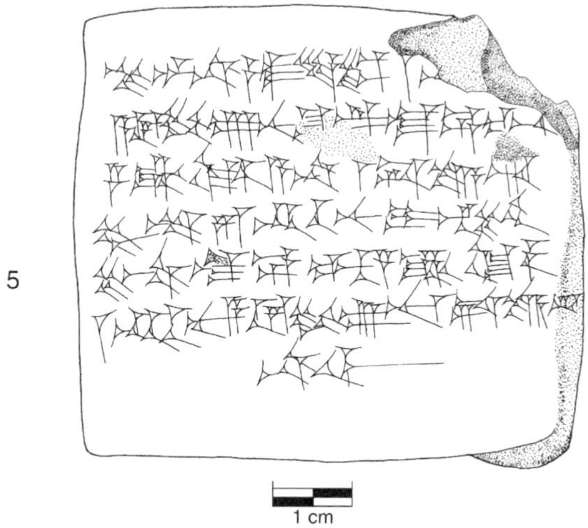

Figure 9. *Oelsner AV* 469 (YBC 11560)

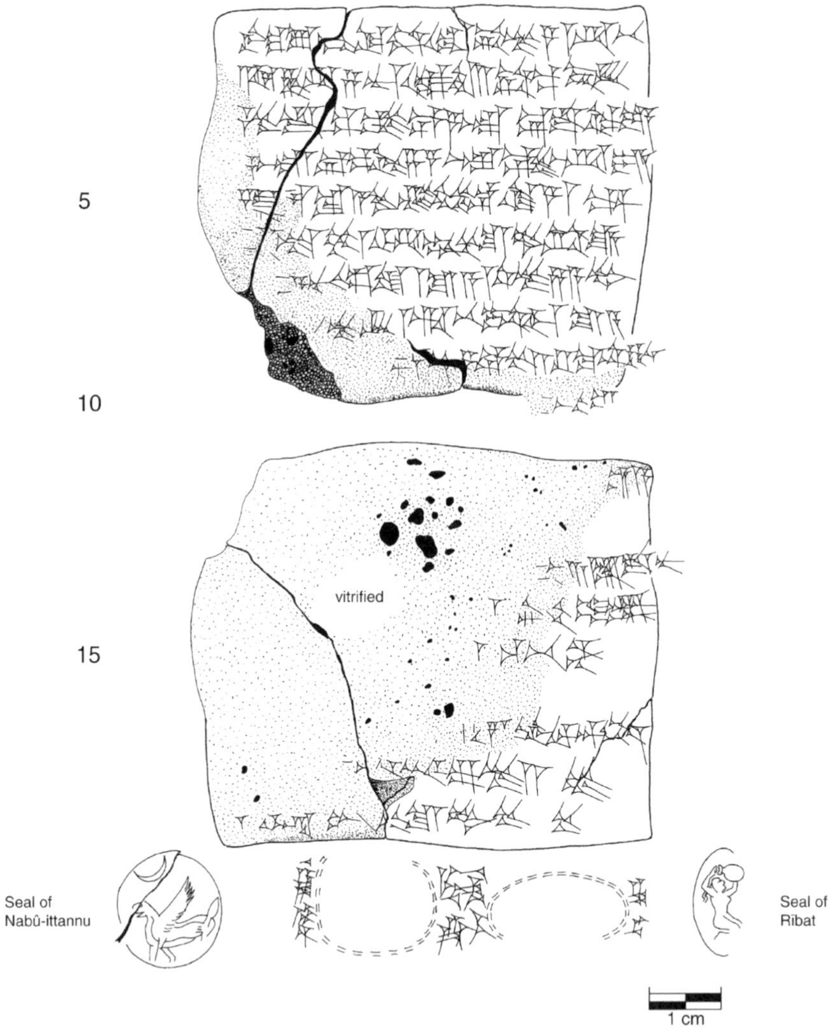

Figure 10. YBC 11554

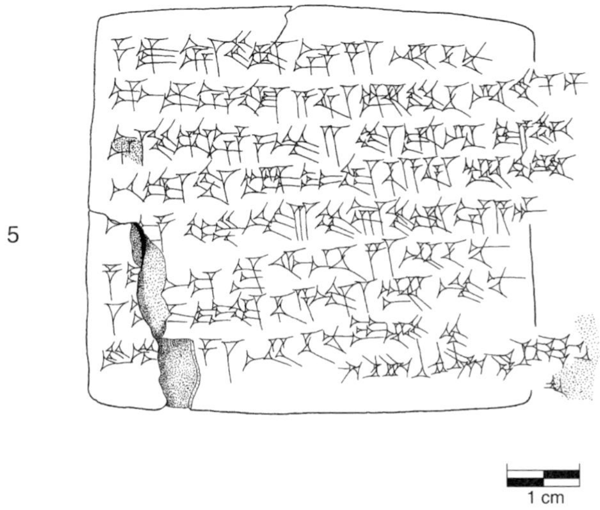

Figure 11. YBC 11550

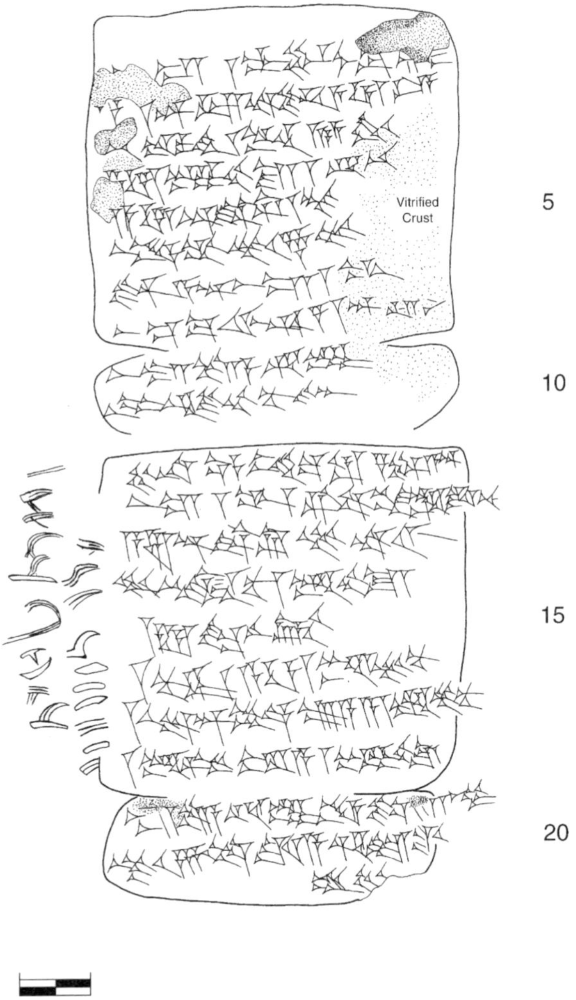

Figure 12. YBC 11532

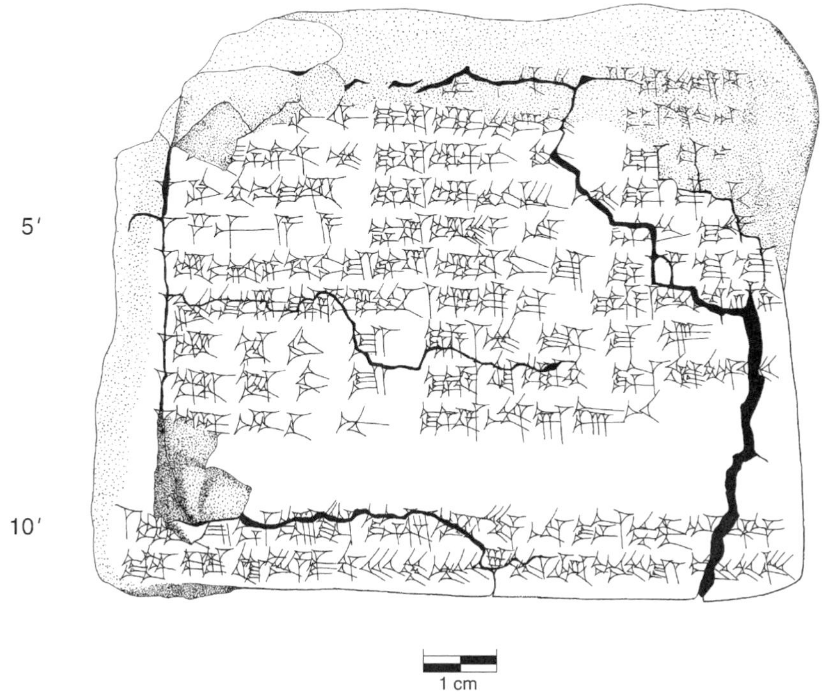

Figure 13. YBC 11600

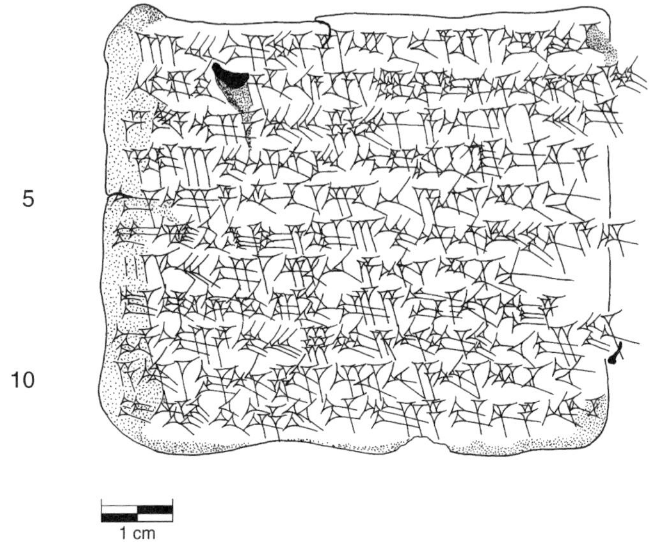

Figure 14. NBC 8394

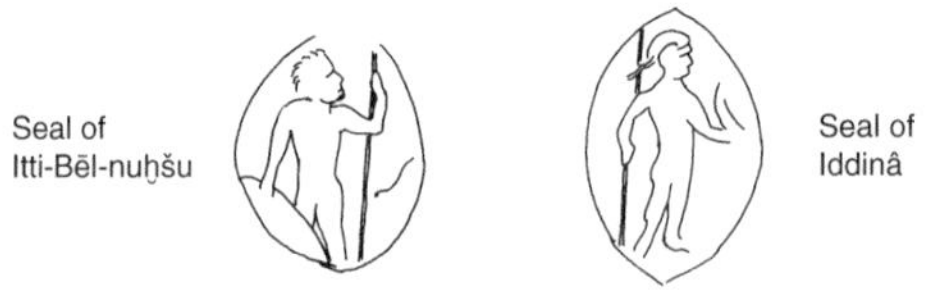

Figure 15. Moore Michigan Coll. 43, Upper Edge, Right Edge

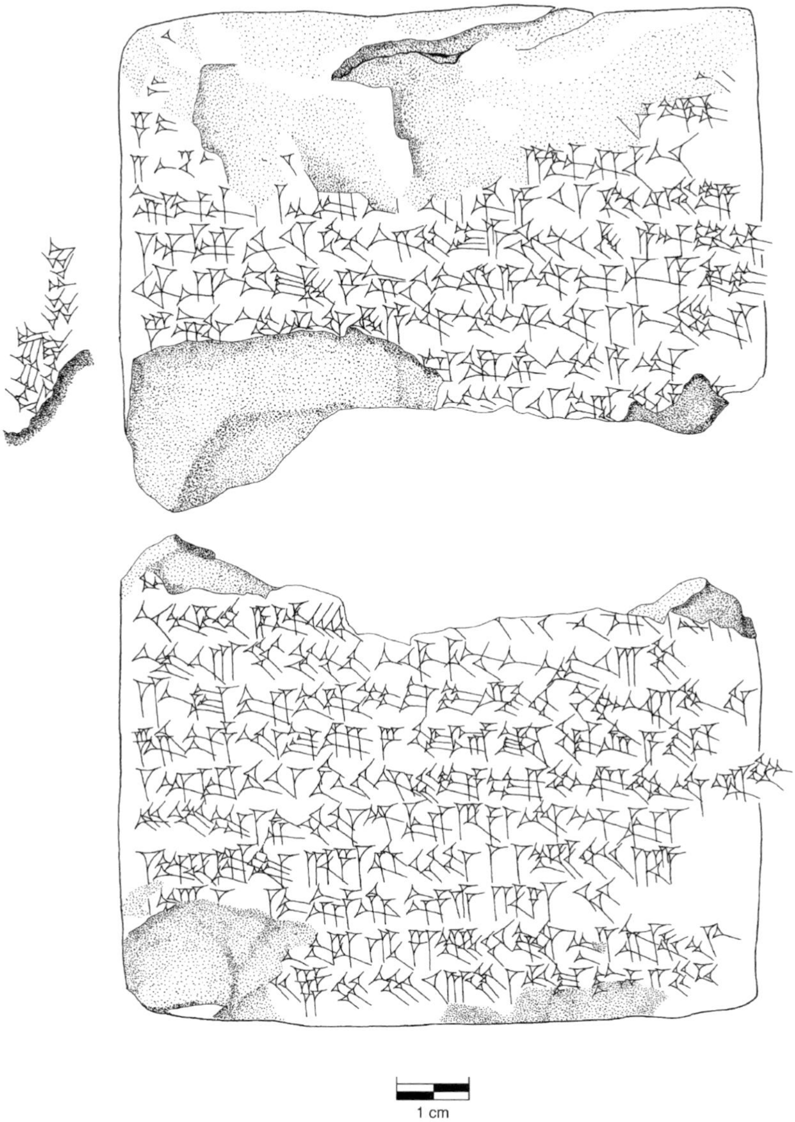

Figure 16. BM 116622

SISTERLY ADVICE ON AN ENDANGERED MARRIAGE IN AN OLD ASSYRIAN LETTER*

K. R. Veenhof, Universiteit Leiden

I. INTRODUCTION

Most of the tablets found in the archives of the Old Assyrian traders settled in the commercial district of the ancient Anatolian city of Kanesh concern their business, overland trade. Because the traders belonged to family firms, relatives also appear in their records, including mothers, wives, sisters, daughters, and daughters-in-law. Many references to the latter reflect their involvement in trade, notably as producers of woolen textiles, which they sent to Anatolia; thus women took part in and supported their husbands' and fathers' businesses and were also able to earn some silver for their own purses.[1] Moreover, letters show that during the frequent, and at times prolonged, absence of their husbands, wives of traders had to manage their households and were often burdened by financial or legal problems.[2]

---

* Abbreviations of works cited in this article that are not found in the *Chicago Assyrian Dictionary* are:

AMMY	*Anadolu Medeniyetleri Müzesi Yıllığı* (Ankara, 1986–).
EL	G. Eisser and J. Lewy, *Die altassyrischen Rechtsurkunden von Kültepe*, MVAG 33 and 35/3 (Leipzig, 1930 and 1935).
POAT	W. C. Gwaltney, Jr. *The Pennsylvania Old Assyrian Texts*, HUCA, Supplement 3 (Cincinnati, 1983).
KEL	Kültepe Eponym List, in K. R. Veenhof, *The Old Assyrian List of Year Eponyms from Karum Kanish and Its Chronological Implications*, Türk Tarih Kurumu Yayınları VI/64 (Ankara, 2003).
OAA 1	M. T. Larsen, *The Aššur-nādā Archive*, Uitgaven van het Nederlands Instituut voor het Nabije Oosten te Leiden, *voorheen* Publications de l'Institut historique-archéologique néerlandais de Stamboul 96, Old Assyrian Archives, 1 (Leiden, 2002).
TC 1	TCL 4.
TC 2	TCL 14.
TC 3	TCL 19–21.

[1] See the data presented in Veenhof *Old Assyrian Trade*, pp. 103–23. Their activities are marked by the word *tadmiqtum*, which denotes an interest-free loan, without fixed or guaranteed profit, usually entrusted to a relative or friend (who will "make the best of it," *dammuqum*); it normally refers to the textiles entrusted as *tadmiqtum*, but it was also used for the amount of silver expected in return.

[2] For a translation of 100 letters written by Old Assyrian women, see C. Michel, *Correspondance des marchands de Kaniš au début du IIe millénaire avant J.-C.*, Littératures anciennes du Proche-Orient 19 (Paris, 2001), chap. 7, "La correspondance féminine."

Women figure also in texts not directly related to trade, however, such as records dealing with marriage, divorce, and wills, which document the legal aspects of the life of well-to-do, literate families, where contracts were made and cases brought before the courts.[3] Other topics, such as houses, children, slaves, health, death, religion, and domestic problems, are mainly attested in the correspondence of women. Differences in the nature and availability of this evidence are due to the status of the women (married wives, widows, unmarried *ugbabtu*-priestesses, daughters) and where they lived. Several wives, especially those married to traders during the early period, stayed behind in Assur when their husbands went to Anatolia, the latter making only occasional visits to Assur. Others lived in Kanesh, having accompanied or later having joined their husbands, who had settled there. Legal records documenting the family life of the former are rare, presumably because the records were kept in Assur, but we know these women through their correspondence with their husbands. Evidence concerned with the women living in Anatolia has generally been found in their husbands' archives in Kanesh and consists of a variety of records. Some of these records were drawn up in connection with important events, such as marriage, death, and inheritance;[4] others reflect the women's usually small-scale business activities (the granting of small loans, dealings with slaves, petty commerce, etc.). In addition, we have letters written by women to their husbands when the latter were on business trips in Anatolia (and which the men apparently took home with them when they returned to Kanesh), and there are also some letters received from or sent to female relatives in Assur.

The letter presented in this article belongs to the last-mentioned category and was written by a woman in Assur called Ummi-Išhara to her sister in Kanesh, most probably Šalimma, in a last attempt to solve the problems between the latter and her unhappy husband, Irma-Aššur, who had moved back to Assur. Written to a sister with problems, the letter is personal and emotional, presents acute observations about the situation and the emotional states of the main characters, and contains pleas, criticism, and warnings. The letter from Ummi-Išhara is meant to convince her sister that the situation is serious and that she must change her mind. Moreover, her rhetoric makes this document also syntactically and lexically interesting. I offer this study as a tribute to Bob Biggs, known for his interest in the intellectual and domestic life of ancient Mesopotamia, as demonstrated by his publication of an interesting Old Assyrian letter containing the plaint of a woman.[5]

[3] For these features, see my recent survey, "Old Assyrian Period," in R. Westbrook, ed., *A History of Ancient Near Eastern Law* (Leiden and Boston, 2003), pp. 450–60, § 5, "Family," and § 6, "Property and Inheritance."

[4] We have the will of a (remarried) Assyrian widow who died in Kanesh (ibid., p. 457, n. 136) and references to those of others, including Lamassatum.

[5] R. D. Biggs, "A Woman's Plaint in an Old Assyrian Letter," *WZKM* 86 (1996): 47–52.

II. Prosopography and Archival Matters

The letter belongs to the archive of the trader Elamma, son of Iddin-Suen, which was excavated in 1991 and given to me for publication by the director of the excavations of Kanesh-Kültepe, Tahsin Özgüç. Some background information is necessary in order to identify the four persons involved and to explain the letter's presence in Elamma's archive; it will illustrate the importance of prosopographical analysis and reconstruction of the family structure but also the problems that emerge, even with officially excavated texts, if we wish to explain their presence in or scattering over different archives and houses.

The letter acquaints us with four persons: its writer, Ummi-Išhara; its addressees, Lamassatum and Šalimma; and a man who is always referred to as "the gentleman" (*awīlum*), who, as the envelope indicates, is Šalimma's husband Irma-Aššur.[6]

Ummi-Išhara was the (eldest?) daughter of Elamma and Lamassatum; she became an *ugbabtu*-priestess and lived permanently in Assur. Kt 91/k 421, which quotes Lamassatum's final dispositions, speaks of Ummi-Išhara as "my daughter, the priestess" (*mer*ʾ*itī* NIN.DINGIR). In kt 91/420 (undated) she concludes an agreement with her three brothers about the division of certain assets left behind by their father, and kt 91/k 377:9 ff. refers to her as "their sister, the *gubabtum*" in a settlement "after (the death of) Lamassatum, her mother" (*warka L. ummiša).*

Lamassatum is Ummi-Išhara's mother, and the fact that her husband Elamma is not mentioned suggests that he had already died, probably in eponymy year 104 or 105,[7] after a career of nearly forty years as a trader in Kanesh. Lamassatum survived him (the latest dated record in which she occurs is from eponymy year 106) and presumably continued to live in his house, which she may have inherited from him. Lamassatum's contacts with her daughter Šalimma's husband, Irma-Aššur, are documented in the letter kt 91/k 455:25 f., which mentions the possibility that his tablets "are with Lamassatum." In kt 91/k 503 (presumably after Elamma's death) a sum of silver belonging to Elamma's (eldest) son has to be sent to Assur and is entrusted to Lamassatum and to Irma-Aššur; kt 91/k 421:15–17 mentions among the assets left behind by Lamassatum: "1 mina of silver that I gave to Irma-Aššur for making purchases (in Assur)."

---

[6] I maintain the conventional renderings of the names: Lamassatum, though forms with (Lamassutum) and without "vowel harmony" are attested, and Irma-Aššur (cf. *Ir-ma-*^{d}IŠKUR in AKT 3 73:19), though this name was pronounced Irmaššur < Irēm-Aššur, or < Irʾam-Aššur (for *irʾam* in theophoric names, see MAD 3 230, with the ideas proposed by M. Hilgert, *Akkadisch in der Ur III-Zeit* [Münster, 2002], pp. 249 ff.).

[7] The eponymy years are counted from the first year of Erišum I, ruler of Assur, on the basis of KEL. A record dated to eponymy year 106 deals with the division of part of his inheritance.

Šalimma, whose father's name is never mentioned, must be one of Lamassatum's daughters. Elamma's son, Ennum-Aššur, in a letter to Irma-Aššur in Assur (kt 91/k 290:33 ff.) quotes the latter's words: "If your sister comes to the city (of Assur), give her the price of the textiles and let her come here." Irma-Aššur's reaction is: "Since there is severe cold here and it is not feasible for her to come, I will therefore not give her the silver. It is up to you, there, to decide what to do."[8] "Your sister" cannot refer to the priestess Ummi-Išhara, who remained in Assur,[9] and hence must be another sister; Šalimma is the only candidate, and we know she indeed did not travel to Assur and while in Kanesh needed money for her expenses. In our letter Irma-Aššur is quoted as saying that she could have asked for the silver she needed from her mother and brothers there (in Kanesh, lines 22–24), apparently from Lamassatum and her sons. One problem is that Šalimma's brother, Ennum-Aššur, in his letter kt 91/k 366:34 f., appeals to Irma-Aššur with the words: "Please, my father, my lord, whom else can I trust but you?" and in lines 7 f., in a more neutral way, writes: "He is my father; he will go and send me from Assur 10 minas of tin and so give me courage." We may explain these lines by assuming that Ennum-Aššur's brother-in-law was his senior (see the observation made in n. 22 below), both in age and in business, and that Ennum-Aššur needed his help.

Šalimma's stay in Kanesh is suggested by the discovery of some of her records in Elamma's archive, a debt-claim on two Anatolians (kt 91/k 518) and the contract kt 91/k 522, wherein she buys a house in Kanesh for $2\frac{1}{2}$ minas of silver from (her aunt) Ištar-lamassi and her brother or her uncle, Aššur-ṭab.[10] It may have been the house where she lived together with her husband when the latter was living in Anatolia. Another legal document, excavated in 1986, kt 86/k 155A/B,[11] may deal with this same house, though it cannot be identified with certainty because neither the seller nor the price are mentioned. This document is a verdict of *kārum* Kanesh, issued when the ownership of the house was disputed, probably by Lamassatum, and states that the house will count as Šalimma's property if Amur-Ištar (Elamma's brother and hence one of Šalimma's un-

[8] *umma attama: šumma* (34) *ahatka ana ālim tallakam kaspam* (35) *šīm ṣubātī diššimma lu tallikam* (36) *annakam kīma kuṣṣū dannūnima la naṭûma* (37) *la tallakanni adi kiam kaspam la uššaršim* (38) *attā ammakam malaka.*

[9] In kt 91/k 366:13–14 Irma-Aššur tells Ennum-Aššur about the silver he had taken to Assur to pay the latter's creditor: "your sister needed the silver, and so I gave it to her in accordance with your letter" (*kaspam ahatka tahšahma ana ša ṭuppika attidiššim*), and this must refer to the *ugbabtu* Ummi-Išhara.

[10] I have edited this text; see G. J. Selz, ed., *Festschrift für Burkhart Kienast zu seinem 70. Geburtstage dargebracht von Freunden, Schülern und Kollegen*, AOAT 274 (Münster, 2003), pp. 693–95. The handing over of the title of the house by the seller to the buyer, mentioned in this contract, makes sense, since the house had originally been sold by its Anatolian owner. Possession of the original deed of sale offered protection to a new owner, who lived in it in Kanesh.

[11] This record is an isolated one in the group of records numbered kt 86/k 153 to 229, the majority of which concern Šu-Suen and Idnaya, sons of Šu-Hubur. This tablet must have been found in debris and may originally have come from a neighboring house, as must also be true of kt 86/k 204, a fragment of the case of the contract kt 87/k 39, an Anatolian slave sale.

cles) swears "that the house was bought with Šalimma's silver and that he does know that it was Lamassatum's silver." If he refuses, "Lamassatum will swear by Ištar's tambourine (? *huppum*[12]) that the house was bought with the silver of Iddin-Suen" (the father of her husband Elamma, from whom she must have inherited money), and thus the house counts as hers.[13] Whichever house the disputed house may be, this document confronts us with the problems that arose in the family, probably after Elamma's death. References to Šalimma in the archival texts of the Elamma family are not numerous, presumably because she had married and thus no longer lived in Elamma's house, was more involved in her husband's business, and did not appear in the records dealing with her father's inheritance because she had been given a dowry when she was married off.

Irma-Aššur, Šalimma's husband, occurs in about twenty texts found in Elamma's archive dated to eponymies ranging from eponymy year 91 to 108. I assume that he was the son of Nidebani (perhaps read *Ì-dí-ba-ni*), a patronymic attested in Dalley *Edinburgh* 7 = EL 93:1 (eponymy 93),[14] AKT 1 40:17 (eponymy 94), and TC 3 213:11 (eponymy 108), where Irma-Aššur figures as a witness.[15] The name of his son most probably occurs as "*Ì-dí-ba-ni*, son of Irma-Aššur," witness to the undated contract kt 91/k 505. He was active in Anatolia, where he traveled, traded, and acted as a witness to a number of contracts, but he also regularly journeyed to Assur, as is clear from kt 91/k 503 and kt 91/k 421, mentioned above. He must have lived in Kanesh for some time but later seems to have settled more permanently in Assur. There he was involved in a legal dispute (kt 91/k 494), and Elamma's son apparently wanted to meet him there, when he wrote (in kt 91/k 366:45 f.): "Allow me to see the eyes of (the god) Assur and your own eyes." There he also, together with Ummi-Išhara and some other young woman, received a dramatic letter written by Lamassatum and her eldest son about the death of three family members.[16] His move from Kanesh to Assur could explain why records involving him have been found in Elamma's archive and,

---

[12] The verdict, referred to in n. 19 below, also obliges women to swear by this symbol.

[13] Lines 3 ff.: *itamma Amur-Ištar ina patrim ša Aššur* (5) *bētū ina kasap Šalimma* (case adds *lū*) *šamūni libbušu la ide'u kīma kasap Lamassitinni* (10) *šumma Amur-Ištar itamma bētū ša Šalimma šumma la itamma tatamma Lamassutum ina huppim ša Ištar* (15) *bētū ina kasap Iddin-Suen lū šamūni* (case: *la šamūni ina kaspiša lū šamūni*) *šumma tatamma bētum bēssa*.

[14] The case alone was edited as EL 93, where in line 1 one should read [KIŠIB *Ir-m*]*a-A-šùr;* the tablet does not give his father's name. It is now clear that seal 2 in Dalley's edition is that of Irma-Aššur, since the same seal occurs on kt a/k 462 (AKT 1 40) and on kt 94/k 179 (courtesy of Cécile Michel), which Irma-Aššur sealed as debtor. Its inscription was discussed by M. V. Tonietti, "Le cas de *mekum*: continuité ou innovation dans la tradition éblaïte entre IIIe et IIe millénaires?" *MARI* 8 (1997): 230, and while the reading of the last two lines, *ša me-ku-um* / *i-ra-mu-šu* is certain, that of the first two, which should identify its owner, is problematic. It does not mention our Irma-Aššur, who must have acquired the seal from someone else.

[15] Irma-Aššur, son of Aššur-malik, who occurs once as witness in another text in the archive (kt 91/k 370:31), must be a different man. There are more than thirty references to Irma-Aššur in texts from other archives, but without knowing the fathers' names it is not easy to distinguish our man from his namesake.

[16] This implies that the letter found in Elamma's archive is a copy kept in Kanesh.

after the latter's death, "are with Lamassatum" (kt 91/k 455:25 f.). Texts of his found in Elamma's archive consist of a few letters, a debt-note in which he was the creditor (kt 91/k 504), a few in which he was the debtor (kt 91/k 523, 525), a sealed quittance (kt 91/k 516), and some texts recording *be'ūlātu*-loans supplied by him (kt 91/k 325, 480). These texts do not constitute an archive but must be records that had been deposited and left behind (in a separate container?) in Elamma's house, perhaps when Irma-Aššur left for Assur.

My introductory remarks could end here, but there is one archival complication that should be mentioned because it sheds further light on our couple, Irma-Aššur and Šalimma. Irma-Aššur figures prominently also in texts excavated in the beginning of the 1994 season, especially in those numbered kt 94/k 119 to 182.[17] They include five letters written to him, ten debt-notes in which he is the creditor (between eponymies 86 and 108), two where he is debtor (eponyms 101 and 102), and one quittance. There are also fifteen legal records, among them a contract by which a certain Aššur-malik marries Irma-Aššur's daughter Suhkana[18] and a verdict by the *kārum* authorizing Irma-Aššur to make some men and women swear an oath in order to obtain information about losses he has suffered.[19] These records also contain references to Irma-Aššur's brother, Aššur-malik; to Elamma's wife, Lamassatum (three debt-notes in which she is the creditor); and to Irma-Aššur's wife, Šalimma. The discovery of records belonging to the same persons in two separate houses (excavated in 1991 and 1994) is remarkable. Speculation on the mixing of texts from two (neighboring?) houses due to destruction and later rebuilding is premature in the absence of a detailed excavation report.[20] The presence of so many of Irma-Aššur's debt-notes and legal documents in the house excavated in 1994 strongly suggests that this was his house, the house where he lived with Šalimma as long as he was in Kanesh (the latest eponymy year attested for him is 108) and the house where later she perhaps lived alone, since its archive also contained a letter, a debt-note, and a contract connected to the purchase of one of her slaves. It may have even been the house bought by Šalimma, mentioned in the (undated) contract kt 91/k 522 discussed above. The close links with Elamma's family may explain that some records belonging to Lamassatum ended up in the house of her daughter Šalimma, perhaps after Lamassatum's death.

Finally, we have a letter written by Šalimma herself, kt 91/k 499, addressed to "my sons" Šu-Ištar and Aššur-imitti, who are asked to take out of the coffers containing

---

[17] I thank Cécile Michel for telling me about these texts.

[18] Kt 94/k 149, edited by C. Michel and P. Garelli, "New Old Assyrian Marriage Contracts," *AMMY* 1995, pp. 298 f.

[19] Kt 94/k 131, edited by C. Michel in "Hommes et femmes prêtent serment à l'époque paléo-assyrienne," *Méditerranées* 10–11 (1997): 111–14.

[20] The house described by Tahsin Özgüç in *Veenhof AV*, pp. 369 f., and whose rooms 5–6 contained 947 texts, as Özgüç has kindly told me, was excavated in 1994. These texts constitute the second archive excavated in that year (kt 94/k 280 ff.) and will be edited by M. T. Larsen.

her tablets, in (her house? in) Kanesh, a particular debt-note and to bring it "here" because the debtor has started a legal dispute.[21] The letter must have been sent from Assur and ended up in Elamma's archive, perhaps because her sons (after the departure of Šalimma's mother) lived in Elamma's family's house. The existence of grown-up sons implies that she must have been married to Irma-Aššur for quite some time, as does the contract found in 1994, whereby Irma-Aššur marries off his (their?) daughter Suhkana.[22] Both texts must reflect circumstances later than our letter, which, instead, speaks of Šalimma's "(young) children" (*šerrū*) in Assur, who suffer because of her absence (lines 31 f. and 46). In any case, Šalimma's letter does show that she eventually returned to Assur, and her stay in that city is also clear from a few texts recording shipments of silver from Kanesh to Assur, where, in three cases, she figures among the (mostly female) recipients of small amounts of silver.[23] This suggests that the crisis responsible for the writing of our letter was finally over.

III. The Letter

A piece of the case kt 91/k 386 (1-240-91; 6.3 × 5.9 cm)

	[KIŠIB *Um-mì-Iš-ha-ra*]	[Seal of Ummi-Išhara]
	[*a-na Lá-ma-sà-tim*]	[To Lamassatum]
	[seal impression A]	
rev.	⌈seal impression A⌉	
	ù Ša-lim-ma	and Šalimma,
	a-ša-at	the wife of
	Ir-ma-A-šur	Irma-Aššur.
	seal impression A	

[21] *annakam ṣaltam* (15) *ištia ēpušma* (16) *libbī* (17) *danniš* (18) *uštamriṣ*.

[22] This marriage (see n. 18 above) must have been concluded in Kanesh, since the contract also mentions that the groom was to marry a girl in Assur, in addition to Suhkana, and that he would be able to take her with him on his journeys. The bride is identified as "the daughter of Irma-Aššur," without mention of her mother, but I am not sure what this implies. The contract is undated, and the marriage might have been concluded after Šalimma's death or even before Irma-Aššur had married her if he had children from a previous marriage. If the latter were the case, he would have been (much) older than Šalimma, possibly one of the reasons for the problems discussed in our letter and perhaps an explanation for Šalimma's brother referring to Irma-Aššur as "my father, my lord."

[23] P. Garelli, "Tablettes cappadociennes de collections diverses (1)," *RA* 58 (1964): 23, no. 4:9; EL 235:34; kt 87/k 386:21 (courtesy of K. Hecker).

Tablet kt 91/k 385 (1-239-91; 5.1 × 5.0 cm; word-dividing wedge indicated by ":")

Text

a-na Lá-ma-sà-tim ú Ša-lim-ma qí-bi-ma
um-ma Um-mì-Iš-ha-<ra>-ma a-dí-i na-áš-pé-er-tim
ša ta-áš-pu-ri-ni um-ma a-tí-ma mì-šu-um
ma-ma-an lá i-ṭa-ra-dam ší-pá-ar-šu
i-li-kam-ma : a-na-ku aṭ-ru-ud : a-dí ma-lá
ú ší-ni-šu aq-bi-šu-ma li-bu-šu : i-ta-na-aṣ-/ra-áp
um-ma šu-ut-ma : a-dí : ma-lá : ú ší-ni-šu
na-áš-pé-er-tí : i-li-ik-ší-im-ma a-lá-kam
*lá ta-mu-a : ša a-ša-pá-ru-ší-ni-*BA *i-ṣé-er*
na-áš-pé-ra-tí-a iš-té-et : ú ší-ta : ša i-li-kà-/ší-ni
a-wi-lúm : a-wa-tim : i-ta-ah-dar
[u]m-ma šu-ut-ma iš-tù a-lá-kam lá ta-mu-ú
lá ta-tù-ri-ma : lá ta-qá-bi-im
šu-ma : a-ha-tí : a-tí : a-wa-tim sà-ra-tim
lá ta-áš-ta-na-pá-ri-im : a-na KÙ.BABBAR *mì-ma*
lá ta-ša-pá-ri-šu-um : a-šu-mì KÙ.BABBAR *aq-bi-šu-ma*
um-ma šu-ut-ma : ma-lá-ma-a : KÙ.BABBAR 1/2 *ma-na*
gám-ri-ša : gi$_5$*-mì-lam*$_5$ *: i-ṣé-er um-mì-ša*
ú-ul a-hi-ša lá-áš-ku-un ú-ul
l. e. *i-na ba-áb-tí-a :* KÙ.BABBAR 10 GÍN *lá i-ba-ší*
ú šu-ma : i-na ba-áb-tí-a lá-šu
rev. KÙ.BABBAR 10 GÍN *: ma-lá : gám-ri-ša*
iš-tí um-mì-ša : ú «ta» a-hi-ša
lu té-ri-iš-ma : a-na-ku a-na-kam : lu-ta-er-šu-ma
lu ta-ta-al-kam : mì-ma : a-wa-tim
ú na-áš-pé-ra-tim : lá ta-áš-ta-na-pá-ri-im
i-na pá-ni : a-wi-lim : tù-uš-ta-zi-zi
um-ma šu-ut-ma iš-tù-ma lá am-tí-ni : ší-it
a-lá-kam lá ta-am-tù-a-ni : lá ta-tù-ar-ma
šu-um-ša : lá ta-za-kà-ri-im : ú a-tí
lá a-ha-tí mì-šu-um šé-re-ki ú É *bé-et-ki*
ša-ni-ú-tum : i-bé-e-lu : ú a-tí : a-ma-kam
wa-áš-ba-tí : a-pu-tum : šé-re-ki : lá tù-ha-li-qí
ú i-a-tí i-na É *a-wi-lim : lá tù-re-qí-ni*
šu-ma : a-lá-ki : i-ba-ší : tí-ib-e-ma a-tal-ki-im
lá-ma a-wi-lúm li-bu-šu : iš-ni-ú
i-na ^{d}UTU*-ši : Pí-lá-ah-Ištar : e-ru-ba-ni*

ki-ma iš-tí-šu lá ta-li-ki-ni : li-bu-šu
im-ra-aṣ-ma : 5 *u_4-me-e : a-na ki-dim*
lá ú-ṣí : šu-ma : mu-tám : ša-ni-a-am
ta-šé-e-i : šu-up-ri-ma : lu i-dé
šu-ma lá ki-a-am : tí-ib-<e>-ma a-tal-ki-/im
u. e. *šu-ma : lá ta-li-ki-im*
i-a-tí : i-na pá-ni : a-wi-lim
tù-ša-zi-zi
le. e. *ú šé-re-ki : tù-ha-li-qí : ú a-na-ku*
lá a-tù-ar-ma : šu-um-ki lá a-za-kà-ar
ú-lá a-ha-tí a-tí ú mì-ma i-a-tí
lá ta-ša-pí-ri-im

Translation

To Lamassatum and Šalimma, thus says Ummi-Išhara.

As for the letter (3) that you sent me, in which you wrote: "Why does he not send someone to me?" A messenger of his (5) did arrive, and it was I who sent him. I talked to him several times, but every time he bursts out, (7) saying: "Several times a letter of mine went to her, but she refused to come here! Could what I should send her then surpass (10) the messages that already reached her several times?"

(11) The gentleman has become very annoyed by the matter and said: "Because she refuses to come, (13) you must not speak to me again." (14) If you are my sister, do not keep writing me things that are not true, and certainly do not write to him for silver. I talked to him because of the silver (17), and he said: "Should I really oblige her mother or her brothers for no less than half a mina of silver for her expenses? Or (19) are there not 10 shekels of silver available from my outstanding claims? (21) And if there are not, let her ask for 10 shekels of silver for her expenses (23) from her mother or her brothers, which I promise I will pay back here, if only (25) she leaves for here." (26) Do not keep writing me all kinds of things and messages. (27) You have brought me into conflict with the gentleman. (28) He tells me: "Since, not being my *amtu*-wife, she refuses to come here, (30) you must not mention her name again to me, lest you will no longer be my sister." Why are others ruling your children and your household, while you are staying there? (33) Please, do not make your children perish, and do not estrange me from the gentleman's house. (35) If you see a possibility to come, get ready and leave for here (36) before the gentleman gets different ideas. (37) The day Pilah-Ištar arrived here, since you had not come with him, (39) he felt very unhappy, and for five days did not leave his house. If you are looking for another husband, write me so; I wish to know it. (42) If not, get ready and leave for here.

(43) If you do not come, you will bring me into conflict with the gentleman, (46) and you will make your children perish, and I, (47) I will never mention your name again; you will no longer be my sister, and (49) you must not write me anymore.

Lexical and Grammatical Notes

4–5 We cannot take *šiparšu* ... *aṭrud* as the continuation of Šalimma's words, "A messenger of his did arrive, and it was I who sent him," since that would flatly contradict the complaint in lines 3–4. I therefore understand it as Ummi-Išhara's reaction to her sister's contention: she herself was instrumental in sending the messenger and hence knows that her sister is not telling the truth (see line 14).

6 *ṣarāpum* is lexically attested and used metaphorically with *kabattum* and *lalûm* as subjects (*CAD* Ṣ s.v. *ṣarāpu* A mng. 2, and *CAD* L s.v. *lalû* A mng. 1b), meaning "to burn with desire, to spend one's emotion" (Lambert's translation in Lambert-Millard *Atra-hasīs*), also "to crave, have a craving for" (with *ana*). The form here is an Ntn and may be compared with the (ingressive?) N-stem in Ludlul I 108, *libbī iṣṣarip* "I had a burning heart," equivalent to *ṣurup libbim rašûm* (*CAD* Ṣ s.v. *ṣurpu* mng. 2b). B. Landsberger, "Über Farben in Sumerisch-Akkadischen," *JCS* 21 (1967): 146, nn. 34–36, pointed out the problems of derivation and meaning of intransitive *ṣarāpum* and *ṣurup libbim* (equated with Sumerian šà.síg.ga), which, in many cases, seem to imply a shrill or loud noise, as made by wailing women.[24] But this is not always obvious; see, for example, Tukulti-Ninurta Epic 'iii' 28 (*CAD* L s.v. *lalû* A mng. 1b) and YOS 11 24:24, where a lover is told *ina ṣēria ṣurup lalâka*, probably something like "vent your passions upon me." In our letter the expression is connected by means of *-ma* with what Irma-Aššur said: his words are the manifestation of his anger.

9–10 The beginning of the sentence *ša ašapparušinni*-BA *iṣṣēr našperātia* ... *ša illikaššinni* is difficult. It contains the postfix -BA, thus far attested only in Old Assyrian, where it is used to express surprise or indignation, to give emphasis to a statement, to express a contrast, or frequently in a question. Identification of the underlying lexeme is difficult, since neither the accusative of *pûm* "mouth" nor the imperative of *bā'ûm* (Old Assyrian, with ventive *ba'am*) is convincing. I would rather compare the Ugaritic conjunctive particle *p* (vocalization unknown), which is also used in letters, with an asseverative and explicative meaning. BA is frequently linked to interrogatives such as *mīnum*, *mannum*, and *miššum*, and occasional spellings of the type *mì-nim/nam*-BA suggest that the final consonant of the interrogative was assimilated to the initial labial -BA, yielding *mīnappa*, *mīnuppa*. Examples of this are Michel

[24] Cf. also von Weiher *Uruk* 225:16, *lallāri ša ṣurrupu nubûša*, comparable to *ṣarpiš nabbûm/bakûm* "to wail/weep bitterly." The Š-stem, with *qubê* as the object, according to the *CAD*, means "to groan loudly."

and Garelli *Kültepe* 1 166:21, *kasapka leqe umma P.-ma mì-na*-BA *kaspam lalqe* "(Š. said:) 'Take your silver!' P. answered: 'What silver then should I take?'"; kt 87/k 551 (courtesy of K. Hecker), *uzanni pete mì-na*-BA *anāku uzakkunu lapte* "(You said:) 'Inform us!' Why should I be the one to inform you?"; CCT 4 27a:15, *mì-nam*-BA *teʾertī lillikakkum* "What instruction of mine then should come to you?"; kt n/k 501:17 (courtesy of C. Günbattı), *a-mì-nim*-BA *ana ṣērišu ettiq* "(He said: 'The silver does not belong to PN), why then should it travel on to him?'"; Matouš *Prag* I 521:12, *mì-šu*-BA *našpertam ... la tublam* "Why then did you not bring me a message?"; kt n/k 94:3 f. (courtesy of S. Bayram), *a-le*-BA *awātuka* (4) *ša umma attāma* (5) *mannum mīnam eppaški* "To what, then, has your (reassurance), 'Who could do you any harm?' come?" (lit. "where, then, are your words?").

In addition, there are some, mostly unpublished, examples of *šu-ma*-BA "if then / really / however..." followed by a perfect tense to express an unexpected, less likely action. Nice examples are found in the letter kt 88/k 97b: 31,[25] where brothers discuss how to finance the expenses for their sister's marriage. One brother offers to borrow the money and asks: *šu-ma*-BA *kaspam ... la alteqe ... ana kaspim la tazzazānim* "If, however, I have been unable to obtain the silver, will you then not accept responsibility for it?" In line 39 his brothers ask him: *kī ma-ṣí*-BA *kaspam tagammar* "How much silver, then, are you going to spend?" Other examples, always in questions, show that the particle can be added to another word, which has emotional emphasis. Cf. P. Garelli, "Tablettes cappadociennes de collections diverses (2)," *RA* 59 (1965): 160, no. 25:34, *nēnu*-BA *ana māti neppaš* "(Since you left PN has now already built two houses), but we, when will we finally build (one)?"; kt 93/k 482:27 (courtesy of Cécile Michel), *anāku*-BA *ana mīnim ... ulappatakkim,* "Why should I keep writing to you?; AKT 3 47:29, *annūti*-BA *ṣubātē* (30) *la ana bēt A. ubbal*, "(A. took the black donkey along, whereupon D. said): 'And these textiles then, should I not bring them to A.'s house?'."

The use of -BA in our letter fits the emotional context and suggests taking lines 9b–10 as a desperate or angry question. The sentence, which compares (*iṣṣēr*) a possible future action (*šapārum* in the present-future tense) with a previous one ("messages that went to her"), is basically a nominal clause with *ša ašapparušinni* as subject: "Could then the message that I am going to send her surpass the ones that have already reached her several times?" We might render it as: "Should/Could I really send her still another message apart from (or: better than) the ones she already received from me?"

---

[25] S. Çeçen, "*mūtānū* in den Kültepe-Texten," *Archivum Anatolicum* 1 (1995): 56; reading -BA makes the emendation of line 39 unnecessary.

12 *ta-mu-ú* is a preterite in the subjunctive (after *illikšimma*), *ta-mu-a* (9) a present describing the current situation ("she refuses"); and *tamtuʾanni* (line 29) is a perfect (see below, notes to lines 28 f.) in the subjunctive with a ventive ending, added because the infinitive *alākam* cannot take one.

17–19 *ma-lá-ma-a* is the first occurrence in Old Assyrian of the enclitic particle with lengthened vowel, *-mā*, always written *-ma-a*, used to mark questions and added to the word that has the main stress (hence not in Hecker *Grammatik* § 128–29;[26] BIN 4 22:28 f., quoted in von Soden *GAG* § 153g, does not have *mannum-ma* but *mannum*-BA). It is common in Old Babylonian and in particular in Mari; cf. von Soden *GAG* § 123b, *AHw*., p. 570b, and my remarks in "Observations on Some Letters from Mari (ARM 2, 124; 10, 4; 43; 84; 114)," *RA* 70 (1976): 156, on line 33.[27] For the use of the precative in questions ("should/could I ..."), see von Soden *GAG* § 153g and Hecker *Grammatik* § 129c. Irma-Aššur's indignation about the amount of money expected from him is further expressed by the inversion of the normal word order: ½ *mana* follows *kaspam*, "silver, no less than half a mina."

27, 44 f. *ina pāni awīlim tuštazzizi*. The verb *izuzzum* combines with various prepositions or prepositional expressions,[28] and with *ana* / *ina pāni* / *mahar* it has various meanings, depending on whether the verb is fientic "to take one's stand" or stative "to stand" and whether *ina pāni* has a neutral, locative meaning or refers to a positive or a negative attitude toward the person confronted. A stative meaning with *ina pāni* matches a fientic one with *ana pāni*, as in, for example, AbB 3 11:5–8. A man who first worked elsewhere is told "At the moment you serve (or: manage) my household" (*ina pāni bītia tazzaz*), since "I have now transferred you (back) to manage my household" (*inanna ana*

[26] Old Assyrian marks questions (not so "ganz vereinzelt" as Hecker *Grammatik* § 128c states) also by vowel lengthening; cf. BIN 6 119:17, *bētāti-ku-nu-ú la tadaggalā*; CCT 5 6a:15, *attūnu la tí-dé-a-a*; CCT 5 11d:9, *hurāṣum ku-a-ú-um*; Michel and Garelli *Kültepe* 1 166:15, *kaspum la* KÙ.BABBAR-*pì-i*; 189:5′, *tù-šé-lá-a-am*; 190:20, *mimma tal-qé-e la tal-qé-e*.

[27] For additional examples, see Lambert-Millard *Atra-hasīs*, p. 107 (OB I) (*jāšimmā*); AbB 6 127:15 (*kalušunumā*); AbB 10 32:4 (*ṭēmmā*, where *-ma* also marks the subject of a verbless clause); AbB 11 106 left edge 2 ([*š*]*ūmā*); AbB 11 112:17 (*ṭurrudumā*); ARMT 13 37:7 (*kīmā*); ARMT 26 148:18′ (*kiʾammā*); ARMT 26 149:6′ (*allikmā*); ARMT 26 171:14 (*matimā*; cf. *OBT Tell Rimah* 145:17); ARMT 26 344:31 (*ana ka-šum-ma-a-a*); ARMT 27 1:18 f. (*išarišmā ... aššummā ...*), etc.

[28] With *išti* or *ina šahat* PN (passim) it means "to assist, to support," and the combination *ina rēš* PN *izēzum* is used for "to serve, to attend to," as in BIN 6 104:15 f., where a lonely bachelor complains that he has nobody "who attends my needs and lays the table for me" (*ša ina rēšia izzazzuma paššūram išakkananni*; see also BIN 6 97:17 f., and Old Babylonian *muzzaz rēš šarri*). In Old Babylonian *ina muhhi izuzzum*, as was noted by Kraus ("Spätaltbabylonische Briefe aus Babylon [VS 22:83–92]," *AoF* 10 [1983]: 60 ad no. 7:6), is not always clear; it could be neutral, as in AbB 2 141:18, "Speak pleasant words when you confront/meet him" or, more aggressive, as in VAS 22 89:6′, "Do not be negligent, lest the creditor get you!"

pāni bītia ut[*tēr*]*ka*) (*sic*). The verb *izuzzum* with *ina pāni* frequently has the neutral meaning of "to be in the service of," as does Sumerian igi—gub. Its Š-stem is used for the appointment of officials who are permitted to serve, are "taken into the entourage" of the Assyrian king (SAA 4 152:7, 154:4, 155:6′, SAA 10 228:5). A clearly positive meaning occurs in AbB 8 102:5, *kīma attī ina pānia tazzizi u tagmilinne* "Since you supported/protected me and did me a favor," and in the Old Assyrian letter ICK 1 14:10, "I sent PN a textile ..., but you did not assist him (IGI-*šu la tazzizā*) and did not sell it as well as you could," where the verb is used with *mahar* with the same meaning. In our text it must be negative because Ummi-Išhara obviously means that her intercession for her sister has annoyed and antagonized the latter's husband, who no longer wants to hear Ummi-Išhara's name mentioned. The same is true in AKT 1 14:17 f., where a woman writes: "Who talked to you with the result that you confronted/opposed my brother Š.?" (*appāni Š. ahia tazzizi*).[29] In AbB 12 45:23 W. van Soldt translates *ana pānišu iziz* with "confront him (as if I myself had come)," but the last words rather suggest a positive reception for the man sent by the writer. This is in line with AbB 8 141:18, where *mādiš ana pānišu iziz* must mean "come to his assistance without any reserve" (fientic, with *ana pāni*). The best parallel for our letter is in AbB 3 2:17, where *ana pāni* is used: *attīma la tadabbubi ana pāniki la tušzazzini*[*āti*] "You, you must not keep complaining, lest you bring us into conflict with you!"

28 *ištuma*, according to *CAD* I/J s.v., means "if indeed, really" and occurs in connection with a prevailing situation (a stative), a future action, and (with a perfect) a past action (also in Old Babylonian, AbB 6 188:32′f. and AbB 14 116:25). But at times its meaning is simply causative, "since," for example, in CCT 2 48:24, kt 94/k 549:15 (with a past tense, courtesy of M. T. Larsen), *ištuma la tublušunni parakannē šāmamma* "Since you have not brought him (the silver), buy for me *parakannu*-textiles" and VAS 26 71:8, *ištuma kaspum ... irtūqannini* "Because silver has become unattainable for me," because being an *amtum* is a fact used as an argument. This argument consists of two asyndetic elements, the second a form of the typically Old Assyrian verb *muʾāum* "to be willing" with a t-infix. *CAD* M/1 s.v. **mâʾu* lists only two examples of such forms and apparently considers CCT 3 49b:8 (*la imtūnim*) a perfect (mng. 2a end) and KTS 1 42a:1 (*ula amtuwa*) a Gt (see the heading

[29] I ignore examples from the legal sphere, such as CCT 5 1a:25, where a disputed slave "should be placed at the disposal (under the control) of the *wabartum* (*ina* IGI *wabartim šazzizāma*), so that nobody can touch him" or kt n/k 1502:8–11, "They have made PN_1 in Kanesh 'stand before' PN_{2-5}" (IGI PN_{2-5} *ušazzizu*), where representation or subsidiary surety is at stake. The use with *warki* in Matouš *KK* 5:4 f.: "Why did you make a servant stand behind me?" (*miššum ṣuhāram warkia tušazziz*; also kt n/k 1139:23) belongs to the same sphere; it is a security measure because the debtor, who is speaking, might disappear.

of the lemma, p. 435); Hecker *Grammatik* § 98b, adding two more examples, takes them as perfects but von Soden, *AHw.*, p. 665a, as Gtn-stems. In an earlier analysis[30] I observed that there is no lexical argument for a Gtn-stem and that a syntactical one for a perfect tense is not that clear, so that a lexical Gt remains a possibility. But in our letter there must be a difference between the forms without infixed *-t-* in lines 9 and 12, and the syntax suggests a connection between Šalimma's status and her refusal to come; *tamtua* in line 29 can only be syntactical, and the latter must be a perfect (which does occur after *ištuma*), which indicates a logical *consecutio*: because she is not an *amtum*, it is possible for Šalimma to refuse to come to Assur (see further below).

30 *u attī* could be taken as the beginning of a new sentence in which Ummi-Išhara begins to speak, her first words abrupt and emotional: "And you, you...." Though syntactically not easy to justify, I prefer to understand this, instead, as the conclusion of Irma-Aššur's words, which spell out what the continuation of Ummi-Išhara's pleading on behalf of her sister might entail for her.

34 *CAD* R s.v. *rêqu* mng. 4 mentions only two Old Assyrian occurrences of *rêqu* in the D-stem, both with an impersonal object (silver), to which we can add L 29-561 = *POAT* 8:51, *kaspam tù-ur*-DÍ-IQ!, and kt 94/k 524:13, *kaspī mādamma tù-ur*-DÍ-IQ. There is also one example with a double accusative, AKT 1 17:25: "By all means prevent the creditor from taking away (the copper), so that it gets out of reach for me" (*e itbalma e tù*-RI-*i-qá-ni*), in line with the frequent use of the G-stem with a personal ablative accusative. But the D-stem *re'uqum* may also have a direct personal object, as it does, for example, in the Old Babylonian letter BIN 7 27:10, *ina ekallia la turēqanni* (with *CAD* R s.v. *rêqu* mng. 4; in contrast to AbB 9 214:9f., which derives it from *riāqum* "to be idle," as in an unpublished Old Babylonian letter, quoted in *CAD* R s.v. *râqu* mng. 6). Another question is how to interpret our form phonetically, for which I profit from some of N. J. C. Kouwenberg's observations. For Old Assyrian *mediae aleph* verbs, the question is (cf. Hecker *Grammatik* § 91) whether we have to assume a strong form (with laryngeal) or a weak form (without one). For the G-stem, Hecker lists several examples of weak forms of the preterite (§ 91c), but not all are convincing, notably those of *be'ālum*, as I pointed out in my *Old Assyrian Trade*, pp. 407 ff. (where some of them were also identified as N-stems). According to him, the D-stem is apparently ("anscheinend") always strong (§ 91f), and this indeed applies to the examples

[30] K. R. Veenhof, "Two Akkadian Auxiliary Verbs, *le'ûm*, to be able and *mu'āum*, to want," in H. L. J. Vanstiphout et al., eds., *Scripta Signa Vocis: Studies about Scripts, Scriptures, Scribes, and Languages in the Near East Presented to J. H. Hospers by His Pupils, Colleagues, and Friends* (Groningen, 1986), pp. 235–51, esp. 239 f.

given, including the present *tù-re-a-aq* in CCT 4 3b:10, where the extra *-a-* indicates the syllable boundary. But it is less clear for the preterites *tù-*RI*-i-qá-ni* in AKT 1 17:25 and (*ba-a-<ba>-tí-a*) *ú-*RI*-i-qú-ma* in kt c/k 443 rev. 4′ and for the two perfects *tù-ur-*DÍ-IQ quoted above. All four could be considered strong, (*t*)*ure'iq*(*anni*), *turte'iq*, or weak, with—as occasionally happens in Old Assyrian—indication of the long, contracted vowel, (*t*)*urêq*(*anni*), *turtêq*. This last interpretation is required for the present tense *tù-re-qí-ni* = *turêqqīni* "do not remove me" in our letter and seems not impossible for the other forms because already during the Ur III period (Hilgert, *Akkadisch in der Ur III-Zeit*, pp. 255 f.) this verb seems to show weak formations or, to put it differently, formations patterned after the *mediae infirmae* verbs. But this does not settle the case for Old Assyrian, since there are phonetic complications and its spelling conventions are equivocal. The form in our letter goes back to a strong **ture'aqīni*, which with Old Assyrian vowel harmony becomes *ture'iqīni* and by contraction *turêqqīni*, due to the vocalic ending after the third radical (which also requires the doubling of the final consonant of the root). The effect of a vocalic ending is indicated by the apparently weak formations of *mediae aleph* verbs in the N-stem: **libbi'il+anni* > *li-bi-lá-ni* = *libbîlanni* (TC 1 26:28), while forms without a vocalic ending remain strong: *li-bi*$_4$*-i-il*$_5$ = *libbi'il* (CCT 2 1:13) and *i-mì-*HI*-id* = *immi'id* "it has become much" (CCT 4 3b:6). *Tù-*RI*-i-qá-ni* and *ú-*RI*-i-qú* have vocalic endings and still write -RI-*i*-, which may indicate strong forms, such as (*t*)*ure'iq*, with indication of the syllable boundary, or weak ones, due to the vocalic ending, with plene writing of the contracted vowel, *turêq-*, as in *tù-re-qí-ni* in our letter, where, however, the long contracted vowel is not marked. The plene writing with -RI-*i* does not necessarily render /*re'i*/, in an attempt to indicate the difference in quality between both vowels (*ture'iq*), since in Old Assyrian there is an indiscriminate use of spellings with *e* and *i*. To assume weak, contracted forms is attractive because it would mean the same phonetic change in all Old Assyrian forms with vocalic endings, but we have to take into account that the spellings allow different interpretations.

36 For Old Assyrian attestations of *šanā'um* with *libbum* as the subject, see *CAD* Š/1 s.v. *šanû* B mng. 2a–3′. "Change of mind" in Jankowska *KTK* 18:4 (D-stem) leads to "fighting" (*teṣētum*) and in line 8′ (G-stem) to "contempt, discredit" (*qulālū*). In TC 3 6:6 the rumor that a man's "mind has changed" is refuted by observing that "he harbors no inimical thoughts; he is your true, reliable brother" (*mimma awatum šanītum* (8) *illibbišu la ibašši* (9) *awīlum ahuka ša kenātimma*).

Interpretation

The issue dealt with in the letter explains the frequent, almost thematic, use of *alākum* "to go" and *atlukum* "to depart" (occasionally preceded by *tabā'um* "to get into motion"), used in various modes, with mention of the possibility (*šumma alākki ibašši*, line 35), failure (line 38), or the refusal (*la muā'um*) to go or depart, with a clear distinction between the forms with and without the ventive (lines 8 f., 12, 25, 29, 35, 38, and 42 f.). Communication in the world of Old Assyrian traders was by letter or messenger, hence the repeated use of the verb *šapārum* and its derivatives *našpertum* "message" (note *awâtim u našperātim* in lines 25 f.) and *šiprum* "messenger" (in lines 2–5, 8, 10, 15, 25 f., 41, and 46). At times the communication as such is at stake (lines 25 f., 48 f.), at times its contents, since Šalimma's messages contain lies (line 14) or make irritating demands on her husband (lines 15 f.).

The letter does not tell us why Šalimma refused to go to Assur. Even her sister seems uncertain (lines 40 f.). One cannot speculate about the reasons for her refusal to go (see n. 22 above), but a letter cited above (kt 91/k 290, if it stems from this period) indicates that weather conditions also played a role. We also do not know how long the problem lasted, but the iteratives (in lines 6, 15, and 26, and "several times" in line 7) imply a lively correspondence. Our letter is the only one preserved, but it was found in Elamma's archive, which could mean that it was the copy delivered to Lamassatum, and it may even have remained unopened, since part of the envelope is preserved.[31] If that is the case (unless we assume that Šalimma had moved in with her widowed mother), we suppose that another copy existed, delivered to Šalimma herself, to her own house. But apparently neither that copy nor any other relevant letter was found in the couple's house, which was excavated in 1994. Letters, of course, may have been discarded after some time, and we do not know what happened when Šalimma eventually returned to Assur.

Ummi-Išhara plays the role of the wise older sister in Assur (particularly after the death of her father?), acting as mediator for the couple and concerned about the family. One may compare her role to that played by Pušuken's daughter Ahaha, who became involved when her brothers had problems with the liquidation of their father's business after he had died and when tensions arose between them.[32] Ummi-Išhara corresponds with her sister in Kanesh and talks to her brother-in-law in Assur (lines 6, 13, 16), interceding for her (lit. "mentions her name," lines 30, 47), a meaning that

[31] For the question of letters in more than one copy, of unopened letters, and of (pieces of) envelopes found together with tablets in an archive, see my remarks in M. Brosius, ed., *Ancient Archives and Archival Traditions* (Oxford, 2003), pp. 90 and 98. I find it hard to believe that incoming letters were opened in an (usually dark!) archive room and that the fragments of their envelopes were simply dropped.

[32] See texts such as CCT 4 31b, CCT 5 8a, Matouš *Prag* I 437, I 652, I 680, *KT Hahn* 7, TC 2 46, and the unpublished letter Ankara 1938. Some of them are translated in Michel, *Correspondance des marchands de Kanesh*, as nos. 312 ff.

šumi PN *zakārum* also has in kt 93/k 145:36 f. (see C. Michel and P. Garelli, "Heurts avec une principauté anatolienne," *WZKM* 86 [1996]: 278), where the representatives of the *kārum* are told by a local Anatolian ruler not to do this on behalf of an Assyrian he had imprisoned. Lines 16 f. suggest that Šalimma approached her angry husband via her sister, and indeed none of her letters to Irma-Aššur are mentioned or preserved. All this irritates Šalimma's husband so much (lines 6, 11) that he tells Ummi-Išhara to stop approaching him on behalf of his wife (her sister) (lines 13, 29 f.); she will follow his wishes if her sister does not come to Assur (lines 47 f.), and she states she will cut off relations with her sister (lines 48 f.) in order to avoid a conflict with her brother-in-law (lines 27, 44 f.), who might otherwise cut off relations with her too (*u attī la ahatī*, lines 30 f.), which would mean that she would no longer be welcome in his home (line 34). I note that Ummi-Išhara never refers to Irma-Aššur by name or as "your husband"[33] but that she always uses the formal *awīlum* "the gentleman" (lines 11, 24, 29, 36, and 44), but I am not certain whether this is a deliberate choice, since the use of *awīlum* and *awīltum* to refer to members of the Old Assyrian trading community was common.

To encourage her sister to change her mind, Ummi-Išhara uses three arguments. In the first place, she states the already mentioned negative consequences for her herself; they are stated emphatically several times by adding a separate first-person-singular personal pronoun to verbal forms already having a pronominal suffix (lines 34, 44, 46, and 48). She then warns her sister that her frustrated husband might "change his mind" (line 36), which is presumably a euphemistic way of saying he might want a divorce. This links up with her own question about whether her sister wants to (divorce and) find a new husband (line 40). Ummi-Išhara's third argument is one that would appeal to her sister in her role as mother and is remarkable in the mouth of a woman who, as a priestess, had to remain unmarried and childless. Šalimma's behavior, she points out, is detrimental for her young children (*šerrū*; we know from other texts that Šalimma had at least two sons), who are living in Assur and being raised without their mother in a household managed by others (lines 31–33, repeated in line 46). "Others" presumably means the family of her husband, since this statement is immediately followed by her fearful remark that she herself will no longer be welcome in Irma-Aššur's house. The letter concludes with lines 43 ff., a summary of her three arguments and a final warning.

Ummi-Išhara vividly describes Irma-Aššur's emotional reactions to his wife's behavior, presumably in order to make clear to her sister that the situation is very serious. She uses three expressions: *libbušu ittanaṣrap* (line 6), *awātim ittahdar* (line 11), and *libbušu imraṣ* (lines 38 f.). Of these, *libbušu ittanaṣrap*, as pointed out above, is unique

[33] The use of such terms in general is rare, and I have noted only a few occurrences of "your husband" (*mutki*) used by a father (VAS 26 33:9), a relative or friend (BIN 6 17:9), and a colleague (EL 292 = CCT 5 17a:6 // TC 3 266) of a married woman.

but probably means that he was consumed by emotions and anger and spoke out. The verb *adārum* in the N-stem, which is not rare in Old Assyrian, according to *CAD* A/1 s.v. *adāru* A mng. 7a, can mean "to become worried" or "to become impatient."[34] Both meanings fit, but the combination with *awātim*, a kind of adverbial accusative, suggests something like "he became worried, annoyed by the affair." The expression *libbušu imraṣ*, used frequently, can express sadness, unhappiness, and disappointment.[35] His feelings are made even clearer by his repetition of what he said before, the emotional and desperate words in lines 9 f., his irritated state in the question in lines 17–19, and his conclusion in lines 28 f. And when he discovers that Šalimma has refused to join the caravan of her brother Pilah-Ištar (lines 37 f.), he becomes utterly frustrated and does not leave his house for five days.

The mention of the possibility of a divorce initiated by Šalimma (lines 40 f.) or her husband (line 36) and Irma-Aššur's use of the words "since, not being my *amtu*-wife, she refused to come" (lines 28 f.) must be understood against the background of Old Assyrian marriage law, for which I refer to my recent survey.[36] Two points are important here. The first is that according to Old Assyrian law, both husband and wife could obtain a divorce, unless there was a question of serious and punishable misconduct, only after paying a certain sum of silver. The second is that Assyrian traders could have two wives but only under two conditions: the wives could not have the same formal status, and they could not live with their husband in the same city or area. One wife was designated as *aššatum* "married wife," the other usually as *amtum*, which does not mean "slave-girl" but apparently does indicate a different status. The wives could be either Assyrian or Anatolian, and there was no rule that the *aššatum* had to be the wife in Assur and the *amtum* the wife in the colonies. What exactly the distinction was is not very clear, since an *amtum* was also officially married, with a formal marriage contract and the requisite provisions (for example, if the wife remained childless), and the legal status of both wives was similar.[37] Possibly one difference may have been that an *amtum* was more closely tied to her husband when he traveled, since only in contracts with an *amtum* (see the contract referred to in n. 35 above) do we find the provision that the husband may take his wife with him on his business trips on the condition that he eventually brings her back home to Kanesh. Perhaps a divorce

[34] The latter meaning is frequent when a period or time limit is mentioned and patience is asked for. The *CAD* for CCT 3 38:27 translates "to become apprehensive," but this is dubious because the sentence "I showed him your letters and up to thirty times I tried to reassure him" follows. If one opts for this meaning, interpreting *adārum* B "to fear," as an N-stem, would be more likely.

[35] See M. T. Larsen, "Affect and Emotion," in *Veenhof AV*, p. 278, with n. 12.

[36] Veenhof, "Old Assyrian Period," pp. 450–55, § 5.1.

[37] See recently also M. T. Larsen, OAA 1, p. xxv, at his text no. 176 (I 490), where a daughter of a prominent Old Assyrian trader, Aššur-nada, born of his *amtu*-marriage with an Anatolian woman in Kanesh, is married off as an *amtum* to the son of another prominent trader, Imdilum.

from an *amtum* in Anatolia was somewhat easier, or at least more acceptable, if a trader wished to return to Assur, where he might also have a wife. For that same reason there may have been differences in the position of the children of both wives regarding inheritance, but this is not yet clear. Irma-Aššur's remark in lines 28 f., read against this background, must mean that since Šalimma had not been married as an *amtu*-wife, she could not be obliged to travel to Assur to join her husband or, perhaps more fundamentally, that as *aššatum* she enjoyed more independence, but we need more evidence to make this assumption. In any case, the situation as described in the letter creates problems, since Šalimma, alone in Kanesh, needs money from her husband to cover her expenses, which he is ready (perhaps even obliged[38]) to give her, but not more than is really necessary. A divorce cost money, money that allowed a divorced wife her freedom and the right to remarry,[39] and, of course, it entailed all kinds of arrangements concerning property and children. With a warning that Irma-Aššur might want to divorce her, Ummi-Išhara encourages her sister to consider the consequences of her behavior very carefully. Her own question of whether Šalimma wants to look for a new husband serves the same purpose but is at the same time presented as the only acceptable alternative, since the present situation cannot continue (line 42).

It would be nice to assume that this honest, emotional, and well-argued letter was responsible for Šalimma's eventual return to her husband in Assur (see above). Written over four thousand years ago, this letter acquaints us with very personal aspects of the lives of Assyrian traders and their families. It is an impressive document, written by a skilled hand, in a small script, but we do not know who in fact wrote this tablet. Perhaps it was Ummi-Išhara herself. Her seal is impressed on the envelope, and as a businesswoman and priestess, just like a so-called *nadītu*, one of the religious women in contemporary Babylonia who were devoted to the sun-god and were businesswomen at the same time, she may have been trained in the writing of cuneiform.

---

[38] The *kārum* verdict kt 88/k 269 (Çeçen, "*mūtānū* in den Kültepe-Texten," pp. 57 f.; cf. the reference in Veenhof, "Old Assyrian Period," p. 453, § 5.1.4) obliges an Assyrian husband to give his wife, who (as a pledge?) is detained somewhere in Anatolia, a monthly allowance in copper (for buying food, oil, and firewood) and a new garment once a year.

[39] "To go after a husband of her choice," as kt 91/k 240 states it. Note that the combination *aššutum šanītum*, as used in Old Assyrian marriage contracts, means a second wife alongside the first one (some contracts use the expression *ina šahātiša šēšubum*). The option open to Šalimma, however, is a second husband after divorcing the first. In this respect, Assyrian women who belonged to the society of traders and businessmen did not enjoy the same rights as men.

THE TRUE SHEPHERD OF URUK

Joan Goodnick Westenholz, Bible Lands Museum Jerusalem

It is a distinct pleasure to have the opportunity to contribute to a volume in honor of Robert D. Biggs. A quiet, erudite scholar, Bob has contributed much to our understanding of the oldest periods of Sumerian and Akkadian literature, the interpretation of medical texts, and the explication of prophetic literature. In this article I hope to add some new insights into a text that Bob has studied and of which he has published a translation.[1]

The unique tablet W 19900,1 was discovered in the palace of Sîn-kāšid during the eighteenth campaign of the archaeological excavations at Warka in the winter of 1959/60.[2] It was found in locus Dc XIV_3, among the Old Babylonian archives containing letters and administrative documents, which were discovered scattered within the palace site, with the greatest number in the neighborhood of the western outer wall, in corridor 12.[3] From the contents of the associated letters, some from the royal correspondence of Anam, it is assumed that W 19900,1 belonged to the palace archives. This palace was apparently destroyed in a conflagration and was not rebuilt.[4]

---

[1] R. D. Biggs, "An Old Babylonian Oracle from Uruk," in Prichard *ANET*, 3d ed., p. 604. For the copy, see J. J. A. van Dijk, "Die Inschriften, III: Die Tontafeln aus dem Palast des Sînkāšid," in *UVB* 18, pp. 61–62 (discussion and treatment of selected lines), pl. 20 (photographs), pl. 28 W 19900,1 (copy); for a recent edition of the text, see K. A. Metzler, *Tempora in altbabylonischen literarischen Texten*, AOAT 279 (Münster, 2002), pp. 866–70; for a partial edition of lines 1–9, see J. G. Westenholz, "Nanaya, Lady of Mystery," in I. L. Finkel and M. J. Geller, eds., *Sumerian Gods and Their Representations* (Groningen, 1997), p. 66; and for the translation, see Biggs, "An Old Babylonian Oracle from Uruk," p. 604; J. J. A. van Dijk, apud L. Ramlot, *Dictionnaire de la Bible*, Suppl. vol. 8, fasc. 45 (Paris, 1972), cols. 877 f.; B. Pongratz-Leisten, "When the Gods Are Speaking," in M. Köcket and M. Nissinen, eds., *Propheten in Mari, Assyrien und Israel* (Göttingen, 2003), pp. 155–56; B. Foster, *Before the Muses: Anthology of Akkadian Literature*, 3d ed. (Bethesda, Maryland, 2004), pp. 122–23. This text is not among the Warka texts in Heidelberg and thus could not be collated.

[2] van Dijk, "Die Inschriften," p. 61.

[3] U. Finkbeiner, *Uruk: Analytisches Register zu den Grabungsberichten; Kampagnen 1912/13 bis 1976/77* (Berlin, 1993), p. 149 § 3.3.4.1 and p. 259 (reference courtesy W. Farber, who also provided several other suggestions and helpful comments while editing the manuscript of this article).

[4] H. J. Lenzen, *UVB* 18, p. 6. It was, however, reoccupied by Rīm-Anum in the 8th year of Samsuiluna; see D. Charpin, "Histoire politique du Proche-Orient amorrite (2002–1595)," in D. Charpin, D. O. Edzard, and M. Stol, eds., *Mesopotamien: Die altbabylonische Zeit*, Orbis Biblicus et Orientalis 160/4 (Fribourg and Göttingen, 2004), p. 113.

The conflagration is attributed to Rīm-Sîn of Larsa, who conquered Uruk in his 20th year. It should be noted that the palace was robbed from antiquity onward, and thus the contents of various rooms had been disturbed.

Tablet W 19900,1 bears reports of oracular statements given by the goddess Nanaya through the medium of an unnamed person who speaks in the first person referring to the "true/legitimate shepherd" and the revival of "dead Uruk." The identity of the intended recipient of the message is not known; he may or may not have been an unnamed ruler (note *bēlu* in line 28). Information about the historical and religious context is utterly lacking. The most peculiar characteristic of this text is that it is written in northern orthography and exhibits late grammatical features.

W 19900,1 is anomalous among Akkadian prophetic texts,[5] since it is the only Old Babylonian oracular text from southern Babylonia alongside the many Mari examples[6] and the two from Ešnunna.[7] It claims to be an oracular message given by the goddess Nanaya through an unspecified medium of prophetic transmission. It is generally assumed from the context that the speaker is a cleric in the service of the Eanna temple.[8] The prophecy is directly related by the prophet rather than being a report of

[5] For the distinction between Akkadian prophecies and Akkadian oracles, see Grayson *BHLT*, pp. 13–14. According to Grayson, the oracle is oral in nature, a single divine utterance, usually through a medium, to a single individual and related to a specific time and event, whereas Akkadian prophecies are literary productions containing generalized predictions usually after the event, concerning unspecified situations and persons and set in unspecified time periods. Under "oracles" Grayson includes our example as well as the Mari and Neo-Assyrian "prophecies." M. deJ. Ellis ("Observations on Mesopotamian Oracles and Prophetic Texts: Literary and Historiographic Considerations," *JCS* 41 [1989]: 127–86) refined these definitions and introduced the new term "literary predictive texts" to refer to the literary prophecies vis-à-vis oracular reports of divine communications. For another usage of the term "oracle" in Assyriological convention, see S. M. Maul, "Omina und Orakel," *RLA* 10, pp. 45–51. Maul defines an unprovoked event as an omen, while a provoked event (i.e., those elicited through the techniques used in various types of divination) is an oracle ("Verfahren, den göttlichen Willen zu erfragen"). According to Maul's definition, if a question was not posed, the answer could not be an oracle.

[6] For recent surveys of this material, see J. M. Sasson, "The Posting of Letters with Divine Messages," in *Birot Mem. Vol.*, pp. 299–316; J.-M. Durand, "Les prophéties des textes de Mari," in J.-G. Heintz, ed., *Oracles et prophéties dans l'antiquité: Actes du Colloque de Strasbourg, 15–17 juin 1995* (Paris, 1997), pp. 115–34; D. Charpin, "Prophètes et rois dans le Proche-Orient amorrite," in A. Lemaire, ed., *Prophètes et rois, Bible et Proche-Orient* (Paris, 2001), pp. 21–53.

[7] M. deJ. Ellis, "The Goddess Kititum Speaks to King Ibalpiel: Oracle Texts from Ishchali," *MARI* 5 (1987): 235–66; see also W. L. Moran, "An Ancient Prophetic Oracle," in G. Braulik, W. Groß, and S. McEvenue, eds., *Biblische Theologie und gesellschaftlicher Wandel: Für Norbert Lohfink SJ* (Freiburg, Basel, and Vienna, 1993), pp. 252–59.

[8] Although Pongratz-Leisten has stated that the king incubated the dream and that the text records the dialogue of the king and the goddess (*Herrschaftswissen in Mesopotamien: Formen der Kommunikation zwischen Gott und König im 2. und 1. Jahrtausend v. Chr.*, SAAS 10 [Helsinki, 1999], pp. 49–50), she implies that the recipient of the divine message was a prophet ("When the Gods Are Speaking," pp. 155–57).

a prophecy heard secondhand as are the prophecies in the Mari corpus. The gender of the prophet of the divine message in W 19900,1 is not apparent. One unusual feature is the narration of the conversations between the cleric and the goddess. The mode of communication is not specified nor whether it was elicited, provoked, or spontaneous. Biggs has suggested that the message was probably communicated through a dream.[9] Messages from a deity are commonly transmitted through dreams or during trances experienced by a person in a temple.[10] Such an experience by the cleric seems to be implied in our text in lines 7 f. A nocturnal vision of the goddess Gula was experienced by the royal letter-writter in the historiographical literary composition, the so-called Weidner Chronicle.[11]

The text of W 19900,1 begins with an invocation to the *rēʾû kīnu* "true/legitimate shepherd." There are two aspects to the riddle of *rēʾû kīnu*—the referent of the term and the term itself. The title *rēʾû kīnu* "true/legitimate shepherd" is a calque on the Sumerian sipa zi "true/legitimate/faithful[12] shepherd," an epithet ascribed to the ruler.[13] This epithet first occurs in an Early Dynastic period personal name En-an-na-túm-sipa-zi "Enannatum(king of Lagash)-is-the-true-shepherd."[14] Among the Sumerian kings who assume this epithet are Gudea, who is chosen sipa-zi-šè kalam-ma "as the legitimate shepherd in the land" (Statue B iii 9; see Edzard, RIME 3/1, p. 32); Šulgi, who is the sipa-zi-ki-en-gi-ra "faithful shepherd of Sumer" (see, for example, Šulgi D refrain in lines 287–320, "With Šulgi the faithful shepherd of Sumer, he [a deity] walks on the road"; see Klein, *Šulgi*, p. 54); and Išme-Dagan, who is the sipa-zi tu-da-ni "the true shepherd whom he (Enlil) engendered" (Išme-Dagan S 28, Ludwig,

---

9 Biggs, "An Old Babylonian Oracle from Uruk," p. 604; see most recently Charpin, "Prophètes et rois," p. 43.

10 For the incubation of dreams in the temple, see A. Zgoll, "Die Welt im Schlaf sehen," *WO* 32 (2002): 86–88.

11 F. N. H. Al-Rawi, "Tablets from the Sippar Library, I. The 'Weidner Chronicle': A Supposititious Royal Letter Concerning a Vision," *Iraq* 52 (1990): 1–13.

12 On the question of the translation of zi, an exact one-to-one equivalent of zi in our languages is impossible, since it covers a range of meanings—true, faithful, righteous, legitimate. It is "true" in the sense of "in accordance with the divine order" and "reliable," "steadfast" in social relationships. In the idiom sipa-zi, it has been mistranslated "good shepherd" in conformity with biblical phraseology.

13 The utilization of the shepherd motif in Mesopotamia was gradual and evolved especially during the Ur III period and the following second millennium; see J. G. Westenholz, "The Good Shepherd," in A. Panaino and A. Piras, eds., *Schools of Oriental Studies and the Development of Modern Historiography*, Melammu Symposia 4 (Milan, 2004), pp. 281–310.

14 There are two occurrences of this personal name: *a*) Sollberger *Corpus* 46 vii 4 = Enz. 1 vii 4; see J.-P. Grégoire, *La province méridionale de l'état de Lagash* (Luxembourg, 1962), pp. 9–11 (who dates the letter to the fifth year of Enannatum II); Michalowski *Letters*, pp. 11–12, no. 1:36; Kienast-Volk *SAB*, pp. 25–29 (both date the letter to the fifth year of Ukg.), and *b*) Cros *Tello*, p. 181, AO 4156 iii 1′ (time of Entemena). If both occurrences relate to the same individual, then the individual could be named after Enannatum I (see the discussion in J. Bauer "Der vorsargonische Abschnitt der mesopotamischen Geschichte," in J. Bauer, R. K. Englund, and M. Krebernik, eds., *Mesopotamien: Späturuk-Zeit und frühdynastische Zeit*, Orbis Biblicus et Orientalis 160/1 [Fribourg and Göttingen, 1998], p. 474).

Išme-Dagan, pp. 88 f.).[15] In the city of Larsa, an unusual new epithet, sipa níg-gi-na "shepherd of righteousness," is borne by two kings: Nūr-Adad ([sipa níg-g]i-na, see Frayne, RIME 4, p. 148, E4.2.8.7:18) and Sîn-iddinam (a contemporary of Sîn-kāšid; Frayne, RIME 4, p. 176, E4.2.9.14:33). The first known instance of the epithet sipa gi-na, the exact Sumerian equivalent of *rēʾû kīnu*, is that of Rīm-Sîn of Larsa, who bears it in his year-dates 26 and 28.[16]

In Akkadian, the adjective *kīnu* is more commonly attached to *šarru* "king." The royal image, *šarru kīnu* "the true (and legitimate) king" is the traditional epithet going back to the name of Sargon of Akkade. An innovative title, *ikkarum kīnum* occurs in an inscription of Lipit-Ištar of Isin: *ikkarum kīnum ša Urim* "the true farmer of Ur."[17] Remarkably, the epithet *rēʾû kīnu* "the true shepherd" occurs for the first time in this composition and does not reappear until Middle Babylonian and Middle Assyrian royal inscriptions.[18] This epithet, for instance, was the leitmotiv of the inscriptions of Nebuchadnezzar I. He used it in the bilingual literary text Seed of Kingship.[19] This leitmotiv was further developed in the hymn to Enlil in a contemporaneous *kudurru*. In this hymn, Enlil bears the title *nābû rēʾû kīnu* "the one who calls by name the faithful shepherd" (Hinke *Kudurru* i 21 [Nbk. I]), and Nebuchadnezzar I is referred to as *rēʾû kīnu* (Hinke *Kudurru* ii 15), which reiterates his function of shepherding Sumer and Akkad (*ana rēʾût māt Šumeri u Akkadî*, ii 1).[20] Thus the epithet *rēʾû kīnu* is a *topos* of royal legitimation, the divine selection of the king, which is a major theme of the oracular and prophetic texts.[21]

Why, however, is the king in our text unnamed? Contemporaneous and Sargonid prophecies designate the royal recipient, whereas later literary prophecies are vague as to the name of the king. On the basis of the context of the find, the referent of the "true shepherd" should be Sîn-kāšid, since he came to the throne by less than legitimate means and thus needed legitimation.[22] Foster has supported this identification by

---

[15] Klein, *Šulgi* = J. Klein, *Three Šulgi Hymns: Sumerian Royal Hymns Glorifying King Šulgi of Ur* (Ramat-Gan, 1981); Ludwig, *Išme-Dagan* = M.-C. Ludwig, *Untersuchungen zu den Hymnen des Išme-Dagan von Isin*, SANTAG 2 (Wiesbaden, 1990).

[16] M. Sigrist, *Larsa Year Names* (Berrien Springs, Michigan, 1990), pp. 54 and 56.

[17] ^{d}Lipit-Eštar sipa-sun$_5$-na Nibru^{ki} engar-zi Uri$_5$^{ki}-ma : ^{d}*Lipit-Eštar rējûm pāliḫ Nibru ikkarum kīnum ša Urim* "Lipit-Ištar, humble shepherd of Nippur (Sum.) / shepherd who is reverent towards Nippur (Akk.), true farmer of Ur" (Frayne, RIME 4, p. 48, E4.1.5.1:1–5 [Sum.]; p. 51, E4.1.5.3:1–7 [Akk.]).

[18] M.-J. Seux, *Epithètes royales akkadiennes et sumériennes* (Paris, 1967), pp. 245 f.

[19] W. G. Lambert, "Enmeduranki and Related Matters," *JCS* 21 (1967): 128, line 11.

[20] V. A. Hurowitz, *Divine Service and Its Rewards: Ideology and Poetics in the Hinke Kudurru*, Beer Sheva 10 (Beer Sheva, 1997), p. 62.

[21] Ellis, "Mesopotamian Oracles and Prophetic Texts," pp. 161, 175–78, 184.

[22] This is the common opinion; see van Dijk ("Die Inschriften," pp. 61–62), Biggs ("An Old Babylonian Oracle from Uruk," p. 604), Ellis ("The Goddess Kititum Speaks," p.138), Pongratz-Leisten ("When the Gods Are Speaking," pp. 156–57), and Foster (*Before the Muses*, p. 122), whereas Metzler (*Tempora*, p. 866, n. 15) suggests the first section may be addressed to an official of the Sîn temple.

etymologizing the king's name to mean "The-God-Sin-Is-Arriving (in triumph)" by rendering poetic allusions in line 15 to the arrival of the true shepherd and by reading in line 19 that the promised ruler came out of the city of Sîn (Ur). There are, however, at least two other possible candidates for the unnamed ruler: Anam (see possible restoration in line 21) and Hammurabi (cf. *bēlum muballiṭ Uruk* CH ii 37–38). Hammurabi is also *mušēpû kīnātim* (CH iv 53, B vi 12, C rev. "ii" 7!),[23] and this attribution might explain the northern orthography in which this text is written. One might imagine a scribe from Uruk sending this oracle to his Babylonian overlord and using the Babylonian way of writing. The tablet we have might then be a file copy or a draft.

Another strange aspect of the prophecy of W 19900,1 is the dating of the beginning of the blessed reign of the "true shepherd" from the day he entered the Eanna. The entering or passing over the threshold may express a rite of passage. Perhaps this refers to a coronation ceremony that may have included a "sacred marriage" ritual. Ellis has suggested that there was a proclamation of an oracular message at the coronation of the king.[24] On the basis of our tablet, Pongratz-Leisten proposed that the kings of the Sîn-kāšid dynasty chose the framework of prophecy to convey their close relationship with Inanna/Ištar and the divine world in place of the ritual of the "sacred marriage."[25] Another probability is that the entrance of the king into the temple refers to his involvement in specific religious rites. Certain livestock were designated in Sumerian as lugal ku_4-ra "the king having entered," which can be understood as animals for sacrifices performed in the presence of the king or by the king.[26] These offerings were presented in the Inanna temple in Uruk as well as in Nippur.

In the introduction to the oracular text W 19900,1, the goddess Nanaya is also said to have made an entrance. In the city of Ur in the Ur III period the cult of Annunītum and Ulmašītum included observances called the u_4 *erubbatum* "Day (of) Entering."[27]

---

[23] See the comparison of these lines by N. Wasserman, "A Bilingual Report of an Oracle with a Royal Hymn of Hammurabi," *RA* 86 (1992): 7–8.

[24] Ellis, "Mesopotamian Oracles and Prophetic Texts," pp. 174, 177, and 181. Moran ("An Ancient Prophetic Oracle," p. 254) also suggests that the temporal context of the Kitītum oracle might be the accession of the king. For a similar proposal, i.e., that the oracles were delivered at the coronation ceremonies of Esarhaddon, see S. Parpola, *Assyrian Prophecies*, SAA 9 (Helsinki, 1997), p. lxiv.

[25] See Pongratz-Leisten, "When the Gods Are Speaking," p. 147, who defines the role of Inanna/Ištar as a prophesying deity for the crown prince and future king but builds her argument on this text, which is less than supportive.

[26] W. Sallaberger, *Der kultische Kalender der Ur III-Zeit* (Berlin, 1993), Teil 1, p. 30 and n. 124 (where he negates the idea that lugal ku_4-ra refers to a specific ritual) and p. 113. Note also the Ur III ritual text, UET 3 57 (see J. J. A. van Dijk, "VAT 8382: Ein zweisprachiges Königsritual," *Studien Falkenstein*, pp. 235–36), which describes a ritual in which the king enters various temples.

[27] M. E. Cohen, *The Cultic Calendars of the Ancient Near East* (Bethesda, Maryland, 1993), p. 138; Sallaberger, *Kalender*, Teil 1, p. 201.

Such an observance was also held in the temple of Dagan and Išhara.[28] Although it is not clearly stated, it can be deduced from the context that the place where Nanaya entered is also the Eanna. The Eanna was the traditional precinct of Inanna, but it was shared with Nanaya before and even after the building of her separate temple.[29] This can be seen in the words of a tigi-song to Nanaya by Išbi-Erra of Isin (Išbi-Erra C, lines 2–4):

> ^{d}na-na-a me-te é-an-ka in-nin-ra túm-ma
> gal zu nu-u_8-gig-ge nin kur-kur-ra zi-dè-eš-šè pà-da
> ^{d}na-na-a kalam é-an-ka igi-gál šúm-mu ba-e-zu
>
> Nanaya, ornament of Eanna, worthy of the Lady!
> Wise one, correctly chosen as lady of all the lands by the "hierodule":
> Nanaya, you instruct the Land, bestowing wisdom in Eanna.[30]

We have royal dedications of various cultic installations to Nanaya from the members of the Sîn-kāšid dynasty—Sîn-kāšid built an ib-oval for her,[31] Sîn-gāmil built her first temple in Uruk, the $É_2$-me-ur_4-ur_4,[32] which was completed by his successor Anam.[33] The close relationship among the kings of Uruk, Nanaya, and the Eanna finds the following expression in the royal hymn of Anam (lines 34–36):

> [bí]-in-dug_4 an-ki-a ig-é-an-na-ka
> nin ummeda-a ^{d}na-na-a bàd-gal ba-gub-bu?
> zi numun hi-li giš-šub-zu-šè mu-e-gar
>
> The lady, the nurse, Nanaya, who stands there like a great wall at the door of Eanna, has decreed throughout heaven and earth and she has fixed life, progeny, and luxury as your lot.[34]

It is interesting to note again that Nanaya is standing at the liminal location of the doorway.

---

[28] M. Hilgert, "*erubbatum* im Tempel des Dagān—eine Ur III-zeitliche Urkunde aus Drēhim," *JCS* 46 (1994): 29–32.

[29] Nanaya's chapel in the Eanna, the é-ḫi-li-an-na, is first mentioned by the Kassite king Nazi-Maruttaš; see George *Temples*, pp. 98 f., no. 459.

[30] For an edition of this tigi-song to Nanaya for Išbi-Erra (Išbi-Erra C), see W. W. Hallo, "New Hymns to the Kings of Isin," *BiOr* 23 (1966): 243, YBC 9859.

[31] Frayne, RIME 4, pp. 451–52, E4.4.1.6.

[32] Ibid., pp. 466–67, E4.4.3.1.

[33] Related in his royal hymn, W 20477, in which he not only completes the Emeurur for Nanaya, but also dedicates a statue of her. See A. Falkenstein, "Zu den Inschriftenfunden der Grabung in Uruk-Warka 1960–1961," *Bagh. Mitt.* 2 (1963): 80–82.

[34] For this royal hymn of Anam, see ibid., p. 81.

The genealogy of Nanaya is now known—she is the daughter of An[35] and Inanna.[36] While Inanna is the daughter of Sîn (specified first in Old Babylonian), Nanaya becomes the daughter of Sîn only in first-millennium texts as a result of her syncretism with Inanna. Thus, Sargon II in his hymn declaims: "Hear O regions of the world, the praise of queen Nanaya ... daughter-in-law of the Esagil, spouse of Muati,... daughter of Sîn."[37] Consequently, an explanation is needed to answer the question of why Nanaya waits at the gate of Sîn, "her father" in this Warka text. Other than it being a scribal error, there seems to be only one justification for this unusual filiation—that "father" is used here to designate "ancestor." In other words, Nanaya's mother's father, her grandfather, the god Sîn, is replacing her father, An. While a gate of Sîn might be found in Uruk,[38] a heavenly gate of Sîn is known from the composition Etana, in which Etana dreams of passing through the gate of Sîn, Šamaš, Adad, and Ištar before proceeding to the palace of Ištar.[39] Thus the vision of the prophet in W 19900,1 might be one of a scene in heaven rather than on earth.

One of the central questions in this oracular text is its divine source, that is, whether it is imparted by one or two goddesses. Because of the confusion in the writing of the logogram U.DAR and of the conjunctive particle *ù*, the reading depends on the subjective analysis of the text with one exception. In line 27, *a-wa-tim ša* U.DAR *iq-ta-bi-a* is the only possible reading. The question is whether to read U.DAR as a proper noun, the name of the goddess Ištar, or as a common noun, the generic word for goddess, which could refer back to Nanaya. In references to this text in the secondary literature,

---

[35] For her genealogy in relation to An, see Richter *Panthea*, p. 281, and Beaulieu *Uruk*, p. 183.

[36] G. Pettinato, "Lipit-Eštar e la dea Nanaja," in M. Dietrich and O. Loretz, eds., *dubsar antamen, Studien zur Altorientalistik: Festschrift für Willem H. Ph. Römer zur Vollendung seines 70. Lebensjahres mit Beiträgen von Freunden, Schülern und Kollegen*, AOAT 253 (Münster, 1998), pp. 267–79.

[37] A. Livingstone, *Court Poetry and Literary Miscellanea*, SAA 3 (Helsinki, 1989), p. 14, no. 4.

[38] Other references to KÁ of ^{d}Sîn are: W 20472,199 (cited by Falkenstein, "Inschriftenfunde," p. 12, n. 40 in list of gates) and the problematic W 20472,95:4 (see S. Sanati-Müller, "Texte aus dem Sînkāšid Palast, III," *Bagh. Mitt.* 21 [1990]: 145, no. 94, and Richter *Panthea*, p. 267). For Sîn in Uruk, see Richter *Panthea*, pp. 267–68. In this connection, it may be noteworthy to point out the confusion of Uruk and Ur in the Ur III period; cf. nam-lugal Kiš^{ki}-ta UNUG^{ki}(var. ŠEŠ.UNUG^{ki})-šè {x} àm-mi-túm ⌈Kul-aba$_4$⌉^{ki} uru [^{d}S]în ù-tu-da pa im-ma-ni-è "You brought kingship from Kiš to Uruk (var. Ur). You made resplendent Kullab, the city of Sîn's birth" (Šulgi O 60–61; see J. Klein, "Šulgi and Gilgameš: Two Brother-Peers (Šulgi O)," *Kramer AV*, p. 278). On this passage, see also D. O. Edzard, "Enmebaragesi von Kiš," *ZA* 53 (1959): 19–23, and C. Wilcke, in "Genealogical and Geographical Thought in the Sumerian King List," in H. Behrens, D. Loding, and M. T. Roth, eds., *DUMU-E$_2$-DUB-BA-A: Studies in Honor of Åke W. Sjöberg* (Philadelphia, 1989), pp. 561–62.

[39] Kinnier-Wilson *Etana* IV 5 = M. Haul, *Das Etana-Epos: Ein Mythos von der Himmelfahrt des Königs von Kiš*, Göttinger Arbeitshefte zur altorientalischen Literatur 1 (Göttingen, 2000), III rev. 5, also J. Novotny, *The Standard Babylonian Etana Epic*, SAA Cuneiform Texts 2 (Helsinki, 2001), III 104.

some scholars believe that the goddess who divulges the oracle is the goddess Ištar,[40] while others think that it is Nanaya.[41] As already pointed out by Bob Biggs, Nanaya is probably to be preferred, since she is specified by name and it is possible to refer to her under the sobriquet "goddess" *ištaru*.[42] The designation *ištaru* as a common noun, the generic word for goddess, is already found in Early Dynastic texts in which the name inanna could be applied to other manifestations of female goddesses.[43] An Old Babylonian example of *ištaru* as a common noun in the singular is:

> *lizziz ina muttiki ilu abīja*
> *lišann[iak]k[im] iš-ta-ri-i a-la-ak-ti limdi*
>
> Let the god of my father stand before you,
> let him tell you, my goddess, learn my way.
>
> (Groneberg *Ištar*, p. 110:13–14; see Streck, *Wilcke AV*, p. 305, and A. Cavigneaux, *NABU* 2005/54)

Note the contrast between the named goddess and the generic use of *ištaru* in the plural:

> U.DAR *rittušša ṣerret nišī uki᾿al*
> *[iq]ullā iš-ta-ra-ta-ši-in [siqr]ušša*
>
> Ištar holds in her hand the nose-rope of the people,
> their goddesses attend to her word.
>
> (Groneberg *Ištar*, p. 75 ii 10–13 [Agušaya])

[40] van Dijk, "Die Inschriften," pp. 61–62; Metzler, *Tempora*, p. 867; Pongratz-Leisten, *Herrschaftswissen in Mesopotamien*, p. 49; Pongratz-Leisten, "When the Gods Are Speaking," p. 155. One reason for this assumption is the close connection between Assyrian prophecy and the cult of Ištar (of Arbela!); see Parpola, SAA 9, pp. xlvii f. Among the many prophecies given in Mari, however, there is only one single mention of an Ištar figure, Ištar of Ninêt (Nineveh?) (ARMT 26/1 192:16).

[41] Charpin, "Prophètes et rois," p. 43; Ellis, "Mesopotamian Oracles and Prophetic Texts," p. 138; Beaulieu *Uruk*, p. 184; and Foster, *Before the Muses*, p. 122.

[42] Biggs, "An Old Babylonian Oracle from Uruk," p. 604, n. 2.

[43] In the Early Dynastic collection of praise-hymns, the praise-hymn to Inanna of Zabalam addresses her as Inanna-kur, Inanna of Uruk, and Inanna-ḫu-ud but in the final line invokes her as ^{d}Nin-um; in the praise hymn to Inanna of Dilmun, the name Inanna is used parallel with the name of the goddess of Dilmun, Nin-ab-KID.KID (lines 143–44). For a discussion, see J. G. Westenholz, "Great Goddesses in Mesopotamia: The Female Aspect of Divinity," *Bulletin of the Canadian Society for Mesopotamian Studies* 37 (2002): 18–20.

A similar example is seen in a late second-millennium composition:

kamsāši kullassin ^{d}*Iš-tar*.ME *nišīma*

All the goddesses of the peoples bow down to her.

(Lambert, *Kraus AV*, p. 202 iv 21 [Šarrat-Nippuri Hymn])

Of the many examples of *ištaru* as a common noun in first-millennium texts, note this parallelism from Gilgamesh:

išassi ^{d}*Iš-tar kīma ālitti*
unambi Bēlet-ilī ṭābat rigma

The goddess began screaming like a woman in childbirth,
Bēlet-ilī wailed, so sweet of voice.

(George *Gilg*. XI 117 f.)[44]

The Old Babylonian flood story contains a similar couplet, with the Akkadian word *iltum* "goddess" in the first line and the mother goddess ^{d}Mami in the second.[45] In Mari rituals, the named goddess is also commonly designated by the generic term *iltum*.[46] In the last line of this Uruk text, the goddess is simply referred to as DINGIR "god," a term unmarked for gender (but see the discussion in the notes to line 30 below).

The words uttered by the goddess contain allusions to "dead Uruk" and wishes for its brighter future. The phrase *Uruk mītum* "dead Uruk" is an extraordinary designation and an expression apparently unique to Uruk. There are two periods in the history of the city of Uruk in which it could be said to be "dead." The first and earlier period of demise was after the fall of the Ur III dynasty, when the city of Uruk seems to have suffered more than any other urban center—it was destroyed and then abandoned for almost a century. During that period, Uruk endured the hegemony of Isin through the reign of Lipit-Ištar, after which it gained independence. Following a short-lived Amorite dynasty that left no records in Uruk, the Sîn-kāšid dynasty arose in the mid-

[44] See also the comments George *Gilg*., p. 886.

[45] Lambert-Millard *Atra-hasīs*, pp. 94–95 iii 32 f.

[46] J.-M. Durand and M. Guichard, "Les rituels de Mari," *Florilegium marianum III: recueil d'études à la mémoire de Marie-Thérèse Barrelet* (Paris, 1997), p. 46. In the ritual of Eštar, *iltum* replaces the goddess Eštar in the second half of the tablet (pp. 52–57 iii 10, 19, iv 3, 4, 5, 25), and in the ritual of Eštar of Irradān, *iltum* occurs throughout (pp. 59–61 i 4′, 5′, 14′, 16′, 20′, iv 18′, 23′) with one sole reference to Eštar (iv 21′ besides the colophon). Note that it has been suggested that these two fragmentary tablets should join (suggested by Charpin apud Durand and Guichard, "Les rituels de Mari," p. 28, and supported by D. E. Fleming, "Recent Work on Mari," *RA* 93 [1999]: 160).

nineteenth century to reclaim Uruk. As far as we know, however, the theme of the revival of dead Uruk occurs with only one Old Babylonian king—Hammurabi—who according to his stele was *bēlum muballiṭ Uruk* "lord who revives Uruk (Hammurabi stele, CH ii 37–38). The second period of demise occurred after the post-Samsuiluna disintegration of the southern Mesopotamian cities, resulting in centuries of abandonment. During this later period, wishes for the revival of Uruk are encountered in late Old Babylonian personal names from Kiš, such as *Uruk-libluṭ*.[47]

While the term "dead city" is found once in Akkadian (TIM 2 16:63; see further, notes to lines 11 and 17 below), the Sumerian adjective most commonly given in relation to uru "city" is gul "destroyed" (see, for example, Nippur Lament 43 and passim).[48] The refrain in the Lamentation over the Destruction of Sumer and Ur put into the mouths of the goddesses is: a uru gul-la é gul-la-mu "Alas, the destroyed city, my destroyed temple!" (line 118 and passim).[49]

To revive dead Uruk, the "true shepherd" in this Uruk prophecy is accompanied by *šulmu* and *balāṭu* "well-being and life." A similar promise is made at the end of the Uruk Lament:

> lú-uru-bi nam-ti níg-du$_{10}$-ge
> gù zìg-mu-na-ni-ib me-téš ḫé-i-i
> zi-da gùb-bu-na ḫé-bí-in-dirig
> ^{d}lamma gá-la nu-dag-ge sag-gá-na tuku-bí-ib
> nam-tar-⌈ra⌉-[ni] ⌈inim$^{?}$⌉-zid du$_{11}$-ga-a-ba
> inim an-[n]a$^{?}$ ^{d}en-líl-lá-šè sud-da-šè nu-kúr-ru
>
> Man and city! Life and well-being!—
> Proclaim it for him. Let praises ring out!
> Let him be made surpassing above all, to his right or left!
> Tireless lamma deity, take hold of his head,
> pronounce his fate in charitable words—
> By the command of An and Enlil it will remain forever unaltered!
>
> (Uruk Lament 12.33–38)[50]

Note, moreover, that in the Uruk Lament, Uruk is referred to as ki-gig-ga "the aggrieved place" (Green, "Uruk Lament," p. 276, 12.26), a description that may reflect

---

[47] R. Pientka, *Die spätaltbabylonische Zeit*, Imgula 2 (Münster, 1998), p. 183.

[48] S. Tinney, *The Nippur Lament*, Occasional Publications of the Samuel Noah Kramer Fund 16 (Philadelphia, 1996).

[49] P. Michalowski, *The Lamentation over the Destruction of Sumer and Ur* (Winona Lake, Indiana, 1989), p. 82, note to line 118. For other examples, see Tinney, *Nippur Lament*, p. 139, note to line 43.

[50] M. W. Green, "The Uruk Lament," *JAOS* 104 (1984): 277, 12.33–38.

its suffering and destruction at the end of the Ur III period. This composition is dated to the reign of Išme-Dagan of Isin, who is mentioned in line 12.14 and who bears the epithet sipa-zi in his hymns and inscriptions.

The major issue concerning the contents of the oracle is the message it brings. Commonly, messages contained in oracles deal with specific public matters, affairs of cult and temple or king and state. Is the message the promise of a rosy future for Uruk or just a pledge for the continuous presence and support of Nanaya?[51] Does the oracle convey instructions for the restoration of the cult of the goddess, be it of Ištar or of Nanaya?[52] The message is unfortunately partially destroyed.

The uncertainties of the contents of the text are mirrored in the problems of its form—its paleography, orthography, grammar, and vocabulary. Regarding paleography, for example, the scribe wrote the sign ù and the logogram U.DAR identically (see above).[53]

The northern orthography of this early text from Uruk can be seen in the following examples: BI for both /bi/ and /pi/ (*bi-tim*, line 3; *pí-ki*, line 19); TU for /ṭu/ (*ba-la-ṭú*, line 5; *ú-ba-al-la-ṭú*, line 11). For comparison, note the orthography of the letter of Anam to Sinmuballiṭ of Babylon, *bi-tum* (*Bagh. Mitt.* 2 56 ii 2), *pi-i-im* (ibid., iii 28), *na-ṭù-ú* (ibid., 57 ii 6). Another peculiarity is the use of DI for /ṭe/ (*te-ṭe-en*, line 12) rather than TE, which is the common Old Babylonian trait; cf. *ṭe*$_4$*-ma-am* (ibid., 56 i 23 [Uruk], CT 52 3:30 [north], Tell Rimah 20:15) and *ṭe*$_4$*-em-ka* (YOS 13 161:13 [Dilbat]), but note the mixture in Šamaš-ḫāzir letters: *ša-ṭe*$_4$*-er* (OECT 3 52:21) and *i-ṭe-eḫ-ḫi* (OECT 3 52:27). TE for /ṭe/ occurs even in late Old Babylonian letters from Babylon (the period of Samsuditana): *ip-ṭe*$_4$*-er* (VAS 22 84:29). The orthography gives no evidence, however, of the typical Middle Babylonian shifts, such as š > l before a dental (*ištu* vis-à-vis *ultu*; see line 4), w > m in intervocalic position (*a-wa-tim*, line 27), or w > Ø in initial position (*wa-ar-ki-šu*, line 5). The Old Babylonian spelling convention of the type V_1-V_1C is found in this text to write monosyllables of the type VC (*i-ib-ta-lu-uṭ*, line 17) and monosyllabic alternants of disyllabic words, such as *ú-ul* (line 27)[54]—supporting the Old Babylonian dating of the text. As is common in Old Babylonian and Middle Babylonian orthography, the double consonants are consistently indicated in the script, but as expected in Old Babylonian, the final vowels i + a are not contracted (*ú*?*-ṣi-a-am*, line 19; *iq-ta-bi-a*, line 27). There is, however, an utter lack of consistency in the handling of mimation (*a-di ra-a-am ki-na* [line 10] as opposed to *aš-šum ri-i ki-nim* [line 22]). The absence of mimation is unambiguous as

[51] Metzler, *Tempora*, p. 866.

[52] van Dijk, "Die Inschriften," pp. 61–62; Foster, *Before the Muses*, p. 122.

[53] Cf. lines 7 and 27, and for a discussion of the problem, see Metzler, *Tempora*, pp. 866–67, n. 18.

[54] E. Reiner, "The Phonological Interpretation of a Subsystem," in *Studies Oppenheim*, p. 172.

seen in the use of VC and V signs but may be even more prevalent, since it is difficult to assess its absence because of the conventional use of CVm signs as the final sign of a word. Thus, *-nim*, *-qum*, *-tum*, and *-tim* are commonly disregarded in studies of mimation.[55] The poor quality of the writing and the variations in orthography are, according to Pongratz-Leisten, due to the prophet's lack of training in writing.[56]

The grammatical rules of nominal declension, nominal and verbal agreement, and verbal sequence are kept. The vocabulary is restricted and words are repeated for effect. Poetic devices include the fronting of the *nomen rectum* of the inverted genitive (see line 1), parallelism (see lines 4–5), and literary repetition. This same type of simplicity of diction and repetition of phrases is to be found in the oracle of Kitītum of Nerebtum (modern Ishchali).[57] Note the inverted repetition and expansion of lines 10–11 in lines 17–20.

The structure of the composition can be outlined as follows:

Lines 1–5 (prophet addresses the king in praise)

Lines 6–14 (prophet tells of first vision)

Lines 15–20 (prophet tells of first vision fulfilled)

Lines 21–27 (prophet tells of second vision)

Lines 28–30 (prophet addresses the king directly)

Metzler breaks down the structure of this text differently because of his assessment of the language: he believes that the beginning lines (1–6) and the final lines (28–30) of the text are poetic in form, while the middle section (lines 7–27) was composed in prose.[58] He analyzes lines 1–6 as two distichs, leaving the subordinate clause of line 6 hanging.

Thus this oracular text is problematic: it is rare to find a literary text with a definite archaeological find-spot whose orthography and language seemingly contradict that archaeological information. If the archaeological details were lacking, this oracular text would be dated to the late Old Babylonian or perhaps even to the early Kassite period, conceivably related to the revival of Uruk under Kara-indaš. It is, consequently, difficult to place this text in its literary context and to determine its political agenda and historical value.

---

[55] Certain forms with mimation could be explained as pausal forms, such as those found in the first two lines of W 19900,1. On the other hand, Sh. Izre'el ("Linguistics and Poetics in Old Babylonian Literature: Mimation and Meter in Etana," *ANES* 27 [2000]: 57–68) analyzed the apparent mimation problem in Etana and concluded that mimation is not rendered consistently in pausal forms, indicating mimation in pausal forms is deleted, whereas it is retained in other environments. He based his conclusions solely on the distribution of forms using final -Vm signs to render mimation. See also K. A. Metzler, "Restitution der Mimation im altbabylonischen Atram-ḫasīs-Epos," *UF* 26 (1994): 369–72.

[56] "When the Gods Are Speaking," p. 157.

[57] See discussion by Moran, "An Ancient Prophetic Oracle," pp. 255–57.

[58] Metzler, *Tempora*, p. 867.

TEXT

1 *re-e-ú ki-nu šum-šu dam-qum*

2 *la-ma-sà-šu da-ri-tum*

3 *a-na bi-tim é-an-na i-te-ru-ub*

4 *iš-tu i-na-an-na a-na pa-ni-šu šu-ul-mu*

5 *a-na wa-ar-ki-šu ba-la-ṭú*

6 *iš-tu u$_4$-um ^{d}Na-na-a i-ru-ba-am$^{!}$*

7 *ù$^{!}$ i-na* KÁ ^{d}EN.ZU *a-bi-ša*

8 *ú-še-ši-ba-an-ni-ma*

9 *um-ma ši-(i)-ma*

10 *a-di ra-a-am ki-na a-ša-ak-ka-nu*

11 *ù$^{!}$* URUK.KI *mi-ta-am ú-ba-al-la-ṭú*

12 *su-ut* URUK.KI *te-ṭe-en*

13 URUK.KI *ra-bu-ú i-na-aṭ-ṭa-la$^{!}$-an-ni*

14 *a-la-am ù bi-tam ú-za-k[a]*

15 *ki-ma re-ḫu-ú ki-nu a-na ma-ti* ⸢*ša$^{?}$-ak$^{?}$-nu$^{?}$*⸣

16 *um-ma a-na-ku-ma*

17 URUK.KI *mi-tum i-ib-ta-lu-uṭ*

18 *ù re-ḫu-ú ki-nu*

19 *ša i-na pí-ki a-w[a]-t[um] ú$^{?}$-ṣi-a-am*

20 *i-ta-aš-ka-an ša$^{!}$-la-am-[š]u tu$^{!!}$-uš$^{!}$-te-eš$_{15}$$^{!}$-še-ri*

21 *um-ma ši-ma i-nu-ma a x x An-a$^{!}$-an Uruk^{ki}-a-am* (or: *A-nim* (^{d})INANNA$^{!}$ DINGIR.URU DINGIR *ad-ki-a-am*)

22 *ù aš-šum re-i ki-nim a-[ša-al-šu-nu]-ti*

23 *ir-bi-ta i-id-na-a ki a-ši$^{?}$-ra-ni* (or: *a-na i-si-ni*)

24 *i-na mu-uḫ-ḫi-ia i-*⸢*ta-na-ap-ḫu*⸣*-ur*

25 *ta-ša-ab la ta-na-aš a-wa-[tu]-ú-a ú-ut$^{!}$-ra*

26 *ú-ṣú-úr-tu eṣ-ra-at*$^{!}$(wr. *am*)*-m[a x]* ⸢*x x (x)*⸣

27 *ú-ul a-la-ak a-wa-tim ša* U.DAR *iq-ta-bi-a*

28 *be-lí pí-ia li-iš-me-e-ma*

29 *a-wa-ti-ia i-na qá-ti li-ki-il*

30 *ù ṣi-bu-ut* DINGIR *li-ik-šu-ud*

TRANSLATION

(prophet addresses the king in praise):

1 True shepherd—his repute is good,
2 his guardian angel is everlasting—
3 he has entered the Temple Eanna.
4 From now on well-being is before him,
5 health behind him.

(prophet tells of first vision):

6 From the day when Nanaya entered
7 and! in the gate of Sîn, her father,
8 had me sit down and
9 spoke:
10 "Until I shall establish a true shepherd
11 and revive dead Uruk,
12 you will grind the *sūtu*-measure of Uruk.
13 Great Uruk will look toward me.
14 Town and temple I will liberate/free."

(prophet tells of vision fulfilled):

15 When the faithful shepherd was established for the land,
16 I spoke saying,
17 "Dead Uruk has revived
18 and the faithful shepherd,
19 about whom the word (oracle) was promulgated from your mouth,
20 has been established. You ensure that his welfare prospers!"

(prophet tells of second vision):

21 She spoke saying, "When ... Anam the Urukean (or: I summoned Anu and Inanna, gods of the city)
22 and regarding the faithful shepherd I asked them.
23 Give the team of four as helpers(?)! (or: as for my festival)
24 Around me, it continually will assemble.
25 Sit down! Do not shake/move! My words are preeminent,
26 the plan is drawn for you and ...
27 I will not go."

(prophet addresses the king directly):

The words (pl. oblique) that the goddess spoke to me
28 let my lord hear (from) my mouth, and
29 let him retain my words,
30 so he may fulfill the wish of the deity.

PHILOLOGICAL NOTES

1 The writings of *rēʾûm* in this text show a variety of renderings: *re-e-ú, ra-a-am, re-ḫu-ú, re-i.* Old Babylonian writings vary between *rēʾûm* (*re-i-im* Gilg. P ii 33) and *rējûm* (*re-iu-um* CH i 51), but *re-ḫu-tim* (YOS 12 438:8) and *re-e-ú-tim* (Szlechter *Tablettes*, p. 90, MAH 16431:7) both occur for the abstract.

For *šumum damqum*, commonly used in wishes in the greeting formulas of Old Babylonian letters, see W. Sallaberger, *"Wenn Du mein Bruder bist,..." : Interaktion und Textgestaltung in altbabylonischen Alltagsbriefen*, Cuneiform Monographs 16 (Groningen, 1999), p. 85.

2 For the importance of the *lamassum* of the king, cf. *lamassam nāṣirtam aštaknakkum* "with a protective spirit I have provided you," FLP 1674:24b-5; see Ellis, "The Goddess Kititum Speaks," pp. 265–66. For the phrase *lamassum darītum* in Old Babylonian letters, cf. *ša ilšu bānīšu lamassam darītam iddinušum* "to whom the god who created him gave a permanent protective spirit," TCL 17 37:1–2. In the late Uruk prophecy, the guiding spirit of the city is called *lamassu* (wr. ^{d}LAMA) *Uruk*^{ki} *darītu*, Hunger *Uruk*, 3:4f.; see H. Hunger and S. Kaufman, "A New Akkadian Prophecy Text," *JAOS* 95 (1975): 371–75, who suggest that the *lamassu* is that of Ištar in the Eanna. In Old Babylonian letters, *lamassum* and *šumum damqum* can occur in parallel phrases; see, for example, Kraus AbB 1 15:1–4 and, further, Sallaberger, *"Wenn Du mein Bruder bist,"* p. 82.

3 The most laudable feat of the reign of Sîn-kāšid was the restoration of the Eanna temple in Uruk; see Frayne, RIME 4, p. 440. There is no extant dedication of the Eanna but only short brick inscriptions (ibid., pp. 440–41, E4.4.1.1) with no mention of the goddess or any deities of the Eanna. He did build separate temples both for An and Inanna and for Nanaya. For Nanaya, he built the Ešahulla (ibid., pp. 451–52, E4.4.1.6), and for An and Inanna, he built the Epapah, possibly a *papāḫum* cella adjacent to the courtyard of the Eanna (ibid., pp. 452–53, E4.4.1.7).

For the form of the verb as a Gt preterite "für die Dauer eintreten," see Metzler, *Tempora*, p. 869.

4–5 For *šulmu* and *balāṭu* as parallel terms in greeting formulas of Old Babylonian letters, see Sallaberger, *"Wenn Du mein Bruder bist,"* pp. 78–81. An enigmatic administrative text listing expenditures for various rites (IM 10135:11–12) contains the words níg.šu *ina šēpīšu šulmu u ina šēpīšu balāṭu*; see J. J. A. van Dijk, "VAT 8382: Ein zweisprachiges Königsritual," *Studien Falkenstein*, p. 241 and n. 43, where he relates the phrase to the legal clause *šalmu-balṭu*. In the lines of the present text, however, *šulmu* and *balāṭu* are personified as if they were the divine bodyguard of the king; cf. V. Hurowitz and J. G. Westenholz, "LKA 63: A Heroic Poem in Celebration of Tiglath-Pileser I's Muṣru-Qumanu Campaign," *JCS* 42 (1990): 30–33.

6 While I earlier read the last sign as *-kum* "to you" (J. G. Westenholz, "Nanaya, Lady of Mystery," p. 66), the sign seems rather to be *-am* (compare *-kum* in line 1 with *-am* in line 10). Such a reading seems to fit the context better and avoids the introduction of a second person. See, however, the discussion in Metzler, *Tempora,* p. 867 and n. 19.

9 The reason for the scribe's erasure of the *i* in *ši-*(*i*)*-ma* indicated in the copy by van Dijk is not evident, but he was consistent in regarding the vowel as short. In line 21, he wrote *ši-ma* without the addition of the *-i-*.

11, 17 For the phrase *Uruk mītum*, cf. the occurrence of *ālam mītam* (TIM 2 16:63) in a text recording the vitriolic diplomatic exchange between the official representative of Rīm-Sîn in the Diyala region, Šamaš-magir, and the local authority, Ibqu-Ištar, the *šakkanakku* of the city of Diniktum, regarding a fugitive who abducted two slave-girls. The immediate context for the phrase *ālam mītam* is at the conclusion of the affair. The text reads: *rabiānum ša Maškan-šāpir ana kīma jâtî iškunu ālam mītam Maškan-šāpir ana kīma Diniktum tašakkan*, which is translated by the *CAD* as "have they made the r. [*rabiānum*] of Maškan-šāpir as (important as) I am? – you want to turn(?) a dead city, GN [Maškan-šāpir], into the semblance(?) of Diniktum" (*CAD* R s.v. *rabiānu* usage a-3′). While the *CAD* clearly assumes that the "dead city" stands in apposition to Maškan-šāpir, this is most unlikely. Not only does it seem not to follow from the preceding records, since Maškan-šāpir is not mentioned except in these lines, but also during this period Maškan-šāpir was enjoying the heyday of its existence.[59] Perhaps "dead city" is a proverbial phrase whose meaning has been lost in the passage of time.

12 For a metaphorical interpretation of this line, which relates the lowly task of grinding to the kingly duty of taxing the country, see M. Stol, "State and Private Business in Larsa," *JCS* 34 (1982): 155. See further W. R. Mayer, "Akkadische Lexikographie: CAD S, I. Babylonisch," *Or.*, n.s., 60 (1991): 116, who suggests the translation: "du wirst die Uruk (auferlegte) Abgabe zermalmen." The figurative image is not obvious. The equation could be with subservience or with hard labor. A pledged slave-girl had to grind one *sūtu* per day (UET 5 366:9–11), while in Old Babylonian marriage contracts, the junior wife is obligated to grind a *sūtu* of barley flour for the senior wife (see, for example, CT 2 44:25). The divine dictate enjoined on the prophet(ess?) is that she will be the submissive attendant of Nanaya until the revival of Uruk under the true shepherd.

---

[59] P. Steinkeller, "A History of Mashkan-shapir and Its Role in the Kingdom of Larsa," in E. C. Stone and P. Zimansky, eds., *The Anatomy of a Mesopotamian City: Survey and Soundings at Mashkan-shapir* (Winona Lake, Indiana, 2004), pp. 26–42.

13 *Uruk rabû* is a rather unusual appellative. The more common designations are *ribītum* or *supūrum*. Uruk is also referred to as uru-ul "primeval city" and úru-sag / *āli rēšti* "first (foremost) city" (for references, see George *Topographical Texts*, pp. 245–46). The adjective *rabû* does occur with cities, especially *Sippar rabûm*, now identified with Sippar-Amnānum (Tell ed-Dēr); see Harris *Sippar*, p. 13; D. Charpin, "Sippar: deux villes jumelles," *RA* 82 (1988): 13–32; D. Charpin, "Le point sur les deux Sippar," *NABU* 1992/114; C. Janssen et al., "Du chantier à la tablette: Ur-Utu et l'histoire de sa maison à Sippar-Amnānum," in H. Gasche et al., eds., *Cinquante-deux réflexions sur le Proche-Orient ancien offertes en hommage à Léon De Meyer*, MHEO 2 (Leuven, 1994), p. 102. The question here is whether the designation *rabû* in relation to Uruk reflects the type of specificity as that of Sippar. Another possibility is that *Uruk rabû* should be understood in the context of the oracle in which it parallels *Uruk mītum*. Thus a meaning such as "risen Uruk" might be appealing, but the source of such meaning for *rabû* is elusive; according to *CAD* R, *rabû* B is "to set, to disappear (said of celestial bodies)."

As for the verb, there is a problem concerning the reading of the third from last sign, which is misformed. The suggested reading *i-na-ad-da-na*$^{?}$*-an-ni* "wird mir gegeben werden" by Metzler, *Tempora*, p. 866, is grammatically impossible. The correct form of the -i- class verb in the N-stem with dative suffix would have been *innaddinam*. For this reason, the reading *i-na-aṭ-ṭa-la*$^{!}$*-an-ni* is offered. For the use of the verb *naṭālu* in the sense of looking toward the deity, cf. *šātu kīma arḫim annaṭālim* "she (Nanaya) is like the moon to look upon," VAS 10 215:3 (Old Babylonian Hymn to Nanaya).

Foster (*Before the Muses*, p. 122) translates: "A great man will give me Uruk." While "great man" as the subject is very appropriate, the verb *nadānu* cannot take a double accusative. The first-person indirect object should be a dative form.

14 While *ú-ṣa-ba-*[*at*] (Metzler, *Tempora*, p. 866) is a possible reading, the sense of *ṣubbutu* "to conquer a city" or "to seize" (as given in all the translations) does not seem to fit the context. Perhaps a nuance such as "to take possession of" might be possible, referring to the return of the goddess after her abandonment of the city. This withdrawal of the deity and of his/her favor leaves any city vulnerable to its destruction—a common motif of the Sumerian city laments. The range of meanings of the D-form are limited compared to that of the G-form. Other possible meanings of the G-form range from the Old Akkadian phrase "to take a stand in GN"[60] to the Neo-Assyrian phrase *ālu šuātu aṣbat*, meaning "I (re)organized the city" (*CAD* s.v. *ṣabātu* mng. 3f), which co-

[60] Aage Westenholz (personal communication).

occurs with an *ana* phrase (for example, *ana eššūti, ana āl šarrūti*), as well as "to take up a position" (mng. 4a).

There is a problem with this reading, however, because there seems to be no space for the [*-at*] at the end of the line, according to the photograph on *UVB* 18, pl. 20. Thus, van Dijk's translation "je libérerai" (*Dictionnaire de la Bible*), probably reading *ú-za-k*[*a*], seems more appropriate. Most likely reading, similarly, *ú-za-ku-*[(x)], Foster (*Before the Muses*, p. 122) translates: "They will purify(?)."

15 Foster's translation (*Before the Muses*, p. 122), "Since the true shepherd has 'arrived' in this land," is based on *ikšudu* in the traces at the end of this line (see Foster, *NABU* 2002/82, on wordplay in this text).

19 This clause is awkward. While the space is seemingly too short for a phrase *ana* + noun before the verb, the traces match the signs of line 15. Metzler (*Tempora*, p. 866) reads *a-w*[*a*]*-s*[*u*]$^{?}$ ("bezüglich dessen ein Wort aus deinem Mund erging"), while van Dijk (*Dictionnaire de la Bible*) translated "que sur ton ordre An [a fait sor]tir" and Foster (*Before the Muses*, p. 122) "he who came out hither from the city of the god Sîn to [Uruk?]" (reading *ina Urim*^{ki} *ú-ṣi-a-am*, Foster, *NABU* 2002/82). Another possibility might be that this clause may refer back to Nanaya's command to the prophet in line 12, and the traces would fit *a-na-k*[*u*]. Perhaps the best restoration would be *a-w*[*a*]*-t*[*um*], although a problem does exist regarding the space for the signs. A comparable example is: *amat ippīša uṣṣia* "the word that comes out of her mouth," VAS 10 214 vi 13 (Old Babylonian Agušaja).

20 The traces in the middle of the line do not seem to yield an easy solution. Metzler (*Tempora*, p. 866) reads: *ta-la-*⸢*ka*$^{?}$*-ti*$^{?}$⸣ *x x te-eš*$_{15}$*-še-ri* "Auf den Wegen$^{?}$ von$^{?}$ [oder: auf meinem Weg$^{?}$] ... kommst$^{?}$ du (nun$^{?}$)." Since the sign is clearly *-uš-* rather then *eš*$_{15}$ (IŠ), the last word could be *uš-še-ri* as an imperative feminine expressing a plea to Nanaya by the speaker to release him from the "grinding" imposed on him in line 12, but that does not account for the signs in the middle of the line. I have followed a suggestion made to me by Walter Farber that makes sense of the line, although it calls for seriously emending several signs.

21 The traces of the signs in the subordinate clause depending on *inūma* are also unwieldy. Although the signs could be construed as *a-*⸢*ša*$^{!}$*-ka*⸣*-an* "when I reestablish," this is unlikely, since the verb does not have a subjunctive marker and the object would have to follow the verb. This precludes a translation such as "When I establish Uruk" (Pongratz-Leisten, "When the Gods Are Speaking," p. 156). The traces at the end of the line might be interpreted as *An-a*$^{!}$*-an Uruk*^{ki}*-a-am* "Anam, the Urukean," while van Dijk (*Dictionnaire de la Bible*) suggested reading "Anum, le fort(?) d'Uruk," which would indicate

that he presumably read the signs at the end of the line as *A-nim da-an-na*$^{!}$*-an Uruk*^{ki}*-a-am*. Metzler (*Tempora*, p. 866) does not attempt any reading. The problem is that this clause does not continue onto the next line and so should end in a verb. Thus it is probably better to read *ad-ki-a-am* "I summoned." For the persons summoned, the reading *A-nim* seems most likely. The traces after *A-nim* could give *É*$^{!}$*-an-na*$^{!}$, but "Anum (of/in the) Eanna of divine(?) Uruk" is slightly awkward, and *A-nim* (^{d})INANNA$^{!!}$ DINGIR.URU is perhaps better. A similar phrase is known from a juridical text recording that an oath was sworn by two of the claimants at the gate of AN *ù* ^{d}INANNA *i*$^{?}$*-li a-li-šu-nu* "An and Inanna, gods of their city," AO 5421:48; see C. Wilcke, "Nanāja-šamḫats Rechtsstreit um ihre Freiheit," in B. Pongratz-Leisten, H. Kühne, and P. Xella, eds., *Ana šadî Labnāni lū allik, Beiträge zu altorientalischen und mittelmeerischen Kulturen: Festschrift für Wolfgang Röllig*, AOAT 247 (Kevelaer and Neukirchen-Vluyn, 1997), pp. 413–29. This suggestion, unfortunately, leaves the last DINGIR sign unaccounted for. Metzler offers no solution for the traces. Logically, Nanaya might be relating that she enlisted the help of her father (despite the mention of Sîn in line 7) and mother. Anu is well known as her father, and a new inscription of Lipit-Ištar of Isin (Pettinato, "Lipit-Eštar e la dea Nanaja," pp. 274–75) recognizes Nanaya as the daughter of Inanna in Isin, but whether this is true of Nanaya in Uruk is not yet known.

23 The last phrase seems to be a prepositional phrase dependent on *kî*. For the writing of *kî* with a short *i*, which is found elsewhere in Old Babylonian literature, see J. G. Westenholz *Akkade*, pp. 206–7, to which many other examples could be adduced. Since the preposition *kî* and the suffix *-āni* are both simile markers, a simile might be expected. Metzler (*Tempora*, p. 866) reads the last two signs as one: ⸢LUGAL$^{?}$⸣, while van Dijk (*Dictionnaire de la Bible*) translated "quatre feux(?) comme pour la fête(?)," which would indicate that he presumably read the signs as: *ir-bi-ta i-ša-ti a-ki a-na i-si-ni*. The simile marker *akî*, however, is known only from the first millennium.

24 One possible reading of this line could be: *i-na mu-uḫ-ḫi-ia i-bi-*⸢*ku*$^{?}$⸣ *x* (*x*) *ši-ib* "into my presence, they brought(?) ...." For *nabāku*, possibly a by-form of *abāku*, see *CAD* N/1. Nevertheless, although it seems obvious that the last word should be a form of *wašābu*, the traces do not yield any coherent form. van Dijk (*Dictionnaire de la Bible*) suggested reading "Au-dessus de moi il s'assemble continuellement," which would indicate that he presumably read the signs at the end of the line as: *i-*⸢*ta-na-ap-ḫu*⸣*-ur*, an Ntn present, thus taking into consideration all the signs. It is a most attractive solution.

25 Since *awâtūa* is in the nominative case, it should be followed by a stative or predicate adjective describing the words in parallel with the beginning of the next line. Despite the extra vertical wedge after *ú*, one possible reading of the last three signs yields *ú-ut-ra* for *watrā* (fem. pl.). The lack of the initial *wa-*,

which should have been preserved (cf. *wa-ar-ki-šu*, line 5), and the Assyrian vocalization of the verb could be said to negate this suggestion.

26 For the reference of *uṣurtu*, Metzler (*Tempora*, p. 867) proposes a plan of the temple. van Dijk (*Dictionnaire de la Bible*) rendered this line: "observe! fais approcher ... [ ]," which would indicate that he presumably read the signs at the beginning of the line as: *ú-ṣú-úr tu-qé*[!]*-ra-am-m*[*a*] for *uṣur tuqerrab-ma*.

27 For the form of the verb as an exceptional Gt reciprocal preterite, see Metzler, *Tempora*, pp. 869 f.

28–30 For these lines, see the transcription by van Dijk ("Die Inschriften," p. 61) and note he transcribed DINGIR as *iltim*. Pongratz-Leisten ("When the Gods Are Speaking," p. 157) conjectures that it should have been written either *ištarātu*, denoting the goddess, or DINGIR.MEŠ, alluding to the gods as the divine counsel. She is manipulating this text, however, in order to maintain the thesis of Inanna/Ištar's role as mediatrix between the divine counsel and the king from the Sumerian tradition to the Old Babylonian tradition. Her first interpretation explains *ṣibûtu* as the "wish or objectives of the god (= Ištar)," while her second interpretation construes the " 'wish or objectives of the gods' in the sense of a general 'divine plan in harmony with the cosmic order' " (ibid.). While it is conceivable that DINGIR could signify the goddess, it is not expected that a king can achieve the objectives of the gods. Rather, it is possible that DINGIR does not refer to any specific deity or deities but that it is a general statement to "fulfill the wish of the god," an indispensable part of any successful king's rule.

THE PALEOGRAPHY AND VALUES OF THE SIGN KIB*

Christopher Woods, The University of Chicago

I

When a comprehensive study of cuneiform paleography is eventually undertaken, this ambitious task will depend in large part upon in-depth studies of individual signs which balance the values attributed to a given sign against its graphic evolution. Only in this way will progress be made in elucidating the relationship between the writing systems of the Uruk, Fara/Abu Salabikh, and Pre-Sargonic periods. This particular study of the sign KIB grows out of a larger investigation devoted to the writing of the name of the Euphrates.[1] As it is concerned with early cuneiform writing, it relies in large part upon the cuneiform record from Abu Salabikh, the mere mention of which evokes the name of Robert D. Biggs, who so masterfully presented this important but difficult corpus. It is only fitting that I dedicate this modest contribution to Bob at the time of his retirement.

II

The complex graph that we transliterate as KIB and that, in Sumerian orthography, is quite rare outside of the writing of Zimbir/Buranuna, represents the fusion of at least two distinct third-millennium graphs. In the lexical tradition of the first and second millennia, the signs in question are analyzed as *giš-minabi-gilimû*, i.e., GIŠ×GIŠ (*LAK*, no. 276) and *gána-minabi-gilimû*, i.e., GÁNA×GÁNA (*LAK*, no. 278);[2] the organization of signs in certain lexical lists suggests that GÁNA and GIŠ were interpreted, at this late date, as graphically related, that is, GÁNA serving as a *gunû*-type counterpart

* I am deeply grateful to Piotr Steinkeller for reading several drafts of this paper and making a number of critical observations and corrections. This study has also greatly benefited from a long and continuing correspondence that I have had with Niek Veldhuis concerning matters of third-millenium paleography and writing. I also would like to thank Miguel Civil, Jennie Myers, and Joan Westenholz for their assistance and suggestions. Finally, I would like to acknowledge the assistance of Tonia Sharlach, who generously provided me with the KIB lexical files of the *Pennsylvania Sumerian Dictionary*.

[1] C. Woods, "On the Euphrates," *ZA* 95 (2005): 7–45.

[2] See Y. Gong, *Die Namen der Keilschriftzeichen*, AOAT 268 (Münster, 2000), pp. 124, 129. *LAK* = Deimel *Fara 1, Liste der archäischen Keilschriftzeichen*.

to GIŠ.[3] It is clear that the paleographic analyses of the late lexical lists lack historical merit—based on contemporaneous sign shapes, they cannot accurately reflect paleographic origins. As we shall see, this is obviously the case with *LAK*, no. 278, allegedly GÁNA×GÁNA. Yet for the sake of convenience, I will refer to the two signs in question as KIB (*LAK*, no. 276) and KIB-*gunû* (*LAK*, no. 278) respectively; I reserve KIB in quotation marks, i.e., "KIB," to refer to the two collectively, without distinction.

The important point to be stressed here is that, regardless of label or paleographic origins, these two signs are not mere allographs in early cuneiform writing. Rather, the differences between them are distinctive—or better graphemic—with KIB and KIB-*gunû* being rigorously distinguished in third-millennium sources. It is only in the Old Babylonian period that the two collapse into a single graph. To be sure, this catch-all sign boasts a number of distinct allographs, including *gunû* and non-*gunû* forms, but by this time the values are no longer graphically distinguished.[4]

The sign KIB can be shown to have an Uruk period ancestry—the problem lies in identifying the number of archaic forebears. *ZATU* identifies two signs that belong to the KIB family, *ZATU*, nos. 522 and 290. For the first, *ZATU*, no. 522, two orthographic variants are given: GIŠ×GIŠ×GIŠ, , or ŠENNURa, and a form closer to GIŠ×GIŠ, 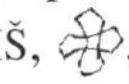, cited as ŠENNURb.[5] It is quite doubtful, however, that these two signs are allographs, as assumed by Green and Nissen. In the archaic copies of the so-called Tribute List[6] all texts agree that the sign form of entry 62 is ŠENNURa,[7] and there are no contexts in which ŠENNURb can be shown to be in free variation with the former. Further, the two graphs are differentiated more than simply by an additional GIŠ element. ŠENNURa displays an oblique 45-degree angle from vertical that is diagnostic of "KIB" in later periods, while ŠENNURb is upright and may be related to EZEN and similar signs.[8] Indeed, further studies of early cuneiform may demonstrate that variations in the orientation of otherwise identical graphs are graphemic rather than merely allographic. Similarly,

---

[3] Note S[b] I 303–07 cited below, where the sequence of signs is GIŠ, GIŠ-*tenû*, KIB(GIŠ×GIŠ), GÁ, GÁNA, GÁNA/GÁNA. Similarly, Proto-Ea (lines 640–41) consecutively lists GIŠ, GÁNA, and GIŠ-*tenû*, followed by GIŠ×GIŠ.

[4] See C. Fossey, *Manuel d'Assyriologie* (Paris, 1926), pp. 504–7. Some of these variants arise already in the Ur III period, leading to misreadings of the sign, for example, UD."ŠEŠ".NUN.KI (Fish *Catalogue* 418) and U.KIB for šennur (TuM 6, no. 20:6; see n. 24 below); note also Hussey's comments in HSS 4, p. 7, n. 7 (the sign in question here is a precursor to the Old Babylonian *šeššig*-type allograph).

[5] Graphs after M. W. Green and H. J. Nissen, *Zeichenliste der archäischen Texte aus Uruk* (Berlin, 1987), no. 522 (hereafter *ZATU*). The indices a, b, c, etc., refer to distinctive, presumably allographic, variants of a given sign (see *ZATU*, pp. 168 and 347).

[6] See R. K. Englund and H. J. Nissen, *Die lexikalischen Listen der archäischen Texte aus Uruk* (Berlin, 1993), pp. 25–29, 112–20 (hereafter *LATU*), and R. K. Englund, "Texts from the Late Uruk Period," in J. Bauer, R. K. Englund, and M. Krebernik, *Mesopotamien: Späturuk-Zeit und frühdynastische Zeit*, Orbis Biblicus et Orientalis 160/1 (Fribourg and Göttingen, 1998), pp. 99–102.

[7] See *LATU*, p. 117.

[8] The *gunû*-form of this graph apparently first occurs in the archaic Ur text VAT 16818, in an obscure context (see the photograph published by the CDLI project: http://cdli.ucla.edu/dl/photo/P005971.jpg).

the identification of *ZATU*, no. 290, , 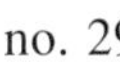, as KIB is doubtful.[9] The sign—which represents an unknown countable item in archaic administrative texts and which occurs also in a Lu forerunner[10]—is likewise written vertically without the distinctive 45-degree tilt. Thus the only certain Uruk predecessor to KIB is GIŠ×GIŠ×GIŠ, which I discuss further below.

KIB-*gunû*, on the other hand, appears by all indications to be an Early Dynastic invention, first attested at Fara. This graph, despite its later interpretation as GÁNA×GÁNA, is actually, in origin, related to KÁR or, more precisely, ŠÈ. As already suggested by Steinkeller, it seems probable that there was no graphic distinction between ŠÈ or, more precisely, ŠÈ-*tenû*$_{90}$ (i.e., horizontal ŠÈ, rotated 90 degrees from vertical and to be distinguished from ŠÈ-*tenû* rotated roughly 45 degrees) and KÁR in the Uruk script.[11] Among the sign forms given in *ZATU*, a number of those claimed for KÁR are indistinguishable from their ŠÈ-*tenû*$_{90}$ counterparts. Moreover, an assumption of a single sign for the early script would clarify the alternation between the two graphs noted by Green and Nissen already for the archaic lexical lists.[12] In this connection, it must be observed that a graph distinct from ŠÈ and representing kár does not occur until the Sargonic period. At Fara, ŠÈ, , and ŠÈ-*tenû*$_{90}$, 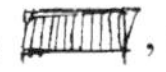, are in free allographic variation, with respect to representing kár.[13] By the Early Dynastic IIIb period, however, ŠÈ-*tenû*$_{90}$ displaced ŠÈ in this role,[14] with the latter sign being maintained only as an archaic feature of the monumental script.[15] With this development, the distinction between ŠÈ-*tenû*$_{90}$ and GÁNA that had been maintained throughout the Early Dynastic period disintegrated, so that by the Sargonic period GÁNA and a *tenû*-graph, identified in the sign lists as KÁR, were used to express kár for the remainder of the third millennium.[16] This latter sign may have been understood paleographically as GÁNA-*tenû* by

[9] Graphs after *ZATU*, no. 290.

[10] W 20421,1; see *LATU*, pl. 23.

[11] P. Steinkeller, review of *ZATU*, in *BiOr* 52 (1995): 702 ad 284, 710 ad 516 and 518.

[12] See the comments to *ZATU*, no. 284. Note, however, that in *LATU* these signs are not counted as variants for the relevant lexical entries—although given the identity or near graphic identity of these signs, the labeling of each is necessarily somewhat arbitrary.

[13] Graphs after Deimel *Fara 2, Schultexte*, no. 13 i 14 and 15 respectively. Observe, for instance, that the Fara-period witnesses of the Tribute List attest me-en-ŠÈ / me-en-zi-ŠÈ (ibid., no. 12 v 7–8; ibid., no. 13 vi 11–12) alongside me-en-ŠÈ-*tenû*$_{90}$ / me-en-zi-ŠÈ-*tenû*$_{90}$ (Shøyen collection MS 2462 v 7–8 [http://www.schoyencollection.com/lexical_files/ms2462.jpg]); compare, from an Old Babylonian witness, me-en-kár / me-en-zi-kár (OIP 11, no. 42 ii 5–6). The two signs share an allographic relationship in other contexts as well; for example, among the Fara witnesses of the Tribute List we find also ⌜zíz⌝-ŠÈ (Deimel *Fara 2, Schultexte*, no. 12 i 15) = zíz-ŠÈ-*tenû*$_{90}$ (ibid., no. 13 i 15). I thank N. Veldhuis for providing me with these references.

[14] Note, for instance, that the Early Dynastic Lagaš PNs Nin-en-šè-nu-$\overset{\text{kár}}{\text{kár}}$ and Nin-uru-ni-nu-$\overset{\text{kár}}{\text{kár}}$ are written with ŠÈ-*tenû*$_{90}$ (for references, see V. V. Struve, *Onomastika rannedinasticheskogo Lagasha* [Moscow, 1984], s.vv.).

[15] As is clearly shown by the writing of ŠÈ for kár in the expression àga-kár—sig$_{10}$ (see *PSD* A/3 s.v.), common in the Lagaš royal inscriptions.

[16] The distribution of these graphs, GÁNA and (for convenience what I will refer to as) GÁNA-*tenû*, is somewhat idiosyncratic for the late third millennium. N. Veldhuis will elaborate upon the distribution of these signs in a forthcoming study. The evidence suggests that ŠÈ-*tenû*$_{90}$ was

the contemporaneous late third-millennium scribal tradition but was historically related to ŠÈ and functionally represented ŠÈ-*tenû*.[17] Interestingly, Ea I (see below) displays a historical consciousness in describing this sign as ŠÈ-*tenû* and attributing to it the values /kara/ and /kiri/. What all of this demonstrates is that ŠÈ, in its various orientations, originally represented kár and that the writing with GÁNA was a secondary development, representing a reanalysis or paleographic drift of kár away from ŠÈ(-*tenû*$_{90}$) and toward GÁNA between the Early Dynastic and Sargonic periods.[18] Many of the values that are later attributed to "KIB," as we shall see, reflect the interwoven histories of ŠÈ and GÁNA in the third millennium.

The precise form of the graph KIB-*gunû* (*LAK*, no. 278) at Fara is uncertain, insofar as it is appropriate to analyze every complex sign as a composite of simpler graphs after the fashion of the analytical apparatus of the first- and second-millennium lexical tradition. Clearly related to ŠÈ and ŠÈ-*tenû*$_{90}$ is a "slanted" ŠÈ,  (note, however, the formal differences from ŠÈ-*tenû*), which is often employed to write zíd and dabin at Fara.[19] In at least one case, KIB-*gunû* resembles the crossing of these signs, ,[20] but, more commonly, the form appears to be based on a *gunû*-form of ŠÈ-*tenû*, e.g., , , , .[21] Indeed it is this second shape that gives rise to the simplified allographs, which make their appearance already in the Abu Salabikh corpus, e.g., , although an allograph derived from ŠÈ-*tenû*$_{90}$, such as, , , is also well attested.[22] In turn, it is this first Abu Salabikh form that is the ancestor of the KIB-*gunû* graph, 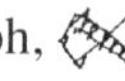, encountered at Nippur and northern Babylonia at the end of the Early Dynastic period.[23] The

replaced by GÁNA in the Sargonic period, which in turn was replaced by Ur III GÁNA-*tenû*; this development, however, is complicated by the writing of GÁNA-har^{ki} for Kár-har^{ki} throughout the Ur III period and beyond.

[17] From a graphic perspective, GÁNA-*tenû* and ŠÈ-*tenû* are necessarily nearly identical; see the comments of M. Civil in MSL 12, p. 12 ad 53. Early evidence that ŠÈ-*tenû* had a value /kar/ or /kir/ is suggested by GÍRID(GÌR×ŠÈ-*tenû*), where ŠÈ-*tenû* likely served as a phonetic complement, reinforcing the reading of GÌR. For the paleographic development of ŠÈ or ŠÈ-*tenû* into GÁNA, note also the evolution of TÙM.

[18] A reflex of ŠÈ = kár may be found in kiri$_7$ and related phonetic values that belong to KEŠDA, which is in origin ŠÈ×ŠÈ. Previous literature concerning the relationship between KÁR and ŠÈ is now cited in R. Borger, *Mesopotamisches Zeichenlexikon*, AOAT 305 (Münster, 2004), p. 83 ad 175.

[19] Graph after *LAK*, no 794. This graph persevered with these meanings at least into the Early Dynastic IIIb period; see *DP*, no. 51 i 6–7, iii 3–4.

[20] Deimel *Fara 3, Wirtschaftstexte*, no. 4 rev. i 3; graph after *LAK*, no. 278. Returning to the point regarding sign orientation, note that in this case the deviation from perpendicular may be graphemic, distinguishing KIB-*gunû* from KEŠDA = ŠÈ×ŠÈ (actually ÉŠ×ÉŠ, two crossed ropes representing kešda "to tie, bind").

[21] Deimel *Fara 3, Wirtschaftstexte*, nos. 53 rev. iv 10; 76 rev. i 10′; 78 rev. iii 4; Deimel *Fara 2, Schultexte*, no. 56 vi 18 [UGN] respectively. Graphs after *LAK*, no. 278.

[22] Graphs after OIP 99, nos. 393 ii′ 4′ (cf. 43 iv 1), 258 iv 1′, and 62 ii 6′ respectively—three instances of the writing of Buranuna.

[23] Graph after TuM 5, no. 56 i 4; this graph also occurs in OIP 104, no. 35 i 2′, Barton MBI 1 xiii 3 and xvii 2 (after "The Barton Cylinder," *Acta Sumerologica [Japan]* 16 [1994]: 15–46 numbering), BiMes 1, no. 31 i 3′; note also D. Charpin and J.-M. Durand, "Tablettes présargoniques de Mari," *MARI* 5 (1987): 72, no. 7 ii 6, written, apparently, without *gunû* marks.

decomposition of the single front wedge into two wedges resulted in the Ur III shape of the sign that begins with a *Winkelhaken*, e.g., [24] (also the GIŠ×GIŠ form [25]). At the end of the Early Dynastic period, the graph assumed a new shape in the south as witnessed in the royal inscriptions, e.g., cursive: [26] and lapidary/monumental: .[27] This graph survived through the Sargonic and Ur III periods as a sign distinct from KIB (GIŠ×GIŠ). No doubt, it is upon this form of the graph that the analysis of KIB-*gunû* as GÁNA×GÁNA, first attested in the Old Babylonian lexical texts, is based. Interestingly, and in no small part owing to the simpler geometry, the prolific paleographic variation exhibited by KIB-*gunû*, apparent already in the Fara period, is not shared by the graphs GIŠ×GIŠ×GIŠ (*LAK*, no. 277), ,[28] and GIŠ×GIŠ (*LAK*, no. 276), ,[29] which, by comparison, are stable in the third millennium.

III

KIB-*gunû* is used consistently in the writing of Buranuna and Zimbir in third-millennium sources with only rare exceptions.[30] It is, in fact, the orthographic root of Buranuna, i.e., ^{UD}buranuna$_{\text{x}}$(KIB-*gunû*)^{nun},[31] with the spelling of the Euphrates, UD.KIB.NUN, employed secondarily to write Sippar. This close association with the Euphrates may have contributed to the understanding, or reanalysis, of the sign as GÁNA×GÁNA, there being a transparent semantic relationship between the river and cultivated land that it makes possible (note that this graph is equated with *qerbetu* "pasture land" and *mērištu* "cultivable land" in the lexical tradition; see below). As will be discussed further, the only other use of this sign is to write a noun with uncertain meaning in the compounds KIB-*gunû*—dím/dug$_4$, which occur in a number of Pre-Sargonic royal inscriptions.

KIB, on the other hand, writes the phonetically related values ùl and hùl. Whether in origin hùl represents the primary lexical item, meaning "reins, leash," and ùl a sec-

---

[24] V. Scheil, *Recueil de signes archaïques* (Paris, 1898), p. 40, no. 96; graph after *LAK*, no. 278. Note also the graph used to write šennur in TuM 6, no. 20:6 (see pl. 48); the *Winkelhaken* is so pronounced that the editors translate ^{giš}šennur(U.KIB).

[25] Graph after W. F. Leemans, "Cuneiform Texts in the Collection of Dr. Ugo Sissa," *JCS* 20 (1966): 35, no. 3:9.

[26] For example, Enmetena: H. Steible, *Die altsumerischen Bau- und Weihinschriften*, Freiburger altorientalische Studien 5/1 (Wiesbaden, 1982), Ent. 44 ii 10; Gudea: Cyl. B xvii 10; graph after TCL 8, pl. 47:10.

[27] For example, Lugalzagesi: BE 1/2, no. 87 ii 7; Narām-Sîn: A. H. Ayish, "Bassetki Statue with an Old Akkadian Royal Inscription of Naram-sin of Agade (B.C. 2291–2255)," *Sumer* 32 (1976): 76 ii 20 (Bassetki Statue, inscribed in metal); graph after *LAK*, no. 278.

[28] Graph after Deimel *Fara 2, Schultexte*, no. 13 iv 4.

[29] Graph after *LAK*, no. 276.

[30] For example, YOS 4, no. 76 rev. 1, where the copy shows Buranuna written with KIB rather than KIB-*gunû*. That by the Old Babylonian period the *gunû* and non-*gunû* forms were merely allographs can be seen in the writing of Zimbir with KIB in CH ii 25.

[31] On the possibility that ^{UD} stands for ^{d} here, see Woods, "On the Euphrates."

ondary syllabic value is difficult to ascertain, given the Sumerian loanwords with these meanings, i.e., *ḫullu* and *ullu*, which are by-forms.[32] Paradoxically, it is KIB and not KIB-*gunû*, the ŠÈ-based graph, which is assigned the meanings "reins, leash." These values occur most commonly in the PN Ìr/Ir$_{11}$-(h)ùl(-la)[33] and syllabically in the writing of the Diyala, Íd-Dur-ùl, and the PN Šu-Dur-ùl.[34] As already observed by Landsberger, the signs GIŠ×GIŠ and GIŠ×GIŠ×GIŠ appear diachronically to be in complementary distribution. GIŠ×GIŠ×GIŠ is attested only through the Sargonic period, where it occurs with the value ùl, for example, Ì-me-Dur-ùl, Šu-dur-ùl, Na-bí-ùl-maš,[35] and Me-ùl-maš,[36] as well as with the value šennur in early lexical texts, while GIŠ×GIŠ cannot be verified for pre-Ur III sources.[37] It is therefore reasonable to assume that GIŠ×GIŠ derives from GIŠ×GIŠ×GIŠ.

The writing of the fruit šennur—identified as a medlar (*Mespilus germanica*) by Thompson and, more convincingly, as a plum by Landsberger[38]—is more complex than the above discussion suggests. The earliest attestation of the lexeme is in the Uruk version of the Tribute List (line 62). There, šennur is written GIŠ×GIŠ×GIŠ;[39] it also occurs with this writing in the Fara version.[40] The identification of the sign in the archaic version of the Tribute List would appear to be assured by the surrounding entries—being immediately preceded by "kišik" and followed by giš[41]—and, moreover, by the Old Babylonian exemplars; the two Old Babylonian texts that sufficiently preserve en-

[32] For lexical and administrative evidence for hùl/ùl(-la) "reins, leash," see P. Steinkeller, "Stars and Stripes in Ancient Mesopotamia: A Note on Two Decorative Elements of Babylonian Doors," *Iranica Antiqua* 37 (2002): 365 and n. 20, to which add giš-(h)ùl-lá (MSL 6, p. 151:106f [Forerunner A to Hh. VI and VII]); for KIB = *ullu*, note also N. Wasserman, "Another Fragment of a Bilingual Hymn to Utu," *Acta Sumerologica (Japan)* 19 (1997): 262:1–2 (reference courtesy of N. Veldhuis). See also the comments of B. Landsberger, MSL 2, p. 79 ad 643 f.

[33] hùl is also used syllabically in the PN Šag$_4$-(h)ùl-la (AnOr 7, no. 153 rev. 4).

[34] MAD 2^2, p. 81 no. 142; note the exception AUCT 1 212:3, where Šu-Dur-ùl is written with KIB-*gunû*.

[35] MAD 2^2, p. 81 no. 142.

[36] A. Parrot, "Les fouilles di Mari, dixième campagne (automne 1954)," *Syria* 32 (1955): pl. 16, no. 1.

[37] MSL 2, pp. 79–80 ad 643f; the Sargonic attestation of the sign cited in REC, no. 170 is uncertain, resting as it does on a text that was unpublished at the time of the appearance of REC.

[38] Thompson *DAB*, pp. 305–7; Landsberger, MSL 3, p. 123 ad 305. J. N. Postgate, "Notes on Fruit in the Cuneiform Sources," *Bulletin on Sumerian Agriculture* 3 (1987): 131, in agreement with Landsberger, identifies *šallūru* as a member of the species *Prunus*; note also the comments of M. Civil, "The Early History of HAR-ra: The Ebla Link," in L. Cagni, ed., *Ebla 1975–1985* (Naples, 1987), p. 150, n. 24. The fact that "KIB" has both the values buranuna and šennur (*šallūru*) likely led to the confusion witnessed in Maqlu II 149–51 (W. von Soden, "Lexikalisches Archiv," *ZA* 9 [1936]: 239), i.e., *ú-ri-ib-šú* (D: *-ḫu*) = *šal-lu-ru*, *bu-ur-ra-nu* = MIN, *bu-ur-ra-nu* = *êru* (GIŠ-MA-NU!), where *burrānu* is taken as a variant of *murrānu* "(a kind of tree)."

[39] The rationale behind the note to *ZATU*, no. 522, namely, that the sign may possibly be read ulul instead of šennur in the Uruk version of the Tribute List, is unclear, since ùl and šennur are distinguished in third-millennium sources.

[40] Deimel *Fara 2, Schultexte*, no. 13 iv 4.

[41] See *LATU*, p. 117.

try 62 again give the writing KIB, i.e., GIŠ×GIŠ.[42] GIŠ×GIŠ×GIŠ as apparently a writing of šennur is also preserved in Ebla Word List B.[43]

Curiously, however, the few extant attestations of šennur from the Ur III period differ in employing KIB-*gunû*.[44] In all likelihood šennur was originally written with GIŠ×GIŠ×GIŠ, and at some point in the third millennium the two signs were confused with regard to this value; KIB-*gunû* came to acquire the value šennur, and the original writing was preserved only in the lexical tradition, as shown not only by the later versions of the Tribute List, but by Proto-Ea as well.[45] The roots of this confusion run as deep as the Fara and Abu Salabikh corpora, as there is evidence that šennur—in addition to the tradition preserving the writing GIŠ×GIŠ×GIŠ—could be written with the same graph as that employed in the writing of Sippar and the Euphrates.[46] Interestingly, in the Waterways lexical list (Deimel *Fara 2, Schultexte*, no. 72), the graph  occurs in the entry ^{giš}KIB SAR.MIN/SAR.MIN (iv 4), while the rotated sign  appears in the same text (iv 14) in the writing of the divine Euphrates, i.e., ^{d}KIB.NUN.MIN.[47] Thus the question may be raised whether in this particular lexical list the 90-degree change in orientation distinguishes the writing of the Euphrates from that of šennur, since the inclusion of GIŠ and SAR in iv 4 strongly suggests the latter reading in this context; cf. GIŠ. KIB-*gunû*.SAR nú "bed of šennur-wood" (Deimel *Fara 2, Schultexte*, no. 20 v 11 // R. D. Biggs, *Inscriptions from Tell Abū Ṣalābīkh*, OIP 99 [Chicago, 1974], no. 34 iv 2′).

---

[42] I thank J. Westenholz, who is preparing an edition of this text, for providing me with these attestations. The two Old Babylonian exemplars have [KI]B KIB (Ni 1597 iv 7′, per M. Civil's copy) and KIB (private collection). According to Westenholz, this entry is broken in the Early Dynastic versions, while that of the Ur III text (6N-T 676 ii 4) is damaged.

[43] GIŠ.GIŠ×GIŠ×GIŠ (MEE 3, nos. 45–46 rev. iv 4 [p. 148] and pl. 18 [see n. 45 below]); the sign, with uncertain reading, also occurs in another Ebla word list in the entry ga-GIŠ×GIŠ×GIŠ (MEE 3, no. 53 iv 11 [p. 207]); it also appears with uncertain reading in several earlier contexts, for instance, the Uruk period Geographical Lists 1, 2, and 3 (*LATU*, pp. 160–61) and the Abu Salabikh word list OIP 99, no. 39 vi 14′ // OIP 99, no. 42 ii′ 5′.

[44] J.-P. Grégoire, *Archives administratives sumériennes* (Paris, 1970), no. 200 v′ 1; Bab. 8, pl. 9 no. 36 rev. 6; MVN 5, no. 289 rev. 10 (quasi-duplicate of Bab. 8, pl. 9, no. 36; see Sollberger's comments on MVN 5, pl. 73) and now TuM 6, nos. 19:6 and 20:6 (see pl. 48, reference courtesy of M. Civil). See also Postgate, "Notes on Fruit," pp. 122, 137, n. 26a; however, in HSS 4, no. 6 rev. i 31 and iii 14 (see HSS 4, p. 7, n. 7) the sign refers to the wood rather than the fruit and is written with *šeššig*- rather than *gunû*-marks—the sign is possibly a precursor to one of the Old Babylonian forms of this sign (see n. 4 above).

[45] še-nu-ur : GIŠ×GIŠ×GIŠ (Proto-Ea 644 [MSL 16, p. 57]).

[46] For example, GIŠ-KIB-*gunû*-SAR nú "bed of šennur-wood" (Deimel *Fara 2, Schultexte*, no. 20 v 11 // OIP 99, no 34 iv 2′ [= Archaic Hh. B; see Civil, "The Early History of HAR-ra," p. 133]; KIB-*gunû* is translated as LAM by Deimel; cf. the photograph provided by the CDLI project: http://cdli.ucla.edu/dl/photo/P010595.jpg). The identical sign for šennur is found in the Ebla Sumerian version of Word List B (MEE 3, nos. 45+46 ii 11′ [p. 144]; read šennur, not peš; see Civil, "The Early History of HAR-ra," p. 143:39; photo = MEE 3/A, pl. 19). The equivalent line in the Ebla Semitic version reads: *ša-lu-ra* (MEE 3, no. 61 iv 1 [p. 248]; photo = MEE 3/A, pl. 34a). But observe that, as pointed out in n. 42 above, this same text elsewhere writes GIŠ.GIŠ×GIŠ×GIŠ, suggesting a meaningful distinction between the two writings in this text.

[47] Graphs after *LAK*, no. 278.

Given that KIB-*gunû* is the logographic base of Buranuna/Zimbir, the question naturally arises whether the fruit(-tree) šennur or the kib-bird[48] enjoys a semantic relationship with the Euphrates or Šamaš—whether the tree or the bird was symbolic or totemic of the river, Šamaš, or his cult center, similar to the origins of the writings for the major southern cities. But this appears not to be the case. In *ZATU* it is claimed that the ancestor of IDIGNA is a sign with clear pictographic origins, specifically representing a bird (*ZATU*, no. 261). While this identification appears at best dubious,[49] clearly for KIB no avian motivation can be posited, however speculatively. Moreover, the graph "KIB" for the spelling of the kib-bird is a post-Old Babylonian development. As Veldhuis has shown, this web-footed water bird is spelled ki in third-millennium sources, ki-ib/íb beginning in the Ur III period, with the CVC spelling kib being a Middle Babylonian development.[50] Quite possibly, the designation /kib/ for the bird is simply onomatopoeic; note *kibkibbu*/*kipkippu*[51] as well as kib-kib-mušen[52] (cf. kab-kab-mušen attested in the Fara and Ebla bird lists).[53] In one religious text a kib-bird is mentioned in connection with the Euphrates, but the reference is vague and not specific to the Euphrates, as the Tigris is also mentioned.[54] In fact, Green connects the kib-bird not with Larsa, Sippar, or the Euphrates but with Eridu, based on a passage from Lugalbanda—ki-ib^{mušen} ki-ib^{mušen}-engur-ra sug-gíd-i-gim "Like a kib-bird, a freshwater kib-bird, as it flies over the marsh"—although here, in all likelihood, the reference to the engur simply refers to freshwater, i.e., a freshwater as opposed to saltwater kib-bird, as already suggested by Wilcke.[55]

48 Appearing in lexical lists as ki-ib^{mušen}, kib$^{\text{[ki]-ib-šú}}$-šu^{mušen} = ŠU (*kibšu*, *kipšu*) = *ṣi-nun-du*, ki-ib-^{d}Nin-kilim^{mušen}, kib-kib^{mušen} = *kibkibbu*, *kipkippu* in Hh. and related forerunners (Hh. XVIII 235–38 [MSL 8/2, pp. 133–34]; Hg. B IV 269 [MSL 8/2, p. 168]; Hh. XVIII 270 [MSL 8/2, p. 140]); the bird sporadically occurs in literary texts; see J. Black, *Reading Sumerian Poetry* (Ithaca, New York, 1998), pp. 94–96; Green, "Eridu in Sumerian Literature," p. 196; A. Salonen, *Vögel und Vogelfang im alten Mesopotamien*, AASF 180 (Helsinki, 1973), pp. 209–10; Wilcke *Lugalbanda*, pp. 177–78. For discussion of this bird, see now N. Veldhuis, *Religion, Literature, and Scholarship: The Sumerian Composition Nanše and the Birds, with a Catalogue of Sumerian Bird Names*, Cuneiform Monographs 22 (Leiden and Boston, 2004), pp. 260–61.

49 See Steinkeller, review of *ZATU*, p. 702 ad 261.

50 See Veldhuis, *Nanše and the Birds*, pp. 260–61. That the bird has webbed feet is suggested by the following passage: ⌈x⌉-mušen-a gìr-ku$_6$-a [ku$_6$-m]u ki-ib^{mušen}-mu šu-šè ba-a-lá-e "(has) the [...] of a bird, the feet of a fish, my kib-bird, will catch you in (his) claws, my fish" (M. Civil, "The Home of the Fish: A New Sumerian Literary Composition," *Iraq* 23 [1961]: 164, lines 145–46 [see the discussion on p. 175]). The kib-bird has been tentatively identified as a gull (Wilcke *Lugalbanda*, p. 178) or cormorant (Heimpel apud Wilcke *Lugalbanda*. Walter Farber, however, notes (personal communication) that neither the gull nor the cormorant hunts with its claws.

51 Written ŠID-mu-BU (Nabnitu XXI [= J] 88 [MSL 16, p. 156]).

52 Hh. XVIII 270 (MSL 8/2, p. 140).

53 MEE 3, no. 39 ii 18 // Deimel *Fara 2, Schultexte*, no. 58 vii 21; see MEE 3, p. 111 ad 36. If not onomatopoeic, possibly related to *kapkapu* "powerful(-bird)" (see *CAD* K s.v.).

54 CT 36, pl. 38 rev. ii 20′–22′.

55 Wilcke *Lugalbanda*, p. 178 ad 159; cf. Black, *Reading Sumerian Poetry*, p. 95.

For the fruit šennur the question has marginally greater validity in light of the ambiguities surrounding the writing of this lexeme and the one tradition, outside of the lexical lists, in which šennur is written KIB-*gunû*. But again, unlike, for instance, the case of the NUN sign—which may have depicted a tree associated with Enki (mes-tree or *kiškanû*-tree?)[56] and thereby became the writing of his epithet and cult center—there is nothing to suggest that the šennur-tree was part of an early Utu or Šamaš mythology.

Ultimately, if the relationship between graph and meaning is more than arbitrary, the writing of the Euphrates, and from there Sippar, with a graph paleographically derived from ŠÈ (ÉŠ) may be based on a metaphor that envisioned the river as a rope—a particularly apt image for the Euphrates, knotted, sinuous, and branching as it is. As we have seen, in at least one Fara attestation of the graph, it appears to consist of "slanted" ŠÈ×ŠÈ, i.e., two crossed ropes, .[57]

IV

What remains to be discussed is the evidence from the first- and second-millennium lexical texts and its correlation with the third-millennium data. Not surprisingly, the later lexical sources are not entirely consistent with the earlier evidence. Many of the older values survive but are supplemented by secondary values that stem from the late interpretation of KIB-*gunû* as GÁNA×GÁNA and, more generally, the semantic and iconic associations that typified scribal erudition. Necessarily, many of these values have a reality only within the lexical tradition.

In Proto-Ea (643–44) the values hu-ul and še-nu-ur are attributed to the GIŠ×GIŠ composition, which is in accord with the third-millennium evidence discussed above. Proto-Aa agrees, adding the respective Akkadian loanwords *šallurum* and *ḫullum*.[58] The form GÁNA×GÁNA does not occur in these lists, but it does appear in an Old Babylonian Ea IV forerunner, which displays a particularly close agreement with canonical Ea.[59] This marks the earliest distinction between GIŠ×GIŠ and GÁNA×GÁNA in the lexical tradition, although here the two signs are not associated through sequential ordering as they are in the later texts. It is to this text that we now turn.

---

[56] See P. Steinkeller, "Inanna's Archaic Symbol," in J. Braun, K. Łyczkowska, M. Popko, and P. Steinkeller, eds., *Written on Clay and Stone: Ancient Near Eastern Studies Presented to Krystyna Szarzyńska on the Occasion of Her 80th Birthday* (Warsaw, 1998), p. 88, n. 8; Green, "Eridu in Sumerian Literature," pp. 186–92.

[57] Deimel *Fara 3, Wirtschaftstexte*, no. 4 rev. i 3; graph after *LAK*, no. 278. This observation stems from a number of conversations I had with Piotr Steinkeller. See Woods, "On the Euphrates," pp. 37–38, n. 139, where it is further suggested that the toponym Buranuna originally referred to the riverain system around Sippar, where the river is particularly dynamic and from whence a number of major branches stem.

[58] Proto-Aa 643–44 (MSL 14, p. 101).

[59] See the comments in MSL 14, p. 107; for this text, see also R. T. Hallock, *The Chicago Syllabary and the Louvre Syllabary AO 7661*, AS 7 (Chicago, 1940), pp. 32 f.

Ea IV forerunner no. 4 (CT 41, pls. 47–48 [MSL 14, pp. 113–16])

1	gu-ru	GIŠ-*tenû*
2	al-al	GIŠ GIŠ
3	hu-ul	GIŠ×GIŠ
4	li-rum	GIŠ×GIŠ

Following the GEŠTIN and GÁ combinations the list continues:

42	e-qé-el	GÁNA
43	ga-na	GÁNA
44	ka-ra	GÁNA-*tenû*
45	gír-re	GÁNA×GÁNA

Continued by KAL forms.

The reduplicated value al-al in line 2 would appear to be related to the primary third-millennium values ùl and hùl.[60] The primacy of the assignment, however, is complicated by evidence presented below for GÁNA×GÁNA.

The value /lirum/ (line 4) is a curious case. The standard writing in Old Babylonian is ŠU.KAL, but in Ur III this value could be written with a crossed sign identified by modern scholars as "KIB," i.e., lìrum. In Šulgi C, with its archaizing orthography, the sign appears without *gunû* marks, according to the copy.[61] At least two Ur III attestations appear to agree, writing KIB for lìrum.[62] But in two other Ur III texts the graph indicating this value is quite different, copied as  and ;[63] the former resembles UR×UR, while the latter is likely a distortion of the former. The appearance of lìrum in the Ur III copy of the Curse of Agade, to judge from the photograph provided by

[60] Cf. ul-ul, al-al : KIB (Ea IV 209f. [MSL 14, p. 363]). See also Hallock's comments in *Chicago Syllabary*, p. 61. Note that in Nik. 2, no. 389 the entries 4 ma-na al-la (4) and 4 ma-na (h)ùl-la (rev. 2) may represent simple variants, although two spellings of the same lexeme in one text would be somewhat unexpected.

[61] Šulgi C 131 (= E. Chiera, *Sumerian Texts of Varied Contents*, OIP 16 [Chicago, 1934], no. 50 rev. 3). See J. Klein, "The Sumerian Word for Monkey," *JCS* 31 (1979): 151, n. 10; the writing KIB for /lirum/ is cited by Klein as an example of the archaizing orthography of the Šulgi Hymns.

[62] MVN 3, no. 331:2; UET 9, no. 1050:2 (N.B.: partially effaced in both cases).

[63] UET 3, no. 191 rev. 9 and UET 3, no. 189 rev. 4 respectively.

Cooper, again suggests a graph that could be interpreted as UR×UR.[64] The interpretation finds support in Ea and Reciprocal Ea, where the graphically similar composites KIB(GIŠ×GIŠ) (GÁNA×GÁNA in Reciprocal Ea, Section C 3′), UR×UR, and KIB.ZA are all claimed to have the value /lirum/.[65] What these assignments in the lexical lists attempt to account for is the various late-third-millennium allographs that wrote lìrum, reanalyzing these complex signs in terms of simpler, well-known graphs.[66] Apparently, lìrum, aside from KIB, could be represented by a distinctive graph; whether this graph was merely an allograph of KIB that was used to write this value (and was later reinterpreted as UR×UR) or was in origin graphically distinct from KIB, perhaps UR×UR, which secondarily merged with "KIB," remains an open question. In favor of the second possibility is the clear semantic association between ur "young man" and lirum "strength"—although UR×UR has not been acknowledged outside of the lexical lists.[67]

In line 45 GÁNA×GÁNA, or KIB-*gunû*, is assigned the reading /giri/. This value is a phonetic variant of /kara/, which belongs to KÁR occurring in line 44[68] and so implicitly preserves the graphic origins of KIB-*gunû* as deriving from KÁR, or better, ŠÈ. Interestingly, in what possibly represents an accurate understanding of the graphic histories of ŠÈ and KÁR—if not simply a confusion between two similarly shaped graphs—Ea I attributes ka-ra and ki-ri to ŠÈ-*tenû*.

Ea I 186–88 (MSL 14, p. 186)

186	ka-ra	ŠÈ-*tenû*	⌈*še*⌉ *te-nu-u*	*ri-ik-su*
187				*ku-ru-su* (var.: *ṭa-pa-lu*)
188	ki-ri	ŠÈ-*tenû*	MIN	*ki-ri-tum šá* GIŠ.MÁ (var.: *ka-ra-su*)

The equation with Akk. *riksu* "binding, knot," *kurussu* "strap," *kirītum ša* GIŠ.MÁ "mooring rope," and *karāsu* "to tie, fasten" is clearly based on éše "rope," the likely pictographic referent of the graph ŠÈ.[69]

---

[64] Line 104 (6N-T 76: 5; see J. Cooper, *The Curse of Agade* [Baltimore, 1983], pl. xix).

[65] See Reciprocal Ea, Tablet A Section C 3′–7′ (MSL 14, p. 530 with notes); Ea IV 216 (MSL 14, p. 363).

[66] In this regard, compare KIB.ZA to UET 3, no. 189 rev. 4 given above.

[67] See the comments of M. Civil, "Lexicography," in S. J. Lieberman, ed., *Sumerological Studies in Honor of Thorkild Jacobsen on His Seventieth Birthday, June 7, 1974*, AS 20 (Chicago, 1976), p. 131. The sign must derive from the third-millennium logogram, with similar semantics, UR.UR, e.g., giš-UR.UR-šè e-da-lá "he fought with him" (Ent. 28–29 iii 10 = iv 1), also giš-UR.UR-e e-da-lá (Ean. I ix 1); see Å. Sjöberg, "Miscellaneous Sumerian Hymns," *ZA* 63 (1973): 12 ad 59.

[68] Of course, the values /kara/ and /kiri/ are also attributed to GÁNA(-*tenû*) in Ea I 186–89 (MSL 14, p. 221) and Ea IV 299 (MSL 14, p. 367), cited below.

[69] Two of the three copies (texts A and B) display the common graphic confusion between KÁR, GÁNA, and ŠÈ, describing the sign as GÁNA and GÁNA-*tenû* respectively.

In canonical Ea distinction between GIŠ×GIŠ and GÁNA×GÁNA is made explicit. KIB—given the sign name *kib-bu* instead of expected *giš-minnabi-gilimû*[70]—is listed as a GIŠ composite, occurring after GIŠ, GIŠ×BAD, and GIŠ-*tenû* and before GEŠTIN; the following values are given:

Ea IV 206–16 (MSL 14, p. 363)

206	ul	KIB(GIŠ×GIŠ)	*kib-bu*	*ul-lu šá kal-bu*
207	a-da-mìn	KIB	MIN	*te-ṣe-e-tú*
208	hu-ul	KIB	MIN	*lem-nu*
209	ul-ul	KIB	MIN	*qer-bi-ti*
210	al-al	KIB	MIN	*me-riš-tú*
211	ki-ib	KIB	MIN	*ki-ib-bu*
212	še-en-nu-ur	KIB	MIN	*šal-lu-rum*
213	du-ru	KIB	MIN	*síḫ!-tum*[71]
214	da-ru	KIB	MIN	*par-ri-ku*
215	pu-uh-rum	KIB	MIN	*pu-uḫ-rum*
216	li-rum	KIB	MIN	*ga-mi-rum*

The value /ul/ for "leash," as in *ullu ša kalbu* "dog leash," is certainly expected in light of the third-millennium evidence discussed above. The crossing of two signs in cuneiform often took on reflexive or negative associations and the composite was interpreted as "one against the other," hence the attaching of the value /adamin/ = *teṣētu* "to contest, quarrel" to KIB. Parallels are found in the equations gu-ug : LUGAL×LUGAL = *nukurtu*;[72] ku-ku : LUGAL×LUGAL = *nu-kur-tu*;[73] [a]-da-mìn : LÚ×LÚ = *te-ṣi-t*[*um*];[74] a-da-mìn : LUGAL×LUGAL = *te-ṣ*[*e-e-tu*];[75] note also [KÁ×KÁ] (sign name) : *šá* KÁ×KÁ = *nak-ri*.[76] Further, the fact that both the signs PAP and BAR are equated with *nakru*(*m*)

[70] See Hallock, *Chicago Syllabary*, p. 68.

[71] MSL 14, p. 363 reads BIT-*tum*, but clearly *siḫtum* "gathered up" must be meant; note du-ru : KU.KIB = *siḫtu*, da-ra : KU.KIB = *parriku* (Diri I 102–03); d[u-ru] : [K]U.KIB = *síh-t*[*um*], d[a-ra] : [K]U.KIB = *par-ri-*[*ku*] (Diri I Ugarit 87–88); giš-KU-$^{du/ṭu-ru}$KIB = *síh-tum* (var. *ki-ib-su*), giš-KU-$^{da-ra/ri}$dara$_5$(KIB) = *par-ri-ka* (Hh. VIIA 143–44 [MSL 6, p. 96; see now N. Veldhuis, "Kassite Exercises: Literary and Lexical Extracts," *JCS* 52 (2000): 77, for a more recent reconstruction]).

[72] Aa VII/2 79 (MSL 14, p. 463).

[73] Ea VII Assur MA Excerpt 8′ (MSL 14, p. 454).

[74] Ea VII ii 5′ (MSL 14, p. 450), partially restored from an unpublished copy (reference courtesy of M. Civil).

[75] Aa VII/2 80 (MSL 14, p. 463).

[76] Ea IV 4 (MSL 16, p. 355).

"foreign, hostile, enemy" speaks to an understanding of these graphs as composed of two crossed AŠ signs, i.e., "one against the other."[77] The association of ideas behind these values finds its counterpart in the metaphorical language of omens, where the notion of crossing often has negative connotations.[78] The attribution of the value /puḫrum/ to KIB perhaps also stems from the graphic composition of the sign—the crossing or doubling of two signs possibly connoting the idea of "assembly" or "gathering"; compare gá-gá = *puḫrum*.[79] The motivations behind the assignment of the values /daru/ and /duru/ to KIB with the meanings *siḫtu* and *parriku* are, however, more uncertain. The equivalences given in Ea IV are related to the fuller entries given in Diri, i.e., du-ru : KU.KIB = *siḫtu*, da-ra : KU.KIB = *parriku* and, particularly, in Hh., i.e., giš-KU-$^{du/ṭu\text{-}ru}$KIB = *síḫ-tum* (var. *ki-ib-su*), giš-KU-$^{da\text{-}ra/ri}$ $dara_5$(KIB) = *par-ri-ka* (see n. 70 above). *parriku* (see *CAD* P s.v. *parriku* B) and *kibsu* "footstrap" are saddle parts; presumably *siḫtu* is synonymous with *kibsu*, although there are difficulties concerning the etymology of the former. As *parriku* derives from *parāku* "to lie across," this object may have resembled a cross, and so this assignment may be graphically motivated as well; if so, the assignment to du-ru = *siḫtum*/*kibsu* could then be explained by homonymy; cf. da-ra and, by semantic similarity, all lexemes belonging to a common semantic field.

According to Ea IV, kib, the flagship value of this graph judging from the sign name *kib-bu*, belongs to the GIŠ×GIŠ rather than GÁNA×GÁNA composition. The attribution of the value kib to GIŠ×GIŠ is also supported by Diri III 75, which reads ki-ib (S_{18}: ùl-ùl) : GIŠ.GIŠ×GIŠ (S_{18}: ⸢GIŠ×GIŠ⸣)[80] = *kippu* (A: MIN *giš min-na-bi igi-lim-mu-u*)—the first GIŠ graph representing, perhaps, either a confusion with ^{giš}šennur or an attempt to analyze the extra GIŠ graph of early GIŠ×GIŠ×GIŠ as a determinative. But in light of the fact that Ea IV 206–16 attributes values to KIB that, as we shall see, are elsewhere, and, perhaps, more convincingly, connected with KIB-*gunû*, specifically ul-ul and al-al (209–10), the primacy of the assignment is open to question. It may be significant that ki-ib directly follows the suspect values ul-ul and al-al. Ea IV 206–12 may represent a catch-all in this regard, incorporating values once attached to archaic KIB-*gunû*.

---

[77] See also Gong, *Die Namen*, pp. 26–27; Hallock, *Chicago Syllabary*, p. 50; A. Poebel, *Studies in Akkadian Grammar*, AS 9 (Chicago, 1939), p. 13.

[78] Relevant, in this regard, is the following pair of omens: *šumma padānū šinā-ma kīma pappi itgurū nakaru ina ri'īti ‹‹ana›› māti būla iḫabbat* "If there are two paths and they are crossed like the sign PAP: the enemy will steal cattle from the pasture land"; *šumma padānū šinā-ma kīma pallurti itgurū rabi sikkati bēlšu ibâr* "If there are two paths crossed like the sign BAR: the general will revolt against his lord" (CT 20, pl. 3:20–21; Koch-Westenholz *Liver Omens*, p. 195).

[79] CT 18, pl. 30 iii 9′.

[80] N.B.: the sign in copies 5R pl. 22 and CT 12, pl. 28 does not closely resemble GIŠ×GIŠ, but it is nonetheless distinguished from the "KIB" of UD.KIB.NUN occurring elsewhere in these texts.

In line 208 the well-known value /hul/, i.e., hùl, is equated with *lemnu* under the homophonous influence of hul = *lemnu* and the semantic influence of a-da-mìn : KIB = *teṣētu*.[81] As already touched upon, the values al-al (cf. Ea IV forerunner no. 4:2) and ul-ul would appear to belong, unremarkably, to GIŠ×GIŠ, based on the third-millennium evidence for (h)ùl and, more directly, Ea IV 209–10 discussed above, but the equation with the near synonyms *qerbetu* "pasture land" and *mērištu* "cultivable land" suggests, on the other hand, a primary association with the graph understood to be GÁNA×GÁNA, i.e., KIB-*gunû*.[82] Indeed, it is with KIB-*gunû* that Ea IV 300–301 (see below) connects these values. What is at work here, evidently, is the free exchange of values between a sign and its *gunû*-counterpart, but the question still remains as to which assignment is primary and which is secondary.

Ea IV 298–301 (MSL 14, p. 367)

298	eq-qel	GÁNA	MIN (*ga-nu-ú*)	MIN (*eq-lu*)
299	ka-ra	GÁNA-*tenû*	*ga-na te-nu-ú*	*na-pa-ḫu ša* A.MEŠ[83]
300	ul-ul	GÁNA×GÁNA	*ga-‹na› min-na-bi gi-li-mu-u*	*qer-bi-tú*
301	al-al	GÁNA×GÁNA	MIN MIN MIN	*mi-riš-tú*

A similar picture emerges from vocabulary S^b, where, as elsewhere, šennur is taken as GIŠ×GIŠ, but, again, the value ulul, equated with *qerbetu*, is attributed to GÁNA×GÁNA.

Vocabulary S^b I 303 f. (MSL 3, p. 123; corrections and additions in MSL 4, p. 207)

303	ge-eš	GIŠ	*i*[*ṣ-ṣ*]*u*
304	gu-ur (var.: gu-ru)	GIŠ-*tenû*	[*na*]-*šú-u*
305	še-en-nu-ur	KIB (= GIŠ×GIŠ)	[*šal-lu-rum*]
306	ga-a	GÁ	[*bi*]-*e-tú*
307	ga-na	GÁNA	*eq-lum*
308	ul-lul (var.: ul-ul)	GÁNA / GÁNA[84]	*qir-bi-tum*

---

[81] A variant to Šulgi O 105 (B) writes hùl as a syllabic spelling for hul (J. Klein, "Šulgi and Gilgameš: Two Brother-Peers (Šulgi O)," in *Kramer AV*, pp. 280:105; p. 292 ad 105). Note also the syllabic use of the sign in the PN Šag$_4$-(h)ùl-la (AnOr 7, no. 153 rev. 4) mentioned above.

[82] See already Hallock, *Chicago Syllabary*, p. 68 ad 282 f.

[83] Note that *šá* ^{d}UTU (or MUL) is expected in place of A.MEŠ, as already pointed out by Hallock, *Chicago Syllabary*, p. 68, noting kár-kár = (*n*[*a-pa-ḫu*]) *šá* M[UL/^{d}UTU?] (Nabnitu XXII 3′ [MSL 16, p. 206]).

[84] The entry is GÁNA/GÁNA and not GÁNA as given in MSL 3 (see the correction in MSL 4, p. 207 ad 308; also OECT 4 37:295).

Finally, in light of the above evidence, I return to the problem of the referent of KIB-*gunû* in the compounds KIB-*gunû*—dím/dug$_4$, which appear in seven royal inscriptions belonging to Enanatum I and Enmetena. Without exception, these inscriptions are written on clay nails, hence the assumption that KIB-*gunû* designates a word meaning clay nail.[85] As obvious as this solution may appear at first glance, it faces a number of obstacles, namely, the limited number of attestations and the restriction of these to the consecutive reigns of two Lagaš rulers—puzzling facts indeed for a word with allegedly as basic a meaning as "clay nail" (cf. the usual term kak = *sikkatu*). The object denoted by KIB-*gunû* is not dedicated *ex voto* (nam-ti-la-ni-šè...a—ru), nor would we expect an unremarkable clay object to be so. Further, with the exception of statues, which fulfill an entirely different function, it is not often the case that the name of the object is noted in the inscription it bears. The phrases KIB-*gunû*—dím and KIB-*gunû*—dug$_4$ denote activities carried out at the conclusion of the building of a temple, conveying meanings along the lines of "to fashion KIB-*gunû* objects" and "to decorate with KIB-*gunû* objects" respectively. Enanatum I assigned this duty to his son or an official, while Enmetena apparently took this cultic responsibility upon himself. The referent of KIB-*gunû* in this compound is possibly part of the temple adornment or furnishing.

As for as the phonetic shape of KIB-*gunû* in this context, the lexical evidence given above yields a number of possibilities, all of which are problematic in light of the historical ambiguities surrounding the sign "KIB." And, of course, there may be other values belonging to this sign that are not preserved by the lexical sources at hand. Based on Ea IV forerunner no. 4 cited above, Hallo suggested that we are to read girri$_x$(KIB) with the meaning "clay nail."[86] This value, /giri/, as we have seen, derives from KÁR (ultimately ŠÈ) and the interpretation of KIB-*gunû* as KÁR×KÁR (cf. the value giri$_{16}$ of KEŠDA, which is in origin ŠÈ×ŠÈ). Unfortunately, it cannot be confirmed by canonical Ea, let alone corroborated, with or without this claimed meaning, by contemporaneous third-millennium sources. Yet the reading remains a possibility. Elsewhere in the lexical tradition, as previously discussed, the sign is assigned the values ul-ul and al-al.

---

85 Steible, *Die altsumerischen Bau- und Weihinschriften*, En. I 10, 28, 30, 32, Ent. 44, 45–73, 80. Incidentally, note that in the Hittite column of Izi Bogh. A kib is equated with Hittite *gangala-* "weigh scale, scale plate," i.e., kib = *kib-bu* = *ga-an-ga-la-aš*, but, as noted by J. Puhvel (*Hittite Etymological Dictionary*, vol. 4 [Berlin, 1997], p. 50), the equivalence may be a mistake based on the phonetically similar *kappu* = Ugar., Heb. *kp* "scale (of a balance)," lit. "hand" (Izi Bogh. A I 308 [MSL 13, p. 142]).

86 W. W. Hallo, "The Royal Inscriptions of Ur: A Typology," *HUCA* 33 (1962): 9–10, n. 67; see also Sollberger and Kupper *Inscriptions Royales*, p. 63. M. Lambert suggested that "KIB"—dug$_4$ is an older writing for še-er-ka-an...dug$_4$ ("Le quartier Lagash," *RSO* 32 [1957]: 137, n. 5), a suggestion doubted by A. Falkenstein, "Sumerische religiöse Texte," *ZA* 56 [1964]: 93, n. 63). J. van Dijk proposed the reading àdamin/lìrum for KIB in this context. Aside from the obvious contextual problems, these values, as has been shown, belong in origin to GIŠ×GIŠ or, in the case of lìrum, to UR×UR (see J. van Dijk, "La 'confusion des langues': Note sur le lexique et sur la morphologie d'Enmerkar," *Or.*, n.s., 39 [1970]: 304–5, n. 2; also A. Alberti, review of Biggs *Al-Hiba* in *Or.*, n.s., 50 [1981]: 254).

But any connection with these values would have to be homophonous, as the meanings certainly do not apply in this context. Finally, there is the value kib. While Ea IV 211 assigns this value to the GIŠ×GIŠ composition, it can be plausibly argued that kib was first attributed to KIB-*gunû*, since the preceding two entries, ul-ul and al-al, may have belonged in origin to the latter graph by virtue of their meanings. Of course, there is the additional hurdle that the sign name *kibbu* is specifically given to GIŠ×GIŠ, but with KIB and KIB-*gunû* collapsing into a single sign by the Old Babylonian period, this too may not be insurmountable.

The one factor that recommends the value kib in this context is the existence, albeit with poorly understood meaning, of the loanword *kibbu*. The earliest evidence for this lexeme is of Old Babylonian date, from Mari, where it apparently denotes some type of ornament cast in gold.[87] In two of the three Enmetena inscriptions referring to KIB-*gunû* objects, the passage immediately follows a mention of decoration in gold and silver.[88] That these objects were manufactured in some numbers is indicated by the reduplicated *ḫamṭu* form KIB-*gunû* mu-dím-dím, which occurs twice.[89] Conceivably, KIB-*gunû* could refer to a specific type of decorative element that was cast—quite fittingly—in gold or silver and applied at the conclusion of a temple construction project. And herein would lie the bond between the text and its bearer, the clay nail, for clay nails are invariably associated with building activities. And if these Early Dynastic clay nails were disposed in a similar manner as their later counterparts, being placed horizontally into the upper walls of temples,[90] then these nails played a decorative function themselves, so again uniting message with medium.

V

The principle conclusions of this study may be summarized as follows:

1. The sign known to second- and first-millennium cuneiform as "KIB" represents the merger of two distinct third-millennium graphs, KIB (*LAK*, no. 276) and KIB-*gunû* (*LAK*, no. 278).

2. The only certain Uruk ancestor of KIB is GIŠ×GIŠ×GIŠ (*LAK*, no. 277), which was simplified to GIŠ×GIŠ, i.e., KIB (*LAK*, no. 276), between the Sargonic and Ur III periods. KIB-*gunû* was apparently an Early Dynastic invention, attested first in the Fara and Abu Salabikh corpora; the sign has its graphic origins in ŠÈ.

---

[87] See *CAD* K s.v. *kibbu* A usage a–1′. Reciprocity may be involved in the graph AL acquiring an equivalence with *kibbu*, i.e., al : AL = *ki-ib-bu* (A VII/4 18 [= *JCS* 13 (1959): 120 i 4]), based on KIB having the value àl (ùl).

[88] Steible, *Die altsumerischen Bau- und Weihinschriften*, Ent. 44–73ii 7–9, Ent. 80: 3–4.

[89] Ibid., En. I. 30 ii 7, En. I. 32 ii′ 3′.

[90] R. S. Ellis, *Foundation Deposits in Ancient Mesopotamia*, Yale Near Eastern Researches 2 (New Haven, 1968), pp. 83–84.

3. In the third millennium KIB writes ùl and hùl, while KIB-*gunû* is used in the writing of Buranuna and Zimbir and first attested in the Early Dynastic IIIb period to represent the object denoted in the compounds KIB-*gunû*—dím/dug_4; šennur was originally written with GIŠ×GIŠ×GIŠ (later KIB), a writing that was preserved in the lexical lists; however, there was a parallel tradition that ascribed this value to KIB-*gunû*.

4. In the lexical tradition of the second and first millennia, KIB-*gunû* was reanalyzed as GÁNA×GÁNA in accord with the development that saw kár drift from ŠE to GÁNA. The reanalysis gave rise to new values and Akkadian equivalences that took their place alongside the primary, third-millennium ones. Additional, presumably late, values are accounted for by a variety of semantic, iconic, and graphic associations, the learned play of scribes.

5. KIB-*gunû* in the compounds KIB-*gunû*—dím/dug_4 in all likelihood does not denote "clay nail" as is often assumed but, rather, some unidentified temple ornamentation. The reading of KIB-*gunû* in this context remains uncertain—/kib/ and /giri/ remain possibilities, although both readings encounter difficulties.

CLAY SEALINGS FROM THE EARLY DYNASTIC I LEVELS OF THE INANNA TEMPLE AT NIPPUR: A PRELIMINARY ANALYSIS*

Richard L. Zettler, University of Pennsylvania

I. INTRODUCTION

The administrative records of Early Dynastic institutions include not only tablets, but also clay sealings that had secured doors, boxes, bags, bundles, ceramic jars, etc. Such records have been found in situ on the floors of buildings but more commonly have been recovered in large numbers from trash dumps represented, for example, by the Ur Seal Impression Strata[1] and the Abu Salabikh 6G Ash-Tip.[2] While written records are often privileged in reconstructing administrative structures and socioeconomic organization, more generally, archaeologists have contributed a number of studies over the last decade or so utilizing clay sealings to the same end.[3] The methodology, pioneered by Enrica Fiandra, involves recording both the seal(s) rolled on the surface of the clay (obverse) and the back (reverse) of the sealings, which preserves an impression of the object on which the clay had been pressed.[4] Correlating

* I would like to thank Donald P. Hansen of the Institute of Fine Arts, New York University, and Holly Pittman of the University of Pennsylvania for their insights into early Mesopotamian (and Iranian) sealing practices as well as for bibliographical references and access to unpublished material from Nippur, al-Hiba, and Malyan.

[1] L. Legrain, *Archaic Seal Impressions*, UE 3 (London and Philadelphia, 1936). At least some of the Ur "Archaic Tablets" may have been found in situ on the floors of structures built of planoconvex bricks. As the buildings were abandoned, they were filled with and in time covered by debris (Sir Leonard Woolley, *The Early Periods*, UE 4 [London and Philadelphia, 1956], pp. 70–71).

[2] H. P. Martin and R. J. Matthews, "Seals and Sealings," in A. Green, ed., *The 6G Ash-Tip and Its Contents: Cultic and Administrative Discard from the Temple?* (London, 1993), pp. 23–81.

[3] Z. Bahrani, "The Administrative Building at Tell al-Hiba, Lagash" (Ph.D. diss., New York University, 1988), pp. 104–15; R. J. Matthews, "Fragments of Officialdom from Fara," *Iraq* 53 (1991): 1–16; and Martin and Matthews, "Seals and Sealings."

[4] E. Fiandra, "A che cosa servivano le cretule di Festòs," *Pepragmena tou B'Diethnous Kritologikon Synderiou*, vol. 1 (Athens, 1968), pp. 383–97; "Ancora a proposito della cretule di Festòs: connessione tra i sistemi amministrativi centralizzati e l'uso delle cretule nell'età del bronzo," *Bollettino d'arte*, Serie 5, 60 (1975): 1–15.

seals and their iconography with objects sealed makes it possible to reconstruct areas of individual or collective administrative responsibility. This article supplements such studies by more fully documenting a small corpus of clay sealings from the Early Dynastic I levels of the Inanna Temple at Nippur.[5]

It is a pleasure—and particularly appropriate—to dedicate this study to Robert D. Biggs at his retirement. The eighth season at Nippur (1962/63), when the sealings analyzed here were found, was his first time in Iraq. As Annual Fellow of the American Schools of Oriental Research's Baghdad School, Bob arrived in the Iraqi capital in November 1962. He was already on the *Chicago Assyrian Dictionary* staff and officially in Baghdad to work on tablets in the Iraq Museum. Still, Bob took the opportunity to visit Nippur and other excavations in Iraq and Iran. In spring 1963 he joined Donald P. Hansen's excavations at Tell Abu Salabikh, a site with which he would become closely identified, and he spent a good part of the rest of his career in the field serving as epigrapher and, not infrequently, supervising excavations. Bob Biggs's contributions to the archaeology of the "cradle of civilization" are as real as his contributions to our understanding of its ancient languages and history, and those of us who spent time with him on site will always recall his unique ability to bring good cheer to life in the field.

II. Early Dynastic I Clay Sealings from the Inanna Temple at Nippur

The Inanna Temple excavations yielded the longest continuous stratigraphic sequence available to date for Mesopotamia, with more than twenty building levels spanning the Middle Uruk through the late Parthian periods. Levels XI–IX date to Early Dynastic I or the first half of the third millennium B.C.[6] Plans and descriptions of those buildings have appeared in various publications.[7] Figure 1 shows an early building phase of the Level IX temple.

Of the forty-three sealings from the Early Dynastic I levels of the temple (table 1), one was from Level XI, thirty-three were from Level IXB, and five were from Level IXA; the remaining four sealings were also from Level IX but were not attributed to a

[5] D. P. Hansen, "Some Early Dynastic I Sealings from Nippur," in D. G. Mitten, J. G. Pedley, and J. A. Scott, eds., *Studies Presented to George M. A. Hanfmann* (Mainz, 1971), pp. 47–54.

[6] E. Porada, D. P. Hansen, and S. Dunham, "The Chronology of Mesopotamia, ca. 7000–1600 B.C.," in R. W. Ehrich, ed., *Chronologies in Old World Archaeology*, 3d ed. (Chicago, 1992), pp. 103–4; for the radiocarbon determinations, see "Additions and Corrections," p. 18, table 1.

[7] R. C. Haines, "The Temple of Inanna at Nippur, the Ancient Holy City of Sumer," *The Illustrated London News*, 9 September 1961, pp. 408–9; D. P. Hansen and G. F. Dales, "The Temple of Inanna Queen of Heaven at Nippur," *Archaeology* 15 (1962): 80–82; Hansen, "Some Early Dynastic I Sealings from Nippur," pp. 47–49; R. L. Zettler, *The Ur III Temple of Inanna at Nippur*, Berliner Beiträge zum Vorderen Orient 11 (Berlin, 1992), pp. 22–27; and M. Gibson, D. P. Hansen, and R. L. Zettler, "Nippur B. Archäologisch," in *RLA* 9, pp. 552–53.

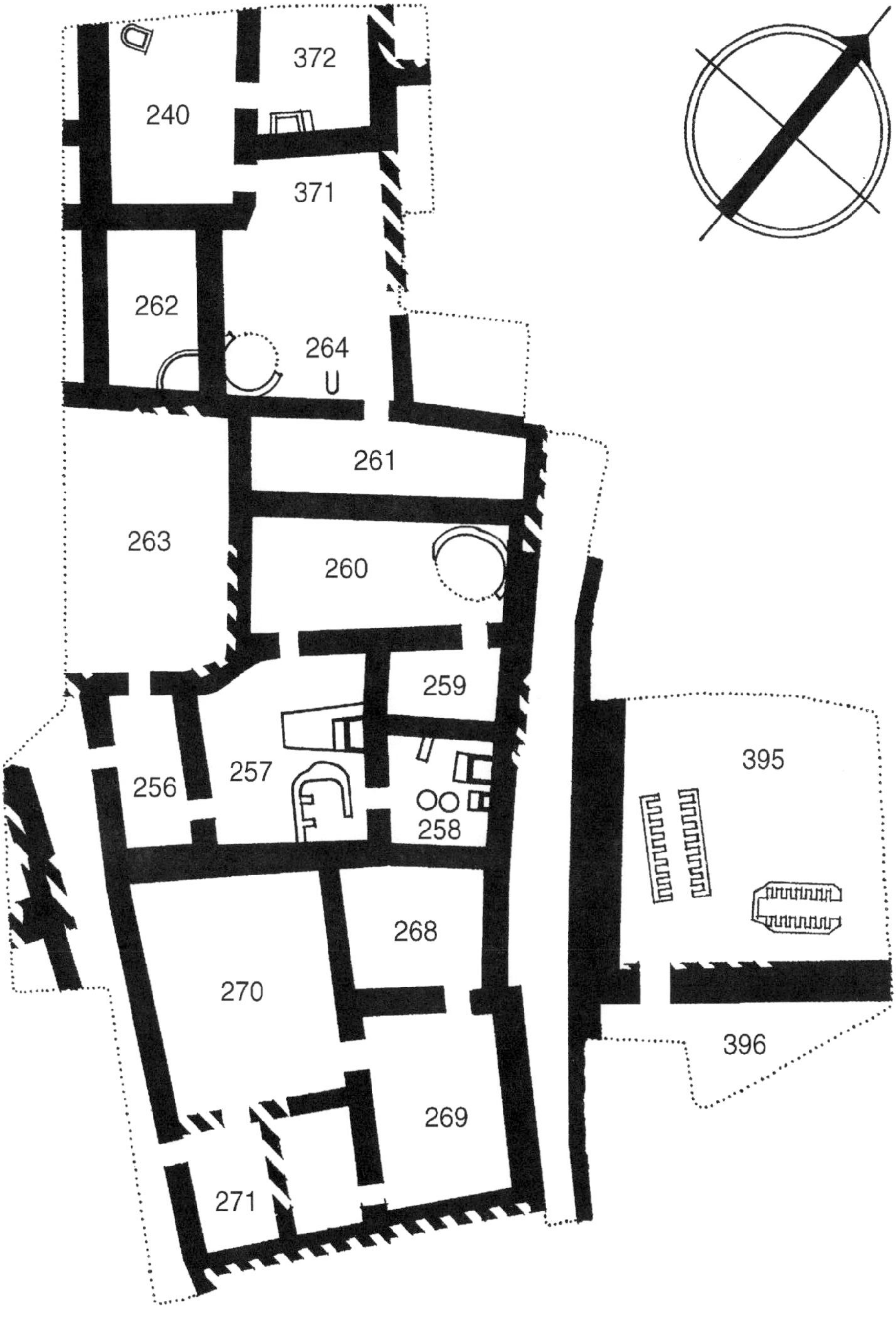

Figure 1. Plan of Inanna Temple, Level IXB

specific building phase. The Level IX sealings were in situ on the floors of two rooms (Loci 395–96) with kilns and ovens to the east of the main temple building. The work area was separated from the cellae complex by a narrow corridor or alley. Since the area of Loci 395–96 was incorporated into the temple precinct in Level VIIA, dated to the end of the Early Dynastic period, the excavators assumed that the rooms were appendices of the earlier temple as well.[8]

TABLE 1. CLAY SEALINGS FROM THE EARLY DYNASTIC I LEVELS OF THE INANNA TEMPLE AT NIPPUR

Field No.	Museum No.	Find-spot	Field No.	Museum No.	Find-spot
8 N 168	Chicago (A32229)	IXB, 395, fl. 2	8 N 190	Chicago (A32244)	IXB, 396, fl. 3
8 N 169	Chicago (A32230)	IXB, 395, fl. 2	8 N 191	Baghdad	IXB, 396, fl. 3
8 N 170	Chicago (A32231)	IXB, 395, fl. 2	8 N 192	Baghdad	IXB, 396, fl. 3
8 N 171	Chicago (A32232)	IXB, 396, fl. 3	8 N 193	Baghdad	IXB, 396, fl. 3
8 N 172	Chicago (A32233)	IXB, 396, fl. 3	8 N 194	Chicago (A32245)	IXB, 396, fl. 3
8 N 173	Baghdad	IXB, 396, fl. 3	8 N 195	Baghdad	IXB, 396, fl. 3
8 N 174	Baghdad	IXA, 395, fl. 3	8 N 196	Baghdad	IXB, 396, fl. 3
8 N 175	Chicago (A32234)	IXA, 395, fl. 3	8 N 197	Baghdad	IXB, 396, fl. 3
8 N 176	Chicago (A32235)	IXA, 395, fl. 3	8 N 198	Chicago (A32246)	IXB, 396, fl. 3
8 N 177	Chicago (A32236)	IX General	8 N 199	Chicago (A32247)	IXB, 396, fl. 3
8 N 178	Chicago (A32237)	IXA, 395, fl. 3	8 N 200	Baghdad	IXB, 396, fl. 3
8 N 179	Baghdad	IXA, 395, fl. 3	8 N 201	Baghdad	IXB, 396, fl. 3
8 N 180	Chicago (A32238)	IX, 395	8 N 202	Baghdad	IXB, 396, fl. 3
8 N 181	Chicago (A32239)	IX, 395	8 N 203	Baghdad	IXB, 396, fl. 3
8 N 182	Baghdad	IXB, 396, fl. 3	8 N 204	Baghdad	IXB, 396, fl. 3
8 N 183	Baghdad	IXB, 396, fl. 3	8 N 205	Baghdad	IXB, 396, fl. 3
8 N 184	Baghdad	IXB, 395, fl. 3	8 N 206	Baghdad	IXB, 396
8 N 185	Chicago (A32240)	IXB, 395, fl. 2	8 N 207	Chicago (A32248)	IXB, 396, fl. 3
8 N 186	Chicago (A32241)	XIB, 391	8 N 208	Baghdad	IXB, 396, fl. 3
8 N 187	Chicago (A32242)	IXB, 396, fl. 3	8 N 209	Chicago (A32249)	IXB, 396, fl. 3
8 N 188	Chicago (A32243)	IXB, 396, fl. 3	8 N 216	Baghdad	IX
8 N 189	Baghdad	IXB, 396, fl. 3			

[8] Hansen, "Some Early Dynastic I Sealings from Nippur," p. 48, n. 3.

a b

Figure 2. Sealings with Impressions (a) Hansen, No. 2 and Stamp B: 8 N 203 and (b) 8 N 200. Scale 1:1

Level IXB, Loci 395–96 were only partially cleared, but three floors (3–1) were traced. A doorway in the south corner of Locus 395 connected the two rooms at all three floors. In Locus 395 two large rectangular ovens or kilns existed at the two lower floors; five sealings were on those floors. In Locus 396 twenty-seven sealings were on floor 3. In Level IXA, four floors (floors 4–1) were recorded. At floor 4 the dividing wall between Loci 395 and 396 was still in existence; at floor 3 the two rooms were a large, presumably open, space (Locus 395). All of the sealings from Level IXA, as well as three tablets (8 NT 14–16), were on floor 3. Two of the tablets probably record distributions; one was poorly preserved.[9] A doorway in Locus 395's northwest wall connected it with unnumbered rooms. A large circular oven stood in the northeastern portion of that space; two troughlike fireplaces were located along the southwestern wall.

The sealings from Level IX carry impressions of nineteen cylinder seals and four stamp seals. Five of the sealings have incised markings. Hansen described the best and most completely preserved cylinder seal impressions.[10] I have given six additional

[9] G. Buccellati, "The Eighth Season," in G. Buccellati and R. D. Biggs, eds., *Cuneiform Texts from Nippur: The Eighth and Ninth Seasons*, AS 17 (Chicago, 1969), p. 5. The text 8 NT 14 is a list of commodities and personal names; 8 NT 16 includes references to professions, including nu-kiri$_6$ (gardener) and nagar (carpenter) on the reverse.

[10] Hansen, "Some Early Dynastic I Sealings from Nippur," pp. 49–53.

sealings numbers (nos. 14–19) that continue Hansen's sequence[11] and have given the four stamp seals letter designations (Stamps A–D). Stamps A–C have roughly similar geometric designs (figs. 2–4). Stamp D is fragmentary but was a round seal depicting animals. Figure 5 shows the sealings with incised markings. As for the sealings' reverses, I examined the twenty-two sealings in Chicago in the Oriental Institute Museum but was not able to gain access to those in Baghdad in the Iraq Museum.

a b

Figure 3. Sealings with Impressions of (a) Stamp B: 8 N 204 and (b) 8 N 198. Scale 2:3

a b

Figure 4. (a) 8 N 208 with Impressions of Stamp C and (b) 8 N 190 with a Single Impression of Stamp A. Scale 2:3

[11] Of the six sealings, I have examined only three (in Chicago); I have worked with photographs of the others: (1) No. 14 (8 N 183) shows heroes with skirts partially pulled up and animals. (2) The photograph of No. 15 (8 N 183) is unclear. I cannot make out the details. (3) No. 16 (8 N 207) shows the head of a horned animal framed by elongated ovals, probably representing the leaves of a bush or tree, and the lower portion of a human figure. (4) No. 17 (8 N 185) preserves two rollings of a single(?) cylinder seal with a combat scene. To the left, a human hero,

a

b

c

d

Figure 5. Sealing with Incised Markings in Place of Cylinder- and/or Stamp Seal Impressions: (a) 8 N 188, (b) 8 N 187, (c) 8 N 173, and (d) 8 N 174. Scale 1:1

The small number of sealings and incomplete documentation of their reverses make an analysis of the corpus such as I completed for the sealings from the later Ur III (Level IV) Temple of Inanna impossible.[12] The sealings nevertheless merit more detailed description.

None of the cylinder or stamp seals impressed on the Inanna Temple sealings were found in more than one building level/building level subphase or locus. Hansen, nos. 3, 6, 17, and Stamp D were in Level IXB, Locus 395; Hansen, nos. 1–2, 4–5, 14–16, and Stamps A–C in Locus 396; and Hansen, nos. 8, 12–13, and 18 in Level IXA. In contrast, sealings with incised markings occurred in all three find-spots.

Table 2 summarizes the data available for sealings that come from Level IXB, Locus 396, floor 3 (or 60 percent of the total number of sealings).

TABLE 2. CLAY SEALINGS FROM THE INANNA TEMPLE AT NIPPUR, LEVEL IXB, LOCUS 396, FLOOR 3

FIELD NO.	SEAL	OBJECT SEALED
8 N 172	Hansen, No. 1	door(?)
8 N 182	Hansen, No. 1	—
8 N 189	Hansen, No. 1	—
8 N 192	Hansen, No. 1	—
8 N 199	Hansen, No. 1	door
8 N 201	Hansen, No. 1	—
8 N 205	Hansen, No. 1	—
8 N 196	Hansen, No. 2	—
8 N 200	Hansen, No. 2/Stamp B	door
8 N 203	Hansen, No. 2/Stamp B	—
8 N 194	Hansen, No. 4	not preserved
8 N 191	Hansen, No. 5	—
8 N 209	Hansen, No. 7	door(?)
8 N 195	Hansen, No. 7(?)	—
8 N 183	No. 14	—
8 N 193	No. 15	—
8 N 207	No. 16	door
8 N 171	Stamp A	door
8 N 190	Stamp A	door
8 N 197	Stamp A	—
8 N 202	Stamp A	—
8 N 198	Stamp B	door
8 N 204	Stamp B	—
8 N 208	Stamp C	—
8 N 173	Incising	—
8 N 187	Incising	door
8 N 188	Incising	not preserved

with skirt partially pulled up, grasps the tail of a lion(?) with his right hand and raises his left arm; a lion's head, shown frontally, is in the field below the lion's body. To the right is a bull-man(?) with one arm raised holding a lance. (5) I cannot make out the details of No. 18 (8 N 179) from the photograph. (6) No. 19 (8 N 177) shows the lower portion of an animal, its front legs bent down.

[12] R. L. Zettler, "Sealings as Artifacts of Institutional Administration," *JCS* 39 (1987): 197–240.

1. Seven (one quarter) of the twenty-seven sealings bear impressions of Hansen, No. 1, a cylinder seal showing two lions attacking a bull and a human hero attacking, in turn, one of the lions with a lance. Two of the seven fragments had sealed a door.
2. Four sealings carry impressions of Stamp A, a rectangular seal with a central diamond in which a cross is inscribed (fig. 4). The diamond is surrounded by hatched triangles. Two of the four sealings had secured a door.
3. Three fragments have impressions of Hansen, No. 2, a seal showing a combat with two "heroes" and two animals alongside a boat carrying two figures, one seated and one standing in the prow with a punting pole(?). The boat moves through water teeming with fish. Two of the three sealings (8 N 200 and 8 N 203) also have one or more impressions of Stamp B over the cylinder seal (fig. 2). Stamp B is a subrectangular seal with a geometric design similar to Stamp A. One of the sealings (8 N 200) had secured a door.

   Two other sealings (8 N 198 and 8 N 204) have impressions only of Stamp B (fig. 3). One (8 N 198) had sealed a door.
4. Of the remaining eleven sealings, two have impressions of Hansen, No. 7, a sealing showing a horned animal leaping. One had secured a door.
5. Hansen, nos. 4–5, 14–16, and Stamp C, a geometric seal with a design similar to the designs of Stamps A–B (fig. 4), each occur on a single sealing.
6. Three sealings have incised designs. One of the three had sealed a door.

The sealings from Level IXB, Locus 396, floor 3 document two unusual sealing practices with parallels in some other Early Dynastic corpora: the use of stamp seals alone and impressed over rollings of cylinder seals and the use of incised markings perhaps in place of seals.

STAMP SEALS AND "OVERSTAMPING"

In the absence of contemporary textual documentation of the practice, our interpretation of stamps struck over cylinder-seal impressions depends largely on intuition and the evidence of comparable practices in roughly contemporary data sets. In the case of the Early Dynastic I Inanna Temple corpus, the occurrence of three stamp seals with nearly identical geometric designs on sealings from a single locus may provide a clue as to their significance. In contrast to cylinder seals' more complex designs, the elementary geometric pattern, as Nissen proposed apropos of simple patterned Uruk seals, would not have identified a specific individual.[13] The seals would

[13] H. J. Nissen, "Aspects of the Development of Early Cylinder Seals," in Gibson-Biggs *Seals*, p. 19.

have been used by multiple parties in instances where sealing had to be traced back to a generic authority, perhaps the institution or some administrative subunit within the institution. If so, the control and use of such seals stand as a key question. Did the stamp seals belong to low-ranking persons, persons whose legal identity was tied to the institution?[14] Or did the stamp seals belong to the temple and were they used by high-ranking administrators or those acting on their behalf? If stamp seals were held and used by low-ranking members of the institution, sealings such as 8 N 200 and 8 N 203 might imply, for example, that a subordinate had used the cylinder seal of a higher-ranking individual in sealing and that he/she had impressed his/her stamp over the cylinder seal to indicate that fact. The action would have been similar to the modern practice of signing a superior's name to a document and initialing it. If, on the other hand, the stamp seals belonged to the temple and were used by high-ranking administrators, a stamp impressed over the rolling of a cylinder seal might be taken as having a validating function.[15] In other words, the stamp seal would have formally "authorized" the sealing activity of the cylinder seal's holder.

The limited functional data available for the Inanna Temple sealings provide little insight into the context(s) in which the stamps were used. Only one (Hansen, No. 2) of the eleven cylinder seals from Level IXB, Locus 396, floor 3 and only two out of three extant impressions were "overstamped." One of the sealings had secured a door. The same stamp seal was used by itself on two other sealings, one of which had secured a door.

Origins of Overstamping and Other Early Dynastic I Corpora

The origins of the practice of overstamping remain uncertain. In the Late Uruk period (ca. 3500–3100 B.C.), stamp seals or the butt ends of cylinder seals were sometimes impressed over cylinder seals on spherical bullae and lenticular sealings from Uruk, Habuba Kebira South, Susa, Chogha Mish, and Tepe Farukhabad.[16] The

---

[14] Ibid., p. 20.

[15] J. N. Postgate, "Excavations at Abu Salabikh, 1978–79," *Iraq* 42 (1980): 91–92.

[16] *Uruk*: R. M. Boehmer, *Uruk: Früheste Siegelabrollungen*, Ausgrabungen in Uruk-Warka, Endberichte 24 (Mainz, 1999), pp. 104–12. *Habuba Kebira*: D. Sürenhagen and E. Töpperwein, "Kleinfunde," in E. Heinrich et al., "Vierter vorläufiger Bericht über die von der Deutschen Orient-Gesellschaft mit Mitteln der Stiftung Volkswagenwerk in Habuba Kebira (Habuba Kebira, Herbstkampagnen 1971 und 1972 sowie Testgrabung Frühjahr 1973) und in Mumbaqat (Tall Mumbaqat, Herbstkampagne 1971) unternommenen archäologischen Untersuchungen," *MDOG* 105 (1973): 31. *Susa*: P. Amiet, *Glyptique susienne des origines à l'époque des Perses achéménides*, MDP 43 (Paris, 1972), nos. 456 + 655; 457 + 580; 460 + 557 + 577; 460 bis; 544 + 649 (lenticular sealing); 548 + 586 + 697; and 680; A. Le Brun and F. Vallat, "L'origine de l'écriture à Suse," *DAFI* 8 (1978): 15, nos. 1–2. *Chogha Mish*: P. Delougaz and H. J. Kantor, *Chogha Mish*, OIP 101 (Chicago, 1996), pp. 135–54. *Tepe Farukhabad*: H. T. Wright, ed., *An Early Town in the Deh Luran Plain: Excavations at Tepe Farukhabad* (Ann Arbor, Michigan, 1981), p. 156.

Clay bullae and lenticular sealings, as well as numerical and inscribed tablets, often bear impres-

butt end of a cylinder seal was used to notch the end of a numerical tablet from Susa. At least at Susa the same cylinder seals impressed on these recording devices were also used to stamp or notch them.[17] Somewhat later in time, a single tablet from Jemdet Nasr has a square stamp with a six-petaled rosette impressed over a cylinder seal.[18]

By Early Dynastic I, written documents apparently ceased to be sealed, but stamp seals continued to be used on clay sealings either by themselves or for overstamping cylinder seals.[19] An Early Dynastic I(?) sealing from Nippur, excavated during the University of Pennsylvania's Fourth Expedition (1899/1900), has a circular stamp with a rosette over an impression of a cylinder seal with an animal combat scene.[20] Many of the sealings from the lower Seal Impression Strata (SIS 8–4) at Ur have stamps impressed over rollings of cylinders.[21] R. J. Matthews has described a subset of the Ur SIS sealings, the so-called city seals, but it would be worthwhile more fully documenting the corpus of sealings from the lower SIS housed in the University of Pennsylvania Museum (hereafter UPM).[22]

Forty-four (or 20 percent) of the roughly two hundred sealings from SIS 8–4 in the UPM have impressions of a stamp or a cylinder and stamp (table 3).[23] The largest

---

sions of multiple cylinder seals (see, for example, Boehmer, *Uruk: Früheste Siegelabrollungen*, pp. 49 and 105; Sürenhagen and Töpperwein, "Kleinfunde," pp. 21–22; and Le Brun and Vallat, "L'origine de l'écriture à Suse," pp. 15–22 and 38–39). How "compound" sealing relates to "overstamping" is an intriguing problem but not one with a ready solution. Since stamps or the butt ends of cylinder seals are not found on large numbers of administrative artifacts, but occur on bullae, lenticular sealings, etc. that have rollings of a single cylinder, as well as those with multiple seals, I assume that overstamping is an administrative action distinct from that (those) represented by the application of two or three cylinder seals on artifacts (see n. 21 below).

[17] Le Brun and Vallat, "L'origine de l'écriture à Suse," p. 22.

[18] R. J. Matthews, *Cities, Seals and Writing: Archaic Seal Impressions from Jemdet Nasr and Ur*, Materialien zu den frühen Schriftzeugnissen des Vorderen Orient 2 (Berlin, 1993), p. 17.

[19] Ibid., p. 26. Even though it died out in southern Mesopotamia, the practice of sealing written documents continued in Iran in the Proto-Elamite period, roughly contemporary with Jemdet Nasr and Early Dynastic I. See R. Dittmann, "Seals, Sealings and Tablets," in U. Finkbeiner and W. Röllig, eds., *Jemdat Nasr, Period or Regional Style?* (Wiesbaden, 1986), pp. 346–50; Matthews, *Cities, Seals and Writing*, p. 27. Stamp seals as well as cylinder seals were impressed on Proto-Elamite tablets (M. W. Stolper, "Proto-Elamite Texts from Tall-i Malyan," *Kadmos* 24 [1985]: 5).

Note also a clay sealing from Susa with impressions of a glazed steatite cylinder seal and the butt end of a seal. The sealing had apparently secured a door (L. Delaporte, *Catalogue des cylindres orientaux, cachets et pierres gravées de style oriental du Musée du Louvre*, vol. 1, Fouilles et missions [Paris, 1920], S54).

[20] L. Legrain, *The Culture of the Babylonians*, PBS 14 (Philadelphia, 1925), no. 48a.

[21] Idem, *Archaic Seal Impressions*, p. 8.

[22] Matthews, *Cities, Seals and Writing*. Matthews's catalogue of the Ur city seals includes seven or so of the sealings in the UPM that have impressions of stamp seals.

[23] In his "Analysis of Decorative Techniques" Legrain records four sealings that have impressions of two cylinder seals (cf. Legrain, *Archaic Seal Impressions*, p. 13). Two of the sealings are in the UPM: U.18400 (889), UE 3, 135 and 169, 33-35-307 and U.18407 (813), UE 3, 160 and 254, 33-35-371 (for an explanation of field and museum catalogue numbers on the Ur SIS sealings, see table 3 below, n. *a*). At n. 15 above I argue that the application of multiple cylinder seals and overstamping on Late Uruk spherical

TABLE 3. UR SIS SEALINGS WITH STAMP-SEAL IMPRESSIONS IN THE UNIVERSITY OF PENNSYLVANIA MUSEUM [a]

	FIELD NO.	PUBLICATION NO.	UPM REG. NO.	FIND-SPOT	MOTIF / SEALING TYPE
1.	U.13912	UE 3, 424	31-16-675	SIS 4	Rosette. Door. Knob and thong?
2.	U.13972	UE 3, 404	31-16-674	SIS 4?	Rosette. Door(?). Knob(?) and cord
3.	U.13982	UE 3, 272	31-16-658[b]	SIS 4	Butt end of unperforated cylinder. Door. Peg and cord
4.	U.14140	UE 3, 198	31-16-619	SIS 4	Butt end of unperforated cylinder. Door. Peg and cord
5.	U.14597	UE 3, 368	31-16-603	SIS 4	Rosette. Door. Peg and cord
6.	U.14625	UE 3, 385	31-16-657	SIS 4	Butt end of perforated cylinder with attached string? Door. Peg and cord
7.	U.14825	UE 3, 281	31-16-671	SIS 4	Rosette. Door. Knob or peg and thong
8.	U.14896A	UE 3, 431	31-16-604	SIS 4	Rosette. Door(?). Reverse broken, but traces of peg
9.	U.14896B	UE 3, 431	31-16-654	SIS 4	Rosette. Door(?). Peg and cord. Peg has squared edge and shows traces of wood grain; base has straw impressions
10.	U.15045	UE 3, 421	31-16-676	SIS 4	Rosette. Door(?). Reverse broken; base flat
11.	U.18397 (918)	UE 3, 395	33-35-290	SIS 4–5	Rosette. Reverse broken
12.	U.18398 (849)	UE 3, 431	33-35-298	SIS 4–5	Indistinct traces of stamp? Door. Knob or peg and cord
13.	U.18402 (753)	UE 3, 382	33-35-323	SIS 4–5	Rosette. Reverse flat. Tag? Bag? Not door sealing
14.	U.18402 (754)	UE 3, 275	33-35-324	SIS 4–5	Geometric design: square inscribed in circle inscribed in square. Impression of cord; reed mat on base
15.	U.18402 (755)	UE 3, 376	33-35-325	SIS 4–5	Animal stamp. Cord and flat base with traces of grass or straw
16.	U.18402 (757)	UE 3, 281	33-35-326	SIS 4–5	Rosette. Door. Knob or peg and thong
17.	U.18402 (767)	—	33-35-327	SIS 4–5	Stamp impressions only: eight-petaled rosette. Dm 2.15 cm. Door. Knob or peg and cord
18.	U.18402 (768)	UE 3, 129	33-35-328	SIS 4–5	Only stamps. Eight-pointed star or eight-petaled rosette. Jar. Leather and cord over mouth, neck, and shoulder of jar
19.	U.18402 (772)	UE 3, 469	33-35-329	SIS 4–5	Rosette. Traces of cord
20.	U.18402 (773)	UE 3, 223	33-35-330	SIS 4–5	Rosette. Door(?). Impression of cord and flat base; cord probably around knob or peg
21.	U.18404 (716)	UE 3, 306	33-35-337	SIS 4–5	Rosette. Door. Knob or peg and cord

[a] Sealings in the UPM from the Seal Impression Strata carry several registration numbers that may vary from sealing to sealing. These include field numbers (prefixed with a "U" and underlined in white ink); what I take to be a preliminary catalogue number, given here in parentheses; Legrain's publication number from *Archaic Seal Impressions*, written in white ink or occasionally the note "Not in Legrain"; and, the UPM's registration number. When I initially sorted the sealings in the late 1980s only a few sealings had museum registration numbers written on them. Since that time, all of them have been assigned museum numbers.

[b] Legrain, *Archaic Seal Impressions*, p. 29, mistakenly lists the UPM registration number as 31-16-858.

TABLE 3. UR SIS SEALINGS WITH STAMP-SEAL IMPRESSIONS IN THE UNIVERSITY OF PENNSYLVANIA MUSEUM (*CONT.*)

	FIELD NO.	PUBLICATION NO.	UPM REG. NO.	FIND-SPOT	MOTIF / SEALING TYPE
22.	U.18404 (734)	UE 3, 351	33-35-346	SIS 4–5	Rosette. Door. Knob or peg and cord
23.	U.18404 (751)	UE 3, 131	33-35-354	SIS 4–5	Rosette. Reverse broken
24.	U.18405 (730)	UE 3, 286	33-35-344	SIS 4–5	Rosette. Door. Knob and cord
25.	U.18406 (749)	UE 3, 192	33-35-355	SIS 4–5	Rosette. Door. Knob or peg and cord
26.	U.18406 (898)	UE 3, 384	33-35-359	SIS 4–5	Stamp with recumbent animal. Boar, spade, and scorpion? Door. Knob or peg and cord
27.	U.18407	UE 3, 248?	33-35-360	SIS 4–5	Butt end of perforated cylinder; cord through perforation visible. Impression of cord
28.	U.18407 (778)	UE 3, 247	33-35-363	SIS 4–5	Indistinct. Animal? Door. Cord around knob
29.	U.18407 (809)	UE 3, 237	33-35-367	SIS 4–5	Rosette. Door. Knob and cord
30.	U.18407 (815)	UE 3, 254	33-35-373	SIS 4–5	Rosette. Impressions of cord; flattened base
31.	U.18410 (859)	UE 3, 297	33-35-387	SIS 4–5	Animal stamp. Boar(?). Door(?). Impression of thong or strap
32.	U.18413 (783)	UE 3, 142	33-25-391	SIS 4	Butt end of seal. Leather and cord. Jar
33.	U.18413 (793)	UE 3, 219	33-35-395	SIS 4–5	Butt end of seal. Door. Peg and cord
34.	U.18413 (797)	UE 3, 378	33-35-394	SIS 4–5	Rosette. Door. Peg and cord
35.	U.18413 (803)	UE 3, 369	33-35-401	SIS 4–5	Butt end of perforated cylinder. Door. Knob or peg and cord
36.	U.18413 (807)	UE 3, 281?	33-35-404	SIS 4–5	Rosette. Door. Knob?
37.	U.18413 (861)	—	33-35-407	SIS 4–5	Cylinder seal impression shows lion attacking bull; bird (eagle) in field. Stamp seal with recumbant calf. Probably UE 3, 215. Door. Knob or peg and cord
38.	U.18413 (863)	UE 3, 281	33-35-408	SIS 4–5	Rosette. Door. Knob or peg and thong
39.	U.18413 (870)	UE 3, 281	33-35-415	SIS 4–5	Rosette. Door. Knob or peg and thong
40.	U.18413 (899)	UE 3, 214	33-35-417	SIS 4–5	Stamp with animal, perhaps a scorpion or spider. Reverse broken; flattened base
41.	U.18413 (913)	UE 3, 393	33-35-427	SIS 4–5	Rosette. Leather and cord. Jar
42.	U.18414 (928)	UE 3, 256	33-35-452	SIS 4–5	Stamp seal design uncertain. Face looks like stamp struck into one impression, with a second rolling made over stamp. Cord impressions on reverse
43.	U.20083	UE 3, 216	35-1-667	SIS 4	Rosette. Door. Knob or peg and cord
44.	U.20083	—	35-1-713	—	Butt end of uperforated cylinder. Door. Knob and cord

number of stamp seals on the Ur sealings are circular and have a rosette or star design.[24] Twenty-seven of the sealings in the UPM have stamp seals with such designs. Six stamps show animals, including a boar carved in high relief, and one has a geometric design; two impressions are indistinct. Eight of the sealings in the UPM have rollings of a cylinder seal and impressions of an uncarved "stamp," probably the butt end of a cylinder, some perforated and others unperforated. Legrain argued that in fact all of the stamp seals on the Ur sealings, including those with rosettes, animals, and geometric designs, were made with the butt ends of cylinder seals.[25]

Though few examples of such cylinder seals survive,[26] Legrain's suggestion is of particular significance for the meaning of overstamping within an administrative system. If he is correct, the occurrence of stamp seals would imply that no more than a single person need have been involved in the sealing activities represented by the SIS sealings.[27] Several observations suggest that the stamp impressions on the SIS sealings could have been made with the butt ends of the cylinder seals over which they were impressed.

Matthews observed that on a sealing in the British Museum the butt end of a cylinder seal had been "pressed deeply enough into the clay to leave the impression of part of the cylinder design on the side,"[28] and Legrain observed that in general the

---

bullae, lenticular sealings, and tablets represented distinct administrative activities. Sealings that had secured doors and various sorts of containers, however, are intrinsically different from such account records, so the question of the relationship between "compound" sealing and "overstamping" needs to be raised again. The large number of SIS sealings with stamps or the butt ends of cylinder seals struck over cylinder impressions as well as the small number of sealings with multiple cylinder seals, and the fact that none of them have evidence of "overstamping" might suggest that in some cases a second cylinder seal could be applied in place of a stamp.

[24] Legrain, *Archaic Seal Impressions*, p. 13 and pls. 34–35.

[25] Ibid., p. 8. Cylinder seals with carvings on their butt ends could not have been bored through. Legrain speculated that such seals would have been suspended by means of a lug or boss carved in the stone at the opposite end, and he cited several examples. Additional examples are known from the Diyala excavation (H. Frankfort, *Stratified Cylinder Seals from the Diyala Region*, OIP 72 [Chicago, 1955], pp. 13–14).

[26] For cylinder seals with designs carved on their butt ends, see *Coll. de Clercq*, vol. 1, pl. 1: 6–6bis, a Jemdet Nasr "brocade"-style seal; Frankfort, *Stratified Cylinder Seals*, pls. 2p and 84, a crude Early Dynastic I cylinder seal from the Diyala; and, Amiet, *Glyptique susienne*, no. 1080, a fragmentary Proto-Elamite cylinder seal from Susa. The latter two seals have drill holes forming a rosette on their butt ends.

[27] Matthews, *Cities, Seals and Writing*, p. 46

[28] Ibid., pp. 46 and 67. I have not examined the sealing in question (U.13902 = P. R. S. Moorey, "Unpublished Early Dynastic Sealings from Ur in the British Museum," *Iraq* 41 [1979]: 109–10, no. 568), but such impressions would likely be rare and could only be created by impressing the end of a cylinder seal down and laterally against the clay. I have examined a number of sealings in the UPM with stamp seals or the butt ends of cylinder seals impressed 5–10 mm deep into the clay but could find no unambiguous traces of designs that might have been carved on the faces of cylinder seals. Instead what I observed—or, more accurately, what I think I observed—on the sides of the stamp impression U.14825 (31-16-671) are remnants of the design of the seal impressed on the clay. The design had been pushed down and distorted when the stamp was applied.

diameters of the stamps struck over cylinder-seal impressions had "some relation to the cylinder itself."[29] I have attempted to confirm Legrain's observation by measuring the length of one complete rolling of various cylinder seals and calculating the circumference of the stamp that had been impressed over them. If the round stamp impressed in the clay was carved on the butt end of the cylinder used to make the impression on the sealing, its circumference ought to be more or less the same as the length of one complete rolling.

I was able to measure the length of one complete rolling of five sealings in the UPM (see table 4). In each case the length is roughly the same as the circumference of the stamp impressed over it. In no case is the difference greater than 6 mm, inconsequential given the distortions caused in rolling seals.

Four—or possibly five—sealings with impressions of the same cylinder seal (UE 3, 281) have impressions of the same stamp, 1.8 cm in diameter, with an eight-pointed star or simplified rosette that looks like the AN/DINGIR-sign. UE 3, 281 is particularly complex, and I was not able to determine the length of a complete rolling from any of the UPM impressions to compare to the circumference of the stamp.[30] The four sealings in the UPM had secured the same door fixture, however, a knob or peg with a smooth surface, ca. 3.6 cm in diameter and wrapped with a leather thong or strip.

TABLE 4. CORRESPONDENCE BETWEEN THE LENGTH OF CYLINDER-SEAL SCENES AND THE CIRCUMFERENCE OF STAMP SEALS IMPRESSED OVER THEM ON UPM SEALINGS

SEALING	UE 3	LENGTH (CM)	CIRCUMFERENCE (CM)	DIFFERENCE (CM)
U.14597/31-16-603	368	6.1	6.4	0.3
U.14625/31-16-657	385	4.9	5.02	0.12
U.18405/33-35-344	286	6.5	7.06	0.56
U.18407/33-35-367	237	5.5	6.1	0.6
U.18413/33-35-401	367	4.15	4.11	0.04

The evidence of the SIS 8–4 sealings, then, would seem to suggest that overstamping had little to do with "initialing" or "authorizing" a sealing activity. If it was not a random activity, then overstamping may have been an administrative practice specific

[29] Legrain, *Archaic Seal Impressions*, p. 8.

[30] U.14825, 31-16-671; U.18402 (757), 33-35-326; U.18413 (863), 33-35-408; and, U.18413, 807, 33-35-415. According to numbers on the artifact, U.18413 (807), 33-35-404 also has impressions of UE 3, 281, but the cylinder- and stamp-seal rollings are indistinct. Cf. Matthews, *Cities, Seals and Writing*, p. 67, no. 39. Matthews lists two of the four or five UPM sealings in his catalogue. He gives the length of a rolling of the seal in question as 5.65 cm; the circumference of the stamp as calculated from its diameter is roughly the same.

to an individual or an individual's administrative responsibilities or perhaps related to a particular sealing context. As for the former, among the Ur SIS sealings in the UPM, overstamping does not appear to correlate with seal iconography, one commonly cited referent of identity or responsibilities.[31] Overstamping occurs with cylinder seals of all the major scene categories among the lower SIS sealings: animal combats, herding scenes, erotic scenes, abstract or geometric designs, cuneiform inscriptions such as the so-called city seals, and so on. As Matthews observed in his study of city seals from the Ur SIS, however, overstamping may have been related to what was sealed.[32] The use of stamp seals on Ur SIS city seals strongly correlated with door sealings, and the overwhelming majority of the SIS 8–4 sealings in the UPM that have a stamp over a cylinder seal had secured doors (see table 3 above). Not all of the Ur SIS door sealings, however, evidence overstamping. More detailed measurement of the reverses of the sealings might be able to determine whether stamp seals or the butt ends of seals were routinely impressed on those that secured a specific door fixture(s) or, by implication, a single storeroom or limited number of magazines.

In contrast to Nippur and Ur, sealings from Early Dynastic I trash pits at Jemdet Nasr[33] and Fara[34] show no evidence of the use of stamp seals or overstamping in administrative activities. The contrast is hard to explain. It might be due to sampling.[35] The overwhelming majority of the more than four hundred Fara sealings Matthews studied had secured doors, so if the practice had been in widespread use there, it might be expected to have been in evidence in that corpus.

Later Early Dynastic Period

The use of stamp seals and overstamping continued at least in some parts of southern Mesopotamia in the later part of the Early Dynastic period. The Early Dynastic III sealings from the Tell Abu Salabikh 6G Ash-Tip, for example, have thirteen or fourteen different stamp seals commonly impressed over cylinder seals. For example, twelve sealings have a rectangular stamp depicting a lion's face impressed over two different cylinder seals, while two sealings have a second stamp with a lion's face impressed by itself.[36] A pyramidal stamp seal (AbS 704) with a lion's face was found at Abu Salabikh in the Southeastern Complex (Area E), Room 52.[37] Three sealings from

---

[31] M. A. Brandes, *Siegelabrollungen aus den archäischen Bauschichten in Uruk-Warka*, Freiburger altorientalische Studien 3 (Wiesbaden, 1979), pp. 93–100; R. Dittmann, "Seals, Sealings and Tablets," pp. 332–66.

[32] Matthews, *Cities, Seals and Writing*, p. 46.

[33] Idem, "Excavations at Jemdet Nasr, 1989," *Iraq* 52 (1990): 32–36.

[34] H. P. Martin, *Fara: A Reconstruction of the Ancient Mesopotamian City of Shuruppak* (Birmingham, England, 1988), p. 66; Matthews, "Fragments of Officialdom from Fara," pp. 2–8.

[35] Martin and Matthews, "Seals and Sealings," p. 26.

[36] Ibid., pp. 26–27, 43–44, and 47–50.

[37] Postgate, "Excavations at Abu Salabikh, 1978–79," pp. 91–92. See Martin and Matthews, "Seals and Sealings," p. 26, for references to other Early Dynastic stamp seals.

the 6G Ash-Tip have impressions of different stamp seals showing a scorpion or scorpions. On one sealing the stamp was impressed over a cylinder seal.[38]

Martin and Matthews offered several possible explanations for the practice at Abu Salabikh: (1) the cylinder seal belonged to the supplier of goods and the stamp to a storeroom supervisor; (2) the cylinder and stamp belonged to storeroom supervisors of different status; or (3) the cylinder seal belonged to the storeroom overseer and the stamp to an official withdrawing goods.[39]

Published sealings from the upper Seal Impression Strata (SIS 2–1) at Ur show no evidence of overstamping nor do sealings from Fara.[40] The largest corpus of Fara sealings was found, along with tablets, on the floor of a large well-preserved and recorded building in XIII f–i. Martin was able to identify more than half of the two hundred forty-three sealings from the building, and Matthews noted that of the seventy or so whose function could be determined, 75 percent had secured doors.

At al-Hiba, ancient Lagash, the late Early Dynastic III Area C Administrative Building yielded more than one hundred fifty sealings.[41] A round stamp seal showing a recumbent(?) animal occurred on a single sealing, but there were no instances of overstamping.[42]

For the following Akkadian period, a number of stamp seals are known.[43] The majority have an abbreviated presentation scene with a standing figure, usually a woman, before a seated deity, in one case identifiable as Inanna/Ishtar or a seated human. No impressions of such stamps exist in the sizable corpus of Akkadian sealings.[44]

In summary, the evidence regarding the use of stamp seals, in particular for overstamping cylinder seals, in Early Dynastic Mesopotamia is perplexing. Stamp seals, perhaps a remnant of protohistoric practices, were apparently in use throughout the period but seem to have been more commonly used at some sites than at others. While this finding could be an artifact of our sample, regional differences on the

---

[38] Ibid., pp. 48–49.

[39] Ibid., p. 27.

[40] Legrain, *Archaic Seal Impressions*; Matthews, "Fragments of Officialdom from Fara"; Martin and Matthews, "Seals and Sealings," p. 27.

[41] D. P. Hansen, "Al-Hiba, 1970–1971: A Preliminary Report," *Artibus Asiae* 35 (1973): 53–64; "The Fantastic World of Sumerian Art: Seal Impressions from Ancient Lagash," in A. E. Farkas, P. O. Harper, and E. B. Harrison, eds., *Monsters and Demons in the Ancient and Medieval World* (Mainz, 1987), pp. 53–63; Bahrani, "The Administrative Building at Tell al-Hiba, Lagash," pp. 104–15.

[42] Donald P. Hansen (personal communication, 14 April 2004).

[43] R. M. Boehmer, *Die Entwicklung der Glyptik während der Akkad-Zeit* (Berlin, 1965), nos. 958, 1532–36, 1596, 1658, and 1675. Note also two Akkadian stamp seals from Umm al-Hafriyat (cf. M. Gibson, "Nippur Regional Project: Umm al-Hafriyat," *The Oriental Institute Annual Report* [Chicago, 1977–78], fig. 2).

[44] The sealing U.15061 (UE 3, 534), from the northeast corner of the Royal Cemetery area, has an impression of what is likely an Akkadian stamp seal. It depicts a female pouring a libation before a seated human, also female. Legrain's drawing of the scene makes its identification as an Akkadian stamp seal tentative; no photograph of it exists, and the original is in the Iraq Museum.

southern floodplain may also have existed in political and socioeconomic organization, as well as in administration. We can only speculate about the significance of the practice of overstamping. The cylinders and stamps used on the Nippur Inanna Temple sealings were separate instruments, and overstamping could have involved multiple parties at differing levels of authority or with discrete responsibilities, whereas the cylinder- and stamp-seal impressions on the Ur SIS 8–4 sealings could have been made by one and the same device, thus not requiring more than an single sealer. Such seemingly contradictory data can be reconciled by assuming, for example, that the stamp seals impressed on the Nippur and Ur sealings encode information extrinsic to specific individuals or administrative hierarchies. Stamps might have been necessary on storerooms housing specific sorts of comestibles or commodities or could have been used as mnemonics to indicate quantities added or removed from magazines on specific occasions, such as religious festivals, to certify the contents of specific storerooms in inventories at the beginning or end of accounting cycles, etc.[45]

CLAY SEALINGS WITH INCISED DESIGNS

The second distinguishing feature of the Early Dynastic I Inanna Temple clay sealings, incised markings, is as puzzling a practice as overstamping. Incised markings might have been made by individuals without seals, but their potential variability suggests that markings would not have served to identify an institution/subunit of an institution or a specific individual as responsible for a particular sealing activity unless they were made in the presence of witnesses.

Incised markings occur not only on the Inanna Temple sealings, but also on the sealings from the lower SIS at Ur. Legrain lists roughly seventy-five incised designs out of the more than four hundred seal designs published, some much more complex than the pattern of incisions on the Inanna Temple sealings.[46] They include incised cuneiform, for example, UE 3, 118 and naturalistic representations, such as UE 3, 475. Seventeen of the more than two hundred sealings at the UPM have incised designs (though in sorting through them I was able to join two fragments). Several of the Ur sealings have both a cylinder-seal impression and an incised design, suggesting some similarity between the practice and overstamping. Four of the sealings with incised markings in the UPM had secured doors; the remainder served as jar stoppers.

In addition to Ur, a single sealing from Fara, whose find-spot is uncertain, appears to have incised lines.[47] Though none of the sealings from the Abu Salabikh 6G Ash-Tip have incised lines, Martin and Matthews noted fingernail marks over cylinder- and stamp-seal impressions on several sealings.[48] The relationship of the practice, if any,

[45] Cf. Brandes, *Siegelabrollungen*, pp. 98–100.

[46] Legrain, *Archaic Seal Impressions*, nos. 21–33, 50–53, and 54–117.

[47] Martin, *Fara*, p. 218, no. 585.

[48] Martin and Matthews, "Seals and Sealings," p. 27.

to the drawings on Proto-Elamite tablets,[49] Abu Salabikh and Fara tablets,[50] and Ebla tablets[51] is unclear.

III. Conclusion

Until Enrica Fiandra's ground-breaking research, clay sealings were consigned to art historians, who focused almost exclusively on the seals impressed on them. Advances have been made over the last thirty-five years in exploiting sealings to reconstruct administrative practices and structures as well as socioeconomic organization. The full documentation of clay sealings is now a routine part of excavation reports as the exemplary publications of sealings uncovered at the key northern Mesopotamian site of Tell Brak demonstrate.[52] But work remains to be done if we are to understand the role of sealing activities in institutional administration, the meaning of specific sealing practices, seal iconography, and so on. For one, the Ur SIS sealings, though found in secondary contexts, remain an underexploited resource. The sealings from that context—those in Baghdad, London, and Philadelphia—need to be reunited, reexamined, and fully documented with the aim of delineating the administrative practices of the institution(s), the Temple of Nanna, whose discarded debris they represent. Furthermore, such studies ought to be carried out in conjunction with a reanalysis of the "Archaic Texts" from the same debris. Along the same lines, detailed analyses need to be undertaken of in situ corpora of sealings from historical periods, where information drawn not only from context, but from names and titles on seals as well as written records can help elucidate institutional organizations and the role of sealings in their administration. As Postgate noted, Mesopotamia's historical—literate—periods provide robust models for explicating behavior in

---

[49] V. Scheil, *Textes de comptabilité proto-élamite*, MDP 17 (Paris, 1923), pp. 67–68.

[50] R. D. Biggs, *Inscriptions from Tell Abū Ṣalābīkh*, OIP 99 (Chicago, 1974), pp. 30–31; Martin, *Fara*, pp. 83–84; cf. P. R. S. Moorey, "Some Aspects of Incised Drawing and Mosaic in the Early Dynastic Period," *Iraq* 29 (1967): 113–14. Note Wiggermann's suggestion that some of the Abu Salabikh and Fara drawings represent cosmic geography (Frans Wiggermann, "Scenes from the Shadow Side," in M. E. Vogelzang and H. L. J. Vanstiphout, eds., *Mesopotamian Poetic Language: Sumerian and Akkadian*, Cuneiform Monographs 6 [Groningen, 1996], pp. 208–9).

[51] G. Pettinato, *Testi lessicali monolingui della Bibliotheca L. 2769*, MEE 3 (Naples, 1981), pp. 243–46, no. 59 (cf. pl. 33b).

[52] J. Oates, "The Evidence of the Sealings," in D. Oates, J. Oates, and H. McDonald, *Excavations at Tell Brak*, vol. 2, *Nagar in the Third Millennium BC* (Cambridge and London, 2001), pp. 121–40; R. J. Matthews, "Image and Function in Early Ninevite 5 Administration," in J. Braun, K. Łyczkowska, M. Popko, and P. Steinkeller, eds., *Written on Clay and Stone: Ancient Near Eastern Studies Presented to Krystyna Szarzyńska on the Occasion of Her 80th Birthday* (Warsaw, 1998), pp. 53–63; H. McDonald, "Art and Artefact: Sealings from the HP Ash Dump," in R. Matthews, ed., *Excavations at Tell Brak*, vol. 4, *Exploring an Upper Mesopotamian Regional Center, 1994–1996* (Cambridge and London, 2003), pp. 212–27.

pre- and protohistoric periods.[53] A secure foundation of such studies, supplemented by cross-cultural comparisons—not limited to "sphragistics" in the Mediterranean or Near Eastern worlds—will help us better understand and exploit the information potential of clay sealings.

---

[53] J. N. Postgate, "Cuneiform Catalysis: The First Information Revolution," *Archaeological Review from Cambridge* 3 (1984): 4–18.